JUDAISM
AS A
CIVILIZATION

Toward a Reconstruction
of American-Jewish Life

MORDECAI M. KAPLAN

Introduction by Arthur Hertzberg

The Jewish Publication Society of America
Reconstructionist Press
Philadelphia and New York 5741/1981

Library of Congress Cataloging in Publication Data

Kaplan, Mordecai Menahem, 1881–
Judaism as a civilization.

Reprint. Originally published: New York:
Reconstructionist Press, 1957.
Includes bibliographical references and index.
1. Reconstructionist Judaism. 2. Judaism—
United States. 3. Jews—United States—
Politics and government. I. Title.
BM197.7.K26   1981   296.8'344   81-6057   AACR2
ISBN 0-8276-0193-X
ISBN 0-8276-0194-8 (pbk.)

" 'Judaism' and 'Jewish religion' are not synonymous terms. 'Judaism' is more comprehensive than 'Jewish religion,' for 'Jewish religion' is only a part of 'Judaism.' Judaism is the composite of the collected thoughts, sentiments and efforts of the Jewish people. In other words, Judaism is the sum total of all the manifestations of the distinctively Jewish national spirit.

"The Jewish religion is, then, only a part of Judaism, though by far its most important part. Among no other people on earth has religion occupied so large, so significant a place in their spiritual life as it has among the Jews. But besides religion there were, and still are, other elements in Judaism."

(BERNARD FELSENTHAL, in Teacher in Israel, by
Emma Felsenthal, New York, 1924, p. 212.)

*　　*　　*　　*

"It was a fatal mistake of the period of emancipation, a mistake which is the real source of all the subsequent disasters in modern Jewish life, that, in order to facilitate the fight for political equality, Judaism was put forward not as a culture, as the full expression of the inner life of the Jewish people, but as a creed, as the summary of a few abstract articles of faith, similar in character to the religion of the surrounding nations."

(ISRAEL FRIEDLAENDER, in Past and Present,
Ark Pub. Co., Cincinnati, 1919, p. 267.)

*　　*　　*　　*

"Is the trend toward placing less emphasis on Judaism as a cult and more emphasis on Judaism as a civilization, i.e., identifying it with all the activities and relations of life?"

(From a questionnaire submitted in 1925 to members
of the Central Conference of American Rabbis.)

REPLIES

	North	South	West	Total
Cult	3	8	4	15
Civilization	20	12	18	50

(Yearbook, C. C. A. R., 1926, p. 320.)

FOREWORD

JUDAISM AS A CIVILIZATION was first published in 1934. Its immediate effect was the formation of a small group of my lay and rabbinic friends, who launched the *Reconstructionist* magazine in January 1935. That started the Reconstructionist movement which is "dedicated to the advancement of Judaism as a religious civilization, to the upbuilding of Eretz Yisrael, and to the furtherance of universal freedom, justice and peace."

The book underwent a second printing in 1935. When a third printing was suggested during my stay in Jerusalem in 1937–39, I advised against it for a number of reasons. In the first place, the description of American Jewish life, as of 1927, given in the first part of the book, began to be outdated. Secondly, the action of the Central Conference of American Rabbis in 1937, in adopting the "Guiding Principles of Reform," necessitated a revision of the chapter on the Reform movement. Thirdly, the concept "nationhood," as applied to the Jews, had come to be closely identified with statehood, and was, therefore, in need of being replaced by the concept "peoplehood." And finally, I had come to realize that it would be a mistake to retain the concept of "Chosen People," even with the interpretation given it in this book. For all these reasons I was reluctant to permit a third printing of the book, intending to bring it up to date in a revised edition. Preoccupation, however, with professional duties, the *Reconstructionist* magazine, and the writing of other books prevented me from carrying out that intention.

In the meantime, the present book went out of print, and no copies of it were obtainable anywhere. The demand for it, however, continued, despite the subsequent appearance of *Judaism in Transition, The Meaning of God in Modern Jewish Religion,* and *The Future of the American Jew,* all of which deal with the problem of Jewish life from the Reconstructionist point of view. Recently an urgent request for a new printing of JUDAISM AS A CIVILIZATION and the undertaking to finance it, came from the Alumni Association of the Teachers Institute of the Jewish Theological Seminary, which I had headed during the first thirty-five years of its existence. This time I finally overcame my resistance to having it reprinted without any revisions. I yielded to the argument that the original text might be of use in serving as a record of a stage in the development of American Jewish thought, as well as in drawing attention to the synoptic view of Judaism, which is still far from being generally accepted. Jews and non-Jews still assume that Judaism is a religion only.

It is, perhaps, not too much to expect that the reappearance of JUDAISM AS A CIVILIZATION will help to vindicate the Reconstructionist movement against those who charge it with being more secular than religious, in that it treats the problem of Judaism as a socio-psychological rather than as a theological problem. It is a fact, however, that the diagnosis of what is wrong with Jewish life, and the prescription of what is necessary to set it right, are as related to what we can learn from the human sciences as the diagnosis and cure of physical disease are related to chemistry and physics. The medicos who opposed Louis Pasteur's interpretation and treatment of physical disease were, no doubt, resentful that a chemist, who was no physician, should instruct them in their own specialty.

The republication of this book might also serve as a reminder that the idea of "Judaism as a civilization" was not intended as a slogan to abet laxity in ritual observances or indifference to religion. It was definitely intended to motivate in Jews a maximum and not a minimum identification with Jewish life. "Judaism as a civilization" is a call to American Jews to attend to the following needs: 1) To reaffirm Jewish peoplehood; 2) to revitalize Jewish religion; 3) to form a network of organic communities; 4) to strengthen the State of Israel; 5) to further Jewish cultural creativity; and 6) to cooperate with the general community in all endeavors in behalf of freedom, justice and peace. May God grant that our People heed the call.

I am deeply grateful to the Alumni Association of the Teachers Institute of the Jewish Theological Seminary for giving the foregoing needs of contemporary Jewish life an additional opportunity to be aired and emphasized.

M. M. K.

March 1957

PREFACE TO THE 1967 EDITION

Characterizing JUDAISM AS A CIVILIZATION as a classic, though meant to be a compliment, is likely to shelve it in a library where it can peacefully gather dust. By the same token, telling its author that he is ahead of his time is likely to serve his contemporaries as an excuse for not taking him seriously. The purpose, therefore, of this Preface to the new edition of his first major work is to disavow either compliment by emphasizing the timeliness of his book and the continued contemporaneity of its author.

Factually, seeing Judaism as a totality, and therefore as more than a religion, was made possible as a result of the latest perspective which the human mind has been able to achieve—that of holistic or organismic thinking. Holistic or organismic thinking is what Matthew Arnold described as "seeing things integrally and seeing them whole," i.e., in their totality.

In other words, when we deal with a living entity like a civilization, we should take cognizance of each of its aspects, to note what it contributes to the entire civilization and what the civilization as a whole does to each of them to render the whole more than the sum of its aspects. That holistic or organismic approach enabled Matthew Arnold to arrive at his classic description of the difference between Hebraism and Hellenism.

Organismic thinking is the latest stage in the maturation of the human mind. First came mythology, then philosophy, then science, and now we are learning to think organismically.

Accordingly, whoever attempts to write about Judaism in organismic terms must take into account the entire Jewish situation at the time he writes, particularly if he writes from a normative point of view, for the purpose of improving the situation. That is why the opening chapter of this book, which was first published in 1934, gives a survey of the American-Jewish situation of that decade.

The worst aspect of the present situation is the alienation from Jewish life and religion of American intellectuals of Jewish parentage —of scientists, writers, and academicians—and the bottomless ignorance of Judaism on the part of some of the leading laity. Due to the

worsening of the situation, the opening chapter of this book is somewhat dated. However, the main body of the book, dealing as it does
with the normative aspects of Judaism, is still timely, for the simple
reason that while the proposed program has been approved by a
considerable number of men and women of light and leading, it has
not yet been translated into action.

MORDECAI M. KAPLAN

March 1967

PREFACE

JUDAISM is a problem to those who have to teach it, and what Jew is exempt from teaching it? Parents who wish to inculcate in their children habits and appreciations which are part of Jewish life can no longer do so as a matter of course, but have to argue about it with themselves no less than with their children. And the problem is by no means confined to parents and children. Nowadays anyone who displays an interest in Jewish activities is challenged and must be prepared to explain what he sees in Judaism. He must be able to communicate his ideas about it in articulate form, if he does not want to be suspected of yielding to blind habit or sentiment. The Sages builded better than they knew when they included in the liturgy a prayer not only for the knowledge of the Torah but also for the ability to teach it. Never was a prayer so much in need of being answered as that one, since it has never been so hard to teach Judaism as it is now. Never did the rising generation so question its value and resent its intrusion into their lives.

The problem, of course, is not with Judaism as a quotation of what our forebears believed and felt; the problem is with the Judaism which the bearers of the future are expected to accept and live by. Formerly the mere knowledge of the past carried with it a categorical imperative for the future. Now anything which claims a place in the future must be justified by all that the future represents at its best. So difficult, indeed, has it become to teach Judaism that only those undertake the task who are too naïve to realize what they have to cope with, or too much committed to Judaism to escape the responsibility of envisaging in concrete terms the future they contemplate for it. That I have been led to formulate a conception of Judaism for our day is probably due to both naïveté and a sense of commitment. In any event, I feel that I owe it to the reader to tell him how I came to hold that conception. For one thing, it is not the product merely of the leisurely play of thought, but rather of the attempt to come to grips with the problem of getting Jews to live a Jewish life and do it wholeheartedly.

xiii

It was undoubtedly in a spirit of naïveté that as a young man I accepted the pulpit of an influential orthodox congregation in New York City. As soon as I found myself drifting away from the traditional interpretation of Judaism, and could no longer conscientiously preach and teach according to orthodox doctrine, I made up my mind to leave the rabbinate. Just as I was about to turn to some other pursuit, I was invited by the Jewish Theological Seminary to take charge of its newly established department for training teachers for religious schools. I seized the opportunity to remain in Jewish work, because I was quite certain that the Jewish ideology which had begun to take shape in my mind was calculated to win and hold the youth. I was confirmed in this belief by the fact that the invitation to head the Teachers Institute came from Dr. Schechter right after he heard me read a paper before the Alumni of the Jewish Theological Seminary. In that paper I developed the thesis that the future of Judaism demanded that all Jewish teaching and practical activity be based on the proposition that the Jewish religion existed for the Jewish people and not the Jewish people for the Jewish religion. That thesis marked a Copernican revolution in my understanding of Judaism.

Not long after having assumed charge of the Teachers Institute I was appointed to the chair of Homiletics at the Seminary. I did not consider it good pedagogy to model the courses in Jewish Homiletics on those given in Christian seminaries. With us Jews, I thought, the question was not so much how to preach, but what to preach. Confining, therefore, the problem of technique for the most part to practical exercises, I found it necessary to devote the rest of the course to the ideas and interpretations, by means of which the spiritual heritage might be made not merely vivid historically, but vital and relevant to present-day needs and aspirations.

As I proceeded with the course, it became apparent to me that the future of Judaism depended on something more than an acceptable ideology. The significance of Jewish milieu and atmosphere, social contact and interaction then began to dawn on me, and I realized that unless the synagogue were more than a place for worship its influence was bound to wane, and the most eloquent preaching in the world would not check its obsolescence. This led me to induce a group of Jews, who were on the point of organizing into a congregation and building the usual type of synagogue, to modify their original purpose and to establish a Jewish Center on such lines as would enable them to conduct in it social, cultural and recreational activities. At the same time I participated in the movement that had been inaugurated in those years to establish a *Kehillah,* and was active in its effort to organize a system of Jewish education in New York City.

These practical efforts, however, did not divert me from my main interest in achieving a satisfactory Jewish ideology for the modern Jew. Together with a number of rabbis and laymen who were in sympathy with my views, I organized The Society for the Renascence of Judaism, which had a short life because it aroused more opposition than its members had anticipated. When some of the Jewish Center members objected not so much to my un-Orthodox views, of which they had known, but to the fact that I had begun to publish them, I left the Center and organized The Society for the Advancement of Judaism for the very purpose of promulgating what I had come to regard as the only valid interpretation of Judaism for our day. A few years after that, the Training School for Jewish Social Workers was established, and I was invited to lecture to the students on the institutions of Jewish life. I found myself in a position where I had to correlate the meaning of Judaism with some of the problems of inner conflict with which Jewish social workers are called upon to deal. Thus, having had to meet the need experienced by the rabbi, the teacher, the social worker and the layman for a consistent and integrated philosophy of Jewish life in America, I was led to formulate the ideology set forth in this volume.

The more I observed the spiritual struggle that went on in the minds of the students and the laity whom I was trying to teach, the more clearly I realized that the present crisis in Judaism spelled unprecedented maladjustment in the spiritual life of Jews. In my search for a way to check the devastation of the Jewish spiritual heritage, I rediscovered Judaism. The eighteenth-century rationalism and nineteenth-century liberalism which progressive Jews so readily assimilated, led them to misconceive the very nature of Judaism. When some interpreted it as nothing more than a revealed religion, and others as nothing more than a religious philosophy, they did so in the hope of fitting it into the framework of a cosmopolitan civilization which they thought was about to be established throughout the world. Not even the penetrating historic sense of the learned men of the Historical School prevented them altogether from accepting the basic fallacy which reduced the Jews to the status of a religious denomination. The rediscovery of Judaism as a civilization I owe to the convergence of various social and cultural influences, many of which I, no doubt, would have missed, had I not been brought up in an American environment. Ahad Ha-Am with his neo-rationalistic and cultural approach to Jewish values, Zionism with its realistic attitude toward the relation of the Jewish people to Palestine, furnished the initial impulse to my thinking. But the direction which that thinking was to take was made plain chiefly by the recent developments in the field of the natural history of religion.

Thanks to the synthesis between Jewish tradition and modernism which the approach to Judaism as a civilization has made it possible for me to effect, I have observed young and old thrill to the beauty of meaning which the Jewish heritage suddenly assumed for them, and rejoice in the creative possibilities which they began to discern in Jewish life.

Although I have occasionally published some of the views expressed in these pages, I have hitherto refrained from setting them forth in integrated form for fear that the strength of the whole might be judged by that of the weakest link. In teaching, it is possible to come at once with hammer and tongs to strengthen the parts that are shown to be weak. Not so with an argument in print. At the least sign of weakness which the reader detects, it crumples up, because the author is not at hand to save it. But now is not the time to be deterred by such scruples. More dangerous to Judaism by far than challenge, opposition and even misinterpretation is the deadening acquiescence of apathy. The lack of controversial writing about Judaism, especially in English, does not mean that there is inward peace in Israel; it betokens the peace of stagnation. This spiritual stagnation in America must be disturbed, and if some of the views expressed in this book will produce the slightest ripple in American-Jewish thinking, the book will have served a useful purpose.

M. M. K.

New York, December 1933.

CONTENTS

PART FOUR. ISRAEL. THE STATUS AND ORGANIZATION OF JEWRY

PART FIVE. GOD. THE DEVELOPMENT OF THE JEWISH RELIGION

PART SIX. TORAH. JUDAISM AS A WAY OF LIFE FOR THE AMERICAN JEW

CONCLUSION

INTRODUCTION TO THE 1981 EDITION

*In celebration of the hundredth birthday of
Mordecai M. Kaplan*

ARTHUR HERTZBERG

SINCE Hellenistic times, and perhaps since the days of Abraham, the history of the Jewish spirit has oscillated between the insistence on Jewish separateness in the name of total authenticity and the desire and need to come to terms with the "spirit of the age" to make Judaism, in all its uniqueness, part of and intelligible to society as a whole.

Abraham broke the idols and separated himself from his father, Terah. The Midrash understood him to be the first Hebrew *(ivri)*, because the whole world was on one side *(ever ehad)* and he was on the other *(ever sheni)*. In a later age the Maccabees stood against the Hellenists in the name of Jewish separatism and purity, but soon their descendants could not dispense with contemporary forms of military and political organization. Even in the Holy Land many Jews spoke Greek. Elsewhere, in Alexandria, the Bible was translated into Greek, probably a century earlier than the Maccabean experience. A whole literature arose to harmonize Greek and Jewish wisdom and to reinterpret the Bible to "prove" that it was the source of all human wisdom, including Greek philosophy. The culminating figure was Philo, a source of both Jewish and Christian philosophical theology.

In the second century in the court of Rabbi Judah ha-Nasi, the decisive figure among the progeny of Hillel and the editor of the Mishnah, there were reputedly five hundred young people who studied Torah and five hundred who studied Greek wisdom. In the Middle Ages, Maimonides was the supreme example of the attempt to bridge the distance between the two cultures; the rabbis of Provence excommunicated his *Guide of the Perplexed.* In the modern age, Moses Mendelssohn and his circle consciously modeled themselves on Maimonides. In the next generation, Moses Sofer, the Rabbi of Bratislava, forbade change, even the slightest, following the rabbis of Provence.

These themes thus have had many replays. The meaning of each has shifted in the course of time. Moses Sofer knew that the body of religious precedent, which he insisted was unchanged and unchanging, existed only in potentia at the time of Rabbi Akiba. Did not the Talmud assert such an estimate of the tradition, in the tale of Moses coming to the heavenly Academy to hear Akiba expounding the Torah and hearing meanings of which Moses himself, who had received the Torah on Sinai, was not aware? Orthodoxies change, but as the nineteenth-century French sociologist Émile Durkheim knew, they change slowly and unconsciously. What changes more, and much more self-consciously, are the formulations of the second theme, the encounter between Judaism and the wider world. Invariably, those who wanted to relate their Judaism to some contemporary scene have been willing and sometimes eager to make modifications, either theoretically or practically. The various environments within which such harmonizations were attempted have changed from age to age, for Hellenistic Alexandria was not medieval southern Spain or nineteenth-century western and central Europe or twentieth-century America.

Mordecai M. Kaplan's *Judaism as a Civilization* thus belongs to a great tradition: that of Philo, Maimonides, and Mendelssohn. His more immediate intellectual ancestors within Jewry were Nachman Krochmal and Ahad Ha-Am. What was new, startling, and of profound historical significance was that such a rational, synthetic approach was taking place for the first time in America. All the Jewish ideologies that preceded Kaplan on these shores, including the American version of Reform Judaism, had been fashioned elsewhere. Even the religious outlook of Isaac Mayer Wise, the chief American Reformer, who celebrated American freedom, owed little to the United States. It is the merit of Kaplan and his historic importance that in him authentic Judaism, the learning and temperament of a Lithuanian *rav*, encountered the dominant philosophy in America of his day, the pragmatism of John Dewey. Kaplan lived among the tensions between strikingly foreign, new immigrants to America—coming by millions before 1914, in the days when he was young—and the "melting pot" doctrine, which the dominant Protestant majority, the descendants of the earlier settlers, were trying to impose.

There is, of course, in every thinker a personal component, that which he brings to his task out of his own character and temper. This element was, and remains, particularly prominent in Kaplan's work. His intellectual honesty is total. Where his mind will lead him he will go; he will not obscure either his conclusions or his actions with any veils to make them acceptable to those more reverent or more afraid. He is a believer, for even in the most rationalist formulations he has never questioned the intrinsic value of Judaism or his commitment to it. That is as much a given for him as it is for any romantic or mystical Hasid. It is possible to discern a deep current of personal mysticism —an echo of Spinoza's awe at moments of immortality in this life, a sense that one's individual life ultimately belongs, at its best and most creative, to the very web of the universe, to its ongoing createdness and creativeness. In his public self Kaplan was the captain of the ship of American Jewish life, the one who defined how that vessel was to be built, in which direction it should sail, and the currents toward which it had to head to be part of the joyous regatta of his day and the day thereafter. He was both architect and helmsman, both a builder of new edifices and a rebuilder of old ones that were still habitable. He was therefore sometimes a wrecker of what stood in the way of new creativity, for he was thoroughly American: he had no respect for old hovels that could not accommodate political and spiritual freedom. Kaplan was not at all sentimental about the beauty of the ghetto, of the Sabbath joys in tenements, for the social activist within him wanted space and renewal of all kinds. Did he not belong to the generation of the muckrakers in American politics, of the reformers who fought against child labor and those who opposed exploitation of the immigrants and their exploitation of each other?

When Kaplan was young, "progress" and "social engineering" were good words whose value no one doubted; certainly Kaplan did not doubt them. To be sure, Freud was also young in those days, and increasingly in Europe parts of the intelligentsia were turning away from social change to contemplate the inner demons of human nature. But until the 1930s, or even later, depth psychology was more of a European than an American concern. Kaplan never encountered the Freudian doctrine in any but a passing way. He was at once too Jewish and too American for such turning in on one's self. Although Kaplan knew much about woe and pain, his anodynes were not the analyst's couch. At the center of his world were society and action; the individual existed primarily in his relationship to the group and to action in the here and now.

He borrowed from Israel of Salant, an older Lithuanian teacher, the doctrine that the salvation of the soul of the individual was in doing something for someone else's body. This Lithuanian Jewish objectivity and activism were consonant with a burgeoning, expanding America, one that was remaking itself and soon the world in the decades at the height of Kaplan's career, the fifty years from the early 1900s to the early 1950s. Despite the Great Depression, this was by and large an optimistic, forward-looking period for America. In Jewish experience even before Hitler, this age had moments of great tragedy, such as the murder of tens of thousands of Jews in the 1919–21 border war between Russia and Poland and the ongoing anti-Semitism thereafter in Europe. But in America, Jews continued to hope for and believe in progress, in the power of good men to better themselves and the world. Kaplan stood at the center of this era as its most characteristic Jewish figure.

Mordecai Menahem Kaplan was born in Svencionys, Lithuania, on June 11, 1881, to a family with generations of tradition of talmudic learning. Seven years later, his father, Israel Kaplan, was invited to New York by Jacob Joseph, who had become the chief rabbi of a growing East European community, to join the bet din (rabbinic court) that Joseph established. A year later, at the age of eight, young Mordecai sailed with the rest of his family to the United States. He was thus part of the great stream of migration from eastern Europe and czarist Russia that brought some two million Jews to the United States between 1881 and 1914 and totally transformed the American Jewish community. Jews represented nearly a tenth of the total migration to American shores in that quarter century. Because these millions came primarily from central, eastern, and southern Europe, they were more "foreign" than the immigrants from England and Scandinavia who had dominated the earlier migrations. The newest arrivals turned a largely Anglo-Saxon, Protestant America into a more complicated country.

Kaplan, like the bulk of his contemporaries, gloried in the opportunities that American freedom offered; from his earliest education he was never entirely at one with them, however. His father insisted on raising him in America as close as possible to the Lithuanian custom that they had just left. For the first three years in New York, Mordecai did not attend public school; he studied at the Yeshiva Aitz Hayim. His all-day program there was enriched by private tutors, who came early in the morning and late at night to instruct him further in Talmud. At the age of eleven, Kaplan was enrolled in a public school, where he went for three years. In the next eight years, while completing high school and receiving a B.A. from the College of the City of New York in 1900 and an M.A. from Columbia University in 1902, Kaplan also studied at the Jewish Theological Seminary. He was ordained in 1902 at the age of twenty-one, in the first class to be graduated at the seminary after its reorganization by Solomon Schechter, recently arrived in New York from Cambridge University.

Schechter reputedly said upon his arrival that he had come "to make traditional Judaism fashionable in New York." One of his first graduates was the young Mordecai Kaplan, the son of a *rav* who had been raised in that tradition even in America, who spoke English faultlessly, and who had acquired in the thirteen years since his arrival an excellent Western education. Kaplan was ready for a career in the fashionable Orthodox congregations of the day.

Right after ordination, Kaplan became the rabbi of the wealthiest East European congregation in New York, Kehillat Jeshurun, then and now located on East 85th Street. The seminary degree was not the Orthodox ordination, the *smikha*, which entitles those who hold it to decide cases in Jewish law and ritual. It was rather an ordination like the degrees granted by Jews' College in England, the training ground for the Anglo-Jewish ministry; it prepared those who held it to lead a congregation and preach to it, but not necessarily to be its sole ritual guide. The recently organized Union of Orthodox Rabbis attacked this appointment. The result of the battle was that a rabbi of the old school, a Yiddish-speaking, Lithuanian yeshiva-trained personality, Moses E. Margolis, was called from Boston to be the rabbi of the congregation. Kaplan's title was changed from "rabbi" to "minister."

By 1908, Kaplan had regularized his own situation. He ceased being a bachelor. On his honeymoon in Europe he made a side trip to receive *smikha* from Rabbi Isaac Jacob Reines, the founder of the Mizrachi organization, which represented a marriage of religious Orthodoxy and Zionism. Still, Kaplan remained unhappy in his job. The personal slings never ended; the intellectual arrows were more fundamental. Kaplan essentially had ceased being an Orthodox believer in his seminary days. Arnold B. Ehrlich, a biblical scholar and a most radical secularist, was part of Kaplan's father's personal circle. The positive historical school in Judaism, founded by Zacharias Frankel in Germany in the 1840s, was willing to apply the tools of historical criticism to Jewish literature after the Bible, but in its American form (which soon would be called Conservative Judaism) it hesitated to approach the Bible with those same tools. In his student days Kaplan had no such scruples. He took to quoting Ehrlich and the whole literature toward which Ehrlich had pointed him in seminary class. He accepted the documentary hypothesis, thus denying that Moses had been the sole author of the Torah.

At Columbia, Kaplan studied sociology and anthropology, the disciplines most concerned with comparative culture; they were relativistic, seeing the practices and rituals of all faiths and cultures as manmade. Despite his doubts and his increasingly non-Orthodox convictions, Kaplan had to preach Sabbath after Sabbath in such fashion as to avoid antagonizing the conventionally Orthodox nouveaux riches who were his congregation. The burden upon him became ever greater; he kept looking for ways to leave the congregation. The opportunity came in the summer of 1909, when the Teachers' Institute of the Jewish Theological Seminary was established by a contribution from Jacob Schiff. Solomon Schechter offered the job of heading it to Kaplan. Schechter knew exactly what he was doing. He was aware of Kaplan's movement away from Orthodoxy; nonetheless, he entrusted Kaplan with the Teachers' Institute. Schechter even protected Kaplan's right to teach biblical criticism there.

Schechter was different, by origin and temperament, from Kaplan. Schechter had grown up among Hasidim in Romania; Kaplan was of Lithuanian rationalist stock. There was also a difference in age and authority, for Schechter was world famous and Kaplan a young beginner. Schechter recognized a kindred spirit, however. He wrote in the first edition of his *Studies in Judaism* that his own historic romanticism would do perhaps for one generation as an explanation of Judaism but the next generation would require other models and other defenses for its commitment to Judaism. Kaplan was that next generation, transplanted to America out of the strongest Jewish soil there was, the rabbinic tradition of eastern Europe.

Schechter promoted Kaplan to a permanent post as professor of homiletics at the Rabbinical School of the Jewish Theological Seminary, the only American appointment Schechter ever made to that school. Kaplan perceived his role to be not merely formal, the teaching of the style of preaching, but substantive, the teaching of the proper content of a contemporary sermon. This allowed him to use his classroom as a platform.

For three decades, the period including both world wars, Mordecai Kaplan was the dominant intellectual influence on the students of the Jewish Theological Seminary. Even those few who later would free themselves of his influence were mostly under his spell in their younger years. The easy explanation in institutional terms is that Kaplan's influence dominated the interregnum between the death of Schechter in 1915 and the accession of Louis Finkelstein to the presidency of the seminary in 1940. Cyrus Adler, the president during this period, a man of large political consequence, was the adviser and often the executive agent on Jewish affairs to the Schiffs and the Warburgs. He was conventionally traditional and observant in a way he had learned from Orthodox Sephardi teachers in Philadelphia when he was young. He disliked Kaplan, both in style and substance, and fought against him, but Adler was not a man of great Jewish learning, nor did he pretend to religious leadership.

The trouble with this explanation is that in those decades there were countermodels at the seminary of far greater Jewish learning and far more impressive classical authority than Kaplan possessed, chief among them Louis Ginzberg, by common consent the greatest authority of his day on the Talmud. Ginzberg was indeed the heir of "positive-historical Judaism," the romantic historical outlook that was the root of Conservative Judaism. He was the supreme incarnation in those decades of the notion of Jewish Law as ultimately of divine origin, moving like some majestic river through changing landscapes of time and place. Ginzberg was even more of a Lithuanian hidalgo in classic terms than Kaplan, for he was descended from the great Elijah of Vilna; it could be argued that with an admixture of substantial modern knowledge he was as learned as his ancestor. In older rabbinic terms, there could have been no contest between Kaplan and

Ginzberg. The seminary students, committed as they were to tradition, should have followed Ginzberg—but they did not. For all his
awe-inspiring learning, Ginzberg belonged to Europe and the nineteenth century; he was the heir of Lithuanian yeshivot and of "the
scientific study of Judaism," which had been invented in central
Europe in the early 1800s. For Ginzberg, learning was a kind of
authority. For Kaplan, the pragmatic American, learning was a tool
to be used for the enhancement of life. Ancestors did not make up a
corporate totem to be worshiped. They were a "usable past," to be
rethought and adjusted to make the present richer and more viable.
The totality of the Jewish heritage was not an accusing finger that
pointed at the present and found it wanting; it was a treasure house,
most of which could be used as material for a contemporary Jewish
building. If Ginzberg wanted to live in the old Jewish castle and make
a few renovations to make it more livable, Kaplan insisted that the
castle was drafty and moldy and could not be transplanted as it was
to America.

Those who studied under Ginzberg knew he was the authentic
interpreter of the Jewish past. He brought to his task an unparalleled,
dazzling blend of old and modern insights. Hours later they would go
to Kaplan, often to the same classroom, to learn about themselves,
about their own times, and how they could function as rabbis in
America in ways that they could defend to themselves—to their own
intellects and consciences—and thus to their contemporaries. Why,
then, did Kaplan's influence in the seminary wane by the mid-1940s?
Louis Finkelstein, who came to head that institution in 1940, once had
been a young disciple of Kaplan's; in the 1920s they prepared sermons
together when Finkelstein was the rabbi of a modern Orthodox synagogue in the Bronx. Finkelstein, however, from the very beginning
opposed Kaplan's naturalism and his willingness, even eagerness, to
make changes in the tradition. Finkelstein remained profoundly conservative in religious matters and tried to lead the seminary away
from Kaplan's influence. Why did he succeed where Ginzberg failed?

The essential change was generational. The seminary class to
which Kaplan appealed did not represent its earliest students; before
World War I these were mostly young people who had come in their
teens to the United States from European yeshivot. For them the
seminary was a place in which they became Americanized rather than

a source of new theology. Students after the mid-1940s increasingly represented the third generation, grandchildren of the immigrants of 1881, whose Jewish orientations were quite different from those of their predecessors. They came to the seminary not to wrestle with the Judaism of their parents but to discover an unknown territory.

Kaplan's audience was his own generation: it was the seminary student of the interwar period whose parents had come in the great wave of migration. The usual biographies of such people were like Kaplan's own. They had gone to some yeshiva or had received equivalent training at home and then had come to the seminary not to Americanize—that is, to learn English and American customs—but to Westernize, to find a way of harmonizing their classic Jewish selves with the American environment in which they wanted to live and function.

These men were all Zionists; Cyrus Adler, the president of the seminary, was not. At the core of their Jewish commitment, even as they had begun to harbor large theological doubts, was a devotion to the Jewish people and its culture. Many of them no longer believed in the divine origin of the texts (as the young Kaplan had concluded at a comparable time in his life twenty or thirty years before), but they cared about the older Jewish learning and did not simply consign it to the rubbish heap as a thing unworthy of the attention of men thinking of universalist values. These students reflected their own generation in their social concern. The bulk of the Jewish intelligentsia was then at least parlor socialist and at most very left-wing indeed; European Jewry was in the 1920s and 1930s an increasing problem; and the Zionist settlement in Palestine, the new *yishuv*, though embattled, was growing creatively. All this evoked sympathy, concern, and action among those younger Jews, and not only among the seminary students, who were more or less equally balanced between their deep Jewish commitment and their desire for intellectual freedom and social justice. For this generation, Kaplan was at once the role model and the teacher.

With the waning of this generation, new voices began to be heard. The last of his important disciples, Milton Steinberg, who died tragically young in 1950, followed Kaplan with great devotion, but in his last decade, Steinberg, very contemporary to his own time, could not accept Kaplan's naturalism. Steinberg already was thinking—as were a number of younger people, such as Arthur A. Cohen, who came briefly under Kaplan's influence—in supernaturalist terms. They were willing to assert again some version of the idea of the chosenness of Israel, the notion that Kaplan had opposed more vehemently than any of the other ideas that Jews had inherited from their past.

In the years encompassing the two world wars and the period between, Kaplan was not the political leader of the American Jewish community, not even of those elements most under the influence of his thinking, for this was the era of Stephen S. Wise, Abba Hillel Silver, and a variety of lesser figures who spent their energies in the political arena, primarily in the service of Zionism. Kaplan had almost no relationship of consequence with the fund-raising establishments. Nonetheless, his influence was pervasive. In the direct sense, many of the leaders in both these endeavors were his friends and disciples; more fundamentally, it was Kaplan's thinking that provided the rationale for many of these efforts in their American version. At the height of his influence, Kaplan almost was crowned as the official thinker who was defining American Jewry as it was and ought to be.

Precisely because his influence was so pervasive and out of deep personal loyalty to the seminary, Kaplan resisted attempts to persuade him to organize a Reconstructionist movement as a separate denomination. When Stephen Wise founded the Jewish Institute of Religion in 1922 as a nondenominational, liberal, rabbinical seminary that affirmed Zionism, this platform was almost a carbon copy of Kaplan's own views. Nevertheless, despite Wise's repeated requests, Kaplan refused to leave the Jewish Theological Seminary to become the academic and spiritual head of the new school. Nor was he the principal architect of the Reconstructionist Rabbinical College, founded in Philadelphia by his disciples in 1967, or of the Federation of Reconstructionist Congregations and Havurot, founded in 1954. Those steps were taken under the leadership of Ira Eisenstein, who in 1959 assumed the direction of the Jewish Reconstructionist Foundation and who succeeded Kaplan as editor of the *Reconstructionist,* which Kaplan had founded in 1935. They occurred after it became clear that, no matter how influential Kaplan had been in the whole spectrum of American Jewish life, especially in all its forms to the left of Orthodoxy, the Reconstructionist outlook was not and would not be adopted in any formal sense as a spiritual position.

It is an almost bizarre result of a unique career. Like Molière's gentleman, Conservative and Reform Judaism spoke and have continued to speak the prose that Kaplan wrote for them. Once, some decades ago, they knew it; now both these religious movements seem to be engaged in trying to forget it. Kaplan taught that the ritual tradition is to be respected but is subject to human choices and especially to collective decision. He emphasized that Jews are a people tied together by group history and feeling; thus, a coalition among various kind of believers and unbelievers was the only way to guard Jewish unity. He defined Zionism as the noblest task of American Jewry and was a proponent of aliyah, but he clearly denied the dominant Zionist doctrine that the Diaspora was sinful and doomed to uncreativity and disappearance. On the contrary, it was Kaplan who defined Zionism in America very early as the central task of American Jews, a task that would provide them with the élan necessary to their own survival in America. Zionism for Kaplan became a kind of Jewish "social gospel," the this-worldly task on which Jews would concentrate in order to continue their basic religion, much as the Christians of Kaplan's youth had seen in such tasks as creating settlement houses and helping the advance of labor the true contemporary expressions of the Christian gospel.

To this day, the Kaplan definition is what American Zionism is, especially in Conservative and Reform circles and in the whole complex of Zionist and Israel-oriented fund-raising establishments. The very institutional fabric of American Jewish life is Kaplanian. He was the founder of the Jewish Center movement and the founding rabbi in 1917 of the first synagogue center, the Jewish Center (still located on Manhattan's West Side), which he defined and created. This endeavor gave concreteness to Kaplan's notion that an American synagogue needed to be a new version of an old idea: just as the classic synagogue was not the Jewish version of a Protestant church—it was not a conventicle of prayer but a place where the whole of life was housed, including study, feasts, and various organizations such as charitable groups and burial societies—so the modern American synagogue needed to provide the contemporary Jew with cultural and recreational activities that would make it the center of much, or perhaps most, of his leisure time. Balanced between his Western education and the redefined synagogue, the Jew would live thus in "two civilizations," the American and the Jewish. In this model, which all contemporary American synagogues of all persuasions have adopted and followed, Kaplan's definitions dominate, even among his opponents.

The specific endeavor of the Jewish Center soon came to a bad end for Kaplan. Because his increasing theological heterodoxy could not continue to coexist with his Orthodox laymen, Kaplan left the Jewish Center to found, in 1921, an organization known as the Society for the Advancement of Judaism. Some who followed Kaplan out of the Jewish Center to help him found the society were led more by his personal charisma than by his ideas; even here there was opposition to his radicalism, but it was muted and generally passive. Just one block down the street from his former pulpit, Kaplan now had a personal instrument, a platform from which he could speak his total mind, a congregation within which he could experiment with program and ritual, and a center to which thinking people who shared his concerns could come, and not only from the neighborhood.

His magnum opus, *Judaism as a Civilization,* first published in 1934, did not spring upon the world totally new. Many parts of it had been prefigured in articles across many years; more important, the views he was expressing had been lived and defined in his synagogue through the 1920s and early 1930s. Here he had to redefine the Jewish religion more seriously than had those for whom it was, as on the surface it was for Kaplan, an aspect, or even the prime aspect, of Jewish nationalism.

Ahad Ha-Am, from whom Kaplan learned much, could content himself with extolling the role of religion in the past and making its meaning in the present a blend of moral passion and mystique about the utter uniqueness of the Jews. Horace Kallen, Kaplan's contemporary, had an even greater share in insisting that America ought to be a country of plural cultures; for him, contemporary Jewishness meant a thoroughly secular ethnicity. Kallen's Jewish definitions were close to those of Simon Dubnow, the older contemporary who was then rewriting Jewish history as the story of a secular nation that, at its most authentic, was a worldwide Diaspora.

Much as Kaplan learned from both such contemporaries (a historian is awed by the memory that the living man, now reaching one hundred, was writing in his diary, already a professor, in reaction to some of the newer essays of Ahad Ha-Am), Kaplan had no Jewish models for the redefining of his theological position. Even the most radical of the mid-nineteenth-century Reformers—those who had been willing to dispense with all Jewish rituals, including the Sabbath and circumcision, as determined by the customs of an older time— nonetheless insisted that something—at the very least "ethical mono-theism"—had been revealed divinely by a supernatural being.

The great task of Jewish theologians toward the end of the nine-teenth century was to try to define the content of this unique morality. It was a task in which they inevitably failed. It is possible to argue that in the course of history Jews have made different moral choices from non-Jews. It may be maintained that these choices were not accidents by powerlessness (Jews "relaxed" no one; they constructed no auto-da-fés in the Middle Ages because the synagogues did not control a secular arm with power to burn heretics) or that the Jews simply chose different modes of conduct. Why Jews have behaved differently morally from non-Jews, or indeed whether they always have, makes an interesting and probably insoluble historical problem. That Judaism is by its nature morally other from universal norms no more admits of philosophical proof than does the doctrine of incarna-tion in Christianity. In the nineteenth century, the doctrine of the "chosenness of the Jews" therefore was redefined by the Reformers not as content but as task. Jews have a particular role as the teachers to the world of universal morality. This was the barricade that Abraham Geiger, the greatest figure of classic Reform Judaism, erected, behind which at least a Jewish synagogue, if not a Jewish people, could continue to exist. In Geiger's view, this barricade would serve for a generation or two; then it would become irrelevant, be-cause by then the world would have reached the level of universal morality and the messianic age of truth and justice would have ar-rived. In the Geiger version, this day of the Messiah looked very much like the world the Enlightenment had dreamt of.

The trouble with this construction is that some young people soon appeared in these circles to suggest that such a consummation de-voutly to be wished by their elders could be furthered if Jews—and for that matter, non-Jews—decided they could prefigure this univer-salism by living it immediately and thus acting as the paradigm for the new age. One of the most devout disciples of Geiger was Samuel

Adler, the most distinguished Reform rabbi of the mid-nineteenth century in New York. His son, Felix Adler, who had been sent back to Germany for rabbinic training, took the inevitable next step and founded the Society for Ethical Culture in New York in the 1870s. Here Jews and non-Jews of the high-minded bourgeoisie together celebrated universal morality without any theological or dogmatic trammels, in the accents of Ralph Waldo Emerson's transcendentalism and with ideas that descended ultimately from Spinoza.

It is to this intellectual and social situation that Mordecai Kaplan addressed himself. He accepted Spinoza: yes, morality was universal, and the true knowledge of it was not a monopoly of any historic group. Yes, religions were historic constructs created out of specific and partial experiences of communities; they differed not in their ultimate content but in their concrete experiences. Yes, rituals were man-made and theological structures, and dogmas were elaborate rationalizations. These revolutionary assertions led Spinoza to deny the importance of specific religions and traditions. He was willing to accept only particular, discrete, political structures. Nearly two and a half centuries later, aided by John Dewey's pragmatism (from which Kaplan derived the notion that every value and ideal must be expressed concretely in the present and preferably in community), Kaplan was able to construct a version of the Jewish religion without supernaturalism. He rejected the path he had tried earlier to redefine the ancient texts and change them by redefinition in favor of the bold, honest venture to accept the whole of modernity—especially its fundamentally relativist notions about all human cultures—and find a way of asserting the significance of Judaism.

The given for Kaplan was the fact that Jews in the present continued to harbor "a blind urge to live as Jews." What needed to be done for this "urge for Jewish survival" was "the formulation of a program which, reckoning with every phase of the contemporary challenge, will set up a goal so desirable that it will enable the Jews to resist the temptation to escape Judaism." Here, in a nutshell, in an early page (84) of *Judaism as a Civilization*, are the main themes of Kaplan's endeavor: since the emancipation there is an open society that offers the Jews the possibility and temptation to escape. There continues to exist within Jews a desire to remain, but supernatural religion—the old religious guilt—cannot contain Jews indefinitely within Judaism. Contemporary Jewish life therefore must be made so attractive that Jews will find rich, positive meaning in their Jewishness.

A few paragraphs later in the same passage, Kaplan goes on to argue another of his favorite themes, that the America he loves is best served by the continuing presence of subgroups and not by their disappearance. All of them together add richness and verve to America as a whole. Kaplan thus has constructed a Judaism without heavenly reward or guilt on this earth. It is rather the Judaism of a vibrant, contemporary community that rewards one with a joyous self and a creative, extended family—the Jews—and punishes with the loss experienced by those who abandon those joys, even if they are insensitive to their own self-inflicted deprivations. In Kaplan's recension the religious commandments cannot possibly be a set of "thou shalts"; they become in several redefinitions a set of "oughts," of norms toward which men and women in this world would be best off striving.

Though Kaplan did not confront anti-Semitism, he feared it. On one hand, he was bold enough to say that of the "forces that make for the conservation of Jewish life . . . the greatest of these is anti-Semitism" (p. 70). On the other hand, it is an obvious premise in his lifelong battle against the doctrine of the "chosenness" of Israel. In largest part, he denied this doctrine because he had abandoned the supernaturalism on which it is based, but there were concrete issues at stake. The anti-Semite, in all his permutations, pronounced the Jew to be "other" and therefore a merited target. The very meaning of the emancipation and of American democracy was that the Jew wanted to cease being other and alien; the only way to end the negative confrontation was, in Kaplan's view, to make an end of the positive assertion. The synagogue of Satan of the medieval anti-Semites is the negative mirror image, in Kaplan's view, of the Jew of Judah Halevi, who was a different order of being than all other humans. Kaplan, in due course, rewrote the liturgy in light of these naturalist, democratic, communitarian convictions.

Almost to this very day, his hundredth year, Mordecai Kaplan has continued to write books and articles. He has explicated further the theological side of his doctrine in *The Meaning of God in Modern Jewish Religion;* after the creation of the State of Israel, he published a short book on *The New Zionism.* Nonetheless, the essential Kaplan is in *Judaism as a Civilization.* All the rest, even his own writing, is commentary and further elucidation of the themes with which he dealt in this, his magnum opus.

Inevitably the question must be asked: what has this book handed on to times to come? The questions Kaplan asks are the recurrent ones of the era of emancipation. How is Judaism to live in an open society, especially among Jews who do not close their doors and their minds? His answers are in the key of an America still on the way to its most optimistic crest. But America today is in a different, more self-questioning mood. His religious outlook was fashioned at a time when the most advanced religious leaders believed that God could be found through human efforts to improve society; indeed, God was, in Kaplan's term, "the power that makes for salvation."

Those who have spent an additional generation tinkering with society and even radically reordering it are rather less convinced that the City of Man is really perfectible, even by man's best efforts. There is a mood in the very circles to which Kaplan talked that salvation may mean, at least for some, how to deal with themselves in a society that does not necessarily offer itself, as a whole or the individuals within it, a very satisfying time in this world.

Kaplan's Zionism is being challenged increasingly by the reality that the complex he helped to create, the American Jewish community oriented to Israel's needs and culture, is not proof against the ravages of assimilation. At least the Israelis—and some American Jews—are beginning now to think of America as an ultimately unfavorable environment for the existence of a creative Jewish community. Kaplan was too American ever to let the word *galut* pass his lips in reference to this country, which he celebrated with religious fervor. Even some of his disciples have started to wonder whether such radical Zionists as Jacob Klatzkin (who insisted, when both he and Kaplan were young in the 1910s, that *galut* was indivisible) were right.

In Jewish theology as a whole, questions of theodicy, of God's justice, are back at the center in the wake of the Holocaust, and supernaturalism is not as out of fashion among men and women who consider themselves contemporary as it was half a century ago. The issues that Kaplan raised must be discussed once more; like all important issues, they have to be rethought and redefined again and again.

The community that is concerned with them has, indeed, to be reconstructed, not once but again and again.

In every important work, even of liberalism, there is an element of dogma. Kaplan himself, whose thought is open and plural, retained in his personal character something of the authority—and even the certainty—of his Lithuanian forebears, but his intellectual openness and a basic optimism were, and remain, the dominant elements in his persona.

For Kaplan's hundredth birthday, when *Judaism as a Civilization* is being reprinted and presented again to its author and to those who continue to read him, let it be read now for the questions that have not changed, for the answers that remain courageous and profound, and for his personal example: to take nothing on authority.

INTRODUCTORY

CHAPTER I

THE PRESENT CRISIS IN JUDAISM

The change in the Jew's attitude toward Judaism—The ancient world-outlook the chief factor of conservation in the past—Faith in other-worldly salvation a force for solidarity and uniformity—The effect of enlightenment upon belief in other-worldly salvation—The life of the Jew marred nowadays by a sense of frustration—Needed: a substitute for the traditional conception of salvation.

BEFORE the beginning of the nineteenth century all Jews regarded Judaism as a privilege; since then most Jews have come to regard it as a burden. The first intimation of that change is recorded in a letter which Moses Mendelssohn wrote to Herder in 1780, explaining what had moved him to translate the Pentateuch into German. It was, he said, to teach his children to accept their fate with patience and resignation, especially their fate as Jews.[1] Before long many of the Jews who might have accepted their fate with patience and resignation rebelled against it, and sought to escape it by the road of apostasy. The most prominent among them was Heinrich Heine, who coined the famous quip about Judaism not being a religion but a misfortune.[2] From Germany the crisis in Judaism has spread to all countries where Jews have come in contact with modern thought and life. At its mildest, that crisis manifests itself as a sullen feeling of helplessness; at its worst, as bitter resentment and revolt.[3] Not even the Jewries of eastern Europe which until recently seemed strongly intrenched in their traditions have been spared. In Russia, whatever Jewish historical continuity and identity with the rest of world-Jewry the Communist régime might have tolerated the Jewish Communists have fanatically sought to destroy, and in a large measure have succeeded. In the west European countries, it is only anti-Semitism, which refuses to recognize even intermarriage and baptism as sufficiently dejudaizing, that prevents Judaism from disappearing completely.

When we direct our attention to the American-Jewish scene, we note that it, too, abounds in signs of ill omen for the future of Judaism." [4] The number of Jews who regret they are not Gentiles is legion. "If I had my choice," a prominent American-Jewish woman is quoted as saying, "I would have asked God to make me a Gentile, but since I had no choice I pray to Him to help me be a good Jewess." [5] Such a woman would scarcely approve of the traditional benediction, "Praised be thou, O Lord our God, King of the universe, that thou hast not made me a Gentile." [6] She is at least determined to make the best out of what she views as a bad situation. But most of those, who feel as she does, succumb to what they regard as an inescapable misfortune. "The great majority of Jewish youths at the colleges," writes a Harvard graduate, "consider their Jewish birth the real tragedy of their lives. They constantly seek to be taken for Gentiles and endeavor to assimilate as fast as their physiognomy will allow." [7] In *Escaping Judaism,* [8] the author describes vividly the sense of frustration and rootlessness which gnaws at the heart of many young Jews, and the wistful yearnings by which they are tortured as they contrast what they consider the rich and colorful life of their Christian neighbors with the drab existence of their own people. He then comes to the conclusion that Jews should reconcile themselves to their fate on the ground that "all men are not born equal; some are born blind, some deaf, some lame, and some are born Jews." That an entire chapter in *Jewish Experiences in America* [9] has to be devoted to the problem, "How to Combat Anti-Semitism Among Jewish Children," indicates how widespread is the disease of self-hate among American Jews.

In accounting for this sense of inferiority and self-contempt which is eating like a canker into the Jewish soul, it is usual to point to the fact that Jews find their Jewishness a handicap to them in all walks of life. As a minority group they are a shining mark for all mob viciousness and xenophobia. Since their Jewish origin stands in the way of their happiness and ambition, how can they help deploring it? However plausible this may sound, it cannot possibly be the true explanation of the way Jews nowadays feel toward Judaism. Jews have always had to bear the vexations and indignities which are the lot of a minority group. Ever since they have been dispersed among the nations of the world, they have been treated as defenseless aliens and compelled to migrate from land to land. Yet, until recently, there existed among the scattered fragments of the

Jewish people more of common life and singleness of purpose than among the members of peoples living in their own lands and under their own governments. This unparalleled sense of unity was accompanied by an implicit confidence in the validity of that which kept them united, and by a self-esteem which rendered them impervious to the derision heaped upon them. Nothing short of a spiritual cataclysm could so radically have changed the Jew's attitude toward his heritage. The forces at work in the present-day environment must have completely shattered the foundations of his faith in the worthwhileness of being a Jew.

On what was that faith based? The answer to that question would solve the mystery of Jewish survival in the past. It would also indicate to what extent the force or forces that made for Jewish survival in the past can be counted on to check the present disintegration of Jewish life.

As a rule, the answer to that question is: the Jew never doubted the advantage of being a Jew because he believed implicitly in the religion which had been transmitted to him by his forebears and which united all Jews into a common brotherhood. It is, therefore, assumed that, since Jews no longer subscribe wholeheartedly to that religion, they see no reason for continuing as a group apart. But, unless we can understand what in that religion imparted such self-confidence to the Jew and such solidarity to the group, we are back to our original question. Why did Jews in the past hold on so tenaciously to their religion in the face of universal opposition? Why are they now so responsive to environmental influences as to be ready to abandon their faith at the first opportunity? Throughout the past, Jews surely felt the impact of surrounding antagonism to their religion, yet that did not in the least weaken their loyalty to it. Consequently, we are merely deluding ourselves, if we believe that by resorting to the usual commonplaces about religion having been the source of Jewish self-confidence in the past, and the environment having undermined that self-confidence, we have diagnosed the spiritual maladjustment of the Jew of today.

To get to the root of Jewish survival in the past, it is necessary to take into account a highly significant leverage which the Jewish religion possessed during the pre-enlightenment period, and which it has since lost. That leverage consisted in the fact that, *before the*

enlightenment, the religion of the greater part of mankind was based
on the same world-outlook as was the religion of the Jews. Christians and Mohammedans accepted as axiomatic three such basic and
far-reaching assumptions as the following: 1. The Old Testament
account of the creation of the world and of the beginnings of the
human race is not only authentic, but constitutes the premise of all
that man should believe in and strive for. 2. Human life on this
earth, being full of sin and travail and ending in death, can attain its
fulfillment or achieve salvation only in that perfect world which is
known as the world to come. 3. The only way man can attain such
salvation is by conducting himself in accordance with the supernaturally revealed will of God. It is, therefore, a mistake to assume
that in the past the Jews were able to ignore or defy their environment. They were, on the whole, just as responsive to it then as
they are now, though they lived entirely segregated from their neighbors. But to be responsive to environment, formerly meant to be
confirmed in one's adherence to Judaism. To be responsive to it
now, means to be perplexed by doubt and torn by inner conflict.

Before the enlightenment the one dominant concern of human
beings was their fate in the hereafter. Salvation meant to them the
fulfillment of their destiny in the life beyond the grave. Men and
women were so dissatisfied with their lives, with the imperfections
of the physical order and of human nature, that they despaired of
ever attaining salvation in this world. It was only the hope of enjoying in the hereafter a life free from fear and death that reconciled
them to the trials of this life, to the frequent wars and plagues and
famines, to the ruthlessness of nature and the cruelty of man. No
wonder then that the Jews, who had even better reason than the
rest of mankind to be dissatisfied with what this life offered them,
had all their thoughts centered upon their destiny in the hereafter.
The prospect of attaining bliss in the world to come, which constituted the Jews' conception of salvation, was thus in keeping with the
conception of salvation which until recently prevailed throughout
the world with which Jews came in contact.

The main point at issue among the three great religious groups
had little to do with the nature of salvation, or with the general
method of attaining it. It turned entirely upon a question of fact;
namely, which group was in possession of the authoritative revela-

tion of God's will? [10] The church maintained that having been founded by Christ, who was God incarnate, it alone, through its bishops, was the final and authoritative instrument of divine revelation. Allegiance to the church and obedience to its ordinances were the sole means to salvation. No salvation was therefore possible to anyone who remained outside the church—*nulla salus extra ecclesiam*. Likewise, Islam placed the main emphasis upon the Koran as the final revelation of God's will. Adherence to the teachings of the Koran, together with the recognition of Allah as God, and Mohammed as the greatest of prophets, constituted for the Moslems the *sine qua non* of salvation.

The Jews were not quite as emphatic as were the Christians and the Moslems in declaring the rest of mankind ineligible to salvation. Rabbinic teaching was inclined to concede that Gentiles, who were righteous or saintly, had a share in the world to come. [11] The Jewish religion made this concession because, from its point of view, the Gentiles had the opportunity of achieving salvation by conforming to the laws contained in the revelation supposed to have been vouchsafed to Noah. That revelation was the source of the seven Noahidian laws which, with the exception of the one law which prohibited idolatry, dealt with matters of universal moral import. Hence there was room in the Jewish scheme of salvation for those Gentiles who, in addition to abrogating the worship of idols, conformed to the fundamental laws of the moral life.

But other things being equal, the Jews were confident they stood a far greater chance of attaining salvation than the rest of the world. "*All* Israel have a share in the world to come," the Mishnah teaches. [12] They also derived considerable self-assurance from the fact that both Christians and Mohammedans had to admit that originally the Jews were the only people in possession of the means of salvation. [13] For a Jew, therefore, to forfeit that privilege by renouncing Judaism for the sake of worldly advantage, was to exchange life eternal for a temporary good. Accordingly, no earthly temptation could lure the Jew away from Judaism, nor threat compel him to renounce it. No Jew could possibly conceive the validity of the claim advanced by either of the rival groups. Salvation was inconceivable, except as a reward of obedience to the will of God, and where was the will of God set forth so clearly as in the Torah?

Only on the rack of torment was the Jew likely to surrender his religion.

The only way in which the Jew believed it was possible for him to achieve salvation was by remaining loyal to his people, for it was only by sharing their life in this world that he was certain to share their life in the next world. This belief was the great cohesive force of Jewish life in the past. Jews conceived their salvation in terms both national and individual. The coming of the Messiah meant the advent of a scion of the House of David, who would establish the spiritual hegemony of Israel. The main advantage which that hegemony held out to the Jew was the opportunity to worship God and meditate upon the teachings of the Torah in tranquillity, thereby achieving a share in the world to come.[14] The hope of national restoration and glory imbued the Jew with the courage to withstand the tortures and humiliations to which he was subjected. The reward of a life of obedience to the will of God, as made known through the Torah, was to be meted out in the world to come. That world to come, *olam ha-ba*, meant to those whose outlook had been formed entirely by rabbinic lore, the creation of a new world-order, a new heaven and a new earth, in which death would be abolished. To the few who had come under the influence of the philosophers, it meant the immortality of the soul freed of its bodily vesture and transfigured through its union with God. Thus was the Jew in olden times animated by the twofold hope: the hope of national restoration and individual salvation. This is borne out by the prayer recited after each meal, "May the All-merciful make us worthy of the days of the Messiah and of the life of the world to come."[15] And the Jew well knew that the only way he could prove worthy was by casting his lot with his people and doing his utmost to obey the laws which God had revealed to them.

We are so far removed from the world-outlook and thought-habits of pre-enlightenment days that, with the best of intentions to know and understand the past, we find it hard not to read into it our own ideas. We are habituated to the modern emphasis upon improvement of life in this world as the only aim worthy of our endeavors. We take for granted that, if we do our best here, we can afford to let the hereafter take care of itself. So much a part of our thinking has this modern conception of human life become that we can scarcely conceive that not so long ago the center of gravity of human existence for Jews, Christians and Mohammedans alike, lay not in this world, but in the world to come. They differed considerably as to what a human being must do in the here and now to deserve a share in that world to come; but they all agreed that this world was a mere prelude to the hereafter. Judaism may have emphasized more than did Christianity the opportunities for worthy action presented by the life in this present world; nevertheless, even in Judaism, the worth and significance of those opportunities consisted chiefly in their being a preparation for the hereafter.

The term "other-worldliness" has a twofold connotation; hence the ambiguity to which it gives rise. It denotes both the goal of human striving and the method of attaining that goal. In the latter sense, it is synonymous with asceticism or abstinence. Christianity quite uniformly stressed asceticism as the surest way of achieving bliss in the hereafter. Judaism, on the other hand, may be said to have deprecated asceticism as a method of living in this world. It rather stressed the importance of utilizing the opportunities afforded by this life as a means of achieving salvation or life in the hereafter. But that in no way detracts from the consistency with which Judaism in the past upheld other-worldly salvation as the true goal of human life.

To prove that for traditional Judaism the center of gravity of human existence lay not in this life but in the hereafter is both as simple and as difficult as proving that to the ancients the earth was the center of the universe. The entire rabbinic literature is based on an other-worldly orientation. Moses Hayyim Luzzatto (1707-1747), who wrote the ethical code *Mesillat Yesharim* in the spirit of rabbinic Judaism, opens the first chapter, which is entitled "Of Man's Duty in the World," with the following:

It is fundamentally necessary both for saintliness and for the perfect worship of God to realize clearly what constitutes man's duty in this world, and what goal is worthy of his endeavors throughout all the days of his life. Our Sages have taught that man was created only to find delight in the Lord, and to bask in the radiance of His Presence. But the real place for such happiness is the world to come, which has been created for that very purpose. The present world is only a path to that goal. 'This world,' said our Sages, 'is like a vestibule before the world to come.' Therefore, has God, blessed be His name, given us the *miswot*. For this world is the

only place where the *miṣwot* can be observed. Man is put here in order
to earn with the means at his command the place that has been prepared
for him in the world to come.

The foregoing was not the esoteric doctrine of isolated mystics
but a truism with the rank and file of Jewry. The autobiography of
Glückel von Hameln reveals exactly the same attitude. Even in
Jewish folk songs and lullabies which may be heard in our own
day there is frequent allusion to the hereafter as the goal of life.
One need only come in contact with the survivals of traditional
Jewish life, which have not been influenced by occidental ideas, to be
convinced that, in the past, Judaism was decidedly regarded as a
means to the salvation of the soul in the world to come. Even
Mendelssohn, apostle of the enlightenment though he was, could
not altogether escape the momentum of tradition, as is evident from
the following statement in his *Jerusalem*:

It is essential that man should be constantly reminded that with death
there is not a complete end of him; on the contrary, an interminable
futurity awaits him, to which his earthly life is only a preparation; the
same as all through Nature every present is a preparation for the future.
The rabbins liken this life to a lobby, in which we are to fit ourselves in
the manner in which we wish to appear in the inner-room. Then take
heed you no longer put this life as the opposite of futurity, and lead men
to think that their true welfare in this world is not all one with their
eternal welfare in the next.[16]

Since all Jews had but one conception of salvation and regulated
their conduct in accordance with that conception, the life they led
was bound to be conspicuously uniform in content and mode of self-
expression. Although they did not lack the variety of dispositions
and opinions that naturally springs from differences in character, in
abilities and in station, their way of life, their interests and aspirations which resulted from their status as a people apart, were fundamentally the same. Philosophic dissent or social ambition never
impelled the Jew to break away from his people, for the salvation
he regarded as worthwhile could be achieved only by participating
in its life. Thus did the belief in other-worldliness sustain the
solidarity of the Jewish people.

The very same belief in the other-worldly salvation which acted
as a cohesive influence on the Jews, was used by the peoples among

whom they lived as a reason for excluding the Jews from all the rights and privileges accorded only to believers. So long as the doctrine of salvation as a privilege limited to believers was accepted by the generality of mankind, only those who professed Christianity could be eligible to civic status. For how could those who were doomed to perish and who, therefore, belonged to a lower order of creation, be treated on a par with those who were destined for life eternal? They were not merely excluded from civic and social intercourse; they were treated as an inferior species of humans. Dissenters were everywhere regarded as *deterioris conditionis*.[17] It took the genius of a Shakespeare to discover that a Jew was as human as a Christian.[18]

As a result of the generally accepted notions with regard to other-worldly salvation, the Jew needed his people not only to achieve life eternal but also to be able to live in this world. The Gentile populations treated him at all times as an alien, and often as an outlaw. If they allowed him to live among them, it was only because they needed him for such uses as money-lending, itinerant trading, or, at best, tax farming—occupations which only served to render the Jew even more odious. There was no ground where Jew and Gentile could meet on a footing of equality.

The Jew, however, was amply compensated for the hostility and contempt he encountered in the outer world by the sympathy, understanding and help he found in his own Jewish world. It was from his fellow-Jews that he received all that made life worthwhile and that crowned his life with a share in the world to come. A well-known poem by Heine depicts what the Sabbath did for the Jew who, during the week, went about peddling his wares among the Gentiles, and who returned for the Sabbath to his home in the ghetto.[19] It was the Sabbath, the holy day which God had given to his people and in which the uncircumcised had no portion,[20] that performed the miracle of transforming the Jew from a dog into a prince. This transformation came about through his contact with his people and participation in their life. It was thus that he received a foretaste of the salvation [21] for which he prayed on the Sabbath. "May the All-merciful let us inherit the day which shall be wholly a Sabbath and rest in the life everlasting." [22] No wonder, then, that whatever he may have thought of the individual fellow-

Jews of his acquaintance, the Jewish people as a whole was to him not an abstract or invisible entity which demanded loyalty and gave little or nothing in return, but a living nation which conferred upon him a privileged status in the order of creation, believed in him, and assured him bliss eternal. The Torah was to him the *lettres patentes* which bestowed nobility upon his people, and, therefore, upon him. "Blessed be Thou, O Lord our God, King of the universe," the Jew would recite every time he was called up to the reading of the Torah, "who hast given us the Law of truth, and hast planted everlasting life [salvation] in our midst." [23]

The revolutionary philosophies of men like Locke and the Deists in England, and of Rousseau, Voltaire and the Encyclopædists in France, gave rise to the modern conception of religion as based upon human experience and reason. Lessing's drama, *Nathan the Wise,* published in 1779, in which he made use of Boccaccio's *The Three Rings,* may be said to mark the turning point in the western world's conception of salvation. Though by no means denying that objectively there can be only one true religion, the parable implies that all men who seek to live in accordance with the will of God are eligible for salvation. This meant the final undermining of the assumption that salvation was the exclusive privilege of any one particular group of believers. Simultaneously, Mendelssohn taught that the prerequisite to immortality was not conformity with any supernaturally revealed teaching, but a life based upon the highest dictates of reason. This is the main thesis of his *Jerusalem.* The eternal truths which are essential to human salvation, he argues, must necessarily be accessible to all human beings, for it would be contrary to the goodness of God for him to reveal only to a portion of mankind such truth as is indispensable to all men. [24]

The denial of the traditional assumptions with regard to the nature and means of salvation paved the way for what is generally termed "the enlightenment," which identified man's salvation with his self-realization in this world. The effect of the enlightenment was to do away with the theory that one had to be qualified for life eternal to be eligible for citizenship in the state. Church and state began to drift apart. The Christian, who no longer took literally or seriously the doctrine of exclusive salvation taught by the church, saw no reason why he should treat the Jew as an inferior being. It was thus inevitable for the Jew to be granted political and civic rights. As a consequence of his emancipation, new and manifold opportunities for the utilization of his long-suppressed energies and talents were opened to him, and he has availed himself of these opportunities with all the avidity of a starved man.

But the more the abilities of the Jew find a field for expression in his new milieu, the less does he need the Jewish community and its spiritual heritage. The average Jew has come to feel that his immediate interests lie far less with the rest of Jewry than with whatever group, political, economic or cultural, enables him to achieve the salvation which is of this world. To most Jews, salvation has come to mean self-expression in industrial, commercial, artistic or social endeavor. Their attachment to any group other than the nation of which they are citizens is therefore conditioned by the opportunity it offers for self-expression and creative effort. The traditional scheme of salvation has become meaningless particularly to the large body of the wage-earning class. If they are socially minded, they look for salvation to some program of social reform or upheaval. For the most part, however, they are too much absorbed in the problem of earning a livelihood and in securing themselves against sickness and old age to be worried about anything but their own immediate future.

Had the Jews been accorded not merely political but also social and economic equality, they would long ago have disappeared as a distinct group. The universal breakdown of traditional religion among the Gentiles would have facilitated the process of complete assimilation. But the prospect of the Jew's attaining social and economic equality is a very remote one. They experience all the tortures of Sisyphus. Brought to the point where they see the chance of bettering their condition, of attaining social standing and a relative degree of economic security, they are told these things are not for them. For the Jew, the primary need of earning a livelihood is beset with humiliating obstacles.

The fact that being a Jew is coming to mean more and more of a hindrance in the effort to find gainful employment is an indication of a very ominous trend to crowd the Jew from the economic framework of society. In the Middle Ages the Jew had no civic rights, and was therefore at a disadvantage economically; but then the economic order in general was still inchoate. As an itinerant people, the Jews were able to fill a gap in the processes of exchange, and so managed to eke out a place for themselves in the interstices, as it were, of the economic order. In addition, there was in those days no uniform policy toward aliens. If the Jews were driven from one country, they could usually find refuge in another. Today all this is changed—for the worst. Nominally the Jews have been admitted into the political framework of the Gentile world, but economically in many parts of the world they are as badly off as in the Middle Ages, in other parts worse, and in no country on a footing of security. With the growing scarcity of economic opportunities, due to the substitution of machinery for manual labor, to the gradual elimination of foreign markets, and to competition in the domestic market, and with the resulting formation of all kinds of collectives for the sake of mutual help in the struggle for a share in the diminishing number of opportunities, the Jew is in danger of being deprived of all opportunity to earn a livelihood.

In addition, the Jew is snubbed socially. Whether he tries to send his child to a private school, to rent a better class apartment, to register at a country hotel, or to join a club or a fraternity, he is given to understand that he is not wanted. This hurts him to the quick. He has grown far more sensitive to social discrimination than was his ancestor to brutal persecution. In the past, the Jew submitted resignedly to the indignities inflicted on him by Christian potentates and mobs. He accepted such treatment as part of what a conquered people must expect from its conquerors. But mentally and spiritually he was lord in his own demesne. Living in a world altogether his own, he was immune to the demoralizing influence of hate and derision. The loss of human rights and privileges could not in the least lower the Jew's self-respect. Ostracism from the social life of the Gentiles found its compensations in the assurance that in the hereafter his would be the privileged rank. Solomon Maimon, in his autobiography, recalls that as a child he was dazzled by the sight of a princess Radziwill. His father, noticing this, remarked, "Little fool, in the other world the *duksel* will kindle the *persure* [stove] for us." [25]

But now that the aura of divine election has departed from his people, and his Jewish origin brings with it nothing but economic handicaps and social inferiority, the Jew rebels against his fate. This is the fundamental reason for the change in his attitude toward Judaism. It is not merely that Judaism as a world-outlook or system of life is in danger of extinction, but that the Jew is maladjusted morally and spiritually as a result of losing the traditional conception of salvation. He has to evolve some new purpose in life as a Jew, a purpose that will direct his energies into such lines of creativity as will bring him spiritual redemption. That purpose will have to constitute his salvation. It is only then that he will gladly identify himself with Jewish life.

Before we can attempt to formulate any such purpose, there are a number of considerations to be taken into account. First, we have to familiarize ourselves with the specific nature of the present-day challenge to Judaism. The passing of the belief in other-worldly salvation is both the effect and the cause of the changes which have taken place in the ideological, the economic and the political order of mankind. A survey of these changes will help us realize the true character of the predicament in which Judaism finds itself. Second, this will be followed by a survey of the reserve energy and the still functioning resources which we shall have to fall back upon in our efforts to bring order out of the chaos of Jewish life. Such efforts have been made during the last century. Why have they not proved successful? We must answer this question before proceeding to formulate that conception of Judaism which, we believe, will enable Jewish life to evolve as satisfying a substitute for the traditional conception of salvation as is possible in an age like ours.

PART ONE

THE FACTORS IN THE CRISIS

A. The Factors of Disintegration
B. The Factors of Conservation
C. The Decisive Factor

A. THE FACTORS OF DISINTEGRATION

CHAPTER II

THE MODERN POLITICAL ORDER

The place of the Jew in the modern political order undefined—The principles of the modern political order—The conflict between these principles and some of the traditional Jewish conceptions—The conflict between the principles of the modern state and traditional Jewish practice.

THE change which has taken place in the status of the Jew within the last century and a half, from that of alien to that of citizen, has given rise to a host of problems for the solution of which the past offers no precedent. The occasional efforts which Jews made at various times to attain the status of equality with their non-Jewish neighbors, belong to a political set-up which was radically different from the one which has obtained in the world since the American Revolution. The rights of Roman citizenship, for example, which the Jews enjoyed in Alexandria, did not imply their incorporation into the body-politic of the non-Jews, and was perfectly compatible with their considering Alexandria "a foreign city." The theory upon which political entities in ancient and in pre-emancipation days were organized, was essentially that of corporate rights. Not the individual human being as such was the ultimate political unit, but the "corporation," or legally recognized unit, like the guild, township or feudal order to which he belonged. It is for that reason that citizenship in a modern nation carries with it political implications which could not possibly have been foreseen, much less provided for, by those who molded Jewish life in the past. Hence the uncertainties and timidities which beset the task of defining the relation of the Jews to the other elements of the population.

Throughout the Middle Ages, the Jews as a group were reckoned with as a nation, and each local Jewry as a fragment of that nation. Neither tolerance nor persecution had any effect on the conception of their place in the political framework of human society.

The very fact of their being Jews meant that they constituted a culturally autonomous group. It was generally taken for granted that the only way they could live as Jews was by being permitted to foster entirely all such institutions as are usually associated with national life. Whatever government was in power did not deal with the Jews individually, but through those who represented them as a group.

Now, however, any such intimate connection between Judaism and complete cultural autonomy is precluded by the prevalent forms of civic life. Every modern nation expects all its citizens to identify themselves completely with it, to accept its cultural values and to further its social aims and ideals.[1] Is it possible to square this expectation with at least some measure of communal autonomy which the Jews must possess if they are to retain their Jewish individuality? Assuming that it is possible, what constitutes the right measure of autonomy? These questions have never been thought out in detail.

Among the first to plead the cause of Jewish emancipation was Christian Wilhelm Dohm,[2] the Prussian councillor of state and contemporary of Mendelssohn. His arguments indicate that he advocated the granting of the rights of citizenship to the Jews from a purely humanitarian point of view. He went so far as to state that the Jews were entitled to group rights and to the exercise of communal authority. Those who called the modern state into being found themselves constrained by the logic of their position to grant the Jew freedom from all civic and political disabilities. They proceeded from the assumption that the state must be established upon the principle of human equality, and that ancestry and religion should not constitute either a privilege or a handicap. By the same token that Protestants were eligible for emancipation in France and Catholics in England, Jews were eligible in both countries. When the National Assembly of France in 1789 included among the Rights of Man the freedom of worship, Comte de Mirabeau and Abbé Gregoire were conspicuous among those who urged that similar freedom be extended to the Jews.[3] Yet neither the statesmen who fought most vigorously for the emancipation, nor the Jews who hailed it as the promised millennium, were fully aware of all that was involved in this change of status.[5] When, as in Holland, the issues centering about the emancipation were more sharply defined, many of the leading statesmen were opposed to its being granted, and many of the Jewish communal leaders were loath to accept it, even if it were granted.* It was then that the question was raised, whether the Jews constituted a nation or a religious sect.

But although the question was clearly articulated, the terms used in it were by no means fully understood. What is a religious sect, and wherein does it differ from a nation or an ethnic group? Is a religious sect merely a group of people who profess the same religious beliefs? Must not such a group necessarily act as a unit also for other than specifically religious purposes? Can a religious community get along without some kind of social organization? These considerations were beyond the scope of the political thinking of that day, because men had not yet learned that "differences in religion were differences in life itself, and life is organized in community." At times, in fact, liberal statesmen forgot that they had expected the Jews to give up their nationhood, and fell back into the habit of referring to them as a nation. "I wish your nation may be admitted to all the privileges of citizens in every country of the world," wrote John Adams in a letter to Mordecai M. Noah, dated July 31, 1818. Nor was Mordecai M. Noah apprehensive that his Americanism might be impugned by his attempt to found a Jewish colony for the purpose of training Jews to settle ultimately in Palestine.

It will be a long time before the functions of the political and of the religious group in relation to each other will be clearly defined. No such demarcation is, in fact, possible until we understand more clearly the nature of religion and its place in human life. It has fallen to the lot of the Jew to ascertain precisely the respective functions of the state and the church, because he is more seriously affected in his spiritual life by the maladjustment of those functions than any other citizen of the state.

In the modern political order of western Europe and America, the formative spirit which is gradually welding together the various elements of the population into a political unit has been rightly designated "democratic nationalism." The outstanding principles of democratic nationalism are the following:

1. The unit of government should be a geographic group, and not a racial, historical or religious group.

2. The sovereignty of a geographic group should be vested in all adults who constitute that group.

3. The interests of the geographic group as a whole should take precedence over the interests of any other group within or without the geographic group.

4. The welfare of the geographic group demands unrestricted economic and social intercourse among its constituents.

Pertinent to the present inquiry is the fact that the political equality of all citizens in the modern state hinges upon the principle that the individual citizen should not permit the interest of any outside group to influence his political action. Otherwise he would be likely to treat the interests of his geographic group as subordinate to those of some other group with which he may be affiliated. That the welfare of the geographic group demands unrestricted intercourse among its constituents follows necessarily from the principle that the interests of the geographic group as a whole should take precedence over those of any group within or without the geographic group. Only by insisting upon such precedence can a nation achieve unhampered social and economic intercourse among its citizens. The far-reaching implications of these principles of democratic nationalism seem to have escaped the minds of those who have engineered the contemporary political order. This explains why the relation of the state to the religious life of its citizens abounds in so many anomalous situations and unsolved problems.

Let us see to what extent, if any, citizenship in a modern state necessitates modification in the traditional Jewish beliefs and institutions. Apparently, neither the principle that the unit of government should be a geographic group, nor the principle that the sovereignty of the group should be vested in all its adults, presents any point of conflict with the traditional mode of Jewish life and thought. Is that true, however, of the two other principles of democratic nationalism, the subordination of all group interests to those of the state, and the freedom of intercourse among its citizens unhindered by barriers of any other loyalty? If what has hitherto been regarded as the Jewish conception of God be taken from a purely formal standpoint, there is nothing in any of the constituent elements of democratic nationalism, including the last two mentioned, that comes into conflict with it. This is implied in the refusal of the modern state to commit itself to any specific conception of God, or to any supernatural scheme of salvation. Had the state demanded adherence to Christianity, citizenship in it would be incompatible with any conception of God other than the Christian. Such a demand, however, is unthinkable in the modern state. Nothing, therefore, in the principle of organization which underlies the modern state in any way interferes with the conception of God as promulgated by traditional Judaism.

But traditional Judaism does not stop with the conception of God. It includes a definite evaluation of the Jewish people, and a number of specific practices which have grown out of that evaluation. Do the principles, that the interests of the geographic group have to take precedence over those of all other groups, and that the welfare of the geographic group demands unrestricted economic and social intercourse among its constituents, present any point of conflict with the traditional evaluation of the Jewish people? They apparently do, since it is impossible to comply with them without colliding with the traditional doctrine that the Jews are God's chosen people.[7] If one's people is God's chosen, then its interests must surely take precedence over those of any secular nation. This conclusion is accepted in every encyclical of the Pope, which touches upon the relation of the church to the state. For the Catholics, the church is the "chosen people."

The Jews, however, have found it necessary to retreat from the stand taken by them in the past with regard to their being God's chosen people. They realize intuitively that, if they were to persist in the literal acceptance of that doctrine, they would have to exclude themselves from complete self-identification with the state. For, according to the literal interpretation of that doctrine, it is the destiny of the *entire* Jewish people to be restored to Palestine. The traditional liturgy reads: "O bring us in peace from the four corners of the earth." To argue that the fulfillment of such a destiny does not belong to the natural order of events, and must therefore be left out of the reckoning in any practical consideration of political problems, is to betray an attitude of cynicism. The traditional evaluation of the Jewish people is bound up with the attachment to Palestine as the most sacred country in all the world, whither the Jew must strive to return. For there alone can he experience the presence of God. The attitude toward Palestine, which was characteristic of Judaism before the emancipation, led to the assertion that any other country in which the Jew lives is not good enough to be a means to his highest spiritual attainment. Were the Jew to believe this seriously, he would have to consider himself an alien everywhere in the diaspora. This he once did, but nothing in the world will induce him to do so any longer.

What has actually happened is that all Jews who have come in contact with modern life have tacitly adopted some kind of metaphorical rendering of the doctrine that they are God's chosen people. Thus as a result of the new conception of the state, a highly important traditional evaluation of the Jewish people has undergone a radical change. But because the change has taken place tacitly rather than explicitly, it has escaped observation. This is why so many Jews make the mistake of believing that, as far as the emancipation itself is concerned, traditional Judaism might have remained intact.

The altered conception of the Jewish people is bound to have as one of its practical consequences the weakening of Jewish solidarity. Competition between the Jewish people and the state for the Jew's active participation in public undertakings is inevitable. Since the Jewish people no longer has for the Jew the transcendent significance it had for his forebears, what besides a rapidly weakening sentimental attachment is there to hold him to it? Will he not seek to avail himself of the opportunities for leadership in the many walks of life which take him far from Jewish associations and interests? On the other hand, what opportunity does affiliation with the Jewish people give the average Jew to feel that he is an efficient cause, that he counts for something in the world, that he is one of a social unit which is making history? What sense of augmented power does he experience as a member of the Jewish people? Thus are the Jews bereft of capable leadership. Without such leaders a people cannot long survive.

Yet this danger is negligible compared to the one which lurks in the principle of democratic nationalism, that the welfare of the geographic group demands unrestricted economic and social intercourse among its constituents. This implies that the Jew as a citizen of a modern state should not countenance the separatist tendencies which inhere in traditional Judaism. He should not encourage any activity, educational or social, that is likely to act as a barrier to free social and economic intercourse. Carried out to its logical conclusion, this should lead to the removal of the interdict against intermarriage.

Among themselves, however, it would seem that Jews ought to feel perfectly free to live their traditional mode of life. There is apparently nothing in the modern political order as such that should come into conflict with the regimen of conduct prescribed by the Torah. This, indeed, accounts for the illusion that citizenship in the modern state is compatible, at least in theory, with as comprehensive and intensive a Jewish life as was possible in the past. "If renunciation of our Law," said Mendelssohn, "were the sole condition upon which we might enter the European State as fellow-citizens and real equals, we should have to decline." We forget, however, that at the basis of the traditional mode of Jewish life is the assumption that the Torah, whence are derived the laws by which that life is regulated, is of supernatural origin. That assumption is no mere rhetorical flourish. It was intended to lead to practical consequences, the most important of which was that its precepts and ordinances were meant for all time and must be observed at all costs. When the least of them is at stake, one should rather suffer martyrdom than disobey.[8]

In the past, when Jews enjoyed a goodly measure of communal autonomy, the Torah functioned not only in its ritual precepts but to an even greater degree in its civil ordinances as interpreted and expounded by the Sages. On the basis, however, of the fourth principle of democratic nationalism, no group within a nation, except its regularly constituted political subdivisions, such as the "states" in America, has a right to maintain its own civil system. This has meant the abolition of the Jewish *bet din,* and the abrogation of that part of the Torah which played a vital part in bringing under control the social relationships and the economic interests of the Jew. The only way in which the Torah can make itself perceptibly felt in the life of the Jew nowadays is by his observance of its ritual precepts.

The fact that in ritual precepts the God-consciousness plays a more important rôle than in civil laws contributes to the illusion that the Torah can occupy just as important a place in the life of the Jew as it did formerly. So long as the civil code of the Torah functioned in Jewish life, the Jews took that code for granted and hardly realized how indispensable it was to their spiritual life. The ancient interdict against resorting for legal redress to non-Jewish courts is perhaps the only evidence of conscious recognition, in the past, of the significance of the civil war. *But the elimination of the civil code from Jewish life has, in fact, administered as severe a blow to Judaism as the destruction of the Jewish commonwealth.* The abrogation of the Jewish civil law has destroyed the *raison d'être* of Jewish communal organization, except for purposes of charity, and has transformed the function of the rabbi from that of spiritual leader, who was in touch with the economic life of the people and thereby was in a position to influence it ethically, to that of lecturer and orator.

The least that the Jew might expect from the improvement in his political status should be the unhampered right to give his child a Jewish training. Yet it is by reason of that very improvement that he finds himself most hampered in the exercise of the right to bring up his child as a Jew. He finds himself under the necessity of giving priority and predominance in the education of his child to the cultural interests of the country of which he is a citizen. To obey this necessity is not merely part of practical wisdom but of his duty to the state. For it is only by having its citizens acquire a common cultural consciousness that a modern state can hope to achieve any degree of integration and solidarity. In the meantime, however, the Jewish education of the child assumes a position of secondary importance, and is continually in need of adjusting itself to the insistent priority of the educational agencies of the state. How rapidly Jewish education under the stress of democratic nationalism falls, with the majority of Jews, from a position of secondary to a position of no importance is evidenced by the small percentage of Jewish children in this country who are receiving a Jewish training, and by the inadequacy of the time given to Jewish subject matter, even by those who acquire what usually passes for a Jewish training.

Such, in outline, is the effect of the political realities upon Judaism in its present environment.

CHAPTER III

THE MODERN ECONOMIC ORDER

Interest in Judaism displaced by the industrial revolution—Traditional values undermined by the new economic order—The high cost of living a Jewish life—Interest in the Jewish people eclipsed by class struggle—The middle class also hampered in living a Jewish life.

THE economic realities of our day are even more of a challenge to Judaism than the political.[1] The whole spiritual life of mankind has been upset by the machine and the technological economy. Contemporary literature in any country of western civilization is one long witness to the possession of men's minds by the problem of what to do with spiritual values shattered by the impact of the machine. If the industrialization of society has had this effect upon peoples and cultures that have remained rooted in their native soils, it is not hard to imagine the effect of that process upon a people and culture that have had no soil since ancient times, and have of late even been compelled to migrate from lands where they had found a temporary asylum.

Historians have generally overlooked the case of the Jews as an item in what is commonly designated the "industrial revolution." Yet the Jews might well have served as a classic example of how the economic reorganization that goes by that name has revolutionized human life. The industrial revolution, being a phenomenon of urban life, has affected the Jews more completely and more suddenly than any other people, for the Jews have been almost exclusively city-dwellers. Over seventy percent of the Jews in the United States live in the ten largest cities.[2] No stratum of the Jewish population has at any time escaped the effects of the process. A medieval economy might survive the industrial revolution in out-of-the-way places in the Old World, but it could never survive in those centers where Jewish communities were established, not, at least, after the ghetto walls were broken down. The Jew had no

28

chance to adapt his Judaism to the new order. As soon as he emerged from the ghetto, he was forced to live on the plane of development established by the modern economic system. As artisan and petty trader, the Jew needed little capital and knew no economic problem other than that of getting enough work. The change from this status to that of manufacturer, merchant, white-collar slave and worker, took place almost overnight. As manufacturer and merchant, the Jew now had to adapt himself to the intricacies and treacheries of the credit system. He had to learn to defend himself against competition, and to adjust himself to a vast complex of commercial relationships whose very vocabulary was until then unknown to him. As a white-collar employee he was caught in precisely the same system, with the added disadvantage that his freedom of economic movement was seriously curtailed, and his independence as a human being much lessened. As a worker he was faced with the constant threat of extortion and exploitation, and had to wage a long battle for the right to forge his only weapon of defence; namely, cooperation with his fellow-workers.[*]

The most obvious hindrances to living a Jewish life under the present economic order are those which are due to preoccupation and strain. There is no time for Judaism, and there are no energies left for it. The worker's preoccupation does not only attack it in the physical sense of taking up the time that he might devote to Judaism, but also involves the active substitution of non-Jewish or un-Jewish interests for Jewish interests. Thus the economic life requires Jews to cooperate with non-Jews to an immeasurably larger extent than was formerly the case, and in the course of this cooperation the Jews inevitably assimilate the customs and manners of non-Jews. The holidays are striking examples of this. Christmas and Easter have acquired an important industrial significance in recent times, and the industries affected are largely those—the personal-articles industries—in which Jews are heavily involved. The Christmas and Easter holidays have, accordingly, come to be far more important occasions in the lives of many Jews than their own holidays. Although the observance of the Jewish Sabbath and festivals has been rendered difficult or impossible by economic necessity, under normal conditions one would not expect to find them actually supplanted by non-Jewish festivals. Yet that phenomenon is in the present-day environment a striking and obvious one. It does not matter that Jews do not, on the whole, observe Christmas and Easter; it is significant that such occasions have come to be among the most important in their year.

But of even larger consequence than the fact of preoccupation and strain is the fact that the whole mental outlook of modern Jews has been radically altered by the new economic order. It is a truism that the increase of capital sets men to seek new uses for it. As a consequence, the large and small capitalists of modern times, and the Jews among them, have come to see their lives wholly in terms of economic enterprise. The life of a contemporary society may be described in terms of the struggle either for economic necessities or for economic power. Accumulation becomes a good in itself, and the struggle to accumulate increasingly gives men the sense of satisfaction and fulfillment that they formerly found in other ways of life. The few Jewish institutions, like the synagogue, that are still active, are sustained exclusively by men engaged in this acquisitive process; namely, the middle-class capitalists and the professionals. But even among these the struggle for economic power is the primary concern of their lives, and all Jewish spiritual interests are totally neglected. Thus, among the more favored members of society, economic interests have eclipsed all others, and have in large measure become ends in themselves.

The change is even more striking in the case of the workers. Industrialism has called into being a large class of wage-earners whose livelihood is less secure than was that of the artisan of former days. But since industrialism has also made economic opportunity more accessible to the wage-earner than it was to the petty trader or artisan of former days, the wage-earner is no longer content with the assumption that his status at the bottom of society is part of the divine plan. The wage-earner no longer takes his economic subordination for granted. He is engaged in the endeavor to create new social machinery, like unions and protective laws, to offset the power which the few, through their ownership of machinery, are able to exercise over him. The improvement of life in this world becomes an urgent necessity and a genuine possibility. Men's minds are thus sharply diverted from supernatural and other-worldly conceptions of salvation, and they begin to look to the improvement of their life in this world as the sole means of their salvation.

Along with the salvation taught by the traditional religions, the workers reject also the superficial consolations offered by such religions. For the industrial system, which has made life both freer and more precarious for the worker, has also created recreational facilities which are much better adapted to satisfy the tired senses of harassed wage-earners than is most religious ceremonial. This is not to say, as "prosperity" preachers sometimes say, that the new comforts and amusements of industrialism amply compensate for the cruelties it otherwise visits upon the worker. The point is that the new forms of recreation made available by industrialism, and the new comforts, have been sufficient to divert the minds of the workers from the more contemplative exercise of religious practices and from the rather attenuated comforts of religious life. These new comforts and amusements have created a demand for more of the same kind. Thus, the non-Jewish worker does not flock in large masses to his church on Sunday. For the same reason, among others, it is doubtful whether even the five-day week would bring the Jewish worker to the synagogue for the kind of stimulation, or boredom, it now offers him.

An important aspect of the change in the mental makeup of men brought about by industrialism is the notion, dear to the laborers and sometimes developed into elaborate philosophies of history, that religion has been employed by the exploiting class as a means of holding its victims under control. When ideals are identified by traditional religion with remote unrealities, it is but natural that such ideals should come to be regarded by the working classes as little more than a means of diverting the minds of the disinherited from their true interests. So that not only has economic necessity made men indifferent to religion, but economic philosophy, coined into catch-phrases like "economic determinism," has made men hostile to religion. This is why the economic factors of our time have contributed, perhaps more than any other, to the undermining of traditional Judaism.[4]

At the present time, those who hold to the traditions or have achieved some reinterpretation of them, belong almost wholly to the middle class. Since the mass of industrial workers are preoccupied with measures of self-protection against the forces of capitalism, the only ones who have been able to turn their thoughts to the perpetuation of Jewish life are those who have escaped from the more relentless phases of the economic struggle. This is the worst calamity that can befall any social or spiritual heritage. No way of life or world-outlook can long survive the stigma of being a class affair.

The maintenance of Jewish life today involves a duplication of cost which only the more favorably situated can afford. The Jews are taxed like other members of the community for the civic institutions and, if they would maintain Jewish life, they must in addition support a system of schools, synagogues and centers that are a considerable economic burden. Obviously the workers cannot support such additional burdens, and Jewish institutions, therefore, become clubs for the middle classes. The Jewish community once did feel the responsibility of maintaining Jewish institutions for all classes of its society, and did so in a manner which was as free from the taint of charity as is the maintenance of a public school system by the state. This sense of responsibility has evidently disappeared from Jewish life. The worker takes his revenge upon Judaism by looking elsewhere for the cultural satisfactions he needs, and which, incidentally, industrial society has enabled him to find.

One might suppose that even if workers cannot afford, or do not desire, to be interested in Judaism either as a way of life or as a world-outlook, they would in some way reckon with the fact that they are aware of themselves as Jews. They are still bound to their fellow-Jews by what has been termed "consciousness of kind," a consciousness in their case traceable to a common national ancestry. But with the Jewish workers, as with all other wage-earners, class-consciousness takes precedence over national or community con-sciousness.[5] They look to their labor organizations, or to the Social-ist movement, to improve their lot. Suspicious of nationhood in any form at all, why should they countenance it when, in addition, it lays claim to transcendental and supernatural sanctions, as traditional Judaism does for Jewish nationhood?

In keeping with this antagonism to the national aspirations of the Jewish people, the wage-earning classes among the Jews have for the most part taken little or no interest in the effort to upbuild Palestine and in the Hebraic renascence. The extreme form of the effect of the modern economic development upon the Jew's attitude toward his traditional religion is to be seen in the ruthlessness with which the Jewish Communists of Russia disown and persecute those Jews who try to express their attachment to their fellow-Jews in terms of religious or national endeavor. Such expression is treated as counter-revolutionary, and considered as being on the same plane with anti-Semitism on the part of the non-Jew. It thus appears that the majority of Jewish workers are either indifferent or antipathetic to Jewish religion and Jewish collective endeavor.

Of the middle-class Jews, a goodly number still adhere to the traditional emphasis upon religion, and to the traditional conception of Israel's unique place in the world. One might therefore suppose that Judaism is safe with them, free as they are from the more bitter aspects of the economic struggle. But further examination shows that the disintegrating influence of economic conditions extends decidedly into the ranks of the middle class. Primarily in this case, the object of attack is the system of ritual observances. In considering the political factor we had occasion to note that the modern state does not interfere with the ceremonial or ritual element of Judaism. But even this last defence has to give way before the economic factors in contemporary life. Those who might otherwise have observed the ritual practices are forced to abandon them, one by one, as they enter the economic world, because they prove to be a handicap in the struggle against non-Jewish competitors. Even when circumstances become more favorable, the practices are rarely resumed. Very few would find it possible to compete with the non-Jewish neighbors, if they were to observe the Jewish Sabbath and festivals. With the breaking down of these institutions, the home loses its Jewish character and ceases to be a source of Jewish influence. For a while the habit of observing the dietary laws hangs on in the home, but as the other distinctively Jewish habits and practices disappear, this too soon succumbs.

The middle-class family itself, which was once the mainstay of

Jewish life and which, unlike the non-Jewish family with its practice of hereditary crafts, was not sustained by economic interests, has suffered serious attack from the multiplication of opportunities and the increasing diversity of social relationships incident to industrialization. It no longer possesses authority, even if its circumstances inclined or permitted it to hold its sons and daughters to Judaism as a matter of course. Ritual Judaism, which ought to have its best chances for perpetuation in the family, is today at its weakest in the majority of Jewish families.

Accordingly, the factors involved in the economic attack upon Judaism are the following: 1. the preoccupation and strain that the economic struggle signifies, 2. the change of recreational interests and comforts brought about by industrialism, rendering traditional "spiritual" satisfactions insubstantial and inadequate, 3. the supremacy of economic values which have an immediate relationship to human needs in a complex and swift modern world. We have seen that these factors affect, in greater or lesser degree, both the workers and the middle class.

So much for the economic attack upon Judaism. What has Judaism done to meet this attack? What has Judaism done to correct the supreme disadvantage in which it finds itself before the realities of the modern economic situation? We find that Judaism has, up to the present, done practically nothing, and that as a result it has only confirmed its disadvantage. Neither Jewish life nor Jewish law has responded to the situation, so that Judaism seems to have reconciled itself to the fact that it becomes increasingly hard to be a Jew. By Jewish life we mean the communal organization which would concern itself with the economic welfare of the Jewish masses and which would take up the cudgels for social justice. By Jewish law we mean Jewish ethical standards for the regulation of economic relationships among Jews, and a system of jurisprudence which, though not backed by police power, would have the sanction of Jewish life, and would be effective to settle difficulties when they arise. When neither Jewish life nor Jewish law comes to the assistance of the laborer in his difficulties, both become irrelevant to him.

The difficulties of the middle-class Jew are not so acute, but those who look beneath the surface will find that not even he is content with the relationship of Judaism to his economic life. He does not find anything in Judaism with which he has to reckon in his economic life, and he has come to feel the lack. From the bitterness of the Jewish workers toward the institutions of Judaism, and from the increasing negligence which characterizes the attitude of middle-class Jews toward Judaism, we may infer that Judaism no longer occupies its erstwhile place in their lives.

CHAPTER IV

THE MODERN IDEOLOGY

Modern ideology defined—The conflict between science and traditional religion—The traditional view of revelation no longer tenable—The effect of the humanist approach—The traditional conception of the history and significance of the Jewish people challenged—The authority of the Torah questioned—The Torah's system of laws obsolescent.

THE impact of modernism has shaken the Jew's faith in his spiritual heritage. To realize the full force of that impact, it is necessary to note especially the distinctive elements in the modern ideology which have been chiefly responsible for the radical change in the spiritual outlook of the Jew. Once the structure of traditional Jewish values has been weakened through the loss of so fundamental a principle as the belief in other-worldly salvation, it is shaken violently by every advance in modern thought. Whether we mean to fortify or to reconstruct Jewish life, we must know definitely with what aspects of the modern ideology we shall have to reckon.

For the sake of clearness in the analysis, we should disengage from the complex of modern thought the three tendencies which, despite the great diversity of beliefs, opinions and theories on every conceivable subject, stand out as essentially those which distinguish modernism from medievalism.

1. *The tendency to adopt the scientific approach as the most reliable method of ascertaining the truth concerning all matters of human interest.* That approach involves recourse to direct observation of facts and careful weighing of testimony put forward in behalf of every assumption or statement of belief. The function of modern education is not to indoctrinate the mind and accustom it to defer to authority, as was the practice of traditional education, but to train the mind to think for itself, and to form opinions on the basis of sufficient evidence.

2. *The tendency to set up human welfare in a socialized sense as the criterion of the good.* Formerly whatever tradition declared

to be the revealed will of God constituted the criterion of what was good for man. We may designate the change as one from theocentrism to humanism.

3. *The tendency to regard esthetic experience and creativity as essential to the life of the spirit.* Instead of being viewed as incidental and even neligible, esthetic enjoyment and self-expression have risen in the scale of spiritual values to the position of ultimates.

The foregoing tendencies represent fundamental attitudes and habits of mind. This does not imply that all who are brought up in a modern environment necessarily acquire these habits of mind; it indicates the direction in which modern thought is moving. The majority of mankind, to be sure, are not inclined to think for themselves, and prefer to follow blindly those whom they consider as leaders. It still remains true that the so-called unthinking masses exercise a decisive influence upon the intellectual tendencies of the day, insofar as they determine the type of intellectual leaders who shall do the thinking for them. The important fact is that nowadays the choice has fallen upon those whose mental career is shaped by the assumptions which underlie the modern ideology. Thus far, very few Jews who have achieved distinction in the world of science, social philosophy or art, have been able to do so as adherents of traditional Judaism. Therein lies the chief element of challenge in the modern ideology.

The medieval mind, like the modern, also professed adherence to the ideal of the true, the good and the beautiful. From that we might infer that the problem of intellectual adjustment has already been lived through by Judaism, or that it has been successfully ignored. But the resemblance is only on the surface. The main question is what kind of ideas and activities are to be identified with these categories. The fact is that the modern standards of what is true, good or beautiful clash far more violently with the traditional Jewish values than did the medieval standards. The intellectual challenge today is thus quite without precedent, and Judaism has no experience wherewith to meet it.

The challenge that is implied in the modern ideology to the traditional conception of God should not be confused with the so-called conflict between religion and science. Strictly speaking, there can be no conflict between religion and science as such. The function of science is merely to study the sequences of phenomena, and so to report and classify those sequences that we might be in a position to foretell them. The moment science generalizes about the meaning of those sequences and tries to interpret them in relation to existence as a whole, it is no longer science but philosophy. Science thus never gets anywhere within reach of the question of the objective existence of God, and therefore cannot come into conflict with it.

Philosophy which derives from science can and does deal with reality as a whole. It has not always seen eye to eye with religion, especially of the traditional type, but in its greatest representatives it has seldom failed to arrive at some conception of God. Whether it was Plato or Aristotle in ancient times, or Spinoza or Kant in modern times, a conception of God was central to the interpretation of reality. Hence, whatever philosophical inferences we may care to draw from modern science may be reconciled not only with the conception of God in general, but even with the actual account given in the Bible of the way he made himself known to Israel. To the Jews, this type of harmonization is not new. The worst that philosophy could do to the conception of God in general, and even to the specific affirmations made in the sacred writings, has proved harmless.

Modern science pushes back, so to speak, the roof and walls of the universe, and reduces man to an infinitesimal atom. Yet it cannot make man less at home in the universe than philosophy had done with its affirmation of an absolute, perfect and unknowable God. It cannot make greater inroads into the traditional view which conceived God as exercising individual providence, and revealing his will by means of a created voice, or mediatorial agency, than did the Aristotelian philosophy into the faith which Maimonides had in the traditional account of revelation. All the facts that the science of nature may adduce as to the incorrectness of the account of creation, and the impossibility of the miracles, would, of themselves, never embarrass anyone who is determined to uphold the traditional conception of God. All that he would have to do would be to resort to the method of allegorization employed by Philo, or of harmonization employed by Maimonides, to overcome the contradictions between the science of nature and the teachings of tradition.

We often fail to grasp the seriousness of the menace to the Jewish heritage involved in the modern ideology because we use the term "traditional conception of God" loosely. If we use it in the sense of the belief in the existence of a supreme being as defined by the most advanced Jewish thinkers in the past, there is nothing in that belief which cannot be made compatible with views held by many a modern thinker of note. But if by the term "traditional conception of God" we mean the specific facts recorded in the Bible about the way God revealed himself and intervened in the affairs of men, then tradition and the modern ideology are irreconcilable.

The chief opposition to the traditional conception of God in that sense arises not from the scientific approach to the study of nature in general, or even man in general. It arises from the objective study of history. The natural sciences like physics and chemistry cannot disprove the possibility of miracles, though they may assert their improbability. But the objective study of history has established the fact that the records of miracles are unreliable, and that the stories about them are merely the product of the popular imagination. The traditional conception of God is challenged by history, anthropology and psychology; these prove that beliefs similar to those found in the Bible about God arise among all peoples at a certain stage of mental and social development, and pass through a process of evolution which is entirely conditioned by the development of the other elements in their civilization.

There can be no question that the study of comparative religion undermines the traditional belief that the Jews have been from the very beginning of their history in possession of the only true conception of God. The history of the idea of God shows that all races have been groping toward the light, some making a little more headway than the rest, but that all are very far from having attained it. It furthermore proves that the tendency to interpret certain experiences as theophany, or the self-revelation of some deity, and as the communication of his will, is current among all peoples at a certain stage of intellectual development. From the standpoint of comparative religion, therefore, the conception of God, which was the basis of traditional Jewish life and in which the fact of his self-revelation is pivotal, must be regarded as the interpretation given to natural occurrences by men of limited experience and knowledge, and not as a reliable record of supernatural events.

If the fact of supernatural revelation is challenged by what we accept as historical evidence, the logic of supernatural revelation is challenged by our sense of values. That logic clashes with the second essential of the modern ideology, that human welfare be the sole criterion and determinant of what is good. To accept revelation of God's will through supernatural experience as a fact means that whatever is thus commanded must be obeyed implicitly, and that we have no right to determine, on the basis of a criterion such as social utility, what is more important or what is less important. It is only when a conflict of duties arises that we are forced to choose; but judged *seriatim* one law is as obligatory and may entail as serious consequences as any other.. This logic is carried out with unwavering consistency in rabbinic Judaism.

Some attempts were made during the Middle Ages to evaluate the *miswot* in terms of human welfare, but they were neither thorough-going nor consistent. In any event, it is only when another source of truth and authority is recognized; namely, reason, that considerations of human welfare as a justification for certain duties are tacitly introduced into the scheme of Jewish law.

Neither does the traditional idea of God square with the present-day emphasis upon man as the standard of values. According to the traditional idea, man exists for the purpose of glorifying God. Man's *summum bonum* consists in being worthy of communion with God. The psychological effect of such a conception of man's destiny is to make religious worship or communion with God an end in itself, to the neglect, very often, of the rights of one's fellow-men.

In keeping with this emphasis upon the theocentric conception of life, the traditional view of God makes God's will the determinant of what is right. A thing is right and good because God wills it. Metaphysically it may be possible to equate this teaching with the one that God wills only that which is right and good. But historically, the traditional idea that whatever God wills is right has deprived the human being of initiative in the determination of what is right, and left him entirely at the mercy of tradition. Modern humanism rejects as socially injurious any such determinant of the right.

The belief that the cultivation of esthetic values is essential to the life of the spirit, has made decided inroads into the values based upon the traditional conception of God. The antithesis to the importance of esthetic values is the belief in other-worldliness, for that belief declares the fulfillments of this world to be vanity. Analyzing the nature of art, A. N. Whitehead maintains that "it exhibits for consciousness a finite fragment of human effort achieving its own perfection within its own limits. . . . Art heightens the sense of humanity. It gives an elation of feeling which is supernatural. . . . It requires Art to evoke into consciousness the finite perfections which lie ready for human achievement." [1] Because mankind developed some of its greatest art forms under the stimulus of religion, it was never conscious of satisfying some inner human craving for self-expression and creativity in producing or enjoying those art forms. They were usually dedicated to the gods or demi-gods that men worshipped, and all thought of them as ends in themselves incorporating ultimate human satisfactions was almost sacrilege. All this is altered, now that man is no longer wary of ministering to his own needs entirely in his own name, instead of in the name of some deity or overlord, and the cultivation of beauty has become integral to all civilization.

Modern estheticism, though it has no direct bearing on abstract conceptions of God, has become so enlarged in scope and enriched in content that it offers a far greater variety of opportunities for the satisfaction of the human spirit than the limited range of beliefs and practices identified as traditional Judaism. It seems to render traditional religion superfluous by means of its capacity to engage the entire personality and genius of the most gifted men and women, and to elicit from them creative works that delight and thrill the rest of mankind. One has only to note the effect of the cult of estheticism upon many Jews of artistic talent or temperament. They have become devotees of modern estheticism to an extent which has destroyed in them the capacity to think in social and religious terms. As a reaction from the traditional tendency to restrict all modes of esthetic self-expression to that which was specifically religious, and to exclude the graphic and plastic arts altogether, many of the younger generation of Jews have become veritable "pagans" in their aversion to moral and religious values. The wealth of productivity in the fine arts which the emancipation has released in the Jew is in striking contrast to the conspicuous absence of religious and ethical genius, or even talent displayed by Jews who have come under the influence of western civilization.

The modern ideology comes into conflict not only with the traditional conception of God, but also with the traditional conception of the Jewish people. First, in point of fact. The modernist refuses to accept as historic fact the traditional account of the origin of the Jewish people. Research has brought to light that traditional accounts of Israel's beginnings are nothing but a construct of the popular and uncritical imagination. The biblical version of Israel's ancestry can no longer be treated as history. It is essentially an idealization of the past, unconsciously motivated by the desire to represent the nation as a unity. The ancients considered blood kinship the chief ground for social unity. Whenever they beheld a group of human beings acting collectively and transmitting from generation to generation the obligation to act collectively, they were convinced that it was because those human beings had a common ancestry. In reality, however, the people of Israel began its life as did every other nation. Like them, it originated in a loose collection of tribes. The process of amalgamation went on for a number of centuries, during which a goodly part of the native population of Canaan was absorbed. Certainly such a notion as that advanced by Judah Ha-Levi that Israel is a pure race, which has inherited the special gift of prophecy from Adam,' can be treated as nothing more than a poetic idealization of the Jewish people.

So also the modern ideology treats as unhistorical the various accounts of the theophanies and miraculous events in which the traditionalist finds the main proof of Israel's superiority to the other nations. Those traditions are not regarded as deliberate attempts to misrepresent the truth, but as the product of the popular imagination which brooded for centuries upon the ancient glories of Israel. These stories have, no doubt, a high value as historical material, not so much for the facts which they contain as for what we may learn from them concerning the life and outlook of the age in which they arose. But what we thus learn from them is at considerable variance with the traditional conception of Israel's origin and subsequent experiences. The Jewish traditional doctrine concerning Israel corresponds to the present-day doctrine of Catholicism concerning the church.

Now there are three necessary societies distinct from one another, says Pope Pius XI, and yet harmoniously combined by God, into which a man is born: two, namely, the family and civil society, belong to the natural order; the third, the Church, to the supernatural order. The third society into which man is born when through Baptism he receives the divine life of grace, is the Church; a society of the supernatural order and of unusual extent; a perfect society, because it has in itself all the means required for its own end, which is the eternal salvation of mankind; hence it is supreme in its own domain.[*]

Israel, in traditional Judaism, is likewise accounted as belonging to the supernatural order.

The modern man who is used to thinking in terms of humanity as a whole can no longer reconcile himself to the notion of any people, or body of believers, constituting a type of society which may be described as belonging to a supernatural order. This is essentially what the doctrine of "election" has hitherto implied. As a psychological defense to counteract the humiliation to which the Jewish people was subjected, the doctrine of "election" had its value. As an expression of the sense of spiritual achievement in the past, it had some justification in fact. But nowadays, when only present achievement tends to satisfy the human spirit, the doctrine of Israel's election, in its traditional sense, cannot be expected to make the slightest difference in the behavior or outlook of the Jew. From an ethical standpoint, it is deemed inadvisable, to say the least, to keep alive ideas of race or national superiority, inasmuch as they are known to exercise a divisive influence, generating suspicion and hatred. The harm which results from upholding the doctrine of "election" is not counterbalanced by the good it is supposed to do in inculcating a sense of self-respect. There are so many other ways of developing self-respect—ways that look to the future instead of to the past, to personal accomplishment rather than to collective pride—that there is no need of inviting the undesirable consequences of belief in the superiority of one's people, whichever people that be.

The effect of the present ideology upon the traditional attitude toward the Torah is entirely of a negative character. It deprives the Jew of that ardor for the Torah which marked his life in the past. The scientific habit of mind is not compatible with the view that knowledge of God is based on man's experience of God's supernatural self-revelation. It makes man's knowledge of God identical with man's search for the divine through the medium of human intuition and experience. The historical approach to the study of the Bible starts out with the hypothesis that the Torah, or Pentateuch, cannot be regarded as literally dictated by God. This hypothesis has thrown an entirely new light upon the contradictions, repetitions and diversities of style in the Torah. Instead of having to be explained away, so that the infallibility of the Torah shall not be called into question, they are now taken as pointing to its composite character. The so-called "higher criticism" of the Bible abounds in wild guesses and fanciful reconstructions of text and history, but it has definitely displaced the traditional belief that the Pentateuch, which is the authoritative text of Jewish life, was dictated in its present form by God to Moses.

The modern view that the Torah is the product of a long, historical process implies that its teachings cannot be more than a reflection of the moral and spiritual attainments of its authors. These attainments may have been ethically superior to those of their contemporaries, but they certainly cannot be expected to be set up as standards of belief and action for all times. In fact, a study of the religions and civilizations contemporary with early Israel reveals considerable borrowings, both of narrative content and religious practices, though, to be sure, as with the Greeks who borrowed their art forms from the Egyptians and Phœnicians, the borrowed material is so transformed as hardly to be recognizable. But all of this knowledge concerning Israel's Torah is bound to undermine the belief in the infallibility of its teachings. Studying Torah can no longer mean what it formerly meant to the Jew—reliving the experience of divine revelation. Furthermore, with the desuetude of belief in the supernatural origin of the Torah, the very ground is removed from the entire structure of rabbinic thought, since it is only on the assumption of such origin that rabbinism was justified in drawing numerous inferences from the minutest variations in the text.

When, instead of reckoning with the Jewish regimen of conduct in general, we take into consideration its specific laws and principles for the purpose of testing their applicability today, we find ourselves hampered at every step by conceptions that have long become obsolete. Nothing can be done with the entire system of punishment for ritual transgressions, since no civilized state would treat the violation of a religious practice as a capital offense. In the civil laws of the *Shulḥan Aruk*, the status of woman and the conceptions of property belong to a state of society which has long been outgrown. Worst of all, no provision is contained in the traditional interpretation of the Torah for any abrogation or amendment by any power on earth. The very notion of law which establishes man's relation to God and man's relation to man as fixed and eternal, is repellent to the modern mind, while the tendency to consider the law as made for man and not man as made for the law, becomes more pronounced. Nowadays, it is almost axiomatic that as man's circumstances change and shift, any law that remains fixed works harm rather than good, and a law that does harm to human life cannot be a just law.

These trends of social and intellectual development contribute to the solvent effect which the modern ethical outlook has upon the traditional conception of the Jewish way of life. To that may be added, also, the circumstance that the ritual observances are in theory, as in practice, ranked on a par with the civil laws and ethical principles. Jewish tradition, the preaching of the Prophets notwithstanding, deprecated the tendency to attach more importance to some *miṣwot* than to others. "Be as careful in the performance of a light *miṣwah* as in the performance of a rigorous *miṣwah*, because thou knowest not what the reward of the different *miṣwot* is." [4] Judah Ha-Levi considers the religious practices as the purpose to which the ethical duties are the means. [5] The average layman who adheres to traditionalism finds it difficult, from the Jewish standpoint, to attach as much significance to the ethical as to the ritual *miṣwot*. The latter seem to him to be a truer criterion of Jewishness.

Such evaluation of conduct offends the modern conception of ethical values. Though we cannot deny a certain moral significance to ritual practices, especially if they be given a symbolic interpretation, such duties as speaking the truth, giving honest weights and measures, and treating the stranger kindly, cannot be placed on the same level of importance as the prohibition of sowing mixed seeds or of wearing linen mixed with wool. Social well-being has come to be the highest criterion by which we have learned to appraise any duty.

This, in sum, is the nature of the intellectual challenge which the ideology of the modern world offers to the traditional values of Judaism.

B. THE FACTORS OF CONSERVATION

CHAPTER V

INHERENT FACTORS OF CONSERVATION

The inner momentum evolved by the Jewish past—Tendencies and activities which hold promise of a Jewish future—1. The tendency to aggregation—2. The strong sentiment against intermarriage—3. Jewish communal centers—4. Religious activities—5. Jewish education—6. Philanthropic activities—7. Cultural activities—8. The upbuilding of Palestine—9. Jewish Secular-Nationalist movement—10. Fraternal organizations.

IF Jewish life were completely unresponsive to the various forces that are undermining it, and made no effort to resist them, its end would be within sight. But this is far from being the case. The Jewish people has been unconsciously generating, during the centuries of oppression, new energies and spiritual potencies, and these are now coming into play. The very forces of destruction are overreaching themselves and producing the most unexpected results. Besides, there are many incalculable resources which a living being, individual or collective, has a way of falling back upon in a time of stress. These must now be fully explored and turned to account, if Judaism is to survive.

Although the primary cohesive force which held the Jewish people together—the traditional conception of other-worldly salvation—has practically become inoperative, there has developed in the course of the centuries of living, thinking and suffering together, a *secondary* cohesive force which manifests itself in the will to maintain and perpetuate Jewish life as something desirable in and for itself. It is a law of human nature that, when people are engaged in a common enterprise for any length of time, they develop a mutual attachment which persists, no matter what becomes of the enterprise. The highly intensive unity fostered by the Jews themselves and reenforced by the persecutions they endured during the last twenty centuries, has caused Jewish life to evolve a momentum of its own. So powerful is this momentum with a great many Jews that the

47

motive of earning a share in the world to come no longer seems to be essential to Jewish loyalty. In fact, the majority of Jews seem to have completely forgotten that it was the belief in exclusive eligibility for salvation that formerly held their people together. This momentum has given rise to institutions, undertakings and commitments, and these in turn have augmented the force of the momentum.

The mere fact that within the last century (1830-1930) the population of world-Jewry has increased fivefold, should be sufficient to make one pause before engaging in prophecies as to the ultimate outcome of the present crisis. *The chances of Judaism surviving in America are augmented by the very increase in the Jewish population, irrespective of locality, since the presence of Jews anywhere in the world is likely at one time or another to be an object of consciousness to Jews everywhere else.* But the chief factor upon which we may count for survival of Jewish life in America is of course the large influx of Jews, which has taken place within the last quarter of a century. In 1907 the Jews in America numbered 1,776,885; in 1927, they numbered 4,228,029.[1] Even if we confine ourselves to the consideration of communal endeavor in American Jewry, we become convinced that the will-to-live as Jews is far from succumbing to the forces assailing it. During the decade of 1916-1925, the number of Jewish organizations nation-wide in scope almost doubled. Expenditures for Jewish philanthropy which totalled $1,686,213 in 1916, reached the sum of $11,234,755 in 1925.[2] The will to Jewish life is evolving new means of self-preservation. It is finding expression in a number of movements and institutions which, if permitted to attain clarity of purpose and an understanding of realities, might enable American Jewry to emerge from the present crisis not merely unscathed, but revivified.

Much of the pessimism about American-Jewish life is due to its low visibility. An effective antidote is a survey of the present tendencies and activities which make for the conservation of Jewish life. Some of these tendencies and activities, when itemized, may appear to overlap. Each of them is sufficiently important a contribution to the preservation of Jewish life in this country to deserve emphasis. They may be listed as follows:

1. *The tendency to aggregation.* The majority of the Jews in this country live in a few of the largest cities. In those cities they reside in such close proximity to one another as to render entire neighborhoods distinctively Jewish. This is true not only of the first generation of immigrant Jews, but even of their children. This tendency is not the result of any deliberate purpose or plan. It is due in part to momentum, and in part to concern for the future of Judaism.

Aside from the historic reason that the Jew has been constantly driven off the soil and has been prevented for centuries from owning and cultivating land, writes Mordecai Soltes, additional deterring factors are discussed frankly in the editorial columns of the Yiddish Press. One of the causes of the reluctance of Jewish parents to settle upon the farm has been the lack of adequate educational facilities—both general and Jewish—for the young children in the sparsely populated agricultural sections, as well as the limited opportunities for social intercourse for the young men and women. This lack of spiritual anchorage has prevented those Jews who are anxious to continue Jewish life and who are deeply concerned about the education of their children from carrying into effect their desire to settle upon the land.

It is natural for immigrants to seek out in the new country those with whom they have most in common. Hence, large cities have their little Italys or little Polands. The Jews who have immigrated to this country have had even less in common with the general population, and are likely to experience greater difficulty in being accepted by the community than the non-Jewish immigrants. This accounts for the greater persistence with which Jews keep in close proximity to one another. Jews themselves are not altogether happy about it, and often express themselves as deeply concerned over what they consider the continuation of the Old World ghetto life. But whether the fact that Jews gravitate to the larger cities and to particular neighborhoods in those cities meets, or does not meet, with the approval of those who mold Jewish opinion, the consequences of that fact for the continuation of Judaism cannot be disregarded. The inevitable and frequent contact of Jew with Jew, which comes out of living in the same neighborhood, must lead to the intensification of Jewish life, since it gives rise to institutions and organizations which inevitably reenforce whatever like-mindedness the Jews brought with them.

2. *The sentiment against intermarriage.*[6] Jewish life may be said to owe its conservation chiefly to a deeply ingrained mental and emotional resistance to marriages between Jews and Gentiles. This sentiment, like most of what goes into the complex of Jewish living, is the product of centuries of habituation, and is therefore charged with a high degree of emotionalism. But unlike many other factors that make for the continuance of Jewish life, it is deliberately fostered with the avowed purpose of preventing the Jews from disappearing.[7] It is the one sentiment which may be said to form the common denominator of all Jews who have not definitely made up their minds to break with the Jewish people. Even those who have abandoned all Jewish religious beliefs and observances think twice before they give their sanction to intermarriage. Though not condemned as vehemently as apostasy, intermarriage is regarded as equivalent in a measure to deserting the Jewish people. The fact that the Jews are the immigrant group among whom the resistance to intermarriage is greatest indicates that that sentiment stems from a determined will to survive as Jews.

The last statement, however, must be qualified by what we know of the specific reasons which frequently restrain Jewish young people from marrying Gentiles. What leads them to make the sacrifice is not regard for the future of the Jewish people but loyalty to their family. The fear of rendering their parents unhappy is often the chief deterrent. Such loyalty is a phase of a type of family cohesion and devotion distinctive of the Jewish people. An intense family loyalty is characteristic of persecuted peoples. The family alone affords the refuge to which the individual can resort from the ill-treatment at the hands of a hostile world. The interest which Jewish parents display in the welfare of their children is scarcely equalled by parents of any other group. It is true that family life among Jews shows the effects of migrations and of the industrial revolution, but by no means to the same degree as the family life of other peoples. "The migration of Jews," writes Israel Cohen, "has a distinctive character of its own. . . . Among Jews it is not young or individual or male members of the family who emigrate, but entire families." [8] In the process of adjustment to the American environment, there is a marked tendency on the part of parents and children to accommodate themselves to one another's ways and ideas.[9] The affectional and protective functions have survived the disintegration of the economic, educational and recreational functions in the case of the Jewish family.[10]

Consequently, the majority of the younger generation are likely to yield to the sentiments of their elders, even in so personal a matter as marriage, especially when the sentiment against marriage with non-Jews is so deeply charged with emotion. Thus Jewish group life is bound to continue for a long time, long after its specific values and aims have become rather vague in the minds of the individual men and women identified with it.[11] Some time ago, an inquiry was conducted among fifty prominent Jewish social workers to ascertain their attitude toward problems of intermarriage, which arose in the course of their ministrations. Of the forty-four who replied, thirty-seven maintained that whether intermarriage be or be not desirable from the standpoint of good social work, it is contrary to the policy of the community and to the spirit of Jewish communal work, and therefore should not be encouraged. Only six ventured the opinion that they would be governed in their attitude entirely by the circumstances in each individual case.[12]

3. *Jewish communal centers.* However, if the only obstacle in the way of intermarriage with non-Jews were loyalty to parents, the Jews would disappear in this country in the course of two or three generations. Those in whom the will-to-live as Jews still pulsates vigorously clearly realize the inevitability of this outcome, unless some effective means be forthwith evolved that will check the increase of intermarriage. This is how the Jewish center, or Jewish communal center, a type of institution which is the unique creation of American Jewry in its struggle to survive, has come into being.

Before 1918, the very term "Jewish center" as applied to a local institution was scarcely known in the vocabulary of Jewish life. Since then, Jewish centers have been springing up in every important Jewish community. The survey made in 1927 showed that every one of the eleven communities numbering 50,000 Jews or more possessed such organizations. Of the twelve communities numbering between 20,000 and 50,000, ten had Jewish centers, and of the thirty-three communities numbering 8,000 to 20,000, twenty-three had Jewish centers. Even communities with only 500 Jews have established such institutions. In 1930, the Jewish Welfare Board included 308 constituent organizations which for the most part maintained communal centers. In 1929, twelve new centers were dedicated, and in 1930 eight new centers were in process of construction. These institutions then ministered to a membership of over 300,000. Over $100,000 was being spent on Jewish center publications which not only publicized various activities, but helped to make the center indispensable to Jewish living. All this activity was developed within little more than a decade.

A phenomenon such as this calls for explanation. Some deep-seated emotional spring must have been tapped to have made possible such an expenditure of resources and energy. Was it a stirring religious ideal, or a new enthusiasm for the conservation of Jewish values that has generated this prodigious activity?

The Jewish communal center appears at first sight to be merely a Jewish replica of what is known in America as the institutional church. This might, indeed, be said of the temple houses established by the largest Reformist congregations in this country about a quarter of a century ago. But those institutions cannot be regarded as the forerunners of the Jewish center, since the impulse behind them was mainly philanthropic. The well-to-do members wanted to supply the Jewish poor with facilities for social and intellectual activities. But they would as soon consider making use of those facilities for themselves as they would consider resorting to the home for the aged, which they also supported.

It is likewise erroneous to trace an historical connection between the communal center and the movement to establish Young Men's Hebrew Associations. The first organization which bore the name Y.M.H.A. was founded in 1874 by a group of young men who felt that they would be more at ease socially among their own people than among Gentiles, who generally showed little warmth in their social intercourse with Jews. The purposes of the organization as formulated in that year do not even contain the word "Jewish" or "Hebrew." All that it aimed to do was of a general cultural character, such as establishing reading-rooms, giving lectures on scientific, historical and literary topics, holding debates, and securing employment for members.[11] Not even as late as 1900, when the New York Y.M.H.A. issued a call to a number of similar institutions, do we discern an interest in the furtherance of Jewish life. The purpose of cooperation among them was stated as being "in order that they may be bound together in a great common cause of philanthropy and education throughout the Union such as the various Y.M.C.A.'s are" (sic!)[14] By 1911, a change takes place, and we hear faint sounds of an awakening Jewishness in those institutions.

There seems to be growing sentiment, reported an eye-witness of what was then taking place, in favor of specifically Jewish centers, but in a great number of instances the non-sectarian character is strongly emphasized and the mention of anything Jewish is carefully avoided. A striking exception in this respect presents itself in the Chicago Hebrew Institute, which boldly announced that it is Jewish and American; its purpose is to blend the strong individuality of the Jew with the noble features of the American, to help him become an American Jew.[15]

When in 1913 there was formed the Council of the Y.M.H.A. and Kindred Associations, the purpose announced was "to make of their members better Jews, and therefore better citizens."

The growing emphasis on Jewishness in these social institutions was due entirely to the fact that those who had immigrated from eastern Europe since 1881, or their children, had become sufficiently Americanized by the middle of the first decade in this country to look for something else than Americanization. There awoke in them the desire to reorient themselves as Jews. During the second decade this emphasis was further intensified. In 1917, the New York Y.M.H.A., which set the tone for the other organizations of similar character throughout the country, had its membership cards bear the following motto: "The aim of the 'Y' is to develop among Jewish men Jewish consciousness as a means to the highest type of spiritual life."[16] By 1922, when the Y.M.H.A. and Kindred Associations was absorbed by the Jewish Welfare Board, which had its origin in the large funds provided by the war department during the war years, Jewishness became the keynote of all the speeches and resolutions at all conventions of the Welfare Board workers.[17]

It was about this time that Jewish sentiment had become definitely crystallized in demanding the type of Jewish institution which is deliberately dedicated to the furtherance of Jewish life. Just what it was that caused this Jewish demand for genuinely Jewish centers is nowhere clearly indicated. The truth is that the large body of immigrant Jews had come to sense danger of complete absorption by the dominant majority. There began to be felt the need for something that would forestall the increase of intermarriage with non-Jews. A purpose of this kind does not lend itself to publicity; it therefore does not figure in the literature which sets forth the aims of the communal center. But that purpose becomes apparent to anyone who comes in direct contact with those who are active in the establishment and maintenance of these institutions.

The communal center as it now exists [18] aims to be affirmatively Jewish without committing itself to any specific type of Jewish religion. It strives to unite on an equal plane all types of Jews, Orthodox, Reformist and Conservative, believers and non-believers, Zionists and non-Zionists, the recent immigrant as well as the Americanized Jew. While it seeks to avert all controversies, it does not want to be colorless or coldly neutral in matters of Jewish interest. It tries to minister to all the legitimate social and recreational needs of the Jew, and to call forth and meet his higher cultural needs. It offers the best that can be obtained in education, music, art and literature, and even makes provision for dances, banquets and entertainments. Its avowed aim is to furnish a common meeting ground for all the Jews of the community and maintain those activities which would contribute to their welfare and development and to the strengthening of their Jewish consciousness as a constructive force in American life.[19] This aim renders the Jewish center the most constructive measure recently devised against the menace that faces Jewish life—intermarriage with Gentiles who refuse to accept Judaism.

4. *Religious activities.* In spite of the inroads of secularism, religion not only continues to function among Jews, but is regarded by some as the only justification for the preservation of Jewish life. The effectiveness of religion in maintaining Jewish solidarity can be measured (a) by the extent to which religion is the basis of organization, and (b) by the prevalence of those practices which are performed in its name.

According to the survey published in the American Jewish Year Book (1930) there were in 1927, 3,118 congregations in the United States. Of these, 2,348 had their own buildings, with an equity of more than $100,000,000. The annual expenditure is given as $33,-391,295. Associated with the congregation, as subdivisions of it, are young people's societies, sisterhoods and brotherhoods, whose purpose is to supply the membership more frequent opportunity for social contact than mere worship offers. Yet, if it were not for worship, these auxiliary societies would not have come into being. Out of 912 Jewish youth societies, 401, or nearly forty-four percent, were affiliated with congregations. While the overwhelming majority of these societies are organized chiefly for social purposes, the initial impulse comes from the congregation. Likewise, with the sisterhoods and brotherhoods which conduct activities of a philanthropic and cultural character, the fact that the congregational unit furnishes the personnel and occasion for their functioning justifies us in regarding them as the product of Jewish religious activity.

A further development of organized religious life in American Jewry is the combination of congregations into national organizations for the purpose of fostering religious activities that demand material support on a large scale. The Union of American Hebrew Congregations was organized in 1873, "to maintain the Hebrew Union College, to promote religious instruction, and to encourage the study of the tenets and history of Judaism." The Union of Orthodox Congregations of America was organized in 1898 "to foster the observance of the practices as prescribed by the *Shulhan Aruk*." The United Synagogue of America was organized in 1913 "for the promotion of traditional Judaism in America." Each of these national organizations is engaged in bringing about the formation of congregations of the type already affiliated with it, in the establishment of schools that teach in accordance with its spirit, and in the publication of literature that interprets Jewish religion from the particular point of view officially recognized by it.

Congregational activities could not be carried on without specially qualified functionaries, such as rabbis, teachers and cantors. Formerly, these functionaries received their training abroad, but within the last fifty years the number of institutions engaged in training rabbis and teachers has been on the increase. These functionaries are formed into various associations for the purpose of raising the standards, both material and professional, of their respective callings.

The existence of Jewish religious organizations on so extensive a scale implies the prevalence of religious observances which are fostered by these organizations. As a rule, these religious customs constitute the principal objective of congregational organization. Chief among these is, of course, worship. Those who join congregations, as a rule, subscribe to the hitherto unquestioned assumption that worship must be carried on by people in groups, and in a manner prescribed, or at least largely determined, by tradition. It is not necessary to discuss at this point the function of worship. Suffice it to say that the average person who regards worship, whether frequent or occasional, as a necessary part of his life, usually joins a congregation, and worships by means of formulas of prayer which have the sanction of tradition, or of some authoritative body.

Daily attendance at synagogue services is rare. It is at present confined to a limited number of immigrant Jews and to those who observe in the traditional manner the eleven months of mourning for a deceased parent. Even Sabbath and holiday services are sparsely attended. But *Rosh ha-Shanah* and *Yom Kippur* are still observed by all Jews who have the least religious attachment to Jewish life. The services on those days are far too complicated for the untrained person to follow without guidance, and are, therefore, unsuited for private devotion. Attendance at services on the holidays is so large that the established synagogues cannot accommodate the worshippers, and additional places of worship have to be improvised. The crowded synagogues on High Holidays may be interpreted as an indication that, for those who are identified with Jewish religious life, worship would normally be a frequent mode of Jewish self-expression. It is only because they must yield to the economic necessity of working on the Sabbath and holidays that Jews cannot join in public worship on those days.

The turning points in the life of the individual have always been invested with solemnity, and are signalized by the majority of Jews in religious fashion. Circumcision is still largely practiced. The *bar miṣwah* and confirmation ceremonies are used as means of formally inducting the child into membership in the Jewish faith. Marriages are consecrated by religious rites. Among the orthodox, divorces granted by the state are not valid unless supplemented by a divorce according to Jewish religious law. At funerals, Jewish religion finds expression even among those who are otherwise out of touch with religious life. The rites of mourning, *yahrzeit* and memorial services are observed in one form or another even by those who have only a tenuous attachment to the Jewish religion.[20]

Those who observe the dietary laws—and they no doubt constitute a very substantial minority—render necessary the maintenance of rabbis and supervisors and ritual slaughterers. With the supervision of slaughter houses, butcher shops, restaurants and dairies, and with the preparation of food for Passover diet, millions of dollars are spent to observe the laws of *kashrut*. So important an item is this that it constitutes the principal activity of the many rabbis who have come to this country from abroad, and whose training is confined to the traditional discipline of the east-European *yeshibah*.

A study was made of a large group of orthodox Jewish young people, nearly 1,800 in number, to determine to what extent they still adhered to the traditional customs, ceremonies and beliefs of Jewish life. The results, which were published in 1929, are summed up in the following statement:

> While the young people studied are no longer strictly observant, they have not abandoned any customs because of a desire to escape the Jewish fold. Witness the observance of the fast on *Yom Kippur*, which could very easily be avoided by unwilling people, or observance of the prohibition of leaven on the Passover. . . . The young people feel positively disposed toward and strongly attached to their people. They still keep the large majority of the customs. They plan to join a synagogue, to marry in accordance with the Jewish religious requirement, to perform the proper ceremonies at childbirth and adolescence. Friday evening is a general substitute for the Sabbath. . . . There is no unanimity, even in the most deep-rooted customs, nor is there any indication that there will be no further relaxation of observance. But there is a very significant change of attitude from that of the past decade. Ten years ago a spirit of antagonism to Jewish ceremonial observance was prevalent. Today the active revolt against tradition has evidently subsided. . . . At the present time, the religious organization is in the ascendancy and the anti-religious movement as an organized effort is losing ground.[21]

5. *Jewish education.* Avowedly the major part of Jewish educational endeavor is carried on in the name of religion. We should therefore class this endeavor with those which find expression in

congregational organization. But were we to follow the popular appraisal of Jewish education, we should disregard a very important factor which operates in Jewish life, a factor which must be central to any program which looks to a Jewish future. We see in the process of Jewish education a great deal more than the desire to transmit to the child certain religious habits and beliefs. It is essentially a means of transmitting to the child the entire Jewish heritage, whatever that heritage may be. Before all else, the parent who gives his child a Jewish training wants his child to grow up as a Jew. It is a gross mistake to assume that being a Jew is solely a matter of religion, and that in giving a Jewish training to one's child, one qualifies him for a specific type of religion. These assumptions will have to be corrected. The most casual examination of what the Jewish child is being taught will show that religion proper forms but a very small part of his studies. He learns for the most part language, history, literature and current events. There is no systematic presentation of the idea of God. The only element of instruction that properly belongs to religion is that in prayers and ceremonies. But these, the child acquires from his home environment rather than from the school. We must also take into account a type of Jewish education which is being fostered by a considerable group known as Secular-Nationalist Jews. They conceive Jewish education as entirely non-religious. For these reasons Jewish education should be identified as a distinct item in the list of conserving influences in Jewish life instead of being included among the religious activities.

It is not necessary to touch here upon the inadequacies of Jewish educational endeavor. The important fact is that such endeavor is made, and that it proceeds from a desire to conserve and develop Jewish life. From the standpoint of commitment to Judaism, the short-lived attendance at a Hebrew school, or the mere preparation for the bar miṣwah ceremony, may have a determining influence. A commitment based upon so casual a contact with Jewish knowledge may be a source of spiritual chaos, but we are not at present concerned with the success or failure of Jewish education. The question to be answered is whether or not Jews still feel the urge of bringing up their children as Jews. This is why the fact that within the last quarter of a century there has been a definite falling off in the number of hours per week which Jewish children devote to their Jewish training is not so significant as the recent increases in the number of Jewish schools, and of children attending them.[21] The calculation that seventy-five percent of the Jewish child population attend a Jewish school during some period of their elementary school life is probably correct, though it is also true that only about thirty percent of the child population between seven and fourteen years of age are enrolled at any one time. It is estimated that the annual budget for elementary Jewish education in the United States is $6,000,000.

The tendency to lessen the number of hours of Jewish schooling should not be attributed entirely to a growing indifference to the child's Jewish training. The gradual encroachment upon the child's time and energies by the secular school, and the distraction of interests which increase as the parents attain a larger competence, are the main causes for the reduction of hours at the Jewish school. Efforts are being made to raise the standard of admission to confirmation rites, to introduce methods that will render the studies intrinsically interesting, and to get the state authorities to absolve Jewish pupils from public school attendance one or two hours a week in order that they might attend religious schools.[22]

6. *Philanthropic activities.* The unifying aspect of each of the factors of Jewish life thus far enumerated is liable to be neutralized by some drawback. Segregation is apt to lead to cultural and spiritual inbreeding, and is therefore deprecated by many a Jewish leader who otherwise favors the fostering of Jewish individuality. The ban against marriage with non-Jews is in itself merely negative. Both religion and education certainly intensify Jewish consciousness, but they also exercise a divisive influence, dividing Orthodox from Conservative, and both from the Reformists. Philanthropy, however, seems to furnish a common denominator to all who want to be identified as Jews.

It is not so easy to live down the odium usually associated with "charity," which is often practiced to cover a multitude of social sins. But, if philanthropy can really manage to be a form of service performed in the spirit of social justice, with due regard for the sensibilities of those who are to be helped, it may arouse a sense of communal responsibility in those who practice it. Once a Jew recognizes in a practical form that he is bound by ties of service to other Jews, Jewish life can no longer remain a matter of indifference to him. A distinguished social worker has well described the effect of philanthropy upon Jewish life.

Our charitable work, he says, has been one of the chief factors in maintaining and strengthening the solidarity of the Jewish community. We have no organized church. Each of our synagogues is a separate unit. That which has most bound our people together has been our shoulder-to-shoulder work in the cause of philanthropy. Our repeated charity drives have been our great social events, using 'social' in the best and highest sense of that word. They have developed among us feelings of affection and comaraderie that have been more impelling perhaps than those derived from any other source. The collateral by-products of our fund-gathering efforts, whether they have manifested themselves in drives, or otherwise, have had a stimulating effect on communal endeavor.[11]

The number of Jewish organizations and institutions engaged in philanthropic endeavor and social service, such as agencies for giving relief, providing family welfare, medical care, child care, care of the aged, recreation, rehabilitation of the maladjusted, etc., is on the increase, not to mention the vast sums which have been spent for stricken Jewry in Europe and for Palestinian colonization. As the agencies multiply, there arises the need for a unifying organization such as "federation." These federations begin their career as collecting agencies. In time they enlarge their scope and not only take charge of campaigns and distribution of funds, but also become "a community organization in the broadest sense of that term, engaged in a great constructive community enterprise, aiming especially at the building of Jewish character and self-respect."[14] Federations are growing in number as well as in the complexity of their activities. By 1926, in fifty-eight cities the greater number of Jewish organizations engaged in relief and social work were federated. Their annual budget amounted to $13,537,000.[15] By 1930, out of a total of 168 Jewish communities in the United States, sixty-nine had federations.[16]

It is only natural that as the work of Jewish philanthropy advances, it should become more self-conscious as an integrating factor of Jewish life. As early as 1908, social workers recommended the inclusion of religious and educational activities in federation, and even made a plea for *kashrut* in the various institutions connected with it."' In more recent years the most prominent executives in federation work have visioned far greater possibilities for federation than have as yet been realized."' The mere fact that social service tends to be carried on in a scientific spirit leads to the recognition that the specific Jewish background of the one to be helped must be reckoned with. The trained social service worker will henceforth find that the more affirmative he will be in his attitude toward Jewish life, the more effective will be his activities. Whereas the Jewish social worker formerly took a negative attitude toward things Jewish, he now acquires in the course of his training, and later expresses in practice and theory, a constructive outlook upon Jewish life as a whole. Had the question, "Should community chests supersede Jewish federation?" been asked in former years, the answer would have been in favor of community chests, on the ground that they would forestall the tendency to emphasize Jewish individuality. Now that very reason is advanced for not permitting federation to give way to the community chests."' This does not mean that federations refuse to engage in the philanthropic endeavor of the general community. All that it implies is that, whenever Jewish federations have the opportunity of cooperating with non-Jewish public agencies, they see to it that the Jewishness of the institutions affiliated with them shall not suffer through such cooperation.

The campaign for funds to help east-European Jewry recover from the effects of the war and to adjust itself to the new environment created by the post-war political and social changes have taught the American Jews a practical lesson in Jewish world-solidarity. They have shown that any doubt about the possibility of Jews acting unitedly for a constructive purpose is unwarranted, and have thus prepared the way for the united action which finds expression in the establishment of a Jewish national home in Palestine.

7. *Cultural activities.* There is a tendency in certain quarters to minimize the significance of the part played by cultural interests other than religion in any program looking to a Jewish future. How mistaken that tendency is becomes apparent when we take stock of the non-religious cultural interests.

a. *The Jewish press.*[20] Periodicals published for Jews, and dealing mainly with Jewish interests, appear in three languages, Yiddish, English and Hebrew. In 1925 those published in Yiddish numbered almost 700,000 readers, in English about 150,000 and in Hebrew about 6,000. Although there were no Yiddish periodicals in this country before 1871, their influence in conserving Jewish life must be accounted as the most potent among non-religious cultural factors. One need not agree with Zhitlowsky, who maintains that the Yiddish press has been the most effective means of conserving Jewish life in America, but it is, no doubt, true that it has served in keeping alive the Jewish consciousness of the non-religious, cosmopolitan and radical labor elements among the Jews.

The principal Yiddish dailies are not merely newspapers in the generally accepted sense, but also magazines. Much space is given to signed articles which interpret current events, stories, literary and dramatic criticism, essays on every phase of human life and popular scientific articles. The varied activities of organized Jewish life, Zionist, religious and secular, the problems of labor groups, philanthropic agencies and cultural movements are discussed at great length. Attention is focussed upon prominent Jewish personalities. In all of its features, the Jewish press deals not with local but with world-Jewry. It is thus not only the medium of expression for all the tendencies that integrate and intensify Jewish life, but is itself a powerful instrument for quickening Jewish consciousness by supplying it with a rich and varied content.

The Anglo-Jewish press addresses itself for the most part to that element of Jewry whose vernacular is English. Virtually all of these periodicals are weeklies. The range of their interests is very much more limited than that of the Yiddish press. In spite of their shortcomings, they undoubtedly exercise an influence in keeping alive the Jewish consciousness of their readers. The few monthly and quarterly magazines are of greater value both in range of interest and in quality of writing, but they have a much more limited circulation.

In recent years efforts have been made to utilize the radio for specifically Jewish purposes. The broadcasting of Jewish music, especially on festivals, of religious services, Yiddish lectures and plays, and English lectures of Jewish interest, is coming to be recognized as an important factor in fostering Jewish consciousness.

b. *Literature*. Literature in a more permanent form than that of the press, capable of keeping alive the Jewish consciousness and strengthening Jewish solidarity, is not wanting in American-Jewish life, although it is far from that standard in quality, or quantity of output, which is commensurate with the needs of a minority group seeking to maintain itself against overwhelming odds. As with the press, so with the Jewish literary output; of the three languages used, it is the Yiddish writing which ranks highest in the fields of fiction, poetry, drama and essay writing. America has produced but few literary works in Hebrew. Even in English, there has appeared very little of genuine literary merit that sets forth the experiences and problems of American-Jewish life. Hardly any Jewish literary work in this country reflects the inner life or manners of a generation, or articulates some compelling human need. The chief reason, no doubt, for the lack of such literature is that Jewish life has not yet found itself.

That there is a need for a rich and varied literary food has been sensed even by that section of American Jewry which is quite emphatic in its insistence upon religion as the only differentia of the Jew. With an inconsistency which betrays a will-to-live as Jews in more ways than their creed would seem to indicate, the Jewish Publication Society has set on foot a movement to stimulate production in English of literature of Jewish interest. That society began auspiciously with the publication of a work like Zangwill's *Children of the Ghetto*, but has not continued to elicit original literary works of high merit because it has gradually shifted its aim from that of fostering creative expression to "instructing the Jew in his history, literature and tradition so as to produce a cultured Jewry and a sympathetic public."[31] Nothwithstanding, it would be amiss not to credit the society with actually helping to build up Jewish life in a measure far beyond other agencies of a more conspicuous character. In having published annually a number of volumes containing useful Jewish information, and having made possible the publication of a new authoritative translation of the Bible, the Society has contributed to the fashioning of the American-Jewish consciousness.

An outstanding achievement of American Jews is the publication of the *Jewish Encyclopedia* in twelve volumes. It is the first systematic attempt to collect in encyclopedic form the salient facts and factors of Jewish life in the past and present.

c. *The arts.* With a Jewish milieu in this country still in its formative stage, it is impossible to expect any notable achievements in the fine arts; yet here and there one may descry unmistakable signs of Jewish life seeking an outlet in painting, etching, sculpture, architecture, music and drama. For the present, most of those qualified to produce works of art animated by a Jewish spirit have been nurtured in other than the American-Jewish milieu, but they are also beginning to find patronage and an audience among the Jews of this country. Synagogues are nowadays planned on architectural lines that indicate a desire to develop esthetic individuality. In some of the community centers, an attempt is made to establish Jewish art classes. A few art clubs have already been formed in some of the larger cities, exhibitions have been arranged, and there are already two associations whose purposes are to establish museums for greater cooperation between Jewish artists and their public, and to bring about a better cultural understanding and a more concerted effort to beautify Jewish life. Many Jewish schools realize the importance of creative effort as a means of cultivating in the child an appreciation of that which is unique in Judaism, and are introducing the teaching of Jewish arts and crafts. This spirit is penetrating the home. Pictures on the wall, style of furniture and hangings, are beginning to show evidences of an esthetic grasp of Jewish life.

The stage and dramatic art[9] have played an important rôle in the maintenance of Jewish consciousness. So far, however, they have thrived entirely on the cultural background of the Yiddish-speaking immigrants in this country. With the disappearance of that background, the days of the Jewish theater seem numbered. Yet it has put up a brave fight for existence in the face of the most difficult odds. Realizing that it must compete with the native theater, it seeks to attain a high level of artistry, and hopes to survive through its effort to interpret Jewish life and lore to the rising generation of American Jews. Its sponsors count upon the Jews ultimately coming to regard the theater as an indispensable vehicle of their cultural expression.

A less spectacular, though none the less courageous effort, is being made by those who insist upon fostering Jewish music in American-

Jewish life. In community centers and elsewhere, choral societies have spontaneously arisen for the purpose of rendering programs of Jewish music. Music contests have been staged by some of the larger Jewish organizations. Of late there has been a very decided attempt made in religious circles to have the musical part of the service in the synagogue as Jewish in spirit as in content. Even the idea of having talented Jewish musicians write special liturgical music for the synagogue has already taken root. All this points unmistakably to music as one of the cultural media in which Jewish life in this country is expressing itself.

8. *The upbuilding of Palestine.* The activities which have thus far been enumerated are not new in Jewish life. Religion, education, philanthropy and cultural interests were never lacking. Their continuance might simply mean that American Jewry still lives on the momentum of the past, and is not producing any new means of counteracting the various corroding forces of our environment.

But all doubts as to the emergence of new conserving influences are dispelled when we take into account the growth of interest in the upbuilding of Palestine. The Zionist movement in America arose, for the most part, in response to a spiritual need keenly felt by those who had been reared in orthodox Jewish homes, and to whom Judaism as traditionally lived appeared inadequate and powerless to cope with the challenge of contemporaneous life and belief. Without any clear understanding of what was wrong with traditional Judaism, or how Zionism could set it right, a number of Jewish young men, feeling instinctively that a Jewish Palestine meant a complete renascence of the Jewish spirit, established in 1897 the Zionist Organization of America.

Within twenty years the Zionist movement had made such headway that its leaders were able to assume the functions of the International Zionist Organization which the World War had disrupted.[19] When the War came to an end and the Jews were confronted with the practical task of supplying the resources necessary for the rebuilding of Palestine, the Zionist Organization conducted the *Keren Hayesod* campaigns. During the years 1920-1930, about 100,000 men and women contributed of their means to the various Palestine funds. In spite of the stereotyped propaganda that was carried on in the various campaigns, important ideas and new values undoubtedly found their way into the Jewish consciousness. Thanks to the varied appeals that had to be made to obtain the vast sums needed for the work in Palestine, Zionist propaganda has taught the Jew to think in terms of world-Jewry, to appreciate his spiritual heritage, to become aware of the perils that menace his spiritual existence, and to hope and plan for his people's future. This was accomplished chiefly through the periodical literature which was subsidized by the Zionist Organization.

Of especial significance from an educational standpoint is the extent to which the Zionist movement has reclaimed Jewish womanhood and Jewish youth for an interest not alone in the rebuilding of Palestine, but in all matters Jewish. The Hadassah organization is noted for its success in arousing thousands of American-Jewish women to a sense of responsibility to the Jewish people, no less than for its effective health work in Palestine. Young Judaea, established in 1909, Junior Hadassah, and Avukah, established in 1925, have rendered invaluable service in cultivating in American-Jewish youth a loyalty to the Jewish people and its heritage.

Although the implications of the Zionist movement for American-Jewish life have seldom been made fully articulate, and are hardly grasped by the majority of those who have contributed to the various funds, they have nevertheless colored the various Jewish activities and have given them new purpose and content. If it were not for the fructifying effect of the interest in the upbuilding of Palestine, the work of the communal centers, synagogues, philanthropic and educational institutions might have gone on, but it would have become soulless and spiritless. As evidence of Zionism's power to supply Jewish life with new inspiration and vigor, we might point to the fact that Jews who had become totally alienated from Jewish life have for the first time found themselves spiritually, and are giving the best of their thought and energy to the Palestinian movement.

Even a more convincing proof of the spiritual potency of the movement is that the Reformists who, by virtue of their ideology, have been definitely set against Palestine, are now beginning to abandon that ideology, and are incorporating the upbuilding of Palestine into their program for the Jewish future.[14] At their conference in 1930, they voted to include the song, Ha-Tikwah, in the

Union Hymnal. The majority of the Reformists in this country could not help discerning in the movement to upbuild a Jewish national home in Palestine immense potentialities for the conservation of Judaism.

9. *Jewish Secular-Nationalist Movement.* In discussing the cultural elements of Jewish life which contribute to its conservation, we had occasion to refer to the large number of publications in Yiddish and to the growth of the Yiddish theater. While the larger portion of that cultural activity represents the momentum of the life of east-European Jews before they emigrated to America, a considerable share of that activity is due to the Secular-Nationalist movement, which may be said to have been inaugurated at the conference which took place in Czernowitz in 1908. This is a movement which aims to combat the assimilation of the Jewish people and its culture, and to reconstruct that culture on purely secular lines, with Yiddish as its language and with Socialism as its ideal.

This movement should not be confused with the cultural and educational activities conducted by Yiddish-speaking groups which have no other aim but that of spreading Socialist and Communist propaganda among the Jewish workers. The spirit in which this latter propaganda is conducted is avowedly hostile to the conservation of Jewish life. The Secular-Nationalists synthesize the Jewish struggle for corporate existence with the so-called class struggle. The left Socialist and Communist Jews use Yiddish cultural media to carry on the so-called class struggle. To them, the Jewish national existence is merely a phase of the capitalistic order which they purpose to destroy.

With this distinction in mind, the Jewish Secular-Nationalist movement may be included among the conserving influences in Jewish life. It is headed by a distinguished group of eminent thinkers, journalists, literateurs, playwrights, artists and scientists. It has a definite philosophy of Jewish life, a philosophy that reckons with the ideological, social and political realities of the day. It is reaching out to increasing numbers of the working classes, who would otherwise be rapidly lost to an affirmative Jewish life, and it imbues them with the conscious purpose of remaining Jews by rendering their life as Jews culturally satisfying and creative. In the short period of its existence there have been established a large number of cultural groups dedicated to the furtherance of its aims. The most noteworthy achievement is the translation of the movement into an educational program. At present Secular-Nationalist schools exist wherever there are considerable numbers of recent immigrants. These schools are conducted as supplementary to the public school system, like most of the communal religious schools and those conducted by the congregations.

This is the merest beginning of what the leaders of the movement are planning to do. In 1928 there was established in this country an organization known as the Yiddish Culture Society. It aims to spread the Secular-Nationalist movement among the Jewish masses, to establish schools, libraries and museums, to establish agencies that make for a Yiddish environment, and to foster a fraternal spirit among Yiddishists. This organization stands in active relationship with all other Yiddish organizations in eastern Europe which function in the same spirit. It seeks to cooperate especially with the Yiddish Scientific Institute of Wilna, which is conducting scientific research into the various phases of Jewish life,—social, economic and cultural.[15]

10. *Fraternal organizations.* The most striking illustration of the potency of historic momentum as a conserving influence in Jewish life is the widespread network of Jewish fraternal orders. These fraternal organizations satisfy the need of the Jew for association with his kind, regardless of religious views and affiliations. The very spirit in which the oldest of them, the Independent Order of B'nai B'rith, was conceived shows how Jewish life began to evolve new forms of organization as soon as it found the old religious framework unable to hold together all who wished to live as Jews. The B'nai B'rith was founded in New York in 1843 by a number of German Jews uniting "on a platform upon which all could stand regardless of dogma and ceremonial custom. Political and religious discussions were to be barred forever in order that harmony and peace might be preserved in the deliberations of the Order."[16] Since religion was thus excluded from the activities of the Order, and no other cultural expression of Jewish character was either known or recognized, there were only two other functions which might justify

the existence of the Order, social and philanthropic. A common social life among a group depends upon so many factors which are unstable in character, such as common background or financial status, that the philanthropic outlet was bound to become the more conspicuous one for the activities of the Order. Orphan homes, free employment bureaus, infirmaries and hospitals, homes for the aged, immigrant schools, social service camps, and similar institutions are maintained by the B'nai B'rith. Latterly, when the philanthropic endeavor was found to duplicate the work carried on by local federations, it branched out into new fields with the establishment of the Hillel Foundation whose purpose is to instil a Jewish spirit in Jewish college students.

When new waves of immigration brought large numbers of Jews from eastern Europe, they also found the synagogue unsatisfactory as a medium of Jewish affiliation. They, therefore, formed fraternal organizations very largely modeled after the B'nai B'rith. Soon there emerged the *Landsmanschaften*, in which the common nativity of the members or of their parents constituted the basis of affiliation. Mutual aid in the form of sick and insurance benefits, free loans, and similar activities figure more prominently in these more recent fraternal orders and *Landsmanschaften* than in the B'nai B'rith, though philanthropic undertakings and communal endeavor in behalf of Jews in general are not wanting in their program.

A third class of fraternal organizations are those which are not content with mere "consciousness of kind" as the basis of affiliation, and accept some definite economic or social philosophy instead of a religious creed as their platform. This is the case with organizations like the Jewish National Workers' Alliance, and the Workmen's Circle. The last-named categories of fraternal organizations differ from the two preceding types in being for their members more than a casual outlet for the desire to belong. Based upon a social philosophy which recognizes the economic struggle for existence, these organizations serve their members by voicing their economic needs and protecting them from actual or alleged exploitation. In addition, they provide opportunities for the cultural growth of their members, and for the children of those members a schooling in cultural and social values which they consider essential and which are not obtained in the public schools."

CHAPTER VI

ENVIRONMENTAL FACTORS OF CONSERVATION

1. Anti-Semitism: a new type of Jew-hatred—Anti-Semitism directed at economic integration of the Jew—The Jewish renascence a reaction to anti-Semitism—2. Catholicism—The position of the Catholics in the body politic analogous to that of the Jews —Cultural homogeneity which would crowd out Jewish life prevented by Catholicism.

1. ANTI-SEMITISM

THE forces that make for the conservation of Jewish life are not limited to those which arise from the momentum inherent in the Jewish people. They are to be found also in the environment outside of the Jewish people. The greatest of these is anti-Semitism. This may sound paradoxical, yet it is no more paradoxical than the assertion that the inclemencies of nature which seem bent upon the destruction of man have forced him to develop the very means of his life. Those who are constitutionally frail succumb to the many natural dangers that lurk in the most normal environment. Likewise, Jews who are too remote from Jewish life to see anything in it but a burden, who have never experienced the magnetism of its memories and ideals, or who are physically or morally too weak to endure the struggle for existence, or the severer struggle for comfort and position, find it too difficult to bear the brunt of anti-Semitism. They try to deny or hide their Jewish origin. Many of them, finding themselves driven to the wall, realize that they will save their self-respect by abandoning the attempt to play the Gentile, so they return to Judaism in the hope of finding in it a spiritual haven.

To understand the cause of their return to Judaism, we have to take into account the new type of Jew-hatred which has developed within the last century. There have been many species of Jew-hatred, of which anti-Semitism is the last and most virulent. From the days of Apion down to modern times, the Jew was hated because he insisted upon remaining separate. However, as soon as he gave up his separatism and was willing to share all the interests, purposes and enjoyments of his neighbors, he was accepted by them.

70

The ancient Greeks and Romans resented the separatism of the Jew. They interpreted it as due to pride and a feeling of superiority. The ill will that prevailed against the Jews would, no doubt, have subsided had they mingled freely with their neighbors and participated in their feasts, games and sacrifices. In the Middle Ages, too, if the Jews had accepted the dominant faith, whether Christian or Mohammedan, they would have been accepted by their neighbors on a basis of equality. During the first decades of the emancipation in Austria and Russia, the governments made strenuous efforts to have the Jews surrender their distinctive language, habits and customs in the hope of rendering them eligible for unrestricted amalgamation with the Christian population. They even invited Jewish scholars to help them in the process of dejudaizing the Jews. Christian liberal thinkers and scholars continually urged the Jews to remove the last obstacle to their complete fusion with the general population—their religion.[1] Anti-Semitism, on the other hand, resents nothing so much in the Jew as his striving to become like the Gentile. It may forgive the Jew who makes no pretense at being anything else than a Jew,[2] though it has no compunctions whatever about destroying him. But its bitterest denunciations fall upon the heads of those Jews who have succeeded in eliminating from their lives the last vestige of whatever is distinctively Jewish.

The old form of Jew-hatred was associated with the assumption that it was within the power of the Jew to redeem himself and become a worthy member of society; he needed only to repudiate that which made him different from his neighbors. It was taken for granted that he could easily divest himself of the traits, customs and beliefs that made him a Jew. The very intensity of the ill will against him was due to what his neighbors considered as sheer stubbornness on his part in refusing to perform the rite, or say the word that might have freed him of his Jewishness. Anti-Semitism[3] takes an entirely different attitude toward the Jew. It regards him as irredeemable. His origin has condemned him to an inferiority which no effort on his part can possibly alter. The slogan of modern anti-Semitism is *"Was der Jude glaubt ist einerlei, in der Rasse liegt die Schweinerei."* He should be prevented, warns anti-Semitism, from becoming outwardly like the Gentile, otherwise he is certain to break into Gentile society and taint it with the poison of his inferior social and spiritual qualities. He should be quarantined, otherwise he is sure to corrupt the politics, the religion, the commerce, the press, and the arts of the country. Since, however, he refuses to be quarantined, there is only one remedy, extermination.

This volte-face *of Jew-hatred, from persecution of the Jew because he refused to be like his neighbor to persecution of him because he insists upon being like his neighbor, is due entirely to the new political and civic status granted him by the emancipation, and to his desire to avail himself of that status.*' As long as Jews had to remain aliens because political and civic rights were accorded only to those who professed the religion of the state, the prejudice against them was principally psychological. They were excluded from the craft guilds and the marts so that they did not have the chance to offer serious competition to the general population. Those among them who succeeded in amassing considerable wealth through money-lending performed a much needed service, since Christians were not permitted by the law of the church to lend money on interest. Kings, nobles and potentates of the church found Jewish money-lenders helpful in financing their political schemes and afforded them a measure of protection against the violence of the mobs. Undoubtedly, the hope of plunder or the desire to be exempted from payment moved both rulers and mob to pogromize the Jews. Nevertheless, had the Jews given the slightest indication of accepting the dominant faith—which was the only way they could become identified with the majority—they would not have been molested.

When, with the granting of civic and political rights, Jews entered into competition for economic goods and services with their non-Jewish neighbors, the prejudice against them took on the form of that hatred which the interloper or the poacher provokes. That prejudice is no longer "the dislike of the unlike." It is the dislike of the uninvited stranger who makes himself at home, of the one who, without any warrant, asserts his claim upon a share of the necessities and luxuries of life on an equal footing with his masters and superiors, and by dint of cleverness succeeds in getting more than what they think he has a right to.

Anti-Semitism owes its existence mainly to the circumstance that the Jew insists upon taking the emancipation seriously and assuming that he has a right to avail himself of every opportunity for economic and social advancement that inheres in the life of his country, equally with all other citizens. In the expositions of anti-Semitism featured in the German newspapers after the Nazi régime had begun to declass the Jews, Wilhelm Stapel, an anti-Semite of the intellectual type, maintained that "where the Jew disregards and transgresses the boundaries that separate him from the non-Jews— that is the point at which anti-Semitism comes into being."[5]

To make sure that their bid for opportunity will, so to say, be considered, some Jews make every possible effort to delete all traces of differences between themselves and their Gentile competitors. But there is the rub. By eliminating every trace of Jewishness from their lives, they are in a position to compete with the Gentile on a plane of equality. In the mind of the anti-Semite this renders the assimilated Jew, the Jew who changes his name, denies his origin, and wants to push his way into Gentile society, a menace to the rest of the population. In a survey entitled, *Jewish Handicaps in the Employment Market*, based on a careful study of the facts, the writer comes to the conclusion that "dislike [of Jews in America] springs from too rapid an adaptation of the Jewish immigrant and his children to American life."[6]

In the struggle in which human beings engage for economic opportunity, all available means are used to eliminate as many rivals as possible. The principal reason advanced in the process of elimination is that the rival, not having enough in common with the majority of those who are entered in the competition, is an interloper. Formerly, a difference in religion was sufficient to exclude anyone from the right of competing as an equal. With the increase of religious divisions to such an extent that insistence upon conformity is no longer practicable, and with religion in general in a state of eclipse among large numbers of people, excuses based on other than religious grounds are utilized to keep out possible competitors.[7]

National and race divisions now supply the main stock arguments against those whose goods and services are to be kept out of the market. Pseudo-scientific racial theories have been elaborated, the dangers of contamination of racial stock by lower human breeds have been luridly depicted, and the protection of national welfare and prosperity against the incursions of "foreigners" who, it is alleged, can never be thoroughly and completely assimilated is being preached as the foremost patriotic duty of the citizen.

The Jew of the Consensus, says Oswald Spengler, follows the history of the present (which is nothing but that of the Faustian Civilization spread over continents and oceans) with the fundamental feelings of Magian mankind, even when he himself is firmly convinced of the Western character of his thought. . . . The word 'international,' whether it be coupled with socialism, pacifism or capitalism, can excite him to enthusiasm, but what he hears in that word is the *essence of his landless and boundless Consensus.* . . . Even when the force of the Consensus in him is broken and the life of his host-people exercises an outward attraction upon him to the point of an induced patriotism, yet the party that he supports is always that of which the aims are most nearly comparable with the Magian essence. . . . If there is inward relationship, a man affirms even where he destroys; if inward alienness, his effect is negative even where his desire is to be constructive.[8]

In an atmosphere such as this, it is to be expected that the Jews would present a shining mark for attack. In his play *Loyalties,* in which anti-Semitism figures as the cause of inner conflict in some of the characters, John Galsworthy gets at the heart of the matter when he attributes anti-Semitism in the Gentile girl to group loyalty and in the Gentile grocer to economic envy. "I know lots of Jews, and I rather like little Ferdie," says the girl. "But when it comes to the point—they all stick together; why shouldn't we? It's in the blood. . . . Prejudices—or are they loyalties—I don't know—crisscross—we all cut each other's throats from the best of motives."

The English grocer of the lower middle class puts it thus: "To tell you the truth I don't like—well not to put too fine a point on it—'ebrews. They work harder, they're more sober, they're honest, and they're everywhere. I've nothing against them—but the fact is—they get on so."

Anti-Semitism in America has not that self-consciousness and systematic pursuit of its aims which it has attained in Germany, the motherland of modern Jew-hatred. But there can be no doubt that it is growing in extent and intensity. This is due to the process of urbanization which is going on apace in this country. As the young people who were brought up on the farms crowd into the cities, the competition for the available economic opportunities is bound to become keener. "Who are these Jews that their presence should retard the absorption of the rural population?" is the question which then occurs to the mind of the non-Jew. Thus begins the silent boycott which is crowding out Jews not only from the economic but also from the cultural life of the country.

Anyone who is familiar with economic realities is aware that nothing can be more shortsighted than the assumption that the interests of the majority are best served by depriving the minority of economic equality. When the minority is industrious and given to a high standard of living, the less it is restricted in its economic development the greater the benefit which ultimately accrues to the majority. But very few are inclined to go to the trouble of exposing the economic fallacy of anti-Semitism. So long as that fallacy prevails, it will neutralize the various efforts on the part of well-meaning Christians to bring about good will between Jews and Christians. Those efforts proceed from the assumption that the prejudice against Jews is due to wrong notions about the religion or the character of the Jew. To be sure, all kinds of prejudices are exploited to the utmost in the boycott that is waged against the Jew. The goodwill work may help somewhat toward exposing many of the lies and slanders against the Jew that still form part of the Christian psychology, but the underlying cause of economic and social discrimination will continue to operate.

It is because Jew-hatred has taken in our day the new direction of preventing the Jew from becoming Gentilized that it has focussed its attack chiefly against the one thing in the Jew which he cannot possibly alter, namely, his ancestry. Bent upon frustrating the efforts of the Jews to hide their identity, the anti-Semite displays an uncanny sense for detecting the least trace of Jewishness in one of Jewish descent. He notes the nervous interest anyone who is of Jewish descent takes in his ancestral people, however little he may have to do with its life and religion. He observes in him a secret preference for Jewish associations, for pride in Jewish achievements, and a sensitiveness to discrimination against Jews. Such symptoms are enough to prove to the mind of the anti-Semite that the remotest descendant of Jews always keeps in touch and conspires with members of the Jewish people to advance its fortune and prestige at the expense of the Gentile population. It is this mania for persecuting the assimilated Jew to the tenth generation that has made a failure of Jewish assimilation.

The inevitable consequence of being confronted by an enemy who will give no quarter is to put up a much braver fight for existence than when confronted by one who proposes terms of surrender. As the Jews begin to realize that anti-Semitism will be satisfied with nothing less than their extermination, they exhibit qualities of heroism which they have never shown before. Modern anti-Semitism has, no doubt, served as the chief stimulus to the renascence of the Jewish spirit, which is evident in the movement to establish a Jewish national home, in the renewal of the Hebrew language and literature, and in the herculean efforts to reconstruct the shattered Jewish communities. These manifestations of renascence generate new values and meanings for the whole complex of activities and institutions which are for the most part being maintained by the momentum of the past. Jews gifted with creative powers, who had abandoned their people, are returning like prodigal sons, and devote at least a portion of their gifts to the replenishment of Israel's spiritual resources.

It is altogether beside the point to disparage the present-day Jewish renascence on the ground that it is largely the reaction to anti-Semitism. All growth and development result from the struggle with a hostile environment. Whatever differentiates man from the subhuman—intelligence, memory, self-consciousness—owes its existence to forces that threatened his destruction. The mind functions most intensely when it has to extricate itself from intolerable conditions. When the Jew displays a more concentrated social energy and a finer spirituality as a defense against the dangers of demoralization to which anti-Semitism exposes him, no one will hold it against him that he makes a virtue of necessity and is impelled to rise to new heights of spiritual achievement because of the threat of annihilation.

2. CATHOLICISM

A second environmental factor which indirectly yet effectively makes for the conservation of Jewish life in America is the presence in the body politic of a large and powerful group that insists upon remaining unassimilable. The Catholics constitute a minority of the American people, but a minority too large, too well organized and too safely intrenched to have any apprehension about succumbing to attrition by the majority.

To understand how the presence of this large group in the body politic affects the future of the Jewish people in America, it is necessary to recall that the tendency of national democracy to break down group distinctions is a challenge to Jewish life. Against this tendency the various national groups like the Irish, Germans, Italians hold out for a short time, but within a generation or two they are absorbed in the rest of the population.

Certain Jewish writers have included the Jews in a plea for the conservation of national minority groups.* They seem to overlook the fact that the Jewish group varies fundamentally from the minority groups in regard to the inherent forces which help to conserve it and in regard to its relationship to its parent people. The other minority groups lack the interdict against intermarriage; they are bound, therefore, to be absorbed by the rest of the population within a generation or two. Furthermore, in case of war, the parent peoples of the other minority groups may at any time become the enemies of America. Potentially, therefore, they are always subject to a conflict of loyalties. No such contingency can arise between the parent people of the Jews and the American nation. Even the potentiality of a conflict of loyalties is wanting in the case of the Jewish group.

If we want to find in any other group a situation more nearly parallel to that of the Jews, we have to look to the Catholics. The Catholics have, of course, an incomparably stronger bond of unity which is re-enforced by all the prestige, authority and skill in organization and education characteristic of the church of Rome. They still operate with a powerfully cohesive force, a force whose decline in Jewish life has created the present problem of Judaism. The belief in other-worldly salvation and in its availability exclusively to adherents of the church, functions just as vigorously among the Catholics today as before the Protestant revolt. Notwithstanding, there are latent cohesive energies in Jewish life which make up for the lack of homogeneity and for the absence of that authority which is wielded by the Catholic church.

The presence of so powerful a minority as the Catholics in the body of the American people has its repercussion upon Jewish life. Their homogeneity and habits of obedience to their ecclesiastical superiors arouse apprehensions in the minds of the Protestants that they might get control of the political institutions. These apprehensions help to keep the Protestants more militant than they would otherwise be. Thanks to this militancy, as well as to the power and influence of American Catholicism, American civilization is long destined to remain aggressively Christian, despite the efforts of certain modernists to evolve an American civilization that shall be non-Christian. The Catholics do not hesitate, both in theory, and to a large extent also in practice, to place the interests of the church above all other interests in life, including those of the country.[10] They feel no need for apology in taking this attitude, because they maintain that the church is the indispensable means to spiritual salvation and to the attainment of life in the world to come. Since the church only is a means to life in the hereafter, no worldly agency, institution or government is to be considered on a par with it. The Catholics, therefore, do not consider it prejudicial to the welfare of the state to give priority to the interests of the church. Proceeding from that premise, they have no scruples about establishing parochial school systems in which loyalty to the church is taught as the highest duty in life. But whatever the justification be, the parochial schooling, the interdict against intermarriage, and the teachings, both direct and indirect, with regard to disbelievers, cannot but have the effect of placing obstacles in the way of free social and economic intercourse between Catholics and non-Catholics, thus countering the trend toward homogeneity which is the goal of democratic nationalism.

It is difficult to surmise how America will ever achieve unhindered social and economic intercourse among all the elements of its population—which after all is the most important aim of democratic nationalism—with a group so definitely unassimilable as the Catholics. In America, the non-Catholic majority will accentuate its Protestantism by keeping at arm's length not only Catholics but also Jews. In spite of the formal separation of state from church, the American state will for a long time to come be subject to church influence.[11] That influence will be largely Protestant in national affairs and Catholic in the localities where the Catholics are in the majority. This rivalry between Catholics and Protestants will keep the United States sufficiently Christian to make Jews realize that by merging with the general population they will not advance one whit the cause of democratic nationalism, nor further appreciably the complete integration of the American people. The only effect of such merging is to augment the ranks of the two churches that divide the American people.

If the American nation can manage to thrive without being the closely knit and spiritually integrated people that the French nation, for instance, has almost succeeded in becoming, it is due to the difference between the two nations in the proportion of Protestants and Catholics that make up their respective populations. The *modus vivendi* between the Protestants and Catholics is bound to encourage the Jews to retain their group individuality, and to see in it nothing that is contrary to the American spirit. Perhaps America is destined to depart from the strict logic of democratic nationalism and to achieve a new cultural constellation in which historical civilizations, or churches, may be permitted to conserve the finest products of their experience and contribute them to the sum total of American culture and civilization.

C. THE DECISIVE FACTOR

CHAPTER VII

NEEDED: A PROGRAM OF RECONSTRUCTION

The realization of the unprecedented nature of the crisis—The present aimlessness due to lack of integrated idea of Jewish life as a whole—A program of reconstruction to be based on an affirmative and realistic philosophy of Jewish life.

THE foregoing description of the present-day situation in American-Jewish life discloses that the forces of dissolution and conservation are almost equally balanced. On the one hand, the obsolescence of the traditional conception of salvation as the exclusive privilege of the Jewish people, the granting of civic rights to the Jews with the expectation that they would surrender their corporate status, the impact of the industrial revolution, the upset in the Jewish way of life owing to the exigencies of the modern economic order, and, finally, the challenge of modern ideology with its humanist outlook and its tendency to substitute reason and experiment for the authority of tradition; on the other hand, the momentum of a common past, the interdict against intermarriage, the manifold of institutions and activities through which Jewish life still continues to function, and the environmental factors that have given new impetus to the will-to-live as Jews. These two sets of forces possess almost equal potency. This accounts for the uncertainty and perplexity which characterizes the state of mind of the American Jew.[1]

Judaism is passing through a crisis which is without precedent in its entire career. The Jew who regards Judaism as indispensable to the mental and spiritual well-being of his people cannot afford to console himself with the thought that there was seldom a time when Judaism was not in danger. He should not allow the remembrance of Judaism's miraculous escapes at critical junctures in the past to lull him into the blind confidence that something is bound to turn up which will extricate it from the present difficulties. It is true that even in the land of its nativity Judaism was frequently in danger of being submerged by alien cultures and religions, and succeeded nevertheless not only in holding its own, but in achieving universal scope. In the diaspora it displayed throughout the centuries preceding the era of enlightenment almost superhuman endurance in withstanding the unbroken siege against it. When the remembrance of the spiritual vigor displayed by the Jews in the past is not merely employed to serve as an incentive to keep up the struggle, but is used to provide the plan and strategy of battle at the present time, then the sooner Jews realize how little they can save Judaism by the means and methods of former times, the better. Instead of indulging in the conventional platitudes about Israel having survived so many of the ancient nations and civilizations, Jewish leadership should assume the responsibility for indicating specifically what Judaism must do today in order to survive.

It is by no means a foregone conclusion that Judaism in America is destined to live. It all depends upon what the Jews of this and the next generation will do. Already the maelstrom of life is about to tear up Judaism by the roots, and nothing less than a heroic effort will prevent it from being swept away completely. If Jewish endeavor be merely haphazard and impelled by blind habit, Judaism's day in America is done. But, if that endeavor be directed by an alert intelligence and a high idealism, Judaism will live. The passive and inert faith in the continued existence of Judaism is about as reasonable as the conclusion that, because a man has managed to attain the age of ninety, he is certain to live to a hundred. If Jews will not take heed, Judaism will meet the fate of the Chinese emperor who died from an overdose of the elixir of immortality.

There were, undoubtedly, trying times in the history of the Jews, when the end of Judaism seemed imminent. There were periods when, through the loss of morale and spiritual stamina, Jewish life seemed to be on the verge of disintegration. We need only think of the events that led to the Maccabean struggle. The Jewish Hellenists and apostates of those days bear a striking resemblance to the Jewish assimilationists of today. Then, too, many influential Jews in high positions were anxious to efface their Jewishness. They were ashamed of the political insignificance of their people and of their people's lack of cultural and military prestige. They chafed at the austerity of their laws which frowned upon idolatry and sensuality, and which interfered with their endeavors to curry the favor of their foreign overlords. If ever Judaism was sorely pressed, it surely was then. Yet that experience can only yield the inspiration that all heroism arouses. It offers small guidance in the present plight. In the Maccabean struggle various factors were present which neutralized the danger to Judaism; these factors are missing in the present crisis. Then the Jews still lived in their own land. They had just become a self-conscious priest-people, consecrated to the Torah which, they firmly believed, had been revealed to their ancestors by God, the one and only creator of the universe. Where, except in the ever-narrowing circle of Jews who have kept themselves insulated against Western civilization, can there be found, nowadays, such a sense of superiority to the rest of the world, such confidence in being divinely chosen and divinely protected?

It does not require acumen to note that the change in political status, a change that has opened to the Jew new opportunities for self-expression and social contact, has given a new turn to the problem of Judaism. But this does not daunt the optimists. They point to the golden era in Spain. The Jews then enjoyed a respite from the spoliation and oppression that had been their lot since they had been exiled from their land. During that respite they attained a high degree of prosperity and power. The temptation to abandon the faith for the sake of being accounted the complete equals of the ruling class was overpowering. Some yielded, it is true, but the Jewish people as a whole remained loyal to its heritage. At that time Judaism blossomed into new life. It found expression in a new dialectic and a new poetry. Have not the Jews thus shown themselves able to withstand the debilitating effect of peace and security? Why then, it is argued, may not the present political freedom accorded to the Jews, which is more comprehensive and more permanent, and the present opportunities for their self-advancement, which are infinitely more manifold, prove the occasion for another golden era in Judaism?'

Abstractly speaking, there is no reason why such a wish should be disappointed. But in actuality there are many new, unforeseen and unprovided for elements in the present situation. In the first place, a totally different conception of the national state has injected itself into the problem. Formerly, Jews were expected to lead their own cultural life, to dwell apart from the Gentile population, and to constitute themselves a quasi-political though subordinate group. This alone should prevent the Spanish era of Jewish history from serving as a precedent from which any inference might be drawn with regard to present difficulties. The resemblance between Jewish life in twentieth-century America and Jewish life in medieval Spain is only on the surface, and is nothing less than misleading if it tends to abate one iota of the effort which must now be expended to save Judaism. Not every Jew is willing, or perhaps in a position, to pay the cost in energy, courage, and idealism involved in cultivating Judaism. This renders it all the more essential that Judaism be made spiritually rewarding to those who are expected to sacrifice their material comfort and advantage for its sake.

Does the Jew find his heritage spiritually adequate and rewarding? This question is the crux of the problem of Judaism. The Jew who has been brought up amidst Jewish surroundings finds himself in a quandary today. Western civilization has become as necessary to him as breathing. But as he acquires that civilization and becomes imbued with its spirit, he finds much of his heritage crowded out or rendered irrelevant. If he is permeated with the higher ideals that have found expression in the western civilization, he is no longer satisfied with a Judaism which merely survives as a vestigial organ in the life of society. He expects it to function normally and healthily as a form of social energy that makes a perceptible contribution to human progress. Every thinking Jew today is thus torn between the claims of the Jewish past and the pressing and immediate claims of the complex life about him.

Judaism is a problem mainly to those who find that they cannot be spiritually whole and happy if they repudiate their Jewish heritage, and who, at the same time, are fairly convinced that to expect that heritage to function in the manner in which it did in the past is neither desirable nor practicable. The Jews who represent the most vital and promising element in Jewry today are those to whom Judaism is a problem. It is just out of such dilemmas that there have always emerged new spiritual values. If this dilemma will be met with wisdom, Judaism will no doubt undergo a renascence similar to that which it experienced during the first Babylonian exile.

In order that Judaism shall survive, Jews must focus their mind and heart upon the task of giving purpose and direction to what is at present little more than a blind urge to live as Jews. The urge to Jewish survival must be given an inspiring and irresistible motive, and supplied with a definite method of self-expression. This calls for the formulation of a program which, reckoning with every phase of the contemporary challenge, will set up a goal so desirable that it will enable the Jew to resist the temptation to escape Judaism, a program which will so map out the possibilities of Jewish self-fulfillment that the average Jew will at last be able to find his way in the maze of spiritual problems.

Jewish life at present abounds in superficially conceived ideologies usually improvised *ad hoc,* when funds have to be gathered for new buildings, or drives are undertaken to obtain the necessary means to support those in need both here and abroad. Institutions of Jewish learning avoid any statement of principle for fear of raising issues that might alienate supporters. Even a new type of institution like the communal center has been permitted to enter into Jewish life without any clear idea as to what it is all about. One might expect to find in the platforms of the various religious organizations and in the propaganda of the Zionist movement at least an attempt to set forth the meaning of Jewish life and the direction it should take. All that one encounters, however, is a mass of vague and fragmentary sentiments which, while perfectly innocuous, only help to accentuate the aimlessness of Jewish life.

To make any headway with the solution of the problem of Judaism, it is necessary to formulate a philosophy of Jewish life as a whole, to orient oneself at least to the salient facts and factors in the struggle of the Jewish people for survival. It must be a philosophy that discerns an organic connection among the experiences and needs of Jewry, its dispersion and its diversity, its past and its future, its religious commitments, its manifold expressions, its many traits and tendencies, its need for self-adjustment and its prerogative to mold environment. Practical projects, like the construction of synagogues, collecting funds for Palestine, or for the Jews who are the victims of war and persecution, organizing federations, fraternal orders and social clubs, are undoubtedly an indispensable part of living as a Jew. But, if those efforts are carried on without the least notion of their relation to the meaning of Jewish life in its totality and the direction which it should be made to take, before long they are bound to slacken, and ultimately to languish completely for lack of interest. The initial energy is bound to be spent before it has had a chance to activate any latent source of energy that can be relied upon to be permanent.

Never were Jews so much in need of taking thought as they are today. In general life, the nineteenth-century doctrine of salvation through planlessness is yielding to the conviction that the only way to forestall chaos in the days ahead of us is to develop a sense of responsibility for the consequences in terms of human welfare, of the assumptions, habits, institutions and social arrangements by which men and nations have lived hitherto. Such a sense of responsibility must lead to social planning. Likewise, Jews must acquire a sense of responsibility for the consequences of their thoughts, as well as their thoughtlessness, with regard to Judaism, and learn to look upon the task of planning Judaism's future as the foremost Jewish duty of the present day.

To meet that responsibility, Jews will have to reopen the discussion of the fundamental questions with which the whole problem of Jewish survival is bound up. Differences of opinion are unavoidable. But that should be the last reason in the world for deterring Jews from bringing those questions into the open forum. If Jews have so little confidence in themselves that they are afraid of free discussion, silence will only augment their self-distrust and lessen their self-respect. It is entirely unnecessary to count upon all Jews agreeing on any one plan or program. No such like-mindedness should be expected of them. All that is necessary is that, whatever the program suggested, it grow out of an integrated conception of the totality of Jewish life instead of being merely some idea-less organizational scheme. Accordingly, a number of such programs corresponding with the number of current philosophies of Jewish life will have to be formulated. The one with the greatest survival-value will naturally win in the end.

Whence is that survival-value to come if not from the basic principles which constitute the particular version of Judaism implied in the program? It is evident, therefore, that it is impossible to plan Jewish life intelligently without committing oneself to some specific version or interpretation of that which differentiates Jews from non-Jews. There are at present three distinct conceptions of the Jewish differentia. According to the Reformists, the Jews are a religious community united by their adherence to ethical monotheism, which their ancestors evolved in the course of centuries. There are others besides Jews who profess ethical monotheism, but the Jews profess ethical monotheism in its truest form. According to the Neo-Orthodox, the Jews are the people to whose ancestors God revealed himself and made known the teachings contained in the Torah. The Jews are thus in possession of the only true religion, since a religion to be genuine must be supernaturally revealed. Those who belong to neither group and yet take an affirmative attitude toward Jewish life and wish to see it thrive may be said to regard the Jews as bound together by the ties of nationhood, differing from the rest of the world by virtue of their inherited culture or civilization.

Each of these conceptions of the Jewish differentia has its variants. There is a conservative Judaism which is the left wing of Orthodoxy, and there is a conservative Judaism which is the right wing of Reformism. The version of those who regard the Jews as possessing a common culture or civilization has been given three different interpretations. According to the one extreme view, Palestine is the only country in which Jewish civilization can survive. According to another extreme view, the survival of the Jewish civilization is contingent upon its thorough secularization and its adoption of Yiddish as its vernacular and literary medium.

The program advocated in this book is based on the cultural version of Judaism, as accepted by those who take the central position that Jewish civilization can function in varying degrees in the diaspora, provided it have its home in Palestine and retain both its Hebraic and religious character. Before proceeding with a description of the version of Judaism which has here been selected as the basis of a program for Jewish life in America, I shall give a survey of the two principal interpretations of Judaism that stand out most conspicuously in American-Jewish life, the Reformist and the Neo-Orthodox, together with their variants, and point out wherein they are inadequate and unacceptable to those to whom Jewish life is not worth saving, unless it be a creative Jewish life.

PART TWO

THE CURRENT VERSIONS OF JUDAISM

CHAPTER VIII

THE REFORMIST * VERSION OF JUDAISM

The needs of the age taken into account by Reformist Judaism—The platform of the Pittsburgh Conference—The God-idea regarded as the fundamental element in Judaism—The attributes Judaism ascribes to God—The election of Israel reinterpreted in the light of the spiritual conception of history—Revelation reinterpreted as refer- ring to Israel's genius for religion—Jewish nationhood surrendered and replaced by the ideal of the Jewish mission—The concept of "Torah" replaced by the concept of "moral law"—The function of religious ceremonies.

REFORMIST Judaism represents the first deliberate and organized effort to adjust traditional Judaism to the exigencies of modern political and economic conditions and to reckon with the modern world-outlook. Reformism takes for granted that, in spite of the recrudescence of reactionary tendencies, the changes which in modern times have taken place in the social and intellectual life of mankind mark a definite spiritual advance on the past. It considers democratic nationalism, which has bestowed citizenship on the Jew and has granted him political and civic rights—though it asks, more or less insistently, for the surrender of his nationhood—as an important phase of the moral progress which mankind has made within the last century or two. The Jews, think the Reformists, should be the last to impede that progress by refusing to surrender their historic status as a nation. That status, in their opinion, is bound to give rise to misunderstanding of the purpose for which the Jews choose to remain a distinct group.

Reformism sees in the shifting of the center of gravity from interest in the hereafter to interest in transforming the world we live in, and in the substitution of the authority of reason for the

---

* The term "Reform Judaism" has remained a Germanism despite its frequent use. "Reformed Judaism" does not convey what the originators of the German expression *"Reform Judentum"* had in mind. They implied that in their interpretation of the Jewish religion the process of reform was recognized as legitimate, necessary and continuous. The term "Progressive Judaism" would have been a more exact equivalent of *"Reform Judentum."* "Liberal Judaism," if not a happier designation, is at least good English. The Reformists in England call themselves "Liberals," and their Judaism "Liberal Judaism." On the other hand, the term *"Liberal"* is used by German Jews of the Conservative wing.[1]

authority of tradition, permanent and ineluctable gains of the human spirit. It therefore assumes that Judaism should welcome the necessity which compels it to readjust itself and to reconstruct its teachings in the light of the new developments in human life. For only by meeting these needs of contemporary life can Judaism progress intellectually and spiritually. "The need of the time," declares Samuel Hirsch, the philosopher of the movement, "is the highest law in Judaism. . . . The Jews of the present day must, before all else, participate in the work of the age with all their powers; for their work is the object of Jewish history. Yes, it is the be-all and end-all of Judaism." [2]

The Reformist movement has had its rabbinical synods and conferences called mainly with the view of dealing with the problem of Jewish adjustment. It has by this time formulated a creed; it is articulated in a definite theology, and it has radically transformed the contour of Jewish life. Inaugurated in Germany, it has witnessed a phenomenal growth in America. "The tangle of politico-national and religous ideas," writes Max L. Margolis, "in which our past is enmeshed and which is especially manifested in the doctrine of the Law and the Messiah, has at last been unraveled and the Gordian knot cut: the task has been performed by Geiger's scholarship, Holdheim's logic, Samuel Hirsch's philosophic erudition, Einhorn's inspiration, above all by the foresight, undaunted courage and indomitable will of Isaac M. Wise." [3]

If the success of a movement is to be measured by results in organization and prestige, Reformism would have to be pronounced successful. Over four hundred of the largest and most influential congregations of this country are federated into a well organized body which yields sufficient income to carry on various activities and to maintain the machinery necessary to its functioning. But these are not criteria by which to appraise a spiritual movement. A movement which is intended to bring order into men's inner life should be measured by the extent to which it succeeds in formulating a program that is spiritually compelling and socially practical, and by the degree to which its adherents live up to its professed ideas and ideals.

The first source of Reformist ideology [4] that comes to mind is the declaration of principles adopted at the Pittsburgh convention of the Central Conference of American Rabbis, held in 1885. Although there are a number of rabbis in that organization who refuse to recognize that platform as authoritative, they do so as a matter of individual insurgency, which so far has had very little influence in shaping the policies of the Conference as a whole. Even in their own congregations the insurgent rabbis have not succeeded in disestablishing the principles of the official platform. "It still stands," writes David Philipson, "as the utterance most expressive of the teachings of Reform Judaism." [5] Well-nigh fifty years of preaching and teaching those principles have rendered the Reformist laity practically impervious to any other conception of Jewish life. Owing partly to the personality of the insurgent rabbis and partly to the apathy of the laity to all questions of belief, these rabbis enjoy considerable freedom in expounding whatever views they choose, so long as they draw large attendance and help to increase the membership of the congregation. These anomalous conditions, however, do not negate the fact that Reformist Judaism has definite norms and that these norms are clearly defined in the principles of the Pittsburgh Conference:

1. We recognize in every religion an attempt to grasp the Infinite, and in every mode, source, or book of revelation held sacred in any religious system the consciousness of the indwelling of God in man. We hold that Judaism presents the highest conception of the God-idea, as taught in our Holy Scriptures and developed and spiritualized by the Jewish teachers, in accordance with the moral and philosophical progress of their respective ages. We maintain that Judaism preserved and defended amidst continual struggles and trials and under enforced isolation, this God-idea as the central religious truth for the human race.

2. We recognize in the Bible the record of the consecration of the Jewish people to its mission as the priest of the one God, and value it as the most potent instrument of religious and moral instruction. We hold that the modern discoveries of scientific research in the domain of nature and history are not antagonistic to the doctrines of Judaism, the Bible reflecting the primitive ideas of its own age, and at times clothing its conception of divine Providence and Justice dealing with man in miraculous narratives.

3. We recognize in the Mosaic legislation a system of training the Jewish people for its mission during its national life in Palestine, and today we accept as binding only its moral laws, and maintain only such ceremonies as elevate and sanctify our lives, but reject all such as are not adapted to the views and habits of modern civilization.

4. We hold that all such Mosaic and rabbinical laws as regulate diet, priestly purity, and dress, originated in ages, and under the influence of ideas, entirely foreign to our present mental and spiritual state. They fail to impress the modern Jew with a spirit of priestly holiness; their observance in our days is apt rather to obstruct than to further modern spiritual elevation.

5. We recognize, in the modern era of universal culture of heart and intellect, the approaching of the realization of Israel's great Messianic hope for the establishment of the kingdom of truth, justice, and peace among all men. We consider ourselves no longer a nation, but a religious community, and therefore expect neither a return to Palestine, nor a sacrificial worship under the sons of Aaron, nor the restoration of any of the laws concerning the Jewish state.

6. We recognize in Judaism a progressive religion, ever striving to be in accord with the postulates of reason. We are convinced of the utmost necessity of preserving the historical identity with our great past. Christianity and Islam being daughter religions of Judaism, we appreciate their providential mission to aid in the spreading of monotheistic and moral truth. We acknowledge that the spirit of broad humanity of our age is our ally in the fulfillment of our mission, and therefore we extend the hand of fellowship to all who cooperate with us in the establishment of the reign of truth and righteousness among men.

7. We reassert the doctrine of Judaism that the soul is immortal, grounding this belief on the divine nature of the human spirit, which forever finds bliss in righteousness and misery in wickedness. We reject as ideas not rooted in Judaism the beliefs both in bodily resurrection and in Gehenna and Eden (Hell and Paradise) as abodes for everlasting punishment and reward.

8. In full accordance with the spirit of Mosaic legislation, which strives to regulate the relation between rich and poor, we deem it our duty to participate in the great task of modern times, to solve, on the basis of justice and righteousness, the problem presented by the contrasts and evils of the present organization of society.

It is significant that the Pittsburgh Conference, at which the foregoing platform was adopted, had been called by Kaufman Kohler,° and that he took a leading part in formulating the principles of that platform. His *Jewish Theology* which, in a sense, is an elaboration of those principles, may, therefore, be regarded almost as authoritative an interpretation of Reformist Judaism as the platform itself. It may, accordingly, serve in conjunction with the platform as a basis for judging the validity of the Reformist interpretation of Judaism.

The characteristic note of Reformism is struck in the fact that it upsets the equilibrium among the three constitutive groups of values in Judaism, which center respectively about the ideas of Israel, God and Torah. In traditional Judaism, the belief in God, loyalty to the Torah as the revelation of God's will, and participation in the life of Israel, are treated as of co-ordinate importance. The exceptions to this attitude are so few as to be negligible.[7] Reformism, however, breaks definitely with this traditional attitude and deliberately singles out the belief in God as the most significant. From the standpoint of Reformist Judaism, the criterion by which to measure the importance of any element in Judaism is the extent to which it makes for the ethical improvement of mankind. Since the moral law is presumably based upon the idea of God, nothing in Judaism can compare in importance with the fact that it has always promulgated the truest idea of God. If the Jews have contributed more than any other people to the cause of morality, it has been due chiefly to their lofty and spiritual conception of God. This does not mean that the Jewish people attained once and for all a conception of God which, for its truth and effectiveness as a moral force, can stand the test of all time. What is meant is that the most advanced conception of God in each age always found a ready reception among the Jews. There were times when the Jews themselves evolved the most spiritual idea of God. At other times they were willing to deepen their knowledge of God by assimilating such truth as other nations had come upon. But whether knowledge of God was due to native genius or to the spiritual insight of non-Jewish thinkers, the Jews always employed it as a means of validating the most ethical ideals of conduct.

Let us see how this applies to what the Jewish people should believe concerning God at the present time. According to tradition, the existence of God is not a matter of rational proof but is based upon the experience of those to whom God revealed himself, or communicated his will. At first sight, there seems to be an impassable gulf between this assumption of tradition and the attitude of the modern man, to whom the very possibility of God revealing himself as a distinct entity is inconceivable. Yet upon reflection the two are not so far apart. Basically, there is more in common between them than appears on the surface. In the position of the traditionalist, there is the evident implication that the unaided human mind cannot arrive at that certainty of God's existence, which only revelation can convey. The position taken by the modern thinker—Immanuel Kant, for example—while not identical with that of the traditionalist is strikingly analogous. The modern thinker does not deny the existence of God. He merely maintains that the kind of reasoning which is employed in science cannot help us to achieve a knowledge of God. For that kind of knowledge we depend upon intuition, or practical reason. The specific experience, where this intuitive or practical reasoning operates, and which, therefore, constitutes the main source of our awareness of God, is the sense of duty, or the activity of conscience.

This modern approach to religion is advocated by Reformism as inherently compatible with the spirit of Judaism. The continuity of Judaism will in no sense be broken through the surrender of the belief in the supernatural self-manifestation of God, for by accepting the doctrine that it is mainly through conscience that man becomes aware of God, Judaism would now be voicing, knowingly and deliberately, what it has hitherto been struggling to express. That the sense of duty is the true source of our knowledge of God gives added support to moral intuition and sanction to the conscience. By recognizing the conscience as the medium through which God reveals himself, Judaism continues its historical tendency to conceive of God as a god of righteousness, since a god whose existence becomes known through conscience must necessarily be a god whose nature is best expressed in terms of a moral order. The traditional belief, therefore, that revelation is the sole means of knowing God may be so interpreted, say the Reformists, as to square with the current assumption that the human mind in its natural functioning is the sole source of knowledge of God.

Is there, or has there ever been, divine revelation? Kohler would unhesitatingly answer in the affirmative, since in every heightening experience, wherein we are capable of perceiving new truths, God reveals himself to us. Especially whenever we perceive the moral bearings of any truth, "God appears actually to step into the sphere of human life as its moral Ruler." [8] This is how the seers and psalmists of Israel actually experienced divine revelation.

There are other reinterpretations of revelation in Reformist ideology. According to Holdheim, revelation is to be identified with the spirit of the age.[9] Samuel Hirsch identifies it with the needs of the time. Max L. Margolis defines revelation as "the creational stage [which] opens with that mysterious, almost timeless moment when, in the depth of the human soul (which, by Divine selection, becomes the organ of revelation), there is conceived a religious idea which, by virtue of its innate force, will seek embodiment in institutions, in song and prayer and, in due season, in articulate, definite, statement, in a formulated dogma. It were idle," he adds, "even after a religious idea has become fully manifest, to seek to explain its beginnings or its appearance just at this and that moment and in this and that personality. . . . The creative energy by the grace of which religious ideas are conceived is divine, infallible, eternal." [10]

The affirmation of God's existence is not a cold, factual statement. It is the conscious recognition of the ethical import of life. So also, when we ascribe certain attributes to God, we do not merely state something otherwise unknown about God's nature as such; we make avowal of the spiritual significance which we discern both in the universe and in man. There are two kinds of divine attributes, metaphysical and moral. The metaphysical attributes are God's unity, omnipotence, omniscience, omnipresence and eternity. They are metaphysical in the sense that our knowledge of them is derived, for the most part, from the contemplation of God's works in the world. Of these, the attribute of God's unity is of utmost significance for the moral life; for, it is in the light of that unity that we can discern order and harmony in the intellectual and the moral world. There is equal need, from a moral standpoint, for emphasizing the other metaphysical attributes, so as to avoid the mistake of Christianity which brings God into the sphere of the merely human. The danger accruing to the moral life from such a lowering of the conception of God is that it might put a halt to the process of growth in moral ideals. By raising a human being to the status of God, we imply that man has attained the limit of his spiritual powers.

The moral attributes of God are holiness, justice, mercy, love and faithfulness. The knowledge of these is derived from the ideals for which men strive. In ascribing such attributes to God, we imply that God is the ideal, the pattern and inspirer of all morality. According to Kohler, the emphasis upon these attributes is bound to lead to a balanced moral life. Judaism is thus afforded the opportunity to make good Christianity's failure to set proper store by the attribute of justice, and Islam's failure to emphasize the attribute of mercy.

As against errors to which the modern man is liable, Judaism must uphold the attributes of God as creator and as possessing self-conscious will. Both have far-reaching moral implications. That God is creator means that the world is not governed by blind necessity. What can exercise a more blighting effect upon all moral endeavor than the notion that there is no meaning or purpose to the world, and that it is soulless in its mechanistic perfection. This does not constrain us to subscribe to the traditional conception of creation as a sudden act. We may accept without reservation the Darwinian conception of evolution, so long as we consider the divine impulsion or initiative as the origin of the process.

We may likewise accept the principle of uniformity of nature. "The maintenance of the entire household of nature is one continuous act of God which can neither be interrupted nor limited in time. God in His infinite wisdom works forever through the same laws which were in force in the beginning and which shall continue through all the realms of time and space." [11] This excludes the necessity of maintaining the historicity of the miracles. "The whole cosmic order is *one* miracle. No room is left for single or exceptional miracles." [12] The stories of the miracles must be read as reflecting the purpose of the ancient authors to prove and illustrate God's power and goodness.

That God is a self-conscious being is a doctrine which Judaism should emphasize in view of the tendency in certain quarters to teach a kind of naturalism which grants the possession of mind or self-consciousness only to the most highly developed human beings. This conception of God would give support and sanction to the teaching that the history of mankind is directed by God into channels that make for progress socially, intellectually, morally and spiritually. Man, as man, is godlike, insofar as he possesses free will and self-consciousness, faculties which are not actually, but potentially, present in all human beings. By obeying the divine law, these potentialities are realized. Such a conception of universal ethical progress is possible only with the basic doctrine of God as a self-conscious being.

Thus, according to Kohler, the ethical conception of God's existence and attributes—or ethical monotheism—may be summed up in the teachings of Judaism that God is one and holy; that humanity is one; and that God's kingdom of truth, justice and peace will be universally established.

In dealing with the conception of Israel as God's elect, Reformism finds it necessary to reinterpret the traditional conception of what caused Israel to be singled out as a unique people in the past, and to alter the corporate status of the Jewish people *vis-à-vis* the nations of the modern world.

Traditionally, Israel was regarded as the only one among the nations to whom God had revealed himself. No greater distinction is possible than experiencing the reality of God in the warm immediacy of his supernatural self-manifestation. True, such experience was accorded to Israel only for a brief moment at Sinai. But that glimpse of the divine was enough to consecrate Israel for all time. Add to that the fact that for many generations after Israel's stay in the wilderness God communicated his will to Israel's Prophets and Sages, and we can no longer question Israel's spiritual supremacy.

Thus far, tradition. But since the truths established by the various sciences of human nature and history no longer permit us to concede that Israel received a type of revelation or communication that was outside the order of nature, we are compelled to find a rational basis for Israel's claim to distinction. That basis is to be found in the spiritual conception of human history as a whole. Assuming that human history is not blind and purposeless, but a progressive movement in the direction of ever-increasing truth, justice and peace, a progressive movement toward the kingdom of God, Israel's part in that movement is so prominent that we must concede to Israel the right to call itself God's chosen. Human progress and sensitivity to the moral order are contingent upon a true conception of God. The two religions which have helped to give two-thirds of mankind a truer conception of God—Christianity and

Mohammedanism—and which have been instrumental in advancing mankind toward its ultimate goal, have stemmed from Israel.

In a sense, every great people that has contributed to enlightenment and progress is the chosen of God. The world would not be as far advanced in knowledge if it were not for Greece, nor in government if it were not for Rome. But both nations, and others before and since, played their part in the progress of mankind, unaware of their function. They were unconscious instruments in the divine plan. Israel, however, stepped into history fully aware of the mission it had to perform, and was prepared to suffer the antagonism of the nations because of its loyalty to that mission. This consciousness of purpose made Israel the chosen of God in a far truer and deeper sense than the one in which we can apply that term to the other great historic peoples. Moreover, the very nature of the contribution which Israel made to the world's progress entitles it to be called the chosen of God in a sense that is unique. The idea of God is of greater importance to human welfare than science, art or government, and it is as the most illustrious bearer of that idea, contends Kohler, that Israel has figured in history. But, even granting that the Jews in giving monotheism to the world have conferred upon it the greatest blessing of all, that does not prove that they are still indispensable to the cause of religion.

Claude G. Montefiore deals with the question which naturally suggests itself at this point. Greece and Rome made their contribution to civilization and passed off the stage of history. The Jews evolved monotheism and produced the Bible. Have not these achievements become sufficiently externalized to function without them? Montefiore's reply to this question is that a people which is "chosen" for the sake of religion is chosen not merely to diffuse knowledge through a book or through the inculcation of doctrines, but to diffuse *experience*. Religion is taught by living it. Hence only a living people can teach it.[13]

Thus, without recourse to the theurgic world-outlook of tradition, Reformism is able to conserve much of the cluster of mental and moral associations which Judaism has built around the idea "Israel." It goes even further. It not only retains in a reinterpreted form the conception of Israel as having made a unique and surpassing contribution to human progress; it also insists on calling Israel "the people of revelation." It regards "revelation" as too important a concept to be dropped from the vocabulary of Judaism. By eliminating the connotation of supernaturalism from the concept of revelation, Kohler feels free to use "revelation" as a synonym for spiritual genius, on the assumption that all forms of genius are manifestations of the more intense activity of the divine principle in man. It is not at all straining the point, therefore, to designate Israel's special genius for religion as revelation. "It is an indisputable fact of history that the Jewish people, on account of its peculiar religious bent, was predestined to be the people of revelation." [14]

Kohler does not hesitate to assert as an empirical fact that the Jewish people possesses "a special capacity of soul and a tendency of intellect which fit it for the divine task." [15] These faculties are hereditary. He makes this assertion not only on the basis of results actually achieved by the Jewish people in influencing the spiritual history of two-thirds of the human race, but on the basis of distinctive traits which the Jewish people has exhibited throughout its history. Kohler ascribes the religious tendency of the Jew to the peculiar mingling in him of contrasting traits. Both the individualistic and the group spirit are strongly developed in the Jew. On the one hand, he is tenacious in retaining what is traditional; on the other, he is eager to assimilate the newest and the latest. At times, he is swayed by materialistic self-interest; at other times, he is ready to sacrifice his life for an ideal. His very obstinacy is a point in his favor, for without it he would never be able to defend his religion. Yet coupled with that obstinacy is a surpassing readiness to obey the call to duty. The traits which the rabbis ascribed to the Jews—chastity, purity and benevolence—account for their extraordinary religious development. These traits have in turn been reinforced by the Law which kept the entire people and the entire life of Judaism consecrated to the great spiritual task of disseminating the truth. [16] It is not only in the past, however, that the Jews distinguished themselves by their contribution to religion. They still give evidence of being able to bring religion into accord with the highest ideals of justice and truth.

This remarkable genius for religion is concentrated to an unparalleled degree in "the little tribe of Judah," the survivors of the original stock of Israel. It is the duty, therefore, of each Jew to maintain the integrity and identity of this group. Judaism must not only defend and make known the truth about God. It must also guard the group in which exists that unique capacity for giving that truth new meaning and new scope. This duty devolves upon the individual Jew, not as a matter of option, but as an obligation to which he is committed by the mere fact of his being born a Jew. "It is birth, not confession," says Kohler, "that imposes on the Jew the obligation to work and strive for the eternal verities of Israel." [17]

It is in the interest of these eternal verities, he continues, that the Jewish people must "avoid intermarrying with the members of other sects, unless they espouse the Jewish faith " [18] In the past, the Jewish people resorted to extreme measures to maintain its racial and religious purity. Its law of holiness which developed its consciousness of being a priest-people abounded in numerous ritual laws that acted as a wall between Jews and Gentiles. In the past that was probably justified. But nowadays such measures must be abandoned because they are liable to foster an "unhealthy clannishness and self-adulation." Our problem is to find a method of preserving Israel as an identifiable group without being charged with clannishness. It is evident, of course, that marriage with non-Jews cannot be permitted, for that would mean the disappearance of the Jews within two or three generations.

Reformism does not regard the nationhood of the Jewish people as indispensable to Jewish survival. It looks with intense disfavor upon Jewish nationhood, which it considers as a hindrance to Jewish emancipation. "We consider ourselves no longer a nation but a religious community," the Pittsburgh platform reads. The belief in Jewish nationhood was bound up with the doctrine that Israel was exiled from Palestine because of its sins, and that it remained in the state of dispersion among the nations, because it had not yet made full amends for its sins. Such doctrine is no longer acceptable. Since Israel did not return to Palestine during all these centuries, and since there is small likelihood that it will ever resume any fully developed national life there, Jews are justified in accepting the dispersion of their co-religionists among the nations of the world as a permanent condition. Moreover, by accepting the terms of the emancipation, Jews have surrendered all claims to nationhood and all expectations to return to Palestine, or "to restore any of the laws concerning a Jewish state." The problem of Jewish survival can be solved through the avoidance of intermarriage with non-Jews. The abrogation of Jewish nationhood, the Reformists maintain, is essential as a means of bringing the Jews into whole-hearted co-operation with the national democratic state of which they are citizens. It will remove the main obstacle which formerly stood in the way of the cooperation of Jew and Gentile for the betterment of mankind.

The Jews can afford to dispense with national status as a bond of unity, since they possess an equally cohesive force in the common consciousness of being entrusted with a religious mission. The mission idea, which was first distinctly promulgated by the Prophets, has fallen into abeyance on account of the centuries of persecution. The emancipation affords the Jewish people an opportunity "to clarify and deepen the truths committed to its keeping, by assimilating the wisdom and culture of the very nations." The Jewish people should feel impelled to dedicate itself with all its energy to the task of bringing about the realization of the highest ideals of a united humanity based upon its teaching of the unity and holiness of God.[19] Thus the messianic hope, which hitherto was limited and narrow in its scope, is given a universality and idealism that are worthy of man's highest powers.[20] Does the world need the Jewish people and its mission? The obscurantism of the dominant religions, the materialism and individualism which have resulted from the superficial interpretation of the meaning of science, the existence of oppression, exploitation and war, make the contribution of the Jew indispensable to the world. With a goal such as this, which is nothing less than "a divine covenant comprising all humanity," what Jew need complain that he has no great cause to live for, or that his present is unworthy of his past? In comparison with the task of furthering "the completion of the divine kingdom in truth and justice," all that the Jew may achieve in the various fields of general culture sinks into insignificance.

Although Reformism departs radically from the traditional conceptions of God and Israel, it considers those conceptions in their modernized form, and all that they imply in terms of belief and practice as constituting the very substance of Judaism. But with regard to the concept "Torah" and to all that it implies concerning the form and authority of Judaism's social and cultural institutions, traditional Judaism and Reformism seem to have nothing in common. Reformism practically dispenses with the concept of "Torah." In the platform of the Pittsburgh Conference the very mention of Torah is omitted, and all that is remembered of the part it played in Judaism is referred to by the colorless term "Mosaic legislation."

The main reason for this attitude of Reformism toward Torah is, no doubt, the loss of credence in its supernatural origin. With critical and historical research proving that the Pentateuch is a composite document which began to function as a single code not earlier than in the days of Ezra, the laws and institutions contained in the Pentateuch are deprived at one blow of the infallibility and permanent validity which traditional Judaism was wont to ascribe to them. From the standpoint of modern thought, all the laws and institutions dealt with in the Pentateuch cannot but be viewed as the spiritual response of various generations of the Jewish people to the needs which those generations experienced. Far from being static, the laws changed with each age under the pressure of shifting circumstances. It is this very capacity for development and adaptation that has constituted the vitality of Judaism.

But nowadays it is not any particular law in the Torah that has grown obsolete. In giving up its nationhood, Israel has given up the very prerogative of law-making. It can exercise only moral suasion over its constituents. It has neither need nor occasion for framing civil or criminal laws. And as for ritual laws, their validity as laws is gone the moment their divine origin is not conceded. Some of them may survive as customs, because they are useful as reminders or symbols of certain truths or historic events. But there is nothing particularly binding or authoritative about the manner of their observance. By eliminating from Jewish life all occasion for any kind of civic or communal authority, Reformism has struck out the most characteristic element of the Torah, and is therefore consistent in allowing the concept of Torah to fall out of its vocabulary. We might poetically or homiletically speak of Torah as "the unwritten moral law which underlies the precepts of both the written law and its oral interpretation." [21] But as a matter of prosaic actuality, such use of the term "Torah" has little in common with the system of unique, social and religious institutions of the Jewish people, originally designated by that term. All religions and philosophies render homage to the "unwritten moral law," but that does not render them upholders of the Torah.

Reformist Judaism does not underestimate the important rôle played in the past by the legalistic element of the Torah in educating the Jewish people for its task as the priest-people of the world. It was legalism that imbued the people with a sense of duty, that left the impress of holiness upon every aspect of its life, and that evoked from the Jewish people its marvelous endurance and resistance. Yet Kohler holds legalism responsible for preventing the growth of the spiritual and ethical elements in Judaism. Though in abrogating the legal force of the Torah the Jews may have lost the spiritual discipline which it afforded, he insists, they have gained the larger liberty of being able to mold and adjust their religion in accordance with the needs of the time. [22]

There is one aspect of Torah, as traditionally conceived, which Reformism considers worthwhile preserving. That is the aspect of prophetic universalism which suffuses the legalistic elements of the Torah. Even the ritualism and the hair-splitting casuistry to which the laws of the Torah gave rise are informed by a spirit of ethical and humane idealism. But while the spirit of prophecy should save the Torah from becoming altogether obsolete, it is in the writings of the great Prophets themselves that it blazes forth in all its brilliance. Those are the parts of Holy Scriptures to which Judaism should henceforth give primacy. There, prophecy is not marred by the priestly spirit which could not contemplate life beyond the borders of Israel, nor free itself from the yoke of custom.

Jews cannot, however, Kohler reminds us, always be expected to live on the high plane of prophetic teaching. Those truths are too general for the needs of the workaday life of the average man and woman. For everyday use, Judaism has its ethical principles, which permeate its wisdom literature and the *aggadic* portions of the Talmud and Midrash.

Through its ethics, no less than through its conception of God, Judaism has its unique contribution to make. It avoids the complete annihilation of self, which Buddhism holds up as man's highest goal, it deprecates the hedonism which we associate with Hellenism, and it keeps clear of the other-worldliness of Christianity. The sanity, the moderation and the rootedness in life, which mark Jewish ethics [22] are reflected in the saying of Hillel, "If I am not for myself, who will be for me? But if I am for myself alone, what am I? And if not now, when?"

Perhaps more distinctive of Jewish ethics than even the foregoing traits, is its emphasis upon purity and holiness, chastity and modesty. No religion was so successful as Judaism in making the home a training school for virtue. The influence of the home life extended to all other activities and relationships. How "to restore the home to its pristine glory as a sanctuary of God, amid our present allurements of luxury and pleasure," says Kohler, "is the greatest problem of modern Israel." [24]

Another fact which Reformism takes into consideration is that doctrines alone are not sufficient to insure the stability of a religion. After all, there is such a wide diversity of knowledge and opinion, and each age so modifies men's ideas that no doctrine can be relied upon to serve as a means of permanently giving distinctive character to a religion. This is why every religion has to develop certain forms, institutions and ceremonies which give it both individuality and continuity. It is impossible for the Jews of today to experience the feeling that the religion to which they adhere is actually the same as that for which their fathers lived and died, unless they observe some of the principal ceremonies with which Judaism has always been identified.[25] Jews must retain the synagogue, with its collective worship, and even some of the ancient liturgies, though they will have to eliminate from those liturgies everything that is out of keeping with the highest spiritual ideals of the age. They should observe the traditional Sabbath, though not with all of the traditional "dont's", but they should retain the injunction to abstain from one's routine week-day work. The three great festivals, with their rich historical meanings, the New Year and the Day of Atonement with their call each year to spiritual regeneration, cannot be omitted without impoverishing the moral content of Judaism and jeopardizing its continuity.

There are other religious observances which, having come down from the past, might give permanence to Judaism, but Reformism is not altogether certain of their inherent spiritual value. However, it is not only the retention of old forms that can keep a religion alive. New forms have to be created. The ceremony of confirmation, for example, which Reformism has introduced as part of the observance of the *Shabuot* festival, is calculated to keep alive the memory of Israel's covenant with God at Sinai.

Reformism is well aware that its ethical and ceremonial program will have to undergo considerable revision and emendation to afford adequate guidance and inspiration to the modern Jew. It deplores the religious indifference and materialism of the majority of those who call themselves its adherents.[*] But it does not have the least doubt as to the ultimate accomplishment of its larger aims.

CHAPTER IX

CRITIQUE OF THE REFORMIST VERSION OF JUDAISM

A serious attempt to save Judaism by reckoning with the realities—Reformism incapable of holding the Jews or eliciting spiritual creativity—The attempt to reduce Judaism to a religious philosophy a mistake—The attributes Judaism ascribes to God— The ethical implications of the God-idea too vague to constitute a basis for a mission —The claim that the Jews possess a hereditary genius for religion highly question-able—Reformism's repudiation of Israel's nationhood unwarranted—A handful of cere-monies and moral precepts a poor substitute for Torah.

No fair-minded opponent of Reformism would venture to assert that it has been a complete failure. Judging the movement objec-tively, one must admit that it has prevented thousands of Jews in western Europe and America from severing all connections with their people. Many, who would otherwise have found Judaism entirely incompatible with modern thought and superfluous in a world which teems with opportunities for idealistic self-expression, have been enabled to discover in it an unsuspected plasticity which rendered it capable of meeting the requirements of the complex age in which we live. Reformism has, no doubt, offered a practical alternative to many honest but distraught Jews who otherwise would have been forced to choose between an anomalous adherence to the past and a complete abandonment of Judaism. It has eased the well-nigh fatal pressure of the forces released by the enlightenment and the emancipation. For this relief alone, it deserves the gratitude of those who, wishing to see Judaism live, realize that the first step must be to prevent Jewish life from being stampeded. This Reform-ism has done.

Nor is it fair to assert that Reformism is governed mainly by expediency [1] and motivated solely by the desire to occidentalize the Jew. We must judge a movement not by its camp followers but by its leaders. The first sponsors of the Reformist movement un-doubtedly proceeded from deep conviction, true courage, and a fine sense of spiritual values when they recognized and acknowledged in the intellectual and moral aspirations of the age a more depend-

able revelation of God than in the uninterpreted teachings of tradition. Whether that attitude to modern intellectual and social tendencies be warranted or not, such at least are the traits one expects of
those upon whom devolves spiritual leadership in times of rapid
social and cultural change.

To subject Judaism to a process of unsparing revision in the
light of the modern ideology required on the part of the pioneers
of the movement a more than ordinary faith in its worth. We must
remember that they were no longer upheld by the sustaining conviction of the Jewish philosophers of the Middle Ages, that Judaism
was of supernatural origin and, therefore, could not possibly be
superseded by any truth that man might discover. In accordance
with this conviction, the medieval philosophers had only to read
into Judaism any newly discovered truth. But such procedure was
impossible for the pioneers of Reformism. Reformists like Holdheim, Geiger, and Samuel Hirsch had to feel convinced of the
permanent worth of Judaism, independently of the belief in its
supernatural origin. This means that they had to reformulate the
traditional values in terms of contemporary needs. The chief significance of the Reformist movement lies in the fact that it represents a deliberate and purposeful effort in social and spiritual adjustment. While natural selection may be depended upon to operate
in the world of nature, it is man's prerogative to speed improvement
by the use of his intelligence. Yet in the field of human and cosmic
relationships man seldom avails himself of that prerogative. This
is all the more reason why Jews should feel indebted to the Reformist movement for having substituted in Judaism the method of
intelligent direction for that of aimless drifting.

Another important contribution is the renewal of the prophetic
emphasis upon the ethical aspect of Judaism. In the struggle for
existence waged by the Jewish people throughout the centuries, no
opportunity for translating the prophetic ideals into a program of
Jewish life ever presented itself. Ritualism, purified, to be sure, of
its pagan connotations, continued to possess a degree of importance
far beyond its intrinsic value. From the traditional or rabbinic point
of view, the ethical values are regarded as indispensable, but are not
granted the primacy accorded them by the prophets. Regardless of
theory, ritualism acquired a dominant place in practice by reason

of the exaggerated amount of attention paid to it in the literature. Compare, for example, the extent of the material in the Talmud dealing with ritual with the amount of material therein that is devoted to the discussion of the civil law. This legalistic treatment of ritual observance has caused it to bulk large in the consciousness of the Jew, and has laid him open to the charge of being a legalist. From that disproportionate emphasis on ritual the Reformist movement might have saved Judaism, if it had not at the same time committed the fatal mistake of destroying the collective life in which alone Judaism could function.

Reformism must also be credited with having directed the attention of the Jew to the need not merely of continuing but also of developing his religion. From the standpoint of a practical program, the separation of religion from the texture of Jewish life is unworkable. But for the purpose of focussing attention upon the need of bringing Jewish religion into line with contemporary outlook and aspiration, the Reformist approach to the Jewish religion as such has been highly serviceable. One may not agree with the particular type of development Reformism proposes, but one must concede that there is a great deal of force to the claim advanced by Reformism that the very complexities of modern life offer the Jews an unprecedented opportunity to unfold spiritual energies latent in their religion.

If Reformism, however, has rendered invaluable service to the cause of Judaism, it has also made serious mistakes which have tended to counteract the good it has achieved. Though it has halted what might have proved a veritable stampede from Judaism, it has failed to check the process of gradual self-elimination of Jews from Jewish life. Apostasy has not been checked; only its tempo has been changed. Reformism has not succeeded in enabling Judaism to survive more than two, or at most three generations. The serried appearance which its ranks present in this country is due not to the constancy of its own adherents but rather to a continual replenishment by the Orthodox and Conservative Jews who, in most cases, join Reformist congregations to advance themselves socially. Its spiritual leaders are for the most part drawn not from Reformist homes but from homes where Judaism of the traditional type still prevails. The rate of intermarriage with Gentiles among Reformist Jews is unquestionably on the increase, and in the overwhelming majority of cases the children of such intermarriages are not brought up as Jews. In the western and southern states, Reformist Jews in large numbers are affiliated with the Christian Science church. These signs certainly do not point to Reformist power to hold the Jew very long.

The success of the Reformist movement is qualified not only by its uncertain practical prospect, but also by its present spiritual poverty. It is confined to one stratum of society—the so-called upper middle class. Since the prerequisites to the proper functioning of Reformist Judaism are magnificent temples, highly paid rabbis, and expensive choirs, the large mass of wage-earners stand outside its pale. To be sure, while nothing in its program makes these outward appurtenances indispensable, nothing in its program suggests a fitting substitute. Traditional Judaism still impels sweat-shop workers in the cities, poor farmers and bus drivers in farm villages, to establish congregations and to make provision for the religious upbringing of their children. Reformist Judaism, on the other hand, seems to be confined to those who are comfortably situated. By fostering congregational affiliation, it no doubt helps its adherents to live up to the conventional moral standards and to keep alive a sense of communal responsibility, however limited. Without such affiliation to prevent the horizon of their interests from being limited to their own immediate family and friends, there is no telling how spiritually callous they might become. But beyond being the mainstay of respectability for a very limited class of Jews, Reformist Judaism has not stimulated intellectual or moral activity of a high order.

With the freedom from traditional prepossessions which marks Reformism, one would expect that some of the outstanding Jews of great intellectual power would be found among its adherents. With its continual stress on the prophetic message in Judaism as the essential element to which we must return, Reformism should have been ethically creative. It should have given rise to a distinctively ethical type of Jew, or it should have evolved some specific means of enabling the Jew to evince a spirit of faith and piety. With its emphasis upon the God-idea as Judaism's main contribution to the world, a century of Reformism should have produced at least one great book on the meaning of God in human experience.

The least one might expect from a movement which claims to be chiefly concerned with the religion of the Jew is an inspiring prayer-book. Instead, this is what many Reformist rabbis themselves think of the Union Prayer-Book:

The Union Prayer-book unconsciously reflects the present apathy and skepticism toward prayer. Therein lies its chief distinction from the traditional Book of Prayer. . . . The Sabbath and Holy Day services are so arranged as to turn the worshipper into an auditor. They are—with but few exceptions—formal in character. In many synagogues they are consciously used as a mere introduction to the rabbi's discourse.[2]

In a footnote in the same article, the author adds "The Union Prayer-book conveys the impression that it was especially written for a people of retired philanthropists and amateur social workers." "Many changes," reports a Reformist rabbi in a survey of religious conditions, "will have to be made before we shall be able to make our services safe for religion." [3]

Probably a great many factors beyond the control of those who have sponsored the Reformist movement are responsible for this spiritual sterility. Yet we cannot absolve the movement itself of all blame. There must be something basically wrong with its ideology; is it, perhaps, too plausible? The program of a movement must ask much and give much. It must demand great sacrifice, and hold out some great reward in return. Traditionalism required nothing less than the surrender of reason to authority and tradition. This is an audacious but challenging demand. It offered, in return, reward in the hereafter, and the satisfaction of having performed the will of God. Of Reformism it is very difficult to say whether it asks much or little. It talks big, so big, indeed, that to take it seriously one would have to belong to the world's chosen spirits. That is a discouraging fact which has led someone to describe Reformism as "a way of speaking."

What Reformism asks of the Jew today is, in short, that he be the apostle of what is essentially a religious philosophy. Having eliminated from Judaism all else that might be satisfying, intriguing or challenging, Reformism proposes to set up the mission of promulgating the truest and purest conception of God, of which the human mind is capable, as the sum and substance of Judaism. Waiving for the moment the question whether the idea of a mission is consistent with the Reformist conception of the Jewish people, and whether such a rôle is a sufficiently valid reason for remaining a people apart,‘ it is questionable whether there is anything in the career of the Jewish people, outside the few passages in the prophetic literature, to qualify it for such a mission.

The basic assumption of the Reformist ideology is that the Jews have always, as a people, been in advance of other nations and religious groups in the purity and spirituality of their God-idea. Reformism, finding itself under the necessity of accepting the conclusions of scientific historical research, abandons the traditional basis for the claim of the Jews that they alone possessed the true knowledge of God. It cannot concede the historicity of supernatural revelation. By thus refusing to resort to supernaturalism for proof of the Jew's qualification as the upholder of the God-idea in its truest form, Reformism should be prepared to verify that assumption by means of historical facts.

But does history corroborate the generalization that the Jews have always subscribed to what in their own day was the truest conception of God? There were, no doubt, periods in the history of the Jewish people when, under the influence of great religious geniuses like the Prophets, the Jewish people as a whole was won over to a truer conception of God than that held by any contemporary group or individual. But to assert that at all times the God-idea as taught by Judaism was in advance of that held by the rest of the world is to examine Jewish history against the background of its immediate oriental environment alone. Truth, indeed, compels us to engage a wider horizon. Even if the Jewish God-idea was always more spiritual and in greater accord with the truth than the God-idea of other nations, it is open to serious question whether it was truer or more spiritual than that entertained by various philosophers or philosophic groups, at one time or another. It is doubtful whether the Stoics or the Neo-Platonists had a conception of God inferior to that of the Jewish people. As for individual philosophers, Xenophanes, among the first to object to the anthropomorphic representation of deity, heads a long line of thinkers who gave the world the various metaphysical conceptions of God that have been embodied in the three great religions of the world, Judaism included.

Reformism admits that the God-idea, as taught in Scriptures, has always been "developed and spiritualized by the Jewish teachers in accordance with the moral and philosophical progress of their respective ages." ⁶ If this be true, then it was not always the Jews who evolved the most spiritual conception of God. On the contrary, they found it necessary to bring their traditional teachings in line with the moral and philosophical progress achieved by others. Such progress, according to the Reformist way of thinking, necessarily involves a better understanding of what God means and a deeper insight into his nature. The conclusion is therefore inescapable that there were frequent periods in the history of the God-idea when the Jews had to learn from the Gentiles.

If there is any doubt as to this implicit admission on the part of Reformism, that doubt is dispelled by its repudiation of the traditional conception of God in favor of that which modern philosophy proposes. By adopting the modern assumption that God could never have manifested himself as a distinct entity to any human being, and by teaching that the only way God has revealed himself has been through the inner experience of the human soul, Reformist Judaism frankly plays the rôle of disciple and not of master, as far as the God-idea is concerned. There is nothing more praiseworthy than the willingness to learn truth from whatever source is available. But why should the fact that the Jews are apt and willing learners of the truth impose upon them the duty of communicating it to the rest of the world? One would imagine that such a duty would rest upon those who were the first to come into possession of the truth, whether they were Jews or Gentiles.

The fundamental fallacy into which Reformism is forced by its habit of playing up the God-idea as the essence of Judaism is that of crediting the Jewish people as a whole with conscious self-dedication to a conception of God, which only its foremost thinkers were capable of achieving. This is nothing more than a fanciful idealization of the Jewish people, which dissolves at the first contact with historic fact. A realistic description of what went on in the minds of the average men and women who constituted the Jewish people would have to record as wide a range of ideas concerning

God as existed among other religious bodies. There have always been Jews who were intellectually unable to grasp all the intricacies of abstract thinking, and whose ideas of deity, the soul and immortality were more naïve and primitive than those professed by Christian or Mohammedan theologians. Yet no one would dream of denying the name Judaism to the religious faith of the former, or of giving the name Judaism to the religious faith of the latter. The identification of Judaism essentially with the highest development of the God-idea may be legitimate as a wish, but lies beyond the domain of historical fact.

The untenability of the Reformist thesis becomes apparent the moment it is admitted that Judaism's God-idea has not been static, and that even contemporaneous Jewish thinkers and leaders differ among themselves as to how God should be conceived. R. Abraham ben David of Posquières, for example, took violent exception to Maimonides, who characterized as an idolater anyone that regarded the Divine Being as having form.[6] In justifying ceremonies and institutions, Kohler points out that "the maintenance of religion does not rest upon doctrine, which must differ according to the intellectual capacity of the people and the prevailing views of each age."[7] Judaism's idea of God, which at no time is interpreted uniformly, and which is subject to change from age to age, can scarcely live up to the claim made for it by Reformism that it is "the central religious truth for the human race."

In a work on theology, we should naturally expect that first place would be given to the problem of evil. After all, the main purpose of theology should be to reconcile the belief in God with the dominance of evil in the world. The question of evil is therefore the last thing in the world that Judaism as a religion ought to ignore. Yet we miss in Kohler's interpretation of Judaism any allusion to the difficulties presented to religion by the problem of evil. Kohler would hardly go so far as to imply that the modern Jew can find in Jewish tradition an adequate solution of those difficulties. It is therefore surprising that, with all his emphasis upon the God-idea as basic to human conduct, Kohler should have nothing to say on what our attitude should be toward the existence of evil, whence arises the very need for the God-idea. The fact is that not only Kohler but the Reformist movement as such lacks either the philo-

sophic vigor or the spiritual insight to make any courageous affirmation with regard to the problem of evil. Claude G. Montefiore, in
his *Outlines of Liberal Judaism*, says very frankly: "To these
terrible questions, there is and there can be upon earth, no satisfactory answer. We do not know. We can think of a few answers . . .
which explain a very little, but we cannot explain the difficulties
properly or entirely." [8] *In other words, we are called upon to be
martyrs for a religion which fails in its raison d'être, that of enabling
us to adjust ourselves constructively to the evil in ourselves and in
the world.*

It might, perhaps, be argued that what distinguishes the Jewish
conception of God is not its close approximation to theological or
metaphysical truth, but its rich ethical content. This contention
makes of the God-idea chiefly a means to ethical conduct. Is
Reformism, however, prepared to commit itself to the assumption
that ethical conduct is inconceivable without the God-idea, all scientific evidence to the contrary notwithstanding? But apart from this
questionable dependence of morality on religion, nothing of practical consequence is gained from this connection for the concrete
conduct of human affairs, and it is the practical outcome of Judaism's conception of God that Reformism emphasizes. Such outcome
depends not so much upon theoretic motivation, as upon the specific
means and measures which men employ to attain the ethical ideals
they cherish. [9]
Abstract ethical ideals may have a certain contemplative charm
or inspirational value, but they certainly are not substantial enough
to serve as a base from which to attack the evils of the world, nor
even as a shelter to which one may withdraw when beset by the forces
of the world. The mission to teach universal brotherhood can be taken
seriously only when it is translated into a definite program like the
abolition of chauvinistic nationalism, the outlawry of war, the
establishment of economic justice [10] or greater equality of opportunity. But the Reformist movement would not venture to commit
itself to any of these causes. Nor would it even dare urge that it is
the duty of its adherents to throw in their lot with some specific
movement for social reform. The philosophy of Reformism furnishes
an excellent illustration of the truth that one of the superstitions

current even among cultivated persons is the supposition that, if the right *end* is pointed out to them, all that is required to bring about the accomplishment of that end is will or wish on the part of the one who is to act. Such a belief "is on a par with primitive magic in its neglect of attention to the means which are involved in reaching an end." [11]

If pressed for a definite pronouncement as to how it would have the Jew further the cause of human brotherhood, Reformism would probably answer that it expects him to lead an exemplary life by living in accordance with the teaching of the prophet Micah who said, "What doth the Lord require of thee? Only to do justly and to love mercy, and to walk humbly with the Lord." Reformism forgets that, if these words of Micah influenced a few of his contemporaries to live more ethically and spiritually, it was because they denoted for his hearers a specific course of action which was to wean Israel from definite evil habits. Micah's message was a message of means as well as of ends. It is thus that all true prophets speak. If the Jews really intended to be the prophet-people of mankind, they would have to exemplify by their mode of life the efficacy of the specific social measures and religious institutions by which they strive to do justly and to express their love of mercy, and their pious communion with God.

One cannot but sympathize with the efforts of the Reformist spokesmen to square the apparent ambitiousness of the newly assumed mission—for in the sense in which the mission is now interpreted it is newly assumed—with the given realities which bespeak inactivity on the part of the Jews and unawareness on the part of the Gentiles.

Meanwhile, writes Claude G. Montefiore, the mere existence of the Jews is not without its value and its influence. A more active period of influence may perhaps at no distant period begin. Already in the United States there is much interchange of pulpits, much mingling of thoughts. Jews, especially liberal Jews, are indubitably doing something in that vast country towards the development of religious belief. In the religious ferment which is there going on, they are playing a part. [12]

Distance evidently lends enchantment.

The Reformist hypothesis that Jews have a native gift for

religion, a gift which is hereditary, should be attributed to the workings of the compensatory mechanism. So long as Jews had implicit faith in the tradition that God had actually revealed himself to their ancestors, one can understand how they came to conclude that they alone possessed the means to salvation. But once Jews give up the belief in that tradition, they cannot replace that belief with a categorical claim of being a race endowed with an inborn sensitiveness for things spiritual.[13] To make such an assertion in the face of the thousand and one problems of heredity and environment, and of the difficulties involved in making generalizations about any race or people, is to betray a sense of inferiority. Even when some ethnologists admit that we may ascribe certain inner tendencies to races or peoples, they always have in mind the fact that a special geographic environment and certain historical forces are required for those tendencies to come into play.[14] The great social and religious ideals were not evolved in a void. Had not the Prophets lived amidst national events which placed them upon a pinnacle whence they could command large vistas of the human scene, no one would ever have been the wiser as to whether or not they possessed spiritual genius.

The statement that the Jews possess a special capacity for religion is far from being a rhetorical flourish. How literally and seriously it is taken is evident from the fact that it is the premise in the Reformist argument against intermarriage with adherents of other religious groups. Since Jews possess this native gift for true religion, intermarriage is undesirable. By diluting the pure Jewish strain, intermarriage would weaken the inherent religious genius of the Jew. Suppose, however, someone should question the validity of the Reformist claim that the Jews are more talented religiously than the rest of mankind, or the assumption that religion is a hereditary trait, the door would then be thrown wide open to intermarriage.

As a matter of fact, Reformism does not make any herculean efforts to stem the increasing tide of intermarriage. It merely advises "to avoid intermarriage." [15] In that kind of advice there breathes very little fervor or zeal. Moreover, it is against "members of other sects" that such advice is directed. Are we to infer that intermarriage with those who have no religious affiliations, though they belong to other races, is not to be avoided? It is no wonder that some of the Reformist spokesmen are beginning to demand the complete removal of the restriction. The element of "racialism" which Kohler regarded as inseparably interwoven with the religious doctrine of Judaism is bound to appear out of place in a program of life which is based on a philosophy of religion. Sooner or later Reformism will be driven to accept the logical conclusion of its basic assumption that Judaism is essentially the God-idea in its truest form, and permit intermarriage. With the elimination of the belief that there is anything in the racial heredity of a human being which disposes him to a particular kind of idea or world-outlook, there remains no plausible ground for opposing intermarriage. Having reduced Judaism to a religious philosophy, it will have to go a step farther and give up the idea to which it still holds that "the Jew is born into it [Judaism] and cannot extricate himself from it even by a renunciation of his faith." [16] The adherent of a philosophy should be free to give it up as soon as he finds it unacceptable, for at no time should the element of constraint be a factor in a loyalty whose chief value depends upon its being a matter of choice. Reformism might thus eventually have proved to be merely an excellent shock absorber, absorbing the shock to social life that usually accompanies too rapid an amalgamation of different cultural and religious groups.

There were religious philosophies in the past. Stoicism was a religious philosophy, and so was Neo-Platonism, which for a time threatened to prove a successful rival of Christianity. But religious philosophies are, as a rule, self-sufficient, sure of the strength and richness of their own content. The children of their adherents do not automatically become adherents. A religious philosophy that lays claim to truth based on reason should insist upon that truth being accepted only by those who are sufficiently mature to judge for themselves. What has truth to do with blood relationship? The right procedure should be to acquaint the child with various religious and non-religious philosophies, and then allow him to choose. But the insistence that merely because one is born to Jewish parents he is duty-bound to remain a Jew, is certainly not consistent with the declaration that Judaism is the truest form of religious truth,[17] intended to preach the unity of God and the brotherhood of man.

The fact is that Reformism has by no means found a satisfactory formula for the Jewish people; it has not found a self-consistent and intelligible interpretation of the traditional conception of Jewish nationhood which it professes to abjure and which, in certain vestiges, it is constrained to preserve. By repudiating Israel's status as a nation, Reformism has to give Israel a status that shall, in a sense, be a continuation of that held in the past, and yet fit into the framework of the modern state. The kind of social organism which Reformism has tried to make out of the Jews is without a parallel in human society. It is based on blood relationship plus consensus of belief. The raciality of the Jew is awkwardly and irrationally forced into the conception of a religion that is meant to be universal. It is as though a family were to organize itself into a philosophical society. Sociologically, such an organism is absurd. From its very nature it cannot function.

Reformism might well consider whether it was justified in the precipitate haste with which it repudiated Jewish nationhood. Has it at all weighed carefully the psychological and spiritual factors involved in nationhood? Since nationhood and religion were always intimately interwoven in Judaism, the Reformists might have suspected that by removing the element of nationhood they would at the same time render the religion as useless as the warp is without the woof. With all one's desire to find nothing but disinterested devotion to truth as the chief motivating force in the Reformist program, one cannot but discover an ulterior prudential motive in the surrender of Jewish nationhood. For it is not nationalism or patriotism in general that Reformism deprecates. On the contrary, some of its outstanding adherents have a tendency to shout their patriotism from the housetops. It is only *Jewish* nationhood that has been thus summarily disqualified and despatched. Does it not look a little like trying to placate those who would withhold from the Jews the full benefits of the emancipation?

This surrender of Jewish nationhood is a new kind of suicide, suicide on a national scale. Considered objectively, one may ask: what right has an individual Jew or a group of Jews officially to change the status of all the Jews in the world? For the last three thousand years all Jews have regarded themselves, and have been regarded by the rest of the world, as primarily a nation. The only way, perhaps, they might change their status would be by electing representatives with full power to decide upon the Jewish status. Even then, it is a question whether the representatives could legally rule out of existence a fact which is too patent to be denied. The Sanhedrin (Assembly of Jewish Notables) convoked in 1806-1807 by Napoleon I, was terrorized into declaring that the Jews of France were no longer part of a nationality, *un corps de nation,* but a religious community, or Frenchmen of the Mosaic persuasion. In doing that they legislated only for themselves and not for Jewry as a whole.

Suppose there were an immigration law to the effect that, if a number of members of one family wanted to gain admission into the country at the same time, they should not be permitted to enter. Let us say that a family by the name of Cohen, which had not heard of the law, happens to arrive. What is to be done? One of them hits upon a capital idea. From now on they shall no longer regard themselves as a family. Their status shall henceforth be that of a society. But a society must have a purpose. That purpose shall be to practice Cohenism; i.e., coming together periodically and performing the ritual of blessing the world. In that way, the immigration law can be circumvented. Such, practically, has been the procedure of Reformism on the question of Jewish nationhood. Assuming that the emancipation precludes the granting of civic rights to those who declare themselves members of the Jewish nationality, that difficulty is circumvented by voting that the Jews are no longer a nation. The only proper thing, it seems, for the Jew to do when he finds Jewish nationhood irksome to him is to read himself out of it, but not to read the Jewish nationality out of existence. Whether Judaism has gained by the action of Reformism in the matter of Jewish nationhood is questionable, but it is certain that Jews throughout the world who refuse to accept Reformism have been embarrassed by that action. The inevitable effect of declaring that Judaism has nothing to do with Jewish nationhood is to cast a reflection on the civic patriotism and loyalty of those who insist upon retaining their Jewish nationhood.

By the same token that Reformism has etherealized Israel, the nation, into Israel, the religious community, it has sublimated Torah, the all-embracing system of concrete guidance, into Torah, the vague abstraction known as moral law. The function of being a source of specific legal sanctions and prescriptions cannot be dissociated from Torah without destroying its fundamental character. Those who cannot subscribe to the traditional belief that specific ritual, civil and criminal laws came directly from God, may nevertheless regard all such laws as an important part of Judaism, believing that the Jews are a nation, or nationality, and therefore a law-making and law-enforcing body. But if the Jewish nationhood is to be repudiated, Judaism can have nothing to do with laws, the very essence of which implies a degree of social coercion which the Jews waive when they surrender their nationhood. Reformism realizes the void created when we eliminate the law from Judaism. What it proposes to put in its place is calculated to emphasize the void rather than to fill it. A few ceremonies centering about the institution of the synagogue, and a pale ghost of an ethical system, can hardly serve as a substitute for Torah.

The ceremonies that are preserved from the past have scant reason for being part of the Reformist program. Kohler's argument for their retention reveals how apprehensive, and justly so, Reformism has been of carrying out its program to its logical conclusion. In his defense of ceremonies, Kohler gives away the entire case of Reformism. "The maintenance of a religion does not rest upon its doctrines, which must differ according to the intellectual capacity of the people and the prevailing view of each age." [18] Hence, the need for ceremonies and institutions. If this statement means anything, it implies that there is much more to a religion than a God-idea. If religion were confined to that, how could people who hold different doctrines, or who understand the God-idea differently, be said to belong to the same religion? Probably this statement is no more than a *lapsus calami*, and should be overlooked. But we are left in the dark as to the why and wherefore of the traditional ceremonies.

How is it that even as much as a single Hebrew phrase has been retained in the prayer-book? One can hardly attach any serious significance to the paradoxical argument advanced by Ludwig Philippson at the Conference at Brunswick (1844) when he said: "Every nation has its historical mission, and the Jews have theirs. They are a nation dedicated to religion. For the sake of such a mission, it has needed a special language. Hebrew is the ideal language for religion." [19] Geiger was far more consistent when at the second conference at Frankfort a.M. in 1845 he argued that "if the Hebrew language were to be recognized as an integral part of Judaism, Judaism would thereby be acknowledged as being a national religion, since a distinctive language is a conspicuous trait of a people that leads a segregated life." [20] Of late, however, there has been a tendency to increase the amount of printed Hebrew in the prayer-book, though less of it is actually recited. [21] It is, indeed, paradoxical that not only is the original Aramaic of the *Kaddish* retained but that an entire paragraph in Aramaic should be added to it. One almost begins to suspect a deliberate purpose to cast a mystic spell upon the worshippers, for they surely cannot be expected to understand Aramaic.

But it is in the moral law, chiefly, that the best of what was associated with the ideal of Torah deserves to survive. Though lacking the concreteness necessary to render it an effective challenge to the moral evils of present-day life, Torah as moral law might at least be made to point to some worthwhile spiritual goal. But even in that respect Jewish ethics, as formulated by Reformism, falls short. It is colorless, uninspiring, and definable for the most part by what it negates rather than by what it affirms. Its chief boast seems to be that it negates Greek ethics with its emphasis upon expansiveness, Buddhist ethics with its belief in Nirvana, and Christian ethics with its other-worldly sanctions. Imitation of God as a principle of ethics, which Kohler declares to be characteristic of Judaism, reduces itself to a vague metaphor, when it is taken for granted that the only way man can know God is through the functioning of the conscience. The positive ethical teachings of Reformism are mostly of the platitudinarian type usually designated as copybook morality. Surely, very poor substitutes for Israel's ancient Torah.

The weakness and the inconsistency of the Reformist movement are most apparent in its educational program for the young. The real test of any religion, movement or civilization is in the process of education to which it gives rise. If that process is rich in content, colorful and stirring, the movement or religion which it transmits is answering a real need, and is bound to live. But when it is as thin, meager and unappealing as the process of religious training identified with Reformist Judaism, there can be no doubt that the movement is a mistake.[22] The traditional "four ells of the law" represented a lifelong educational process. Reformist Judaism has not enough content to occupy young children for a few years, sixty hours a year. The mere inability of Reformism to employ the thought, energy and enthusiasm of its lay adherents should be proof of its irrelevance.

Reformism's greatest failing is in that which is supposed to be its main contribution, the cause of religion. From the standpoint of religion as a personal reaction to life, it is a mistake to confine oneself to the results achieved by one's own people or religious community. The characteristic tendency in advanced religious thought is to recognize that the time-spirit has brought to the fore new issues and ideals which all the historic religions have to take into account. "Over all the world today," says E. Eustace Haydon, "the leaders of the great religions are thinking the same thoughts and turning their faces toward the same ideals. . . . There is a recognition of the solidarity of the human race. They realize now that no one race or religion can save the world. Since religion is a way of life and all races are now entangled in the maze of common problems, the realization of a world made hospitable to the higher values must be the result of the united labors of all the religions of mankind." [23]

The entire program of Reformism is based on a misconception of the very nature of a religion like that of the Jewish people. Such a religion never existed apart from the people that evolved it, and cannot be treated as a system of ideas and practices which might be fostered by a religio-philosophical group. The religion of a people is but a phase of the entire life of that people and determined by the forces, social, economic and cultural, inherent in its life, as well as by the fortunes attending it. What a noted writer has had to say of Christianity in speaking of the failure to treat religion as a phase of civilization applies with even greater truth to the Jewish religion:

Such a method ignores the fact that doctrines have not sprung up as independent systems of truth. In this respect, they do not resemble philosophy as much as they do law and especially the common law of England and the constitution, of the United States. Strictly speaking, there is no history of doctrine; there is only the history of the people who made doctrines. A theology is a function of the religious life of a given period, and this in turn is the expression of a social order conditioned not only by elements of culture, like philosophy, literature and science, but also by the creative forces which were engaged in the production of the social order itself.[24]

The resemblance to law is borne out by the fact that in Jewish literature, until the medieval period, there was no special term for religion—quite a paradox from the Reformist viewpoint. The term that passed for what now corresponds to religion was Torah, which at once suggests the aspect of law. Even the relatively recent term "*dat*," specifically reserved for religion, means law.

Only in Wonderland can there be a cat which leaves its grin behind it. In the world of reality it is not feasible to try to have the grin without the cat. That experiment has been undertaken by Reformism in trying to have the Jewish religion without the living entity to which that religion belongs—without a living, functioning Jewish people.

CHAPTER X

CONSERVATIVE JUDAISM (RIGHT WING OF REFORMISM)

Conservative Judaism merely a variant of Reformism—Contends Reformist principles are no innovation—The attitude of Conservative Judaism to ceremonial observances based on sentiment.

WHATEVER fault one may find with the Reformist movement as promulgated by outstanding leaders like Geiger, Kohler and Montefiore, one cannot charge it with being inconsistent in its philosophy or half-hearted in the changes it advocates: Its theory is, on the whole, coherent, and the practice it recommends keeps pace with the theory. As was to be expected, however, there have been many Jews who, though dissatisfied with traditional Judaism, were not quite prepared to go the entire length with Reformism. They may have been in sympathy with the major premises of the movement, but finding that the conclusion to which it led was such as to reduce Jewish life to a vanishing point, they have refused to subscribe to its minor premises. Those who have taken this attitude constitute the Conservative element, or the right wing of the Reformist movement. They should not be confused with another group that has differentiated itself from the Neo-Orthodox constituency, as its left wing, and has also come to be known as Conservative.

Laboring under the handicap of vagueness of purpose and lacking aggressive leadership, Conservative Reformism has not been able to attract a large following, or effect extensive organization. In America it was much more influential a generation ago, when it had men of the stamp of Marcus Jastrow and Benjamin Szold among its leaders. In Germany in 1899 a number of rabbis organized themselves into the "Union of Liberal Rabbis of Germany." [1] The term "liberal" in this instance has a different connotation from what it has in English Jewry where it is synonymous with unqualified Reformism. In England, Conservative Reformism did not make much headway, but it found an able spokesman in Morris Joseph. His book on *Judaism as Creed and Life* ² is the clearest statement of the Conservative point of view, and the exposition it gives of Judaism may well serve as basis for evaluating the tenability of Conservative Reformism.

Morris Joseph describes his position as intermediate between that of M. Friedlander whose interpretation of Judaism as set forth in his book *The Jewish Religion* ³ is definitely Neo-Orthodox, and that of C. G. Montefiore whose *Liberal Judaism* expounds the doctrine and practice of the Reformist movement. In Morris Joseph's own words, *Judaism as Creed and Life* is an attempt "to give a comprehensive account of Jewish belief and practice as they are conceived by men of moderate views." ⁴ If we are to take M. Joseph's exposition of Judaism as representing the Conservative Reformist point of view, we are warranted in concluding that basically the philosophy of Conservative Reformism is identical with that of unqualified Reformism. It is only in the matter of religious practices that Conservatism refuses to accept the logical consequences of that philosophy. To prove this point, it will suffice to touch upon the outstanding ideas in *Judaism as Creed and Life*.

Morris Joseph takes for granted that "the great intellectual and social movements of this age" preclude the complete acceptance of what has come down to us from the past. Jews have to select only those elements of their spiritual heritage which can be synthesized with the great intellectual and social movements·of this age.⁵ What is the principle of selection? His unequivocal answer is: Reason.⁶ Even the faith in God which Judaism demands of us is faith based on reason.⁷ While it is true that not everything that transpires in the world and in human life confirms the belief in divine providence, there are sufficient evidences of godhood to justify us in inferring that God is everywhere in the great domain.⁸ According to M. Joseph, the human mind acts just as normally in postulating the existence of God as when it postulates the existence of ether or electrons. In the one case it performs an act of faith in order to comprehend the universe as a whole, in the other, it performs an act of reason in order to account for certain physical phenomena. But, fundamentally, there is little difference between the two methods of orienting oneself to life.⁹ In fact, the substance of his argument concerning the belief in God is that God's existence may be inferred from the universe, from history, and from the life of the individual,¹⁰ and is therefore essentially a matter of human experience, and not of supernatural revelation.

In taking this position, however, Morris Joseph breaks with tradition, though he refuses to admit that he does so. He makes it a point to deny that he advances anything new in Judaism. In this respect he displays the attitude characteristic of Conservatism. He does not propound an idea without at once proving that it is not new, as though it was sure to be wrong if no authority could be quoted in support of it. But, viewed objectively, the basis for the belief in God was in olden times unquestionably the tradition that he had revealed himself in person, as it were, and indirectly through miracles. Only the few who came under the influence of philosophy took it for granted that man could not help believing in God, if he allowed himself to be guided by his reason. From the traditional standpoint, therefore, the difference between Jewish religion and the other religions was not a matter of degree but of kind. The Jewish religion was the only one that was regarded as true, because it alone was based upon what was considered the indisputable event of God's self-revelation. But when M. Joseph describes the Jewish religion as "the truest form of truth" he implies that the difference between the Jewish and the other religions is only a matter of degree. His reasoning is consistent with his assumption that all religion is based on human experience and is not imposed from without in some transcendent fashion; but it is, nevertheless, a decided departure from traditional Judaism. This he cannot bring himself to admit, though there is nothing to indicate that he takes the tradition concerning the theophany at Sinai to be historic fact. The tendency to represent his exposition of the Jewish conception of God as being in line with traditional teaching is bound to distort his idea of traditional Judaism,¹¹ and to give the wrong perspective on the Jewish religious problem of our day. All that it does is to impair the principle of progress, which Reformism has sought to inject into Judaism.

An examination of the universal truths which M. Joseph holds up as constituting Judaism's chief contribution to religion reveals that they are none other than those professed by all Theists. He realizes that this must give rise to the question:[12] why can we not teach the same truth about God as Theists instead of as Jews? In the answer which he gives there emerges a new principle for which there is no preparation whatever in the body of his argument. "The Jew," he says, "owes allegiance to Judaism as well as to his mission, just as every Englishman owes loyalty not only to England's civilizing task but to England herself."[13] This parallel between England and Judaism is far from clarifying. All through the book we are led to believe that the Jews are not a nation. To all intents, the attitude taken toward nationhood is exactly the same as that of the Reformists. What, therefore, can be the meaning of this comparison of Judaism to England? The England which claims the Englishman's allegiance is surely a nation. Perhaps M. Joseph is in accord with Kohler who maintains that Judaism is a matter of race as well as of religion. But if that is what he has in mind, it is nowhere clearly stated. With half-thoughts like these, Conservative Reformism expects to overcome the absurd inferences to which one is led by its assumptions.

On no question, however, does there seem to be such complete agreement between Conservatism and Reformism as on that of Zionism. They agree even in their misunderstanding of the Zionist movement. While latterly Reformism has been inclined to oppose it on the ground that it is secularist and anti-religious, in the official Reformist literature Zionism is classed with the traditional belief in the advent of a personal Messiah, as though they belonged to the same type of ideas. The revolutionary character of Zionism, its implied revaluation of traditional concepts, are not even suspected. This mistake of Reformism is blindly accepted by Morris Joseph, together with the stereotyped arguments advanced by Reformism against the Zionist movement. "There are many Jews," he writes, ". . . who do not and cannot believe in these things. They cannot believe in the Restoration of the Jewish State, for they hold that such an event would impede rather than promote the fulfillment of the great purpose for which Israel exists. The moral and religious education of the world, they maintain, can best be promoted by close contact between Jew and Gentile."[14] The two overworked rabbinic sayings that the dispersion of the Jews was providentially designed as

a means of making proselytes,[16] and that the Messiah was born on
the day the Temple fell,[16] are hauled out and misinterpreted so as
to lend support to the doctrine of the denationalization of the Jewish people. We are, indeed, informed that "we can be equally good
Jews whatever view we hold on these points." Yet one must confess
that this complaisance is rather paradoxical, coming after the statement that the restoration would impede the mission of Israel.

It is obvious that the principles which Conservative Reformism
lays down concerning the belief in God and the status of the Jewish
people coincide entirely with those of Reformism proper. The difference—and it is by no means weighty—appears in the matter of
religious observances. As to the Torah from which these observances
emanate, there is further coincidence between Conservatism and
Reformism. Conservatism can have no compunction in adopting the
fundamental conclusions of modern biblical scholarship which prove
that the Torah is a composite work. There is no qualitative difference
between the Pentateuch and the rest of the Bible from the standpoint of authoritativeness, for Morris Joseph holds that it is only
the intrinsic character of the teaching that determines the authority
of any part of Scripture. Hence it makes no difference in which
part of Scripture that teaching occurs.

The teachings of Scripture deal with the idea of God, with morality, and with ceremonial observances. There is nothing in the idea
of God as expounded by Conservatism to which any Theist might
not subscribe. As for morality, that too has nothing distinctive
except that God is set up as the pattern of the moral perfection to
be striven after. According to Morris Joseph, "As systems of morality, Judaism and Christianity may be said to be practically identical." [17] It is only in their applications that they differ. One urges taking Jews as patterns and the other one has to protect the reputation
of the church. He characterizes ceremonial observances as ranking
lowest in importance among the constituent elements of religion.[18]
"We can imagine," he writes, "a religion without a scrap of ceremonial." That being the case, it is a questionable advantage that
he ascribes to Judaism when he says that "no religion has more
clearly recognized the value of ceremonial than Judaism." [19] Incidentally, this statement is contradicted by all the information

furnished us concerning every ancient religion. And it is in this lowest among the constituents of religion, in the one that gives the Jew the greatest amount of trouble, that all of this type of Conservatism is centered.

We are bidden to observe dietary laws, Sabbaths, feasts and fasts, abstain from marriage with Gentiles, retain Hebrew in the ritual, and even study in order to understand it. The specific recommendations with regard to the observances would be declared by the Neo-Orthodox as nugatory, and by the Liberals as arbitrary. Thus he advocates the complete abandonment of the rabbinic interpretation of the dietary laws, and would retain only the pentateuchal prohibitions of certain animals and shellfish. Why make a distinction which, from the premises of this kind of Conservatism, must appear rather arbitrary and trivial? Why incur the hostility of Gentiles by flaunting Jewish separateness for the sake of what "ranks lowest in importance among the constituents of religion?"

The conception of Judaism set forth in the *Religio Laici Judaici*[20] by Laurie Magnus has much in common with that elaborated by Morris Joseph. He, too, negates the supernatural origin of the Torah and the nationhood of Israel. Nevertheless, he strenuously opposes any changes in the ritual that must logically follow these negations. He enters into a lengthy argument to prove why, despite higher criticism, it is perfectly proper for the congregation to proclaim when the scroll is raised, "This is the Torah which Moses placed before Israel according to the command of the Lord." In the same spirit he argues for the retention of the prayer for the restoration of Zion on the ground that we might interpret it symbolically as referring to the ultimate fulfillment of the Jewish mission.[21] On the other hand, Laurie Magnus, unlike Morris Joseph, sees no justifiable reason for maintaining the dietary laws.[22] This vacillation which is characteristic of all middle-of-the-road systems is accentuated in the case of Conservative Reformism by a vague sentimentalism which hankers after a tangible residue of Jewish life without knowing exactly why.

The main weakness of Conservative Reformism is that, in a situation in which there is no way of telling what the extremes are, it makes a principle of moderateness. It may even be that the nature of the situation is such that the very purpose of being moderate is out of place. When a person is drowning, moderateness in the means taken to save him is scarcely a virtue. Collective Jewish life is obviously in danger of disintegration unless something immediate and drastic be done to save it. The problem is to find an objective in living as a Jew that shall be sufficiently stimulating and inspiring. That one can be a Jew without doing violence to reason and without too severe a wrench from sentimental attachments to tradition is by no means sufficient reason for being a Jew. As we have seen, in the last resort, Morris Joseph has to appeal to the Jew's sense of loyalty. But England, which has a claim on the Englishman's loyalty, is not merely a state of mind. It is a living, interacting society to which the Englishman is bound by ties of personal interest. What does Judaism do for the individual Jew that he should owe it loyalty? Does it offer him at least such means and opportunities for salvation as he cannot get elsewhere? According to the answer of Conservative Reformism, it would seem that the philosophy of life it offers him is nothing that he cannot learn from any textbook on Theism. As to a program of practice, he is left to choose between that of Morris Joseph and that of Laurie Magnus. Very few Jews are likely to feel morally bound to render allegiance to a Judaism which makes no attempt to re-establish that corporate Jewish life whereby the individual might be made to feel that his interests are shared to some extent by the Jewish aggregate. "England" is to the individual Englishman a living, corporate entity. The "Judaism" to which Conservative Reformism asks the Jew to be loyal is nothing more than a memory of a people that once had body, but is now a mere haunting ghost.

CHAPTER XI

THE NEO-ORTHODOX VERSION OF JUDAISM

Neo-Orthodoxy as a mode of adjustment—Neo-Orthodoxy's retort to the spirit of the age—Revelation the main source of our knowledge of God and of the destiny of man—No alternative to the belief in the supernatural origin of the Torah—No interpretation of Torah valid unless from the standpoint of the Torah's teachings—The *miswot* to be observed in a spirit of implicit obedience to the will of God—Allegiance to the Torah the sole basis of Jewish nationhood—Israel's mission to exemplify obedience to the laws of God.

THE changes in the habitual modes of Jewish life and thought, which began to make their appearance toward the end of the eighteenth century and beginning of the nineteenth, were due to the contacts with non-Jews which arose out of the gradual extension of civic and political rights. The opposition which those changes encountered were originally animated by sheer apprehension of the consequences to which such contacts might lead. Even when no specific traditional belief or law was impugned, the mere fact that any social measure or cultural undertaking implied a *rapprochement* between Jew and Gentile was enough to condemn it. When Mendelssohn published his translation of the Pentateuch, Rabbi Ezekiel Landau of Prague pronounced a ban against it. When Hartwig Wessely urged the establishment of Jewish schools where secular studies would be taught, the rabbis of his day denounced him as a traitor to Judaism.[1] Soon, however, the discontent with ghetto Judaism grew to proportions that found expression in attempts to introduce innovations in codified rabbinic law, and in the enunciation of views at variance with tradition. This stung the spokesmen of rabbinic Judaism into embittered and determined resistance. Every time any of the Reformist group inaugurated some new undertaking, or made an attempt to mobilize the existing forces of Reformism, the defenders of the old order answered with a counter mobilization. At times the latter even resorted to governmental aid to check the Reformist advance. Nevertheless their warfare was on the whole defensive. It merely tried to hold the fortresses of rabbinism against attack. There was no counter move made to reckon with the new conditions which the changed political status and cultural opportunities created for the Jew.

But before long a new type of opposition to Reformism developed. Instead of combating the introduction of European culture, the new spokesmen of rabbinic Judaism took the position that it was possible for the Jews not only to escape the negative influences which inhered in European culture, but even to enlist that culture in the cause of traditional Judaism, provided it was approached in what they considered the proper spirit. Most of these new spokesmen had acquired a modern training in the leading universities of Europe and were well-versed in modern methods of science and research. Far from shaking their faith in rabbinic Judaism, this training made them all the more confident that traditional Judaism had nothing to fear from contact with western civilization. On the contrary, only by becoming part of it and realizing what it has to offer can the Jew fully appreciate the deeper meanings of his own spiritual heritage, and make its challenge to mankind effective. Although Solomon Rapoport, Samuel David Luzzatto, Nathan Marcus Adler and Samson Raphael Hirsch who led the forces of opposition to Reformism came to the aid of the rabbinic leaders of the old school who refused to make peace with European culture, they themselves waged the war for traditional Judaism by means of entirely different strategy and tactics.

This aggressive type of Orthodoxy is so different from the Orthodoxy of the rabbis of the old school who represented rabbinic or traditional Judaism of the pre-enlightenment age, that the name Neo-Orthodoxy by which it is sometimes called should be regarded as more than a casual designation. The term Neo-Orthodoxy should be systematically employed not only to register a historic truth which is already becoming blurred, but to focus attention upon the essential fact in this new type of opposition to Reformism. That fact is that instead of trying to avoid the conflict with European civilization, by retaining as much of the past social and cultural separatism as possible, Neo-Orthodoxy is only too ready to come to grips with the western outlook and mode of life. Neo-Orthodoxy, in contrast with the Orthodoxy of traditional Judaism, is thus decidedly one of the present-day versions of Judaism which are programs of adjustment.

The literature of the Neo-Orthodox movement reveals the wide front upon which it has conducted its campaign against the tendencies it deems dangerous to Judaism. Samuel David Luzzatto combated the modern spirit as atheistic and unmoral. David Hoffmann wrestled valiantly with higher criticism. Zeeb Yabetz wrote a history of the Jews in which the traditional conception of the past is given all possible semblance of historicity, and Yizhak Isaak Ha-Levi combated point for point every intimation that rabbinic law was a gradual growth answering to the spiritual needs of the various periods during which it developed. Samson Raphael Hirsch is practically the only one who made an effort to restate the philosophy underlying traditional Judaism as a whole in terms that reckoned with the challenge of modern thought and life.[2] Hence a summary of his views is the best means of judging the merits of the program whereby Neo-Orthodoxy hopes to meet successfully the forces that threaten to undermine Judaism.

Hirsch wrote prolifically, but the one work of his which contains the most comprehensive statement of his philosophy of Judaism is *The Nineteen Letters of Ben Uzziel*.[3] That will serve as the basic text in the exposition of Neo-Orthodoxy, and will be supplemented by relevant passages from Hirsch's other writings; other spokesmen of Neo-Orthodoxy add little to his exposition.

As a piece of pleading, *The Nineteen Letters of Ben Uzziel* deserves to take its place by the side of Ha-Levi's *Al Khazari*. Like that famous apologia for rabbinic Judaism when it was menaced by the Karaites, Hirsch's book resorts to a literary device to state his case for the traditional conception of Judaism. Hirsch addresses himself to a friend by the name of Benjamin[4] whom he is supposed to have known as a pious youth, but who has now entirely changed his religious views and practices as a result of his reading and contact with the world since leaving home and parents, and bears suppressed ill will against Judaism. Hirsch attributes this attitude on the part of Benjamin to his inadequate understanding of Judaism. On the one hand, whatever knowledge of Judaism Benjamin possesses is based, for the most part, upon a few mechanical practices which he was taught to perform in his parents' home, and upon a few ill-digested fragments of the Bible and the Talmud which he learned from some "Polish *rebbe*." In contrast, he was dazzled by the ideas of Christian writers and Jewish Reformists, and allured by the love of comfort and ease to which the modern spirit panders. Hirsch thus implies that the hope of traditional Judaism rests upon a proper understanding of it. He expects the letters that follow to further that understanding. Neo-Orthodoxy boldly accepts the challenge of the modern world. Far from urging that Judaism withdraw into its own shell, the Neo-Orthodox defenders invite a fair-minded examination of its claims.

Neo-Orthodoxy, however, frankly refuses to be placed in a position where it would have to defend its claims before the court of reason. It regards the submission of its case to reason as taking a stand outside Judaism. The principle that to interpret Judaism correctly one must not take the neutral attitude of an outsider, but view its teachings and institutions from the standpoint of their character as divinely revealed, is set up by the Neo-Orthodox school of thought as a norm which they would apply to any apologia, no matter who its author be. Samuel David Luzzatto did not hesitate to take Maimonides to task for finding it necessary to reconcile Jewish tradition to Aristotelian metaphysics. Samson Raphael Hirsch in the introduction to his *Horeb* frankly disavows all intention of coming to terms with reason. "If you, my reader," he says, "expect a defense of the divine commandments that would reckon with your inclinations, views and general assumptions concerning life, if you intend to take this book with the attitude of a judge who wants to find in it the pros and cons concerning our most sacred interests, and then make up your mind whether you are going to accept or repudiate the divine commandments, better leave my book unread; it was not meant for you." * Divine teaching, and not investigation and study, is the only soil out of which the life of the spirit can blossom. Wherever any of our views is in conflict with a teaching of the Torah, it is that view which must yield and not the teaching of the Torah. Had we learned to reckon with the Torah in its entirety as an instrument of supernatural revelation instead of approaching its contents critically and in piecemeal fashion, we would never come to hold such troublesome views, laments Hirsch.

In the *Nineteen Letters,* Hirsch opens his argument with a statement of the Jewish outlook upon the world as embodied in the traditional Jewish conception of God. He launches his attack against the spirit of the age by questioning the humanistic assumption which underlies the ideology of our day, that the salvation of the human being consists in the attainment of happiness and self-perfection. Of what good is it to accept such an aim, he asks, since it in no way helps us to decide what to do, and how to live. To make happiness a criterion of conduct is to encourage anarchy. The pleasure seeker and the criminal find happiness in conduct which must lead to the destruction of society. The goal of self-perfection, on the other hand, is attainable only by those whose intellect is of the very highest order, since it presupposes a high degree of intellectual development and a keen sensitiveness to truth. That cannot be set up as a goal for the generality of mankind.

Although man is incapable of discovering the true purpose of his existence, he knows enough to realize that he must avoid everything that is likely to bring him into clash with the inherent trend of life as a whole. Whatever aim he adopts must be in line with the destiny of mankind as manifest in its history. If he is a Jew, the destiny of Israel should determine his choice. But neither mankind nor Israel could be said to disclose any inherent trend or destiny unless viewed as the creation of God, who confers meaning and purpose on whatever he creates.

How shall we conceive God? It does not even occur to Hirsch to engage in speculative reasoning in order to find an answer. He turns directly to what to him is the incontestable revelation of God, the Torah.[1] Why philosophize about God when God himself tells us all that he wants us to know, all that it is humanly possible to know about him? Read the story of creation and you will know all that the human mind can comprehend of God. The account of creation, for example, teaches that everything which you behold of nature is the work of the one omnipotent creator. Everything has its special purpose assigned to it by God. The matter, form, force and dimensions of each object are arranged in such a way as to further that purpose. This fact points to God's infinite wisdom. Science, the study of nature which enables you to discover the forces at work and the laws by which they work, helps you to comprehend the will of God with regard to every object in the world. That a stone falls according to the law of gravitation is God's will manifesting itself in the stone.

In the same story of creation, the Torah indicates the harmonious arrangement whereby each thing in the universe cooperates with every other so as to constitute that universe. All things are interdependent. There is not a single thing which is self-sufficient, which contains the conditions of its existence and activity in itself. One continuous process of giving and receiving unites all creatures. Therein we behold God's love. But in order that such harmony be achieved, each object and force has its measure and limitation beyond which it cannot go. Therein we behold God's justice: God is not only creator of the universe, but also its upholder. It is he who maintains it and gives it permanence.

All of these truths are not the achievements of reason. You can find them in the Torah if you only know how to read and interpret it. Whatever you learn about the specific nature of the world through scientific research, you do so at the bidding of the Torah itself, which gives you sufficient incentive to spur you on in your investigation of reality. But when you want to penetrate into the inner meaning of what you discover, you must come back to the Torah, to the word of God himself, and steep yourself in its study. The truths about God's love and God's justice are not the only ones that the Torah teaches. Other significant truths, such as those which pertain to his unity, his illimitable greatness, his unchangeable will, and his faithfulness, and what they imply for our conduct and world outlook, can be learned only from the Torah.

This revelation of the nature of God gives us the true clue to the destiny of man. If God's relation to the world is such as has been described, then the world is divine. All objects and forces in the world, including man and his powers, are God's servants, ministering angels whose one destiny is to carry out God's will or be witness to his nature as the Torah reveals it. Since everything serves God and obeys his will, should man be the exception and serve himself? Man is not called merely to enjoy and suffer, but to obey the will of God and to testify to the nature of God by working out the ends of love and justice. A truly human deed, a deed in which man fulfills the humanity that is in him to the highest degree, is a deed whereby he serves God. It is for that purpose that God has endowed man with all those powers which entitle him to be called the crown of creation. Man cannot waste those powers without having to give an accounting. "Compare yourself with a grassblade or with the rolling thunder peal, and you will be ashamed of your selfishness."

In a passage of stirring eloquence, Hirsch sets forth the following as the destiny of the human being:

> Whoever in his time, with his equipment of powers and means, in his condition, fulfills the will of God toward the creatures that enter into his circle, who injures none and assists every one according to his power, to reach the goal marked out for it by God—he is a man! He practices righteousness and love in his existence here below. His whole life, his whole being, his thoughts and feelings, his speech and action, even his business transactions and enjoyments—all of these are service of God. Such a life is exalted above all mutation.*

Since man's destiny is to obey the will of God, we have a standard of what constitutes goodness. That standard is not to be found in man's happiness or perfection. The only criterion of excellence is conformity with the divine will. That is good which conforms with the disposition fixed for it by the wisdom of God.

The argument as developed so far is strongly reminiscent of the religious philosophy which held sway over some of the most influential thinkers in the ancient world. We seem to hear the voice of Stoicism again urging man to live in accordance with the law of his nature, that nature which God implanted within him. But this is only a passing suspicion, for as we read further we are recalled to what is unmistakably Judaism. And this gives us the opportunity to note wherein Judaism is incommensurate with any religious philosophy, whether ancient or modern. Religious philosophy sees the law of God in the nature of every being, human and otherwise. It therefore leaves it to man to decipher for himself that law of his nature which for him must spell the law of God. Not so Judaism, which beholds man's superiority to all other creatures in the fact that God articulated his will to man in revealed teaching. The existence of subhuman creatures is governed entirely by the will of God, but lacking power of mind or spirit they are unaware of what causes them to function the way they do. It is man's glory and privilege to know what God would have him do. Furthermore, whereas other creatures are by the very limitation of their nature compelled to obey God's will, man, having the freedom to choose, is in a position to obey God's will voluntarily. If, however, he would have to grope and fumble for the knowledge of God's will, the freedom to choose would be wasted on him.

Hence the teaching that God has made his will articulate and that man has had no part in rendering that will articulate—for the Torah, which sets forth plainly what God wants of man, is entirely the work of God—is what Judaism only and no humanly evolved philosophy could promulgate.

With this as a premise, all our human criteria as to the true, the good and the beautiful fall to the ground. Inasmuch as we know definitely what God expects of us, man's highest wisdom consists in living up to the will of God, keenly aware that it is the will of God. "To be willing to fulfill the behests of that will," writes Hirsch, "only when or because they appear also to us right and wise and good, could that be called obedience to God? Would not that rather be obedience to oneself?" [9]

The crux of the entire apologia for traditional Judaism is the question whether or not the Torah is divinely revealed. It is upon the belief in the supernatural origin of the Torah that the modern ideology has concentrated its attack. If the arguments against that belief can be met successfully, Judaism would have little to fear from the bitterest opposition. Surely the word of God can survive all influences that would nullify it and withstand all the contrivings of man to resist its fulfillment. How then shall the modern assault against the Torah be repulsed? David Hoffmann proceeds to build up an elaborate system of defenses by resorting to the slow and scientific method of patient research. He displays all the acumen of the biblical critics to disprove their conclusions. But Hirsch is by temperament too little of the historian and the scholar, and too much of the impassioned pleader, to resort to a plodding refutation of higher criticism. In one of his essays in the *Jeschurun*,[10] he states his position in the following terms:

Let us not delude ourselves: The entire matter reduces itself to this question. Is the statement, 'And the Lord spoke unto Moses saying,' which introduces all the laws of the Torah, true or not? Do we or do we not believe that God, the almighty and all-holy God, spoke thus to Moses? Do we mean what we say when, in the circle of fellow-worshippers, we point to the written word of the Torah and declare that God gave us these teachings, that these are his teachings, the teachings of truth and that he thereby implanted in us everlasting life? Is all this a mere mouthing of high sounding phrases? If not, then we must keep those commandments, fulfill them in their original and unabbreviated form. We must observe them under all circumstances and at all times. This word of God must be accepted by us as an eternal standard, transcending all human judgment, as the standard according to which we must fashion all our doings, and instead of complaining that it is no longer in conformity with the times, we should rather complain that the times are no longer in conformity with it.

With equal fervidness he announces his implicit faith in the divine origin of the oral law. He did not engage in the difficult research to which Yizhak Ha-Levi devoted the greater part of his life in trying to discredit the thesis of Graetz, Frankel and Weiss that the oral law was the result of gradual development. But he wrote an extensive commentary on the Pentateuch to prove that Judaism cannot be divided into different stages and distinct periods of development. He there tries to prove that the traditional laws and interpretations transmitted by the *Tannaim* and *Amoraim* are the logical and necessary postulates of biblical revelation.

It is as divine tradition, says Hirsch, as having been orally transmitted by God, the same almighty God who gave the written law to Moses, that we regard the teachings and interpretations handed down to us by the Sages. If this be untrue tradition, if this be only the mask under which pious priestcraft got the people to accept what is regarded as the meaning of the word received from God, then the fathers deceived their children and grandchildren and allowed them to live and suffer, endure and perish, for an illusion and a deceit. We should forthwith each become his own oracle, and model the law of the Bible according to our own views and ideas. Then it is not, cannot, it need not be, any more the word of God. Then God did not speak to Moses, then have we not the teaching of God in our hands. Then are we, and all mankind with us, whose hope for salvation is based upon these words, nothing but deluded deceivers. Then it is high time to throw off this miserable burden. These are the alternatives; there is no other. If Judaism is a divine institution, then it is appointed to influence the times and not to allow itself to be influenced by the times. . . . From the very beginning, God appointed Judaism and its devotees as a protest against the spirit of the times.¹¹

The last sentence in the foregoing indicates how pointless it is, according to Neo-Orthodoxy, to try to come to terms with the spirit of the times. Hirsch believed that this was the mistake made by both Maimonides and Mendelssohn. They showed too much consideration for the ideology which threatened Judaism, with the result that they executed their strategy in defense of Judaism far from the place where it was being attacked. It is, says Hirsch, as though a garrison tried to defend a fortress by carrying on operations at a point far removed from it.

Since the Torah is the only true source of our knowledge of God's nature and of his will, it is essential to make the study of it the principal occupation of our lives. All work should be carried on with a view of ultimately affording sufficient leisure to engage in the study of Torah. All other study and research should serve as prerequisite disciplines for it. Even the most scrupulous observance of the *miṣwot* cannot render the study of Torah superfluous, for it is only through study that we acquire the right spirit and attitude so essential to a proper observance of them. Only through study of the Torah do we acquire the proper perspective upon life, are we aroused and stimulated to those thoughts that lead to proper actions. Hirsch deprecates in the strongest terms the identification of religion with mechanical observance. "Judaism," he says, "must be lived and handed down not as a habit; only through the spirit can it be properly transmitted."

The study which yields the knowledge of God's nature and of his will is not attained by a superficial reading of the text, nor by arbitrarily reading into the text any hypothesis which one considers important, nor by assuming that there are in it mystic implications intended only for the initiated. We must study the Torah entirely from its own standpoint in order to gain a true knowledge of one's self, in order to realize what we are and what we should strive to be in this earthly existence. This kind of study presupposes a thorough knowledge of Hebrew. Since the Hebrew language is rich in symbolic connotations, it has to be properly understood, if it is to yield the deeper significance which lies hidden beneath the surface of the words. As a further aid to the study of the Torah, Hirsch urges the development of a methodology known as symbolism.[12]

By means of this methodology, the various commandments will become alive with meaning.

In his collected writings he gives considerable space to the elucidation of his methodology, which is based upon the following three principles:

1. Symbolism derives from the assumption that ideas are most emphatically and permanently expressed through outward actions. This applies especially to ideas which are intended as a means of uniting a group and fostering in them a collective consciousness.

2. The meaning which is to be read into those actions must not be arbitrary, but must be inferred from the nature of the circumstances, the intent of the individual performing the action, and the nature of the individual for whom the action is performed.

3. The ideas and ideals thus symbolized must be of a simple and popular character.

Important as is the study of the Torah, we must not overlook the fact that unless it find expression in action, that is, in the observance of the *miṣwot*, the purpose of study is defeated. "In spite of the purest sentiments, life may be a failure if the deeds done are not right." The knowledge of the Torah should lead to a more devout observance of the *miṣwot*, an observance which would tend to curb man's natural arrogance, and which would counteract the development of the animal side of his being. Lest we become too insistent in our demand to understand the idea underlying each *miṣwah* before we are ready to obey it, we are reminded of the analogy that exists between Torah and nature. In nature we accept the facts, whether or not we can fit them into the scheme of science. Likewise, we have to fulfill the divine precepts—which are ineluctable laws in the Torah—whether we have succeeded in finding out their inner meaning or not.

Were every divine command a riddle which calls up innumerable questions that we are unable to answer, its obligatory character would in no way be diminished. There is but one answer to the question, 'Why do I have to do this or omit that?' Because it is the will of God, and it is for you to be the servant of God with all your power and resources, and with every breath of life. This answer is not merely sufficient but is the only possible one. It would be the only answer even if we were able to penetrate into the reason for every one of the precepts, or if God had revealed to us the reasons for his various ordinances.[13]

No difference should be made between ritual and moral laws. All are equally divine precepts. The laws of Sabbath, dietary laws, laws of ritual purity, are wrongly described as ceremonies, as though to imply that any excuse is good enough to have us dispense with them, and that scrupulousness in observing them is entirely misdirected energy.

Neo-Orthodoxy is fully aware of the difficulty of trying to live in accordance with traditional Jewish practice now that the Jew must accommodate his work days and his rest days to the habits of his non-Jewish neighbors. It reckons with this fact by advising the Jew to do nothing about it and to trust in God. It insists that a Jew should be able to transcend the problem of earning a livelihood, for loyalty to the law of God places one within the domain of life where natural law can work no harm since it is subordinate to the higher law of God.

"Is not the God who ordained the Sabbath," asks Hirsch, "the same as the one who provides us with the means to live by? Did he not prove by giving a double portion of manna on the sixth day, and none on the Sabbath day, that no one need be anxious lest through the observance of the Sabbath he be left without a livelihood?" [14]

Hirsch classifies the *miṣwot* as follows: judgments, statutes, commandments, symbolic observances, service or worship.[15] The purpose of the *miṣwot* is to foster the traits of justice and love, and to further moral growth.

The cultivation of the Torah in this spirit will win for the Jew the respect of the rest of the world much more than the cultivation of the arts and sciences. "Through estrangement from the Torah we defeat the very purpose for which we have become estranged from the Torah." Loyalty to the Torah would not inhibit the development of esthetic values, though it would no doubt prevent the artist from lending his talent or genius to anything that might stir impure imagination or rouse the animal in man.

And now, my dear Benjamin, Hirsch pleads, a law which bids us recognize God in the world and in mankind, which teaches that the fulfillment of His will is our mission, which shows us in Him the Father of all beings, of all men and in every creature, every human being, our brother; a law which makes our whole life service of God through the practice of righteousness and love toward all beings and the proclaiming of these truths for ourselves and others; can this be a law which stunts the mind and the heart, limits every joy of life and turns men into secluded monks? Can it be that the study of this law, when pursued earnestly and intelligently, perverts and deadens the mind, narrows or restricts the impulses of the heart? [16]

Thus in the face of all that history, anthropology and comparative religion may maintain, Neo-Orthodoxy reasserts its fundamental credo that the Torah is "an eternal code set up for all ages by the God of eternity."

Finally, there is the traditional conception of Israel to be taken into account. Israel is a creation of God in a twofold sense: it is part of his handiwork, and it has been created for a special purpose in relation to the rest of humanity. Israel is the instrument which God has created for the education of mankind.

It is notably in its conception of Jewish nationhood that we may observe how Neo-Orthodoxy differs from traditional Judaism, how it is essentially a reinterpretation of traditional Judaism to meet challenge—and thus a mode of adjustment.

The Neo-Orthodox conception of Israel, though presumably a reiteration of the traditional view of Israel, turns out, upon examination, to be a decided recasting of that view in a number of ways. The traditional belief as formulated by Judah Ha-Levi is that Israel was privileged to come into the possession of the Torah on account of the inherent superiority which it had inherited from Adam, Noah and the Patriarchs, and which marked it off as a higher human species. [17] According to Neo-Orthodoxy, it is for the sake of the Torah, for the sake of preserving and propagating the teachings of that Torah, and not because of any hereditary superiority, that God chose Israel. Tradition declares that the Torah is principally a means of maintaining Israel's inborn superiority so that at no time shall Israel descend to the level of the nations. Neo-Orthodoxy declares that Israel is meant to be essentially an instrument for the promulgation of the Torah to the nations. Tradition takes Israel's nationhood for granted. Neo-Orthodoxy feels that it has to explain why God uses a nation instead of a voluntary group as a medium for the propagation of the Torah. The significance of Israel's nationhood, according to Hirsch, consists in the fact that only in a collective group can there be found a sufficient variety of spiritual abilities, physical powers and material resources working together for the attainment of the sacred purposes which the Torah would have Israel attain.

It is evident that Neo-Orthodoxy is not prepared to retain the traditional belief in the inherent superiority of Israel, for that would mean challenging the growing conviction that spiritual attainment is a social acquisition, and neither a biological nor a supernatural endowment. Unlike Christianity, which affirms that no salvation can be achieved outside the church, Neo-Orthodoxy goes so far as to maintain that Judaism does not teach "No salvation outside of Israel." Have we not been told that the pious of all nations have a share in the world to come? Do not the Sages comment upon the Scripture which describes the ordinances and the statutes of the Torah as those "which if a man do, he shall live by them," by adding that it is not only Priests, Levites and Israelites who are expected to attain life everlasting through the observance of the ordinances, but all men regardless of rank or nationality? [18] Israel has not even the sole prerogative to divine revelation, since in giving laws to Noah and his sons God had revealed his will to all mankind. Far from seeing anything contrary to the spirit of traditional Judaism in the modern stress upon the worth of the human being, Neo-Orthodoxy maintains that the present emphasis upon the value of man is indicative of a general acceptance of the teachings of the Torah, that man was made in the image of God, that mankind as a whole has a divine mission to perform.

There can be no doubt that Neo-Orthodoxy assigns to the Jewish people a different status from the one which pre-emancipation Judaism assigned to it. It does not consider the Jewish people as a unique group or community intrinsically endowed with high worth. Its only distinction is that of being the bearer of the Torah. The Jewish people, according to this Neo-Orthodox conception of it, is nothing more than a vessel or instrument for the fulfillment of a certain purpose. Would anyone attach any inherent significance to the parchment upon which the text of the Torah is written? The

Jewish people is only a kind of living parchment. What quarrel can anyone have with an Israel which consents to such self-effacement for the purpose to which it is dedicated? When it calls itself a holy nation, it does not lay claim to being intrinsically holier than any other nation. All that it asserts is that it is consecrated to the task of proving by its mode of life the possibilities of holiness that inhere in the human being.

What did R. Saadya mean when he said: "Our nation is only a nation by reason of its Torah." [19] He surely did not mean to negate the mass of rabbinic teaching which developed the biblical conception that Israel was an eternally "chosen people" and that nothing it might ever do would cause God to repudiate it. He was also well aware of the mystic apotheosis of Israel in rabbinic writings, an apotheosis that ill accords with the idea that the Jewish people considered by itself is just an ordinary group of human beings. What he evidently meant to imply was that the transcendent quality of the Jewish people was the result of its acceptance of the Torah. But to Neo-Orthodoxy, transcendence is a quality which can pertain only to a super-mundane object like the Torah, but not to a group of human beings, even if that group be dedicated to the promulgation of the Torah. What is of interest to us is that Neo-Orthodoxy, in spite of its protestations that it does not deviate even by a hair's breadth from tradition, actually substitutes a prosaically sober conception of Israel for the mystical one of tradition.

The real difference between the ardent idea of Israel as conceived by the Sages and the cold matter-of-fact idea of Israel as conceived by Neo-Orthodoxy, becomes apparent when we learn what attitude Neo-Orthodoxy takes toward the nationhood of the Jewish people. It would never have occurred to a Saadya so to stress the primacy of the Torah as to minimize Israel's need of a land of its own. Yet that is exactly what Hirsch does. He argues that the possession of a land and of a government, without which no other group can be said to constitute a nation, is a mere incident in the life of Israel whose nationhood arises solely out of its relation to the Torah. For a time, to be sure, Israel possessed a land and even constituted a state. But that was only through the Torah, and for the sake of the Torah. Actually Israel was a nation long before it possessed a land, and has therefore remained a nation for centuries without a land. The ordinary worldly attributes of nationality would only detract from the true character of Israel as a nation. It is best for the mission with which Israel has been entrusted that it has on the whole been "poor in everything upon which the rest of mankind reared the edifices of its greatness and its power; externally subordinated to the nations armed with proud reliance on self, but fortified by direct reliance upon God. . . . Despite its political subordination, however, this people was to receive from the hands of its Creator all the means of individual human and national prosperity in order that it might dedicate all its wealth of resources to the one purpose—fulfillment of the divine will." [20]

And what is that divine will? That Israel be a witness unto the nations of the truth that obedience to God's law can give the firmest stability and most permanent security to human existence. This is Israel's mission to the world. Israel's self-realization consists in the faithful discharge of the task which God imposes upon it for the good of mankind. Mankind would, probably, in course of time, have benefited by its own experiences, and, after a great deal of tragic blundering, might have learned to know God and become aware of its own true destiny. But God has saved mankind age-long effort that would have resulted in very slow spiritual progress, by introducing into its midst a nation "which through its history and life should declare God the only creative cause of existence, fulfillment of His will the only aim of life." [21] Israel should serve as an example, an inspiration and a guide to the rest of the world. There need be no fear that the consciousness of having been entrusted with a mission from God is liable to arouse in the Jews a sense of pride and to encourage a holier-than-thou attitude, for the nature of the mission and the responsibility of carrying it out are such as to leave no room for vanity or self-righteousness.

To carry out this mission, the Jewish people must be isolated from the other nations. The other nations are addicted to the worship of wealth and power, and identify happiness with the pursuit of pleasure. The Jewish people could not merge its life with theirs without adopting their standards of life. "It must remain alone and aloof, must do its work and live its life in separation, until, refined and purified by its teachings and its example, universal humanity might turn to God and acknowledge in Him the only

Creator and Ruler. That attained, Israel's mission will have been accomplished." [22] While this isolation demands racial purity and precludes intermarriage, social segregation is strongly deprecated as narrowing the mind and life of the Jew.

A corollary of this novel interpretation of the traditional conception of the Jewish people is Neo-Orthodoxy's conception of the diaspora. The dispersion of Israel among the nations is by no means an unqualified evil. When God deprived Israel of its land, he did not merely punish it for its transgression, but he removed from Israel something that diverted it from its mission. Of what use to Israel was a land, if the possession of that land only distracted it from the accomplishment of its task—the fulfillment of the laws of the Torah? The very fact that Israel committed no worse sins than many a nation that retains its land and enjoys prosperity proves that the deprivation of its country was not simply punishment, but part of God's plan with Israel, so as to prevent the Jews from being engrossed in the pursuit of worldly aims. "The dispersion opened a new, great and wide-extended field for the fulfillment of its mission. . . . Israel has accomplished its task better in exile than in the full possession of good fortune." [23] In the first place, the dispersion taught Israel a true sense of values, that wealth and power constituted but temporary goods. When the Jews saw for how short a time prestige and power endured, when they saw state after state disappear from the stage of history, they learned how ephemeral were wealth and power. Secondly, the dispersion, in teaching the Jews to withstand both the persecutions and the allurements of the nations which sought to sever the alliance between Israel and the Torah, served as a training school in the exercise of true heroism. The story of Israel's martyrdom "is written with Israel's heart blood on all the pages of history." [24] This martyrdom has surely not been in vain.

And what of the emancipation? That certainly is an unqualified blessing. For now that the Jews are everywhere "tolerated and protected and even accepted as citizens," [25] for the first time since they have been dispersed, they have the opportunity to live the Israel-life in all its grandeur. Now most effectively can Israel teach the world by example the beauty of a life lived according to the Torah. If mankind were to behold the beautiful and serene home life of the Jews, the upright and kindly characters of the men and women in Israel, would it be able to resist the beneficent influence of such example? Would not the nations in time abandon their evil ways, their glorification of power, their indulgence in lust? Would they not adopt the teachings of love and righteousness as set forth in the Torah?

"In the centuries of passion and scorn, our mission was but imperfectly attainable, but the ages of mildness and justice, now begun, beckon us to that glorious goal, that every Jew and every Jewess should be in his or her own life a modest and unassuming priest or priestess of God and true humanity. When such an ideal and such a mission await us, can we still, my Benjamin, lament our fate?" [26] But all this is true only when the emancipation is regarded not as the end of the *Galut*, not as the attainment of the goal of Israel's history, nor as the means for the acquisition of long-sought gain and pleasure. In a sense, the emancipation is a severer trial than the centuries of oppression. But, if properly utilized, it is bound in the end to bring about the final redemption when God will see fit to unite Israel again in one land. This realization of the future promised us by the Prophets will come about in due time, and for it we must pray and hope. "But actively to accelerate its coming were sin, and is prohibited to us." [27]

It is on this basis that Neo-Orthodoxy takes its stand to face the challenge of the modern world.

CHAPTER XII

CRITIQUE OF NEO-ORTHODOXY [1]

Impressive character of Neo-Orthodoxy's defiance of reason—Neo-Orthodoxy's argument for belief in supernatural origin of Torah based upon an artificial dilemma—Neo-Orthodoxy's failure to stress other-worldly salvation a surrender to the spirit of the times—Neo-Orthodoxy inconsistent in permitting Jewish civil law to become defunct.

THE striking characteristic of the reply offered by Neo-Orthodoxy to the challenge of the modern spirit is its boldness. The boldness of this reply seems commensurate with the magnitude of the challenge, and gives the apologia the force of a counter attack. Neo-Orthodoxy's eloquent reaffirmation of the traditional conception of Torah which is the basis of its apologia is overwhelming, and one's first disconcerting impression is that it is the "spirit of the times" rather than traditional Judaism which is on the defensive. The vista which Neo-Orthodoxy opens up before the troubled eyes of the modern Jew is alluring; the whole difficulty of being a Jew seems to have been dissolved. If this reaffirmed supernaturalism is acceptable, then the problem of Judaism is settled. Even if it is hard to be a Jew, what does that signify when so great a prize is at stake, the prize of life everlasting and of shining progress on paths clearly and unmistakably marked out by God? With the assumption of a supernaturally revealed Torah, all the contemporary political, economic and intellectual realities which have attacked the integrity of Jewish life and Jewish destiny no longer seriously affect the issue.

The whole point is contained in the following question which Neo-Orthodoxy, by implication, poses: will you conform to the will of God or will you reject it and commit moral suicide? The choice we ought to make seems clear. We cannot ignore the fact that there are people who in all sincerity disavow the canons of logic and experience when they deal with what to them is religion. Since the defiance of all rational standards is for them the main characteristic of religion, how can they be expected to treat deferentially the evident objection to a program like that of Neo-Orthodoxy on the ground that it cannot be integrated with the world-outlook of the majority of thoughtful men and women? What God commands must be obeyed and not weighed. Results in terms of visible influence in self-adjustment, material or spiritual, are of secondary consideration. Whatever is divinely revealed transcends human ken or power to alter.

It must be recognized that however impossible it may seem to most of us to accept the type of reasoning upon which Neo-Orthodoxy bases its program, orthodoxy as such possesses a fascination for certain types of mind. Among these may even be found those who are temperamentally sceptical. Their very scepticism, ending as it usually does in a failure of nerve, drives them into the arms of a faith that is free from all doubt. In the flux of beliefs and ideals, it is good to be able to lean upon some truth which may be regarded as eternal and changeless. They may possess brilliant intellects and be gifted with fine sensibilities. But the one thing they cannot and will not endure is a world hanging on nothing. They crave fixity, permanence, order, and they will achieve it at all costs, at the price of the most audacious intellectual somersaults. They delight in the very daring of the mind's defiance of reality. It is to them a sort of proof that the mind is inspired to this negation of experience by a reality that transcends experience. *Credo quia absurdum est* is no mere paradoxical epigram. It is the revolt of the human mind against its limitations and its avowal of allegiance to some transcendent and unfailing source of truth. That is the secret of orthodoxy's appeal to minds like Tertullian, Cardinal Newman,[2] Chesterton, Belloc, Santayana and the modern school of Royalist French Catholics. In the brilliant publicist, Nathan Birnbaum, the Jews have had an outstanding example of that type of mind. He started out as an adherent of historic materialism, changed into a Zionist, then became a radical Yiddishist, and finally embraced strict orthodoxy.[3]

But though we may be carried away in the beginning by Neo-Orthodoxy's glorious boldness, we are constrained to pause and inquire whether this boldness be genuine. We are constrained to ask: is this boldness candid? Is it fully aware of its implications for the mind of man? Or is it the result of a kind of self-hypnosis which derives its assurance from a deliberate evasion of certain facts and the determination to ignore them? The test of Neo-Orthodoxy's ultimate sincerity will be the extent to which it is willing to abide by the implications of its position, the extent to which the cardinal items in its adjustment are found to be consistent with the whole of its reactions to the modern world. We shall see in the following analysis how this test applies, and with what results.

The clue to the understanding of the psychology of Neo-Orthodoxy is the fact that Neo-Orthodoxy is not traditional Judaism speaking with its own voice, but rather a reaffirmation of traditional Judaism by spokesmen who are aware that alternatives now exist. The Neo-Orthodox acceptance of supernaturalism is a reaffirmation of the spiritual sufficiency and truth of supernaturalism, which means that belief in supernaturalism has under these circumstances wider connotations in thought and attitude than the ancient assumption that God had revealed himself in person to the Patriarchs and to Israel.

In ancient times, the proposition which described the social heritage of Israel as the product of supernatural revelation was not arrived at by a process of selection from intellectual alternatives; the proposition was the first unreflective reaction to experience, and the limited experience of the race did not allow for alternative reactions. It is hardly necessary to emphasize the difference between the primitive reaction in its native state and the sophisticated insistence that this reaction is the only true one, long after other and more plausible explanations of the same experience have been developed. To believe with the author of Genesis, who was, of course, unaware even of Greek geodetic speculation, that the earth is flat, is to believe what was sensible enough for the uses and experiences of the ancient world. But to reaffirm today the proposition that the earth is flat, when it has been more plausibly shown that it is round, is to take eccentric refuge in a proposition that flies in the face of our accumulated experience, and which, if seriously maintained, will do profound intellectual damage to the adherent. So also, the facts formerly accounted for by "supernatural revelation" have long been more plausibly interpreted in the light of well-known psychological and social forces which have universally produced similar phenomena. Modern research is not constrained to deny any ultimate divine significance that may reside in such facts, but it provides us with another method of approaching, abstracting, and utilizing any such possible divine significance, with a method that will not involve the denial of all other truths dearly bought with experience.

The dilemma in which Neo-Orthodoxy would like to place those who accept the spirit of the times is thus no dilemma at all. The choice between complete acceptance of the received tradition as literal truth and complete rejection of it as a tissue of lies is not the only one, and it is the third choice that Hirsch completely ignores. It is the achievement of historical science since its progress from the iconoclasm of the eighteenth century that it has shown how it is possible for ancient peoples to construct, without ulterior or fraudulent motives, a version of experience which they believed to be true. In order to avoid the dilemma into which Neo-Orthodoxy would like to thrust us and in order to preserve the necessary belief in the integrity of our ancestors, all we need do is to accept the teaching of historical science that the stories purporting to describe facts of theophany grew up long after the period of history to which they refer. Hence, the fact that the Torah is not a tissue of lies does not necessarily imply that it is literal historical truth, and the modern man cannot be bullied into Neo-Orthodoxy by the threat that he would be considered an atheist if he refused to subscribe to its version of Judaism.

The boldness of Neo-Orthodoxy is thus seen to be partly the boldness shown toward an adversary of straw. Neo-Orthodoxy has not truly represented the "spirit of the times" and has therefore not faced it at all, so far as the intellectual challenge is concerned.

Indeed, it is not the Neo-Orthodox but the historical view of the Torah as a composite of various literary strata that can account for the different levels of ethical outlook that one finds in it. It is not necessary to multiply examples, since it is by this method that unimaginative men destroy the moral worth of the Torah altogether. But since the point is crucial for Neo-Orthodoxy, which holds that each word of the Torah is literally the word of God, a few examples of the facts with which Neo-Orthodoxy refuses to reckon must be cited. Briefly, then, these questions may be fairly addressed to

Neo-Orthodoxy: is there no distinction between the God who reasoned with Abraham about the wickedness of Sodom and stated the conditions on which he would spare the city, and the God who commands the ruthless extermination of the Midianites? Is the God who ordered the execution of the Sabbath gatherer of sticks, the God of Israel's highest spiritual development or the God of its primitive stage? Again, to depart from the Pentateuch—since the whole of the Bible is equally Torah—was it divine command which moved David to hang the remaining posterity of Saul in order to relieve the land from famine? Did God really send a plague upon Israel in punishment for the taking of a census which he himself had commanded? No commentary produced by any kind of Orthodoxy, either new or old, has yet resolved these questions, which is to say that Neo-Orthodoxy has hardly begun to face the problem of Judaism. In the intellectual aspects of the problem of Judaism, these questions are fundamental.

Although Neo-Orthodoxy claims to be merely a reaffirmation of traditional Judaism, it has tacitly made some serious compromises with the times. Before the enlightenment, Judaism spoke entirely in terms of other-worldliness. The traditional interpretation of the Scripture, "Ye shall therefore keep my statutes, and mine ordinances which if a man do, he shall live by them" (Leviticus 18, 5), is that the statutes and ordinances are a means to life in the world to come. "Since we die, how can they be a means to life in this world?" argues Rashi. Neo-Orthodoxy has certainly said nothing that is in conflict with this traditional interpretation of the function of the *miṣwot*. But neither has it said anything that can be taken as unmistakable evidence of a vital interest in that traditional interpretation and of a desire to uphold it in the face of challenge. It has in effect permitted the conception of other-worldly salvation to remain inert by neglecting to dwell upon the consequences and implications of that conception.

Imperceptibly the center of interest has been shifted from life in the world to come to life in this world. By thus "mummifying" what was in traditional Judaism a vital and functioning belief, Neo-Orthodoxy has managed to make a very significant concession to the spirit of modern times without attracting any notice. It is only when we realize how prominently other-worldly salvation still figures in traditional Christianity that we cannot help but infer what a thoroughgoing, though silent, transformation must have taken place in traditional Judaism to make it possible to relegate so important a belief to the background.

But what Neo-Orthodoxy gains by evading the issue, it loses in authoritativeness. Traditional Judaism at least grappled with the problem of reward and punishment. It realized the frequent incongruity between men's deserts and their fate, and made an attempt to harmonize the realities of life with the fundamental truths of religious teachings. Neo-Orthodoxy, on the other hand, assumes that we can manage to live complacently without even being troubled by this problem. We can perform the *miswot* without having in mind the particular nature of the desirable consequences to which they are presumed to lead. The truth, however, is that it is no longer possible to have any ordinance obeyed merely on the ground that it is commanded by God. The demand to know its social utility has become too insistent to be silenced.

Neo-Orthodoxy's answer to the charge of evasion would probably be that the one who observes the *miswot* as commanded by God experiences a form of spiritual satisfaction that is the equivalent of faith in *olam ha-ba,* salvation, or immortality. Neo-Orthodoxy regards itself exempt from the necessity of granting to the traditional conception of *olam ha-ba* the place which that conception formerly held in the consciousness of the Jew. Such reasoning, however, is little less than sophistry. If it be true that the belief in the supernatural origin of the *miswot* is bound to create in the mind of the Jew that spiritual satisfaction which he formerly obtained from the belief in the world to come, why did the Jews in olden times find it essential to focus so much attention on other-worldly salvation? Why did the *Tannaim* and the *Amoraim* dwell with such fondness upon the theme of reward that awaited the righteous in the world to come? Believing as they did in the divine origin of the *miswot,* they should have regarded the observance of them as its own reward. If the experience of communing with God could render superfluous all striving after bliss in the world to come, they should have been the last to give any thought to the world to come, since the study of the Torah undoubtedly afforded them that experience. Yet, neither their devout performance of the *miṣwot,* nor their ecstatic devotion to the study of the Torah, displaced the need of accentuating the other-worldly bliss to which they looked forward.

If Neo-Orthodoxy were consistent in its reaffirmation of traditional Judaism, it would not be content merely with restating the traditional emphasis on *olam ha-ba.* The spirit of the times, which treats other-worldly salvation as meaningless, should have caused Neo-Orthodoxy to stress the belief in *olam ha-ba* all the more militantly. If Neo-Orthodoxy were actually as much at war with the spirit of the times as it leads one to believe, the abandonment of other-worldly salvation would be the chief *casus belli.* Fortunately for the cause of spiritual progress, this is not the case.

In the last analysis, submission to Jewish law is the essential requirement. Then it is fair to inquire: how far is submission to Jewish law a reality in the practice of Neo-Orthodoxy? The answer to this question will show to what extent Neo-Orthodoxy is willing to abide by the implications of its commitment to the Torah as supernaturally revealed and eternally binding truth and duty. *We are amazed to discover that the most important elements of Jewish law are as obsolete in Neo-Orthodoxy as they are in Reformism.* We learn that Neo-Orthodoxy accepts with equanimity the elimination of the whole civil code of Jewish law, and is content to confine the scope of Jewish law to ritual observance. Neo-Orthodoxy's acceptance of the emancipation has been no less glad-hearted than Reformism's. Which is to say that Neo-Orthodoxy, in effect, has suffered no more qualms than has Reformism about the whole extirpation of the civil code from the law of God. The *Shulḥan Aruk,* by which Neo-Orthodoxy swears, is honored in the breach by the nullification of those manifold laws which deal with the adjustment of conflicting interests. When these laws cease to function, they cease to be studied. In spite of all protestations to the contrary, both the study and the practice of the law of God have become identified mainly with ceremony and ritual, with the decorative aspects of religion. In the curriculum of Neo-Orthodoxy, *Ḥoshen ha-mishpat,* the code of civil law, once fundamental in the equipment of a rabbi, has practically fallen into neglect. A crucial differentia of Neo-Orthodox thought is its inconsolable sorrow over the loss of the sanctuary and the disappearance of the sacrificial system. Yet there is never a word about the desuetude of the civil code, and no thought of how much more a Jew has lost of his Jewishness by having eliminated it from his life.

It is perhaps not quite accurate to say that Neo-Orthodoxy is altogether silent on this matter. It has occasionally taken notice of the effect which the new political status of the Jew is bound to have upon the Jewish civil code. To quote the following foreword from the Wilna editions of the *Shulḥan Aruk* printed before the World War, as an example of the occasional illumination that has burst upon Neo-Orthodoxy:

Everyone knows that many of the laws contained in these volumes are not actually observed in our time, such laws, e.g., as pertain to buying and selling, larceny, lost articles, inheritance, oaths, testimony, corporal punishment, usury, fines, excommunication, collection of debts, etc. All those laws were in vogue in the past, but are not at present. In all the aforementioned matters we conduct ourselves according to the laws of the various countries which afford us protection. We must bear in mind and obey the Talmudic decision that the law of the government is law.

It should also be known that wherever mention is made of an idolater, gentile or alien, the reference is only to those who belonged to nations which did not acknowledge the true God, which did not believe in the revelation of God on Mt. Sinai, nor in the Ten Commandments, and which were far from morality, purity and philanthropy. But the nations in whose lands we live and whose rulers grant us effective protection, believe in the creator of the universe and in the revelation of God on Mt. Sinai. They possess righteous statutes and ordinances. Touching these nations our teachers and guides have commanded us to conduct ourselves kindly, justly and truthfully at all times and on all occasions.[4]

It is true that this amazing surrender is partly in compulsory deference to the censor, but that objection loses its force when we remember that Neo-Orthodoxy actually lives in conformity with such disavowals even when it is under no compulsion to do so. *Dina demalkuta dina*, "The law of the government is law," [5] says Neo-Orthodoxy, quoting a statement of the *Amora* Samuel in the third century, which merely recognizes the duty of conforming to the civil law of the land, including the payment of taxes, but which certainly did not contemplate the nullification of Jewish law or the abolition of Jewish law-courts. If Neo-Orthodoxy can stretch this statement to mean that the Jews are subject to all the legal *mores* of the state in which they dwell, why does it strenuously object to having government law supersede Jewish law in marriage and divorce? What, in short, is this law of God which no longer regulates our workaday life, and which, outside of marriage and divorce laws, functions only in matters which least affect social relationships and the adjustment of conflicting interests.

If in respect to the conception of Torah, or Jewish cultural and social institutions, Neo-Orthodoxy's deviation from traditional Judaism is unconscious, and is the result rather of an inner inconsistency than of insincerity, its departure from the traditional conception of Jewish nationhood is quite deliberate. We miss in Neo-Orthodoxy the rabbinic idealization of Israel as the nation in whose midst God dwelt "despite their uncleanness." To Neo-Orthodoxy, Israel is little more than a community of men and women banded together for the observance of the Torah, a rôle which it has in serious and fundamental aspects largely surrendered. Neo-Orthodoxy, like the Reformist movement which it is combating, regards all the institutions of national life as quite secondary in importance, if not altogether superfluous. It substitutes for Jewish nationhood a mission of its own, the messianic program of propagating the teachings of the Torah, and it envisages the ultimate realization of this program. It is obvious, however, that Neo-Orthodoxy does not take its messianism seriously, for characteristically enough it refuses to press the point of Israel's future. When messianism is a potent spiritual urge, it produces messianic movements, as it once did in Israel. But Neo-Orthodoxy is too sophisticated to produce messiahs.

It is clear that Neo-Orthodoxy's boldness speaks louder in words than in deeds, in protestations of belief than in any program of action.

CHAPTER XIII

CONSERVATIVE JUDAISM (LEFT WING OF
NEO-ORTHODOXY)

The origins of the Conservative movement—Conservative Judaism subject to inconsistencies and evasions—Attitude of Conservative Judaism toward Torah ambiguous—The emphasis of Conservative Judaism upon ceremonial observances—The traditional conception of Israel's future set aside without warrant in the premises of Conservative Judaism.

AT the second meeting of the Conference of the Rabbis of Germany which took place in Frankfort-on-the-Main in 1845,[1] Zacharias Frankel sought to stem the tide of Reformism by proposing a formula which he hoped would direct the course of Jewish life in consonance with both the needs of the times and the postulate of continuity with the past. That formula was "positive historical Judaism." Just what he meant to convey by it has to be inferred from the discussion in the course of which he stated his attitude toward Reformism and from his opening article in *Zeitschrift für die religiösen Interessen des Judenthums,* entitled "Concerning Reforms in Judaism," in which he advocated "moderate reform." The following are the guiding principles which emerge from his discussions of Reformism:

1. The spirit of the age should not be relied upon as a guide in dealing with any phase of the problem of Judaism.

2. Any organized attempt to adjust Judaism to our day should omit the consideration of beliefs and confine itself to practices.

3. The purpose should be to strengthen Jewish practice.

4. No practice should be considered obsolete because there happen to be a number who do not observe it. The criterion should be the attitude of the community as a whole.

5. The cultivation of the science of Judaism will furnish the only dependable criteria for Jewish life.

6. Avoid creating factions in Judaism.

These principles at first give the impression of being helpful in resolving the conflict between loyalty to tradition and response to the exigencies of the times. But closer examination proves them quite nebulous and self-contradictory. The spirit of the age, which is cavalierly dismissed as of no account in dealing with the problem of Judaism, is of necessity reckoned with in the scientific study of Judaism where, according to Frankel, Judaism's salvation lies. For what else is the scientific study of Judaism if not the application of modern methods of research to the whole mass of tradition? If it is to be real science, then it must not be afraid of coming into conflict with authoritative teaching. And if it is ready to overthrow authoritative teaching, it has made such teaching yield to the spirit of the age. On the one hand, he thunders against any organized attempt to readjust Jewish life without first arriving at a clear understanding of principles, and, on the other hand, he enunciates the principle that no such attempt should tamper with beliefs, but concern itself only with practices. What he urged the members of the Conference of Rabbis to do is like the feat which God asked Satan to perform on Job and which is satirized in the Talmud as tantamount to asking one to smash the bottle but to take care not to spill the wine it contains.

Equally puzzling is his advice concerning changes in Jewish practice. The criterion which he suggests as a means of determining when any practice has become obsolete is "the attitude of the community as a whole." This principle has come to figure very prominently in the philosophy of the Conservative movement, but withal has remained just as vague as when Frankel first stated it. The statement in the Talmud (Abodah Zarah 36a) upon which he bases this principle is one which definitely precludes any kind of reform. It implies that not a single one of the "eighteen decrees" which were ordained to prevent social intercourse between Jews and Gentiles dare be abrogated under any circumstances. Would Frankel have maintained that bread baked by Gentiles should not be used? That is one of the "eighteen decrees" which the Talmud implies "had become generally adopted," and therefore not even Elijah and his *bet din* would have the authority to annul it. The forthright interpretation of the Talmudic statement leaves no room whatever for any kind of reform.

But apart from rabbinic sanction, the principle of consulting "the attitude of the community as a whole" is meaningless.' Any practice or prohibition which some have come to regard as being in need of modification or abrogation is undoubtedly one which is no longer observed by the entire community. Those who raise the question of whether a certain practice or prohibition should be observed are on the verge of joining those who have broken with it, and with whom they are probably more like-minded than with those who still uphold it. Why should they not rather follow the example of those with whom they have much more in common than of those with whom they have less in common? The fact that at the time the latter are in the majority is no argument, since, in all likelihood, they are a rapidly dwindling majority. In periods of transition and change like ours, to be told to lean on "the attitude of the community as a whole" is poor advice. It is to lean upon a broken reed.

But none of the principles advocated by Frankel met with so ironic a refutation as the one that those who undertook to deal with the problem of Judaism should avoid creating new factions. It goes without saying ,that those who opposed his views on Judaism constituted themselves into the Reformist party. But even those who agreed with him did not agree among themselves, and in time became divided into two Conservative parties, one the right wing of the Reformist and the other the left wing of the Neo-Orthodox group.

Having discussed Conservative Reformism in a previous chapter, I shall now touch upon the ideology of the more conservative Conservatism. Like the Reformist movement, the latter kind of Conservatism has witnessed its most extensive growth in America where it was transplanted by Solomon Schechter. By virtue of his scholarship and dominant personality, he was able to set forces at work that have called into being a Conservative group which has already proved much stronger and influential than the Neo-Orthodox, of which it constitutes the left wing. With the fidelity of an ardent disciple, Schechter promulgated every one of the six principles of Frankel almost in the very terms in which Frankel himself formulated them, except that for the phrase "the attitude of the community as a whole" he substituted the slogan "Catholic Israel." In keeping with Frankel's advice not to form any new party in

Judaism, Schechter emphatically deprecated all attempts to have the movement which he inaugurated labelled "Conservative." But the logic of events has compelled those who are now identified with the movement to accept that label.

Reluctant to be identified as a distinct group, the leaders of this movement have not been inclined to set forth any systematic ideology which would define their position. Only from occasional sallies of wit or satire in Schechter's more popular writings can one gather the main trend of his thinking about some of the burning questions in Jewish life. The question of supernatural revelation which Neo-Orthodoxy properly treats as the crux of the problem in Judaism is nowhere elaborately dealt with. Schechter justly attacked "higher criticism" on the ground that much of it was animated by a spirit of anti-Semitism, yet he was too much of a modern scholar to subscribe to the traditional view of the Torah.

We have thus been left without any systematic presentation of this type of Conservatism as a means of judging what promise it holds out of furnishing a consistent and comprehensive program for American-Jewish life. We have to fall back upon a text which was not meant to serve as a statement of the ideology of Conservatism. I refer to Julius H. Greenstone's book, *The Jewish Religion*. Greenstone intended his book to be used merely as an aid to teachers in the interpretation of Judaism. This necessitated his organizing into a unit the main ideas which have been reckoned with in considering the problem of Judaism. But he is so imbued with the philosophy of the Conservative school, and states it with such fervor, that he well deserves to be regarded by the Conservative school in this country as its leading spokesman. The spirit in which Greenstone wrote his book is fully described in these words: "Without consciously suppressing my own conservative point of view, I still hope I have succeeded in my attempt to deal fairly and sympathetically with many other points of view regarding Jewish faith and practice. All polemics have been studiously avoided. I aimed especially to give the attitude of the great body of Israel towards the various principles of belief and the many ceremonies of Judaism, and the reason for such an attitude."

The fact that the book is not written in the spirit of a party program should prove the authenticity of the point of view which, apparently, Greenstone cannot help articulating. How little he can avoid the Conservative point of view is evident in the very way he conceives his task. He aims, he says, "to give the attitude of the great body of Israel." We at once recognize the influence of Frankel and Schechter. Its very virtue of not being fragmentary is the reason for its being selected for this criticism. It is a sufficiently comprehensive statement of the Conservative (left wing Neo-Orthodox) position to constitute a basis for the analysis which follows.

In common with Neo-Orthodoxy, Conservatism emphasizes the traditional belief in the supernatural origin of the Torah, but, unlike Neo-Orthodoxy, it treats reason with respect. In common with Maimonides, with whom Neo-Orthodox spokesmen are wont to find fault, it assumes that both revelation and reason, or conscience, are equally authoritative. It ignores, however, the fact that reason nowadays speaks in terms of comparative religion, ethnology, biblical science, and instead of reconciling these with the revelational view of the Torah, Conservative Judaism rests content with the compromise arrived at by the ancient Jewish Sages and philosophers. If the medieval Jewish thinkers could harmonize the truths which God had revealed with those which man discovered, why should we not be able to make peace between tradition and science?

The archæologist or ethnologist, says Greenstone, may indulge in speculations about the origin of certain religious symbols and build his theories upon them. Such investigations are extremely interesting and may even lead to valuable discoveries in the domain of history and anthropology. The religious teacher, however, should avoid such discussions in the classroom, for they are entirely irrelevant to the present observance of such symbols and ceremonies. What concerns him mostly is what certain symbols meant and still mean to the great majority of the Jews.[3]

Greenstone seems to overlook one of the "valuable discoveries" of ethnology, that the claim of supernatural origin has been made by every people for its religious laws, beliefs and customs. Unless the Jewish religion, therefore, can make that claim good by means of evidence whose validity can be established by the modern canons of history, that claim will become irrelevant for an increasing number of Jews. Should not the effect of those "valuable discoveries" upon the teacher himself be taken into account? Is it possible for the teacher to ignore them and go on telling his pupils "what the symbol meant and still means to the great majority of the Jews?" What the teachers are to think is after all the ultimate question and the preface to everything else.

The outstanding trait of this type of Conservatism is a gift for the evasion of fundamental issues. Neo-Orthodoxy is outspoken in its conception of supernatural revelation as the main sanction of Judaism. And there is no equivocation in its use of the term "supernatural." Conservatism is no less emphatic in its insistence upon supernatural revelation as the main sanction of Judaism, but the meaning of the two words "supernatural revelation" is blurred and shifting. At times "revelation" is made to appear as nothing more than a more sensitive conscience, a greater ability to distinguish between right and wrong. "While this power," says Greenstone, "is common to all men, it is not developed to the same degree in all and consequently does not function in the same manner in all persons." [4] That reduces revelation to a phenomenon of an extraordinary but not supernatural character. In line with this conception is the statement that the Bible is not infallible, because the prophet was after all the product of his age, and, therefore, circumscribed in his knowledge of the truth. [5] Even the critical study of the Bible is conceded as serving a useful purpose. But that concession is immediately qualified by the statement that the results of such study "are matters of little consequence to the person who seeks for religious truth and moral guidance." [6] It seems that in order to feel at home in Conservative Judaism, it is necessary to divide the mind into idea-tight compartments.

It is by no means easy to get to the bottom of what Conservative Judaism actually affirms concerning the basic texts of Judaism. It is clear that Conservative Judaism is at one with Neo-Orthodoxy in giving primacy to the Pentateuch and in accepting the traditional estimate of Moses as the greatest of all Prophets. But it is by no means so unequivocal in its reasons for holding those beliefs. Instead of accepting on the authority of tradition as Orthodoxy does, that "God dictated to Moses as one dictates to an amanuensis," [7] Greenstone makes the primacy of the Torah depend upon the supreme significance of its contents, and not as Neo-Orthodoxy does, upon the unique supernatural manner in which God revealed the Torah to Moses. The manner of revelation is for Greenstone "purely a speculative matter." [8] He seems to forget that hitherto it was solely the unique manner of revelation that rendered the Torah supremely authoritative. If the manner of revelation is no longer a criterion, we need some other criterion by which to evaluate the contents of the different parts of the Bible. So far Conservative Judaism has not produced any new criterion.

Unquestionably the central dogma of Neo-Orthodoxy is the historicity of the theophany at Sinai. Greenstone, writing in the spirit of Conservative Judaism, gives apparently unqualified assent to that dogma. He says, "The children of Israel, gathered at the foot of Sinai, at a given moment all became conscious of a message from God. . . . All of them were, for the time being, endowed with the prophetic gift, all heard the divine voice proclaiming these eternal laws." [9] This picture is inconsistent with the attenuated conception of revelation as the highest degree of "the refinement of conscience." It is conceivable that one, or a few people, may attain a high degree of spiritual sensitivity, but that three million people can do so at one stroke is beyond the grasp of the human mind. It is usual for those who take this Conservative attitude to argue that the revelation at Sinai is one of the mysteries which we are not supposed to fathom. [10] Then why labor in the first place to identify the conception of supernatural revelation with extraordinary power of moral insight, or refinement of conscience?

One would imagine that though Conservatism is not logically consistent in its attitude toward the sanction of the laws and beliefs in the Torah, it is at least consistent in its attitude toward the laws and beliefs themselves. But there, too, we encounter the same tendency to vacillate. On the one hand we are told that "the message entrusted to Moses contained a standard of living for all times, laws and regulations that shall guide the Jewish people throughout all centuries. . . ." [11] On the other hand we are told that "important changes in the life of the Jewish people also made many of the Biblical laws inapplicable or entirely obsolete. . . . The whole system of sacrifices and temple worship, as prescribed by the Torah, fell into desuetude with the destruction of the Temple. All the agrarian laws of the Bible, as well as the laws of ritual purity, became impractical after the Jews were driven from their land and began the life of a wandering nation." [12] The position of Neo-Orthodoxy in the matter of animal sacrifice, agrarian laws, and the laws of ritual purity is unequivocal. It makes no secret of its hope to have all of them restored. Would Conservative Judaism admit as much? Its reply is as evasive as usual. "When the Temple will be restored, we shall see. At present such a question has only academic interest." This is not true. What we hope for in the future, as much as what we believe concerning the past, determines the present. Or, are we to infer that the oft-repeated prayer for the restoration of Temple and sacrifice is only a matter of academic interest?

What makes Conservatism so expert at playing fast and loose with ideas is its tendency to abstract from reality some of its aspects and to treat those abstractions as though they were significant entities. Thus it insists that the attitude toward a law in the Torah need not be influenced by the conception of its origin nor by its relevance for the future. With the same deftness it introduces a wedge between truth and the form in which the truth is stated. It asserts that "the truths are divine and eternal, while the form in which they are given in the Bible bears the marks of the scientific knowledge of the age in which these truths were uttered. In its narrative portions also it reflects the moral standards of the time in which the respective authors lived. The divine truth passing through human media may be imperfect in form, but perfect and eternal in essence." [13] One is inclined to ask: what is the perfect and eternal essence of the commandment to slay the captive Midianites "every male among the little ones, and every woman that hath known man by lying with him?" [14]

What Conservatism has to say about God lacks the vigor which is characteristic of the Neo-Orthodox version of Judaism, because it has not the courage to go so far as the latter in making our knowledge of the existence of God depend entirely upon his self-revelation to the Patriarchs, to Moses and to Israel at Sinai. "The idea of God, however crude and hazy, is inherent in the soul of every child." [15] This implies that our knowledge of God is after all a matter of human experience. But what experience? "The very idea of God, of which we are conscious, carries with it certain qualities and attributes. Unable to think of God in any other way but in the light of our knowledge and experience, we ascribe to him the perfection of all the power and wisdom which are manifested in our personalities and in the world around us." [16] There is then spun out of the idea of God a series of other ideas about his attributes. These other ideas have been developed "in a distinct and definite manner and formulated in a set of doctrines which are regarded essential to an adherence to the Jewish faith." [17] But later we are reminded that in Judaism "dogmas and creeds are necessary, but ceremonies and observances are essential." [18] In other words, what we think concerning God is really not so important as whether or not, let us say, we observe the dietary laws. In this respect Conservatism parts company with the Reformist version of Judaism, according to which the conception of God is the most important fact in the life of man because upon it depends his moral and spiritual life.

In the conception of Israel, Conservative Judaism merely restates the Neo-Orthodox version, which is itself nothing but the Reformist version with the theurgic element kept intact. It contains the traditional belief concerning miracles as proof of the intervention of God in the career of the nation. [19] Conservatism strongly deprecates as secularism the tendency to have the Jews develop a sense of nationality that has anything in common with the nationality of other peoples.

It is conceivable, says Greenstone, to have an entirely secular Jewish nation, established in Palestine or elsewhere, working out its destinies in the same manner as other nations do. Such a survival, however, will not serve God's purpose for Israel, the purpose expressed in the revelation handed down to us and in the course of our history. [20]

Although Conservatism assumes the historicity of miracles in the early development of Israel, it takes a different attitude when dealing with the picture of Israel as envisaged in the messianic hope. Greenstone deliberately quotes the traditional view with regard to the Messiah only to take issue with it. Thus we read:

Under the guidance of a great leader, appointed by God, a scion of the house of David, the ideal king of the Jewish people, all Jews will be gathered back to Palestine and there establish a great power, based on the exalted principles of righteousness and peace, rebuild the Temple and reinstitute the ancient Jewish form of worship. . . . It is at that time that the dead will be resurrected, all past generations participating in the supreme happiness that will come to the human race through his advent.[21]

For a moment it would seem as though this is what Conservatism taught, but then we are told that these were some of "the fanciful pictures which the Jew's imagination, let loose, created."

What Conservatism retains of all these beliefs is the same as that to which "the more sober-minded and more rational Jewish thinkers and writers" are said to have subscribed. They "conceived of the Messiah as a man, a descendant of the Davidic dynasty, 'divine only in the greatness of the natural gifts,' " [23] who will guide the destinies of a rejuvenated Israel and establish an ideal kingdom in Palestine which will serve as a model of government to all nations. "The Messianic age will differ from the present age only in this, that Israel will then have regained its sovereignty, and that the world will have become converted to the fundamental ideals of the Jewish religion." [24] In other words, the Temple with the ancient forms of worship and the resurrection, to say nothing of the Day of Judgment—all that is tacitly omitted from the picture.

Such, in brief, is the version that the left wing of Neo-Orthodoxy gives of "the religious truths, moral injunctions and ceremonial observances which together constitute Judaism." [25]

Notwithstanding that Conservatism is regarded by Neo-Orthodoxy as un-Jewish, untraditional, and even more dangerous than Reformism, its own sympathies and leanings entitle it to be classed as another orthodoxy. That is why, though it may conceivably progress toward a far sounder adjustment than Neo-Orthodoxy has reached, it is subject to the same drawbacks as Neo-Orthodoxy. There is little to choose between the Conservatism which is a timid Reformism and the Conservatism which is a tepid Orthodoxy.

PART THREE

THE PROPOSED VERSION OF JUDAISM

CHAPTER XIV

JUDAISM AS A CIVILIZATION

The inadequacy of the current versions of Judaism—Analysis of what is meant by the Jewish differentia—The need of having the right kind of category for that differentia—Judaism as a civilization, an end in itself.

THE versions of Judaism which have thus far been reviewed hold in common the assumption that Jews differ from non-Jews essentially in the matter of religion. They therefore envisage the problem of Jewish survival as a problem either of so interpreting the religious beliefs and practices, or of so adapting them to the exigencies of the times, as to ward off from Jewry the menace of being absorbed by the environment.

It is true that to the Neo-Orthodox, Jewish survival is not a matter of doubt, since they regard the very existence of the Jewish people and of the Torah, which constitutes its *raison d'être*, as supernaturally founded, and therefore not subject to the natural laws of growth and decay. Nevertheless they cannot be blind to the fact that individually, Jews are being dejudaized by their surroundings. To prevent that process from making headway, Neo-Orthodoxy reminds the Jew of the exalted origin of the Torah and the inner meaning of its teachings. He is called upon to appreciate the significance of Judaism as a revealed religion. On the other hand, the other versions of Judaism do, by implication, take cognizance of the possible disappearance of Jewish life as a whole, unless Jews be fortified by a stronger faith in its worthwhileness. To provide that faith, they stress the specific beliefs and practices which show wherein Judaism, as a historically evolved religion, is truer than other religions.

We have noted the shortcomings of all those versions of Judaism when analyzed from the standpoint of what they actually teach. But their most conspicuous failure is in what they omit to teach. Their inadequacy is such that they have nothing to contribute to

vast areas of Jewish life which are in need of planning and direction. *The most vital issues which confront the Jews today do not
even figure in the theoretic background of Neo-Orthodoxy, Reformism and their variants.*

The upbuilding of Palestine as a homeland and spiritual center
of the Jewish people has been agitated for the last two generations.
Neo-Orthodoxy, Reformism and its conservative variant at first
vigorously attacked the Zionist movement. The Conservative wing
—the left of the Neo-Orthodox—in America was the only one that
viewed the movement sympathetically. That is as far as it went.
It did nothing to incorporate in its philosophy any teaching which
might illuminate the relationship of the upbuilding of Palestine to
the rest of Jewish life in the diaspora. To this day Neo-Orthodoxy,
as consistently represented by the *Agudat Yisrael,* is opposed to the
Zionist movement and refuses to enter the *Jewish Agency.* The *Miz-
rahi* organization which is orthodox in its constituency, is devoid of
any systematic philosophy of Judaism. Its members are impelled to
support the movement by the intuitive realization of its significance
for Jewish life. The Reformists have relented in their opposition
as a result of the urgent need for utilizing whatever colonization
facilities Palestine offers, since the doors of other countries have
been shut against Jews fleeing from persecution. But whatever the
attitude of these groups may be today, there can be no question
that the Zionist movement did not arise from anything they advocated in their programs. It owes them nothing, for they had nothing
to do with taking the initiative in declaring that the existence of the
Jews as a people is no longer possible without a Jewish homeland
in Palestine. *If it is a fact that the Zionist movement has brought
about a renascence in Jewish thought and activity and has helped
to render Jewish life creative, could there be any graver indictment
of the current versions of Judaism than that they neither originated
nor sponsored that movement?*

Again, let us take the diversity in outlook and mode of life
which prevails among Jews who wish to foster Jewish life. Even
if we do not take into account those who advocate the complete
secularization of Jewish life, there is enough diversity among those
who regard religion as indispensable to create a problem which
cannot be ignored. Yet what is there in the theory of any of the

religious groups to point to a permanent *modus vivendi* with those who hold other views and practice a different regimen of observances?

With anti-Semitism becoming too dangerous to be met merely with passive resistance on the part of the Jews, there arises the need for organized effort to counteract its malicious propaganda. What shall be the nature of the organization? If it is to have any permanence, it must derive from some philosophy of collective Jewish life. Shall the Jews throughout the world be represented by a world congress, or shall the Jewry of each country attend to its own anti-Semitic evil independently of the rest of Jewry? Even more important, though at first it may seem to have only a theoretical bearing, is the formulation of a philosophy to counter anti-Semitism and all its works. Such a counter-philosophy would have to include general principles about the rights of minority groups, nationalism, internationalism, tolerance and cognate issues. All that would have to form part of any program which aims to set forth the kind of adjustment Jewish life demands.

Equally in need of finding a place in any comprehensive version of Judaism is the communal organization of each local Jewry. The various versions which have been considered seem to contemplate only the congregational form of organization. Yet it is a fact that the bulk of activity which makes for the conservation of Jewish life is carried on outside of the congregation. Philanthropy and social work among Jews cannot be carried on without communal organization. With each new need that arises, new machinery is set up to meet it. There is undue duplication of effort. Many Jews escape communal responsibility altogether. All these abnormalities exist because the various religious groups conceive their Judaism so narrowly as to leave no room for any philosophy of Jewish organization as such. In the past there was no occasion for stressing the principle of Jewish organization. The non-Jewish world isolated the Jewish group so that it was forced to organize its own communal life. But now that Jews do not have to belong to any Jewish community, the whole problem of communal organization ought to be canvassed as thoroughly as any traditional belief or practice in Judaism, and some definite declaration enunciated with regard to it.

No less basic a problem than the foregoing, is that of Jewish education. In the past the Jewish training included whatever general education the child needed to escape illiteracy. Now that such education is transmitted as part of the activities of the general community whose life the parents share, the entire purpose and function of Jewish training have had to be reorganized, and the responsibility for it assumed by the community; otherwise, the very need for such training is bound to wane. Nor is the problem of Jewish education one that affects the child only. With so much of the life of the adult necessarily pre-empted under modern conditions by the general cultural and recreational opportunities, what incentive is there for making the study of things Jewish part of the cultural interests of the adult? The most convincing proof of the inadequacy of the conceptions of Judaism developed by each of the four groups discussed is furnished by the futility of the Jewish educational efforts carried on by all of them and their seeming inability to find a fulcrum, as it were, with which to lift the dead weight of ignorance which obtains in their ranks.

How is it that each of the four outstanding groups in Jewish life could have so misconceived the problem of Jewish adjustment as to omit from its conception of Judaism principles that would guide the Jew in meeting some of his most pressing needs? It is no answer to say that they all assume that the Jew would know enough to apply the general ideas with regard to Judaism as the specific situations demand. The fact that there is a need for restating what Judaism should mean to the Jew of today, indicates that he wants a program that will help him to apply the general principles of Judaism to the manifold problems created by the new conditions of the contemporary world. The Golden Rule and the Ten Commandments are excellent criteria for the good life, yet the need for specific laws and regulations is not obviated by them.

When Zacharias Frankel charged the Reformists of his day with not having their proposals informed by any principle, he intuitively put his finger on the weak spot in their very approach to the problem of adjustment. But he did not realize clearly what kind of a principle it was that a proper approach demanded. This is why when it came to enunciating one, he was not much more successful. The concept "a positive historical Judaism" which he suggested might have furnished the much needed guidance in formulating the process of Jewish adjustment, had he met the following two conditions: first, had he been clear as to the kind of principle that is needed; and secondly, had he pursued the adopted principle to its logical conclusion. But both are hard conditions to meet, and it must be remembered that Frankel lived at too early a stage in the process of Jewish readjustment to have been able to do so. It is only after all that has happened since his day that we are in a position to view the problem more comprehensively and to be more daring in its solution.

The way to arrive at the kind of principle which Frankel was groping after is to view Judaism in its totality, and to avoid the mistake of identifying it merely with some particular phase of its functioning. That requires a clear grasp of what it is that differentiates the life of the Jews from that of the non-Jews. To begin with, we have to analyze the very notion of difference. *To be different may mean to be both other and unlike, or, to be other only.* Otherness is difference in entity, unlikeness is difference in quality. Unlikeness presupposes otherness, but otherness is compatible with either likeness or unlikeness. Otherness may therefore be considered primary, and unlikeness only secondary. Hence, when Jewish life is endangered and we try to conserve it, we necessarily try to conserve that which differentiates it from non-Jewish life. But here a fallacy insinuates itself. We make the mistake of believing that what we chiefly try to conserve is that wherein Jewish life is unlike non-Jewish life, or what may be termed its differential. We concentrate on the religious aspect of Jewish life, because it is that aspect which is conspicuously most unlike, and because we assume it to be the least troublesome to justify. But the truth of the matter is that what is at stake in our day is the very maintenance of Jewish life as a distinct societal entity. Its very otherness is in jeopardy.

The Jew's religion is but one element in his life that is challenged by the present environment. It is a mistake, therefore, to conceive the task of conserving Jewish life as essentially a task of saving the Jew's religion. When a person is about to abandon a house for fear that it might fall about his ears at any moment, it is folly to try to convince him that he ought to remain in it because of the beautiful frescoes on its walls. Jewish life is becoming uninhabitable because it is in danger of collapse. The problem is how to make it habitable. To drop the metaphor and return to the more abstract method of viewing the problem of Judaism, *the task now before the Jew is to save the otherness of Jewish life; the element of unlikeness will take care of itself.*

Put more specifically, this means that apart from the life which, as a citizen, the Jew shares with the non-Jews, his life should consist of certain social relationships to maintain, cultural interests to foster, activities to engage in, organizations to belong to, amenities to conform to, moral and social standards to live up to as a Jew. All this constitutes the element of otherness. *Judaism as otherness is thus something far more comprehensive than Jewish religion. It includes that nexus of a history, literature, language, social organization, folk sanctions, standards of conduct, social and spiritual ideals, esthetic values, which in their totality form a civilization.* It is not only Judaism, the religion, that is threatened but Judaism, the civilization. What endangers that civilization is not only the preoccupation with the civilizations of other peoples but also the irrelevance, remoteness and vacuity of Jewish life. There is little at present in Jewish life that offers a field for self-expression to the average man and woman who is not engaged either as rabbi, educator, or social worker. If one does not have a taste for praying three times a day and studying the Bible and rabbinic writings, there is nothing in any of the current versions of Judaism to hold one's interest as a Jew. Activities that might hold one's interest, and through which one might express oneself as a Jew, have not been recognized as part of Jewish life because there has been found no concept which might integrate them into it. Lacking that integration, they are bound to remain sterile, and Jewish life is apt to become an empty shell.

The Reformists, it is true, recognize this fact of otherness but they mistake its very nature and make only a limited and negative use of it in their reconstruction of Judaism. In the teaching that "the racial community formed and still forms the basis of religious community," [1] the otherness of Jewish life is identified as a matter of race, or of physiological heredity, and the main practical corollary to which it gives rise is the deprecation of intermarriage. Jews will never extricate themselves from their spiritual difficulties unless they have the courage to accept fully and frankly the element of otherness involved in their being Jews, and base their efforts as Jews upon an honest recognition of its true character. They must learn to accept Judaism in the future, as they did in the past, as a social and not as a physiological heritage. It is a social heritage because it is the sum of characteristic usages, ideas, standards and codes by which the Jewish people is differentiated and individualized in character from the other peoples.[2]

The categories under which it has been customary to subsume Judaism have proved inadequate.[3] It can no longer be confined within the terms of revealed religion or ethical monotheism. Both its own nature and the temper of the time preclude its being classified with either the one or the other. We must, therefore, find for it a category which will do justice to the whole of it. Those who try to interpret Judaism to the outside world are in the habit of describing it in terms which they imagine would justify its existence in the opinion of their audience. This is why Philo and Josephus found it necessary to represent Judaism to the Gentiles of their day as a philosophy, and this is why modern Jewish apologists deem it necessary to represent Judaism as a religion. But what may reconcile non-Jews to the existence of Judaism does not necessarily help the Jews in solving the problems to which it gives rise. Now that it is in need of intelligent planning and direction Jews should learn Judaism's essential character so that they might know what to do with it in times of stress.

The term "civilization" is usually applied to the accumulation of knowledge, skills, tools, arts, literatures, laws, religions and philosophies which stands between man and external nature, and which serves as a bulwark against the hostility of forces that would otherwise destroy him. If we contemplate that accumulation as it works in the life process, we realize that it does not function as a whole, but in blocks. Each block of that accumulation is *a* civilization, which is sharply differentiated from every other. Each block or unit of civilization can exist and flourish, even if every other should become extinct. This fact indicates that a civilization is a complete and self-contained entity. *Civilization* is an abstract term.

The actuality is civilizations; e.g., the civilizations of Babylonia, of Egypt, of Palestine.

Not all elements of a civilization constitute its otherness. Each civilization possesses elements which it shares with other civilizations, and which are transferable *in toto* to other civilizations. Among these would be included mechanical developments, inventions, the funded discoveries of science. But it would be wrong to assume that these improvements in the mechanics of living constitute a civilization. The elements which give it otherness and individuality are those which produce the human differentia in the individuals that are raised in it. The development of the human differentia is due mainly to non-transferable elements like language, literature, arts, religion, and laws. They are non-transferable in the sense that they cannot be adopted by other civilizations without essential changes in their character.

By placing Judaism within the category of civilizations we shall know how to fit it into the framework of the modern social order. That classification should help us identify in the complex thing called Judaism, all of the elements and characteristics which go to make up its substance, and which can be properly appraised in terms of present-day values and desiderata, because they can be studied as the reactions of human nature to social environment. Judaism is but one of a number of unique national civilizations guiding humanity toward its spiritual destiny. It has functioned as a civilization throughout its career, and it is only in that capacity that it can function in the future.

If Judaism is to be preserved amidst the new conditions, said the late Israel Friedlaender, if, lacking as it does, all outward support, it is still to withstand the pressure of the surrounding influences, it must again break the narrow frame of a creed and resume its original function as a culture, as the expression of the Jewish spirit and the whole life of the Jews. It will not confine itself to a few metaphysical doctrines, which affect the head and not the heart, and a few official ceremonies which affect neither the head nor the heart, but will encircle the whole life of the Jew and give content and color to its highest functions and activities.[5]

A civilization is not a deliberate creation. It is as spontaneous a growth as any living organism. Once it exists it can be guided and directed, but its existence must be determined by the imperative of a national tradition and the will-to-live as a nation. Civilization arises not out of planned cooperation, but out of centuries of inevitable living, working and striving together. Its transmission takes place by the method of suggestion, imitation, and education of the young, sanctioned by public opinion and authority. The operation of these forces is postulated by the existence of the social institutions of the family, school, religious organization and communal self-government. The process cannot wait until the child reaches the age of choice. Civilizations live by the inherent right to direct the child into their ways. It is only thus that the whole course of human development has been made possible.

Being a Jew is thus primarily a matter of momentum, and does not turn upon the choice between two equally balanced alternatives. This does not mean that Jewish life is impelled merely by a blind *vis a tergo*. The momentum that inheres in a civilization may with the application of intelligent purpose be transformed into creative social energy. But that is entirely different from expecting Judaism to validate its existence on purely rational grounds, that is to say, on the ground of being an indispensable means to some universal good. As a civilization, Judaism possesses the prerogative of being justly an end in itself. It is questionable whether the approach to Judaism as a phenomenon demanding continual justification can ever prove satisfying. This method has honorable motives, but its phychological effects on the life and character of the Jews often prove highly undesirable. *In a world of competitive values, it is an honorable thing to seek a rationale for the particular value that one lives by, and for the Jew "values" are especially competitive. Yet when the tendency is carried to excess, Judaism becomes a complex rather than a way of life. The necessity for continual self-justification ceases to be stimulating and becomes a depressant.*

Even if we admit for the moment that the attempt to find a justification for being a Jew is legitimate, it is obvious that to find this justification in Jewish contributions to universal values is paradoxical. The logical social structure for the expression and propagation of universal values is not a group of people who have an hereditary interest in the system of values, but a society based on voluntary affiliation. At those times in Jewish history when there was high degree of awareness of the strictly ethical and religious values which might be found in Judaism, such societies actually flourished as, for example, in the case of the Essenes. A classical example outside of Judaism is the Stoics. If the *raison d'être* of the Jewish people is the system of universals which it has created, then Jewishness ought to mean deliberate affiliation with a kind of religio-philosophical sect, and Jewish life ought to become sharply and sincerely sectarian, according to the various interpretations placed on these universals by various groups of Jews. This is neither the desideratum we commonly envisage, nor the actual state of affairs. What we usually seek is the refinement of Jewish otherness and its exploitation for good, rather than its attenuation.

With this approach, the question of "why be a Jew?" loses its relevance. If Jewish life is a unique way of experience, it needs no further justification. We may call this approach to Judaism the intuitional approach, in contrast with the traditional approach of Neo-Orthodoxy and the rational approach of Reformist Judaism. Such an approach would bring about a profound psychological difference in Jewish living. Jewish life would no longer have to be lived for the purpose of exemplifying certain universal truths. Neither would it have to be pruned and clipped into conformity with a complex of abstract values whose very universality precludes their adoption as the purpose and rationale of an entire nation. Attachment to Judaism has always been derived from just such an intuitional attitude toward it. The various interpretations of Jewish doctrine and practice, the abstract values and concepts, are but the formal afterthoughts of that intuitional attitude. The recital of the *Shema Yisrael* was traditionally one of the most dramatically meaningful practices of Judaism, not because of the abstract idea of absolute monotheism which it is supposed to express, but simply because it provided an occasion for experiencing the thrill of being a Jew. The idea of abstract monotheism is hardly contained in the proposition; implicit or explicit, it was an abstraction the Jew did not constantly hold in mind. And even when he was aware of the idea of abstract monotheism, it hovered over the experience and did not constitute its chief value.

The religious observances, too, claimed the fervent loyalty of the Jew primarily because they were a unique way of collective self expression. What often passes for orthodoxy is a mode of Jewish life that is not at all motivated by a conviction of the supernatural origin of those observances. If that mode of life were properly analyzed, it would be found that its chief purpose was to be identified with the Jewish people, a purpose that is just as ultimate as the will-to-live. In *A Plea for Orthodoxy*, a noted Jewish scientist, whose interest in Judaism was due to an intensive Jewish upbringing, pursues an entirely different line of argument in defense of the religious observances from that which a protagonist of Neo-Orthodoxy like Hirsch would advance.

In contrast to not a few of our co-religionists who have no occasion for weeks and months together . . . to bestow a thought on their creed or their people, the Jew who keeps *Kashruth* has to think of his religious and communal allegiance on the occasion of every meal . . . and on every such occasion the observance of the laws constitutes a renewal of acquiescence in the fact that he is a Jew and a deliberate acknowledgment of that fact. . . .

The labor and care required for carrying out our religious laws not only do not justify any attempt to simplify or abrogate them, but constitute one of the essential objects of our endeavor in carrying them out in their integrity. For it is in the performance of obligations calling for thought and effort that the character of men and their loyalty are trained and tested, and the object of their loyalty is made dear to them and bound up with their lives. . . .

. . . It may appear a minute matter, for instance, to teach one's children the Hebrew blessing of the bread and to accustom them to pronounce that blessing on the necessary occasions. . . . For if a Jew remembers, at the time of partaking of food, and makes the benediction in the authentic words used by his fellow-Jews since time immemorial the world over, he revives in himself, wherever he be at the moment, communion with his unyielding and imperishable race. . . .[6]

To one who argues thus Judaism is not merely a revealed religion but a civilization.

It is true, no doubt, that in Judaism the religious practices were for a long time interpreted as constituting the means of attaining a share in the world to come, or salvation. This conception of the religious practices operated as a powerfully motivating force in Jewish life, but it would never have succeeded in gaining its traditional importance in the Jewish consciousness, if there had not already existed the need for self-identification with the Jewish people. That need met with fulfillment in the very practice of the *miṣwot* apart from any end which they were regarded as serving. This fact renders the survival of Jewish civilization independent of the traditional belief in other-worldly salvation.

The most important inference to be drawn from the intuitional approach relates to the manner of our response to the need for adjustment as Jews to the changed conditions of life. The Neo-Orthodox Jew meets the challenge of the modern environment by a reaffirmation of his faith in tradition. He bases his veneration of the content of Judaism on the high authority of those from whom that content is derived. Their authority, in turn, it is assumed, is validated by the supernatural revelation of God's will. The Reformist Jew rejoices to find in Judaism truths of universal application, the unity of God, the brotherhood of man, the supremacy of righteousness. But for the Jew who approaches Judaism as a civilization, the test for any form of adjustment will not be whether it conforms to the accepted teachings of revelation, nor whether it is consistent with the universal aims of mankind. His criterion will be: does that adjustment proceed from the essential nature of Judaism? Will it lead to the enrichment of the content of Judaism? Is it inherently interesting? The thing that makes Judaism a vital reality for him is not a regimen of conduct or a system of thought. He realizes that the force of a social heritage lies not in its abstract and universal values, but in its individuality, in its being unalterably itself, and no other. This individuality he knows from within. It is an immediate and untransferable experience. It is as interesting to him as anything that is part of his own personality can be.

It is the feature of interest, rather than that of supernatural origin or rationality, which is—which must be—the essential factor in the approach to Judaism. That interest can be achieved only if Judaism is intensely related to one's own personality. The Jew must so identify himself with every facet of Jewish life that all aspects of it find their reflection in him. The Jew cannot live Judaism as a civilization unless the past of his people becomes his own past, unless his entire being becomes a nerve that reaches out to the life of his people, and is aware of their every experience. The one who is actively and recognizably interested in Judaism, though he may reserve his judgment as to the absolute or final worth of the particular Jewish meanings to which he has for the time attached his interest, makes a valuable contribution to Jewish life in his very attitude.[7]

Accepting Judaism as a unique form of experience does not preclude the admission of non-indigenous elements. Jews will be justified in seeking to heighten that very uniqueness by leaving the way open for the assimilation of forms and values that Judaism may not now possess. None of the arts in past Jewish life had a scope sufficient to fix definitively the limits of these arts as they may develop in Jewish civilization in the future. The way is thus left open for Jewish artists to assimilate the forms of other civilizations for their own uses, as Jewish painters without waiting for the sanction have already done. There must obviously be some criterion for the difference between healthful assimilation of non-indigenous forms and the passionless and sterile imitation of such forms. Ahad Ha-Am[8] has dwelt on the difference, but no criterion has yet emerged.

Ultimately, the difference between a uniqueness that is trivial and abnormal and a uniqueness that is spiritual fulfillment is determinable only empirically. We cannot say before the fact whether a particular attempt to intensify Jewish experience will produce results that are outlandish or those that enrich Jewish life. In this respect, we can proceed only from faith, and from the desire to make Jewish experience spiritually satisfying. *When Jewish life shall have developed a law of its being, we shall have some criterion for determining the spiritual value of the aspects and elements of Jewish experience.* And this law will emerge only when Jewish life becomes an experience of infinite variety.

CHAPTER XV

CONSTITUENT ELEMENTS OF JUDAISM AS A CIVILIZATION

A land—A language and literature—Mores, laws and folkways—Folk sanctions—Folk arts—Social structure.

I. A LAND

A *sine qua non* of a civilization is a place in the sun. A civilization is the product of social interaction of a group commonly known as a nation, whose life is rooted in a specific part of the earth. The landscape of the particular part of the earth where a civilization arises and flourishes is as essential to a civilization as shelter is to a living being. It figures as the *locus* of the civilization, and gives it concreteness and visibility. Each civilization has its own landscape which it conceptualizes and thus makes an object of consciousness. Those who are identified with the civilization share the psychological values of that landscape, even if they be far removed from it.

Judaism could neither have arisen, nor continued to exist apart from the land that gave it birth. To appreciate what *Ereṣ Yisrael* has meant to Judaism, it is necessary to understand the intimate relation that exists between a people's country and its social and spiritual life. A common country molds an aggregate of human beings into a people. It serves as the physical basis of a people's life and civilization. Mere physical propinquity is sufficient to give rise to common interests which in turn find expression in a social framework, a common language, common customs, laws, forms of worship, ethical standards and social aspirations. What soil is to the life of a tree, a land is to the civilization of a people.

Judaism, not being a religion, did not spring into existence at a particular moment in history. The pattern of life we now call Judaism developed gradually and imperceptibly as the outcome of collective life. The process of living together in Palestine molded the various invading Israelitish tribes into the people that in time evolved the civilization which has come to be known as Judaism. So imperceptible was the development of Judaism, that before long there arose traditions which assigned to it a theurgic origin and an idealized history. Such at least are the conclusions of historical research which the thinking man of today finds it impossible to ignore.

Neo-Orthodoxy refuses to admit these conclusions. Israel was a nation long before it possessed land and state, says Samson Raphael Hirsch, and has therefore remained a nation for centuries without a land and state.[1] But from the standpoint of a scientific reading of Scriptures, the stories in the Pentateuch which represent Israel as having been formed into a nation in Egypt, from which it emerged to take possession of the land promised to the Patriarchs, is Israel's idealization of its beginnings—an idealization that arose after it became a nation in Palestine. A careful study of the various texts in the Bible that throw light upon the actual beginnings of Israel verify what has been borne out a thousand times in history; namely, that it takes the physical propinquity of a land to mold an aggregate of human beings into a nation.

But even if there remain a doubt as to the part played by Palestine in bringing the *nation* Israel into being, no one will gainsay the fact that during the fifteen centuries of Israel's stay in Palestine—the period during which Israel constituted the majority population—there unfolded that unique drama of national life in which all the forces, ideas and strivings that go to make up Judaism came into play. Even on the traditional assumption that the Torah was given on Mount Sinai, it cannot be denied that the laws in the Torah assume the occupation of the Promised Land as a condition of their observance. Certainly the actual struggle against the corrupting Canaanite civilization—the struggle which elicited the prophetic revelation of God as a God of righteousness, the lyrical ecstasy of the Psalmists, and the practical wisdom of the Sages—all this found its motif in the life of the nation living in one land. The history of the Second Commonwealth, during the existence of which Judaism was consolidated into a highly self-conscious and almost fixed civilization, is a history of the forces that played upon the Jewish people by reason of its occupying a common territory. Without Palestine, Israel could never have been molded into a people with a common culture.

But was Palestine necessary to keep Israel a people? S. R. Hirsch, the protagonist of Neo-Orthodoxy, would maintain that since Israel remained a nation without a land or state, Palestine contributed nothing to the preservation of Israel's national being during the nineteen centuries of exile. This is not in accord with the facts. Philo, in referring to the dispersion of the Jews, says that "they look upon the holy city as their metropolis in which is erected the sacred temple of the most high God." [2] It does not need a practiced eye to discern the hope for the recovery of Palestine in every move and turn of Jewish life and thought since the destruction of the Second Commonwealth. The Jews did not merely retain the customs and traditions which had arisen and were developed in Palestine, but used those customs and traditions as a means of keeping alive their memory of Palestine. Hearing the messianic call was not a remote possibility, but something that entered into the practical reckoning of the average Jew.

Even when the belief in a return was countered by all actualities, it colored the Jews' entire social and religious conduct, and constituted their principal hope during the incessant persecutions endured in the diaspora. No matter where the Jews lived, culturally and spiritually they moved in a Palestinian milieu. Even the climate and other physical conditions of the countries they lived in did not seem to interest them. We do not find that they prayed for rain or dew for the countries of their dispersion. It did not matter to them that Palestine was in the possession of Bedouin or Turks; the petition that her crops might prosper went up three times daily, as though the Jews lived there in undisturbed possession. After each meal, the Jew gave thanks for the Land as though he were still living in it and enjoying its produce. The memory of having once lived in Palestine, and the certainty of occupying it again, could not be considered the equivalent of actually living there, but they were at least effective anodynes for his *Heimweh*. The Jew remembered that he was in exile and bitterly deplored his condition. On the most joyous days of the year he still reiterates the plaint, "And because of our sins we were exiled from our land and removed from our country."

However, not even the most ardent aspiration to return to *Ereṣ Yisrael* could have enabled Judaism to survive, if the Jews had not managed to live in large communities which were kept in constant touch with one another. The measure of autonomy and freedom from non-Jewish interference in its internal affairs each local Jewry enjoyed was of more than local significance. It made possible the cultural and spiritual interaction of world-Jewry. Living together in groups as a result of voluntary or enforced segregation enabled the Jews to cultivate their own mode of life, to develop their own institutions, to conduct their own system of child training, and to govern themselves in matters economic and judicial as an autonomous community. Just as the Jewish captives in Babylon were permitted to settle in groups and to reproduce the mode of life they brought with them from *Eres Yisrael,* so throughout Jewish history wherever Jews migrated, they sought each other out and formed themselves into self-governing communities. In Alexandria, in Rome, in the cities of Moorish Spain, in the Rhine region, in England, or in Poland,[3] the Jews were always a "state within a state." [4] This fact, which is the most fundamental commonplace of Jewish history, is seldom viewed from the standpoint of its true significance for the survival of Judaism. The connection between the segregation of the Jews and the continuance of Judaism throughout the centuries is treated as purely accidental, when, as a matter of fact, it is that of cause and effect. Without segregation there could have been no collective self-determination, and without that, there could have been no Judaism.

Thus, until the emancipation the Jews were, to all intents, a territorial group. The philosopher Kant speaks of the Jews as the "Palestinians who sojourn among us." [5] The fact that they did not all occupy a continuous stretch of territory, or that they were not confined to one single pale or ghetto but were distributed in a number of pales or ghettos, did not render a common territory less of a factor in their lives. The remarkable uniformity in all matters pertaining to Jewish life that prevailed within the various Jewries, and the unparalleled discipline and obedience to authority that obtained everywhere among the Jews, made of them a nation in a truer sense than were those who lived in one country under their own government. Though they regarded themselves as exiles in the lands where they sojourned because the nations among whom they lived never gave them a chance to forget their homelessness; yet because the Jews in all lands wanted to be a nation in their own land, they really had a far stronger bond of unity and cooperation to serve as a basis of a common life and civilization than any people living unmolested on its own native soil. As a result, the Jews managed to maintain enough of a civilization during the many centuries of dispersion to feel that their identity as Jews had grown dependent upon their perpetuating that civilization.

2. LANGUAGE

A language is pre-eminently the distinctive mark of a civilization. That a common language gives a people individuality seems to have been recognized at a very early date. It is assumed in the biblical legend that YHWH broke up the unity of mankind into nations by confusing men's tongues. A language enables the individuals of a nation to enter into communication with one another and, at the same time, develops in each a consciousness of his people as distinct from other peoples—or of his people's otherness. Whereas a common land is an indispensable condition to a civilization, a common language is an indispensable vehicle of a civilization, and the most conspicuous element in it. A human group, at however primitive a stage of development, possesses a mode of speech. When that mode of speech begins to serve as a medium for communicating not alone the immediate wants and reactions of the group, but also its conscious approvals and disapprovals, it becomes the vehicle of a civilization. Every language is a storehouse of a particular cluster of ideas and experiences which are common to the members of the group and distinguish the group from other groups.

A language is not a series of disconnected symbols, corresponding to certain "areas of experience" which in a different language might be denoted by other symbols. The "areas of experience" of one people are never exactly co-extensive with those of another. This is why the most sacred and intimate experiences of a people cannot be faithfully reproduced in a foreign tongue. "It is impossible that the quality of one language should be preserved in another," states Roger Bacon, in his *Opus Majus*,[6] to prove that Hebrew is a prerequisite to the understanding of the Bible. Each language has not only its idioms but also its specific and haunting overtones which give it individual timbre. It is in that psychic timbre that we can discern the mental and spiritual characteristics of a people.[6]

A language thus helps to keep alive the collective consciousness of a people. In the words of Zangwill: "Language is the chief index of life. As no man is dead so long as the mirror put to his lips reveals a breath, so no race is extinct so long as there comes from its lips the breath of speech. A people that speaks is not dead; a people that is not dead speaks." [7]

English civilization dates from the time that the Anglo-Saxon fused with the Norman French to form the English language. French civilization did not exist before the Latin was so modified through the mingling of the Germanic Franks with the Latinized Gauls as to give rise to a new language called French. The fate of a civilization is usually reflected in the fate of the language which serves as its medium. The last century has witnessed the renascence of a host of languages in Europe and Asia. The modern Greek, the Polish, the Irish, the Norwegian, the Lithuanian and the Catalonian are a few of the languages which have more or less succeeded in establishing themselves as literary media. These languages represent the rise of new civilizations, or the revival of old civilizations that had long been repressed by tyrannous conquerors. In modern times, imperialist nations have generally reckoned with the power exercised by the language of the conquered people in keeping its spirit alive. Accordingly, among the first measures adopted to stamp out the national spirit of a conquered race or nation has been the prohibition of its language in the public schools. France, Germany, Russia, Poland, have all had their turn in being oppressor and oppressed in the matter of language. If world-peace is to be secured not through the suppression of national groups but rather by directing their individual energies into useful channels, any people whose civilization is of consequence to it is entitled to insist upon the survival of its own language.

Judaism probably represents the first instance of a language conflict. Spengler is mistaken when he says, "Piety towards the mother tongue—the very term testifies to deep ethical forces, and accounts for the bitterness of our ever-recurring language battles— is a trait of the *Late* Western soul, almost unknowable for men of other Cultures and entirely so for the primitive." [8] During the first seven hundred years of its existence, Judaism was engaged in acquiring the Hebrew language and building up a rich literature. During that time, Hebrew developed into the medium in which the other elements of the civilization, the codes and the mores, the folkways and the folk values, were given permanent form. Then came the destruction of the two kingdoms, the Northern and the Southern. The land was settled by neighboring tribes and by those brought from distant regions by the Assyrian and Babylonian conquerors. Before long Hebrew fell into disuse, and its place was taken by the languages of the neighboring peoples. This irritated Nehemiah, for he apprehended that it would prove a menace to the spiritual life of the community. In the disuse of Hebrew he saw the consequence of mixed marriages. "In those days saw I also Jews that had married women of Ashdod, of Ammon and of Moab; and their children spoke half in the speech of Ashdod, and could not speak in the Jews' language, but according to the language of each people." [9] About the same time that Nehemiah deplored the decadence of Hebrew in Palestine, an unknown visionary foretold the time when Jews would be settled in Egypt, and not only maintain their religious rites there, but also their Hebrew tongue.[10]

Despite the wishes of the Jewish zealots, Hebrew was unable to hold its own against Aramaic which, prior to the Greek conquest, seems to have become the official language of the entire western half of the Persian empire. At that time there began a unique procedure which has characterized Judaism ever since, that of retaining Hebrew as the language of worship, of the elementary school and the *bet ha-midrash,* while developing the foreign vernacular into a Jewish dialect for use in the home and in the street. When the competition of other languages was too strong to be withstood, Hebrew did not succumb, but retired to the inner sanctuaries of Jewish life, where it continued not as the esoteric language of a few pedants, but as the medium in which the most vital interests of the people found expression. The Rabbis of the Talmudic period considered the use of the Hebrew language so essential that they accounted it as one of the chief merits for which the Israelites were redeemed from Egyptian bondage.[11]

It has been correctly observed that after the Hebrew language ceased to be the language of communication among the Jewish masses, it did not pass into the category of dead languages because it retained the power of individual expression and style. In contrast with medieval Latin which maintained a uniform style, though it was the international language of Europe for a number of centuries, Hebrew has seen the rise of one style after another. The vernacular, which was usually some Jewish dialect of an alien tongue, came also to contribute to an individualization of the Jewish people, and helped to differentiate it from other peoples no less effectively than did the Hebrew language.

To understand the part that language played in the history of Judaism, we must bear in mind that since the fifth century B.C.E. Judaism has not been monolingual, as is the case with most civilizations, but bi-lingual.[12] Instead of having one language to give it individuality, it has always had two. Thus, later, there developed alongside the Hebrew, Jewish dialects of the Aramaic, the Persian, the Arabic, the Ethiopic, the Spanish, and the German language.[13] These dialects not only included a large number of Hebrew words and idioms, but they were also written in Hebrew script.[14] Each of these dialects was so colored by the rest of the Jewish social heritage that parting with it was an occasion for vehement protest, and it seemed as though with its relinquishment an essential element of Judaism were being sacrificed. Jews from eastern Europe, who have not come under the influence of occidental civilization, can scarcely think it possible for anyone who is not able to understand the Yiddish language to be a "real" Jew. There are Jewish pulpits where preaching in any language but Yiddish is forbidden. Among the ultra-orthodox Jews in Jerusalem, the substitution of Hebrew for Yiddish is resented not only because of the secular use of Hebrew thus involved, but also because the disuse of Yiddish is regarded as an alienation from the true spirit of Judaism.[15]

Of the two languages which Judaism as a civilization has had to cultivate by reason of the exigencies of history, Hebrew has been by far the more indispensable one. In the first place, it has supplied the elements of historic continuity and present solidarity. More than a million Jews lived in Egypt during the time of Philo. In spite of persecution, massacre and forced conversion to Christianity and later to Mohammedanism, a remnant would probably have survived had these Jews not dispensed with Hebrew altogether, nor contented themselves with translations of their literary heritage. Their zeal for the teachings and institutions of Judaism is attested by the numerous writings they left behind, and by their efforts to convert the heathen population about them. Yet they disappeared completely because they lacked one of the fundamental elements of the Jewish civilization—the Hebrew language. The rebirth of the Hebrew language is a modern miracle of the spirit. It is almost incredible that a language which had ceased to function as a vernacular for thousands of years should spring into life at the deliberate fiat of a handful of enthusiasts.[16]

3. MORES, LAWS AND FOLKWAYS

In a civilization it is scarcely possible to distinguish form or mode of expression from content. That distinction is usually made in the interests of priority in importance. But for purposes of discussion, we find it necessary to treat the content of a civilization as, in a sense, different from its form, and to reckon with the fact that it is chiefly through its content that a civilization comes to possess individual character.

The main content of a civilization consists of folk habits and folk sanctions which have the twofold effect of producing like-mindedness among those who belong to the same people, and a consciousness of difference from other peoples. Social habits include the actions and inhibitions which are habitual to any folk or people. They are social in the sense that the causes leading to their adoption are to be found in the collective life of the group as a whole, and not merely in the lives of the individuals who practice them. The impulse to perform those actions, or to yield to those inhibitions, partakes of the nature of both an inward and outward pressure. The outward pressure may come directly from one's immediate circle, but indirectly it is felt to come from the entire people. Social habits cover the entire range of human conduct, insofar as one is expected to conform to certain prescribed rules. They, therefore, include folkways, social etiquette, moral standards, civil and criminal laws, and religious practices.

We find represented in the Torah, both in the written and in the oral, every one of these types of social habits. Even a superficial examination discloses wherein these social habits differ from those of the other civilizations. There is in the Torah, to be sure, an abundance of religious precepts, of social habits which regulate the conduct of the individual toward God, but that is no reason for regarding Judaism as nothing more than a religion, any more than we ought to consider the Roman civilization a religion because it, too, abounded in religious practices to an extent perhaps even greater than the Jewish civilization.[17]

The main question is: did Judaism in the past possess enough mores, laws and folkways to direct the individual in the various adjustments that he was called upon to make to friend and foe, to stranger and kinsman, to employer, employee, litigant, etc.? Did Judaism embrace social standards in ethics, laws for marriage and property, and all the other institutions that human society has developed? One has only to take a casual glance at the contents of the written and oral Torah to be convinced that it sought to provide for all the contingencies of human life. What is more remarkable about the Torah is that it reflects conscious recognition on the part of the Jewish people that these laws give it individuality and distinction. "Observe therefore and do them; for this is your wisdom and your understanding in the sight of the peoples, that when they hear all these statutes, they shall say: Surely this great nation is a wise and understanding people!"[18]

When the Jews both in Palestine and in the diaspora were ready to sacrifice all for the Torah, it was the Torah in its entirety that they tried to save. They could not contemplate with equanimity a Torah in which one or more groups of its legal enactments would remain inoperative. When the destruction of the Temple rendered sacrificial laws defunct, the Jews were inconsolable. To have made the social customs and civil law inoperative would have meant to them the complete destruction of the Torah. A Jew who brought litigation against a fellow-Jew into a Gentile court committed an act of treason against Judaism. Although the Jewish community could not administer criminal law to the full extent, it had the power of corporal punishment and of excommunication. The autonomous life which all Jewish communities led throughout the diaspora afforded the Jews an opportunity to live their Judaism as a civilization.[19]

Among the *mores* which a civilization can least forego are those which have to do with the rearing of the child. *A civilization*

*demands that the foundations of personality in the child be laid
with the materials which the civilization itself supplies.* The more
self-conscious a civilization is, the more it insists upon having its
content transmitted through the process of education. No ancient
civilization can offer a parallel comparable in intensity with Judaism's insistence upon teaching the young and inculcating in them
the traditions and customs of their people.

Judaism functioned as a civilization throughout the centuries insofar as it had a monopoly on the first years of the child's upbringing.
There was no competing civilization to inculcate in the child other
traditions and customs. This is the true significance of the resistance which western civilization for a long time encountered on the
part of the Jewish school. The resistance took on a religious expression. Essentially it was the last stand against the effort to deprive
Judaism of the prerogative of giving to the child in his formative
years that which was to civilize him.

When in the face of these facts Judaism is identified in the
minds of some, merely with a system of beliefs dealing with the idea
of God and consisting of practices intended to bring the human
being into conscious relationship with God, it is due, no doubt, to
the circumstance that in the past every element of Jewish life was
related to the God-idea. Does it follow, however, that because
the Jewish people related all of its social habits to the God-idea,
its main interest in living its Torah or civilization was the God-idea?
We might as well argue that because a person would not eat a meal
without reciting grace, his main purpose in eating his meals is to
recite grace. The main object of the Jewish people in maintaining
the Torah is summed up in the Torah itself, "Ye shall therefore
keep my statutes, and mine ordinances, which if a man do he shall
live by them." [20] Accordingly, Judaism functions only so long as
it is coextensive with the whole of the Jew's life. To be that, it has
to consist of the entire range of social habits, from the most artless
folkways to the most formal legislative decree and the most self-
conscious ethical standards.

4. FOLK SANCTIONS

The *inner* aspect of the mores, laws and folkways which give
character to a people consists of specific folk sanctions. No custom,

duty or ritual is ever performed without having some kind of sanction implied or expressed, since no voluntary act or inhibition is conceivable without some awareness of purpose or reason. The ideas which validate the customs, usages, laws and standards should be termed "values" because their main purpose is not to express judgments of fact, but judgments as to the importance of the social habits and attitudes to which they refer, and the reasons for such importance. They are folk creations because the judgments they imply are not individual but collective. The ideas expressed in sanctions are not bloodless abstractions but are "charged with the motor urgent force of habit." They have been aptly termed *idées forces*. Hence the folk sanctions of a civilization include the traditions, both oral and written, which motivate its folk habits.

The type of social sanction which is likely to be evolved in the civilization of a savage people is of a very crude nature. When in answer to the question put to the Australian savage, "Why do you perform the war-dance?" he answers, "Because we always did so," he expresses a folk judgment which establishes for him and the other members of his clan the validity of the war-dance. His answer contains a very definite implication: since the custom has come down from the past, that is *ipso facto* a sufficient reason for its continued observance. When the members of a group become accustomed to suppress their impulses, and can articulate some kind of an explanation for what they do or refrain from doing, they are, to some extent, civilized. As soon as we come upon peoples with any degree of culture, we encounter elaborate reflection upon the social usages and institutions. Such reflection results in a complex of folk sanctions, which include beliefs elaborated into stories about gods and heroes, about the world of man and of nature. In addition, the people as a whole also becomes the object of reflection so that the origin, purpose and nature of the social usages and institutions are interpreted in terms of the people's experience and interests.

Thus arise formulas of tabu, religious beliefs, ethical standards and national ideals which give coherence and continuity to a civilization. These constitute what may be termed "folk ideology," insofar as they are ideas which are not only subscribed to by the entire folk, but refer to the interests and the welfare of the entire folk. Those ideas express in articulate form why certain places, objects, persons, events, laws, customs, are important. The adjective in folk ideology that corresponds to "important" is "sacred." The attitudes that anything important or sacred evokes are awe, reverence, fear, love and devotion.

It is by means of these *sancta* that a folk attains the state of self-awareness. The folk sanctions thus form the element of self-consciousness in the civilization. They provide the folk with memory of its past and aspirations for the future, and so create the human differentia of group continuity and group history. In all early civilizations the folk sanctions are related to deities, who are supposed to inhabit the particular environment in which the folk resides, and to be solicitous of its welfare. The existence of these deities is not questioned. They are the ultimates, or last point of reference, in validating the things, persons, laws and relationships considered sacred and important for the welfare of the folk. Whether the matter in question affects the welfare of certain individual members of the group or the group as a whole, its validity must derive from some god or gods. At that stage of human development, no authority outside that derived from superhuman origin is recognized or even conceived as possible.

As civilizations progress there begin to emerge two additional sources of validation, the folk or nation as a whole, and individual reason. That is to say, the national being becomes an object of reflection, and its survival and welfare become ends worthwhile in themselves distinct from the divine sanction that usually sustains those ends. Not until modern times, however, does the national being attain such importance as to be able, in the opinion of many, to dispense with all further sanctions derived from a supernatural or divine source.

Until modern times, individual reason, even when acknowledged as worthy of authority apart from all relation to or verification by divine sanction, nevertheless, preferred to maintain its attachment to such divine sanction. This is illustrated in the deference paid to reason in the Middle Ages. The Stoics, who were nearer in their outlook to modern thought than were the medieval theologians, likewise found it necessary to identify reason with the will of God. The tendency to treat reason as an ultimate source of validation apart from all reference to God is seeking to assert itself nowadays in various quarters. That religious sanctions, however, will be indispensable both to the national being and to individual reason as sources of validation in the future, as they have been in the past, will be pointed out in the chapter dealing with the trend of religion.

The Jewish civilization differs from all except the Hindu and Far Eastern civilizations in deriving both the religious and the national sanctions from one and the same historic background, and that altogether its own. The English nation, for example, has two kinds of folk sanctions to lend authority to the different usages, customs and institutions that constitute the English civilization. It has the Christian folk sanctions which lean for the most part upon the experiences of the Jewish people. Its God is the God of Israel, its ideals of social righteousness are related to the character of the God of Israel, and its conception of purpose in human history is based upon the idea of purpose displayed in the history of Israel. On the other hand, obedience to the specific laws of the state, payment of taxes, enrollment in the army, are all sanctioned by allegiance to the country and people of England. The experiences of the English people furnish the social values for these patriotic duties. Thus the English civilization which is also largely religio-national is religious on the basis of Israel's experiences, and national on the basis of the experiences of the English people. The same is true of every modern civilization, whether Christian or Mohammedan. It is otherwise with the Jewish civilization. In this, the religious and national sanctions coincide. As a consequence of this coincidence of two orders of sanctions, we should naturally expect a more self-conscious attitude toward the social habits fortified by them, and a greater tenacity in maintaining the integrity of the civilization as a whole.

The coincidence of religious and national sanctions in the case of the Jewish civilization is one of the most significant facts about that civilization. This is the case not only because the religious sanctions are thereby prevented from being contentless abstractions, and the national sanctions are prevented from degenerating into expressions of national egotism. The coincidence of the two categories of authority or validation, religion and nationalism, fulfils a psychological need; otherwise religion tends to become formal, abstract and separated from life.

In primitive society there prevailed conditions which favored vital and relevant religion. The individual was then entirely dependent upon the social group, in which he was born, for the safety of his person, for the provision of his material wants and for the defense of his possessions. All his basic interests were thus bound up with those of his group. The beliefs and practices of a religion that arose under those circumstances, crude as they were, had the advantage of being rooted in the basic interests of the group. The festivals and ceremonies voiced the various religious sentiments of joy, thanksgiving or prayer called forth by periodic or noteworthy facts incident to their daily pursuits. Whether it was the preparation for some hunt, or the shearing of the sheep, or the ingathering of the crops that was celebrated by religious ceremonies, the religion was living and creative of such cultural values as men are capable of in that state of intellectual development.

With the growth and shift of populations, the progress of democracy and the resultant redistribution of human society, the historic social groups are dissolving and new ones are forming in their place. The process of redistribution and reorganization is being carried on at the expense of personal equilibrium. These conditions are by no means favorable to the flourishing of a religion that is indigenous and relevant. Today, the Jewish, Christian and Mohammedan religions may be considered as being in a state of suspended animation.

At the present time, the creeds, ritual and ceremonies of the various historic religions are not vitally significant even to the majority of those who observe them. This is true not merely because they are out of harmony with the enlarged human experience of the modern man, but primarily because they are detached from the basic interests of the life of the individual. Instead of being rooted in the things which make up the work and play of the modern man, they are based upon the work and play of the ancient man. During the last twenty centuries religion sought to divert man's attention from the ephemeral interests of this world, and taught him to look for God elsewhere than in his workaday cares and joys. This was why man was satisfied to ruminate over the religious experiences of his forebears, and in doing so, translated them into the regrets and wish-thoughts that belonged to the sphere of other-worldly aspirations. Nowadays, however, man looks to present-day realities for evidence of the divine in the world. If those realities prove disappointing or disillusioning, he turns atheist.

Thus, every difficulty or necessity for reinterpretation that the surviving religions encounter in modern times confirms the truth that a living religion is not universal abstract truth but local and concrete experience, which is interpreted in terms of universal human interest. The religions of today, the Jewish religion included, no longer conform to this principle. The group civilization and the professed group religion are today indifferent to each other, or even antagonistic to each other. The once living interaction between the social values and the other constituents of a civilization has been interrupted. An idealism and spirituality that are abstracted from the immediate actualities of life, that derive from a way of life and a mode of thought alien to these actual realities, divorce religion from life, with consequent harm to both.

While this description of present-day religions may run counter to the popular notions of religion, it is in complete harmony with our deeper intuitions. Do we not look forward to the establishment of the kingdom of God among men? Do we not speak of the day when the Lord shall be one and his name one? Does not this imply that as life is constituted at present, the sovereignty of God is not manifest? In other words, that very hope is an admission that we are in need of vital, functioning religion, a need which the historical religions in their present form do not satisfy.

Since a civilization is the unique ensemble of group interests, habits and ideals, it cannot exist without evoking all the emotions and actions that we usually associate with religion—obedience, hope, faith, loyalty, self-sacrifice, and even rites and ceremonies. Can what we ordinarily term religion elicit more? Is its main business to impose upon civilizations some shallow metaphysics, some pseudo-science, or some ill-conceived mysticism?

The truth is that a religion is a quality inherent in the very substance of a civilization. We can no more separate a religion from a civilization than we can separate whiteness from snow, or redness from blood. If we want to have a religion that is relevant to life, we must of necessity accept the civilization that goes along with it. It is a deep-rooted error of the human mind to believe that whatever can be talked about must have individual existence. Religion has certainly been talked about, hence the notion that religion, which is a mere abstraction when considered apart from a civilization, is something that can by itself influence life, save souls and build mansions in heaven. Whether a man recognizes it or not, he finds his real religion in his civilization.

But if religion is a quality that is inseparable from a civilization, it follows that, like a civilization, its existence and growth are entirely dependent upon people who lead a common life, because they are near each other, and have the same basic interests. They must actually live together and have some form of social autonomy. A certain minimum of social autonomy which is indispensable to the development of a civilization is equally indispensable to a religion. The assumption that a religion can be made the aim of a group of individuals that have only religion in common is altogether untenable.

5. FOLK ARTS

There is a current assumption that the artist works in solitariness, and that he is aloof from the interests and desires that agitate common mortals. Although the actual process of creation must necessarily go on in solitude, the artist derives his impetus toward creativity and most of his material from the actual life about him. To achieve work of any vitality, the artist must breathe the mental atmosphere of contemporary life. He must be permeated with the spirit of his time and use the current symbols. He must be rooted in locality. Before any art can be produced, a civilization must exist which that art can express, and essential to the growth of civilization is some degree of social and economic stability. Only then can it produce those institutions and symbols which the artist draws upon for his creative work; only then does the civilization evolve those conditions of life in the midst of which men may function creatively.

The fact that certain types of art, chiefly literature, painting and sculpture, require very little direct and immediate social cooperation toward their production has obscured this inalienable relationship that art as a whole bears to the social life of the group, and the meaninglessness of any art which is without relation to the group life. It has been pointed out that art is the individual's means of identifying himself with the life and thought and aspirations of his group. Works of art give expression to the group emotions and provide occasions for participating in them. Art forms may thus be understood as the rhythms into which the emotions of a civilization fall at their moments of highest power and intensity, and correspond to the heightened speech-rhythms of emotional excitement. What is significant for the perpetuation of civilizations is that their characteristic ways of feeling are preserved only in the heightened forms and the accentuated rhythms of art. A civilization cannot endure on a high plane without the preservation and cultivation of its arts. The art creations become part of the social heritage which is the driving force of the civilization, and come to be the means of calling forth from the group the civilization's characteristic emotional reactions.

Jewish civilization has conformed to this principle. It is true that Judaism did not develop the plastic arts, but it compensated for this lack by the development of music, literature and dance to a remarkably high degree. The Bible is replete with evidence which points to the mature development that music and the dance had achieved in the earliest days of the Hebrew Commonwealth. Music, both instrumental and vocal, was an integral part of the public life. That this music had a complex and rich tradition is made clear by the full musical terminology that we find in the Bible. "They must have been a people of an unusually musical temperament," writes C. H. Cornill, "whose daily nourishment was song and sound. . . . Everywhere and at all times were song and music to be found in ancient Israel. Every festival occasion, every climax of public or private life was celebrated with music and song." [21]

We learn from an Assyrian monument that the chief item in the tribute that Hezekiah on one occasion offered to an Assyrian ruler was a company of men and women singers, a fact which indicates that the musical tradition of Judea had achieved international repute in antiquity. The evidence of Psalm 137, in which the Babylonians demand songs of the captive Jews, is not to be disregarded in this connection. Song was so integral a part of Jewish life that despite its migratory and exposed condition throughout the last two thousand years, we are told "the Jewish people as a whole has never forgotten its original song," [22] which has found expression not only in the devotional music of the synagogue, but also in the lullaby, the love-song, and the satiric ballad. In the *Ḥasidic* movement which arose during the middle of the eighteenth century, song and dance figured as powerful factors in giving expression to the mystic and joyous aspirations of spiritual renascence.

It hardly needs to be said that it is possible to regard the whole of the literary heritage from a purely "esthetic" point of view, and that so regarded, it forms the most generative literary heritage of humanity. As a collection of literature, ranging from the saga to the incipient drama, from lyric poetry to philosophic meditation, the Bible is without parallel in the literature of the world. Its shaping influence on the literature of many nations, and its fascination for the mind of man, cannot be attributed to a human craving for cosmological speculation and moral instruction. The enchantment which the Bible wields arises from its haunting implications, from its strange and compelling cadences, from its power to arouse the imagination of men to white heat. Nor is the literary art of Judaism wholly contained within the canonical Scriptures. The literature of the Apocrypha, which exhibits some of the earliest forms of the *novelle*, testifies to the fact that literary inspiration never died out in ancient Judaism and never ceased to find an audience even after the highest national genius had for the time exhausted itself. The critical investigations into the Bible have made it fairly certain that literary movements were strong enough in the ancient Hebrew civilization to create schools for their maintenance, and the Bible itself has many references to works of history that are lost. In the Middle Ages the Bible was the starting point for Jewish imaginative literature. It inspired a vast body of creative expression in the form of *piyyut*, devotional literature and lyric poetry.

Although the interdict against the reproduction of the human form severely restricted Jewish sculpture, it is not to be supposed that Jewish art was without its plastic expression. With religion as the chief interest in Jewish life, it became the occasion for a rich tradition of plastic adornment, at first in the Temple and later in the synagogue. The verse from the Song of Moses, "This is my God and I will glorify Him," [22] was interpreted by the Sages as a scriptural injunction to make the objects used in ritualistic practices notable for their beauty. The injunction was taken seriously in Jewish life of the past. The prayer-book and the sacred writings, the case for the *etrog*, the wine cup and the candelabra, the ark and its hangings, the scroll and its ornaments came to be symbols of the group emotions and the group aspirations. Wherever the interdict did not apply, Jews cultivated the art of graphic design, as in the ornamental writing of their *megillot.*

In short, the notion that Judaism had not and need not have significant and characteristic art, is an illusion. The facts of the Jewish past confirm this, and the logic of civilization, in general, makes it clear that the illusion is dangerous to the perpetuation of Judaism. A civilization implies a specific esthetic mood, and a unique content of sensuous and imaginative beauty. The art of a civilization is its individual interpretation of the world in color, sound and image, an interpretation that is familiar and profoundly interesting to the people of that civilization. This art contributes a unique expressive value to each object of the spiritual life of that people. The creators of this art endow the landscape of the civilization with rare color, its language with original and unique beauty, and the remembered personalities of its past with heroic mold.

6. SOCIAL STRUCTURE

The elements of civilization that have thus far been discussed— language, laws, folk sanctions, folk arts—cannot come into being except in the milieu of collective life. They presuppose the life of a group which contains enough social machinery to articulate the general will. A living civilization must include a general will which makes itself felt in the consciousness of the individual, either as a form of authority, capable of physical coercion, or as that more subtle form of authority which reveals itself in what may be called social expectation. In civilizations, as we are ordinarily familiar with them, the state is the mechanism which the people creates in order to articulate the form and content of its collective life, as well as to bring to bear on each individual the weight of its authority. It must be remembered that the dictator or the despot is as much an instrument of the general will as the parliament of the most enlightened democracy. The general will exists and is made manifest, whatever the form of government which is operative.

In the matter of language, there is under ordinary circumstances little need for having any public pressure to have its use made general, since the language which the child is likely to learn is that of the civilization into which he is born. It is only when two civilizations compete for the possession of the child that each will exert its authority or influence to have the child learn its language. In self-conscious civilizations the primacy of language is stressed by pressure upon the individual through the organized school system. Laws and folkways also presuppose the functioning of the general will. The fact that the individual will is often sufficiently moralized to abide by the laws and folkways without coercion means little more than that the general will has become operative within the individual will itself, and requires no outer pressure. When the folkways interfere with one's convenience, there occurs the conflict between the individual and authority. Without a social structure, without teachers and officials, whose authority is recognized, to indicate what is ·important and sacred, the maintenance of the folk sanctions is inconceivable. In the arts, even when the artist resents the pressure of the general will, he cannot be creative except within the social structure. There would have been no temples, and none of the arts associated with worship in those temples, had there not been a priesthood. Most of the cultural wealth developed during the Middle Ages was conditioned by the social structure of the church wherein the painters, the sculptors, the musicians and the poets could find scope for their activity. The same holds true of the modern state. Although very few states officially encourage the arts, their administration and spirit undoubtedly play a part in the progress of the arts.

In early society the social structure, like all the other elements of the civilization, was related to the God-idea. It followed, therefore, that only those wielded authority who were in close contact with the religious life and its expression. Those in authority did not content themselves with appeal to the power of the gods to whom they could legitimately resort, but they also employed human agencies to obtain obedience. In early society authority expressed itself through the double sanction of religion and physical force. This was later known as the combination of state and church. In a theocracy like that of the Second Jewish Commonwealth, authority was, for the most part, centered in the high priest. The Jews carried out on a small scale what the Catholic church attempted on a larger scale when, under Hildebrand, it tried to give to Christian civilization a social structure that might derive its authority directly from God. Nominally, the church disclaimed the sanction of physical force, but in reality it commanded the secular arm of the state and could not function without that sanction.

As a result of religious and political revolutions, the church has become separated from the state. It has had to abandon the sanction of physical force and to rely upon the sanction of social expectation. But even that sanction cannot be exerted without some kind of social machinery. Whatever influence Christianity exercises in the lives of its adherents is unthinkable without the church organizations. The more closely knit and the better disciplined the organization, the more penetrating and enduring the influence. The fact that an American Catholic cannot be made to feel the force of Catholic civilization through any physical compulsion does not preclude the operation of a machinery that brings the general will of the Catholic civilization to function in the form of social expectation. When an individual fails to live up to that expectation, he is made to feel as an outsider, either by excommunication or disapproval. In the case of the Catholic church, the power which these instruments of expectation or disapproval wield is concentrated within a well-defined organization headed by the Pope. Hence allegiance to the Catholic church is allegiance to an authority which emanates from a central source, and reaches Catholics of all parts of the world. Its authority is so far-reaching that it very often has the effect of setting Catholics in opposition to the authority of the countries in which they live. This is illustrated by the resentment some Catholics evince at what they consider the unjust dealing of the American government in taxing them for education even when they conduct their own parochial schools.

As long as the Jews were in their own land, they were in a position to evolve the usual instruments of authority whereby their general will could make itself felt. They had to reckon only with the limitations imposed upon them by their status of vassalage. But within that status they evolved a theocracy, and brought it to an extraordinary state of development. Even then, however, there were enough Jews in the dispersion to make the matter of Jewish unity a problem. They began to feel the lack of the necessary structure to maintain life in the scattered members of the community. It was the absence of an adequate social structure that led the Jews, since the era of the Second Commonwealth, to pray for the day when all Jews could be gathered back to the same land. That seemed the only way all Jews could be made to feel the functioning of their collective will. But since the return to Palestine could not be realized, the Jews evolved a type of social structure whereby not only the solidarity of each local community was retained but the unity of all Jewries as well. The Jewish people achieved a unity much stronger than that of the Catholic church, without the aid of secular government, by relying solely upon what may be called the instrument of social expectation.[14] Not only within each local community was excommunication used effectively, but it is significant to note that excommunication pronounced in one community was operative in all.

The social structure of Jewish life was hitherto of the ecclesiastical type, for though the rabbi exercised his authority with the consent of those to whom he ministered, the Torah, the supernatural revelation of God's will, was the sanction of the laws he enunciated. It was by virtue of that sanction that the rabbi could apply the weapon of excommunication. With the rise of modern ideology and the denial of the validity of the supernatural sanction, the exercise of the power of excommunication was eliminated from Jewish life.

The problem of Jewish life at the present time is, accordingly, a twofold one: to find the proper type of social structure which would animate the form and content of the Jewish civilization, and to integrate this structure within the life of the various nations with whom Jews have come to identify themselves.

CHAPTER XVI

IMPLICATIONS OF THE PROPOSED VERSION OF JUDAISM

Judaism enters upon a new stage of development—A uniform pattern of life for all Jews henceforth precluded—The organic character of Judaism—Wherein the new approach reckons with the truth in Neo-Orthodoxy and Reformism—Room for diversity of belief and practice.

As a civilization, Judaism is not a static system of beliefs and practices but a living and dynamic social process, the manifestations of which are conditioned by the nature of the environment. The Judaism in Maimonides' time was as different from the Judaism in Ezra's day as Maimonides' world was different from Ezra's; and the differences between King David's world and Ezra's were reflected in the Judaism of their respective periods. In the light of this evolutionary conception of Judaism, the present crisis assumes a new significance. It means that Judaism is now entering upon an entirely new stage of development. So far, the Reformists are right. But their mistake consists in conceiving this new development incorrectly. They assume that Judaism must undergo a complete metamorphosis and transform itself from a civilization into a religion. They do not realize that Judaism can cope with the changes which have taken place in the social and intellectual life of mankind, not by giving up its character as a civilization, but by transforming itself from an ancient into a modern civilization.

The phase of existence upon which Judaism is about to enter will undoubtedly contain much that is totally new in form, content and organization. That implies transformation, an experience by no means new to Judaism. So many have been the changes that have taken place in Judaism that in their cumulative effect they disclose three distinct stages in its career. To discern these stages we have to take cognizance of the development of the Jewish religion, for though religion is but one element in a civilization, it is the most self-conscious one and therefore the truest index of its character.

The three types of Jewish religion by which we can distinguish the three past stages of the Jewish civilization will be discussed in a subsequent chapter.* For the present, only the outstanding trait of each of these stages will be mentioned.

The henotheistic stage. The first stage of the civilization which later became Judaism should properly be designated as *Israelitism.* It may be said to date from about 1200 B.C.E., by which time, it is conjectured, all the tribes identified as the *Bene Yisrael* had entered Palestine. As a henotheistic civilization, Israelitism had its social and religious values center about the God YHWH. In that stage the social habits, sanctions, institutions and whatever there was of literature and arts in Israel were permeated with the assumption that YHWH was wont to manifest himself to his people in direct and perceivable ways and was ever ready to make his will known to them. Theophany or the experience of the self-revelation of the deity, while an extraordinary experience, was counted upon as part of the scheme of life. Deeply embedded in the consciousness of all the tribes in Canaan answering to the name Israel, was the tradition that before they entered the land they had jointly made a covenant with YHWH, whose habitat had been the mountain range of Sinai. According to the terms of the covenant, YHWH was to be their God and they were to be his people.

The belief that YHWH was the only God had not yet been evolved, though it was assumed that he was mightier than the other gods and more to be feared—more truly a god. "Who is like unto thee among the gods, O YHWH, who is like unto thee, glorious in holiness, fearful in praises, doing wonders?" [1] YHWH was identified as the god who had led the Israelites out of Egypt, given them laws in the wilderness of Sinai and enabled them to conquer the land of Canaan. These beliefs constituted the nuclear religious values around which were built up traditions and legends which took as their theme the supremacy of YHWH. The motif in all these stories was to impress upon the Israelites the importance of recognizing YHWH as their God and the necessity of obeying his laws. These laws were ordained from time to time by the priests, judges and elders who governed as the representatives of YHWH. But since the date of the formulation of these laws was unrecorded, they came to be regarded

* Chapter XXV.

as part of the divine law which YHWH had given to his people in the wilderness, through Moses. The outcome of the efforts exerted by Israel's spiritual leaders was that the nature of YHWH was conceived in terms of power and holiness such as no other people was wont to ascribe to any of its deities. Thus did the Prophets initiate the development which later culminated in the second stage of Jewish civilization, and thus was Israelitism, the henotheistic civilization, transformed into Judaism, the theocratic civilization.

The theocratic stage. We may define a theocracy as that form of social organization in which the instruments for the expression of the people's will are conceived to have been given directly by God and to operate under his direct providence. In a theocratic civilization, it is further assumed that an instrument of this kind, whether it exist in the form of a written document or of some kind of organization, is fixed and unchangeable.

In theocratic religion, there was no longer any need of oracle or prophecy to make the will of God known. It was probably felt that this method of making his will known at intervals, and only upon request, was fitting for a pagan deity who was really not a god; but for God, the king of the universe, the more appropriate method was a series of *torot* which were to be interpreted as his will by the priests and the judges. As a means of affording that continual contact with a divine being, without which the ancient man would have felt helpless, Judaism now had the Torah. It dealt with all aspects of the intercourse of men with their fellow-men and of men with God. Lest the sense of relationship to God be weakened through preoccupation with daily needs, which do not always make one conscious of God's law and providence, Judaism gave place in its Torah to the sacrificial system and laws of ritual purity. These were direct means of keeping alive the consciousness of God's presence. In addition, there was developed the institution of public prayer.

In the theocratic stage of the Jewish civilization, the individual attained a higher degree of self-consciousness than he possessed in the henotheistic stage. He began to expect a definite correlation between his happiness and conformity to the laws and requirements of the state or society to which he belonged. The cultural development of the Jews, however, was such that they found but little difficulty in assuming a connection between obedience to the law of

God and their personal vicissitudes. The promise of reward for conformity, and the threats of retribution for disobedience were taken
literally.² To be sure, there were some who began to question
this view. But the popular sentiment overruled the occasional
objections and, in the main, the traditional view that virtue was
rewarded and evil punished in this life was vigorously upheld.

It was otherwise with the ideal of well-being which concerned
the nation. The hopes which had been raised by the Prophets who
had pictured the future of Israel after the fall of Babylon in the most
glowing colors, were still far from realization. In those visions
Israel was promised prestige and power. It was to be an Israel
gathered again into its own land and in the enjoyment of such rare
blessings of peace and security as would compel the other nations to
realize the greatness of Israel's God and transfer to him the allegiance they yielded to false gods. This vision of the future was in
utter contrast to the actual situation. The greater part of Israel
was dispersed among the nations, while the remnant in Palestine was
in humble vassalage to Persia, and later to the successors of Alexander. The paradox of being the special people of God, the creator
of the world, and at the same time in complete political eclipse, had
to be resolved.

Before this paradox was completely resolved, Judaism had
passed into the third phase of its civilization, the other-worldly
stage. The impulses and the stirrings which culminated in other-
worldliness were already discernible some centuries before it became
the distinct mark of Jewish civilization. These find expression in
the apocalyptic literature that flourished during this period, a literature which has been correctly described as the successor to
prophecy.

The other-worldly stage. The faith in the advent of a new
world-order or in the creation of a new heaven and new earth completely dominated Jewish thought during the eighteen centuries of
traditional Judaism. That modern Jewish theologians have either
passed over the significance of that faith, or have deliberately denied
its existence, shows how great their anxiety is to reconcile Judaism
with current thought. Current thought is opposed to other-worldliness as a guiding principle of life, ergo, Judaism never had much to
do with other-worldliness. The only plausible excuse for failing to

recognize the predominance of other-worldliness in Judaism is that it fills Judaism like an atmosphere, and is so ubiquitous as to escape notice.

The belief in a world to come, when it actually functions as it did both in Judaism and in Christianity, and as it still functions in Catholicism, revolutionizes all standards and values of everyday existence. It affects not merely a person's religion, but his entire conduct. It determines the character of social organization and institutions. It transfers the *summum bonum* from the present earthly environment to an environment which God will create at some future time. "This world is like unto a vestibule before the world to come," [3] is the ruling principle of human existence. To be qualified for that divinely created world-order, or to achieve other-worldly salvation, becomes the most worthwhile aim of all activity, individual and national. During this stage, the Torah with its *miṣwot* becomes the means of this salvation. There is no way of qualifying for it except by meeting the conditions which God himself has laid down in the Torah. Maimonides sets forth the authoritative conception of the world to come in the following words: "As for the messianic period, the Prophets and Sages looked forward to it only in order that they might have respite from the yoke of foreign governments which do not allow them to engage adequately in Torah and *miswot*, and that they might have the leisure to accumulate wisdom wherewith to attain the life of the world to come. Such attainment is the highest reward; there can be no greater good." [4]

By thus taking a survey of the whole of Judaism, do we become aware of its power of self-transformation, the like of which no ancient culture possessed. We then realize that only spiritual vitality of exceptional vigor could have enabled the Jewish people to remake itself from a henotheistic kingdom into a monotheistic theocracy, and from a monotheistic theocracy into an other-worldly ecclesia. Such transformation in the case of any other people would have meant the substitution of one civilization for another. By some divine gift, the Jewish people managed to bridge the gaps between the different stages of its history so that it did not experience the least break in the continuity of its life. Each crisis in its career brought about an adjustment which was creative of new spiritual values. The struggle against Canaanism elicited Prophetism. The effort to survive in the midst of a world politically and culturally subservient to Hellenism brought out in the Jews Torah-conscious-ness, with its apotheosis of the moral law. In striving to hold its own against a humanity obsessed with a desire to escape the respon-sibilities of this world by securing salvation in the hereafter, the Jews formulated a version of other-worldliness which was free from all tendencies to escape responsibility in the here and the now.

The next stage. Judaism is now on the threshold of a fourth stage in its development, and the civilization into which it will grow will be humanistic and spiritual. In discussing the program for Jewish life in the modern world it will become evident that the next phase of Jewish civilization will constitute, in some respects, a return on a higher level to the first stage; the center of gravity of the spir-itual interests will again be the here and the now, and communion with God will again be a possible normal experience for the Jew. Instead, however, of being an outward visible experience, com-munion with God will be realized in the inwardness of mind and heart.

Modern Jewish civilization will be more than merely a return. It will be an adventure into the unexplored possibilities of creative living. It will avail itself to the full of the hitherto dormant impli-cations of its own teaching, that man reflects the image of God. It will revaluate theocentrism in terms of anthropocentrism, and iden-tify the striving after righteousness, the discovery of truth and the revelation of beauty as obedience to God's will.

Like all other ancient civilizations, the Jewish civilization was structurally undifferentiated, with religion as the all-dominating factor. The various aspects into which the Jewish civilization may be analyzed were little more than "the application of the religious point of view to the functions of daily life." But as a modern civilization, each aspect of Judaism, its language and literature, its ethics, its art, its social organization, will acquire not independence but its own structural reality, apart from religion. Religion will still occupy a position of primacy, but it will be a *primus inter pares*. In considering the other elements of life as mature enough to be self-sufficient amid inter-relationship, religion will become more humanized.

As a civilization, Judaism can continue vigorously in the spirit of modern thought, and can discard its theurgic character without discontinuity or loss of vitality. The conception of a dynamic civilization enables us to view the ideas of the past as having arisen in conformity with the laws of human nature and social development, and suggests the method of revaluation by which our spiritual heritage can be brought into conformity with the social development of modern times.

The survival of Judaism can no longer mean that all Jews throughout the world are to live in accordance with a uniform regimen of conduct. *No uniform pattern of Jewish life can meet the needs of the different Jewries any longer.* The former policy which invariably treated the Jews in all lands as aliens is now replaced by a franchise which varies with the political and civic institutions of the countries in which the Jews live. Some countries reckon with Jews only as individual citizens, others reckon, in addition, with their corporate interests, civic, cultural and religious. In the political institutions of France and America, the Jews have no corporate status whatever. In Poland, Roumania, Czecho-Slovakia, the Jews have minority rights which cover the political as well as the cultural status. In England and Italy, Jews enjoy corporate rights of a religious character. It therefore devolves upon the Jewry of each country to reckon with its particular milieu and to create the frame most congenial to its development.

Judged by its capacity to live Judaism as a civilization, Jewry will have to be divided into three zones:

1. The first zone of Jewish life is Palestine, where the Jews are to be given an opportunity to develop their own civilization on the same terms as any other nation. In Palestine only will it be possible for the Jew, if he so chooses, to live entirely within his people's civilization. There the Jew will be able to lead a normal life, as a member of a community which functions as an integrated entity, and evolves the institutions and the arts organically related to its needs. Whatever he may want to acquire of the cultural life

of other peoples will naturally increase his social vision and adaptability, but it is not indispensable. A Jewish National Home means therefore a place where it will be possible to live Judaism as a primary civilization.

2. The second zone of Jewish life will extend over those countries where they are granted the rights of a culturally autonomous minority people. There it ought to be possible to live Judaism to the same degree that one lives the civilization of the majority. It is understood, of course, that the development of Jewish civic and educational institutions will not be such as to crowd out the life and institutions which the Jews must share with the majority. Survival of Judaism in those countries must therefore mean survival of the civilization of the Jew on a basis co-ordinate with the native civilization.

3. The third zone of Jewish life would include countries like France and America, where the only civic status recognized by the state is that of individual citizens, and where Judaism can survive only as a subordinate civilization. Since the civilization that can satisfy the primary interests of the Jew must necessarily be the civilization of the country he lives in, the Jew in America will be first and foremost an American, and only secondarily a Jew. That he cannot avoid whether he will live his Judaism as a civilization or as a religion. But the difference between the two modes of life is like that between the substance and its shadow.

The Jew who is satisfied to live in two civilizations, in his own and in that of the country of his adoption, but wants the two civilizations to play an equal part in his life, would have to live in a country where Jews are granted minority rights. If he wants to live as a Jew only, and to be free of the need of reckoning with the civilization of any other people, he will have to go to Palestine. These alternatives may sound hard, but they are inevitable and conditioned by the entire trend of modern political life which it were futile to resist. Even in one's wildest dreams it is impossible to conceive of the return of all or even of the majority of Jews to one Jewish homeland. Neither can we contemplate the possibility of living a completely Jewish life in any other country in total disregard of the non-Jewish civilization. In a country like America, Jewish life cannot possibly occupy in the consciousness and activities of the Jew a place co-ordinate with that of American life. The majority of Jews are prepared to retain their Jewish individuality provided they can do so without surrendering the primary place in their lives held by Americanism. This condition can be met. No civilization has a right to monopolize the life of its adherent when he cannot find self-fulfillment, or express himself completely, through it. These considerations confirm the possibility of Jewish survival outside Palestine.

This constitutes a radically new approach to the apparently insoluble problem: under what modern political concept or category can the Jews be integrated into the nation of which they are citizens and at the same time remain sufficiently autonomous to be identifiable as a group? The Reformists have sought to solve that problem by declaring that the Jews constitute a religious community whose individual members differ from the other citizens of the state in the matter of religion only. We have seen how unworkable that conception of the Jewish group has proved to be. No less inoperative is the attempt of the segregationists who ask for the Jews minority rights analogous to the minority rights accorded to the autochthonous European minorities. Even should the concessions to minorities granted in the Versailles Treaty prove feasible for the Jews of eastern Europe—which is far from certain—the Jews in America, France, England and most of the other countries of the world will not be helped by them.

For the Jews who live among nations which do not share their sovereignty with minorities, there has not yet been articulated any frankly avowed group category. The only group category that can render their position tenable is one that will recognize the moral and spiritual right to cultural hyphenisms. It is not for the Jews alone that such a category should be created. There is the large group of Catholics who are just as unassimilable in a Protestant country like America as are the Jews. They not only refuse to intermarry but they conduct their own educational system, and are far more solidly united in acting for their welfare than the Jews can ever dream of being. They go much further than the Jews in taking exception to the very theory upon which the modern political state is founded. The Catholics cannot possibly make peace with the conception of the strict cultural homogeneity of the state. They, even more than the Jews, are in need of a conception of the state that frankly grants to its citizens the right to hyphenate with the civilization of the majority that other civilization which they find necessary to their complete development as persons.

The claim that such right can be conceded only in the case of a religion but not in the case of a civilization cannot be taken seriously. What meaning could the right to practice one's own religion have, if those who grant the right were to reserve to themselves the power to define religion. They might then say that only Christianity is entitled to the appellation "religion" and that Judaism and Mohammedanism are superstitions and may, therefore, not be practiced by any citizen of the state. Religious freedom means not only the freedom to practice any religion, but also to practice none. It surely ought to include the freedom to foster whatever other civilization besides the one of the majority, which affords consolation or supports the human spirit in the same way as does conventional religion. That being the case, the Catholics should have the same right as they have at present to practice Catholicism even if they were to consider it, as they well might, a civilization. And the Jews should have as much right to live their Judaism as a civilization as they have to live it as a religion. Fundamentally, Catholics and Jews are hyphenates. What is needed to normalize their status in the state is to have the cultural hyphenism of minority groups accepted as legitimate.

There are minimum requirements, however, which anyone who wants to live as a Jew must meet. These are the requirements which arise out of the very nature of a civilization. The main elements of a civilization are organically inter-related. It is this essential and organic inter-relation that differentiates a civilization from a religion, a religious philosophy, or a literary culture. For the purposes of planning a program, we may identify separate elements of Jewish civilization. Language is a vehicle of the group memories and devotions, literature and other arts their storehouse. Law and mores are the social cement among contemporaries and generate the sense of continuity with preceding generations. The religious elements of a civilization constitute the sanctions of the ideals and purposes of the group. They heighten the values of the civilization and protect it against absorption or destruction. But though these elements are distinguishable, they are organically related to each other, and *the organic character of Judaism is the crucial fact about it*. The pattern of each part determines the whole. A program of Jewish life must enable Jews to see and live Judaism steadily, organically and completely.

No single Jewish activity or interest can serve for the whole of Judaism. Worship, or philanthropy, or ethical idealism, or the up-building of Palestine, or the cultivation of Hebrew, or the fostering of Jewish art, is often singled out as the equivalent of Judaism. While philanthropy or Zionism is never seriously considered as exhaustive of all that Judaism connotes, religion or ethical idealism is very definitely upheld as synonymous with Judaism. Some argue that under circumstances which make a full Jewish life impossible, Jews ought to be satisfied with the cultivation of their religion or ethical idealism. They forget that religion and ethical idealism mean nothing apart from the particular civilization through which they find expression. Where they do not arise from concrete realities, spirituality and idealism become pale and bloodless platitudes.

Where religion has no specific group to mold, where there is no vital interaction between it and life, religion may become the protégé of esoteric cults, the subject of much abstruse cerebration. It does not affect the active thought and conduct of man. The very self-consciousness of religion is ominous. The higher life of man should be lived to the rhythm of alternation. It should alternate between self-consciousness and oblivion of self. Far more potent than in the articulated and self-conscious ideals of a civilization is religion's subtle and invasive power in the unself-conscious habits and the secret and mysterious strata of being that are beyond verbalization. It is the absence of unself-consciousness that makes for the weakness of present programs of Jewish life. They do not reckon with the force of all those things which do not achieve exact expression. The elimination of every element of Jewishness not strictly included within the category of highly self-conscious religious aims is bound to lead to the elimination of those very aims. This is the fate of programs which tend to reduce all cultural expressions of Jewish life to a minimum.

"Judaism asks—this is a mistake of the clever people—not intelligence but, in the first instance, obedience," writes Laurie Magnus, "Wisdom is its reward not its entrance qualification. Obey the law—fully, if you will, with understanding, if you can, partially and blindly if you cannot, but—obey the law. A hard saying, but not harder than many human demands, and infinitely safer of its rewards." [5] It would not have appeared such a hard saying, if Magnus had treated Judaism not as a religion but as a civilization. In the setting of a civilization, we may expect non-understandable conventions, but not in a religion which claims to be rational. If Magnus noted so important a characteristic in Judaism, it was because he felt, even if he did not clearly realize, that there was something more to Judaism than what is usually associated with the term religion. "For one thing," he writes elsewhere, "I am a Jew by birth. Hebraism is in my blood, and commits me straightway to a definite inheritance of potential action and thought." [6]

The acceptance of Judaism as a civilization, even though it be of ancillary status, calls for a maximum program, that is, *a maximum program of Jewishness compatible with one's abilities and circumstances*. What constitutes such a maximum must be left to the judgment and conscience of the individual Jew, guided by the standards and ideals that will be evolved.

When Neo-Orthodoxy and Reformism offer such radically opposed solutions to the problem of Judaism, one is tempted to conclude that the truth must lie somewhere midway between the two. Conservative Jews—whether they belong to the left wing of Neo-Orthodoxy or the right wing of Reformism—have actually fallen into this error, and we have seen what confusion and inconsistency mark their programs. Nevertheless, there must be something in Neo-Orthodoxy that answers to the spiritual yearning of its adherents; and the same is, no doubt, true of Reformism. The wise procedure, however, is not to aim at some haphazard synthesis of what appear to be the elements of strength in both. After having found both versions inadequate, the logical procedure is to approach the problem of Judaism from an entirely new angle. But now that this requirement has been met by reckoning with Judaism as with a civilization, it is of interest to know whether this new approach includes the constructive tendencies in Neo-Orthodoxy and in Reformism. If the conception of Judaism as a civilization remains free of the half measures and compromises of Neo-Orthodoxy and Reformism, and yet succeeds in conserving whatever inherent strength they possess by conforming to the spirit of Judaism and to the spirit of the time, we are encouraged to believe that we are on the right track.

Neo-Orthodoxy seems to imply that being a Jew is not solely, or even chiefly, a matter of rational conviction of the plausibility of Judaism's teachings. There are many Jews who are in sympathy with Neo-Orthodoxy, not because of what it expressly affirms but because of what it implicitly denies. They interpret the belief in the supernatural origin of the Torah, not as a theological doctrine to be taken in strict literalness, but rather as a way of stressing the futility of trying to rationalize the customs and folkways of Jewish life through adherence to a series of abstract truths. It is probably in this spirit that Moses Mendelssohn spoke of Judaism as revealed legislation rather than as a revealed creed.

This interpretation of Neo-Orthodoxy would be disavowed and deprecated most violently by Samson Raphael Hirsch and his followers. But that does not alter the fact that psychologically there is good ground for this interpretation, since what it amounts to is that Judaism must be worthwhile in and for itself, and not merely a means to universal salvation. There are religions and philosophies in abundance that claim to be roads to universal salvation, and the average Jew would be hard put to prove that this was the best and most direct road to universal salvation. Hitherto the only way the Jew felt he could evade the necessity of such proof was by claiming supernatural origin for the "Torah," which he regarded as the only instrument of eternal bliss. Now he can be released from that necessity by conceiving Judaism as a civilization and availing himself of its spiritually redemptive potentialities.

On the other hand, the Reformist movement has contributed to the solution of the problem of Judaism the notion of spiritual evolution. Reformism assumes that the process of evolution functioned unconsciously throughout the history of Judaism, and it urges that henceforth this evolution should not be left to chance, but consciously planned and directed. The idea of spiritual evolution is invaluable for the achievement of that mental plasticity which is essential for an orientation to so complex a world.

The conception of Judaism as a civilization should dispel the imaginary fear which inhibits all spiritual progress, the fear that innovations, by destroying the uniformity of Jewish life, would destroy its unity. Time and again, Jews become convinced that their tradition abounds in laws, customs and beliefs which have outlived their usefulness, and which today only obstruct Jewish life and menace its survival. But they refrain from taking action and making the necessary changes because they are afraid of the resulting disunity in the ranks of Jewry. To take but one instance: many Jews realize the absurdity of praying for the restoration of the sacrificial system, yet they refrain from eliminating that prayer from the liturgy, so long as there is a large number of Jews who refuse to admit that the sacrificial system has become obsolete. Their favorite remedy for all such predicaments is the convocation of a synod of duly authorized rabbis who will find some way of abrogating those practices.[7] But to postpone changes until a synod arise—an unwieldly body at best—cannot be but postponement *sine die*. Judaism must permit progress to take its course, and must somehow retain its unity without imposing a uniform regimen of conduct upon its adherents. Progress in any phase of life takes place when some individual or group inaugurates a needed change. If that change justifies itself, it wins general acquiescence. It is only when we conceive Judaism as a developing civilization, which can retain its individual character, despite great latitude in belief and practice, that there can be any room for progress.

However, the immediate need is for some conception of Judaism broad enough to include within its scope all who want to remain Jews, whatever the reason or motive be. That is not merely an academic need but a practical one. Some basis of creative unity among Jews has to be found that will not require anyone to surrender his convictions, or to do violence to his conscience. Such a basis, it would seem, can be found in the conception of Judaism as a civilization, because that conception allows for diversity of belief and practice, for all forms of socially useful activity and all types of group associations, without in any way impairing the organic character of Jewish life.

Both Neo-Orthodoxy and Reformism are in their nature sectarian. The one purports to represent the only true Judaism, the other, Judaism at its best. Either contention must be a divisive influence in Jewish life. But Judaism as a civilization admits of more than one religious viewpoint. Orthodox Jews may continue to insist that Jewish civilization is supernaturally revealed, and Reformists may cultivate the modernist attitude toward the content of Judaism, without thereby altering the nature of Judaism as a civilization, or denying themselves that place in the life and future of the civilization which they may earn and deserve. The orthodox Jew may condemn as heretical the conception here proposed because it is latitudinarian, but his Jewish outlook could not logically be denied a place in Judaism as a civilization. The Reformist may regard this conception as impracticable because it comes into conflict with some of the current political ideas, or as visionary because it implies the possibility of reviving and modernizing an ancient civilization. But if the cultural conception of Judaism is the correct one, the Reformists are carrying out many of its important implications in spite of themselves. They therefore have a place in Judaism as a civilization. For those who subscribe to the extreme view that the Jews are destined to be transformed into a secularized Yiddish-speaking group in the diaspora, living as a Jew can mean nothing less than having one's entire mentality shaped by all the influences that constitute a Jewish civilization.[8]

The important point to remember is that the survival of Jewish life is by no means dependent upon unity among Jews or uniformity in Judaism. What a noted sociologist has said of the family applies with equal truth to the Jewish people. "The family does not depend for its survival," writes E. W. Burgess, "on the harmonious relations of its members, nor does it necessarily disintegrate as a result of conflicts between its members. The family lives as long as interaction is taking place and only dies when it ceases."[9] The advantage of a category like "civilization" as descriptive of Jewish life is that it suggests the basis of and material for interaction among the most divergent elements of Jewry, by reason of the large consensus of Jewish interests and purposes which it connotes. Perhaps, like the modern family, Jewish life is henceforth destined to be "an experiment in antagonistic co-operation." But one thing is certain: The sooner Jews will come to think of that which unites them as a civilization, the sooner will they overcome the process of disorganization which is reducing them to the status of a human detritus, the rubble of a once unique society.

PART FOUR

ISRAEL

THE STATUS AND ORGANIZATION OF JEWRY

CHAPTER XVII

THE NATIONHOOD OF ISRAEL *

The theurgic conception of Israel to be replaced by a conception relevant to the modern outlook and political framework—Neither the Neo-Orthodox nor the Reformists have arrived at a formula for the status of Jewry—The Jews forced to rethink the national idea—Nationalism as an instrument of freedom from tyranny—Nationhood not to be suppressed but disciplined in the interest of internationalism—The significance of the Balfour Declaration.

IN any deliberate endeavor to maintain the continuity of ·the Jewish civilization in the face of such challenging conditions as those of today, the first question that comes to mind is: what shall henceforth be the status of Jewry as a collective entity *vis-à-vis* the rest of the world? Before the emancipation the Jews regarded themselves and were regarded by the rest of the world as a nation in exile. This meant that they considered their sojourn outside of Palestine as temporary; that they retained a sense of unity despite their dispersion; that every local Jewry in relation to the nation as a whole occupied a status analogous to that of the ancient colony in relation to its mother country.

But this entire conception of the Jews as a nation belongs to the theurgic universe of discourse. The term "nation," applied to the Jews by themselves and others, did not convey the same meaning as that which it conveys today, but rather that which is implied in the term "church," in the sense of a collective body of transcendent character or a society called into being and sustained by supernatural intervention. The frequent designation of Jewry in rabbinic literature as *Keneset Yisrael*, the ecclesia of Israel, points to the emphasis upon the element of supernaturalism as the factor which accounts for the corporate character of the Jewish people. This must not be confused with the modern attempt to identify the Jews

* The term "nationhood" is used in these chapters to denote a *form* of associated life, "nation" or "nationality" the *group* which is held together by that form of associated life, and "nationalism" the *national idea* which approves that form of associated life.

227

as a religious community. A religious community is less than a nation. A religious community has none of the organizational features and agencies of a nation. A church, provided it is a visible one, or an ecclesia such as the Jews said they were, is more than a nation. It not only has the organizational features and agencies of a nation; it regards them as divinely ordained and supported.

We might possibly derive from the traditional theurgic conception of the Jewish nation interesting implications for our own way of thinking, but in its original and uninterpreted form that conception is today entirely inoperative. The reconstruction of Jewish life depends upon the ability of the Jews to evolve a humanist interpretation of the concept "Israel." That achievement is dependent on the ability to realize that a humanist interpretation is bound to constitute a *novum* in the Jewish ideology. Jews should not expect much aid and comfort from the traditional ideology in their effort to formulate the status of the Jewish people as a natural or historical social formation. Nor should they minimize the wide gap between the traditional conception of "Israel" and the one which they must achieve at the present time. The tendency to treat the gap as non-existent, or even as negligible, will not in the least facilitate the process of readjustment which has to take place in the mind of the Jew, if he is to orient himself anew to his people. It will only prevent the organic synthesis between the elements of the past which are worth preserving and those in the present which must be accepted.

The traditional conception of Israel contributed to the preservation of the Jewish people because it constituted an effective answer to the challenge of the Gentile world. That answer could be expressed only in the theurgic idiom of those days. Then Gentiles took for granted the biblical account of Israel's origin. They admitted that the history of the Jewish people was a phase of the career of God, a phase which was of utmost significance to humanity as a whole. To the Gentiles, Jewry as a whole constituted a nation which God had created and fostered, and which retained its status as a nation despite its rejection of what the Gentiles regarded as the gospel meant for the Jews as well as for the rest of the world. So long as the Gentiles accepted that interpretation of history, according to which the Jewish people in its collective capacity played an important rôle in the scheme of human salvation, it really did not matter by what specific designation the Jews were identified. The important fact is that as a distinct group the Jews possessed status.

It is no longer possible for the Jews to maintain their collective life without relating it in some way to the political and civic structure of the contemporary social order from which all theurgic elements have been eliminated. That order is based on humanist and rational principles of government. The traditional conception of "Israel," therefore, as a people that transcends the natural laws of environment and social life, can be of but little assistance in helping the Jews to adjust their status in terms of the political and social realities of the time.

Accordingly, the Neo-Orthodox interpretation of Israel as given by Samson Raphael Hirsch and others can be of no practical help in directing the policies of collective Jewish life. Neo-Orthodoxy may be justified in defining the place of Israel among the nations in the idiom of theurgy. It may regard the Jewish people in very much the same light as Catholicism does the church since, consistently with its general outlook on life, it treats the nationhood of the Jews as a supernatural rather than as a natural fact. But by maintaining this attitude, Neo-Orthodoxy in reality evades the problem of adjusting the Jew to the social and political structure of the Gentile world. Why keep on insisting that the Jews are a nation of a supernatural order of being, when no one is seriously concerned with supernatural sanction or support? The Catholic church, to be sure, still holds fast to that kind of sanction, but it no longer possesses the power to challenge the existence of the Jewish people. That power is now in the hands of the nations which are governed by considerations of human law. Furthermore, the main trouble with the Neo-Orthodox conception of the Jews as a people is not that the conception is obsolete, but that it is held in a formal and inert fashion which robs it of creative social significance. It merely serves as a sentimental aura for the punctilious observance of a few ritual practices. All it does is to reduce Jewish life to a negligible backwater.

On the other hand, the Reformist movement in Judaism has made a deliberate attempt to reckon with the political and civic arrangements of the modern world, but it has made the mistake of thinking itself under the obligation to regard those arrangements as final and infallible. This mistaken sense of obligation explains why Reformism has failed to make a careful study of the conditions which are indispensable to Jewish survival, and why it has so light-heartedly repudiated the national status of the Jews and declared them to be merely a religious community. It is true that religion based on the belief in the supernatural self-revelation of God can act as a bond of unity among large masses of mankind. But the modern man's religion which admits the spirit of inquiry and investigation can scarcely be depended upon to act by itself as a force for social solidarity. The Reformists have to some extent apprehended the danger of basing the unity and continuity of Jewish collective life upon religion solely, and have therefore sought to bolster up that unity by means of the theory of Jewish racialism. But racialism, apart from being inconsistent with both anthropological and historical truth, carries with it all of the dangerous implications of nationalism and none of its redeeming traits.

When Jews try to pass off either as a religious group or as a distinct race, they only stultify themselves in their attempt. They continually give the lie to the claim that they are a religious group; the very Jews who make it a point to speak of their fellow-Jews as their co-religionists and who stress that religion is the only bond that unites all Jews, are the first to disclaim any responsibility other than that of philanthropy in relation to their less fortunate "co-religionists." They strenuously oppose making Jewish education and the teaching of Jewish religion to the young an important item of large-scale Jewish collective effort. This attitude is not merely a sporadic manifestation of the failure to live up to what they profess. It is the inevitable outcome of the paradoxical attempt to crowd the Jews with their wide diversity of religion into the narrow category of a religious sect or denomination. Those who act on a theory which defies objective reality must necessarily do many things that contradict that theory. In the matter of religion, there is more in common between the liberal Jew and the liberal Christian, or between the orthodox Jew and the orthodox Christian, than there is between the liberal and the orthodox either in the Jewish or in the Christian group. Furthermore, to what category do the large number of Jews belong who are agnostic or atheistic, and yet want to remain Jews and perpetuate Jewish life? Their ideas on religion may be all wrong, but who other than a traditionalist—and for that matter not even he—has a right to read them out of Jewry?

The attempt on the part of the Jews to pass off as a distinct race, that is, as a branch of mankind which has been endogamous for a long period and has developed distinct traits, is equally anomalous. The concept "race" may describe what set off Jews from the rest of the world in the past, but it suggests no program for the future. The fact that Jews have developed common traits is no guarantee that they will retain them, or even that they want to retain them. The colored people constitute a race in a far truer and deeper sense than the Jews, yet some of its members would give half their lives to be absorbed by the whites. There is nothing in the concept of physical or historical race to give the slightest hint of the institutions Jews intend to establish, or objectives and ideals they mean to pursue. Status gives direction to the strivings of a person or group. So long as Jews do not know what their corporate status is, they cannot know what direction their group life should take.

The lack of corporate status puts Jews in the category of foundlings left, as it were, by fate upon the doorstep of the nations that they might take pity on them, and provide them with food and shelter. To be a Jew under these circumstances is not conducive to peace of mind, nor compatible with human dignity and moral stamina. It is impossible for the Jew to be true to himself, or to the part for which life has cast him, so long as he does not know to what kind of group he belongs as a Jew.

The present situation calls for a conception of the Jewish people which shall reckon with the humanist outlook of the modern world and with its political and civic arrangements. But there are two ways of reckoning with current views and institutions. One is to accept these views as final and authoritative and submit to them without further question; the other is to realize that, while they may contain much that is good, they still fall short of the highest good to which they should be raised. The necessity for Jewish life to reckon with the present environment need not be made synonymous with the uncritical acceptance of the political dogmas of the day.

No one would venture to maintain that the political development of mankind has reached its final stage. In reckoning with the environment, we must include those incipient social forces and ideals which not even reactionism can entirely suppress. Jewish life will survive not as a result of passive self-adaptation to the *status quo*, but of identification with those movements which are intended to increase the measure of freedom, justice and peace in the world. No such movement can possibly oppose the aspirations of the Jews to develop the forms and institutions of national life. On the contrary, any movement which aims at a higher level of associated life should welcome the effort of the Jews to retain their national status, because it is only through such retention that Jews can energize the good latent in their consciousness of a common past, and work for collective purposes which are bound to coincide with the common good of the human race as a whole.

Any conception of the Jewish people which will help the Jew adjust himself to the modern world must be inherently in accord with the highest ethical standards of human individuality and cooperation. Such a conception may come into conflict with some of the current political assumptions. But so long as its validity can be demonstrated on rational and ethical grounds, it is entitled to a hearing that it may prove its compatibility with democratic nationalism at its best. If democratic nationalism is to heed fully the claims of justice and reason, it must concede the right of the Jews throughout the world to retain their status as a nation, though the retention of such status involves their becoming a new type of nation—an international nation with a national home to give them cultural and spiritual unity. In the very process of conceding this right to the Jews, democratic nationalism will be living up to its own more ethical conception which has recently emerged, the conception which sees in internationalism the only hope of civilization.

As long as current political concepts will be taken for granted, Jewish nationhood will no doubt continue to be challenged. Gentiles will challenge it as inconsistent with citizenship of the countries in which Jews live on a plane of equality with the rest of the population, and some Jews will concur in this challenge. Other Jews, again, will contest Jewish nationhood on the ground that all nationhood is undesirable and inconsistent with world-citizenship. If Jews would realize that nationhood in general, and Jewish nationhood in particular, is not only consistent with the highest moral aspirations but essential to them, there would be no need for frantic appeals to Jewish loyalty. A unique history and an unusual combination of difficulties have conspired to place upon the Jewish people the task of demonstrating the spiritual potentialities of nationhood. The problems which have arisen in the wake of nationalism are among the most perplexing of the time. If the Jewish people, in working out its own adjustment, will succeed in formulating an ethical philosophy of nationalism, it will render a much needed service to the cause of world amity.

The Jew may readily accept this necessity of redefining the meaning and function of nationhood because the tendency to speculate about it is almost as old as Jewish tradition. The division of mankind into nations, which did not seem to arouse the curiosity of the other peoples of the ancient world, struck the Jews very early in their career as a phenomenon that called for explanation. The story of the tower of Babel and of the differentiation of peoples and languages may be said to be an attempt at this explanation. It accounted for the emergence of nations as a preventive measure to which God resorted in order to check the rising tide of human arrogance and self-sufficiency. An undivided humanity would have believed itself potent enough to violate God's laws with impunity. This assumption was developed by the Prophets into the inference that nationhood was a positive instrument for the realization of God's kingdom.[1] Though this ancient speculation may seem fanciful, it reveals how aware the Jews were of the significance of nationhood for the spiritual life of mankind. That awareness should qualify the Jews to achieve a conception of nationalism which would entitle it to be numbered among the spiritual values destined to emerge from the present welter of purposes and ideals.

To justify their status as a national entity, Jews must rethink the meaning of the national idea, both from the psychological and the sociological point of view. The current conception of nationalism, based upon the misleading assumption that nationhood is synonymous with statehood, makes it impossible for a people to be considered a nation unless it is represented by a state. Furthermore, it is assumed that since no one can be a citizen of more than one state, no one can belong to more than one nation. Such assumptions will have to yield to the more ethical conception of nationhood fundamentally as a cultural rather than as a political relationship. The rights of the Jew to citizenship are based upon his readiness to bear the burdens equally with all other citizens, perform the duties, and make the sacrifices that are the concomitants of national life. In claiming the right to foster his Jewish nationhood, he does not seek exemption from the responsibilities of citizenship. There is no disguising the fact that insofar as the Jew has to be integrated into the life of the Gentile nation to which he belongs, his life is largely pre-empted by Gentilism. All that he asks is that Gentilism shall not so monopolize his life as to leave no room in it for the Jewish civilization. He should be free to cultivate that group consciousness which is for him both historic background and the promise of a better world. Such a consciousness is a conscience, and the right to live by its dictates is no more and no less than the right to religious freedom. Religious freedom is not merely freedom to entertain any or no conception of God. It is essentially the freedom to remain loyal to one's historic culture. *The notion that allegiance to a state precludes identification with more than one nation will therefore have to be scrapped.*

Nationhood as a dynamic factor in the life of mankind may be traced to the very beginnings of history. It is true that the political condition implied by the word nation did not exist in the ancient world, but the ideal implied by that word did exist. In a sense, every large group, be it tribe, clan or federation of clans, which was aware of common interests, possessed something of that cluster of sentiments and ideas out of which nationhood ultimately developed. In ancient times, this group self-awareness always took on a religious form. Loyalty to the nation and its purposes expressed itself as loyalty to the nation's gods. It is only in modern times that the nation as such has come to be regarded as possessing an inherent claim on the loyalty of its members. This is the significance of the common observation that patriotism plays a part in the modern world analogous to that of religion in the ancient world. It is, undoubtedly, today a far more vital factor in the affairs of men than any of the historical religions.[2] If any interest that is deemed sufficiently worthy for a man to give his life for it is, in a sense, his religion, patriotism may surely be said to be the religion of the greater part of mankind.

This does not mean that in practice the cause of nationalism actually serves the highest interests of human life as a whole. Though it possesses tremendous potencies, no way has as yet been found to prevent these powers from being used for evil purposes. It is hardly necessary to labor the point that nationalism can be, and has been, put to the most vicious uses. The fear and distrust with which it is regarded are warranted when we consider the crimes which have been perpetrated in its name. The Jews themselves have been its most unfortunate victims ever since the rise of "national" monarchies,[3] and have continued so to be to the rise of Nazism in our own day. It has been and is still exploited by those who command large capital resources for the purpose of raising artificial tariff walls, keeping out foreign competitors, protecting investments in foreign lands, and coercing backward peoples to accept surplus goods and surplus population. Nationalism run riot embroiled the European peoples in the late war. These abuses have led many to conclude that nationalism is a survival of barbarism rather than a promise of civilization, that it harbors volcanic energies which may erupt at any time and devastate the earth. Its idealistic allure renders it all the more dangerous.

Moreover, in recent times there have sprung up philosophies which frankly preach a belligerent nationalism. The gospel which for a long time has been preached in Germany, and which has been taken up by the patrioteers of other countries, is that a nation is first and foremost a fighting unit. According to this teaching, the main purpose of a national culture is to foster war-mindedness. *"A people is only really such in relation to other peoples,"* says Oswald Spengler. "and the substance of this actuality comes out in natural and ineradicable oppositions, in attack and defence, hostility and war. War is the creator of all great things. All that is meaningful in the stream of life has emerged through victory and defeat."

These misapplications and false interpretations of nationhood should not blind us to its creative potentialities. The arguments which may be used to prove the dangers of nationhood may also be used with equal cogency to prove the danger of selfhood or indi-

viduality. By admitting the right of the individual human being
to bring his powers to fruition, we waken dormant energies that
create infinite occasions for conflict where originally there was the
undisturbed peace of herd unity. Likewise, when we turn to that
other manifestation of collective will—religion. There is not a
nefarious deed which has not used religion as a cloak or banner.
Yet even the most militant opponent of religion must admit that, if
religion has been thus used, it is not due to anything inherently evil
in religion, but rather to human perversity which is capable of corrupting the finest products of the human soul. We must not forget
that in nationalism, as well as in religion, we are dealing with
tendencies which are rooted in human nature and in the circumstances out of which it has been shaped. Nothing will be gained by
advocating their suppression. *It is just as possible to eliminate
chauvinism from nationalism as it was possible to eliminate human
sacrifice and phallic worship from religion.* Since Jews are placed
in a position where their own highest interests can be served only
by nationhood freed of all taint of barbarism, they should welcome
the opportunity to direct this form of associated life into channels
where it can yield the maximum of individual self-realization and
social cooperation.

Any doubt as to the potentialities for good inherent in the
national idea should be dissipated by the realization of the part it
has played in the overthrow of tyranny. Whatever form group
oppression took in the past, whether it was usurpation of power by
some foreign invader or a domineering aristocracy which monopolized the economic resources of the country, or ecclesiastical domination which invoked supernatural sanctions, freedom from that oppression always intensified national consciousness. The emergence of
European nationalism coincides both with the revolt against the dominion of the feudal aristocracies and with the breaking away from
the imperialistic sway of the Roman Catholic church. The commercial revolution of the fifteenth and sixteenth centuries due to the discovery of new continents, the revival of trade and the contact of
cultures, as well as the intellectual curiosity stimulated by the discoveries, brought to the front the middle class, the burghers and the
merchants with whose aid the kings deprived the feudatories of

power and established the dynastic national states. Political central-
ization, mercantilism, vernacular language and literature, led to the
development of national cultures.

The French became nationally conscious when they freed themselves from English dominion in the beginning of the fifteenth century. The epoch-making events in the growth of English nationhood are the granting of the Magna Carta, the break with Rome, the
beheading of Charles I. The French Revolution was followed by
the nationalistic reconstruction of Europe. The war against dynastic
tyrannies led to the emergence of the German nation, and eventually
of the Italian. In addition to the establishment of larger national
states, historical groups like the Poles, the Irish and the Czechs,
claimed the status of nationhood. Although in each case the old form
of oppression was succeeded by some new form, yet with each advance
of national solidarity the accountability of the ruling class to those
whom they ruled increased. If the mercantile class which led in
the overthrow of the feudal aristocracies merely replaced the latter
in the process of exploitation, they have at least had to be more
subtle about it. In building up a national economy of which they
were to be the chief beneficiaries, the leaders of commerce and
industry have had to appeal to national sentiment. Ultimately that
must lead to a sense of power on the part of the masses which will
put an end to their exploitation. The proletarian revolution in
Russia would not have succeeded had it not appealed to the national
spirit of the Russian people as a whole and of the subject peoples
whose nationhood it has since restored and fostered. Nationalism
perhaps even more than the doctrine of class struggle has been
instrumental in releasing the Russian peoples from a corrupt
domination which was a survival from the days when statehood
meant the subjugation of the weaker by the stronger. All these
manifestations of nationalism point to it as a force which makes
for the substitution of commonwealth for the domination of some
ruling class, and confirm the statement that "the basis of nationalism in all cases, in spite of additional elements, is revolt against
political and cultural imperialism." [5] Present-day national reactionism notwithstanding, Herbert Croly was not wrong when he said:
"A people which becomes more of a nation has a tendency to become
for that very reason more of a democracy." [6]

Nationalism is very much complicated by the legacy from the past, a legacy of wrongs committed by the nations against one another, of usurpation and oppression of the weak by the strong. That entail will continue to plague mankind unless some of the prevailing assumptions concerning national prerogatives be abandoned, and unless each nation be compelled to submit to an international code of law. All nations nowadays in their relations to one another are selfish, imperialistic and predatory. They act as though they were complete and self-sufficient entities and reject all supernational standards except those which interest or expediency prompt them to respect. Statesmen and writers of note still promulgate the doctrine that a state has an inalienable right to independence of any higher authority. It is generally assumed that a nation loses something of its essential character by submitting to a higher authority. Such an assumption is not only unwarranted but also destructive and immoral. It is because nations refuse to subordinate themselves to a supernational code and organization that nationhood is prevented from being a means to the highest self-fulfillment of the individual and the common good of mankind.

If the individual nation is to express fully its capacity for good, it is just as much in need of a society of nations as the individual human being is in need of associated life as a means of the fullest self-expression. When, therefore, we expect nationhood to exert a spiritual influence, it is only because we envisage a United States of the World which shall exercise the same authority over each of its constituent states as each nation now exercises over the individuals and internal groups within its borders. It is taken for granted that so long as anarchy prevails within any nation, the individual cannot be expected to lead a normal life. It will likewise be understood that so long as anarchy prevails among nations in their relation to one another, the good that lies dormant in nationhood cannot come to fruition. A *civitas maxima* may seem utopian but, unless it be brought within the sphere of reality, it will not be long before the human race will destroy itself. With nations becoming more and more economically-minded, and seeing in one another competitors in an ever-shrinking field of economic opportunity, the tension of human life is bound to grow so intolerable as to drive men into suicidal war. It is the very menace of such war that has led to the establishment of the League of Nations. Unless the League become coextensive with mankind and develops into a world-government which will compel the nations to submit to an economic code of world-wide scope, nationalism will prove to be the death-knell of civilization.

The continued existence of the Jewish people as a national entity consisting of scattered groups throughout the world must, therefore, be predicated upon the hope that mankind will ultimately abandon the political and economic nationalism which is threatening to embroil the nations in internecine war. Faint as are the rays of the new nationalism, controlled and disciplined in the interests of international unity, which are dawning upon the world, Jews should be the first to descry them and help to usher in the new day which they herald. There can be no doubt that a new and more ethical type of nationalism has already begun to find embodiment in the law of nations. The League of Nations, despite its present inadequacy and ineffectiveness in preventing war, is significant as an attempt to implement two principles concerning nationhood which are calculated to minimize its dangers and promote its wholesome functioning. One principle is that nationhood does not confer the right to absolute self-determination. The other is that nationhood does not entitle any majority people to deprive minority groups, racial, religious or cultural, of the right to some measure of self-determination.[7] Both principles follow naturally from the surrender of the conception of nations as monads or complete entities which are subject to no higher law than that of their own will. In the very effort to bring offending nations to court, in granting political status to minority groups and in the system of mandates, the League has broken with the narrow interpretation of democratic nationalism, which has been responsible for all the ills which modern nationalism has inflicted upon mankind.

The likelihood that, as an outcome of a more humane and liberal interpretation of nationalism, the Jews will be accorded national status is not so remote as it may seem. This is borne out by a transaction which implies nothing less than that the Jews have had their national status restored to them in international law. It has been correctly pointed out [8] that the British government, in offering the territory of Uganda to the Jewish people in 1903, performed an act which implied the national status of the Jews as a body. Of course, a more explicit recognition of the national status of the Jew is contained in the Balfour Declaration. In stating that the British government favors the establishment of a national home for the Jewish people, the Declaration takes it for granted that the Jewish people is entitled to the status of nationhood. No public act in modern times can equal the Declaration in its importance for the future of the Jewish people. A further step was taken when the principal nations of the world gave their formal assent to the establishment of a national home for the Jewish people and incorporated the Declaration in the statutes of the League of Nations. With that the status of the Jews as a nation was written into international law.° So dominant, however, are the current political concepts in the minds of most people that these significant moves to reckon with the Jews as a collective entity have made little impression. If the Jews as a body are to play any part in releasing the tremendous energies for good latent in the national idea, they must be permitted to foster their own nationhood.¹° That means that they should be permitted to regard Palestine as the source and inspiration of that cluster of institutions, language, literature, art, law and religion which constitutes the Jewish civilization. They must further be permitted to foster that civilization wherever they happen to live and retain the sense of Jewish nationhood that derives from it.

Nevertheless, we cannot overlook the radical difference between what the status of nationhood meant for the Jews in the past and what it must mean henceforth, and accustom the Jewish consciousness to effect the transition without too great a shock. In the past the Jews expected to recover Palestine through some supernatural event concurrent with the advent of the Messiah who would be recognized by his power to work miracles. Repentance, prayer and fasting were regarded as the means of bringing about that miracle. They now view the recovery of Palestine as a project in colonization, industrialization and education, and as such contingent upon the consent of the non-Jewish peoples whose interests will be affected by the execution of the project. The other difference is in the attitude toward the diaspora. Whereas in the past the Jews regarded their dispersion among the nations as a form of divine punishment and as a state of exile from which they were to be redeemed as soon as God saw fit, such a view is now altogether precluded by the eagerness with which the Jews have availed themselves of the process of enfranchisement. They look upon their dispersion as permanent. It is not divine punishment but an outcome of historical circumstances, an outcome which must be accepted as unalterable.

The restoration of the Jews to national status will contribute to, rather than detract from, international-mindedness. For, as an international nation they are bound to demonstrate the possibility of grasping with equal integrity the two poles of the contradiction which inheres in present-day life, the contradiction between loyalty to nation and loyalty to mankind. Simultaneously with striving to retrieve and reorganize their own nationhood and foster the nationhood of the peoples with which they are united in citizenship, Jews should promulgate all forms of international-mindedness. Such promulgation must henceforth constitute an integral phase of their religious and social idealism.

CHAPTER XVIII

NATIONALISM AS A CULTURAL CONCEPT

The Jews compelled to contribute to the revaluation of nationalism—Nationalism as a cultural concept based on the will-to-civilize—Cultural groupings ineradicable and inviolable—The separation of church from state essentially a concession to cultural hyphenism—The implications of cultural nationalism for the status of the Jews.

WE HAVE seen how the present enigmatic status of the Jews as a group would naturally impel them to explore the creative potentialities of nationhood which is the only status they can henceforth occupy as a collective entity. Being more exposed than any other group to the effects of the widespread intensification of national consciousness in the world, they have a ready criterion for judging when it is a blessing and when a curse. *If the national sentiment is such as to furnish the majority population with reasons for discriminating against any minority element, whether racial, religious or cultural, then it is undoubtedly a menace not only to the particular groups that are victimized but to civilization in general.* Injustice and violence cannot flourish anywhere in the world today without poisoning the springs of human life everywhere. Any conception of nationalism which demands that Jews break with their past, and commit spiritual suicide by repudiating a three-thousand-year-old tradition and ancestry, undoubtedly harbors dangers for people other than Jews. On the other hand, if the national idea is translated into institutions which permit the Jews to maintain at least the most valuable elements of their group life, it is evidently of the type that makes for group cooperation and for the peaceful solution of the problems that arise from the conflict of group interests.

Nationhood will never be purged of its glorified selfishness and its cruel propensities, unless the hitherto accepted doctrine expressed in the Spenglerian maxim "A people is only really such in relation to other peoples," be extirpated from the consciousness of mankind. Nationhood must henceforth be based on the principle that a people is mainly such in relation to its individual members. Its field of operation must be regarded as fundamentally the relationships among the individual members to one another and to the people as a whole. Only secondarily and under stress of attack should nationhood operate *vis-à-vis* other peoples. The inwardness and substance of national life should least of all be sought in the *extrovert* political forms and measures. Nationhood at its best is to be found in the cultural content which arises from the round of normal activities.

Such social framework as is integral to Judaism as a civilization should be entirely introvert in its operation. The distribution of the Jews in various countries, and their integration into the political framework of the other nations, precludes their developing political machinery *vis-à-vis* the other nations. Jews in the diaspora most emphatically renounce any kind of fighting allegiance to a central authority, whether it be in Palestine or elsewhere. The only bond of unity is to be that derived from the exercise of their civilization. International conferences called together *ad hoc* to solve specific problems or to meet specific emergencies will represent the maximum of political framework that Jews will call into being to meet their problems *vis-à-vis* the rest of the world. Even Palestine, where a political framework similar to that developed by other nations would have to be instituted, must be counted on as ultimately to be included in and subordinated to a World State.

The main idea which Jews should stress with regard to nationhood is that it is a form of associated life in which the principal element of cohesion is culture or civilization. That is the element through which what would otherwise be a mere aggregate is molded into an organism. The successive generations are united to each other through the social heritage which the earlier generations accumulate and the later take over. Understood thus, nationhood begins to function in the life of the child from the moment of birth as the process whereby he is supplied with the basic layer of personality. Personality in the individual human being—the whole of that differentia by which the human is distinguished from the non-human being—can be mediated only through a social heritage. As an infant, the human being is only potentially human; the human differentia begins to emerge as he learns to speak. The first words that he uses are not part of a universal language but of the specific cultural group to which he belongs. As such they forthwith mirror the particular interests and values of that group. In acquiring the vernacular of his people, the child acquires not only the means of identifying objects and events and the capacity for generalization, but also the evaluation of those same objects and events, evaluations that are on the whole as distinctive of the group as is the vernacular in which they are conveyed. In the very act of selecting particular objects, persons and situations as subject matter for words, the aspect of value is implied. These evaluations constitute the substance of the cultural heritage which is to a nation what the soul is to the body.

If we will learn to recognize in the personality of the human being the extent to which it is the product of nationhood, we shall appreciate the cogency of Renan's definition of a nation. "A nation," said Renan, "is a spiritual principle made by two things—the one in the present, the other in the past: the one the possession in common of a rich bequest of memories; the other a present sense of agreement, a desire to live together, a will to continue to make effective the heritage received as an undivided unity." [1] It is in that sense that the Jews must insist they are a nation, and it is in that sense also that they should regard the nationhood of the people to whom they are united by the bond of citizenship.

The fact that every basic culture must bear a specific character does not imply that the primary purpose of the basic culture is to inculcate in the child particularistic tendencies and loyalties. The primary purpose of that basic layer of culture is to elicit the human potentialities of the child, to render him as completely human as possible. When the Eskimo mother trains her child, she is not conscious of bringing him up as an Eskimo first and foremost, but as a human being according to her lights. The particularistic aspect of national cultures is an incidental phase, a reaction to the hostility displayed by other groups. The natural tendency of every national culture, and therefore of the basic layer in a person's development, is extrovert and refers to humanity as such. Nationhood qualifies the human being not only for the group but for human life, and, though the means are necessarily particularistic, the aim is universal.

There is another vital factor in nationhood which calls for emphasis. The process of communicating to the child the basic values that enter into the shaping of personality does not take place in a void. The medium which has thus far proved the most effective in the transmission of national culture has been the family. Although latterly the state has taken upon itself the major part of the task, the initial and determinative part of the process has to be left to the family. Only in exceptional cases have child-rearing institutions taken the place of the family. It remains true, nevertheless, that the human family is not a self-contained unit, but always requires some larger group to validate it, to give it recognition and status. That group in turn usually forms part of a larger group, and so on, until we reach what may be termed "the limits of validation." All who are included within those limits know themselves as members of one nation. The family or unit which transmits the basic layer of culture to the child may be said to derive its sanction from, and in turn give life to, the nation.

The relation between the family and the nation is, thus, one of reciprocity, like that between the living cell and the tissue of which it is a part. The family owes its stability to the civilization of the nation of which it is a part. The marriage laws by which it is given status and permanence are not of its own making, but are the product of the national life. On the other hand, the nation depends upon the family as the initial medium for transmitting its accumulated cultural heritage.[2] It is not only the biological phase of the family which renders it of such vital import to the life of the nation but also its educational function.

Since a nation derives its life essentially from the family unit, which it uses as a means of transmitting the cultural product of its life process, nationalism is not a political but a cultural concept. Its fundamental purpose is to humanize and civilize. Many a misunderstanding and misapplication of so potent an instrument for human development as nationhood could be avoided if this, its fundamental purpose, were more widely recognized.

The division of mankind into nations has produced lasting accumulations of culture, and the individual who is a member of a nation inherits its culture as surely as he gets the color of his eyes from his parents. No generation can begin the process of human development *de novo*. It must take over the social heritage which is transmitted to it by its forebears. Consequently, as far as we can reasonably prognosticate, civilization in the concrete will consist of many civilizations. It is inconceivable that as long as there will be Frenchmen, Germans or Englishmen, the civilization of any of these national groups will be permitted to die out. As long as these civilizations remain alive, there will be national groups to cultivate them. The Great Society will always have to reckon with the manifold civilizations which it has inherited from the past. Though that manifoldness complicate matters, it is inevitable. As a rule, men are not daunted by the increased complexity of living, when such complexity opens up new horizons. The trend has thus far been not to lessen the number of civilizations, but to revive those that were moribund, and to foster those which are in an embryonic state.

Once a group has reached the degree of collective consciousness when it possesses the *will-to-civilize*, it has established a right to existence which no one can question any more than one can question the right of a human being to live, once he has come into the world. There is something ultimate about the will-to-civilize which carries its own justification. If we deny to any group the right to transmit its language, its experiences, its *sancta*, its beliefs and its desiderata, we rob all its members of the elementary right to exercise their most human, as distinct from subhuman, function—that of eliciting the humanity inherent in the child.

"But," it will be said, "why must the medium of the process of humanization necessarily be the culture of one's own people? If by reason of political dominance the parent is prevented from transmitting his own language, literature, religion and ethical standards to his child, he can have his child brought up in the culture of the dominant group. Why insist upon one's own inherited culture as a means of civilizing one's child?" They who argue thus would, in effect, counsel submission to the civilization of the majority. Such advice is based on expediency, not on justice. Jews now gladly submit to the necessity of imparting to their children the civilization of the country in which they live. The cultural substance which forms the texture of their children's personality is derived in the main from the civilization of the majority. The question is: shall it be derived *exclusively* from that civilization? Shall the majority population have the right to prevent the Jews or any other minority group from imparting in addition to the majority civilization its own historic civilization? *Shall democratic nationalism spell, in a sense, greater intolerance than medieval ecclesiasticism?*

A submission which involves the surrender of the most elementary and instinctive right of a human being to express his selfhood runs counter to the most deeply rooted biological instinct. To yield without protest to the arbitrary will of anyone who happens to possess greater power is as subversive of moral law as the act of violence, for the basic assumption of all moral law is the inviolability of the person, and complacent submission to greater force negates that assumption. It is the very purpose of Jewish nationhood to evolve those cultural values which help to humanize the child by developing his sense of self-respect through resistance to domination by superior force.

Another challenge to Jewish nationhood comes from those who envisage the Great Society of the future as organized chiefly on vocational or functional lines. Functionalism claims that the group with whom the individual is in close contact or relationship through the pursuit of a common calling contributes most to his development and self-fulfillment. The nation is too complex an organism to influence the individual profoundly. Its very size precludes the exercise of sufficient mutual influence to make nationhood of much consequence morally and spiritually. Can the stranger who lives in the same city, or even in the same house, matter as much to me as the person in China who has business dealings with me, or is engaged in the same kind of scientific or cultural endeavors as I am? Labor organizations, professional guilds, the numerous fraternal and sport associations, societies organized for the purpose of some intellectual, artistic or social aim, associations which are transnational or international in their scope, seem to play an infinitely more significant part in the lives of their constituents than the nation to which those constituents belong.

This assumption, however, is not borne out by experience. It arises from the tendency to consider the facts and factors of our *self-conscious* life as the chief determinants of our existence. We often forget that the forces which determine a person's life are usually those which lie beneath the threshold of consciousness and are recognized only after long analysis. The basic layer of culture which the human being receives in his home leaves so deep an impress upon his life that its power is second only to the biological force of heredity. It is during the childhood years spent in the home that a person's mentality is formed; it is then that the basis of the prejudices and the sentiments which constitute the disposition is laid. The habits acquired during the first few years of a person's life are those which give final bent to his character and to his capacity for happiness.

If these facts are true, then it is the national group to which a man's family belongs that places its stamp upon his personality. The vernacular which a man employs, and which binds him to his nation, inculcates in him habits of mind that have a profounder influence than the conscious ideas expressed. Even if later in life he tries to suppress the memory of the particular nationality, or the home he came from, he continues to experience the effect of his upbringing in the very endeavor to forget it.

The chief corollary that stems from the cultural conception of nationhood is that the adherents of a civilization have an inalienable right to transmit that civilization to their children. *No state is justified in monopolizing the prerogative of laying the foundation of personality in the young.*

The Catholic church maintains that it is no part of the state's duty to teach; that authority over the child belongs not to the state but to the parent. But this is only half the story. The other half is that the Catholic church, in emancipating the parent from the state, wishes to assert undisputed authority over the parent. The church, in absolving the state of the duty to teach, claims the education of the child as solely its prerogative. The church thus comes out boldly as the rival of the state.

Jews, however, would never venture to question the right of the state to educate the child. On the contrary, in consistency with their own conception of nationhood, they must take the position that the state's chief duty is to teach. But if the state is to permit freedom of conscience and the right of association, it must share that duty or right with the ethnic group, minority, nationality or church that wishes to take part in the education of the child. This principle was, indeed, tacitly accepted by all the enlightened nations when they granted religious freedom to all their citizens. The full significance of that grant has escaped political thinkers and statesmen because they have labored under the illusion that religion is a matter of the individual conscience.*

Were the actual facts concerning religion considered, it would be realized that religious freedom means essentially the right of any group within the nation to maintain its social solidarity and the cultural institutions with which its life is intertwined. The time has now come when the implication of the principle of religious freedom must be made explicit, and extended beyond the province of formal religion. It should be made to include the right of any minority group to foster its language, its folkways and its arts.

The true significance of the separation of state from church is to be found in the changed status of the citizen. As far as his cultural life is concerned, he may be a hyphenate. Before that separation took place, he could live only by the civilization which was represented in the state; he may now live, in addition, by the civilization of whatever other group he chooses. As a matter of fact, that is how the average citizen does live. He derives his political values, his language, literature and the arts, from the civilization embodied in the state; his ethical and spiritual values from that embodied in the church.

The same confusion which prevails in the mind of the average person with regard to the status of the Jewish people and the nature of Judaism prevails also with regard to the status of the church and the nature of Christianity. The same clarification is needed in Christianity as in Judaism. The fact that Christendom is divided into many nations, and that the collective term by which it is usually designated is "the church" has prevented most people from realizing that Christendom was to have constituted the one nation which was to embrace all mankind. As a world-nation, or Catholic nation, Christendom wanted to impose one language, one history and one social structure upon all its adherents. During the Middle Ages, Christianity was a full-fledged civilization. The fact that religion permeated all its constituent elements and that other-worldliness was the characteristic of that religion in no way disproves the cultural character of Christianity. For the Catholic church, Christianity is still more than a special department or phase of human life; it is synonymous with the whole of human life. The Catholic church has never retreated from that position. It has consistently demanded of its adherents that in the education of their children they give priority to its doctrines, sanctions, laws and authority over those of the civilization embodied in the state. It insists upon being regarded not as a voluntary organization but as "a structure of law and government." The Catholics take full advantage of the principle of religious freedom to live as cultural hyphenates.

The Protestants are all in a tangle. Their conception of Christianity as a "purely spiritual" institution is just as illogical and inconsistent as the Reformist conception of Judaism. Once in a while even a liberal Protestant, realizing that the Protestant churches are losing ground, and that Protestant Christianity is fast disintegrating, raises a warning voice to urge his fellow-believers not to yield all prerogatives to the state. "Let the Churches reassert that the state is not a final moral authority for the citizen," writes George A. Coe. "This is an ancient doctrine, but it has fallen into disuse among Protestants. It is high time to recover the old position. . . . A super-political conscience must be developed in and through the church schools." [4]

All this indicates that for a long time to come citizenship in the western world will take the form of hyphenism. Living in two civilizations which yield different types of values is not merely a necessity into which modern nations are driven by historical forces beyond their control; it is a means of warding off the danger of raising the state to a religion. Far from viewing the hyphenated cultural allegiance of the citizen of a modern state with alarm, we should rejoice that there is present in the body politic an influence counteracting the danger of chauvinism. Christianity, in whatever form, is so far the only cultural agency the occidental man has developed to broaden and spiritualize his outlook upon life. The English, the German, the French and the Americans who are loyal to Christianity live in two civilizations. Simple justice requires that the same right be extended to the Jew. The only difference is that, since Christians are in the majority, they require no justification for their right to hyphenate. But since Jews are in the minority, they must define their status clearly. Since they can no longer claim the right to cultivate a corporate Jewish life on the traditional basis of being the sole possessors of supernatural revelation, they must be able to base that right on their interpretation of nationhood. To do that they must learn to interpret nationhood in conformity with the deepest intuitions of their own forebears, intuitions which harmonize with the tendencies to see in nationhood an expression, not of political separatism, but of cultural individuality and spiritual creativity.

The conception of Judaism as a civilization yields two corollaries by which Jews will have to be guided in their efforts to reconstruct Judaism in accordance with the spiritual needs and social conditions of the present time. They are as follows:

1. Only in a Jewish national home is it possible for Judaism to achieve those environmental conditions which are essential to its becoming a modern, creative and spiritual civilization.

2. As long as the modern nations depend upon historic civilizations like Christianity or Mohammedanism for the moral and spiritual values which they cannot find in their own native civilization, the Jews must insist upon the right to cultivate their own historic civilization as a means to their spiritual life. Such cultivation necessarily takes on the twofold form of rebuilding *Eres Yisrael,* and endeavoring to maintain in the diaspora as much social cohesion and organization, and as much of each of the constituent elements of their historic civilization, as are compatible with unqualified loyalty to the countries of which they are citizens.

The status of the Jews which emerges from this program is that of an international nation with its home in Palestine. The fact that at present there exists no social organism like the one which is here proposed for the Jewish people of the future, does not rule it out of the realm of the feasible or the valid. The church, during the first three centuries of its existence, had no precedent for its form of social organization. Yet it managed to grow into a spiritual power that had to be reckoned with.

Now that the social framework which united the Jews in the past is shattered, they must set about at once to reconstruct it. They must not allow themselves to be diverted from that effort by the fear of being charged with divided allegiance. *No allegiance, divided or undivided, dare stand in the way of the right to have one's life motivated by satisfying moral sanctions.* If these sanctions presuppose being rooted in a historic culture which needs a social framework to support it, any political system which interferes with the establishment of such a social framework violates the fundamental law of human freedom. Let us hope that America, at least, will not rob any of her citizens of that freedom.

CHAPTER XIX

CULTURAL NATIONALISM AS THE CALL OF THE SPIRIT

The need of reinterpreting the doctrine concerning Israel as the elect of God—The mission idea advocated by Reformism a wrong reinterpretation—Why the Jews regarded themselves the only true nation—The Jews' way of validating nationhood—The level of self-consciousness attained by Jewish nationhood.

OF the conscious factors which formerly contributed to the survival of the Jews in the face of systematic persecution and oppression, first place is undoubtedly to be assigned to the belief that they were the special object of divine providence, a belief held alike by the sophisticated and the naïve. The Jews could never have displayed such power of endurance had they not been fortified by the doctrine of election. To assume that it is possible for the Jews to maintain their nationhood at the present time without believing that there is something in it of universal significance is to reckon without human nature. Jewish nationalists, who contend that the sense of nationhood requires no justification in any universal purpose, are correct only as far as the challenging outsider is concerned. To be sure, one cannot change one's grandfather, but one's belief does affect one's grandchildren. If they are to be born into a Jewish nation, that nationhood must constitute a high moral asset. Jews must therefore find a meaning in their status as a nation, or, failing this, must construct one that will justify the effort and struggle involved in upholding that status. *Such a meaning would be the equivalent of the traditional belief in Israel's divine election, and, therefore, the functional revaluation of that belief.*[1] It is the purpose of what follows to establish this point.

The Reformists have proposed an equivalent for the traditional doctrine of election. By maintaining that the Jews, as a race, have a genius for religion and are therefore entrusted with the mission of upholding the cause of true religion, the Reformists believe they

253

have saved the doctrine of election from obsolescence. But the trouble with the mission idea is that it has not gone far enough in the process of revaluation. It has stopped midway between the theurgic or semi-anthropomorphic conception of God's choice of Israel as his people and the humanistic conception of groups and individuals living with a sense of purpose. Morris Joseph, for example, believes that he has entirely rationalized the traditional belief in divine election when he says: "It is in no arrogant temper that we claim to be the chosen people. We thereby affirm, not that we are better than others, but that we ought to be better." [2] He is apparently unconscious of the presumption implied in assuming that "we ought to be better" than others. We ought to be better than we are. But to say that we ought to be better than others implies that we regard ourselves as being inherently superior to them. Such notions may have been tenable in the pre-enlightenment outlook, but today seem obsolete or arrogant.

Likewise, the doctrine that the Jews had the task of making God known to the nations was relevant only at a time when the Jews could claim that they alone had received supernatural revelation, and that they alone had been granted an infallible code of laws. As long as they were so minded they had good reason to set up their claims against the claims of other nations. "To make God known" has the ring of an authentic mission that seeks to proclaim a supernatural revelation as an historic event. To an historic event, all can serve as witness, men, women and children, regardless of their intellectual development.

But when the task of making God known depends not upon the affirmation of the historicity, validity and superiority of a specific supernatural revelation, but upon a mode of spiritual life that is calculated to reveal the reality of God in the world, or the meaning of God in human experience, then the mission idea is in no sense a revaluation of the doctrine of Israel's divine election. That task can be fulfilled by anyone, Jew or Gentile, so long as he lives up to that high standard. The career of Israel viewed as a manifestation of the divine in the world may, no doubt, act as an incentive to living an exemplary life. But that career as a past event is the spiritual heritage of all men and has been appropriated by the greater part of mankind. It is no longer necessary to be a Jew to be inspired by that career. To be *the descendants* of a nation that once existed, rather than present members of a nation, may bring a glow of self-satisfaction, but imposes no extra burdens or responsibilities.

The "Israel" which the Jews in the past regarded as divinely chosen was a nation in a real and consequential sense. A mission idea which is the psychological offshoot of this doctrine of election must be applied to an entity similar to the one about which the doctrine was conceived. It is in Israel's career as a future reality that the mission idea must find an application. This means that *Jews must find within the scope and functioning of their very nationhood something that would endow it in their own eyes with purpose and value.*

To achieve a pertinent and realistic revaluation of the traditional doctrine of the divine election of Israel, the doctrine must disclose some psychological implication on which to rear an effective rationale for the continuance of Judaism. It should not be difficult to find such an implication, for in our most egoistic self-laudation a tribute to some ideal of excellence is always implied. It has been said that hypocrisy is the tribute which vice pays to virtue. Even in a hypocritical act, some ethical implication is latent. It stands to reason, therefore, that in any claim to superiority, founded or unfounded, the claimant pays homage to that trait or ability by virtue of which he regards himself superior.

When the Jews affirmed that they were God's chosen nation, their claim was tantamount to the assertion that they alone constituted a nation. They meant to emphasize their belief that all the other peoples, including the most powerful, were not really nations. This interpretation of the doctrine of election rests not only on the words of an ancient singer in Israel who said: "Thou art the One (God) and Thy Name is One: and who is there like Thy people, the one nation in the world?"[3] It rests upon the entire outlook of ancient man to whom godhood was but a higher form of kinghood. Godhood was a correlative concept like fatherhood. A spirit was not necessarily a god; it became such when it acquired worshippers. Ancient man was unable to conceive a god without a people any more than he could conceive a king without a people. The converse was equally true. He could not conceive a people or nation without a god any more than he could conceive a nation without a ruler or king. This is analogous to what happens nowadays when a government, which has come into power through the use of force, is regarded as a government *de facto*, but not *de jure*. To be *de jure*, a government must satisfy recognized norms. Therefore, when the Jews arrived at the belief that the gods of the other nations were nonentities, they concluded that the other nations were not nations in the true sense of the term. The other peoples, it was assumed, would attain true nationhood, if they would acknowledge Israel's God who was the only true God.

Whatever other connotations there were in the doctrine of Israel's divine election, apposite to the present discussion is the connotation that Israel regarded itself as the only true nation because it was ruled by the only being who was God, and because it professed allegiance to his code of laws. Though there may be a certain crude "sacred egoism" in this doctrine, its implications are important. It implies not only a tribute to nationhood as the ideal arrangement under which human beings can achieve their highest good, but also the consciousness of a standard which nationhood must attain to fulfill its function.

It is often asserted that many ancient and barbarous peoples regarded themselves as divinely chosen.' For that matter, every ancient people had its gods. Yet no one would deny that the Jews succeeded in giving to the idea of God connotations which have uniquely widened the spiritual boundaries of human life. *Judaism is unique not in having evolved values which were totally unknown to other peoples, but in having carried common values to pragmatic conclusions never dreamt of by other peoples.* Just as Judaism's interpretation of the God-idea was so striking that it displaced the versions given to the God-idea by other nations, so also did it succeed in contributing to the spiritual life of mankind a unique version of the idea of a divinely chosen nation.

Most people, given to reflection, are so used to the process of abstract reasoning inaugurated by the Greeks that they fail to appreciate the significance of any truth or value which is not conveyed formally by way of general propositions, a form practically unknown to oriental thought except in the gnomic literature. This is why the significance which Judaism attaches to nationhood has escaped them. The Jewish mind which has retained its oriental cast down to our own day, the medieval Jewish philosophers notwithstanding, experienced the moral and spiritual importance of nationhood as a factor in the development of human personality to a far more intense degree than any other people. It was not, however, a calmly thought-out conclusion so much as a deeply felt conviction, achieved perhaps as a result of confluent circumstances unparalleled in any other group. Because it was a conviction held by a type of mind not given to abstract thinking, and therefore not transferable, it remained confined to the Jews. The ideal of nationhood became an obsession with the Jews who intuitively sensed the power for good inhering in the ideal. The obsession was translated into the belief that they were the only nation, and this belief in turn derived its sanction from the further belief that the God to whom they gave their allegiance was the only true God.

The ancients could not possibly imagine that their allegiance to a deity had originated entirely with them. They did as a matter of fact choose their gods, but not being fully aware of this process, they reasoned that the gods had chosen them. By this mode of reasoning, the Jews ascribed to their God the act of choice which bound them in allegiance to him. Shelled out of the mode of thought and expression natural to the oriental mind, the kernel idea of the doctrine of the divine election of Israel is that nationhood brings into play forces and events in the life of a group which enable its members to achieve self-fulfillment. The belief that God chose Israel held in latent form the generalization that the possession of true nationhood qualified a people to achieve its highest potentialities.

Although the idea of nationhood never attained in Jewish thought that abstract and generalized form which might have rendered it communicable, or perhaps because of that fact, it found expression as a way of life, not merely as a way of speaking. That God chose Israel to be his people did not remain an inert idea, but gave point and unity to the entire civilization by which the Jews lived. Every element in that civilization was regarded as contributing in some way to that self-realization which, as the chosen of God, they were in a position to achieve. That civilization was symbolized in and delineated by the Torah. There could be no greater incentive to live in accord with that civilization—the Torah—than the knowledge that it was the principal means through which God indicated his special love for Israel. No wonder that, whenever the Jew was about to read from the Torah, the scroll of the Law which represented his national civilization, he praised God in the benediction, "Blessed art Thou, O Lord, our God, King of the universe, who hast chosen us from all the nations, and given us thy Law." ⁵

The concept of divine election as the differentia which distinguished the nationhood of Israel from the nationhood of other peoples has a radically different background of thought and sentiment from that which divine election has, let us say, in Calvinism. The individual does not thank God because he happens to be of those whom God for some reason known to himself has selected for divine favor; he thanks God that through the national civilization at his disposal he is given the opportunity of experiencing God's election. The election is contingent upon his living the civilization of his people, upon his utilizing the nationhood of his people as the sanction of his purposes and the directing principle of their achievement. Thus in the idea of election the Jews were made aware that the nationhood of a people was conditioned by its manner of life or civilization. Throughout rabbinic literature it is assumed that the Torah constitutes the principal instrument which confers nationhood upon the Jews. For them, accordingly, nationhood was synonymous with theocracy. To the Jew of today Torah can mean only a historically evolved civilization, and the nationhood which it validates must find expression in the ideal of democracy.

The specific implications for our own day of the Jewish doctrine of election, or of the ancient belief that the Jews were the only nation in the true sense of the word, may be gathered from the following considerations:

1. It is a matter of recorded and verifiable history that the Torah was a covenant twice formally accepted by the Jews as the authoritative instrument of their collective life; once in the days of Josiah, and the other time in the days of Ezra and Nehemiah. *As a covenant, the Torah is a symbol, representing the truth that a nation becomes such not through the accident of common ancestry or physical propinquity, but through the consent of those who constitute it to live together and to make their common past the inspira-*

tion for a common future. The general will that speaks in such consent is the spiritual bond which unites the members of a nation. Any people that develops a general will of that kind has acquired a collective personality and an inalienable right to existence, limited only by the right to existence of similar groups which have developed a general and articulated will of their own.

2. The Torah, as content, is not merely a code of laws. It is comprehensive in its scope, and includes all the basic elements of human culture. It embraces a philosophy of life and of history; it outlines a national policy; it prescribes ethical and religious conduct; it lays the foundation of a system of jurisprudence; it deals in matters of etiquette. The Torah, especially as developed in practice and interpretation, is the full equivalent of what we understand by a national civilization. *So viewed, the Torah emphasizes the important truth that a nation is not a fighting unit but a cultural group, united not by the instincts that keep together wolf-packs for purposes of offense and defense, but by the urge to develop those human differentiæ and potentialities which only collective life can bring forth.*

3. The Torah, as process, represents teaching, or the communication from one who is in possession of vitally significant knowledge to one who is lacking that knowledge, whether it be from parent to child or from master to disciple. The process of transmitting such knowledge is given primacy among all the duties and obligations of Jewish life. *Torah thus brings into sharp relief the function of education as the one to which all other functions of social organization, of state or government, should be subordinate.* All the machinery of social organization which does not aim at developing to the full the powers that inhere in each individual human being merely impedes human progress, and deserves to be scrapped.

These considerations prove that the question whether Jews shall retain their nationhood is not a political but a moral question. If what makes them a nation is the Torah and all that it represents as symbol, as content and as process, it is their duty to uphold their nationhood, even as their ancestors had to uphold the unity of God, to the point of martyrdom. The division of mankind into nations derives from laws of human nature and geography that cannot be defied. Cosmopolitanism is a vain delusion, and in the mouths of

Jews who deny their Jewish nationhood it often goes together, para-
doxically enough, with an obstreperous patriotism for the countries
of which they are citizens. When not disciplined and brought under
the control of a moral standard such as represented by the Torah
of Israel, nationhood is sure to run amuck, and, driven by the wild
impulses of greed and vanity, is bound to wreak ruin upon all who
come in its path.

*In the face of all this, the Jew should be an active protestant
against the wilful perversion of the creative energy of nationhood.*
He can do so only by being true to the type of nationhood which is
validated and directed by the symbol, the content and the process
of Torah. By fostering his Jewish nationhood together with the
nationhood of the country of which he is a citizen, the Jew demon-
strates in himself that the right of a nation to live must go together
with the duty to let live. By fostering his Jewish nationhood, not
with the aid of engines of war, but by engaging in the undertaking
to build a land and to renew a civilization, he becomes the bearer
of the truth that bayonets do not make a nation. A nation is the
product of a civilization which expresses itself as the will-to-
cooperate for the good of its individual members as well as for the
good of humanity. By fostering their nationhood in the spirit of
Torah, the Jews are bound to develop social agencies which will
demonstrate to the world that the main function of states and governments is not to exercise police power in defense of the economic
and political *status quo*, but to create such laws and institutions as
would enable those who are identified with the nation to bring to
fruition whatever powers for good they possess. Only when the
nations adopt the educational ideal embodied in the Torah will they
evolve the economic and political institutions that will make for
justice and righteousness.

It is evident that the individual Jew can experience the privilege
of divine election only as he identifies himself with the whole of
Israel. The significance of this process of identification becomes
apparent when it is realized that "Israel" does not mean only the
generations contemporaneous with the life of the individual, but
that national being whose origin reaches back into the dim past, and
whose future is endless. It is only when the nationhood of a people

attains the intensity which it acquired among the Jews that the national being becomes objectified into a kind of corporate personality. "Post-exilic Judaism," says Oswald Spengler, "was a juridical person long before anyone had discovered the concept itself." [6]

The background of an individual who relives his people's past and lives in anticipation of his people's future is infinitely vaster and fuller of human experiences than that of the individual whose horizon is limited to the immediate. It is this enlargement of background that nationhood brought into the mental life and conduct of the Jew. This is why it may be said that if other peoples achieved a group *consciousness*, the Jews achieved a group *self-consciousness*, that is, a consciousness in which group memory was long, and group imagination far-reaching. The individual Jew lived and acted under the constant visualization of his people's history. He had a mental picture of Israel's origin as a single patriarchal family which grew into a nation. The career of that nation is traced in all its vicissitudes, from the time it was a slave people in Egypt to the destruction of the First Temple. In this way Judaism came to be the first civilization to have a national history.

The ancient empires had royal annals to perpetuate the glory of their monarchs, and occasionally to celebrate the achievement of some person of distinction. Greece had its epics and odes to sing the praises of gods, demigods and athletes. The sagas of the Norsemen, the Vedas of the Hindus, the poems of Homer and the Æneid of Virgil, celebrate the deeds of heroes. These heroes, though they served to establish like-mindedness among the individuals of a nation, did not succeed in developing collective self-consciousness. History, not in the sense of a chronology of events but as a drama of national life in which there are plot and meaning, was unknown before the historical books of the Bible made their appearance. "For Thucydides, the events of the Persian Wars, for Cæsar those of the Punic Wars, were already devoid of living import." [7] Oswald Spengler senses the significance of the time-aspect of the Jewish consciousness. "The Arabian Culture," he says, "dared the astounding gesture—we see it in the historical thought alike of the Jews and of the Persians from Cyrus's time—of connecting the legend of creation to the present by means of a genuine chronology." [8] Whether the plot which the Jewish people read into the course of the events and experiences of its history be true or not is immaterial. What is significant is that they were at great pains to describe such a plot, to give organization, logic and meaning to their experiences *as a nation*.

The historic sense which is characteristic of the group consciousness implied in the term "Israel" is responsible for another type of social institution which is peculiar to Jewish civilization; namely, days dedicated to the commemoration of epochal national experiences. All the other ancient civilizations had festivals that merely served as a means of expressing man's rapport with nature. The Jewish civilization stands out unique in having festivals to commemorate past events. *Pesah,* the spring festival, became essentially the day whereon Israel was redeemed from Egypt. *Sukkot,* the festival of ingathering, served as a reminder of Israel's sojourn in the wilderness. The process of giving historic significance to festivals continued for a long time. Thus, *Shabuot,* the wheat harvest festival, came to commemorate the giving of the Torah. *Hanukkah* and *Purim,* like *Pesah* and *Sukkot,* were reinterpreted to commemorate historical events significant in the life of the nation Israel.

A second characteristic of self-consciousness is imagination or the power which enables a person to visualize himself in some situation set up as a goal toward which he may strive. Measured also by this criterion, we find that the collective consciousness of Israel attained an unusually high degree of self-awareness. Since its earliest years, Judaism held up to the imagination of the Jew a picture of his people enjoying in the future an extraordinary measure of bliss. To share in that bliss constituted his main ambition in life. It did not matter to him whether he personally would share the good fortune of his descendants. The future was pictured in a divine promise such as that which had been made to Abraham. "I will make of thee a great nation, and I will bless thee and make thy name great." Or it was depicted as the Day of YHWH when he would display his power, a conception that underwent numerous developments until it became the messianic ideal and the vision of a better world. But whatever the form, the Jewish consciousness was always employed in the contemplation of the future. This national self-consciousness inhered in every individual Jew who was humanized and spiritualized through the enlarged mental horizon as he could never have been otherwise. This result was achieved for him by his intense nationhood, although he was incapable of isolating and naming the sense of nationhood itself. Feeling its power, however, he used the only term by which he could identify and explain it: Israel, the chosen of God.

In sum, the Jews must be prepared not only to foster their nationhood but to see in nationhood as such, whether it be their own or that of any other people, the call of the spirit. *By this they will achieve a revaluation of the doctrine of the election of Israel, and realize that their mission is inherent in their very functioning as a nation.* By overcoming all opposition and difficulties to the continuance of its career as a nation, by revealing in its own existence and history the moral and spiritual powers which nationhood evokes, the Jewish people will point the way to the beneficent utilization of the most potent social force in human society.

CHAPTER XX

THE LAND OF ISRAEL

The interpretation of Israel's destiny always in terms of Ereṣ Yisrael—The unquenchable yearning for Ereṣ Yisrael motivated by the Jews' will-to-live as a nation—The Jewish emancipation based on a misunderstanding—Jewish emancipation must include the right to land and nationhood—Right of the Jews to Ereṣ Yisrael compatible with interests of natives—The meaning of the mandate for Palestine—The upbuilding of a Jewish national home an incentive to Jewish revival in diaspora.

JUDAISM has always contemplated Israel's life and destiny in terms of a collective existence associated with a particular land. Nothing in traditional Judaism indicates that Israel is to function in the world as a landless people. The proposal that the Jews reconstitute themselves into a religious organization that would completely omit Palestine from its reckoning, except as an ancient memory, must ultimately lead to a complete severance with the Jewish past. Whatever the religious philosophy or program of action of such an organization, it would not be Judaism.

"Nationality," says Alfred E. Zimmern,[1] "is a form of corporate sentiment." A nation is "a body of people united by a corporate sentiment of peculiar intensity, intimacy and dignity, related to a definite home-country." The Jewish people has always been highly conscious of its relationship to the land where it developed its national life. It did not accept that relationship casually, after the fashion of most nations. Unlike the other ancient peoples, it never considered itself autochthonous; it never forgot that it came to the land from elsewhere, and that only in the land did it begin to function as a nation. *A true reading of the Pentateuch—the basic source of the sanctions, laws and folkways of the Jewish people—would indicate that the Jews have in it a perfectly recorded deed to the possession of Ereṣ Yisrael.*

On the basis of a few *Aggadic* passages which reflect the religious-polemic interests of rabbinic times, the conception arose that Abraham was called by God because he had discovered the oneness and spirituality of God. The Torah knows nothing about Abraham

264

as a religious philosopher or reformer. It is mainly interested in giving an account of the way God went about creating a people that would acknowledge him as its God and obey his laws. It informs us that God chose Abraham to be the founder of that people. To achieve that purpose, he commanded Abraham to leave his home and his kindred—among whom he would naturally have had to worship other gods—and directed him to the land of Canaan, promising to make his descendents into a great nation. Abraham no sooner arrived in the land, than God appeared and said to him: "To thy seed will I give this land." [2] This promise is reiterated ten times in the course of the patriarchal epic.

Why did not the Patriarchs enter into actual possession forthwith? There were two conditions to be met. First, Abraham had to prove his worth as a faithful and obedient vassal of God. Second, the Amorites who held the land had to reach the full measure of sin before they could with justice be deprived of their land. This latter condition necessitated the sojourn of Jacob, his children and their descendants in Egypt. The achievement of God's purpose—the formation of Abraham's descendants into a nation—had to be suspended. When Joseph adjured the children of Israel to take his remains to Canaan, he said: "God will surely remember you, and bring you up out of this land unto the land which he swore to Abraham, to Isaac and to Jacob." [3] According to the biblical narrative, it was in the spirit of waiting to be called to their land that the Israelites lived in Egypt.

When the time came for the exodus, God sent Moses to lead the Israelites out of Egypt into the promised land.

And I am come down to deliver them out of the hand of the Egyptians, and to bring them up out of that land into a good land and a large, unto a land flowing with milk and honey; unto the place of the Canaanite and the Hittite, and the Amorite, and the Perizzite, and the Hivite, and the Jebusite.[4] And I will take you to me for a people, and I will be to you a God; and ye shall know that I am the Lord your God, who brought you out from under the burdens of the Egyptians. And I will bring you in unto the land, concerning which I lifted up my hand to give it to Abraham, to Isaac and to Jacob; and I will give it to you for a heritage: I am the Lord.[5]

In the song which celebrates Israel's victory at the Red Sea, the main purpose of the deliverance is stressed as having been that of enabling the Israelites to enter into possession of the land that is described as God's own.⁶

On their way to the land where they were to live as a nation, they received the laws which were to govern them. Those laws, except for the directions concerning the Tabernacle, contemplate the Israelites in possession of the land. In God's plan, their sojourn in the wilderness would have lasted only long enough to effect the passage between Egypt and Canaan, and to prove by their patience under trial their qualification to be the people of God. They fail in every one of the trials—they violate outright the commandment against making an image of the deity. Yet even then they would have entered the land, had they not committed one sin which, more than any other, called forth the divine wrath. They sent spies to reconnoitre the land, and these spies brought back an evil report which threw the people into a panic. In expiation of that sin, the Israelites had to journey in the wilderness well-nigh forty years until the entire generation that left Egypt after the age of twenty-one, including Moses, Aaron and Miriam, died out. According to the Torah, their one unpardonable sin in the wilderness was that of rejecting their national destiny with regard to the land.

Just as Genesis unfolds the epic of the adventure of Israel's forebears to win the land, so Deuteronomy plays variations on the theme of what their descendants must do to hold the land. From the beginning of Deuteronomy to the end, the one great concern is that Israel shall not forfeit its right to the land. It is as though Moses were bringing to focus the significance of Israel's experiences in the wilderness by pointing out the relation of those experiences to Israel's destiny as a nation in the land.

The first oration in Deuteronomy opens not, as one might expect, with a description of the exodus, but with a reference to the divine command to the Israelites to start on the last stage of the march to their destination. In chapter after chapter, Israel is reminded that the purpose of all its experiences was to train it to attain its goal as a people in the land. The aim and reward of its obedience to the laws of God were to be continued possession of the land and the enjoyment of the wealth of its blessings, which excelled even the watered shores of the Nile. In case of disobedience, on the other hand, the land would be forfeited and every conceivable disaster would befall Israel. Thus, in one uniform strain does Deuteronomy interpret Israel's fortunes and failures in terms of the part that Israel is to play in the land.

If we were to take a survey of the other books of the Bible, we would invariably meet with the same tendency to define Israel's experiences and backslidings, its failures and its hopes, in terms of its relationship to the land. Some of those writings belong to an earlier period than the Torah, some are contemporaneous with it, and some belong to a later period. But no value is so uniformly interpreted and emphasized as the value of the land in its relation to Israel. The Torah, which embodies the teachings of the earlier Prophets and enjoys pre-eminence among the sacred writings of the Jewish people, must be regarded as a most decisive influence in the shaping of Judaism. Since the Torah makes Israel's relationship to the land its principal motif, it is hard to conceive how the Jews could contemplate their functioning as a group apart from the land.

Self-evident as is this integration of Palestine into the Jewish consciousness, it is often ignored. The impression one gathers from the works of Christian scholars is that, when the civilization of the Jewish people entered upon its theocratic stage during the period of the Second Commonwealth, the Jews ceased to be a nation and became a church, an ecclesia. These scholars are accustomed to think of nationhood as essentially a secular form of associated life. Finding that the priesthood exercised political authority during the greater part of the existence of the Second Commonwealth, they conclude that the Jews became a "temple-community" and thereby transformed into a society properly designed as a church. Assuming that a church is a social or spiritual organization upon which territory exercises no determining influence, they conclude that the life, the habits and the hopes of the Jews after the return from Babylon, were those characteristic of a church, since the Jewish conception of God now transcended the limitations of territory and nationhood. Hence they reason that the Jews were an ecclesiastical entity, "a kingdom of priests." This view totally misrepresents the facts. Apart from what may be inferred a priori from the nature of the Torah—that they could not possibly have thought of their future in any other but national-territorial terms—the facts of Jewish history during the entire period of the Second Commonwealth confirm that inference.

The main authority for the assumption that the past supplies a precedent for divorcing the destiny of Israel from its homeland, is the collection of prophecies contained in the latter part of the book of Isaiah. While it may be conceded that, according to the Torah, Israel is inseparable from its land, it is alleged that the author of those prophecies which speak of Israel as the servant of God destined to bring the light of truth and justice to the nations, had in mind an Israel that transcended the limitations of national boundaries and of nationhood. He was far ahead of the times, and his universalism ill comported with the narrow nationalism and legalism of the majority. But now, so runs the argument, the time is ripe for adopting his interpretation of Israel's mission.

This argument quite disregards the circumstances under which the anonymous author enunciated the mission idea. It was during the time when the dispersion of the Jewish people had reached a stage when its dissolution seemed imminent. Family after family had migrated, and the land of Israel swarmed with strangers. Like all the seers and lawgivers of Israel, he viewed the dispersion with deep concern. In the firmness of his faith in the God of Israel, this anonymous Prophet concluded that the dispersion, far from portending the end of the Jewish people, was a means of enabling it to carry out the divine purpose of promulgating among the nations the name and character of YHWH. But that state of dispersion was by no means to be permanent. It was only an interim state preparatory to the attainment of the ultimate goal—Israel's restoration to its land.'

In consonance with the general *Weltanschauung* which prevailed until modern times, the Jewish civilization was other-worldly, and was based entirely on the assumption that everything in this life was of value only as it qualified the human being for a share in the world to come. From that viewpoint, Israel was to the Rabbis an ecclesia, *Keneset Yisrael*. This fact has misled some present-day Jewish thinkers into believing that rabbinism altogether denied the nationhood of the Jewish people, or considered it of secondary importance. The barest acquaintance, however, with rabbinic writings should disabuse one of such an error. We may question the logical consistency of a tradition which considered salvation in the other world as the principal purpose for which Israel was called into being, and yet insisted that Israel must remain a nation held together by the same kind of physical bonds as any other nation. But whether consistent or not, it is an incontestable fact that there is not the slightest hint anywhere in rabbinic literature that *Ereṣ Yisrael*, the holy tongue or messianic government can be omitted from the program of Israel's future.

The rabbis held to the national prerogatives of land, language and group autonomy with such unwavering tenacity that any conception of a denationalized Israel becomes a deliberate subversion and repudiation of the past. It is needless to recall the devotion to *Ereṣ Yisrael* which characterizes rabbinic Judaism. After every meal the Jew recited the prayer, "We thank thee, O Lord our God, because thou didst give as a heritage to our fathers a desirable good and ample land. . . . Blessed art thou, O Lord, for the land and for the food." We have seen how far the Torah goes in reading all of Israel's life and fortunes in terms of Israel's tenure of the land. In keeping with that view, the Torah presents a highly colorful and idealized picture of the land. Yet that picture pales into insignificance beside the glowing idealization which the land receives at the hands of the rabbis,[8] who as long as they found it feasible to retain *Ereṣ Yisrael* as the seat of authority, did so, despite the larger and wealthier communities that existed elsewhere.[9] Long after the destruction of the Second Temple, the Palestinian Rabbis were trying to prohibit emigration from Palestine.[10] They went so far as to say that only he who lives in *Ereṣ Yisrael* can be said to have a God; he who resides elsewhere is as though he had no God.[11]

These citations make clear the true meaning of the oft-quoted statement that "God dispersed Israel among the nations in order that they may receive an accession of proselytes."[12] It implies that the temporary suspension of Israel's life as a nation in its land, could be accounted for only on the assumption that God wanted others besides Israel to enjoy the benefits of salvation. But with that accomplished, Israel would resume its national life in its land. It is obvious that nothing could be further from the truth than to read into this rabbinic saying the abandonment of nationhood. Search as we may in the entire range of traditional Jewish literature for the conception of a denationalized and landless Israel, we shall not find the slightest evidence for it.

It is a mistake to imagine that in the centuries since the destruction of the Second Commonwealth the Jews merely dreamed about Palestine, or found the recitation of prayers an adequate substitute for living there. The fact is that until the Arab occupation in 634, the Jews constituted a majority of the population in Palestine. Except for the hundred years between the First and Second Crusades, Palestine was continuously inhabited by Jews. The number of Jews in Palestine did not depend upon the economic opportunities to be found there, but upon the degree of flexibility of the governmental measures against Jewish immigration.

When Nahmanides in 1267 established the practice of having the Jews in the diaspora support those who migrated to Palestine; the Jewish people indicated its intention of retaining a hold on the land as an essential condition to its continuance as a people in the diaspora. That was, in a way, an answer to Judah Ha-Levi's charge that the Jews merely repeated their prayers for a return as parrots repeat the words that they are taught. Ha-Levi overlooked the fact that it was impossible for the Jews of his day to accompany their prayers with practical action. It would have meant certain death, as it did in his own case. The action of Nahmanides proved that as soon as there was the least chance of re-entering the land, the Jews did so, even though it was impossible to gain economic security there.

The mass of Jewry, however, could not remain content with this tenuous hold on the land. From time to time they forgot all restraining considerations and flung themselves wildly against the closed gates of the land. These were the lost causes, the messianic movements. It is a mistake to estimate the scope of these movements by their tragic culminations. Messianism, as a series of movements to regain the land, should be appraised by the vast activities of those Jews who devoted themselves to mystic lore in all its forms. Mystic lore formed a part of Jewish civilization, as it was part of all other ancient civilizations, because, in its essence, mystic lore develops from man's necessity to adapt his environment to his desires, to render the physical and spiritual forces subservient to his wants. Impelled by the need of transforming their environment, the Jews resorted to mystic lore in the hope of discovering the theurgic formulas and practices that would help to bring about the forcing, as it were, of the hand of God to redeem his people, by sending the Messiah and restoring them to their land. A colony of practicing mystics actually established themselves in Safed to prepare the way for the redemption. They exerted no small influence on the Jews of the diaspora. In the tense spiritual struggle that centered around the *Kabbalah,* the yearning for the return to *Ereṣ Yisrael* and the resumption of national life constituted the most meaningful part of Jewish life during the centuries of exile.

Since the Jewish people so consistently and steadily considered itself appointed by God to work out its destiny in its own land, on what grounds did the liberal-minded Christians in the eighteenth and nineteenth centuries urge the admission of the Jews to citizenship? Did they expect the Jews to surrender their hope of returning to Palestine? If so, on what did they base their expectation?

The following passage from the speech on Jewish disabilities, made in 1833 by Macaulay in the English parliament, will help us understand the attitude of the liberal-minded Christians toward Jewish nationhood:

Another objection which has been made to this motion is that the Jews look forward to the coming of a great deliverer, to their return to Palestine, to the rebuilding of their Temple, to the revival of their ancient worship and that therefore they will always consider England, not their country, but merely as their place of exile.

But surely sir, it would be the grossest ignorance of human nature to imagine that the anticipation of an event which is to happen at some time altogether indefinite, of an event which has been vainly expected during many centuries, of an event which even those who confidently expect that it will happen, do not confidently expect that they or their children or their grandchildren will see, can ever occupy the minds of men to such a degree as to make them regardless of what is near and present and certain.

Indeed, Christians, as well as Jews, believe that the existing order of things will come to an end. Many Christians believe that Jesus will visibly reign on earth during a thousand years. Expositors of prophecy have gone so far as to fix the year when the Millennial period is to commence. The prevailing opinion is, I think, in favor of the year 1856; but according to some commentators, the time is close at hand. Are we to exclude all millennarians from parliament and office, on the ground that they are impatiently looking forward to the miraculous monarchy which is to supersede the present dynasty and the present constitution of England, and that therefore they cannot be heartily loyal to King William? [12]

We gather from this argument that Macaulay classed the hope of a return to Palestine with the belief of the average person, Jew or Christian, in the advent of the new world-order. Since that world-order was to be entirely of God's doing, and its advent was to take place in God's own time and in God's own way, all that man could do was to wait passively. Macaulay, like other Christian liberals, took for granted that the Jews would *not* renounce Palestine. They realized that to demand that they do so would be tantamount to demanding a renunciation of their religion and their past. So the liberals struck a compromise. They would grant the Jews citizenship, provided the Jews would allow their hope of national restoration to remain passive and dormant. Thus Palestine might continue to be the subject of pious wishes in the synagogue, but must in no way affect the practical social conduct of the Jews. This type of argument had been advanced by Comte de Mirabeau [14] and had also been used with effect in the National Assembly of Holland. [15]

The Neo-Orthodox came nearest to fulfilling the expectations of the Christian liberals. [16] But the majority of the Jews who have been engaged in fashioning their lives to meet the new civic requirements have not been satisfied with a dualism which consists in expressing one's yearning for Palestine within the synagogue and suppressing that yearning outside the synagogue. The Reformists healed the dualism by surrendering all Jewish national aspirations, verbal and practical. The Neo-Orthodox have the advantage of having satisfied the expectations of nineteenth-century liberal statesmen. But that does not solve the problem of the continuity of Judaism.

The liberals, who helped to secure civic and political rights for the Jews of the western countries, believed that they secured for the Jewish people all the "emancipation" to which the latter were entitled; they meant well, but they had no understanding of Judaism. To them Judaism was an ancient superstition that had somehow managed to survive, but which was bound to die out with the cessation of persecution and political discrimination. Napoleon I seems to have understood the implications involved in granting political rights to the Jews, when he compelled the Sanhedrin in Paris to renounce the nationhood of the Jews and to permit intermarriage. Nevertheless, Napoleon entertained, for a time, the idea of restoring Palestine to the Jews.¹⁷ His twofold plan with regard to the Jews only brings into bolder relief the shortsightedness of the Jewish leaders themselves, who greeted the removal of political disabilities as the final redemption, and not only abstained from any effort to secure Palestine as a homeland but deliberately surrendered all Jewish claims to it. At all events, we cannot escape the conclusion that the terms on which emancipation was offered to the Jewish people, as well as the terms on which it was accepted by the Jewish leaders of the day, were based on the fictitious assumption that Judaism was a religion only. This constitutes one of the grievous mistakes in Jewish history.

That mistake must now be rectified. Jews must clarify their position both to themselves and to the world. They cannot consider themselves emancipated unless they are granted the opportunity to foster and develop their historic civilization. This means that for the Jews no progressive corporate life anywhere is possible without the establishment of a national home in Palestine.

If Judaism still possesses creative energy, it should regain the only medium through which adequate expression is possible to any civilization—a land of its own. It cannot maintain continuity without an environment where it will be able to exercise a civilization's primary prerogative, that of molding the minds of the young and endowing them with the fundamental traits of human personality. Only those who are thus nurtured by a civilization are its true children, and through them alone it creates values and makes history. Palestine is the only land which can furnish such an environment for the Jewish civilization.

Judaism is unlikely to survive, either as an ancillary or as a co-ordinate civilization, unless it thrive as a primary civilization in Palestine. It is obvious that Palestine can harbor only a limited number of Jews. But a sufficiently large community of Jews must be permitted to lead there a full, normal and creative life. With the resulting enrichment of Judaism's cultural and spiritual content, Jews in the diaspora will then feel themselves members of a minority group that possesses motivation, idea and purpose.

The Jewish people had its rise and growth in Palestine; and Palestine has become a holy land to two-thirds of mankind because of the part the Jews played there. The history which the Jewish people enacted in Palestine has been accepted by the followers of Christianity and Mohammedanism as proof of God's providence in the career of mankind. The Patriarchs, Kings and Prophets of Israel stamped themselves upon the human imagination to a greater degree than the national heroes of any other people. During their stay in Palestine, the Jews produced a literature which has given a common consciousness to the greater part of the human family. A land which forms the very texture of a people's life and genius is not a mere geographical entity that may be easily surrendered, but becomes, as Palestine became to the Jew, an inexorable destiny.

If the Jewish people has earned its right to Palestine through its achievements there, it has doubly earned that land through its unswerving devotion to it after the exile. Its devotion and yearning for the land has had the compelling power of an obsession. The Jew never stood up in prayer, never rose from a meal, never celebrated a Sabbath or festival, never rejoiced at a wedding, never mourned the loss of a beloved, never drew comfort from his religion without invoking the hope of restoration to Zion. The Jews have not omitted a single significant occasion, nor one single day in all the centuries that they have been dispersed among the nations, to reaffirm their right to national existence in Palestine. By that token the Jews have not merely upheld a claim in the face of forcible eviction; they have helped even in their absence to keep that land *spiritually* fruitful. The steadfast hope in their ultimate return to Palestine enabled the Jews to survive as a people. It has engendered whatever spiritual and cultural potentialities they still possess.

The claim of Arab agitators that Palestine belongs to the Arabs was met effectively by M. Van Rees, vice-chairman of the Permanent Mandates Commission of the League of Nations, at the Seventeenth Session of that Commission held at Geneva, from June 3 to June 21, 1930.

The Arabs, he said, maintained that their country belonged to themselves and that they had been masters in it for fourteen centuries. Great Britain, in authorising the establishment of a National Home, had disposed of a country which did not belong to it. This claim was particularly open to refutation. It was not in accordance with most elementary facts of ancient history in Palestine. It would be enough to point out that Palestine had belonged before the war to the Ottoman Empire. That country had been conquered not by Arabs of Palestine, but by the Allies, and had finally been ceded to the Allies and not to the Arabs. Since 1517 Palestine had been under the rule of the Turks. There could be no reference, therefore, to an Arab nation in Palestine, nor could it be claimed that the territory formed part of the patrimony of that nation.

Secondly, the Arabs asserted that Great Britain had failed to carry out its promise, made during the war, tha. they should be granted independence. Was that really the case? . . . the British Government had constantly denied the allegation of the Arabs. The correspondence between Sir Henry MacMahon and the Sherif Hussein, of Mecca, on which the Arab claim was founded, had never been published, which meant that doubts might still subsist. It was nevertheless to be observed that the Sykes-Picot Agreement of May 1916 provided that the administration of Palestine *properly speaking* was to be internationalised; it was reasonable, therefore, to conclude that this arrangement excluded any possibility that there might have been formal promises given assuring the independence of the Arabs inhabiting this territory.[18]

In the face of the incontestable claims of the Jewish people to a national home in Palestine, only one possibility could necessitate the renunciation of those claims. If Palestine were completely, or even for the most part, occupied and developed by its inhabitants, the Jews might have to resign themselves to the loss of their homeland. In actuality, only a fraction of the material and cultural values that Palestine is capable of yielding is utilized and rendered productive by the non-Jewish inhabitants.[19] With an influx of settlers who could render the land productive agriculturally and industrially, it could be brought to a point of economic development sufficient to maintain a population five or six times the present number.

The Jews, driven by an inner necessity which can give them no rest until they have reclaimed Palestine, are prepared to render it fruitful with their sweat and blood. They alone can supply the labor, the patience and the endurance necessary to convert the barren rocks, the infested swamps and the baffling sand dunes into thriving and healthful oases. With the drainage of swamps, the reforestation of the hills, the creation of an adequate system of irrigation, the development of the latent resources, the growth of industries for the manufacture of native and foreign raw materials, there arises the possibility of a land economically stable, culturally creative and capable of supporting three million people.

Such considerations moved Great Britain, while freeing Palestine from Turkish rule, to make the promise to the Jewish people known as the Balfour Declaration. When the war was terminated and the treaties of peace were being arranged, the Balfour Declaration was ratified at San Remo. Finally, when the League of Nations was established and the Covenant drawn up, Great Britain was awarded the mandate for Palestine. In that mandate, the Balfour Declaration was incorporated, thereby becoming a covenant valid not only for Great Britain and world-Jewry, but also for the fifty-two nations associated with the League.[10]

The preamble to the mandate for Palestine states:

The Principal Allied Powers have also agreed that the Mandatory should be responsible for putting into effect the declaration originally made on November 2, 1917 by the Government of His Britannic Majesty, and adopted by the said Powers, in favor of the establishment in Palestine of a national home for the Jewish people, it being clearly understood that nothing should be done which might prejudice the civil and religious rights of existing non-Jewish communities in Palestine, or the rights and political status enjoyed by Jews in any other country.

Recognition has thereby been given to the historical connection of the Jewish people with Palestine and to the grounds for reconstituting their national home in that country.

Article 2 reads:

The Mandatory shall be responsible for placing the country under such political, administrative and economic conditions as will secure the establishment of the Jewish national home, as laid down in the preamble, and the development of self-governing institutions, and also for safeguarding the civil and religious rights of all the inhabitants of Palestine, irrespective of race and religion.

Article 4 reads:

An appropriate Jewish agency shall be recognized as a public body for the purpose of advising and co-operating with the Administration of Palestine in such economic, social and other matters as may affect the establishment of the Jewish national home and the interests of the Jewish population in Palestine, and, subject always to the control of the Administration, to assist and take part in the development of the country.

The Zionist organization, so long as its organization and constitution are in the opinion of the Mandatory appropriate, shall be recognized as such agency. It shall take steps in consultation with His Britannic Majesty's government to secure the co-operation of all Jews who are willing to assist in the establishment of the Jewish national home.

The mandate system is new in the law of nations; it is natural that in its operation unforeseen difficulties should arise. Essential to the solution of the problems in various mandated countries is the realization that the mandate system represents a sincere attempt on the part of civilized mankind to substitute the rule of right for the rule of might. Hitherto a victorious nation could govern and exploit the conquered territory, and the native population had no voice in the matter. In the disposition of the conquered territories after the World War, however, a new principle was taken into account—the principle of national self-determination. Among the conquered territories were some whose populations were either too heterogeneous, or too immature politically, to be entrusted with self-government. These have been placed temporarily under the tutelage of the Allied Powers until the population achieve sufficient political maturity to become qualified for autonomy. Assuming even that the mandate system is only a camouflage for conquered countries as the spoils of war, the very articulation of this new conception of international justice has raised hopes and ambitions that must be reckoned with in future dealings with suppressed peoples.

Palestine was made one of the mandated countries not so much because of the political immaturity of its inhabitants, but mainly to give the Jewish people the opportunity to rebuild its national home there. Later, when Jewish life would be firmly grounded, Palestine could be granted self-determination. In making the covenant with the Jewish people, the nations were not unaware of the existence of a non-Jewish population in Palestine, nor disregardful of their rightful claims and interests. In the very first promise made by the Balfour Declaration, these claims and interests were carefully safeguarded; and in the mandate for Palestine ample provision is made against any possible violation of the rights of the non-Jewish population.

The mandate for Palestine as a covenant between the nations and the entire Jewish people throughout the world gives formal recognition to the national aspirations of the Jewish people. The same spirit which moved the nations of the world to grant rights to subject populations and oppressed minorities caused them to consider the anomalous condition of a people long bereft of its national home. By recognizing the national aspirations of the Jews, international justice took a large stride forward. Hitherto, only peoples occupying a given territory which they could claim as their own were recognized as nations. The Jewish people, deprived of its homeland, lacked even the advantage possessed by other minorities and oppressed peoples. The League of Nations, however, realized that the historical association of the Jews with Palestine and their passionate yearning for it made them as much a nation as actual residence in the land. This resolve on the part of the nations has put new heart and new spirit into the Jews everywhere. It has given back to the Jew his self-respect. It has released in him pent-up moral energies and awakened in him new spiritual powers.

Palestine's contribution to Judaism is not a distant hope but a present reality. Palestine has become to the Jews everywhere "a symbol of corporate existence." All Jewish activity throughout the diaspora which bears a constructive character and has in it the promise of permanence derives from the inspiration of Palestine. It already exerts a cohesive influence among the different Jewries of the world and among the different groups in each of those Jewries. The Jew can remain a Jew without being constrained to follow a uniform regimen of practice. He can cultivate his convictions and preferences without endangering his status as a Jew, or weakening Jewish unity.

But Palestine is not only beginning to emancipate the Jew from sterile uniformity; it is creating a cultural content to which he may apply his released energies. It is transforming Jewish education from the acquisition of values that belong to a dream world—so unreal seem most of the ideas in their traditional form when compared with the realities of present-day life—and from a Jewish replica of Protestant Sunday schooling, into a process of humanizing and spiritualizing the child's mental growth. It is stimulating

Jewish art to change and enrich its media, its subject matter, its style. Its Keneset Yisrael, its efforts to reconstruct Jewish civil law, its "religion of work" and its yearning for a vital religion of faith are symptoms of spiritual gestation which cannot but have a revitalizing effect on the entire organism of world-Jewry. The present influence of Palestine upon the diaspora is but a dim forecast of the incalculable spiritual impetus that Jewish life will acquire when Palestinian civilization shall have grown to its full stature.

If Judaism succeeds in taking up its career in the land of its origin and evolving into a modern civilization, it is bound to enrich the life of mankind with new social and religious values. By demonstrating anew the reality and potency of spiritual values, the sovereignty of righteousness—as the revelation of the divine in man—and the method whereby nationhood may exalt human individuality, Judaism will be doing its share toward advancing the kingdom of God on earth. Then, indeed, will the Jew have both the right and the means to come before the world as the bearer of a noble mission.

CHAPTER XXI

JEWISH COMMUNAL ORGANIZATION

The Jewish people to help the Jew attain this-worldly salvation—Modern nationhood to function as a means of this-worldly salvation to the individual—The basic purpose of Jewish communal organization to be the social and economic welfare of its members—The congregation no longer to be permitted to obstruct the organization of Jews along communal lines—Needed: a *kehillah* type of organization—The ultimate evolution of Jewish federations into *kehillot*.

So long as salvation was regarded as attainable only in the world to come, everyone was welcome to it because human imagination pictured that world ample enough to hold all who wanted to get there. But ever since men began to seek salvation in this world, which impresses them as being limited, they are none too anxious to have too many seekers after such salvation. Therefore, if for any reason a group can be shown to be undesirable, the incentive to exclude them from the world's goods, services and opportunities is never lacking, and the arguments with which to do it are always at hand. It is too much to expect people under present conditions to realize that the wells even of this-worldly salvation are inexhaustible, and that there is no reason for preventing any human being from drawing from them.

We must resign ourselves to the bitter truth that for many generations to come the nations will continue to be obsessed by the fear of diminishing opportunities and growing populations, and will be dominated by the spirit of intolerance and competition. So long as that condition will obtain, they will begrudge the Jew the full benefit of this-worldly salvation, and will refuse to admit him into their corporate life as an economic and social equal. For them to do otherwise would involve not only a complete break with deeply rooted habits and prejudices, but a complete change of heart and mind. It would involve giving up the christological interpretation of human history according to which the Jew plays the part of anti-Christ, or cosmic villain. Furthermore, to admit the Jew on a basis of complete equality, the nations would have to be tolerant of the

280

cultural differences among their own groups instead of trying to cast them into a uniform mold. Finally, they would have to be converted to the principle that the common good is best furthered by economic cooperation and justice. So long, therefore, as traditional Christianity, national intolerance and the competitive economic order reign supreme, the nations will refuse to extend to the Jews the right to avail themselves unrestrictedly of the opportunities to achieve this-worldly salvation.

To be sure the Jew can always worm his way into Gentile life. He can erase all traces of his ancestry, deny his descent, accept Christianity and perhaps even turn anti-Semite. Such salvation is this-worldly in the most abject and contemptible form. To resort to these tactics is to forfeit that self-respect, freedom and undividedness of personality without which life is not worth saving in any world. This-worldly salvation as the new regulative ideal of human life is not a form of cheap expediency to be secured at the cost of one's soul. It is a high adventure of the spirit from which one with a taint of scheming careerism is precluded. Only in the full light of truth and in complete expression of one's selfhood can one enjoy its bliss. How then can the apostate who for material advantage abjures the history and background that are part of his selfhood and pretends to subscribe to a creed which his reason rejects, be eligible to a spiritual redemption which presupposes complete inner harmony and truth? Of late even the alternative of apostasy is being denied to the Jew so that, all in all, the redemption that the Jew expected from emancipation has turned out to be a mirage. He is therefore compelled to return upon his tracks in the arid wilderness of assimilation, and to march once again in the direction of the only promised land in which he will ultimately be redeemed, the promised land of self-emancipation.

Self-emancipation is a term which has by this time become familiar in Jewish life. Leo Pinsker was the one who first coined it in 1886. Although it has gathered about itself a vast body of thought, its far-reaching implications have by no means been exhausted. Interpreted in its broadest sense, it means that since the Jew has set his heart upon this-worldly salvation, and realizes that he cannot fully achieve it by becoming Gentilized, the only honorable alternative is to seek this salvation by turning to his own people and heritage. But when he turns to his people he finds either an ecclesia, a religious community, or the débris of a disintegrated people. As an ecclesia it still invokes the ancient promises about inheriting the world to come; as a human débris it leaves the Jew without a home where he might take shelter from life's vicissitudes. And as for the spiritual heritage, it is full of outgrown truths and anachronisms. Surely no opportunity here for that self-realization which comes from the unfolding of creative powers in the discovery and conquest of new worlds of the spirit. How can the Jewish people, then, become a means to the Jew's this-worldly salvation? The answer is through self-emancipation, through self-reliance and through liberation from the inhibitions and prejudices which have kept the Jew bound to ways of thinking and modes of living that have outgrown their usefulness.

To sense the full significance of self-emancipation, it is necessary to look somewhat more deeply into the meaning of salvation. If we purpose to persuade the individual Jew to cooperate in the reorientation of Jewish thought and the reconstruction of Jewish life—and there surely is no likelihood of individual salvation unless he is so persuaded—we must base our entire argument upon its intimate and personal application to him. The success of any proposed program of Jewish living will depend entirely upon the extent to which it leads to the salvation of the individual.

With all due deference to Ahad Ha-Am, one cannot but regard as chimerical and unpsychologic his effort to bring about the renascence of the Jewish people by urging the substitution of loyalty and devotion to the Jewish national being in place of the individualistic yearning for personal salvation. He contends that such complete identification of the individual with the group existed before other-worldly motivation was introduced into Judaism, and could therefore again become the characteristic of Jewish consciousness. This contention overlooks the progressive self-assertion of the individual which may almost be formulated into a law of human history. Once men have learned to reckon with the individual as an end rather than as a means in appraising the value of any social ideal or program, it is reactionary to ask the individual to sink back into his former subservience.

It is a mistake to see in the growth of modern nationalism the negation of the individual and the affirmation of the group as the measure of all values. That modern nationhood—by which is meant a form of associated life—has been more successful in securing mass cooperation, and has even been instrumental in creating mob-mindedness on a larger scale than ever before, should not be interpreted as implying that the essential purpose of modern nationhood is to submerge the individual in the group. These manifestations of modern nationhood are by no means an outcome of its inherent nature and purpose. Not knowing how to take into account the specific needs of the individual, or to reckon with his highest interests, it resorts to the spurious functions which have turned it into an instrument of evil. But these perversions of modern nationhood should not blind us to the truth that basically it intends to serve the individual. We are therefore in keeping with present-day realities when we treat the well-being of the individual in the most comprehensive and enduring sense of that term as the ultimate criterion of any plan of social or spiritual regeneration.

When we study the quest for salvation and the conditions of its fulfillment, we note that salvation presupposes a community which treats the individual as so organic a part of itself that in promoting his life it is aware that it promotes its own. The chief aim of such a community is to help him attain those objectives which constitute for him his complete self-realization.

These two conditions were met by the Christian and Moslem communities throughout the pre-enlightenment centuries, when salvation meant bliss in the world to come. The Christian church constituted a community which gave its members the status of persons, possessors of souls of unique and immeasurable worth. Each believer was made aware that he was an indispensable part of the living body of the church. It was in exactly the same relationship that the Mohammedan church stood to the individual Mohammedan, and *Keneset Yisrael* to the individual Jew. Furthermore, these three world-communities also helped the individual attain self-realization during all those centuries when other-worldly bliss was accepted as the only form of that self-realization. Had these same communities continued to aid the individual when he came to identify self-realization with this-worldly bliss, they would have retained their hold on him to this day. The very rise of modern nationalism means that the Christian and Mohammedan churches refused to recognize the individual's right to change his objective in his quest for salvation. The modern nation has come forward as the competitor of the church for the soul of the individual. It is not only ready to be a means of his salvation, but it also offers the sense of at-homeness, the sense of indispensability and the status of personality, which had always been in the power of the church to grant. Needless to say, the church has resented this usurpation of its claims and gifts. But the hour when it might have made nationhood superfluous is long past. Its separation from the state is nothing more than a form of euthanasia to which it has condemned itself through the stubbornness and blindness of its leaders.

Modern nationhood is by no means contented with a superficial relationship to the individual. It is gradually penetrating into the innermost recesses of his life. Whereas at first it merely claimed the prerogative of saving him from his enemies within and without the nation, it now wants to help him earn his livelihood, to impart to him the cultural values which are indispensable to his intellectual and esthetic development, and even to develop his character. Had the nation fully and sincerely lived up to this program, it would long ago have displaced the church in the consciousness of the individual. His allegiance to his nation, his loyalty to its institutions and furtherance of its rightful aims would have supplied him with all the religion that he normally needs. Only those who are highly sensitive and introspective would have required the kind of personal religion which transcends the limits of national life.

If this consummation is still in the very remote future, it is because the state—perverting the true purpose of nationhood—has too often betrayed the individual. Its interest in teaching him to earn his livelihood has turned out to be with an eye to furnishing servile hands for the industrial magnates. Its inculcation of cultural and civic ideals has been actuated by the desire to make willing cannon fodder. The aggrandizement of the few through the industrial enslavement of the many has been the thinly veiled aim of the state. It is this hypocrisy which has made men realize that the political set-up of the modern nation, far from being the instrument of salvation, is an instrument of exploitation. Salvation is possible only through a community based upon the pursuit of the common good in a spirit of justice and equality. No wonder that anyone who takes life seriously is nowadays in a state of bewilderment. He doesn't know where to find the community which is so essential to his salvation. The church has failed him and the nation has betrayed him. That the nations exclude the Jews from the opportunities for this-worldly salvation is of a piece with the deception which the states practice on their own citizens. Even if the dominant elements in nations had treated the Jew as a social and economic equal—assuming that such inconsistency with the rest of their self-seeking policy were possible—he would still fail to attain this-worldly salvation, for the simple reason that the nations as at present constituted tend to destroy souls rather than save them.

Under these circumstances, the most reasonable thing for the Jew to do is to concentrate his efforts upon his ancestral people with the view of making it into an instrument of this-worldly salvation. There can be no question that the Jewish people treats the individual as an organic part of itself. It alone, of all peoples, cherishes him as bone of its bone and flesh of its flesh. It confers upon him human worth and dignity, and endows him with that status of personality which is the groundwork of any self-realization. But the question is: what must the Jewish people do to help the individual Jew attain those new objectives which he regards as constituting his salvation, since it can no longer impose upon him the traditional objectives which he considers unreal or abstract? It must at least make a serious attempt to accomplish what under normal conditions a nation ought to do for its citizens in a spirit of justice and peace. Stated concretely, it must come to the assistance of the Jew: first, by obtaining for him a place in the sun; secondly, by helping him make his social and economic adjustments; thirdly, by imparting to him cultural values and habits which can make his life significant. Such a program cannot mean that the individual Jew is to wait passively for the Jewish people to do all these things for him. The Jewish people does not exist apart from the individual Jews who compose it. Such a program therefore implies that as soon as a sufficiently large number of Jews will be aroused to act collectively along the lines suggested, the Jewish people will become for the individual Jew an instrument of this-worldly salvation.

Like all other ethicists, Jewish thinkers, when dealing with the relationship of the individual to the community, have oft taken for granted that the loyalty of the individual to the community must be treated as an ethical absolute in the nature of Kant's categorical imperative. They invariably disregard the aspect of mutuality without which ethical values are impossible. There is nothing mercenary or degrading in the fact that unless the community furthers the well-being of the individual, it has no claim upon his allegiance or cooperation. *It is just as essential for the community to accept responsibility for the welfare of the individual, as for the individual to be responsible, to the extent of his ability, for the welfare of the community.*[1] The community, as the church, was successful in holding the loyalty of the individual mainly because it made itself responsible for securing him a place in the world to come. That was the function which Israel, likewise, as a church community, sought to discharge to the best of its ability. To use a rabbinic metaphor, Israel made it possible for the Jew to win a place above the sun. Now, however, that the problem of securing a place above the sun has become irrelevant, the Jewish people must devote all its energies to help the individual secure a place under the sun.

The primary mistake which Reformism made was to disregard this mutuality between the Jewish people and the individual Jew. When other-worldly salvation became irrelevant and the literal realization of the messianic hope no longer conceivable, Reformist Judaism released the people in its collective capacity from all obligation to the Jew. Whatever duty it owed him, it discharged in having given him its great spiritual heritage, the inspiration of its unique history. But it did not provide him what every other nation supplied its individuals, a place in the sun. Jews might voluntarily organize themselves into an *Alliance Israélite* or a *B'nai B'rith* to protect their own civic rights and those of their fellow-Jews in other countries. *This they did, however, purely on humanitarian and fraternal grounds, and not as an essential part of the philosophy or program of Jewish life.* As far as such philosophy or program was concerned, Reformism regards the Jews as having already found their place in the sun. This is the fatal weakness of the Reformist position. Its theory is based upon a false conception of the realities, and its practice, grounded in the realities, is not accounted for in its theory.

This anomaly must not be permitted to continue. The nations either officially or unofficially refuse the Jew complete social and economic equality. This means that they refuse him a place in the sun. It therefore devolves upon the Jewish people as a collective entity to fill that lack which robs the individual Jew of the fundamental condition of this-worldly salvation. This effort should consist in ceaselessly campaigning against social and economic discrimination wherever Jews live, in upbuilding a national home in Palestine, and in directing their economic life into visibly productive occupations. All these efforts must proceed from the philosophy of Jewish life as a whole, and be sanctioned and supported by all of Israel.

One of the most notorious effects of the emancipation has been to develop in the Jew a panicky fear of giving the impression of Jewish world-unity. There is little that he dreads more than having the anti-Semites charge him with conspiring against the world. To prevent this libel, he is willing to release the Jewish people from any obligation to help him in his fight against being treated, in spite of certain civic rights, as an alien. However, the more he deprecates any international action, the more do the anti-Semites keep on accusing the Jews of engaging in international conspiracy. Should not the Jew by this time have learned from experience that no matter what he will do to ingratiate himself with his enemies, he will only be wasting his energies, besides making himself despicable in his own eyes? He certainly does the Jewish people no favor by exempting it from the duty of helping him find a place in the sun, for he thereby deprives it of the chief opportunity of being an instrument of his salvation. Let the Jew frankly invite his people to help him in his struggle, not only against civic but also against social and economic disabilities, and let the invitation be openly and expressly accepted by the Jewish people as part of the new rôle which it must henceforth play in the life of the individual Jew.

It is evident that we cannot expect the principle of social control to work among the Jews as it does among other people. The latter are usually concentrated in one territory. They are, therefore, free to choose between a centralized and a federated plan of government as a method whereby the nation as a whole discharges its responsibility to the individual. The Jewish people, on the other hand, being divided into a number of Jewries residing in different countries, is compelled to adopt the federated plan by having each local Jewry organized from within, and autonomous as to its local problems. It is to be assumed that those who would be in charge of the affairs of each local Jewry would strive to keep alive the spirit of Jewish world-unity in everything that would be done by their respective communities.

The Jewish people must become an instrument of this-worldly salvation by organizing itself into local communities which would aid the individual Jew in making his economic and social adjustments in relation both to Jews and non-Jews. This statement implies a conception of Jewish community which has rarely been projected in modern times. Yet, unless steps be immediately taken to call that kind of community into being, it is questionable whether Jewish life in a country like America will last more than two or three generations.

The familiar fact that before the emancipation the Jews were organized into self-governing communities is usually viewed as having had merely political significance. Its implications for the cultural and spiritual life of the Jew have been entirely ignored. Yet it was by virtue of that autonomy that the community was able to make itself needed in the everyday life of the individual Jew. Without that concrete service which the community rendered to every Jew, rich or poor, learned or ignorant, Judaism would long ago have disappeared. If the community had to be of practical help to the Jew when the salvation which he hoped for was of the other-world, does it not have to be all the more so now, when the salvation he seeks is of this world? The important point to remember is that this duty of the community to help the Jew make his economic and social adjustments was not something incidental or accidental, but was discharged as essential and integral to the purpose which Judaism sought to achieve in the world. This essentiality was reflected in the carefully elaborated principles of law and equity.

How Jews reconcile themselves to the surrender of all these activities and inner forces of solidarity with complete nonchalance, and pretend that they still have something to live for as a distinct group, illustrates the power of the human mind to believe the absurd, if it only wants to.[2] But absurd it remains, nevertheless, for Jews to claim that Judaism can exist without a Jewish community. The most elaborate temple structures resounding with the music of the most expensive organs and reverberating with the orotund echoes of the most highly paid preachers, will not hold to Judaism the thousands of young typists, stenographers, teachers and clerks who go about from one employment agency to another and are compelled to sign away their Judaism for even a chance at a job. If the Jewish people has something to offer in the way of rendering life worthwhile and holy to these young people, there is no stone it ought to leave unturned in order to prevent them from foreswearing their Jewish heritage for the sake of a livelihood. The Jewish community is up in arms whenever a Jewish infant is adopted by a Christian institution, but it seems to feel not the slightest compunction when thousands of Jewish young people come to detest Judaism through its sheer indifference to their elementary needs.

From time to time, the healthy communal instinct asserts itself and impels a number of public-spirited Jews to engage in a form of endeavor that exemplifies what a Jewish community ought to do, purposefully and continuously. Some years ago, for example, there was established a bureau to divert the stream of Jewish immigration from the few large centers to smaller cities in the land. The sponsors of this bureau were moved by a spirit of responsibility for the best interests of both the resident and the immigrant Jews. If, at the same time, it had been generally recognized that such a task devolved not upon the few who were generously disposed, but upon the community as a whole, we should have had the beginnings of the communal spirit which henceforth will have to be deliberately fostered, if the Jewish people is to survive. Another project, which is still in operation, and which illustrates the same point, is the work of settling Jews on farms. In that, too, there is the beginning of an idea which, if it had been clearly recognized at least in its major implications, would have revolutionized the general conception of the purpose of the Jewish community. The chief implication is that *the economic security of every Jew, who is willing to work, should be as much a part of the communal care and responsibility as is the provision of shelter and food and clothing for those who have been reduced to destitution.*

If the Jewish community would make itself responsible for helping the individual in the struggle against economic insecurity aggravated by his being a Jew, it would find itself engaged in a variety of activities which branch out from this initial one. It would combat the evil of Jews discriminating against their own people. It would seek to deal with conflicts between employers and employees in industries where there is a predominance of Jewish labor. Some years ago, there emerged from the efforts at conciliation in such industries a notable measure of idealism and social justice in the settlement of labor disputes. Some observers then thought that the Jews were about to make an important contribution to industrial peace in American life. Undoubtedly, if the Jews were to act in a communal way in the solution of economic difficulties, they would be rendering a far greater service to the country in general than by merely prating about their mission to teach the unity of God and the brotherhood of man.

The type of organization which American Jews must evolve for their spiritual salvation is a radically different instrument from that upon which they have been taught to depend of late; namely, the congregation. The congregation as constituted at present is likely to prove the most serious obstacle to the creation of a normally functioning Jewish community. To understand how the congregation, which is usually regarded as the mainstay of Jewish life, can stand in the way of its healthy development, it is necessary to become better informed about the true nature of the congregation. We might then be able to determine its proper place in Jewish life.

The delusion under which most Jews labor, whether they be Neo-Orthodox, Reformists or radicals, is that the congregation is the same as the synagogue—that social institution through which the Jewish spirit has made itself articulate during the last twenty centuries. Hence the sacrosanct attitude with which the congregation is regarded by those who are identified with it, and the violent opposition to it on the part of those who have broken with the traditional expression of the Jewish spirit. What both groups should learn is that the congregation is only a recently evolved form of social organization. Jews have come upon it absent-mindedly, as it were, in the course of their efforts to work their way from medieval-ism to modernism. It is a sort of hit-or-miss experiment which the Jews have been trying out in their attempt to adjust themselves to the new social and political conditions resulting from the emancipation.

Two factors have contributed to the rise of the congregation. One has been the political emancipation which was usually accompanied with the understanding, either tacit or expressed, that the Jews would reduce the scope of their communal activity to a minimum. The other factor has been the loss of homogeneity in ideas and practices. Contact with a variety of cultures and with people in different stages of cultural development has changed the Jews into an almost hopelessly heterogeneous human mass. This has narrowed the basis of communal cooperation among them. In their desire, therefore, to conserve their collective life and traditions, Jews have done the next best thing, by organizing themselves into congregations which are homogeneous groups united for the purpose of fostering Jewish life.

The congregation, as the Hebrew equivalent of that term indicates, aims to be a miniature *kehillah,* to fulfill for the Jew all those functions which the *kehillah* fulfilled in the past. This, however, it cannot possibly do, because the principle of homogeneity extends to economic status as well as to background and perspective. That means that the whole nexus of communal interests which constitute Jewish life could never arise within the congregation as such. Accordingly, if a Jew wants to express himself fully as a Jew, he must look elsewhere than to the congregation. Then why not accept the need for extra-congregational organization as inherent in the very nature of Jewish life? Why not proceed to make the principal unit of Jewish interaction not the congregation, but the community which includes all Jews living in a town or in a district of one of the larger cities?

The congregation as a self-contained unit is a detriment to the religious, no less than to the communal welfare. By making the element of religion the main bond of unity among the members, religion becomes highly subject to misunderstanding. It is set up as something apart from other Jewish interests. This is neither wholesome nor in keeping with tradition. In the end, both religion and the other interests suffer. Religion is rendered abstract and contentless, confined in the main to worship and ceremonies, while the other interests are secularized and dejudaized.

It cannot be denied that the congregation has served a useful purpose as a temporary means of warding off the complete disintegration of Jewish life, which was bound to set in with the break-up of the pre-emancipation type of Jewish community. This explains how the congregation has come to eclipse all other types of organized effort as a means to Jewish life. But, when temporary remedies or stop-gaps are relied upon as permanent sources of strength or support, they usually lead to great danger. In a normally organized Jewish community, provision will have to be made for worship and the conduct of religious observances and rites. There will have to be synagogues and rabbis as there were in the *kehillah* of old. But the synagogue must not be the exclusive clubhouse of a homogeneous group, nor must the rabbi be monopolized by those who can pay his salary. Rabbis, as well as social workers, center executives and other functionaries should be appointees of the community as a whole.

Moreover, organization on congregational lines as the social framework of Jewish life in America, contains an intrinsic weakness insofar as it lacks the element of socialized authority. Whether a people expresses its will through the state, which is government by a lay body, or through the church, which is government by an ecclesiastical body, the collective will takes the form of law. The normal individual does not want to be a law unto himself. In his actions and in his impulses, he requires the sanctions and restraints imposed by a will which is supra-individual. Human nature demands that some pressure be brought to bear from without, and does itself create the source of that pressure—community life. Social life has as much need of a measure of involuntarism as physical life.

A person is a member of a nation not by choice, but by virtue of the pressure of the cultural group into which he is born. That pressure is exerted in the first instance through the family. If nationhood has played a useful part in the evolution of the race, it has been due, in no small degree, to this involuntarism which characterizes it. If, then, Jewish nationhood is to function in the diaspora, its principal manifestation must be this very element of involuntarism characteristic of national life. The congregation cannot supply it because it is too small, intimate and transient to be authoritative. There is a growing tendency to treat synagogue affiliation as a luxury to be enjoyed when times are good and money plentiful. But as soon as the financial status of the members slumps, the affiliation is one of the first luxuries to be surrendered, and once dispensed with, it is seldom resumed even with the return of prosperity.*

The needs of Jewish life require a civic type of organization. This means that, if Jewish life is to continue in the diaspora, its nationhood must henceforth find expression chiefly through lay, instead of religious, organization. Not that religious organization need be discontinued or superseded by lay organization, but a social framework must be evolved by means of which all who want to remain Jews, whether they be orthodox or radical in their views, whether they be wealthy or poor, might retain Jewish status.

It is superfluous to reiterate that nothing is further from the mind of the Jew than remaining apart from the general life of his country. On the contrary, nothing less than a vigorous participation in the development of American life will content him. But it is necessary to make clear that loyalty to American ideals does not call for the suppression of the Jew's deep-seated desire to retain the individuality of his Jewish life which is inconceivable without the institutions and machinery of communal organization. Communal organization enables the group to bring pressure upon its constituent members. Without that power, no community can maintain its corporate activities, much less perpetuate itself and its culture. In fact, no democratic state has yet been devised, and probably never will be devised, which can secure the maximum of safety, happiness and moral growth of its citizens without resorting to the aid of the church. The Jewish community must do for the Jews at least what some of the churches do for the non-Jews.

The notion that one who is identified as a Jew is at liberty to repudiate all responsibility for the maintenance of Jewish life should be vigorously combated. Anyone who is born to parents who are American citizens is *ipso facto* an American, and thereby shares the duties and responsibilities of American life. The same attitude must be adopted by Jews with regard to all who are of Jewish parentage. Of course, one can always expatriate oneself. It is easier to expatriate oneself from the Jewish people than from the American people, for it can be accomplished without exile and economic loss. But as long as a Jew does not deliberately read himself out of the Jewish fold or expatriate himself from the Jewish people, he should be considered subject to whatever organized authority the Jewish group may be in a position to exercise. This is one of the Jewish attitudes which must henceforth be taught and preached at every possible occasion. Without it, all efforts to build up Jewish life in America are futile.

The *kehillah* should embrace all classes of Jews, men and women, rich and poor, Orthodox, Reformists, Conservatives and radicals. Their bond of union should be the desire to maintain Jewish life and to enhance and perpetuate its heritage. *The main need at present is to get the American Jews to become communally minded, to appreciate the significance and indispensability of communal organization.* This involves something more than taking immediate steps to establish *kehillot*. It calls for a reconstruction of the agencies, content and methods of the Jewish educational system so that even the child will have an opportunity of sensing the working reality of Jewish collective life. Only by adopting so fundamental an approach to the problem of organized communal life will the Jews finally possess the social structure that will insure the continuance of Judaism in America.

At the time the New York Kehillah ' was in the process of formation, some of its leaders formulated a plan for the establishment of an organization for the study and promotion of Jewish communal work. That plan contains a number of principles and concrete suggestions that are still valid. It reads in part as follows:

The Need: During the last three decades Jewish life in America has grown to great proportions and complexity. An increasingly larger number of men and women have become either professionally engaged as Jewish communal workers or have developed an avocational interest in Jewish affairs. Their outlooks and attitudes upon Jewish communal life have become more and more sharply drawn, until today it is possible to distinguish several fairly clearly marked points of view upon Jewish life in America as a whole.

If these persons, all of whom are striving for progress in their field and in their own way, are to give their best efforts to their work, it is essential that some means be found by which the experiences of one group may be made explicit, so that they may be compared with all other points of view; that the results of their common deliberations be made public, and that upon the basis of those results social measures may be initiated and promoted, which are agreed upon as sound and necessary for the betterment of Jewish life and family, that the problems of the Jewish community be presented effectively to the non-Jewish world.

Underlying Principles: It is believed that such a need could be met by the establishment of an organization for the study and promotion of Jewish communal work. This organization is to consist of a body of persons whose aim is scientific, impartial and comprehensive study of every possible aspect of Jewish life.

But unless there be an aim or a goal toward which the activities of such an organization would tend, the mass of facts gathered and the mass of experiences of the members, would be absolutely inert and meaningless. To make the organization vital, there must be a clear definition of underlying principles by the members. These underlying principles may be stated as follows:

1. The Jews of America form a community.

2. This community has a deep-seated desire to preserve its individuality and to continue developing it.

3. This individuality must continue to develop not apart from the American environment, but as an integral part of it, and in complete harmony with it.

4. In the past the Jews of America have developed a vast network of communal activities, mainly dealing with the negative aspects of their life, such as poverty, disease and crime. Necessarily the positive aspects, such as recreation, education, industry and religion have been less emphasized. It is these that at present need stronger emphasis.

5. Both the positive and the negative aspects, however, must be looked upon as part of one unified Jewish communal life, and all further efforts must be in the direction of the organization of such a communal life.

In harmony with these principles it is proposed to establish in the organization three *general divisions:* a division on local communal affairs; a division on national (American-Jewish affairs); a division on international Jewish affairs. There are to be *sections* dealing with the various phases of the general problem indicated by the name of the section. It is planned to begin with those sections in which a representative group of persons can be gathered, who may agree substantially on the underlying principles stated above.

Significance of the Plan: An organization such as proposed in this plan, if properly organized and kept on a high level of activity, could be of invaluable aid in clarifying many perplexing problems confronting the Jews of America. It would bring together on a common platform persons of divergent experiences and opinions. It would put behind much-needed basic communal enterprises the combined influence and experience of all those who strive for a richer, more effective, more positive Jewish life in this country.[5]

It is evident that if the communal unit is to function effectively, it cannot afford to be too complex and unwieldy. Workable plans of organization have been prepared for the Jews of Pittsburgh and of Harrisburg.[6] In a city like New York,[7] and to a lesser degree in cities like Chicago and Philadelphia, nothing could be more impracticable than to have all Jews form one community or *kehillah*. That, too, was one of the reasons for the failure of the New York Kehillah about fifteen years ago. The only way it will ever be possible to organize the Jews in a city where they are massed in large numbers is to divide the city into districts and to treat the Jews of each district as a separate local community. The beginning should be made with one of the districts. All the Jewish institutions, religious, educational, social and philanthropic, functioning within that district should gradually be brought together to plan and execute all such activities as make for Jewish life. Before long, the other districts would follow suit. The objective of an integrated community for all the districts would have to be postponed until each of the district communities was sufficiently developed, although cooperation for the avoidance of duplication could be begun as soon as more than one district would be organized.

The basic social unit of American-Jewish life should not be the congregation or union of congregations, the lodge or fraternal order, the social club or organization of clubs. That unit should be the community which should consist of all the Jewish institutions and organizations within a given area, federated to foster the normal manifestations of the Jewish spirit as well as to help those who are in need of relief. It should collect funds and make allotments, not only for the local needs and institutions, but also for those of extra-local scope. Membership in the community should be a prerequisite to affiliation with the synagogue, the Jewish club, the cultural group or the fraternal organization. In recognition of such membership, the community should give to the congregation and to the other social bodies representation in its councils. The congregation as such should cherish the ambition to bring to bear upon all communal effort the vision of the wholeness of Jewish life, and imbue all collective endeavor with consciousness and soul.

Fortunately for the future of Jewish life there still survives a crude vestige of the old community idea. Like the dorsal vertebra out of which, according to Jewish legend, the body of the resurrected dead would be reconstructed, so out of this vestige it might be possible to re-form the community idea in its original scope and vigor. The vestigial communal organ is the federation of philanthropic institutions whose purpose it is to take care of the Jewish destitute. It seems surprising that even this communal function should have survived, and that it owes its efficient discharge chiefly to Jews who are of an assimilationist turn of mind. But the answer is not far to seek. The non-Jews, in keeping with their policy not to mingle with the Jews in their social efforts, prefer to carry on a goodly part of their charitable and social work on sectarian lines. It is only because of the inability of sectarian organizations to extend aid in all cases of need that the state is called in to supplement their philanthropy. Jews, even though they be assimilationists or assimilated, do not want to have it said that their poor are a burden to other groups or to the state. It is that fear which accounts for the comparatively high development of philanthropic endeavor among Jews. Once it is no longer a question of relief for those in dire need, "federation" displays toward normal Jewish needs a blindness and insensitiveness that are heartbreaking. But the irony of it is that the state is gradually taking over a greater share of the responsibility for those in want, and all sectarian philanthropy is on the wane. The elaborate communal machinery set up for the Jewish poor will sooner or later become superfluous.

In the nature of things, however, social machinery of any kind refuses to be scrapped so long as there is some function which it might legitimately serve. Before even the question of scrapping the philanthropic machinery built up by Jews in this country need be raised, let attention be directed to the vastly more far-reaching and important uses to which this machinery might be put. This involves educating the Jew into a clear understanding of his position in the world, both materially and spiritually, and getting him to meet his difficulties with intelligence and courage. Only then will he begin to appreciate that the Jewish community is not merely a matter of organization for the purpose of gathering of funds and administration of relief, but a spiritual agency through which all that Jewish life represents might be translated into concrete advantage for the benefit of every Jew.

The Jewish federations, as at present constituted, take at best a benevolently neutral attitude toward all efforts to foster an affirmative Jewish life. Yet they furnish the initial framework for the type of communal structure which Jewish life calls for, provided, of course, they be enlarged in scope and transformed in purpose. With few exceptions, they were established and are still controlled by Reformist Jews. In their present form, they are remote from the *kehillah* type of social organization, and act as fiscal agencies mainly for the purpose of administering relief. To realize how limited their scope is, one need only compare it with that contemplated for the New York Kehillah. The first step to be taken in widening their scope is to democratize them, to make them, as a leading authority on federations has put it, "fully representative of the entire community and inclusive of every demonstrated community need." [9] If the federations or Jewish welfare funds are to win support from the broad masses of Jewry, they must devise a way of giving to all their contributors an opportunity to be represented on their councils.[10] Any Jewish society of a religious, cultural, social or fraternal character that would make affiliation with the local federation or the support of the local welfare fund a prerequisite to membership, should constitute a cell or unit of contributors with power of representation. Instead of having, as at present, the representation confined to the institutions which are the beneficiaries of the local federation or welfare fund, it would be necessary to have an additional group of representatives who would express the interests and point of view of the contributors. This second group of representatives would be like an upper legislative body reviewing the decisions of the lower legislative body, and initiating measures which would in turn be reviewed by the latter. The upper legislative body would make itself responsible for keeping alive the larger aims of communal organization which the beneficiary institutions are only too apt to forget.

In the last instance, the process of progressive unification of Jewish social agencies leading to creative Jewish communal organization will depend upon the extent to which those who give tone to Jewish life are imbued with a workable idea of an integrated Jewry. Just now organization machinery is of the least importance. They who supply the resources and they who are at the helm of Jewish affairs, must possess imagination, social vision and intelligence and passionately yearn to see a Jewish future in this country. Otherwise, all their activities will be short-lived and their achievements insignificant.

PART FIVE

GOD

THE DEVELOPMENT OF THE JEWISH RELIGION

CHAPTER XXII

INTRODUCTORY

THE NEED FOR REORIENTATION TO THE PROBLEM OF RELIGION

Religious tolerance implied in Judaism as a modern civilization—Religion indispensable to Jewish civilization—The relation of religion to science—The wrong deductions from psychological approach to religion.

THE current versions of Judaism as a religion prove to be least helpful and least tenable when we want to know what to make of the diversity of religious belief and practice to which we must resign ourselves as a permanent condition of world-Jewry. Even if the Neo-Orthodox or the Reformist conception of Judaism were theoretically correct, the mere fact that it would limit Jewish life to a specific system of belief and regimen of conduct, departure from which constitutes a departure from the norm, is sufficient to condemn such a version of Judaism as unworkable. The expectation of getting all Jews to submit to one code of law and doctrine is, under modern conditions, nothing less than chimerical. The variety of ideas which obtain in Jewish life is a replica of·that which exists in the world at large. It is difficult to conceive how Jews living in Persia, eastern Europe, Germany and America could hold similar views on religion. To expect, therefore, a single type of religion to unite them is as futile as to expect all mankind to subscribe to one universal religion. On the principle of religious tolerance alone, from which Jews should be the last to recede, Judaism must be so construed as to grant to the individual Jew the right to regard as his religion whatever he conscientiously accepts as such.

Formerly, each civilization was identified with a particular religion. In the days of undisputed Catholic supremacy in Europe, the aim of the church was to bring the various peoples of the world under one civilization and one religion. The national cultures were then still in their infancy. The church produced the enlightenment and esthetic expression which constituted the culture of the European peoples. When, with the advent of the Renaissance and later with the outbreak of the Protestant revolt, the European nations became sufficiently mature to cultivate their own civilizations apart from that which they had inherited from the church, the same principle of intolerance that had existed in the Catholic church was continued in the Protestant states. In modern times, however, the principle of intolerance has yielded to the assumption that civilizations must henceforth recognize the citizen's right to adopt whatever religion his conscience dictates. The outstanding philosophical proponents of religious tolerance whose arguments have laid the foundation of the modern attitude of the state toward the religion of its citizens are Spinoza and Mendelssohn. The former in his *Tractatus Theologico-Politicus* and the latter in his *Jerusalem* were the first to formulate in detail the theory of religious toleration.

This principle of tolerance is integral to the very conception of Judaism as a civilization. That conception implies that we may disagree with Neo-Orthodoxy, either as an interpretation of Judaism or as the only true version of religious truth, but we must concede that it is possible to be an orthodox Jew and yet live Judaism as a civilization. Likewise, whether or not we agree with the theologic assumptions of Reformism, we must admit that one can be a Jew, provided those assumptions are not lived up to so consistently as to prevent one from sharing other Jewish interests besides those of religion. But the conception of Judaism as a civilization does not stop at this point. It addresses itself to those who hold these versions of Judaism, and pleads that they give up their denominational or sectarian spirit, and look upon themselves as parties in a larger Jewish life. *Though theirs may be the correct version of religious truth and practice, they share too many elements in common with the rest of Jewry—elements which are included in the term civilization—to make difference of religion a cause for aloofness.*

But, it will be asked: would the conception of Judaism as a civilization admit of Jews professing Christianity or Mohammedanism? The answer is: by the same token that we must reject the assumption that Judaism is, or can be reduced to, a religion only, we must see in Christianity and Mohammedanism not merely religions but civilizations. A Christian is essentially one who belongs to the church, whether visible or invisible. There would be no paradox in being at the same time both a Christian and a Jew, if it consisted merely in living in two civilizations that are mutually neutral. Indeed, the only way out of the present mêlée of historical civilizations and modern nationalities is to sanction the necessity of living in more than one civilization. That is the inevitable lot of the modern man. But when one of the two civilizations is avowedly antagonistic to the other, a person imposes upon himself an intolerable conflict of loyalties by trying to live in both. The very existence of Judaism is regarded by Christianity and Mohammedanism as a challenge to their authority. The New Testament is no less interested in denouncing Judaism than in advancing its own ideas of what man must do to enter the kingdom of God. It would therefore be the height of absurdity for a Jew to want to remain a Jew while subscribing to Christianity or Mohammedanism, just as it would be absurd for one to be a Christian and a Mohammedan at the same time.

Far more difficult is the question whether a man may consider himself a Jew, though he have no interest whatever in religion. It is assumed, for example, that a person can be a Frenchman, or Englishman, without professing any religion. Upon reflection, however, it becomes evident that the parallel is a misleading one, and is based upon a superficial understanding of the laws of civilization. It is true, no doubt, that modern civilizations have to a large extent divested themselves of historic religions and are committed to a policy of religious tolerance. But this neutral attitude toward religion does not indicate the place of religion in the civilizations of the future. The fact that until recently civilizations were completely identified with religion implies a very intimate association between the two. The divorce of religion from modern civilization should be viewed as temporary. The next stage will find each civilization once again identified with religion, though it will be a different type of religion from that of the past.

Of all civilizations, Judaism can least afford to omit religion. Religion has loomed so large in the entire career of the Jewish people that its elimination would leave Judaism impoverished, especially since its other elements are still in the process of acquiring their own structural reality. If the glory of a civilization consists in the uniqueness of its contribution to human culture, then religion was, and will remain, the glory of the Jewish civilization. Take religion out and Judaism becomes an empty shell. Not by the furthest stretch of the imagination could a secularized life be identified with the spiritual heritage which has shaped the Jewish people into a unique entity. The very fact that Jews are compelled to re-emphasize their status as a nation places upon them the obligation to be a religious nation, for it is only through religion that Jews can recapture the sense of world-unity and the spiritual oneness of mankind.

On the other hand, to urge the retention of religion in Jewish life is to state a problem, not to solve it. The moment we make such a demand we come up against the ideological challenge to the formulated versions of Judaism as a religion. It is not enough to evolve a proper conception of Jewish life and of the social framework necessary to its maintenance. It is equally necessary to formulate a conception of religion for those who are dissatisfied with the conceptions thus far proposed.

The main prerequisite for understanding the place of religion in Judaism as a modern civilization is a reorientation toward religion in general, and toward Jewish religion in particular. The initial and hardest step in the process of religious readjustment at the present time is to grow accustomed to the idea that it is possible to have religion without subscribing to the supernatural character of its origin.

To steer clear both of rigid traditionalism and irreligion, the Jew will have to realize that religion is rooted in human nature, and that the belief in the existence of God, and the attributes ascribed to him, must be derived from and be made to refer to the experience of the average man and woman. The ability to negotiate the transition from the theurgic to the rational conception of religion is but a phase of the larger problem of spiritual readjustment which has prevailed since the days of Copernicus, and which has been accentuated with the acceptance of the Darwinian theory. Whatever his conception of the physical universe may be, assuming that man must come to terms with life and justify his spiritual striving, it should be possible to work out an affirmative spiritual adjustment in Jewish life in terms of the evolutionary conception of religion.

The reorientation which is essential to the survival of the Jewish religion cannot be effected merely by trying to harmonize the traditional teachings of religion with the results achieved by modern science. It calls for nothing less than an approach to the religious interpretation of life with the same unbiased empirical attitude as that which constitutes the spirit of science, that spirit which regards truth not as something absolute and final, but as an active process of the mind whereby error is gradually eliminated. A conflict between science and religion is possible only when we assume that our knowledge of God originates not from our understanding of the universe and of human life, but from some supernatural revelation which is entirely extraneous to the natural powers of the human mind. However, once we take for granted that our knowledge of God is necessarily based upon experience, and develops with it, all conflict between religion and science is precluded; for then all that is necessary to keep religion vital is to permit it to grow concurrently with experience.

The inclusion of religion within the scope of scientific thinking presupposes a much broader conception of science than that of a method of measuring phenomena, or tracing their sequences. The scientific spirit is synonymous with the application of intelligence to everything within the range of human experience, including ends as well as means, social and spiritual life as well as physical existence. So understood, it is to the interest of religion to submit itself to the scientific approach. To state the matter more concretely, it is to our advantage spiritually to submit all our religious ideas, habits and emotions to the scrutiny of intelligence. Emile Durkheim has stated the attitude of science toward religion with matchless clarity.

That which science refuses to grant to religion is not its right to exist, but its right to dogmatize upon the nature of things and the special competence which it claims for itself for knowing man and the world. As a matter of fact, it does not know itself. It does not even know what it is made of, nor to what need it answers. It is itself a subject for science, so far is it from being able to make the law for science. . . . However, it seems destined to transform itself rather than to disappear.[1]

The intelligence to which religion must henceforth learn to submit its content is that inclusive process of thought which views each aspect of reality as part of an inter-related whole. Intelligence does not preclude either intuition or mysticism, but intuition should not be confused with supernatural revelation, nor mysticism with intellectual surrender.

Formerly, when men found the religion of theophany and miracle untenable, they resorted to philosophic reasoning in the hope of discovering universal and eternal truths which were beyond cavil. But the modern thinker has at his disposal the history and psychology of religious experience. The knowledge of the various manifestations of religion among peoples of different stages of development, and of the forces of human nature, both individual and collective, that come into play in the manifold of religious beliefs and activities, makes it possible for him to discover those fundamental needs of human nature to which the God-idea answers. Those needs are far more universal and significant than the logical necessity of assuming a first cause or prime mover, which for the religious philosopher of former days was the main reason for believing in God.

There has, unfortunately, arisen a science of religion which has proved to be a snare and a delusion. It is the kind of approach which, by trespassing upon fields of inquiry beyond its scope, presumes to explain away the reality of God. That however should not prejudice us against the science of religion, which, by keeping strictly within its limitations, confines itself to the task of explaining how the God-idea has functioned in history. Such science is as indispensable to a proper understanding of religion as mathematics is to astronomy. The religion which it enables us to understand is not that of the metaphysician whose problem is the reality of God, but of the group, and of the individual in the group whose concern is with what God means to man and expects of him. The problem of the metaphysician is prior to science; the concern of the religious group or individual can best be understood in the light of science.

It is one thing to identify and name the factors which condition the conception of God—fear, dreams, ghosts, animism, the yearning for protection; it is quite another to infer that the conception of

God can be resolved entirely into the factors which condition it. The inference which reduces the God-idea to an illusion is not logically justified by the psychologic data of religion, but derives rather from an antipathy to religion. Psychologists who reduce the God-idea to an illusion disregard the changing character of the God-idea. They usually attack an outgrown God-idea, and overlook the fact which might have served at least as a psychologic datum, that as soon as one God-idea is discarded, another one, which is regarded as a closer approximation to the truth, emerges. They also forget that the very condemnation of an idea as illusory implies the existence of some reality which is regarded as the norm. *Why may not the quality of godhood reside in that very reality which serves as a criterion for rejecting as illusions the traditional or conventional ideas of God?*

Thus Freud in his recent attack on religion [2] starts out with the unwarranted assumption that "Religion consists of certain dogmas, assertions about facts and conditions of external (or internal) reality which tell one something that one has not oneself discovered and which claim that one should give them credence." [3] Nothing is easier than demolishing a man of straw. Why limit religion to dogmas that must be believed in? To be sure, authority still plays an important rôle in most people's religion. Not so long ago that was the case also with science. Yet no one would think of treating authority as an integral part of science. Just as science entered upon a new stage in its development when it replaced the deductive method with the inductive, so can religion parallel the progress of science by subjecting its own assumptions and processes to analysis. That a man of Freud's intellectual caliber should be guilty of confusing "religion" with a particular type of "religious doctrines" is, indeed, a case for psychoanalysis.

Psychology by itself is not concerned with the validity of the inferences we draw from our knowledge of the origin and nature of religious experience. In utilizing the psychological data to re-define our conception of God, we admittedly go as much beyond the province of psychology as do those who infer that the God-idea is an illusion. Why then should we prefer the inference which validates the God-idea rather than the one which negates it? Because the one indisputable fact which the psychology of religion reveals is that the God-idea is an expression of man's will-to-live. The idea as such may convey a wrong notion of God, but the reality which it seeks to identify or point to is no illusion. *God may not in any way resemble or correspond to the idea we form of him, but he is present in the very will-to-live, the reality of which we experience in every fiber of our being.* We cannot help interpreting this will-to-live as of cosmic significance. The universe, being an organic totality, determines and is determined by the least part within itself, and therefore determines and is determined, in however infinitesimal a way, by the life of man. Such a universe must needs be conceived as in rapport with the will-to-live which functions in every living being. By cooperating with that life urge, the universe has brought it to the point of development attained in man. As we better understand ourselves and our environment, we achieve a clearer knowledge of the circumstances that condition the cooperation between the living universe and our will-to-live. This growth in understanding includes the realization that all religious behavior is an attempt to discover and reckon with the conditions upon which that cooperation depends. We keep on blundering as to those conditions, but there can be no mistake about the reality and imperativeness of that cooperation.

Even the scientific interpretation of reality is a projection of our subjective need for order and unity. There is no way of proving that the picture of reality reconstructed by the physical sciences corresponds to the actual nature of things. Yet we do not become solipsists and conclude that we can never know the truth about the outer world. "What a deep faith in the rationality of the structure of the world," writes Albert Einstein, "and what a longing to understand even a small glimpse of the reason revealed to the world there must have been in Kepler and Newton to enable them to unravel the mechanism of the heavens in long years of lonely work." [4] The faith in the rationality of the structure of the world is but one aspect of the faith that has given rise to religion. Its antithesis is the skepticism which identifies life with unreason.

CHAPTER XXIII

THE PLACE OF RELIGION IN JEWISH LIFE

The relation of religion to the rest of Jewish life as conceived by the different Jewish groups—The dichotomy between the natural and the supernatural assumed in Neo-Orthodoxy—How the non-orthodox religionists view the divine aspect of reality—The meaning of the God-idea in the group religion—The fallacy in the Reformist conception of the Jewish religion—The fallacy in the Secularist conception—Some illustrations of the Religious-Cultural conception—When religion is vital.

It is futile to deplore the loss of credal uniformity which marked Jewish life in the past. The number of Jews no longer content to accept unquestionably the religious traditions of their people is definitely on the increase. They insist upon the right to think for themselves. The only limitation to which that right should be subject, if they want to remain Jews, is at least an unqualified acceptance of Jewish survival. No doubt diversity of belief will put a strain on Jewish unity, but, on the other hand, without the recognition of the right to differ Jewish unity would be disrupted. "A controversy which is for the sake of heaven," say the Sages, "will in the end lead to permanent results." A controversy in which the parties credit one another with well meaning purposes is bound to lead to constructive thinking and fruitful effort.

From the standpoint of the relation of religion to the rest of life, Jews who take an affirmative attitude toward Jewish survival may be divided into four distinct groups whose philosophies of Judaism are herewith given in outline form.

A. *The Neo-Orthodox*

1. The Jews have been in possession of a written and an oral Torah supernaturally revealed to the Israelites through Moses in the course of their journeying to the Promised Land.
2. Only those truths which are supernaturally revealed by God to man constitute true religion.
3. The Jewish differentia must consist henceforth, as it did hitherto, in the possession and cultivation of the religion supernaturally revealed at Sinai.

B. *The Reformists*

1. In the past the Jewish differentia consisted of a distinctive national-cultural life and a unique religion.
2. The national-cultural life was bound up with Palestine and gave rise to a distinctive Jewish civilization.
3. In that civilization the element of religion as the sum of beliefs and practices which center about the relation of man to God developed into ethical monotheism.
4. Though the element of religion was until modern times closely associated with the national-cultural life of the Jews, it achieved sufficient content of its own to be worthy of being fostered in its own right.
5. Now that emancipation makes it necessary for the Jews to surrender their national-cultural life, they can dispense with the cultural elements of their heritage and retain only the element of religion.
6. The Jewish differentia is henceforth to take the form of the historically evolved religion of ethical monotheism.

C. *The Secular-Culturists*

The Secular-Culturists agree with the Reformists in the first three propositions. But they add the following:

4. Now that the enlightenment has taught us to regard religion either as superfluous or as a matter to be left entirely to the individual, the Jews should cultivate their national life along secular lines.
5. The Jewish differentia is henceforth to take the form of secularized national culture.

D. *The Religious-Culturists**

The Religious-Culturists agree with the Reformists in the first three propositions, but add the following:

4. Religion and national-cultural life are so integrally related to each other as to be unable to function separately.
5. The emancipation and enlightenment have necessitated many changes in both concurrently.
6. The Jewish differentia is henceforth to take the form of a historically evolved civilization which is to reckon with the social and spiritual needs of the Jews as individuals and as a national entity.

It is evident from the foregoing outline that the point at issue is the nature of religion and its relation to the rest of human life.

---

* The group which is at present emerging and whose conception of Judaism it is the purpose of this book to crystallize.

The principal division of opinion is that between the Neo-Orthodox group, on the one hand, and the three non-orthodox groups, on the other. Orthodoxy * assumes that religion must be based upon an authentically attested supernatural revelation. That assumption presupposes a sharp dichotomy between the natural and the supernatural. To treat that distinction as relative or unimportant is to misinterpret orthodoxy. This applies especially to the belief with regard to the origin of the Torah. The basic doctrine of Judaism, according to orthodoxy, is that the Torah is *min ha-shamayim,* or supernaturally revealed. There are many who give to the term *min ha-shamayim* a metaphorical meaning. Whether they are right or wrong is not the question. But they cannot identify themselves with those who call themselves "Orthodox" because they deny the fundamental idea in the orthodox outlook when they refuse to abide by the implications of the absolute distinction between the natural and the supernatural.

From the standpoint of the orthodox dichotomy between the natural and the supernatural, it is easy to define the place of the Jewish people in the scheme of things. What differentiates the Jews from the rest of the world is the fact that they have been the sole recipients of direct communication from God. This does not mean that the divine communication was intended solely for them. It simply means that they were chosen to be the priests or mediators between God and mankind. They owe that privilege to the virtue of their ancestors. In their behalf alone did the miracles take place. All other peoples who wish to enjoy the fruits of obedience to the will of God must in some way recognize the more intimate relation of the Jews to the supernatural order.

In the world of today that same dichotomy in all its logical consequences is taken for granted by the Catholic church and by the major Protestant sects. The only difference between them and the Jews turns upon the questions as to what is to be regarded as the final and authoritative revelation of God, and as to which particular group has a right to lay claim to the possession of that final and authoritative revelation.

---

* Orthodoxy is the reaffirmation of traditionalism in the face of challenge. It therefore describes the attitude of a Philo, a Maimonides, or a Samson Raphael Hirsch. For purposes of clarity, the orthodoxy espoused by Hirsch is in this book designated "Neo-Orthodoxy."

The spokesmen of the non-orthodox groups have hardly ever come to grips with the basic principles underlying their respective philosophies of Judaism. This is undoubtedly the cause of much that is paradoxical in their thinking and self-contradictory in their action. One such basic principle has to do with the dichotomy of reality into the natural and supernatural. Although the non-orthodox have seldom had much to say on that question, there can be no doubt that for them the dichotomy does not exist. That fact is indeed the main reason for their taking issue with orthodoxy. But it deserves to be set forth in a more detailed and articulated form than has hitherto been the practice. This is especially true with regard to the Reformist and Religious-Cultural ideologies in which religion figures either as coextensive with Judaism or as its dominant element.

The implication in the Reformist and the Religious-Cultural ideologies is that religion is by no means committed, as is commonly believed, to the division of reality into the natural and the supernatural. It is a common fallacy to regard religion as always having been aware of that distinction. In the experience of those who lived in what might be considered the classic age of religion no such dichotomy can be discovered. Before the advent of philosophy the very contrast between natural and supernatural was inconceivable. A distinction was then noted, to be sure, between the usual everyday occurrences and extraordinary occurrences like storms, earthquakes, pestilences and wars. But they were never conceived as belonging to such different orders of existence as the natural and the supernatural.

The "natural" is more than a synonym for the regular and the usual. Natural has a specific meaning which is intended to correct one of the basic assumptions of the unphilosophic mind. It denotes the fact that the action of each thing is conditioned by the law of its own being. That law cannot be altered by any will acting from without. To the unphilosophic or unscientific mind all things appear as being acted upon extraneously by quasi-human wills or a single quasi-human will. Philosophic apologetics aside, God is conceived in Scriptures and in rabbinic literature more or less anthropomorphically. His will, though infinitely superior in power, justice and goodness to that of man, resembles it in the consciousness of the specific purposes it seeks to achieve. From that viewpoint nothing possesses a law of its own being. All things act in accordance with the will of God, which is conceived as entirely extraneous to their essence or attributes. In such a universe of thought there can be no such thing as supernatural since it lacks the concept of the natural. The attempt to bring the pre-philosophic universe of discourse into harmony with the philosophic universe of discourse inherited from the Greek thinkers engaged the minds of theologians, Jewish, Christian and Mohammedan, for fifteen centuries. *The dichotomy of reality into natural and supernatural is, as a matter of fact, nothing more than the admission of failure on their part to arrive at a satisfactory solution.*

The approach to reality, characteristic of modern thought, has rendered the dichotomy of natural and supernatural irrelevant. The tendency nowadays is to enlarge the concept of the natural so that it might include that *plus* aspect of reality which the traditional outlook did indeed sense but not altogether apprehend. From various quarters there have been launched onslaughts against the oversimplified view of nature as synonymous with the working of blind mechanical forces. All advanced thinking nowadays tends to recognize that the mechanistic interpretation of existence is only a half-truth. The fact that the minutest fraction of reality is determined by the whole of reality, and that each living organism determines as a totality the behavior of every part of itself, introduces the entire cluster of meanings and values which constitute the spiritual aspect of life.

This departure from the mechanistic interpretation of existence has a special bearing on human life and human relationships. In the case of man, there is the added factor of self-consciousness. That factor gives to man the consciousness of his own unity as a person. Through the unity of his person he becomes intuitively aware of that phase of reality with which he has gropingly and blunderingly tried to reckon in his various religions. In the past, however, man always imagined himself as standing outside reality conceived as a whole. When, therefore, he sensed the inter-relatedness which gave to reality that meaning out of which he derived his various notions of godhood, it did not occur to him to look for that same type of meaning in his own personality. Only an occasional gleam of the truth that the human being possesses more of godhood than anything else in his environment flashed across man's mind, as, for instance, when he achieved the notion that he was created in the image of God. But that gleam was only for a moment. It has had to be recaptured by increased self-knowledge for man to realize that he belongs *within* reality, the whole of which determines his life.

Man has come to understand that the act of contemplating reality in its wholeness does not place him outside reality. He now realizes that the inter-relatedness which is the source of his awareness of godhood operates within him, no less than outside him. *Thus is eliminated the very need of making any dichotomy either between the universe of man and the universe of God, or between the natural and the supernatural. There is only one universe within which both man and God exist.* The so-called laws of nature represent the manner of God's immanent functioning. The element of creativity, which is not accounted for by the so-called laws of nature, and which points to the organic character of the universe or its life as a whole, gives us a clue to God's transcendent functioning. God is not an identifiable being who stands outside the universe. *God is the life of the universe, immanent insofar as each part acts upon every other, and transcendent insofar as the whole acts upon each part.*

Whether the modern man's conception of God as here formulated be correct or not, it serves the purpose of illustrating how those who cannot accept the orthodox view of religion manage to find a place for the God-idea within the field of natural experience. They resolve the conflict between religion and science. From their standpoint religion can have reference, not to an aspect of reality which exists entirely outside the order identified as nature, but to an aspect of reality which is not taken into account in what is ordinarily called a naturalistic approach. When the modern man studies reality scientifically, he abstracts from it certain specific aspects, such as the physical, the chemical, the biological, the psychological. When, in addition, he tries to grasp the *significance* of the parts of reality in their relation to the whole, and of the whole in its relation to the parts, there emerges that entire universe of values in which are reflected his yearnings to be at one with life at its best. To recognize this is to sense the divine aspect of reality.

There are many who hold that the belief in God which is based merely upon human experience cannot have the objectivity that we associate with scientific truth. In taking this attitude, they are merely voicing a feeling of homesickness after the belief in supernaturalism which they have not altogether outgrown. There is no reason why a conception of God should be less objective than any other conception that is based on experience. There is a way of checking its validity. It must not only harmonize with other elements in our experience, but must lend to them even greater unity and meaning than they derive from the arts and sciences. The power to help us orient ourselves to life, to elicit the best of which we are capable and to render us immune to the worst that may befall us is the pragmatic test to validate a conception of God. To that extent at least a God-idea based on experience is analogous to a scientific conclusion, and like it possesses objectivity.

Those who intend to cultivate Jewish religion as a normal reaction to life must realize that it is subject to the laws of human nature which determine the relation of religion to the rest of human life. They should resort, therefore, to the empirical sciences of human nature and society for the purpose of noting how the God-idea has actually functioned in the life of men and nations. They would readily discover that the God-idea of group religion is least of all an idea or system of ideas. Ratiocination plays a very minor part in collective religion; emotion and conation practically monopolize the whole of it. The God-idea in every collective religion functions not as an intellectual assent to a proposition, but as an organic acceptance of certain elements in the life and environment of the group, or of reality as a whole in its relation to the group, as contributing to one's self-fulfillment or salvation. Such organic acceptance is articulated in the adjective "holy" which is applied to whatever object is accepted in this spirit.

Long before the human being was able to formulate the idea "God," he was aware that there were elements in his environment, certain animate and inanimate objects, definite places, particular persons upon whose help he depended for the fulfillment of his needs. He ascribed to them power, which he believed he could direct to his advantage by resorting to actions and formulas which we term magic, because they had no intrinsic connection with the results which he wanted to obtain. As he grew in self-consciousness, he also grew more conscious of the clan or tribe to which he belonged. This led to his awareness that the magic practices to which he resorted were shared by the other members of his group. There then dawned upon him the realization that overarching the dependence upon the particular elements in his environment was his dependence upon his group. As a consequence the indispensable elements in the life and environment of the group acquired that additional significance for him which he tried to convey by viewing them and conducting himself toward them as holy. With that the notion of godhood began to emerge, for *psychologically, the notion of godhood is the precipitate of the notion of holiness.* A holy being is synonymous with a divine being. As man developed further, he extended the domain of holiness to include not only visible or picturable objects, events and persons, but also customs, laws, social relationships, truths and ideals.

This natural human trait, which finds expression in the sense of holiness, long antedated the traditional conception of religion as a supernatural phenomenon, and will continue to function long after supernaturalism as a method of interpreting life will have disappeared. It is a mistake to infer from the infrequency of the terms "holy" and "holiness" in the present-day vocabulary that the human mind is growing disaccustomed to the kind of response which those words implied. Psychologically the terms "worth" and "significance" refer to the same type of reaction as holiness. There is fashion in words as well as in dress. People nowadays prefer to speak of objects or persons they consider indispensable to human life as possessing high worth. But there are moments in every person's life, no matter how prosaic or matter of fact, when "holy" is the only word that can adequately express what he feels about certain things, persons or ideals.

The foregoing description of the manner in which the God-idea arose and developed points to the human factor that is common to all religions. At the same time it helps us understand what it is that really differentiates one religion from another. It becomes clear that we are on the wrong track entirely when we try to discover differences in world-outlook between one religion and another. Careful study will reveal surprisingly much in common among religions that are most hostile to each other. Group religions differ from each other mainly by virtue of the fact that they belong to different groups, and therefore refer to different constellations of *sancta*. Each religion has its own objects, persons, places and events that are deemed holy, or occupy a place of supreme value in the collective consciousness of its adherents.

This truth is sufficiently recognizable when we deal with ancient religions, each of which had its own sacred trees, waters, stones and mountains, but escapes us when we deal with the great historical religions. Yet a moment's careful consideration would reveal the same truth with regard to the latter. The beginnings of the Jewish religion are marked by rivalry between the Canaanitish *sancta* and the *sancta* which the Israelites brought with them from the wilderness, between the bull image and the ark of YHWH, between the local sanctuaries and the sanctuary at Jerusalem. In the very process of upholding the claims of the Israelitish *sancta* there emerged the great spiritual conceptions and moral ideals which have rendered them of universal import. It is interesting to note how the mere fact that the Samaritans insisted upon having their sanctuary at Mount Gerizim was enough to constitute them adherents of a different religion from the Jewish. Likewise Christianity branched off from the Jewish religion by adding the person of Jesus to the other Jewish *sancta*, though the early Christians, as is known, conformed to Jewish rites, accepted all the beliefs and honored all the *sancta* of the Jewish religion. It was a correct instinct which guided the church to declare the first instead of the seventh day holy, for if the church had observed the same day, its religion would not have been sufficiently distinct from the religion of the Jews.

In spite, however, of the unmistakable distinctiveness of religions from the standpoint of their *sancta,* there is bound to be considerable overlapping in the domain of social relations and universal truths and ideals. It is this circumstance which often misleads people into believing that all religions are fundamentally one, and the reason we have many religions is that their adherents are too blind and prejudiced to recognize that fact. The individual who contemplates God may experience a kind of "drunken joy and surprise" at the wonder of life. The God-idea may remain with him purely as a state of mind, and does not have to be externalized. But when the God-idea is the outcome of collective experience, then it cannot avoid being externalized. Of the three constitutive elements that enter into any mental reaction, to make a rough estimate, we should say that in a collective God-idea there is a small part of ideation, a larger share of emotion while the largest element is conation. Concretely speaking, this means that a group religion is least of all a *philosophy* of life. Its function primarily is to invest with sanctity not life in general, but specific objects, persons, places, events, days, etc., and specific codes of law, customs and morals.

If we would visualize the rôle of collective religion in this realistic fashion, we would not make the mistake of expecting a collective religion to justify its existence by being logically diverse from other collective religions. Each group religion is different in substance or entity from every other group religion, as one mind is different from another. The *raison d'être* of the existence of separate minds is by no means their logical diversity. Collective religions, likewise, being to the group what self-consciousness is to the individual, derive their justification from their ability to further the existence of the group and to develop its spiritual potentialities.

If these generalizations concerning religion are correct, we possess a criterion whereby we may judge the tenability of the different non-orthodox conceptions of the Jewish religion. The crucial assumption in the Reformist position is that religion and national-cultural life are inherently independent of each other, and that it is, therefore, possible to retain the element of religion without any of the elements which constitute national-cultural life. To do that consistently, Reformism would have to eliminate from Jewish religion all those elements which are of a concrete nature, since their very concreteness identifies them with the substance of national-cultural life. The most conspicuous concrete object which Reformism has consistently eliminated from Jewish religion has been *Ereṣ Yisrael*. But it should have gone much further. It should have so completely denationalized the Jewish religion as not to permit any national event to stand out as significant. The exodus from Egypt, the journey in the wilderness, or the Maccabean revolt may have had an important bearing on the spiritual life of mankind, yet why should those events have been singled out to the exclusion of so many other numberless events in the history of mankind which have contributed to the shaping of human destiny? The same applies to the heroes of Jewish history. A universal religion ought to show no preference for the heroes of any one particular people. It ought to contain a sort of pantheon to which heroes of all nationalities should be admitted. Least warranted is the retention of the Hebrew language as part of Jewish religious practice. It should have been entirely omitted from the Jewish prayer-book. A consistent application of the theory that religion is capable of being completely separated from the national and cultural values of Jewish life would require that religion confine itself to abstract truths about the nature of God, the world and man and to ethical principles of a universal character. It ought not even include such duties as a Jew owes to his fellow-Jews by reason of certain historic, racial or national ties. From the Reformist viewpoint, voluntary choice and not birth ought to constitute the basis of adherence to the Jewish religion.

To be sure, Reformism has sought to account for its inconsistencies by the idea that Jews are not only members of one religion, but also members of one race, and that the retention of many distinctively Jewish practices is to be accounted for not so much on religious as on racial grounds. Fearing, however, that this explanation might not prove satisfactory, Reformism has added another. It claims that while a religion is essentially a system of truths and ideals which must find expression in ethical practice, there is a need of having some concrete rites and ceremonies that might give continuity to that religion. The lameness of this justification is altogether too apparent, since there is nothing in the Reformist conception of the nature of ethical monotheism that calls for the sense of continuity. Continuity is relevant and desirable only from the standpoint of living and changing entities. The Jewish religion as an expression of the Jewish people necessarily demands guarantees of continuity, but as a system of universal truth, it needs no such guarantees.

The fundamental fallacy of the Reformist position is that it confuses religious philosophy with historical religion. A religious philosophy is a world-outlook which is achieved as a result of reflection. It is essentially a matter of personal choice and is generally confined to the selection of certain truths, ideals or principles of conduct supremely important to the salvation of the human being, regardless of race, nationality or historical background. A religious philosophy can be fitted into any civilization because it need not be the outgrowth of any one civilization. It is, as a rule, cosmopolitan in origin, and therefore cosmopolitan in application. Like science, it may serve as a common denominator of all civilizations.

It is far otherwise with a historical religion. A historical religion is a group religion. It consists of group habits before it comes to possess well-defined ideas. It is acquired through the medium of the civilization into which one is born. It is transmitted from parent to child in the same way as language. The child has as little choice in group religion as he has in language. A group religion functions chiefly as a process of sanctifying certain concrete elements of the particular civilization to which it belongs. The process of sanctification consists in treating certain facts, events, places, things, times and human beings that figure prominently in the life of the group as indispensable to the self-fulfillment or salvation of that group. The difference between a philosophic and a historic religion is like the difference between the general principles of symphonic structure and the Ninth Symphony of Beethoven.

This process of sanctification takes place in accordance with what may be termed "the law of particularity." It acts in a reverse manner from that which is characteristic of a religious philosophy. A religious philosophy is a series of generalizations which are abstracted from the varied experiences of mankind and are therefore regarded as applicable to human life as a whole. In group religion, however, the object of concern is a particular milieu to which human beings are committed, generally by reason of birth and heritage. The task of the historical religion consists in rendering that milieu efficacious in eliciting from its adherents the best that is in them. It accomplishes that by attaching high worth and significance to certain concrete elements in the milieu. The cluster of concrete elements thus singled out becomes the content of the historical religion. Jewish religion is the cluster of concrete elements within the civilization, which figure in the consciousness of the Jew as indispensable to his self-fulfillment or salvation. That it shares high ethical and spiritual ideals with other historical religions and religious philosophies cannot be denied. That its value, in the last analysis, depends upon the degree to which it succeeds in rendering the Jews ethical and spiritual in their dealings and relationships with their fellow-men goes without saying. But all this does not minimize one whit the truth that the *unicum* in the Jewish religion, the distinctive and colorful part of it, consists of the nexus of specific *sancta*, heroes, events, things, places, etc., that are inconceivable except as part of a national civilization.

The conception which the Secular-Culturists have of the Jewish religion is, in a sense, an inverted Reformism. It proceeds from the same fallacy that ignores the fundamental distinction between a religious philosophy and an historical religion. With the Secular-Culturists, however, this fallacy serves as a major premise for the conclusion that it is possible, yea necessary, for the Jews to eliminate religion as an expression of their collective life. It is true that they do not make the mistake of the Reformists who fail to realize the implications of the fact that the Jews are committed to a specific social and cultural milieu. On the contrary, the Secular-Culturists go far in their efforts to live up to what is implied in that commitment. To them the Jewish problem is essentially the problem of the happiness of the men and women who constitute the Jewish people. But they claim that the happiness of these men and women can be adequately achieved, and provision for its attainment secured, without religion. If an individual Jew is interested in interpreting the content of Jewish life in terms of the God-idea, he can do so on his own responsibility. But the Jews as a group should not be expected to subscribe to any one interpretation of life in preference to any other.

This contention of the Secular-Culturists seems tenable so long as we think of religion in terms of individual outlook that finds expression in abstract truths and ideals about life and duty. But in the light of the actual nature of historical religion, such a contention ignores the laws of human nature and society. Whenever human beings cooperate for any length of time and develop common interests, they invariably come to regard their salvation as conditioned by those common interests which will inevitably be found to center around specific objects, persons, places and events. In the very assumption that salvation is an achievable goal there is the making of an affirmative attitude toward Reality, an attitude which becomes articulate in some version of the God-idea.

The Secular-Culturists maintain that the trend of modern civilizations is to omit religion from the roster of activities for which any political group, be it city or state, organized on modern lines is ready to assume responsibility. If the Jews want their civilization to take its place among modern civilizations, they should follow the example of the progressive nations which have disestablished their churches. In reasoning thus the Secular-Culturists show themselves victims of half-truths which are based upon a superficial reading of the facts. They misjudge entirely what is actually happening to institutional religion. It is true that among the great nations of the world the historic religions are on the wane. But that is due to the fact that in becoming nations and developing their national life, they sensed the incongruity of depending upon the *sancta* of an ancient oriental civilization for the individual and collective salvation of their citizens. The Christian religion is not native to any of the peoples that live by it, and, therefore, never really became an organic part of any of the European cultures. This is in essence the significance of the *Kulturkampf* which has been going on in the occidental world ever since the establishment of the church, and which will be waged for a long time. Ultimately, however, each civilization will organize its own *sancta* into a collective religion to fill the void left by the shrinking of Christianity.

It is absurd to regard, as the Secular-Culturists do, the changes going on in the inner life of the Jews as an extension of the *Kulturkampf*. The relation of the Jewish religion to the Jewish people is in no way analogous to the relation of the Christian religion to the so-called Christian peoples. The Jewish religion consists of the very substance which went into the creation of the collective consciousness of the Jewish people. Take away the traditional *sancta* from the Christian peoples, and there are revealed the really creative elements in their civilizations. Take away the traditional *sancta* from the Jewish people, and there is nothing left to account for its past. There remains a very small spiritual capital, indeed, on which to build a Jewish future. Changes will undoubtedly take place in the beliefs and practices that have hitherto constituted the Jewish religion, but they will be within the scope of the historical *sancta*. The Jewish religion will never suffer the fate of the Christian religion. It will never have to be replaced by a religion more native and integral to the social heritage of which it is a part.

Whatever may be the outcome of the changes taking place in the spiritual life of other nations, there can be no doubt that in the case of the Jews, their collective life will naturally retain the level of self-consciousness, and will therefore continue to find expression through its historic *sancta*. Of this we may be sure, because the Jews have a religion which was not imposed upon them from without; because the *nisus* to Jewish collective life in the diaspora, deriving mainly from the momentum of the past, functions chiefly through the specific objects, places, personalities and events around which the Jews have built up the mental associations of sanctity.

Bearing in mind that historical religion is the sanctification of specific elements in the group life, and, inversely, that group life naturally gives rise to the sanctification of some of the specific elements in it, we cannot but conclude that historical religion without group life is empty of content, and is merely a way of speaking. *Group life which refuses to be merely a replica of a community of ants is bound to find expression in collective religion.*

From the standpoint of reckoning with the integral relationship that exists between religion and the rest of life, the Religious-Cultural conception of Judaism is at one with the Neo-Orthodox conception. To the oft-quoted dictum about the oneness of God, Israel and Torah the Religious-Cultural group can conscientiously subscribe. This apparent agreement accounts for the tendency to identify the members of that group as orthodox. For the sake of clarity, however, it is necessary to realize that the unanimity with regard to the integral relationship between religion and nationality is compatible with a radical divergence of opinion concerning the practical corollaries emanating from that relationship.

It is possible, for example, both for the Neo-Orthodox and the Religious-Culturists to agree that the Jewish religion is indissolubly bound up with *Ereṣ Yisrael*. But the conclusions to which that agreement leads are a universe apart. To the Neo-Orthodox the bond between Jewish religion and *Ereṣ Yisrael* means the retention of that entire nexus of ideas concerning that land which are found in the Bible and rabbinic literature. Anyone who is imbued with those ideas finds it strictly consistent to do nothing more than continue reciting daily the various prayers thanking God for having given the land to his forefathers. For the Religious-Culturist, however, the consequences which result from the integral relationship between culture and religion would, of necessity, find expression in the serious attempts to engage in all those efforts to rebuild *Ereṣ Yisrael*, which are part of the Zionist movement. In other words, the wide divergence in the consequences following from the same assumption with regard to the interdependence of Jewish nationhood and Jewish religion is evident in the wide chasm that divides the *Agudists* from the Zionists. This exemplifies what contradictory conclusions may be drawn from the acceptance of religion and group life as interdependent. The nature of the conclusion depends entirely upon the interpretation placed upon that interdependence.

If the Religious-Culturists' point of view gives the impression of being at one with Neo-Orthodoxy in its recognition of the interdependence of the national and religious elements of Judaism, it gives the impression of being at one with Reformism in recognizing the evolutionary aspect of both of these elements. It assumes that the form in which Judaism has come down to us is the result of a series of changes and adjustments in the past, and that to readjust, reinterpret and reconstruct both cultural and religious values with a view of making them function under the present totally different conditions is not only legitimate but imperative. The emphasis upon the need for reconstruction implied in the Religious-Cultural conception of Judaism is apt to identify it in the minds of some with Reformism. Many Religious-Culturists who are associated with Reformist congregations delude themselves into believing that they can consistently accept the Reformist ideology. This only adds to the confusion in Jewish life.

Even the freedom from the traditional prepossessions with regard to the supernatural origin of the Jewish religion, and assent to the principle of conscious and deliberate revaluation and adaptation to spiritual needs are not sufficient grounds for identifying the Religious-Cultural with the Reformist conception of Judaism. The two conceptions differ radically in their approach to the practical task of living as a Jew. The Reformists take for granted, that as soon as the Jewish religion is brought up to date, it will be able so to influence the Jew's belief and conduct that he will feel perfectly at home in the world and will be induced to lead the good life. All that the Jew will have to do to achieve salvation will be to expose himself to the Jewish religion in that perfected form. But what is to guarantee that the perfected religion will prove spiritually satisfying? If the primary purpose of the Jewish religion is to satisfy the spiritual hunger of the individual Jew, why condemn him if he finds he can satisfy that hunger far more effectively by becoming a Christian Scientist? The Reformist approach which places upon the Jewish religion the burden of justifying itself cannot avoid coming up against a blind alley of that kind.

From the Religious-Cultural point of view it is not the function of the Jewish heritage to validate itself by providing a fully satisfying religion, but it is the duty of the Jew so to interpret and utilize the elements of that heritage as to fulfill himself through it. As soon as the Jew finds the content of his heritage sufficiently satisfying and exalting to be a means to his salvation, however he may conceive salvation, he has Jewish religion. This shifting of the responsibility for the effectiveness of the heritage sets the moral duty of the Jew in its proper light. Since it devolves upon him to render his heritage capable of yielding salvation, he has no right to repudiate that heritage when he finds it none too easy to cultivate, or none too productive of spiritual values without tremendous exertion on his part. The disparity between the basic assumptions of his heritage and those of the contemporary world is often baffling. None the less, if he wants to remain a Jew and have Jewish religion, he must find some way of making his heritage of supreme import to him.

If, then, we are to understand by Jewish religion such interpretation and utilization of all that goes to make up Jewish life as may render it a means to the self-realization or salvation of the Jews both individually and collectively, we should have no difficulty in formulating concretely the kind of program which their religion at the present time calls for. Taking as our basis the well-known trilogy, God, Israel and Torah, that program would have to indicate what interpretations and uses of Israel and Torah would lead the Jew to experience the reality of God. This presupposes a kind of Jewish nationhood and a form of Jewish civilization that would evoke the maximum of good latent in the individual and in the group. To be a Jew religiously is to go to all lengths in actualizing the potentialities of the Jewish people so that it may attain its moral and spiritual maximum.

The Religious-Cultural program would, in the first place, demand that the Jew bend every possible effort to help his people become a factor for the good life. Social interaction with one's Jewish contemporaries must be made conducive to ethical and spiritual living. That is a radically different approach from the Reformist program in which the source of inspiration to the good life is not the actual give-and-take between the Jew and his people, but the contemplation of an Israel that is more of a memory than a present fact. *From the standpoint of the Religious-Cultural program, whatever helps to produce creative social interaction among Jews rightly belongs to the category of Jewish religion, because it contributes to the salvation of the Jew.* Hence a movement like spiritual Zionism, the purpose of which is to keep the Jews of the world united and creative, is entitled to a place in the Jewish religion.

Spiritual Zionism cannot content itself merely with the rebuilding of Palestine. If the Jews throughout the world are to be united and creative, they must not only have a spiritual center in Palestine; wherever they live in considerable numbers they must organize themselves into vigorous communities. The associated life of a Jewish community should not be regarded as extraneous to Jewish religion. It is the very substance out of which the Jew must strive to evolve religious values. Cooperation on a communal scale is the *sine qua non* of a genuine and sustained interest in Jewish religion. The present anarchic condition of Jewish life gives an air of unreality to any social or spiritual idealism which looks to the Jewish people for its sanction. Jews have to rely altogether too much upon the reputation of their ancestors or the promise of greatness in their descendants to be moved to sacrifice the present for the future. This is far from being a sign of moral health. To raise the present status of the Jews from a disintegrated and fragmented mass of individuals into an organic unity, whether it be the unity of the Jewish people as a whole, or of any part of it, is to create the conditions that make the Jewish religion possible. What the oil and the wick are to the flame, organized Jewish life is to Jewish religion.

So long as the God-idea finds expression in the sanctification of concrete objects, events, ideals, institutions and other elements in the life of a people, it has a chance of being interwoven with the people's needs and interests and therefore of possessing vitality. But as soon as it is abstracted from the texture of *sancta,* it becomes a subject for metaphysics. Medieval theology, failing to appreciate this peculiarity of the God-idea in religion, treated it in its abstract form, as in mathematics we treat numbers apart from existing things. The result was a confusion between religion and metaphysics, with detrimental consequences to both. Thus, for example, the question whether God created the world out of nothing or out of a pre-existing substance became a burning issue in medieval religion among Jews and non-Jews. That this mistake in abstracting the God-idea from the part it played in religion is avoided by modern theologians is evident from the fact that to them the question of *creatio ex nihilo* has lost all relevance.[1]

Medieval theology, likewise, started out with the assumption that God was the one perfect being who was omnipotent and omniscient. It then reasoned backward to fundamental axioms to establish the truth of this assumption, and reasoned forward to square this assumption with the stubborn facts of life. Traditional theology was performing a gratuitous task in trying to justify the suffering and evil of the world. It might go on with that task to the crack of doom and never get one whit further than Job's friends who were asked, after all their labor in defending God: "Will ye speak unrighteously for the Lord, and talk deceitfully for him?" [2] Not only has such theology fallen on evil days; it is dragging religion down with it, that religion which is an affirmation of life's worthwhileness, and which should not be tied up with any particular theology.

The God-idea is not the reasoned allocation of chaos, cruelty, pain and death in some neat logical scheme. It is the passionate refusal of every atom in the human being to be terrified by these ogres. The God-idea is not an idea but the reaction of the entire organism to life, the reaction by which man's will-to-live overcomes the fears and the miseries that only a being of his mental capacity can know. Oswald Spengler correctly describes religion as "the desire for freedom from the anxieties and anguishes of waking consciousness; for relaxation of the tensions of fear-born thought and search; for the obliteration and removal of the consciousness of the Ego's loneliness in the universe, the rigid conditionedness of nature, the prospect of the immovable boundary of all Being in eld and death." [3]

The God-idea in religion is not the product of reasoning, but of the complex of factors in the history of a people which, by revealing to it life's meaning, have become its *sancta*. If the *sancta* which kept religion alive in the past will make for a greater measure of health, goodness, order, reason, beauty and meaning in the world, the religion of the past will undergo a metamorphosis which will give it a new lease of life. *Whether the Jews will be able to vitalize the* sancta *of their religion is still to be seen. If as a people they fail in that, there is nothing else in which they can succeed.*

The hope that there will arise a religion which will be universally acceptable is chimerical. In the future, religion, both group and personal, will be based upon the kind of experience that can be integrated with the modern approach to reality. This implies that a group which will express its life, its memories and aspirations in terms of religion will endeavor to bring its religion into conformity with the highest needs of human nature, which are universal. The particularity of the religion will not be due to the profession of some truth or teaching that is necessarily denied by the religion of some other group, but to the fact that the experiences, upon which the particular religion is based, and in terms of which its liturgical forms are expressed, are peculiar to the group professing that religion. This view is entertained by the average intelligent layman who often displays a more correct intuition into the nature of religion than the learned theologian. Claude G. Montefiore expresses the official view of Reformism when he declares that the ceremonies of Judaism must have as universal a significance as its doctrines. But his critics take a far more correct view of the matter. "True religious doctrines," says one of them, "must ultimately be shared by all men. Truth is universal and not national. But why should not each race preserve its own national ceremonial? Israel, in keeping the Passover, celebrates *Israel's* deliverance from Egypt. Will (or can) the keeping of the Passover ever become general amongst those to whom it is not connected with the same historical associations? Provided there be unity, diversity of ceremonial need not keep races and nations apart. I conceive the Judaism of the future as becoming conscious of itself as a branch of universal religion." [4] Another critic writes, "A denationalized Passover, that is, a religious festival arranged for all nations, with all the national element left out, might be religious in a Theistic sense, but it could not be called Jewish." [5]

If progress means further complexity and differentiation, religion must be many to satisfy man's needs. Religion will be one and universal insofar as it will come to be identified more and more with the experience of life's momentousness and worthwhileness. It will be many and multiform insofar as different individuals and groups will look to different sancta as the symbols and proof of life's worthwhileness. This union of universalism and manifoldness in religion will lead to a type of tolerance which is dictated not by the necessity of common political action but by a deepened understanding of the place of religion in human life.[6] The mutual toleration of religions can come about only through the recognition that each religion must strive to have its beliefs and practices meet the universal needs of human nature, and that each religion must cultivate the uniqueness which arises from the particular civilization constituting its background.

Religion thus conceived will be vital because it will respond not to imaginary but actual needs. It is in this spirit that the Jewish civilization will have to transform, revaluate and augment its traditional religious values and render them vital for our day.

CHAPTER XXIV

THE FOLK ASPECT OF THE JEWISH RELIGION

The relation of religious rites to group consciousness—Folk religion a means to group continuity—Patriotism merely the modern form of folk religion—Christianity an imperialistic patriotism—Folk religion destined to survive—The main implication of folk religions for diaspora Jewry—Public worship an indispensable element of folk religion—The essentials of Jewish public worship.

RELIGION always constitued an integral part of a civilization, insofar as it accentuated the significance and momentousness of the particular social group through which man achieved his personality. To take part in the religious behavior of the group was always obligatory upon each member of a class, tribe or nation. Through such participation the group became an instrument for eliciting the most intense social emotions in the human being, thereby accustoming him to transcend his self-seeking instincts. Whenever a situation arose in which the desires of the individual conflicted with the well-being of the group, he had to make a choice. But since the religion which he shared with his group left little doubt of what his choice should be, it habituated him in envisaging the imperious demand of the group. At first perhaps he yielded reluctantly, but in the end he so identified himself with the group-will that he came to experience through it the sense of self-fulfillment. Thus man entered on the long process of taming himself—a process still in its initial stages.

All such means of control, and occasions for privation and sacrifice, as contribute to the development of personality have their origin in the collective life of the group. In order, however, that the individual shall submit to this group control, even to privation and sacrifice, he must be aware of the pressure of collective life, even when that pressure does not take the form of physical compulsion. This function was performed by his belief in gods. The gods should not be put in the same class with spirits, genii, jinns or devils. The latter were imaginary beings that moved about in the world unbeholden and not responsible to anyone. But the gods, however arbitrary they were believed to be, were considered as the patrons and guardians of man, interested in the welfare of the group that acknowledged them as gods. They thus served to symbolize and represent to the individual what he would otherwise have been unable to grasp—the clan, tribe or nation as an organic entity.

Emile Durkheim, in his study of the elementary forms of religion to determine their relation to social life, clearly indicates the part played by religious rites in the development of group consciousness:

When the Australians scattered in little groups, he says, spend their time in hunting and fishing, they lose sight of whatever concerns their clan or tribe: their only thought is to catch as much game as possible. On feast days, on the contrary, these preoccupations are necessarily eclipsed; being essentially profane, they are excluded from these sacred periods. At this time their thoughts are centered upon their common beliefs, their common traditions, the memory of their great ancestors, the collective ideal of which they are the incarnation; in a word, upon social things. Even the material interests which these great religious ceremonies are designed to satisfy concern the public order and are therefore social. Society as a whole is interested that the harvest be abundant, that the rain fall at the right time and not excessively, that the animals reproduce regularly. So it is society that is in the foreground of every consciousness; it dominates and directs all conduct; that is equivalent to saying that it is more living and active, and consequently more real, than in profane times.[1]

In reflecting the most important group interests by means of rites and symbols derived from the activities by which those interests are furthered, a religion fortifies the collective consciousness. The religious consciousness is, thus, the most intimate phase of the group consciousness.[2]

The universality of initiation ceremonies makes it evident that the function of religion is to hold up to the individual the worth of the group and the importance of his complete identification with it. Those ceremonies necessarily call attention to the advantage of being able to share the life of one's family, tribe or clan, and thus point to a high degree of awareness of the collective unit of which one is a part. That unit includes not only those who are contemporary with the initiate but also his dead forebears. The bond which unites the living with the dead is not only physical but spiritual, for the living regard themselves bound to their ancestors by the traditions and lore handed down to them. The initiation ceremonies do not merely seek to protect the initiate against the mysterious forces that are released by the physiological fact of bodily maturity. They are not merely theurgic practices carried out as a means to some immediate or practical end.

> We see at once, says B. Malinowski, that religion does something more, . . . than the mere 'sacralizing of a crisis of life.' From a natural event it makes a social transition, to the fact of bodily maturity it adds the vast conception of entry into manhood with its duties, privileges, responsibilities, above all with its knowledge of tradition and the communion with sacred things and beings. There is thus a creative element in the rites of a religious nature. The act establishes not only a social event in the life of the individual but also a spiritual metamorphosis, both associated with the biological event but transcending it in importance and significance.[3]

Religion fostered not only the sense of group unity among all the contemporary members of the clan, tribe or nation, but also of group continuity. In the earlier religions of mankind, the gods did not belong to a transcendent order of existence. They were merely a higher order of chieftains or rulers, and part of the society of their worshippers. But since the gods possessed the additional advantage of immortality, they not only limited those of their devotees who were contemporaneous but also many generations of their worshippers. Thus it was through the medium of the gods that the individual grew aware of his people, not only as a group existing in the present, but as one whose life extended far into the past, and was expected to endure eternally.[4]

If we analyze the evident fact that the human species evolved from savagery to civilization through the operation of the social instinct, we find that those groups or cultural units survived in which the individual learned to consider his personal existence less valuable than the existence of the group. This habit of behavior without which civilization is inconceivable, has been bred into the very substance of the mental life of humanity by religion. Through its ideals, customs and traditions, religion has enhanced the importance of the cultural group to which one belonged.

Even religious doctrines and dogmas, which seem to be expressive of general truths, served to consolidate the group and to emphasize its importance. Apart from their content, the fact that religious beliefs had to be accepted unquestioningly, and that to doubt or reject them was to be guilty of sacrilege, indicates their social significance. Judging from the nature of the beliefs usually stressed in the historical religions, it seems that emphasis always went with incredibility, as though their being in conflict with reason enabled them to test the loyalty of the individual to his group. In fact, there seems to be a great deal of truth in the witticism that a religious dogma is a doctrine which people have ceased to believe.

It has been chiefly in advanced religions that the indispensability of the group as a means of salvation has been consciously stressed. Christianity has decreed, "No salvation outside the Church." [5] This ruling is nothing more than a carry-over from the Jewish religion of the requirement of membership in Israel as a prerequisite to salvation. Such a requirement is entirely in keeping with the inescapable law of human nature that only through interaction with his group can the individual achieve personality and self-fulfillment or salvation. Those who flee society do so because of the sense of frustration which they could have acquired only through society. The needs which they expect to satisfy in solitude are those which they never would have experienced apart from their social environment. The tendency of human life is to render the individual human being increasingly dependent upon the group into which he is born and by which he is bred. *This implies that one's people will always constitute one's chief source of salvation, and therefore one's chief medium of religion.*

The religious values which accentuated the significance and worth of the group attained so high a degree of development in the Jewish civilization that they were taken over by other civilizations. The result was the Christian and Mohammedan civilizations. But the time has come when the peoples that adopted the religious values of the Jewish people are beginning to utilize values based upon their own national experience. This means that the church is gradually being superseded by the various nationalities with their self-conscious patriotisms. Indeed, so potent an influence is patriotism in the lives of modern nations that it threatens to displace the church entirely.

The failure to appreciate the social implications of religion is responsible for the mistake commonly made of viewing religion as entirely incommensurate with nationalism. It is a common observation that the subjective satisfaction which the individual formerly derived from religion he now derives from nationalism. But why should that be the case? How does it come that two such apparently dissimilar affiliations should equally afford the individual a sense of self-realization? Somehow, despite Emile Durkheim's illuminating analysis of religious experience, most sociologists miss the truth to which this fact points, namely, that in transferring one's interest and devotion from religion to nationalism, one is transferring his attachment from the church to the state.

It would seem as though the need of a group serving as a medium of one's salvation is now being satisfied in the main by the civic community. How the church, which claims to be the only source of salvation, will deal with the rivalry of the civic community is difficult to foretell. The Jewish people, however, is not troubled by such a problem. It can afford to resign itself to the fact that it is not to be the only group through which the individual Jew can attain self-fulfillment. It is willing to share with the civic community the task of meting out salvation to the Jew. But this willingness, if it is to be more than a yielding to the inevitable, should be based upon a clear recognition of the psychological factor underlying religion, which is loyalty to one's historic community, and patriotism, which is loyalty to one's civic community.

The reason we fail to identify patriotism with religion is that we think of religion essentially as a personal and individual reaction to life, an experience which is the product of complete self-isolation. We shall never find our way in the maze of religious problems, unless we realize that the manner in which religion has functioned hitherto has been neither fortuitous nor imposed from without, but in response to the laws of human behavior. Human nature being constant, religion in the future is bound to take the same course as in the past. The way some of us would like to have it function represents in all probability the emergence of a new and additional human need, which is the outcome of more complex conditions of human life.

This additional need can be met without replacing those religion has served hitherto. Let us keep the distinction in mind and designate the way religion functioned in the past as "folk religion," reserving the term "personal religion" for the additional function it discharged for the few in the past, and which some of us would want to have it discharge for all mankind in the future. This will enable us to study objectively such apparently disparate phenomena as civic loyalty and historic religion, and to discover that *civic loyalty which finds expression in patriotism is fundamentally a continuation of the rôle played by religion in the past. It is in a large measure the modern form of folk religion.*

The ancient pagan religions functioned as folk religions insofar as they were systems of habits and values through which the group life became so significant to the individual that it constituted his principal medium for self-fulfillment. The historic religions still function in that capacity. It is immaterial whether those social habits and values are but a form of accredited, socially approved magic, or constitute an integrated system of spiritual affirmations and symbolic rites. Among primitive folk, or among a civilized people when its life is in a state of equilibrium, there is usually very little occasion for personal religion. The saint or ascetic who leaves his people in order to be able to commune with God, undisturbed by worldly distractions, does not necessarily practice personal religion. He usually accepts the norms of the society he leaves behind. He is dissatisfied with that society because it does not live up to the norms which it professes. His is therefore an individuated form or expression of folk religion, but not personal religion. *Religion is personal when it emphasizes the authority of one's own personality in contrast with, and sometimes in opposition to, the authority of one's group.* When social life begins to disintegrate, those who are spiritually sensitive to the process of disintegration feel the need for reorienting themselves anew to life here and hereafter, and the outcome is personal religion. This personal religion may take the form of new religious insights. Those who experience it become prophets. Or it may lead to a more active use of human reason. Those who show the way become philosophers. In the men and women of mediocre or inferior mental and spiritual capacity, personal religion takes the form of superstitions and mysteries. But ordinarily personal religion is the exception and folk religion the rule.

To understand the place of patriotism in the spiritual life, it is necessary to see it against the background of folk religion, or in relation to the way religions have functioned down to modern times. The religions by which the bulk of mankind have lived, and still do live, have been folk religions, whether the community which gave the individual his folk religion was a tribe, a people, an empire or a universal church. In each case the individual had to accept his community as his entire world, or at least as the central and most important part of the world. "The world was created for the sake of Israel," said Judaism. "The world was created for the sake of the church," said Christianity. To realize in what way a great historical religion like Christianity is essentially a folk religion, and not, as most of its apologists maintain, the religion of the individual human soul, it is necessary to know the historical background which made Christianity possible and which determined the part it played in human life.

In ancient times, when means of communication were limited, and the vast majority of people seldom had opportunity of contact with the world outside their own town or city, the civic group constituted the world of the average person. Since the civic group constituted one's world, religion and group loyalty were coextensive. The gods of antiquity began their careers as local gods, and when their dominion was extended to other localities, the conception of their character was changed to correspond with their enlarged power. *Gods always had their histories, which were in essence the personified forms of the histories of their peoples.'* For a god to acquire hegemony, his worshippers had to subdue the adherents of other gods. Thus it was principally through conquest and disintegration of peoples that a particular god would attain supremacy.

As long as folk and world were coextensive, it was possible to be perfectly adjusted to the environment. But this equilibrium was disturbed upon the awareness of a world of activity beyond the boundaries of one's own folk. As soon as the members of a folk realized that they were but part of the world, their first impulse was to annex that outside world to their own. The only large scale cooperation recognized by early man was that obtained through conquest.

Politically, conquest meant military control and imposition of tribute. Religiously, it meant that the annexed peoples were required to accept the gods of the conquerors and become part of their world. It was not always necessary for the conqueror to impose his religion upon the conquered in the same way as he imposed his rule upon them. The conquered people would frequently, of its own accord, accept the religion of the conquerors. In any event, it was to the interests of the conquering nation that its god should be acknowledged by all its subject peoples as supreme. An ancient empire had to constitute for all its members—both victors and vanquished—the one world in which each one had to work out his salvation, and it was the imperial god or gods presiding over that world which gave it unity. One of the reasons for the rapid disintegration of the Persian empire was that it did not pursue the policy of enforcing religious solidarity. The policy of Alexander the Great, on the other hand, included religious as well as cultural imperialism, and was continued with vigor by the Seleucidæ, the dynasty whence sprang the Antiochus who almost succeeded in destroying Judaism.

The reaction to the existence of a vast and manifold life outside the borders of one's own nation, which gave rise to imperialistic ambition, could be translated into actual conquest only by a few powerful peoples. What of the many nations or folks that were not strong enough to engage in conquest? Since they could not subjugate and annex the world they discovered beyond their own boundaries, they had to submit to subjugation and annexation by that world as a matter of course. They evinced no resistance to being culturally and religiously absorbed by the stronger nations. Sooner or later every nation was drawn into the orbit of some dominant people. Each such change in the constellation of empires was accompanied by a reorganization of the religious affiliations of the constituent peoples. *The only nation in ancient times which, despite its military weakness, refused to fall in with the political and religious imperialism of any of the great empires of which it formed a part, was the Jewish people.*

As the Roman empire grew, it permitted the various countries which it annexed to retain their own worship, but expected, in addition, religious identification with Rome. When the number of coun-

tries became unwieldy, it was found that the original religion of
Rome was too weak to act as a solidifying force; so Rome devised
the religion based on emperor worship. By the beginning of the
fourth century, emperor worship degenerated to such a degree that
it could no longer hold the empire together. There was need for a
more effective religious imperialism. That need was met by the
messianism or spiritual imperialism which had been promulgated by
the Christian sect. "What the acquisition of Roman citizenship
meant for the Gaul or the Greek in Cæsar's time," says Spengler,[8]
"Christian baptism meant for him—entry into the leading nation
of the leading Culture." For a number of centuries thereafter, the
Roman church and the Roman empire became synonymous.[9] It
claimed to be catholic, or universal. The doctrine that no one
could attain salvation except through the church, was tantamount
to the demand that the reorganized Roman empire constitute one's
entire world.[10]

Christianity has always been ambitious of becoming coextensive
with humanity. It has had to limit itself, against its will, to the
western world. It inherited the ambitions of Roman imperialism.
The substitution of the imperial for the national principle in religion led to the attempt to maintain a uniform type of social organization in a most diverse and heterogeneous mass of humanity. "The
Church . . . sought in a double sense, to be universal," says Ernest
Barker. "It would embrace the whole world in its extension as a single Catholic society under a single oecumenical head. It would also
penetrate the whole world by the intensity of its operation, seeking
to bring every walk of life and every human activity under the
control of the law of Christ entrusted to its charge."[11]

As a consequence of the forces, political, economic, social and
intellectual, that have brought into being the modern European
nations, the church is being replaced by competing organizations
that bid fair to supply the individual with the environment and
interests necessary for complete self-realization. In the thirteenth
and fourteenth centuries we note the beginnings of new nations
arising in Europe. Simultaneously with the political attempt to
break away from the hegemony of Rome, there occurred the religious movement, which resulted in the Protestant schism in the
church.

Since mankind began to adjust itself to industrial and economic changes, enlightenment has developed side by side with nationalism. Consequently too many conceptions of God have arisen to make it possible for all those who belong to one nation to subscribe to any one particular religion. The policy set in, therefore, of either disestablishing the church, or recognizing the right of other churches besides the established one to exist. With the disestablishment of the church in nearly all the European countries, the problem of the relation of religion to nationalism has not been solved. The church has been forced to agree that the functions of church and state are different and mutually exclusive. But the agreement has not altered the fact that their functions overlap and interfere with each other. For the modern state tends more and more to offer its citizens a scheme of salvation. Ever since the state assumed responsibility for education, its effect upon the spiritual life of the citizens has become far-reaching, and more significant in character than the influence of the church.

Assuming that the historic churches will dwindle and finally disappear, will not personal religion survive? This is the opinion of those who see the end of organized religion. It would be far more logical to see the end of all religion, than to promise a future to personal religion while pronouncing the doom of folk religion. For, if we assume that the essential function of religion is to facilitate the fulfillment of the individual, we realize that it is unattainable without the cultural background provided by the group. Though personal religion may develop criteria of self-fulfillment, it is evident that the individual depends upon the community for conceiving the very need for self-fulfillment.

The way in which religion functioned in the past conformed with the social needs of human nature. Therefore it will continue to function that way in the future without thereby hindering the growth of personal religion. We may, accordingly, take for granted that it will always retain the form and characteristics of folk expression. It will continue to serve as a means of integrating the aspirations of the individual with the ideals of his community. To be sure, all folk religions will lose their theurgic character. No folk religion will henceforth advance the claim that its adherents are espe-

cially favored by God, or that they alone are qualified for salvation.

*To accept folk religion will be to realize the truth that the basis
of individuality and character is supplied not by the world at large
with its multitudinous culture, but by the section of mankind which
constitutes one's particular folk.* The first encounter of the individual
with the community takes place in the narrow environment of the
home, which exercises its influence for good by transmitting to the
child not universal concepts and loyalties but a specific tradition or
social heritage. Even if the individual is to be trained for world-
citizenship, he must begin as a member of the particular tribe, people
or nation into which he is born.

Since the community is indispensable to the rearing of the individual, it will expect him, when matured, to perpetuate its life
through his adherence and loyalty. In the degree to which that expectation will be met, we shall have folk religion. Each people is
bound to possess all the institutions bearing the earmarks of religion as it is conventionally understood. There will be rituals, festivals, communal gatherings, symbols and glorification of heroes
and martyrs. There will be the affirmation of ideals, the willingness
to sacrifice, and the sense of exaltation, all of which have formed an
integral part of the historic religions. These manifestations of
national life are not a thing of the future. We are so familiar with
them that we have missed their true import, and dismiss them merely
as expressions of patriotism.[11] It does not occur to us that they are
folk religions in the true sense of the term, gradually displacing
the folk religions of the churches. When we shall understand fully
the nature of the changes now taking place in the spiritual life of
mankind, we shall reach the inevitable conclusion that a civilization,
in addition to other outlets, must find expression in folk religion. *It
is through the folk religion that a civilization reaches the point of
self-consciousness essential to its perpetuation.*

This entire analysis is borne out by the career of Communism,
which has become the folk religion of Russia. The economist, J. M.
Keynes, was among the first to recognize that Russian Communism
was a new religion, no less than a new economic system.[12] It has
the main constituent of folk religion, *sancta*. Its *sancta* are the
persons of Marx and Lenin, the various places where it fought its

battles, the texts and the creeds which embody its doctrine, and it promises the reward of redemption, or salvation, through the complete surrender of the individual to the common good.

If the Jewish civilization is to evoke individual potentialities, and to enrich the world of values, it must have folk religion. It is necessary, therefore, first, to reinterpret the traditional beliefs and reconstruct the practices which formerly emphasized the religious aspects of Jewish life, so that instead of being part of a theurgic scheme of salvation they may constitute a modern folk religion, exacting, while not monopolizing, the loyalty of the individual Jew. Secondly, it is essential to lay down plans and formulate criteria for the future course and enrichment of the Jewish folk religion. Thirdly, it is important to stimulate an interest in personal religion analogous to that displayed by other nations in music or the plastic arts.

The Jewish people has the advantage over the church in possessing a method of folk religion that is gradually asserting itself in the national and cultural reconstruction which is taking place in the modern world. The Jewish people has demonstrated the validity of the principle, which has been repeatedly verified by the experience of mankind, that a folk religion retains its relevance and vitality so long as it confines itself to those who have evolved it. A folk religion is like the soul of a human being. As long as the soul is associated with the person who evolved it, it acts normally. But as soon as it is introduced into the body of another person, it becomes, in the language of Jewish legend, a *dybbuk*, and speaks with a voice not its own. Likewise a religion, which is the soul or self-consciousness of a particular folk, performs some of the strangest antics when it is forced upon or adopted by another folk. In refusing to surrender national life and culture as fundamental elements in Judaism, the Jewish people has intuitively struck upon the secret of dynamic religion, an intuition which has been confirmed by anthropological research. Not being given to abstract thinking, the Jews failed to articulate this intuition in their writings.

The outstanding generalization which emerges from the history of Judaism, and from its present struggle to continue, is that all spiritual values, from those of godhood to those of individual salvation, are irrelevant and mischievous unless they are based upon the interests and history of some particular community, and unless they are applied to the life conditions there prevalent. The daily life and activity of a people should constitute the main source of its spiritual values. Unless those activities are transfigured and woven into a pattern of religious values, they leave the human spirit dwarfed, and likewise, unless religion is a product of vital activity, it dries up into an archaism. This is the principle which the Jewish people vindicated by holding its ground stubbornly against the attraction or compulsion of Christianity and Mohammedanism and all other religious traditions with which it came in contact.

An important corollary of this analysis of folk religion is that those who live in two civilizations will tend to give adherence to two folk religions. This is as it should be. *Jews in the diaspora must of necessity live within two civilizations, and will therefore have to adjust themselves to that necessity by participating in both.* By and large they still continue the practice of their own historical folk religion, and are already participating in the folk religions of the countries in which they live. They enter whole-heartedly into the spirit of a Thanksgiving Day celebration, to say nothing of Independence Day and all the other national holidays. Only when the folk festival or sabbath is frankly Christian does the Jew who is loyal to his historical religion hesitate to join his fellow-citizens in celebrating it.

Since it is only in Palestine that the Jewish civilization can be counted on to achieve normal and unhampered expression, it is only there that Jewish religion can be expected to regain that native strength which a folk religion should normally possess. This will constitute the fulfillment of the rabbinic prophecy, "The synagogues in the dispersion will be transferred to Eres Yisrael." [14] But if the Jews will continue to foster their civilization in the diaspora, even if it be only in a form ancillary to the civilizations of the countries in which they live, they will ultimately evolve a type of Jewish folk religion adapted to their own spiritual needs.

In the present situation of Jewish life, one can see a people's creative struggle to fulfill in its own career those conditions which render a religion vital and fruitful. This is what is meant by the statement that the Jewish people has "a genius for religion." *This genius has not manifested itself in the discovery of any single ethical or religious doctrine, but in the fulfillment of the conditions of religious creativity under the most adverse and changing circumstances.*

The problem of the Jewish religion in the diaspora will be to foster the maximum of Jewish civilization possible outside Palestine, so that certain elements of that civilization will stand out as *sancta,* or foci of religious values. This is quite different from having religion become the only expression of the collective life of a group. With the process of differentiation going on apace, religion can no longer serve as the sole basis of Jewish unity. The creative effort to establish a national homeland points to other expressions of collective life besides religion as a means of identifying the Jew with his people. It gives promise of the Jewish religion attaining a more normal development by very reason of its being only one aspect of a manifold life. The subservience of every human interest to religion is understandable from the standpoint of the other-worldly ideology, which assumes that the criterion of everything that man does is the extent to which it qualifies him for a share in the world to come. But from the standpoint of this world as the theater of man's self-realization, religion itself is a call to life abundant and complete, in which all the faculties of the human being are to be brought into play. So viewed, religion's rôle in the life of man is practically the same as that of self-consciousness and, like the latter, must operate not continuously but intermittently. Preoccupation with religion, like preoccupation with oneself, is a form of morbidity.

Normally, religion should take its place by the side of social, economic, scientific and esthetic activities without attempting to overshadow them or subordinate them to its own aims. A religion which is utilized as the sole means of national self-expression is bound to become stunted and ingrown. Its God-idea tends to be congealed, its rites to be formalized, and its traditions to eclipse vital needs of the present. It is imperative, therefore, to find outlets other than religion for the collective life of the Jewish people. *Paradoxical as it may sound, the spiritual regeneration of the Jewish people demands that religion cease to be its sole preoccupation.*

Public worship is believed to be the one element in traditional Jewish religion incapable of being continued and readapted as part of folk religion. To the modern mind, there is something incongruous in treating worship as an integral element of civilization. Yet an objective study of the psychological and social factors in the relation of public worship to the cultural life indicates that the various civilizations of the future will find expression in public worship as did all civilizations of the past. There is a tendency nowadays to treat all religious ritual, and especially prayer, as the concern of the individual. This tendency should not be taken too seriously. Worship is too deeply rooted in the social nature of the human being to be easily discarded. So long as a people will have holidays and festivals to commemorate the events in its career, to recall its victories and to confirm its strivings, the institution of public worship will remain. Public worship is a means of giving a people that collective consciousness which unifies its life and integrates all of its individuals into an organized totality.[16] Though its form may change, it is certain that before long it will be reinstated in all normally functioning civilizations.

Just as we cannot conceive a civilization without literature, music and architecture, so is it impossible to conceive a civilization without public worship. There is no gainsaying the fact that the revolution which has taken place in the human outlook upon life will change our ideas about the purpose and method of worship. That is a normal development, and implies both the rejection of many a traditional belief concerning the nature and effectiveness of prayer and the emergence of new ideas concerning worship. Just now the change expresses itself merely in negation. When people say that the drama, music, and books satisfy the needs which were formerly satisfied by worship, they assume that there is but one philosophy and method of worship and that, the traditional one. They do not realize that worship satisfies a social need which cannot be met by intellectual or esthetic activity.

Public worship is far from incompatible with the modern outlook on life. It has far more exalted uses than that of setting in motion forces that might fulfill one's private desires. Those uses go together with a conception of God which precludes the magical consequences of offering praises addressed to him. Likewise, the authoritarian aspect of ritualism is no longer tenable, for it can no longer be believed that in order to be effective, worship must take on the form laid down by authority, and that the least departure from it is heresy and rebellion. A certain element of uniformity is necessary, because it is the very purpose of worship to arouse a feeling of common consciousness. But to make uniformity an indispensable requisite of worship negates spontaneous self-expression.[16] Least of all should stereotyped liturgical formulas which have ceased to call forth any emotional response, usurp the place of new formulations of spiritual yearnings.

Public worship meets two essential needs of human nature: the need for selecting and retaining those aspects of reality that make life significant, and the need for identifying oneself with a community which aspires to make life significant. Public worship meets this twofold need, because it affirms this meaning of life and the primacy of its moral and spiritual values, and because it gives reality, purpose and self-consciousness to the collective spirit of a people. The usual objection to the traditional liturgy is that it abounds in endless praises of the Deity. But even that objection can easily be overruled. Only a philistine literalism can miss the poetic beauty and majesty of the traditional type of hymnologies. Primitive man, no doubt, resorted to praising his deity as a means of eliciting favors from him. But in the higher civilizations, when the pious sang praises to God they gave utterance to the ineffable delight they derived from communion with him. The modern equivalent of that experience is a glimpse into life's unity, creativity and worthwhileness. To articulate that experience in the midst of a worshipping throng is a spiritual necessity of the normal man. He needs it as a means of affirming the meaning of life and of renewing his spirit.

There are some principles which must be reckoned with in reinstating worship as part of Jewish folk religion. It should intensify one's Jewish consciousness. There should be no mistake about the type of civilization and people with which Jewish public worship identifies the Jew. It should interpret the divine aspect of life as manifest in social idealism. It should emphasize the high worth and potentialities of the individual soul. It should voice the aspiration of Israel to serve the cause of humanity.

To achieve these purposes, Jewish worship will have to conform to the following conditions: *In the first place*, the language and the atmosphere of the worship should be entirely Hebraic. The architecture of the building should symbolize Jewish values. The reading from the scroll, the use of symbols like the *talit*, the *tefilin*, the *shofar*, the *lulab*, the recital of *kiddush* and *habdalah*, though they can no longer have the theurgic significance they had in the past when they were regarded as supernaturally commanded by God, are ritual forms which help to give Jewish worship its distinctive character. The use of Hebrew would make possible far greater latitude and flexibility in the writing of new prayers, so that Jewish worship, instead of being confined to stereotyped formulas and antiquated ideas, would progress with the movement of the mind and of the spirit without becoming any the less Jewish. "Even perfection," writes Whitehead, "will not bear the tedium of indefinite repetition." Furthermore, if the synagogue were to substitute the vernacular for the Hebrew, the Jews of one country could not unite in worship with the Jews of another. *Secondly*, worship must be highly esthetic. Since it is effective mainly through the esthetic appeal, the synagogue should enlist the creative ability of Jews. The talents of the Jewish architect, musician, poet, or dramatist should be encouraged to create forms embodying the ideas expressed in Jewish worship. Folk religion must be translated into poetry, music, drama, and the plastic arts. *Thirdly*, the content of Jewish worship should deal not only with the past but also with the present interests of the Jews, collectively and individually. The renascence of the Jewish spirit and the reclamation of the ancient homeland should have a foremost place in the ritual. Likewise, the yearning for peace, for justice, and for freedom should be given more specific expression than that implied in the various prayers for the establishment of the kingdom of God.

The task of modern Judaism must not end with the readjustment of its folk religion. As the emphasis placed upon its folk religion increases, it is essential to guard against the chief misuse that folk religion is open to—its apotheosis into a consecrated chauvinism. It is evident that however high an ethical standard it may uphold for the members of the group in their relationship to one another, it is not likely to transcend the limitations of folk morality. Personal religion, with its element of universalism, will therefore have to act as a check and corrective. Furthermore, we must remember that folk religion necessarily moves on the plane of popular intelligence and crowd emotions. It cannot breathe in those reaches of mysticism where the more highly developed mind dwells. Since modern mysticism presupposes a highly trained metaphysical grasp of reality, folk religion will lack the metaphysical and mystical elements with which the more advanced mind cannot dispense. Personal religion, however, cannot displace folk religion; it can, and should, supplement it. Thus far no civilization has made any contribution to the problem of so balancing the functions of folk and of personal religion as to insure their reacting beneficially upon each other. Here is an opportunity for the Jewish civilization once again to become creative in a phase of human life which it enriched by its achievement in the past.

CHAPTER XXV

THE PAST STAGES OF THE JEWISH RELIGION

The need for a reorientation to the history of the Jewish religion—The henotheistic stage of the Jewish religion—The contest between the syncretistic and anti-syncretistic tendencies—The origin of the "Day of the Lord"—The prophetic movement—The theocratic stage of Jewish religion—The function of the Temple in Jerusalem—The Torah as the will of God—The growth of eschatology—The other-worldly stage of Jewish religion—Religion the chief outlet of national life—The rabbinic conception of God—The rabbinic conception of Torah—The rabbinic conception of Israel—The meaning of the continuity of the Jewish religion.

THE past is always with us; our idea of it not only influences the present but also conditions the future. In the words of Zangwill, "We shall never get the future straight until we disentangle the past." For most Jews of our day, the past is little more than a chaotic blur. Formerly, every Jew had a fairly definite idea of how Judaism happened, and on the basis of that idea he could envisage and plan a future for Judaism. But now that Jews cannot accept the traditional version of the origin and development of their religion, and know no substitute version that might give them historical perspective, they have no means of gauging the Jewishness of whatever religion they are inclined to foster.

The modern Jew cannot utilize the past as a means of rendering the present significant and the future worthwhile until he reinterpret the traditional ideas about the past, and form a coherent and organized understanding of how his people came to have so unique a religion. In any reconstruction of the past there are bound to be gaps, but so long as they are gaps which can be bridged by intelligible conjecture they cannot be so baffling as when they are closed by accounts of miracles. In the traditional version of the Jewish past, it is held that the Patriarchs, Moses, the Prophets and the Sages entertained essentially the same conception of God and sought to live up to the same law, both moral and ritual. This view conforms with the theurgic conception of Jewish religion, which assumes the intervention of the supernatural in the affairs of men. That conception, the modern Jew finds untenable.

350

To visualize the past of Jewish religion, we must avail ourselves of the reconstruction of history made possible through the scientific study of the Bible and post-biblical literature.[1] The Jewish past has not been restored in all its details. The scientific reconstructions differ among themselves, and are to a large extent hypothetical. For our purpose, however, it will suffice to accept the basic ideas which have been established by scientific research, and concerning which there is unanimity among the investigators. These ideas may be generalized in the form of the proposition that the history of the Jewish religion is a history of three types or stages of religion, each merging so gradually into the next that the changes in the God-idea long remained imperceptible. It is only in recent times that the dynamic character of the continuity of the Jewish religion has been recognized.

What is meant by the dynamic continuity of the Jewish religion can be made clear only by a somewhat detailed account of the metamorphosis of the principal beliefs in the course of the various stages of the Jewish past. The very assumption that religious beliefs can alter their form puts them in a class apart from supernaturally revealed truths, or from rationally acquired truths. Such a view of religious beliefs is based upon the conception of religion as an integral element of a civilization, which undergoes change along with the civilization.

The traditional view of the Jewish religion is derived from the overt account given in the Pentateuch and interpreted by the generations of scribes, teachers and commentators who until recently were the moulders of the Jewish consciousness. According to that account, Israel's ideas of God, its religious emotions and practices had their origin in a series of theophanies. These theophanies were specific events in the lives of individual men. There was one occasion when God made his presence evident to the entire nation and communicated his will to them. In the light of tradition, it is incorrect to speak of the evolution of Jewish religion. Though the religious ideas, emotions and habits of the majority of Israel have undoubtedly varied in the course of the centuries, such variations are interpreted by tradition as having been merely departures from the norm established once and for all when God communicated his law to Moses at Sinai. If we find divergences of opinion in matters of ritual and other laws during the rabbinic period, it is because the laws communicated by God to Moses are assumed to have been forgotten during the many disasters which had befallen the Jewish people.

The traditional belief that the Jewish religion has remained the same since it was promulgated at Sinai is quite untenable and is being superseded by the evolutionary conception of its origin and growth. According to that conception, the complex of ideas and practices centering about the belief in God underwent gradual but thorough-going changes. Lacking as the ancients were in historical grasp and perspective, they always read the records of their past in terms of their present.* Scientific research, armed with the historical method and the means of comparative study, can retrieve from these records enough of the actual mental and social background to illumine the bare facts. The factors which entered into the shaping of the Jewish religion are now generally recognized as having been, first, a substratum of religion which the Israelites had in common with other oriental peoples; secondly, a unique combination of historical circumstances; and thirdly, the religious genius of Israel's spiritual leaders and prophets, beginning with Moses.

The Jewish religion is so far from changeless that a chronological survey reveals three distinct orders of belief and practice so different from each other as almost to appear like different religions. It is only because throughout the history of the Jewish religion most of the *sancta* have been the same, and because there has been an unbroken continuity in the civilization of the Jewish people, that these types so merged into each other as to give the illusion that the Jewish religion is identical in form and content from its beginning to our own day. But if the three orders of religious belief and practice are not three distinct religions they certainly mark three distinct stages of the one religion. It is not possible to fix the exact dates of each stage, but on the whole the period of the First Commonwealth may be identified as the first stage, that of the Second Commonwealth as the second stage, and the eighteen centuries preceding the modern era as the third stage.

When the Israelites entered Canaan they brought with them religious traditions and laws which set them apart from the natives. The traditions had as their main theme the marvels of the God YHWH whose habitat was the region of Sinai or Horeb, and with whom they had made a covenant in the course of their journeyings in the wilderness. The terms of the covenant were that he would be their God, fight their battles and provide them with all they needed; and they in turn would obey his laws and be loyal to him. They brought with them an ark which was the symbol of his presence and the reminder of their covenant with him.

Side by side with these unique elements in their religion, the Israelites shared the religious conceptions and practices common to mankind at that stage of social development. They retained the survivals of animism. They had their sacred trees, sacred waters, sacred stones and mountains; they had their *numina* and myths; they practiced theurgy and the mantic arts; they had their tabus and sacrifices. This entire complex of religious practices, together with the interpretations which they gave to them, at first formed part of the religion of YHWH. When they came to Canaan they found the natives engaged in similar practices, except that the latter invoked the various local *baalim* as authority and sanction for all their customs and laws. There at once set in a twofold process of syncretism and resistance to syncretism. On the one hand, the danger that the individuality of the concept YHWH would merge with that of the *baalim* was imminent. On the other hand, there arose the counter movement to emphasize the individuality of YHWH by denouncing the *baalim* and stressing the mighty deeds which YHWH had performed for the Israelites, and which placed them under eternal indebtedness to him. This counter movement was led by those who had an interest in strengthening the bond of unity among the Israelitish tribes. As the determination to remain in permanent possession of the land grew, they gradually coalesced into a nation that knew itself as the people of YHWH.

Although the Israelites at times realized that YHWH was the deity who had enabled them to overcome their enemies and was entitled to their undivided allegiance, their conception of him during the period of settlement was exceedingly primitive. We find that Jephthah assigns to YHWH a rôle analogous to that which he assigns to Kemosh,[*] and that he considers it obligatory to sacrifice his daughter because he had made a vow to bring as an offering to

YHWH the first living being he met on his return from victory. That images of YHWH were at one time considered legitimate appears evident from the stories of Gideon and Micaiah.[5] The account of the image made by Micaiah gives an illuminating picture of YHWH religion in the days of the Judges.

The Canaanite sanctuaries of Shechem, Hebron, Beth El, Beersheba, gradually passed under the jurisdiction of YHWH.[6] To justify this transfer there arose traditions concerning theophanies, in which YHWH was represented as having revealed himself at those places to the Patriarchs and founders of the nation. In other respects, however, the original *baal* cults were retained almost in their entirety. The sacred poles, sacred stones, the images, probably of the bull form, all originally dedicated to the various *baalim*, were converted into sacred symbols of YHWH.

A very significant intensification of the YHWH concept, determining the entire future of YHWH worship, was the ascription to YHWH of the power to give rain. Such power had to be ascribed to him or else he would have remained solely a war god. YHWH had to take over the functions of the nature deities, if he was to monopolize the obedience of Israel. This tendency to ascribe rain-giving power to YHWH no doubt began with the moment the Israelites integrated the agricultural festivals into the worship of YHWH. But the contest between him and the native gods for the title of rain-giver was not fought to a conclusion before the fall of the First Temple.[7]

During these formative years of Israel's religion, it was mainly the ark that kept alive the distinction between YHWH and the *baalim*. Without the ark, YHWH would have taken on the traits of the Canaanitish deities as completely as he did their worship. The Israelites would in all likelihood have forgotten that they had ever invaded Canaan, and would have come to regard themselves as the original settlers of the land. The fusion with the natives would have become so complete that the Israelites would have ceased to look upon themselves as a distinct people. In ancient times no people could retain its distinctiveness for any length of time, unless the deity, who was the central figure in its life, was able to hold his own against the syncretistic tendency to identify him with some alien deity. Had the specific memories associated with YHWH as the

Sinai deity and as the redeemer of Israel been lost in the growing tendency to assimilate him to Baal, the very name YHWH would soon have been forgotten, and with it the individuality of Israel as a people. One of the agencies which prevented this was the ark, which served as a center and symbol of the collective individuality of Israel.

The ark as the tangible evidence of YHWH's presence served as the occasion for the rise of outstanding personalities who accentuated his uniqueness and the part he had played in redeeming Israel from Egypt. The urge to national unity contributed to the strengthening of loyalty to YHWH. But for the deepening and spiritualization of the idea of YHWH we have to look to the unparalleled religious genius which found expression in a long line of great leaders, warriors and prophets. The first leader after the invasion who gave the initial impetus to the identification of the unity of Israel with loyalty to YHWH was Samuel, who began his career as a seer, or prophet of YHWH at the sanctuary at Shiloh.

King David did more than any other leader during the early years of Israel's history to raise the prestige of the Israelitish nation and of the nation's god, YHWH. He turned what had seemed imminent defeat into resplendent victory. He took a loosely federated group of tribes, torn by jealousies and demoralized by the continual onslaught of a powerful foe, molded them into a victorious nation and extended its boundaries. Having achieved all this in the name of YHWH, David became the synonym of the ideal king, the anointed of YHWH.

The conception of YHWH was in many respects no more spiritual than that which other peoples had of their respective deities. He was then regarded as a powerful deity who made his presence felt by wreaking destruction through storm, earthquake, pestilence, famine or drought.[8] It was not at all unusual to ascribe the evil deeds of men to YHWH's instigation.[9] In his relations to the individual human being, he was conceived as displaying a degree of arbitrariness [10] that made it difficult for man to know what to expect of him, or how to ward off his wrath.[11]

As against these traits, there were two other outstanding ones that made it possible for the spiritually minded in Israel of a later day to identify YHWH as the God of justice and mercy *par excellence*. One was his solicitude for the welfare of Israel, a solicitude that derived from his status as a god; for the godhood of YHWH was based upon his relationship to the nation of Israel. He was not only bound by his self-imposed covenant to defend the nation against its enemies and provide it with its necessities; he did so even more out of the abundance of his grace and loving-kindness. The other trait was that of justice, which was regarded as manifest in YHWH's championship of the weak and the helpless against their exploiters and oppressors and in his laws which commanded fair dealing. These are the two traits of YHWH's character which his devotees continually stressed as a claim on Israel's loyalty and obedience.

The victories of David added a new impetus to the glorification of those events in which the God of Israel had figured as the redeemer of Israel from Egypt. The national consciousness, fostered by the zealots of YHWH through their efforts to prevent the people from being Canaanized, was intensified, and a new hope was born: the hope that the God of Israel would display his power in the potent fashion of the days of the exodus—but on a much larger scale, so that all the kingdoms of the earth would recognize his dominion and accept him as their God. That was to be the "Day of the Lord." An integral phase of this manifestation would be the undisputed supremacy of Israel. After what David had been able to achieve in ridding Israel of all its foes and in widening the boundaries of its land beyond all expectation, the prospect of such supremacy was by no means an idle dream. The division of the kingdom and the subsequent catastrophes further accentuated the yearning for the Day of the Lord. In the reign of the second Jeroboam, when the fortunes of Israel rose for a time so that the glory of the Davidic reign seemed to be revived, the confidence in the advent of the Day of the Lord was renewed.

The conviction, however, that the time must come when the God of Israel was bound to make his godhood manifest to all the world was a double-edged sword. The affirmation that the God of Israel would one day deal with Israel's foes as he had dealt with Pharoah was strangely ironic at a time when Israel's fortunes were low, or when signs of the storm that was to break upon the nation was already evident. It was during these critical periods that the most active zealots of YHWH came forward with a new interpretation of the Day of the Lord. Amos, Hosea, Isaiah, Micah, broke in upon their contemporaries with the astonishing assertion that when the God of Israel would begin this visible world-sovereignty, the first to feel the shock of the new world-order would be his own people. He would cleanse his own people of those who had been disloyal, and of those who had been flouting his laws of justice, righteousness and purity.

It may be said without exaggeration that no single belief contributed so much to the unique development of the Jewish religion as the belief that the God of Israel was some day bound to reveal himself in his full glory and power to all the world. This belief proved to be the main driving force for the prophetic movement. The primary task of the Prophets was not merely to announce this belief—since it was universally assumed to be true—but to interpret in its light whatever disaster seemed imminent. The upshot of their interpretation was that the Day of the Lord was a day of doom for all who rebelled against YHWH, and that only those who would repent and return to YHWH would be spared. Had not their contemporaries taken for granted the advent of the Day of the Lord, the Prophets would have had nothing to which to address themselves. As it was, that postulate proved the most potent vehicle for communicating the moral and spiritual urge by which they were obsessed. What the modern person experiences as a relentless inner urge the ancients experienced as a compulsion coming from some outside mysterious being—usually the god they worshipped. The Prophets, therefore, could do no other than identify as the command of YHWH the urge that drove them to make known what the Day of the Lord had in store for their people.

The religion of the canonical Prophets is not quite identical with what is commonly understood by the term "monotheism." That term usually designates the outcome of an intellectual development which could not possibly have been carried on in early Israel. God, as monotheism conceives him, is a metaphysical being whose traits and attributes have nothing in common with anything in human experience. When we say that God is all-knowing, or all-good, it is with the qualification that we are using a terminology which in strictness is totally inapplicable to God. Why then do we use it? Simply because we have none better. No such sophistication could ever form part of the Prophets' idea of the God of Israel. YHWH still retains his proper name. He is not merely God, but the god *par excellence*, the one being who has more right to be called a god than the deities of the other nations. YHWH, in the estimate of the Prophets, comes up to the standard of what a god should be. The other beings for whom godhood is claimed are not unreal or imaginary, but they have not the qualities essential to being a god. They may be considered evil spirits, or good spirits, but they are not gods because they lack the power and the holiness of YHWH.[11]

There was something paradoxical about the God of Israel. On the one hand, he was conceived as possessing all those traits that made him the God of the whole world, and, on the other, as content to put up with one little rebellious people for his nation. None felt the paradox more keenly than the Prophets. They were at great pains to find some degree of commensurateness in the relationship between God and Israel. They tried, as it were, by a *tour de force* to change Israel from an average people dominated by the blind impulses of superstition and greed into a holy people that might deserve, by virtue of its purity and righteousness, to be the people of YHWH. This is the reason for their unremitting opposition to any entangling alliances with other nations. Israel must remain unique and solitary.

The inevitable conclusion concerning the solity of the God of Israel to which the Prophets felt themselves driven, did not comport in the least with the kind of religion they saw their people live by. In the sanctuaries of Israel were to be found all the paraphernalia of altars, pillars and images, all the feasting and abandon that one could behold at any of the sanctuaries of the false gods. The people's adoption of a syncretic religion, which bore all the earmarks of Canaanitish custom and ritual, indicated no awareness that the God of Israel was totally incomparable with the so-called gods of the nations. Along with their failure to mark the supreme godhood and holiness of the God of Israel in the worship at the sanctuaries, the Israelites actually flouted his supremacy in their daily life, and in their political affairs. They disregarded the laws of justice which had been promulgated in his name in former days when they still retained the simple nomadic customs. Their rulers were continually engaged in political intrigues with the rulers of the neighboring nations. This always led to the aping of foreign customs. Since YHWH was all-powerful, Israel did not need the protection of the great empires, nor did it need to enter into conspiracies with neighboring peoples for the overthrow of those empires. Those who resorted to such measures evidently had not much faith that the God of Israel was able to defend his own people. It was but one step from lack of confidence in the God of Israel to the adoption of other gods with whose peoples Israel sought to form alliances.

The Prophets were not merely social reformers or preachers of morality voicing their protests against the social wrongs of their day in the language of the religion familiar to their hearers. They were primarily believers in, and ardent devotees of YHWH. What rendered them so devoted was that they saw in him the only supernatural being who was truly a god, because, in addition to being all-powerful, he was the patron and defender of the oppressed. They were sensitive to the injustice committed by the strong against the weak. Godhood, therefore, could mean but one thing to them—the will and the power to vindicate the right. They were certain that YHWH had the will to vindicate the right because of the many ordinances and precedents ascribed to him in the interests of justice and purity.[13] None of the deities of the neighbors was known to be so insistent upon righteous dealing. Accordingly, YHWH alone possessed all the attributes of godhood; he alone was truly a god. They were certain that before long, he alone would be acknowledged as God, and to him only would divine honors be rendered.

The crises which betokened oncoming upheavals and which the Prophets interpreted as heralding the Day of the Lord had their beginning in Assyria's resumption of a career of conquest, after having been held to her own borders for almost half a millennium. She sought once more an outlet to the Mediterranean. The peoples of the many small kingdoms that stood in the path of her ambition were thrown into panic. Alliances and counter-alliances against Assyria were the order of the day. The cooperation of Judah and Israel was sought by their neighbors. It was evident that some great catastrophe was impending.

To the devotees of YHWH, it was unthinkable that the gods

either of Assyria or of the little peoples which were seething with fear and unrest could have anything to do with the oncoming calamities. Many in Israel, no doubt, concluded that the gods of the conquering Assyrians were apparently more powerful than the deities of the other peoples, more powerful even than YHWH. Resistance was, therefore, futile; the best policy was either to make alliance with Egypt, or court the favor of Assyria and her gods. The Prophets could not possibly permit such a conclusion to go unchallenged. They would not brook the thought that YHWH was inferior to any other deity. Since YHWH was the only supernal being, who by reason of his power and righteousness could be deemed God, they believed that he alone was the prime mover of the destinies of nations. It was YHWH and no other god, they concluded, who let loose the devastating hordes which were about to sweep over countries and carry away populations. Whether he sends the Assyrian, the Scythian or the Babylonian hordes, it is because the peoples of the invaded countries had aroused his indignation through cruelty or immorality. How will Israel fare in the oncoming doom of the nations? No better than the rest. The Israelites, to be sure, were at one time the object of YHWH's special love and interest. Their history was replete with accounts of the marvelous deeds their God had wrought in their behalf from the time he redeemed them from Egypt. Gratitude should have impelled them to repose implicit faith in YHWH and obey his laws; yet they proved recreant. Nothing, therefore, could save them from the universal disaster.

As much as the Prophets had to contend against those who in their hearts believed that YHWH would have to succumb to alien gods, they had an even more difficult task in combating the patriotic optimism of the "false prophets" and their adherents, who argued, "Is not YHWH among us? No evil will come upon us." [14] One of the popular beliefs which fortified this optimism was that YHWH would some day manifest his power over the nations by granting Israel a spectacular victory over its foes. Such was their interpretation of the long-awaited Day of YHWH. It was at this juncture that the Prophets appeared and warned the Israelites that their God was about to display his glory, but with consequences to them other than those that had been expected. The great cataclysm that would ensue would destroy all enemies of YHWH, those within Israel as well as those without. All who disobeyed the law of YHWH, who oppressed the poor, who grew rich through exploitation or who worshipped strange gods, were his enemies, and would feel the impact of his wrath. "Woe unto you that desire the Day of YHWH," cried the Prophet. "Wherefore would ye have the day of the Lord? It is darkness, and not light . . . even very dark and no brightness in it." [15]

This preoccupation with the belief concerning the Day of YHWH placed the Prophets in the forefront of those who have done most to influence the course of mankind's religious development. They prodded their people into realizing that the attribute of godhood ought not to be bandied about freely and bestowed upon every candidate and claimant, from crawling reptiles to kings and emperors. For the first time in the history of religion, the man of average intellectual and spiritual grasp was called upon to appreciate some of the implications of his idea of God. This was not the product of abstract thought; it was the result of the continual "speaking betimes and often" of the Prophets who proclaimed the belief in the Day of the Lord, and interpreted it in its relation to current events.

Subsequent events proved the truth of the frenzied warnings uttered by the great Prophets. The fall of Samaria was a complete vindication of YHWH's power and character. But it took more than one prophet, and more than one manifestation of YHWH's wrath, to raise him in the minds of his worshippers to the position which he finally attained. Not even the Prophets, aided though they were by the course of events, could have brought about such a result. The work of the Prophets would have remained futile if there had not arisen a band of anonymous zealots, including priests of the Temple at Jerusalem, who not only consolidated the results of the Prophets' preaching, but also laid the foundation of a theocratic commonwealth. These anonymous zealots labored more or less in secrecy during the reign of Manasseh, when the voice of prophecy was silenced and a new influx of foreign religious practices, chiefly from Babylon, presented a new danger to the worship of YHWH. During that period the traditions concerning YHWH were gathered and revised, and the laws attributed to him were reformulated so as to be in accord with his character as a God of righteousness. All of these efforts finally bore fruit. Upon the death of Manasseh, the prophetic party, consisting of Temple priests and disciples of the Prophets, became active again. In the year 621, when the scroll of the Torah was found, a new covenant was made with YHWH. Henceforth there was to be a definitive instrument which was to serve as the criterion of obedience to the will of YHWH, a written Torah.

Although that covenant marks the beginning of the Jewish religion as based upon a written Torah, a long time elapsed before the Torah came to occupy the place of primacy in the life of the Jews. Outside the limited group of priests and prophets, the deeper and more spiritual conception of the God of Israel was still unknown or unpopular. It was only after the stupendous efforts of prophets like Jeremiah and Ezekiel, and of others who have left no writing behind, or whose writings have remained anonymous, and after Jerusalem and the Temple were destroyed and the people had experienced all the horrors of war and exile, that the prophetic conception of the God of Israel and of his dealings with his people came to be generally accepted. It was only then that Jews were animated with a sincere desire to know and obey his Torah. During the century and a half following the destruction of the First Temple, Jewish life was in the process of reorganizing itself as a theocratic civilization. It was as such that Judaism functioned virtually until the destruction of the Second Temple.

The second, or theocratic,[16] stage of the Jewish religion may, on the whole, be said to have been contemporaneous with the period of the Second Commonwealth. The religious ideology of the second stage, which we may identify with that period, was not yet fully developed at its beginning, and came to be somewhat modified by the end of it. The reason for designating this stage of the Jewish religion as theocratic will become apparent in the sequel.

By this time the God of Israel is no longer conceived merely as a god, or as the principal god, but as God, the creator of the world and of all that it contains, the one Being who is *sui generis,* whose power is manifest both in the ordinary and in the extraordinary manifestations of nature and whose will governs the life of every created being. To the category of created beings belong the heavenly bodies, the heavens and the earth, the angels, the spirits and all animal life. God created all these to serve mankind, and mankind in turn was created to serve him. How it came about that only Israel served him is explained in the opening chapters of the Torah. The very term "God of Israel," which is taken over from the henotheistic period, has acquired a new meaning. The notion that he exercised dominion only over Israel had grown obsolete. God is designated the "God of Israel" merely because he had singled out Israel from among the nations to give them his laws. That, however, was not his original intention when he created the world, for he had expected all mankind to be his people and to obey his laws. Only when the human race showed itself recalcitrant did he choose Abraham to be the founder of a nation that would obey his will. But ultimately God's original purpose, to have all mankind serve him, is bound to be realized. This is the story which the first chapters of the Pentateuch tell.

The effect upon the ancient mind of this enlarged cosmic conception of God was to make it far more poignantly God-conscious than it could ever have been when gods were matter-of-course beings like trees and animals. It is not easy to retrieve even in imagination the sense of awe and mystery of those who first became aware of God as the creator of the world, as the one and only God. If we were to realize both the apprehension and the sense of need with which the ancient man approached any deity whatever, and if we could conceive all the emotion that man expended on the many gods that he worshipped, focussed upon the one being who came to be known as God *par excellence,* the sole creator of the world, we might relive the attitude of the Jewish religious devotees during the Second Commonwealth.

In analyzing that attitude, we come upon a paradox which had to be resolved. To the ancients, the more holy a god was, the less approachable could he be. Those who believed there was only one God reasoned that he must be so holy as to be unapproachable. How then is it conceivable that man with all his evil and impurity could enter into communion with him?

It must be recalled that in those days communion with a deity could be conceived only as analogous to the communion of one human being with another. Furthermore the ancients still labored under the magical conception of holiness. They assumed that a deity was charged with deadly power which had to be reckoned with by anyone who wanted to address him. During the theocratic stage of the Jewish religion, with its transfer of allegiance from divers gods to one, this apprehension was greatly augmented, since the Jews had become more God-conscious than they had ever been. It was considered dangerous even to pronounce his name, except on highly important occasions. Had this mode of reasoning not been counteracted by another postulate, the ancients would have hesitated to approach God even in worship.[17] This postulate was that godhood as such necessarily implied solicitude for man's well-being. It was therefore man's duty to worship him.

The paradox inherent in the newly achieved conception of God was resolved for the Jews during the second stage of their religion by the assumption that there was only one place where God had chosen to manifest his presence, the Temple in Jerusalem. With a priesthood and a body of temple-servitors carefully taught and trained in all the rules pertaining to holiness, it was feasible to avoid trespassing upon the rules of propriety when communing with God. If there were more than one sanctuary at which God might be worshipped by means of sacrifices, that privilege might be abused. Although Jews could pray everywhere, they were expected to turn toward the Temple, for there alone did God actually manifest his presence.[18] In this way was the Jew able to reconcile in his mind the two apparently contradictory facts, God's transcendent holiness and his intervention in human affairs.

A similar paradox presented itself with regard to learning the will of God. So long as the difference between a deity and a human being was conceived as a matter merely of degree, it was assumed that whenever a deity wanted to direct the actions of his adherents he would appear to the most devout among them and utter his command, or he would communicate his will by means of certain signs which the priests would interpret. But neither method of directing human conduct altogether comported with the belief in the one God, the creator of the world; it put God on too low a plane. On the other hand, to conclude that God so far transcends human life that he would not deign to instruct man how to conduct himself was absurd, for in the very notion "God" there was the implied postulate that he was a being who was deeply concerned not only with man's well-being but also with man's conduct.

This dilemma was solved by the assumption that God had made his will known for all time through the Torah, the collection of laws contained in the Pentateuch, together with the oral teachings which were regarded as having accompanied the written Torah. It was thus possible to know what God would have man do, and yet to dissociate from theophany that temporality and casualness which were deemed unworthy of a theophany vouchsafed by God, the creator of the world.

The belief that the creator of the world has articulated his will, leads to a far more conscious and ardent absorption in what is promulgated as his Torah or teaching than could have been possible during the henotheistic stage of religion. The privilege of knowing the very commandments communicated by God for all time was all the more keenly felt, since theophanies and oracles were no longer in vogue. The Torah was regarded as the repository of all knowledge and wisdom. Its every teaching was viewed as a mine of inexhaustible treasure of truth. The ecstatic praise of God's Torah found in the Psalms is the beginning of what, in time, grew into a veritable apotheosis.[19] The study of the Torah came to be the chief spiritual vocation of the Jew. In the synagogue he heard it read and interpreted on Sabbaths and festivals. A class of scribes and teachers arose to disseminate the knowledge of it.

The impetus of the belief which had given rise to the prophetic movement had by no means spent itself. The belief in the coming of the Day of the Lord acquired new nuances and implications through the unqualifiedly monotheistic meaning which was now associated with the term "God of Israel." After the many disasters of war and exile had vindicated the truth of the warnings sounded by the earlier Prophets, that the Day of the Lord would be one of severe chastisement for Israel, came the consolatory utterances of the later Prophets depicting in the most glowing colors the advent of a new era of peace for mankind and of great prestige for Israel. Throughout the period of the Second Commonwealth, with the exception of a brief spell, the Jews in Palestine were subject to one or the other of the world-empires. More deplorable even than the lack of political independence in Palestine was the state of affairs which made it necessary for many Jews to live in other lands. Surely no greater eclipse of God's glory was possible than the dispersion of his people in distant lands where they were out of direct communion with him and denied worship at his Temple. Thus throughout the second stage of the Jewish religion the Jews experienced a sense of lack, of unfulfillment and abnormality of relation between God and the world.[20] This consciousness produced a vast eschatological literature, only a small portion of which has been admitted into the Bible —such as is found in the latter parts of Ezekiel, in Zachariah, Psalms and Daniel—while the greater portion was excluded from the canonical writings. In this way the belief in the coming of the Day of the Lord acquired a connotation different from the one prevalent during the henotheistic period. From connoting a feeling of contentment and sense of immunity to national disaster, that belief now afforded an escape, in thought and hope, from the disagreeable realities of the present.

By the middle of the theocratic period, eschatology came to include the newly acquired belief in resurrection. The adoption of that belief is a striking instance of how the Jewish religion, even when it was advanced in its development, continued to assimilate elements of alien religions. Though the evidence against the Jews' having known anything about the doctrine of resurrection before they came under the influence of Persian culture and religion is incontestable, traditional Judaism emphatically denies that the doctrine was a later accession and affirms that it was coeval with the rest of Jewish religion.[21]

Until the fourth century, B.C.E., the Jewish religion, in common with the less developed religions, assumed that man maintained relationship with God only during his lifetime. Theories of what happened to the human being after death, though they provided a rich source for magic, did not become part of the body of religious ideas or practices. Such magic known as necromancy was drastically forbidden and condemned.[22] Israel's ideas about the condition of the dead originally resembled those generally entertained by the peoples of the Near East during the first stages of urban culture. People then thought that death came after the principle or spirit of life left the body, although they had no definite ideas of what happened to the spirit after its departure. The prevalent notion that the shades, or shadowy doubles, of those who died spent the rest of their existence in a subterranean pit known as *Sheol,* seemed to have no practical implications for the human being while alive.

Though ancient man could not believe that death meant complete extinction, he formulated no definite belief in the immortality of the soul as part of religious doctrine.[*] All customs and institutions that in the ancient world attended the burial of royal personages as, for example, in Egypt, and that seem to have been interwoven with the religious life of the people, only prepared the way for the later emphasis upon religion as a means of redeeming the human soul from the power of death. For it must be remembered that royal personages were regarded as gods whose life was necessarily immortal. It was only in its later stages, especially in the traditional form handed down to us, that religion came to look upon the continuance of the ordinary man's relationship with God, even after death, as a matter of course. But the ancient Israelite took it for granted that this relationship was severed at death. The prospect of such severance, rather than that of personal annihilation, was what he dreaded about death. "In death there is no remembrance of thee; in Sheol who shall give thee thanks?"[**] "For Sheol cannot praise thee; they that go down into the pit cannot hope for thy truth."[***] Thus the fact of death, far from entering the circle of beliefs, emotions and practices centering around the conception of God, constituted the cessation of religion as it did of life itself.

Whatever outward influence may have contributed to the adoption of the belief in resurrection during the fourth century, B.C.E., it was undoubtedly concurrent with an important psychological development which took place in Jewish life—the emergence of the individual.[*] Many adumbrations of this development may be found in the Deuteronomic law, in Jeremiah and Ezekiel, but only when the belief in resurrection became a part of the Jewish religion were the claims of the individual recognized, not only in the religion of the few who were spiritually eminent, but also in popular religion. Before then it was assumed that the individual suffered the fate of his people, no matter what his own deserts were. But from now on man was regarded as a being who was judged as an individual, not as an indistinguishable unit in the mass. When God would create the new heaven and new earth, all the dead would rise again, all would be judged, and according to their deeds they would gain the world of the blessed or be destroyed forever.

Apparently the belief in resurrection was accepted when people clearly perceived that, despite all assertions to the contrary, man did not receive his just deserts in this world. The Bible produces sufficient evidence to show that the claims of the individual are asserted with increasing emphasis not long after the reforms introduced by Ezra and Nehemiah. Some of the Psalms,[27] the books of Job and Koheleth, attest the persistent questioning of the then traditional conception of retribution. As a result, some became skeptical and broke with Jewish religion entirely. Others, after an extreme effort of the will to find a solution, acquired serenity. This solution, reflected in Psalms 73 and 92, amounted to a categorical reaffirmation of the belief that the prosperity of the wicked does not endure, and that their end is all the more disastrous because of the unmerited prosperity which they enjoyed. Yet experience belied these brave affirmations. In times of conflict with foreign and Jewish rule, in the tyranny of the powerful over the humbler and more pious members of the population, men saw the triumph of those who were manifestly evil. All too often the wicked ended their days in peace and left behind them numerous progeny who showed not the least tendency to come to terms with those whom their fathers had persecuted. At that critical juncture, the belief in resurrection saved the Jewish religion. For it was possible now to affirm that the time of judgment and retribution was not in the here and now, but at the end of days,[28] when God would become the king of the world, who would judge the quick and the dead. Thus did the faith in the power and justice of God take on new life.

The Jewish religion passed through the third stage [29] of its existence from about the beginning of the common era down to modern times. The difference between the first and second stages is in many respects a difference in the type of religious ideas and practices. The difference between the second and third stages is a difference in emphasis upon the constituent elements of apparently the same religious content. Nor is the resulting variation negligible. *A change in the relative emphasis of spiritual values may transform their character and significance beyond recognition.*

When the destruction of the Jewish commonwealth seemed imminent and the possibility of national extinction all too likely, the Jewish religion was being prepared, both consciously and unconsciously, to play a new and unprecedented rôle in the life of the Jewish people. Until that time religion constituted the principal medium through which the Jewish people found its collective or national self-expression. In that respect the Jewish people differed during the five centuries of the Second Commonwealth from what it itself had been during the First Commonwealth, and from what all other peoples were. All other peoples embodied religion in their life, but did not make it the principal mode of national self-expression. Political activity, and in the case of highly civilized nations also cultural activity, served as a means of national self-expression coordinate with religion. The Jews of the Second Commonwealth enjoyed the distinction of making religion the *principal* medium of collective self-expression. That fact was reflected in the type of religious ideology which prevailed among the Jews of that period.

When the Second Commonwealth was destroyed, the Jewish religion underwent vast changes in emphasis, due to the fact that instead of being the principal means of national self-expression, it became the one and only means. Such a rôle has not been played by any other religion in the world. Because of this unique function served by the Jewish religion, it is by no means an easy task, if not an altogether impossible one, to describe Jewish traditional religion correctly in terms used to describe other religions. Terms like "national" and "universal" do not apply to it. If already in the days of the Second Commonwealth the Jewish religion became *sui generis* by becoming the *principal* national preoccupation, it became infinitely more so when, through the loss of the last vestige of political independence, it became the *only* medium through which the national consciousness and will of the Jewish people found an outlet. All the religious ideas, emotions and habits were very much intensified in order to further the survival of the nation. Not that the conservation of national existence was deliberately professed as an end in itself, but subconsciously the will-to-live as a people henceforth colored every element of the religion, its ideas, attitudes and practices.

The most important result of the fact that religion became the sole outlet of national self-expression was the conservation of the revelational basis of the belief in God. It is evident that no reasoned conception of the existence and nature of God could possibly have formed the basis of Jewish unity. It is impossible for any reasoned conception to gain uniform acceptance, unless it is backed by some authoritative body which can arrogate for its decrees the validity of supernatural revelation. This was what the Christian synods did. But even they would have been ineffective if the emperors, in order to conserve the unity of the Roman empire, had not added the weight of their authority to the synods' decrees.

With the lack of an external force to sanction any reasoned theology, the Jewish religion was compelled to retain as its sole basis the purely revelational conception of God, a conception that remained free of any admixture of philosophical investigation into the problem of God's existence or his nature. The traditional Jewish religion as interpreted by the *Tannaim* and *Amoraim,* and as conceived and lived by the sixty generations of the Jewish people preceding the present era, contributed nothing to the conception of God that had not been known in the era of the Second Commonwealth. On the contrary, that conception was somewhat narrowed because of the national motif interwoven with it. That does not mean that the scope of the God-idea in Judaism was reduced to the needs of Jewish national survival. The danger that God would be conceived once again as a sort of tribal or national deity was long past. But the conception of the universe as a whole shrank to smaller proportions by very reason of the central place which Judaism accorded in it to Israel.

The surest evidence of the narrowed conception of God is the complacent acceptance of the beliefs handed down from the past and the successful repression of all doubt or questioning. In that respect the second stage of the Jewish religion was superior to the third. During the second stage the fundamental belief in a guiding, rewarding and punishing Providence was openly challenged. That challenge found embodiment in an extensive literature of which there have survived books like Job and Koheleth and stray passages in the Psalms. But the third stage is marked by a rigid exclusion of any thought-tendency that deviated in the slightest degree from what was regarded as the norm. There was no time in the history of the Jewish religion when anyone who made light of a religious belief could escape severe rebuke. But not before the religion attained its third stage did questioning become the mortal sin of heresy that cut one off from salvation in the here and the hereafter. As far, therefore, as reflective and experiential grasp of the problem of the existence of God and his nature is concerned, the Jewish religion retrogressed from the point of development it had attained during the Second Commonwealth. Though this narrowing process was necessary for the very conservation of the Jewish religion, without which, in turn, the Jewish people would have disappeared, it was none the less a retrogression. In the terminology current during this stage of Jewish religion, the *galut*, the exile, of Israel may be described as a *galut* of the *Shekinah* as well.

But while from the standpoint of abstract thinking the God-idea was narrowed, from the standpoint of consequences in the life of the Jews it was very much deepened. Every phase of the conception of God presented itself with sufficient simplicity and definiteness to make that conception an effective determinant of conduct. First, God was conceived as an identifiable being whose existence did not have to be inferred, since he had revealed himself at one time to the whole of Israel, and a number of times to Israel's ancestors and Prophets. As an identifiable being God was necessarily conceived as having form.[30] Until Judaism was compelled to reckon with the challenge of Aristotelian philosophy, the philosophic difficulty of ascribing form to God in no way disturbed rabbinic thought. Even the question of God's omnipresence did not trouble them greatly. Although they assumed that God was omnipresent, they nevertheless held the idea of God as moving from place to place, and of heaven as his principal abode. Certain as it was that God was a being perceptible not merely to the mind but also to the senses, traditional Jewish religion could, for practical purposes, afford to leave unsolved the question about the form and substance of the divine nature and its relationship to the visible world. Hence the vagueness and the contradictions which abound in the traditional conception of God with regard to his spatial relationship to the physical universe.

There was no uncertainty, however, concerning those aspects of the divine nature that had a relationship to human conduct; viz., his unity, his justice and his mercy. The unity of God meant that, of the multitude of invisible spirit-beings that populated the world, the one who revealed himself to Abraham, Isaac, Jacob and Moses, and who is addressed as "our God and the God of our fathers," is the only true God. To ascribe to traditional Jewish religion the urge to teach the nations the formal truth of monotheism is to convey an entirely wrong impression of what the Jews conceived to be their place in the world. The God of monotheism is an object of philosophic inference. His existence may be equally inferred from the most insignificant as well as from the most important event of human life. But the God of revelation is an object of sensory response to supernatural stimulus. The Jewish religion taught that the God who revealed himself to Israel was the only being who possessed the power, the justice and the mercy to affect the welfare of mankind. To proclaim this God, the Jews regarded as the sole function of their national existence in their relation to the Gentile world.

The attribute of God's power, which accounted for the creation and maintenance of the visible world, was sufficient guarantee that God was bound to have his will realized in the world. Those who lived in conformity with the will of God relied upon his power to mold the circumstances of life to their advantage. Miracle, the change in the ordinary course of events for the advantage or hurt of the individual and nation, was considered God's normal method of getting man to do his will. People thought that such miracles were wrought at all times in behalf of individuals and communities, but not on a sufficiently large scale in this world to compel universal recognition of God's power. Such was the case in the distant past, and such will again be the case in the future when it will please God to usher in the new world-order. As to the manifestation of God's power in the very acts of creation and maintenance of the world, which is the crux of the God-idea in terms of reason, rabbinic religion has very little to contribute, and what it does is far more poetically conceived and beautifully expressed in the Bible.[31]

The divine attribute proclaimed as most distinctive of God and most significantly related to human conduct was the attribute of justice. That those who lived in accordance with the will of God achieved happiness was accepted as axiomatic; likewise the belief that those who transgressed his will were destined to suffer punishment. God's justice was expected to manifest itself chiefly in the correlation between man's conduct and his fortune. Had the doubts that a frank facing of experience would inevitably have aroused been permitted expression, they might ultimately have led to a revision of the meaning of the attribute of divine justice. But such a revision could not have been accomplished without a great strain upon the inner unity of the Jewish people, a strain which could have been withstood only if the Jews had remained in their own land, and had led at least a quasi-normal group life. The abnormal life which the Jews led as a people, and which drove them to resort to their religion as the only mode of national expression, rendered imperative a definite and satisfying conception of justice which would permit the belief in the correlation between conduct and happiness to remain unshaken. Such a conception was made possible by the unprecedented significance which Jewish religion in the third stage of its development attached to the belief in the world to come.

The doctrine concerning the world to come represents a new and more penetrating version of the ancient belief in the advent of the Day of the Lord. From the viewpoint of implications for conduct, it marks an advance upon the eschatological form which that belief assumed during the Second Commonwealth. Instead of serving merely as a psychic compensation for a state of political vassalage, the doctrine of *olam ha-ba* changed the Jew's entire perspective. He no longer estimated at face value either the good or the ill fortune of this world. He considered the suffering he endured in this world as divinely planned, to make it possible for him to come to the next world with a clean bill of spiritual health, and to increase his ultimate reward. The good fortune which the wicked enjoyed was to pay them off for the little good that they might have done in this world. All the passages in the Bible which definitely assume that well-being and prosperity are the reward of obedience to the will of God, were reinterpreted in the light of the axiom that this world was the vestibule to a better and more normal world. All questionings and doubts about the importance of obeying the will of God were thus dismissed, and religion remained the chief bond of national unity.

The attribute of mercy is an integral part of the very conception of a divine being, since he is supposed to be intimately related to his people and profoundly interested in its welfare. By ascribing the quality of mercy to God, religion makes man at home in the world, and grants him a sense of confidence and security. During the precarious condition of the Jewish people after the destruction of the Second Commonwealth, the attribute of mercy was in special need of being invoked, for then the Jews felt insecure, and looked to the protection which only God could give them. It was natural, however, that their state of helplessness made them dream passionately of the redemption that would restore them to their land and freedom. Aware of their failure to live fully in accordance with God's will and weighted down by a consciousness of sin, the Jewish people's only claim to God's protection and its only hope of redemption could be God's quality of mercy. This accounts for the deepened meaning which the mercy of God acquired in rabbinic literature.

In the Scriptures it is chiefly in God's forgiveness of sin that his quality of mercy is manifest. This is also the case in rabbinic literature. During the third stage of its career, the Jewish people found in the Prophets' call to repentance a constant reminder of what it had to do to earn redemption. Along with *miswot* and good deeds, repentance became the daily duty of a faithful Jew.[32] But the efficacy of repentance, in turn, assumed in God the attribute of mercy, since on grounds of strict justice, according to their way of thinking, punishment should be the inevitable consequence of sin.[33] With repentance thus looming large in the life of the Jew in his national as well as in his less inclusive relationships, the assumption that God necessarily exercises mercy became firmly fixed as an integral part of the Jew's conception of God.

When religion became the exclusive medium for national self-expression, the two values which emerged very much intensified and deepened were Torah and Israel. To the Prophets, the Torah of God was synonymous with a type of civilization which was dominated by the ideals of justice, kindness and piety. In the theocratic period the Torah of God was specifically identified with Pentateuchal law and teaching. The 119th psalm, and the passages in many other Psalms [34] dealing with the Torah of the Lord, reflect an ecstatic devotion to what was regarded as the will of God. The Hellenists' efforts to have the Jews adopt Greek civilization elicited from the loyal Jews a highly conscious appreciation of the Torah, and the conviction that it transcended all other civilizations as a way of life. This estimate of the supreme importance of the Torah was, no doubt, based upon the belief that it represented the articulate will of God.

Yet in comparison with the attitude of the Jews to the Torah during the third stage, all former expressions of appreciation of the Torah appear commonplace. During the third stage, the Jew was completely possessed by the Torah; he had no room in his mind or heart for anything else. In spite of all devotion to the Torah during the period of the Second Commonwealth, no one then could have uttered a statement like that of R. Hiyya bar Abba, [35] who attributed to God the words, "Would that Israel had forsaken me and kept my Torah." Though this may be only a figure of speech, it indicates a trend of thought altogether inconceivable in an earlier stage. If the third stage of Jewish religion afforded the mental background for so paradoxical a statement, it was because, from the standpoint of national self-preservation, to know specifically what was the will of God was considered infinitely more important than to understand the nature of God.

The Jewish people might have made religion a predominant expression of national life in various ways. They might have encouraged the establishment of ecclesiastical orders; they might have placed a spiritual premium upon the cultivation of religious asceticism; or they might have fostered an atmosphere conducive to religio-philosophical and theological schools of thought. Religion, however, was not merely the predominant means of individual self-expression, but the sum total of national self-expression. Therefore, something much more comprehensive than ecclesiastical orders, monasticism or theologic system was needed to fortify the Jewish spirit. The entire civilization by which the Jewish people lived had to be accounted as the will of God. Every mode of social behavior, every form of conduct which answered to the expectation of fellow-Jews, fell under

the category of divine command. It was this inclusion of the entire
regimen of conduct within the range of divinely prescribed ordinances that gave rise to the dogma that the oral Torah was given
simultaneously with the written Torah.[35]

In the oral Torah we may distinguish two types of prescribed
conduct. One type consists of ordinances which are based upon the
rabbinic interpretation of the written Torah. These are designated
as *mideoraita,* or prescribed by the Torah. When a doubt arises about
the application of such a law to a particular instance, the decision
is always on the side of rigor. The second type consists of ordinances
prescribed by the Rabbis themselves, either as a fence to Torah laws,
or as special decrees and enactments. These are designated as
miderabbanan. When their application to a particular instance is
doubtful, the decision is always on the side of leniency. But rabbinic
laws are inherently no less binding than Torah laws, and are, in a
sense, also divinely prescribed, because the Rabbis derive their
authority from the divine command in Deuteronomy concerning
the duty of obeying those who interpret the law in the spirit of the
Torah.[37] In time there arose the legend that all rabbinic teachings
and ordinances had actually been enunciated by God at Sinai.[38]

Because the entire regimen of conduct was placed within the
scope of God's will, the Jews had to turn for guidance and authority
to those who mastered the contents of both the oral and the written
Torah. Although the sway and authority of the rabbinate seems to
indicate that Jewish life possessed the same ecclesiasticism which
dominated the church, a careful analysis reveals an important distinction. The priest or ecclesiastic acted as an intermediary between
God and the individual. The ecclesiastic was in direct line of descent
from the medicine man of old; he followed upon the priest, who
delivered the oracle of the deity to whom the devotee appealed for
answer. *The rabbi was not an intermediary between God and the
people in any sense of the term. He exercised no theurgic function
whatever,*[39] *and rejected all ascription of such functions to him.*[40]
He merely applied the law prescribed by the Torah to the particular
situation that confronted him, and used his moral authority to have
it enforced.

But, though we discount all theurgic connotations in the esteem
with which the rabbi was held by the Jewish people since the destruc-

tion of the Jewish state, the fact remains that one who possessed a knowledge of Torah was regarded as an indispensable guide in the performance of God's will. And since the welfare of the individual and of the nation hinged entirely upon the performance of God's will, the Sages and the "disciples of the wise" enjoyed the prestige usually accorded to those who have control over the welfare of others. Their authority was deferred to at all times. The Jew was expected to place implicit faith in the Rabbis, who were acknowledged masters in the law. One version has it that if the rabbinic authorities tell you that right is left and left is right, you have to obey.[1] However, this is qualified elsewhere [2] by the condition that the Sanhedrin pass decisions that are not contrary to common sense. If a master in the law persists in defying the law as laid down by his colleagues, he is amenable to capital punishment.[3]

We can understand why the study of the Torah became the most important pursuit of the Jew, when we realize to what extent religion became the sole national preoccupation of the Jewish people. R. Johanan b. Zakkai speaks of the study of the Torah as the very purpose for which the human being was created.[4] The well-known discussion, in the academy of Lod, of the question, which is more important, study or practice,[5] together with the decision that study is more important because it leads to practice of the *miṣwot*, appears at first as a denial of the *supreme* value of the study of the Torah. But a closer analysis of the meaning of the decision discloses that it merely emphasizes the importance of practice, and is in no way intended to deprive study of its primacy. There is a sufficient number of rabbinic dicta to verify the interpretation of the decision rendered at Lod: "The whole world is not equal in value to one word of the Torah," says an *Amora* of the third century. "All the *miṣwot* are not equal to one word of the Torah," says his contemporary.[6] This estimate of the study of Torah should not surprise us, since the Torah was considered in all literalness the very word of God. By poring over its contents one actually lived through the experience of communion with God, and thus attained the highest goal of all human striving. It is as though one were present at Sinai when God revealed himself to all Israel. Bertrand Russell said that the study of higher mathematics afforded "the true spirit of delight, the exaltation, the sense of being more than man, which is the touchstone of the highest excellence." The ordinary Jew obtained all that from the study of the Torah.

If we consider that the Jew expected to derive the rare experience of revelation through the study of the Torah, we shall not confuse his passionate absorption in it with the intellectual interest that we associate with the study of objective truth. To arrive at objective truth implies a reliance upon the intellect and upon the validity of the senses. The study of objective truth is based upon the direct observation of the phenomena of the inner and outer world. Authority in such study is simply the authority of greater expertness in observation and inference. On the other hand, the study of the Torah as advocated in rabbinic Judaism is based on the assumption that man can never learn the most important truths by the use of his own intellectual powers. Those truths God alone can make known to him, and those truths have been revealed to him in the Torah. By the same token, authority resides only in those to whom God has revealed his will, or who have thoroughly familiarized themselves with the formulation of his will in the Torah. It is evident that such an attitude to truth would not further the objective study of outward reality, or of human nature, except as it contributed to a clearer understanding, or to a more effective defense of the Torah. It was only with that end in view that science and philosophy were cultivated by the medieval Jewish theologians.

When the entire national life and activity became concentrated upon living in accordance with the will of God as revealed in the Torah, national existence assumed a degree of importance in the consciousness of the Jew which it had never possessed during the preceding stages of the Jewish religion. We must remember that by this time the belief that the present world-order was transitory and altogether inadequate to supply man's essential needs was generally prevalent. The main purpose of human striving in this world was to inherit a portion in the world to come. This constituted salvation. The greater part of mankind uniformly accepted this philosophy of human life. The fact about which they differed was merely which religion, or more accurately expressed, which revelation, contained the final declaration of God's will to man; for only those who acknowledged the authority of that revelation and lived in accord with it could be certain of salvation, or life in the world to come.

The Jewish people, claiming sole possession of the true and final revelation of God's will, thought itself the only people destined to inherit the new world. It was assumed that before the new world-order would be ushered in, a great part of the Gentile world would repudiate its false gods, accept the God of Israel, and obey the teachings of the Torah, thus identifying itself with God's chosen people. It became a prerequisite to salvation, therefore, to be a Jew. This assumption went hand in hand with exaggerated glorification of the proselyte. The few statements,'' generally quoted as typical, which describe the proselytes as undesirable, are not at all characteristic of the Jewish attitude toward them. They are isolated opinions and reflect unpleasant experiences with proselytes; they are entirely out of keeping with the volume of praise accorded to them throughout the rabbinic writings.'⁸ In a prayer repeated thrice daily, the Jew invoked divine blessing upon the proselytes and prayed for the privilege of sharing their good fortune.'⁹ There is even a tendency to hint that God set greater store by the proselytes than he did by the Jews, because the former accepted the yoke of the heavenly kingdom although they had not witnessed the revelation at Sinai.⁵⁰

Augmented by the proselyted Gentiles, and destined to be the sole inhabitants of the world to come, the Jewish people could no longer be conceived as an ordinary nation. Chosen by God for so high a destiny, it became transfigured into the *Keneset Yisrael*, the beloved of God. Coordinate with the ideas of God and of the Torah was the concept of Israel as a people personified, idealized and apotheosized.

In the exhortations of the Pentateuch and in the consolatory utterances of the prophetic writings, we meet with idealized portrayals of Israel the nation. The Prophets, in order to give point to their denunciation of the actual condition of their people, frequently alluded to the perfection and greatness that Israel might have attained. Some of the Prophets found it necessary to picture the future as glorious in order to arouse hope and instill patience when difficulties and dangers threatened the life of Israel. In rabbinic Judaism, the idealization of the Jewish people was motivated, for the most part, by the need of counteracting the contempt in which they were held by the Gentile world. The ideal qualities visioned by the Prophets were no longer considered merely latent and potential, but actual. Instead of projecting those qualities into the Israel of the future, rabbinic Judaism retrojected them into the Israel of the past, even though in the process of retrojection many passages of the Bible had to be interpreted in other than a literal sense, and a new construction had to be placed upon the propriety of the denunciatory attitude assumed by such Prophets as Elijah, Amos, Isaiah and Jeremiah.[51]

The need to feel at home in the world, which religion seeks to satisfy, is a universal one. The Jew, living as he did in an alien and inimical world, could never have achieved the feeling of being at home, had not his own people served as an environment which was impervious to the threats and attacks of enemies. To function as such a haven of refuge, the Jewish people had to be conceived as marked out for a destiny that meant ultimate stability and security for all who were identified with it. It was so conceived by being regarded as the only people destined for the world to come. By harboring the divine presence, even the actual and present condition of the Jewish people met the individual's need for an environment of safety. For though the Jewish people was exiled from the land where it could commune with God as nowhere else, it was not altogether bereft of his presence. The *Shekinah* accompanied Israel in all its wanderings.[52] This gave Israel a sacrosanct character which it did not have in biblical times.

To realize to what extent the glorification of Israel, characteristic of the third stage, advanced beyond the most extravagant idealization of Israel found in the Bible, we need but recall that Israel came to be considered as God's very purpose and intent in creating the world. The creation of the world is no longer taken for granted, as in the Bible, as an ultimate act of God which needs no further accounting. It is now interpreted as having been intended mainly for Israel. Rabbinic Judaism represents largely a reversal of centrality in the spiritual realm analogous to the reversal of centrality effected by the change from the Ptolemaic to the Copernican system of astronomy. Instead of Israel existing for the world, it is the world that exists for Israel. The people of Israel is the *raison d'être* of the world.[53] Were Israel to fail in its allegiance to God by rejecting the Torah, the world would be destroyed. The Israelocentric conception of the universe is carried so far as to lead to the belief that the natural order of events for all mankind is determined by Israel's conduct. It is in no hyperbolic sense that Resh Lakish represents God as saying to Israel, when the latter complains that God seems to have forgotten her, "I have created twelve constellations in heaven, each constellation consists of thirty hosts, etc., and each camp consists of 365 times ten million stars, . . . and all of them I have created only for thy sake." [54]

We are now in a position to understand what actual historical fact is conveyed in the statement that the Jewish religion maintained its continuity for three thousand years. When we speak of the continuity of a religion, we do not mean that its teachings and prescribed modes of conduct have remained unchanged. This is the continuity of a stone, but not of a living organism. The living organism possesses a dynamic identity because of the life principle that animates its constantly changing elements. To comprehend the continuity of a religion, it is necessary to think of the religion not as an abstract entity existing by itself, but as a function of a living people and as an aspect of the civilization of that people. *The common denominator in the different stages of the Jewish civilization is not to be sought in the tenets and practices, but in the continuous life of the Jewish people.* Without the continuity of social life, without the countless generations of men, women and children who lived and cultivated their social and spiritual heritage and transmitted it to the generations following, the religion of the Jews of the Second Commonwealth could not have been continuous with the religion of the Israelites who entered Palestine.

But while the transmission of the spiritual heritage from generation to generation is sufficient to account for its *actual* continuity, it is necessary to point to some factor which operates to prevent the changed outlook and mode of life from destroying the *feeling* of continuity. That factor has been the tendency to reinterpret religious values which have come down from the past so that they can serve as a vehicle for the expression of teachings and ideals which have relevance to contemporaneous ideas and needs. The articulate or symbolic form of those values remains the same; it is the significance that is new. *Reinterpretation of religious values is spir-*

itual metabolism. It is a form of that law of growth which, by an uninterrupted transfer of life from the old to the new, renders vital change a very means to vital sameness and continuity.

We have seen how the Prophets prepared the way for the transformation of the Jewish religion from a henotheistic religion into a theocratic one, and how eschatological speculation transformed it from a theocratic into an other-worldly religion. Likewise, during the other-worldly stage of the Jewish religion there developed a theology which prepared the way for the next and fourth stage of the Jewish religion. The principal function of Jewish theology was to fit the biblical and rabbinic conception of God into the framework of the philosophic concepts which had came to be regarded as setting forth the truth about reality. Although medieval Jewish theology believed it was merely reaffirming the Jew's allegiance to traditional beliefs, it indirectly paid sufficient homage to reason to prepare the way for a type of religion in which reason—in a sense sufficiently large to include our deeper insights and intuitions—is the only guide and authority."

When the anthropomorphic conceptions of God in the Bible were found to clash with the more intellectualized conceptions of God developed in Greek philosophy, there arose the need for reinterpretation. Since it was inevitable that those who came under the influence of Greek thought should prefer the much more rational conception of God therein developed, only one course of action remained whereby the Bible could retain its authority: that was to utilize the allegorical method of interpretation inaugurated in the fourth century, B.C.E., by Euhemerus, in his attempt to save the religious heritage of the Greeks. This method was used by the Jews of Alexandria, who were the first to experience the conflict between the Jewish spiritual heritage and Greek thought; Philo was its most noteworthy protagonist. He gave a new significance to Jewish religion as a whole. His revaluation had the effect of transforming the Jewish religion into a divinely revealed philosophic system. "Philosophy," he said, "is the soul, and ceremonies the body, of Judaism."

Analogous was the experience of the Jews who came in contact once again with Greek thought through the medium of Islamic culture. R. Saadya in the tenth century, with his *Emunot we-Deot,* marks the beginning of a line of Jewish thinkers who applied themselves to the task of restating in terms of the philosophic world-outlook the teachings of the Torah as interpreted by the Rabbis. The principal Jewish theologic text which, until the advent of modern philosophy, has helped the more thoughtful among the Jews to bridge the gap between tradition and rationalism, has been Maimonides' *Guide for the Perplexed.*

Although previous attempts to revaluate the Jewish religion have been useful in their own way, they afford little help in the problem of reconstruction before us. The allegorical method, whereby the content of Judaism was adjusted to contemporaneous thought by the Jewish philosophers, could be acceptable only when the Torah was considered a supernatural phenomenon. Proceeding from the assumption that the Torah was supernaturally revealed, the Jewish philosophers were justified in taking for granted that nothing in it could contradict any of the conclusions of reason which to them was but another form of divine revelation. Since language is used not only literally but metaphorically, one did not violate the supramundane character of the Torah by resorting to metaphorical interpretation, whenever the literal text appeared untenable in the light of the prevalent philosophic ideas. From that standpoint, it was comparatively easy to interpret a text in such a way as to make it yield meanings so anachronistic that its author could not possibly even have implied them.

In the nineteenth century, a heroic attempt was made to revive that method of interpretation. Samson Raphael Hirsch, in his commentaries on the Bible, attempted to interpret symbolically every one of the rites and ceremonies of Jewish life. His efforts have proved sterile because the allegorical method comes into conflict with the modern man's demand for historic truth. The allegorical method is no longer acceptable because it implies the denial of the outstanding fact—deeply ingrained in the mind of modern man—that in ancient times people had some very crude notions of human society and of the world-order, and that those notions found their way into their sacred literatures, and gave rise to many of their social and religious institutions. To this limitation the Jews were no exception. The Jewish philosophers who lacked this historical point of view were in a position to believe sincerely that the thought which they read into the Scriptures was actually implied therein. But nowadays every allegorical rendering of Scripture smacks of jugglery. An entirely different method must be evolved to achieve religious continuity with the past, a method compatible with the evolutionary and historical conception of religion, and based upon needs of the human spirit which cannot be disregarded without danger to man's moral and spiritual health.

CHAPTER XXVI

THE FUNCTIONAL METHOD OF INTERPRETATION

Reinterpretation a means of eliciting latent values—The achievements and short-comings of the historical school—The functional method of interpretation as a means of maintaining the continuity of the Jewish religion—The God-idea in the problem of reinterpretation—The variable God-idea in Jewish history—The emotional and conative aspects of the God-idea—Moral progress as reflected in the God-idea—What is implied in the revaluation of God-idea—The functional interpretation of the divine attributes—The functional interpretation of other-worldliness—Resistance to reinterpretation to be expected.

THE Jewish quality of the religion of the Jews will not depend on claims to supernatural origin or claims to being more rational or more ethical than other religions. Its uniqueness will consist chiefly in the fact that it will be lived by Jews, and will be expressed by them through such cultural media as Jewish civilization will produce. But even before these media are cultivated on a scale commensurate with present spiritual needs, the religion lived by Jews can be given character and individuality by utilizing the vast storehouse of spiritual values that are implicit in its traditions. If the recorded experiences of Jewish prophet and sage, poet and saint will occupy a predominant place in the Jewish consciousness as it strives to adjust itself to life, the resulting adjustment will constitute Jewish religious behavior. The individuality of the Jewish religion cannot be described in advance. Only after a Jewish life or civilization is attained will there emerge a type of religion as unique as that which emerged from the Jewish civilization of the past.

Individuality is at first spontaneous and unshaped, says John Dewey. It is a potentiality, a capacity of development. . . . Since individuality is a distinctive way of feeling the impacts of the world and of showing a preferential bias in response to these impacts, it develops into shape and form only through interaction with actual conditions. . . . The imposition of individuality as something made in advance always gives evidence of a mannerism, not of a manner. For the latter is something original and creative; something formed in the very process of creation.[1]

If the traditional Jewish religion is inherently capable of engendering the most significant human attitudes—faith, hope, courage —if it can lead to social control and improvement and to the development of personality in the individual, it should be capable of revaluation in terms of present-day thought. Whereas in the past the theurgic element of the traditional values often eclipsed the ethical and spiritual consequences, now it will be necessary to stress the ethical and spiritual consequences to such an extent as to make evident their independence of the theurgic element. It may be asked: but why start out with traditional concepts, and then subject yourself to the arduous task of revaluation? Why not begin with utterly new standards and values? The answer is that the tendency to reinterpret derives from the basic human need of feeling that there is some objective truth to the course which human history has taken. If all that man achieved of culture and religion should turn out to be illusory, what meaning can human life have, as a whole? On the other hand, if we can discover some element of continuity between that which we find to be helpful to human life and development and that which was cherished by the ancients, we are fortified in our hopes and aspirations. *The advantage of utilizing traditional concepts is that they carry with them the accumulated momentum and emotional drive of man's previous efforts to attain greater spiritual power.*

To derive that advantage, it is necessary to develop a method of discovering in traditional Jewish religion adumbrations of what we consider an adequate spiritual adjustment to life. We must evolve a method of interpretation which, though it regard the traditional religious teachings and institutions as a product of social life, reflecting the limitations of the various periods of their origin, will yet discover to what extent those teachings and institutions made for faith, salvation and loyalty. By this means the pragmatic implications of the traditional teachings will be revealed and developed. Thus the forgotten mood of a people's civilization can be recaptured and given "a spiritual contemporaneousness."

That method is now being evolved. The principle underlying the work of the Historical School[2] is that Judaism is not a static congeries of beliefs and practices definitely fixed for all time and handed down intact from generation to generation. The Historical School assumes that Judaism represents the changing cultural and spiritual life of a people subject to the vicissitudes of time and place. It expected to put new life into Judaism by interpreting it as a series of social phenomena subject to the natural laws of change that operate in the universe. The Historical School has not treated Judaism, especially since the biblical period, as a supramundane revelation somehow vouchsafed to a single people chosen for that purpose, but as a continual development of a living people adjusting itself to its environment and adjusting the environment to itself. Viewing Judaism as a dynamic process prepares the way for the synthesis of the Jewish social heritage with the best in the civilizations of our day, a synthesis so essential to the spiritual normality of the Jew.

However, the historical method of interpretation, as developed and applied up to now, has fallen short in two respects. In the first place, it has been too limited in its scope. The Historical School has subjected to its method of interpretation the material of the rabbinic period in Judaism, but has contributed little to the study of the Scriptures in the light of scientific research.[3] With the characteristic inconsistency of the Historical School, Henry Malter wrote: "Our religion restrains us from any criticism of the Bible because *torah min ha-shamayim* is one of the main principles of the doctrine of Judaism. No such prohibition exists against criticism of the Talmud. The Bible is the word of God; the Talmud is the work of men, no matter how great or glorious."[4] We can, of course, understand why it has refrained from submitting the Bible to its method of investigation. The Bible has been the Jews' "Holy of Holies." To subject it to scientific analysis before the greater part of Jewry sensed the actuality of the living spirit of the Jewish people would have been to deprive the Jew of his spiritual mainstay. Rabbinic Judaism, the traditional religion of the Jewish people, is popularly regarded as derived from, and dependent for its validity upon, the written word of the Torah. So long as this idea prevails, any attempt to study the Bible from the historical point of view will be considered a blow at the very vitals of Jewish religion. But that reason is no longer valid. The negative implications of biblical criticism have percolated to the general mind, and unless they are countered by a positive intellectual readjustment, they are bound to render the Jewish religion even more inoperative than it is already.

Secondly, the Historical School has fallen short in having failed to reckon with the fact that *the significance of an idea or an institution is to be sought not only in its overt expression but also in its implications.* These implications need not necessarily have been recognized by those who first voiced the idea or evolved the institution. It is only in retrospect as we review the consequences in thought and action of any tradition that we begin to sense its full significance. To identify those consequences which are essential to a comprehension of the larger significance of a traditional belief or custom, it is necessary to approach that belief or custom from the psychological point of view. Had the Historical School utilized that approach in its study of traditional Judaism, it would have inaugurated the spiritual readjustment so essential to Jewish life. It would not merely have piled up archeological data, but would have revealed the elements in Judaism which are of permanent value. It would have brought back to the Jew the spirit that groped after self-expression in the traditional teaching and the aspiration that animated the ritual observance. "It must be admitted," writes I. Elbogen,[5] in his survey of the achievements of the *Jüdische Wissenschaft,* which is the creation of the Historical School, "that the *Jüdische Wissenschaft* made but little effort, when it was in the heyday of its career, to formulate a new world-outlook for Judaism."

The Jewish religion must be so reinterpreted that it will be able to further the values which have become the conscious objects of all higher human striving. These values are the product not of any single religious philosophy, or ethical tendency, but of the various social and intellectual forces that have entered into the shaping of modern civilization. In reinterpreting the traditional values of any spiritual heritage or civilization, we are conserving accumulated energy that would otherwise go to waste. *Revaluation of spiritual values is the conservation of spiritual energy.* It helps to conserve and foster all tendencies, individual and social, which make for the complete development of the individual and the progressive unification of mankind.

The ideas expressed in the ancient Jewish literature, and the institutions that have become identified with Jewish life, should be regarded as attempts to express in terms of beliefs and practices the needs and desiderata of a fuller life than man had been able to attain. What these needs and desiderata were, can be discerned in some of the consequences in thought and action which resulted from those ideas and institutions. The task of reinterpretation consists first in selecting from among the ideational and practical consequences of the traditional values those which are spiritually significant for our day, and then in turning those consequences into motives of thought and conduct. Functional interpretation, therefore, implies a knowledge of the background of the teaching or institution interpreted, of the various contexts in which that teaching or institution occurs, and most of all a knowledge of human nature as it functions in society and in the individual. Reinterpretation is the process of finding equivalents in the civilization to which we belong for values of a past stage of that or another civilization. While there is a qualitative difference between such values, yet in their relation to their respective civilizations or, considered morphologically, they possess equivalence.

Assuming that there has taken place no qualitative change in human nature during the last two or three millennia, we may take for granted that whatever objectives we now accept as worthy and desirable have been anticipated by some of the avowed objectives of the past. For modern ideals to be without ancestry would imply that human nature has altered radically in the past hundred years or so. If we search diligently, we shall find that traditional aspirations are pregnant with implications that are highly significant for our day.

It must be remembered that we are not dealing with questions of fact. To interpret the past functionally does not mean to follow in the footsteps of the traditional harmonizers who tried to prove that the Scriptures had anticipated every recently discovered scientific fact. Functional reinterpretation is concerned with man's yearning to find himself in a universe that is friendly to his highest purpose, to fulfill the most valued potentialities of his nature and to achieve a social order that is founded on justice and peace. These yearnings are as constant as human nature. If it is our purpose to continue any particular spiritual heritage, we can do so by reconstructing mentally the aspirations implied in its teachings and institutions. Every tradition is rich in these aspirations, for it could not have become a tradition without them. By rendering these implications explicit, we supply momentum to all social and spiritual endeavors which have as their aim the unhampered and complete self-fulfillment of the individual and the increasing measure of cooperation among individuals and groups.

This type of interpretation consists chiefly in disengaging from the mass of traditional lore and custom the psychological aspect which testifies to the presence of ethical and spiritual strivings. The effect of discovering the psychological element in a tradition is that the tradition ceases to be regarded as something to be accepted or rejected. A third alternative presents itself, that of employing it as a symbol for a spiritual desideratum in the present. Which desideratum it shall be can best be determined by choosing from among the implications and consequences of the tradition the one relevant for our day.

How necessary it is to apply this type of interpretation to the contents of the Jewish past can best be appreciated, perhaps, when we realize that the values which have been incorporated into other civilizations have been only those of the first two stages of the Jewish civilization. The prophetic ideals evolved during the period of the First Commonwealth, and the messianic ideals crystallized during the period of the Second Commonwealth, have become the common possession of mankind. But the same cannot be said of Talmudism, or of medieval Jewish philosophy and poetry.⁶ So far the only one who has hinted at a value of universal significance to be derived from the last twenty centuries of Jewish suffering and striving has been Simon Dubnow.⁷ He regards the ideal of steadfastness to a cause and the capacity for martyrdom as the universal value which emerges from the third stage of Judaism's history. But even that value is scarcely apparent to the average person of today to whom the greater part of the literary content produced by Judaism during its third stage seems, in its uninterpreted form, completely irrelevant to his own spiritual needs. It is only by means of the functional method of interpretation that all the life and thought that have gone into Judaism since the destruction of the Second Temple can be so rendered that the particularistic and national mode in which they are cast will become transparent enough to permit the universalistic and human to shine through. This has to some extent been attempted by Moritz Lazarus in his *Jewish Ethics* and Hermann Cohen in his *Die Religion der Vernunft*. But while they both succeed in idealizing many of the leading religious and ethical ideas in Judaism, their deductions suffer largely from the absence of historical perspective. They read much more into, than out of, the statements they interpret.

Nothing about the Jewish civilization of the past is so conspicuous as its permeation with the God-idea. Physical phenomena, historical events and moral duties acquire their significance from their relationship to God. As handed down, the conception of God which is the *leitmotif* of the Jewish civilization is theurgic in character; that is, it implies divine interference with the continuity of nature for the sake of man. To some people the elimination of the theurgic element from the God-idea is equivalent to the abandonment of the belief in God, and an act which must lead to the disintegration of the Jewish social heritage. If we approach the Jewish civilization with the purpose of understanding its psychological—not its logical—reality, its conception of God should interest us not for what it seeks to tell concerning the metaphysical nature of the Deity, but for the difference it made in the behavior of the Jew. We should analyze the Jewish conception of God in order to learn how it functioned in the life of the Jewish people. If it in any way made for that justice which spells the fullest possible opportunity for the individual to give play to his highest intellectual and spiritual powers, and for that love which spells the growing capacity to make our common humanity the basis of cooperation, it should be capable of revaluation in terms of present-day thought.

To understand how it is possible for a God-idea to undergo change without producing a break in the continuity of the civilization to which it belongs, we must realize that it does not function by itself, but through that pattern of emotional, volitional and ideational reactions which may be described as religious behavior. Before considering, however, the God-idea in the process of operation with the other elements of religious behavior, it is necessary to note that the human mind has evolved two different types of God-ideas: one consists of both percepts and concepts; the other, much rarer type, consists of concepts only. In the religion of primitive peoples, the God-idea is of the first type for, despite the conceptual ramifications it may later acquire, its fundamental content is always some real or imaginary entity, some object or identifiable being. The primitive man was able to conceive everything, animate or inanimate, as informed with divine qualities. The focal object of his religious behavior might be any being or thing in the heavens above, the earth beneath, or the waters beneath the earth. Only at a comparatively late stage of civilization does the worship of other than the human form come to be abhorred. When this happens, the God-idea already consists to a marked degree of concepts.

Even in the most primitive religions, the God-idea is never altogether free from conceptual thinking, since the object or being regarded as divine is *ipso facto* conceived as endowed with the qualities of power and purposiveness. If purposiveness be the essential characteristic of personality, then we may say that together with the percept which entered into the God-idea—with the focal object of that idea—more or less vague conceptions of power and personality were always present.

Thus far the God-idea as a synthesis of perceptual image and conceptual abstraction. When philosophy invaded the field of religion, all mental representations of God were considered inconsistent with ideal religious behavior. No form, whether that of object or of human being, was deemed compatible with the God-idea. For the more speculatively minded, the perceptual element had to be banished altogether from the God-idea. The God-idea was now an abstraction distilled out of the conceptions of power and personality which had always accompanied the perceptual elements in the God-idea. *The qualities of perfection and infinity which the philosophers ascribed to God were not additional qualities superimposed upon the traditional concepts of power and personality, but were simply the extension, in thought, of those qualities.*

The main contribution of philosophy to religion has thus consisted of a change not merely in the focal object of religious behavior, but in the *type* of focal object. In unphilosophic religion the focal object of religious behavior was always an identifiable being either real or imaginary. In philosophic religion the focal object was treated as far too different from reality as conceived by the human mind to be accounted an entity or identifiable being in the same sense as any known or imagined entity. This gave rise to the tendency in pre-modern philosophy to define the nature of God negatively rather than affirmatively. When it was said, for example, that there was only one God, the philosophers added, "But there is no unity like unto his unity." Likewise every one of the other attributes ascribed to God was interpreted in terms of what God was not. The tendency of philosophic religion in modern times is to be even more emphatic than it was in the Middle Ages in deprecating any identifiable being as the focal object of religious behavior. Nevertheless, modern philosophic religion is more inclined than medieval to define the focal object of religion in affirmative fashion by identifying God with some aspect of reality, or with reality as a whole, viewed from some particular standpoint. It does not hesitate for example, to identify God as the *life* of the universe, or as the *meaning* of reality.

When we trace the history of the religious behavior of the Jewish people, we find that the God-idea which was the source of that behavior varied with the different stages of its civilization. We know that after the Israelites established themselves in Canaan they worshipped YHWH in the image of a bull.* What psychological factors contributed to the attitude of derision and abhorrence which developed against that image in Israel it is difficult to discover. It is possible that what contributed most to the elimination of bull worship was the sacred ark which the Israelites had brought with them from the wilderness.* But whatever percept the earlier Israelites had of YHWH, there can be no doubt that for the Prophets, YHWH was essentially an anthropomorphic being. Some prophets, like Ezekiel, may have had a distinct mental image of YHWH, while others, like Isaiah, pictured his form in vague outline.

When the Jewish religion came into contact with philosophic thought as it did in the case of the Alexandrian school, and later in the Middle Ages beginning with the period of the Geonim, it had completely emancipated itself from the need of any perceptual image of God. In fact, the Jewish philosophers not only treated the perceptual image of God as dispensable, but they very emphatically condemned it as on a par with idolatry. Despite the insistence of the philosophers, however, upon a purely conceptual representation of God, and the expression of that insistence in the formal creed of Maimonides, the vast majority of the Jewish people have not been seriously troubled about the philosophic objections to conceiving God as a magnified being. In fact, the uncompromising tendency of Maimonides and his successors to declare any but a purely conceptual idea of God heretical called forth opposition on the part of the unphilosophic Talmudists.[10]

To this day, there is no intellectually formulated conception which has acquired authoritative recognition in Judaism as the only true idea of God. The inevitable conclusion to which we are led by the consideration of the evolution of the God-idea in the history of the Jewish people, and of the part played by it in civilization in general, is that *the Jewish civilization cannot survive without the God-idea as an integral part of it, but it is in no need of having any specific formulation of that idea authoritative for all Jews.*

The foregoing refers to God only as the focal object, or object of reference, in the pattern of reactions, which in their totality constitute the religious behavior of the Jew. To get the full significance of that behavior, and to appreciate the nature of its functioning, we have to consider also its emotional and conative aspects.

The emotional phase of religious behavior is compounded of the emotions of awe and trust which are the principal ingredients of the sense of holiness. There is, however, a marked difference between the cognitive and the emotional aspects of religious behavior in the degree to which they are affected by cultural development. The cognitive element, as we have seen, may vary from the crudest percept with a minimum of concept, to the most abstract concept with a complete negation of percept; the emotional phase, however, is the same in the most diverse forms of religious behavior. Whether the negative element of fear or the positive element of confidence predominate in the compound, emotion is not a matter of progressive development, but rather the result of individual temperament, or of the outward circumstances which are at times depressing and at times exhilarating. A savage will manifest the same intense religious emotions as the most highly cultivated person. It is evident, then, that the emotional phase in Jewish religious behavior would in no respect be different from the manifestation of that phase in the religious behavior of any other people.

It is chiefly the conative aspect of a people's religion that reveals its distinctive element. This aspect of a religion finds expression in the activities and restraints which are exercised with reference to objects or situations of vital interest to the adherents of that religion. What is of vital interest depends upon the state of cultural development. Under primitive conditions, only those objects and situations which appeal directly to the elementary needs of human nature excite interest. Food, mating and the maintenance of life and well-being are the only interests of savage society. Objects and situations which are directly connected with these ends and which excite interest simultaneously in a number of people evoke communal activities and restraints. In turn these activities and restraints focus further attention upon the objects and situations and bring them to the fore of consciousness. These latter thus become the main sources of the percepts and concepts that are projected into the focal object, or object of reference, in religious behavior; that is, into the object or being which is identified as a god.

As soon as man emerges from the savage state, he tends to develop derivative interests. As William James puts it, "Things not interesting in their own right borrow an interest which becomes as real and as strong as that of any natively interesting thing." The only things interesting in their own right are those which have to do with the satisfaction of the elementary needs. But the activities and restraints connected with objects and situations which are interesting in their own right acquire a derived interest that may attain an intensity not only equal to, but sometimes even greater than some of the elementary interests. *The cultivation of derivative interests is the chief function of a civilization.* If they retain their connection with the basic wants of human nature, they can with advantage serve as the norm of human living. Such a norm constitutes part of the higher life and makes for greater abundance of well-being. When man's elementary needs are stifled or even neglected through overemphasis upon derivative or spiritual interests, religion revenges itself by becoming either ascetic and dehumanized, or romantic and voluptuary.

The pragmatic significance of religious behavior turns upon the nature of the activities and the restraints through which it expresses itself. The pragmatic consequences of any religious idea—the conception of God, the conception of the messiah, or any similar idea—need not be the object of conscious recognition or reflection. If those activities and restraints refer merely to elementary needs, we have a very low type of religious behavior. That is the type of religion whose deities were the concrete and externalized expression of man's elementary needs—they were the gods of rain, of fertility, of war. As soon as these activities and restraints refer to interests which even for a time eclipse the elementary ones with which they are connected, there result two important consequences: first, the activities and restraints are modified to conform with the more developed social and ethical needs that arise; second, the God-idea is made to reflect the modified or more ethical nature of the activities and restraints.

Evidences of this development are discernible in the religions of Babylon, Egypt, Greece and Rome. The social and ethical standards that gave rise to their changing legal codes could not but modify their conception of the deity that was the focal object of the religious behavior. *But in the case of no people did the activities and restraints which constituted religious behavior undergo such a revolutionary change, and bring about so radical a transformation in the conception of the focal object of religious behavior, as in that of Israel.*

This radical transformation of religious behavior was attempted by the Prophets. As a result of their activity, the ethical element in the priestly *torot* was stressed, and God came to be conceived as creator of the universe, and sovereign of all mankind. The unity attributed to God in the Jewish religion has altogether different implications from the unity attributed to God by the Greek philosophers. The *conation* accompanying the concept of the unity of God in Jewish religious behavior consists in treating mankind as one, whereas no such pragmatic consequence is implied in the philosophic conception of divine unity. Though the reconstruction of the religion of Israel, which took place after the return from Babylon, did not altogether reap the fruits of the prophetic revaluation, enough of the prophetic impulse remained to affect Jewish religious behavior ever after. The prophetic inspiration suffused with a sense of high worth or holiness those activities and restraints which made for the holiness of life, for the fostering of human personality, and for the unification of society.

The revaluation of the traditional Jewish religion will be possible, therefore, only if we recognize that its significance does not derive from the cognitive element of its God-idea, but from the *conduct* in which that idea has found expression. Jewish religious behavior requires *an* idea of God, but were it contingent upon a particular idea of God, the continuity of the religious heritage would be broken. Since, however, the Jewish civilization succeeded in retaining its own continuity and that of its religion, despite the changes in the God-idea, it has proved itself exempt from the necessity of commitment to one authoritative conception of God. But though the Jewish civilization is not tied down to the God-idea of the *Tannaim,* the *Amoraim,* or of the Jewish philosophers of the Middle Ages, it cannot afford to become secular and omit the God-idea altogether. The only alternative is to reinterpret the God-idea in such a way as to allow for the differences in intellectual outlook. For some people only perceptual or demonstrable things are real, and of supreme importance. The focal object of their religious behavior might then be some anthropomorphic being. *There is nothing in Judaism viewed as a civilization to preclude an anthropomorphic or any other God-idea, provided its emotional and conative expression in religious behavior make for what are now recognized as the highest ends of human aspiration.* But most rational people today cannot bring an anthropomorphic God-idea to the necessary emotional and conative expression. They prefer to identify God with that aspect of reality which elicits the most serviceable human traits, the traits that enhance individual human worth and further social unity. Since those traits constitute what we value most in human personality, it may be said that the modern thinker tends to base his conception of God upon the cosmic implications of human personality.

It is interesting to note how the foregoing analysis of religious behavior throws light upon the three types of spiritual leaders that the human race has produced—the prophet, the philosopher and the mystic. Whereas the function of the priest has been to maintain the *status quo* of spiritual attainment, the prophet, the philosopher and the mystic have contributed, each in his own way, to the development of moral and spiritual values. The prophets have always concentrated their efforts upon the conative expression; the philosophers upon the cognitive aspect, and the mystics upon the emotional. Whenever an upheaval in social and cultural life makes the traditional religion inoperative, it is necessary for the prophetic type of activity to assert itself in the conative expression of the spiritual life in order to bring about a readjustment in the moral and social standards. The philosopher and the mystic then follow with their activity, and consolidate in intellectual and emotional terms the result of the change that is effected in individual conduct and in social institutions.

Only pedantic literalists would insist that the God-idea can have meaning only in religion based on the acceptance of supernaturalism and other-worldliness. They forget that we are so constituted that we have to keep on using old words and operate with traditional ideas, though with each generation experience is enriched, and the language in which that experience is expressed necessarily acquires new meaning. This is especially true in the case of terms which designate the distillation of social experience. Take, for example, words like justice, liberty, education. At one time, gruesome punishment meted out in a spirit of revenge was the prevalent idea of justice, and the ideal of liberty was so conceived as to be compatible with the institution of slavery. What was once considered education would now pass for learned ignorance. Would it ever occur to us to adopt some other method of designating one's ego than by the use of the personal pronoun "I," because our conception of the entity denoted by it has been completely revolutionized?

Words, like institutions, like life itself, are subject to the law of identity in change. It is entirely appropriate, therefore, to retain the greater part of the ancient religious vocabulary, particularly the term "God." As long as we are struggling to express the same fundamental fact about the cosmos that our ancestors designated by the term "God," the fact of its momentousness or holiness, and are endeavoring to achieve the ideals of human life which derive from that momentousness or holiness, we have a right to retain their mode of expression.

In attempting to deal with living emotions, says John Cowper Powys, with those nameless subjective feelings which underlie such historic words, it seems wiser to direct the introspective mind toward each particular feeling rather by means of the older symbols than by means of the newer ones, just because these traditional names—'will,' 'soul,' 'universe,' 'nature,' 'ego,' and so forth—have by long use on the high roads of human intercourse acquired such a rich thick emotional connotation that, however mythological they may be, they are more suggestive of what lies behind all words than the newer, more logical terms, coined by clever modern thinkers, so puzzlingly obscure except to the initiated, and of necessity so abstract and thin.[11]

One wonders what inhibited the author from adding just one more term, "God."

The reinterpretation of the traditional religious values and concepts is resisted by the enemies [12] of religion as vigorously as by the reactionaries and fundamentalists. This resistance of the so-called rationalists is motivated by an animus hardly compatible with rationalism. It is difficult to understand why religion should not be accorded the same right of revising and correcting itself as science and philosophy. We need only recall the crude guesses that went by the names of science and philosophy in olden times to realize that it is not the results attained that constitute the identity of an intellectual or spiritual discipline, but the impulse behind them. Religion conceived in terms of supernatural origin is the astrology and alchemy stage of religion. The religion which is about to emerge is the astronomy and chemistry stage of religion. Instead of resorting to belief in miracles, theophanies and external authority as the sanction for its teachings, religion will, henceforth, resort to the study of the needs of human nature which have found their satisfaction in the complex of beliefs, practices and emotions that center about the idea of God. Those needs form the common denominator between the religion of the past and the religion of the future.

Once we have learned to reinterpret the God-idea in terms of function, there is no difficulty in applying the same method of reinterpretation to the *attributes* that traditional religion has associated with God. Our chief interest is in the attributes which form part of the religious, and not necessarily of the philosophic consciousness. The attributes of God which were formulated by the Jewish philosophers of the Middle Ages are reinterpretations of the religious conceptions of God in terms of specific systems of thought. Thus the attributes of absoluteness, infinity and incorporeality do not represent original elements in the God-idea of Judaism. They served the purpose of establishing a certain functional identity between the God-idea of Scriptures and that of the philosophies current in the past. Our task is with the qualities ascribed to God in the sacred writings and prayers of the Jewish people, where God is conceived as creator, helper, king, lawgiver.

Much of the wisdom and aspiration of our ancestors is lost upon us because we no longer speak their language, though we may speak to the same purpose. The effort to recover the permanent values inherent in traditional religion is handicapped by the lack of imagination. An inflexible mentality takes every word in texts of ancient origin literally and ignores the *nisus* which created the word. If we disengage from the language of adoration the spiritual desiderata implied therein, we discover that the attributes ascribed to God represented the social and spiritual values formerly regarded as all-important. Those attributes are by no means limited in their meaning and application to the theurgic conception of God.

Just as the God-idea progressed from a perceptual image to a conception like the one which identifies God as the sum of all those factors and relationships in the universe that make for unity, creativity and worthwhileness in human life, so can the attributes of God, which once were externalized and concrete, be translated into modern terms and made relevant to modern thinking and living. Men attributed to God their own highest desires and aspirations. They called him creator, protector, helper, sovereign and redeemer. These terms can now be identified with the highest and most significant aims of human existence, and achieve a new force and vitality through this conscious process of identification. We can no longer believe that God is a mighty sovereign, or that the universe is the work of his hands. In the light of the present development of the God-idea, however, we can see that God is manifest in all creativity and in all forms of sovereignty that make for the enhancement of human life.

Let us take, for example, the attribute of God as creator. Were we to approach it from the standpoint of medieval metaphysics, we would at once involve ourselves in the complicated problem of *creatio ex nihilo,* and land in a philosophic *cul de sac.* If we proceed by the functional method of interpretation, we can discern in the belief that God created the world an expression of the tendency to identify the creative principle in the world with the manifestation of God. This approach to the problem of creation is in keeping with the trend of modern religious metaphysics. In a sense, it is the very antithesis of the approach of traditional theology, yet, emotionally and volitionally, we can deduce the same practical and socially valuable results from the one approach as from the other—from the conception of *God as the creative principle* of the universe as was derived in the past from the conception of *God as the creator* of the universe. For the creative principle is compatible in human life only with intelligence, courage and good-will, and is hindered in its operation by arrogance, greed and uncontrolled sexual desire.

God as helper and protector may be identified with the powers of nature which maintain life, and with the intelligence that transforms environment by subjugating and controlling the natural forces for the common good of humanity. In any act of social cooperation and good-will, in the striving for finer human relations, in man's courage and moral resilience, in his conquest of fear and death, we can discern the operation of the divine principle,—God made manifest. Likewise, whenever we experience a sense of stability and permanence in the midst of the universal flux, we experience the reality of God as helper.

The attributes of God as redeemer and sovereign can also be translated into terms of contemporary needs. According to tradition, when God revealed himself to Israel at Sinai, he made himself known not as the creator of heaven and earth, nor as the sovereign of mankind, but as the redeemer of Israel. In terms of the present world-outlook, man's desire for freedom, his struggles to attain it, reveal the striving of the divine in man. The cosmic life urge is displayed in restiveness under restraint. When the life urge becomes self-aware in man's efforts to shake off intolerable restraint, God as redeemer is manifest.

The sovereignty of God denotes the primacy of spiritual values in human life. That God is sovereign means that those aims, standards and interests which center about the belief in God are ends to which all other aims, standards and interests are subordinate as means. Thus for the individual so to strive after wealth that it becomes to him the standard of all values, is a denial of the sovereignty of God. So are the attainment of power for its own sake and the subservience to power, regardless of the manner in which it was acquired or the purpose to which it is applied. In domestic life, the primacy of the spiritual values means placing love and the spirit of sacrifice above any selfish purpose. In economic life, the primacy of the spiritual means realizing that men count more than things, that production is not an end in itself. In national life, from the standpoint of internal relations, the primacy of the spiritual values implies aiming toward creation of opportunities for the many rather than maintaining privileges for the few; from the standpoint of external relations, it implies that international dealings be motivated by a desire for peace and cooperation rather than for war and domination.

The difficulty in effecting the transition between the last stage of traditional religion and the religion of the future lies in the changed emphasis from other-worldly to this-worldly life. In traditional religion, the sense of at-homeness in the world, the fulfillment of personality and group loyalty were bound up with the belief that the present world was destined to give way to a new heaven and a new earth. Only by believing that this world would be superseded by another did man reconcile himself to life on earth; only the ultimate liberation of the soul from earthly needs rendered this life worthwhile; only that group which helped secure one a share in the world to come was genuinely significant. If we acquire the habit of viewing the traditional belief in the world to come, not from the standpoint of objective truth, but from that of its functional aspect, we can easily discern in it a meaning for our day. Interpreted functionally, the traditional conception of the world to come expresses man's discontent with the things as they are and his yearning for the things as they ought to be. From this viewpoint, the important element in this belief is not the fantastic picture of the ideal world, but the inner urge of which it was an expression; namely, the compulsion to look forward to a condition of human existence which would be free from the physical, spiritual and social ills that detract from life's worthwhileness. In former times, man was not familiar enough with the processes of nature to realize that he himself could effect the desired transformation. Not having observed nature with sufficient care to note its uniformities and plasticities, he was unable to conceive how the ideal world could arise out of the actual world. *The human mind will have to undergo considerable development before it will learn to treat its own initiative in bringing about a better world as part of the process whereby God is actualizing the world to come.*

With all their wisdom and insight the ancients did not arrive at the truth which has been distilled out of the sufferings of the human race, the truth that the kingdom of God is a paradox, an inner contradiction that must somehow be resolved. For ages men have put their faith in conformity and obedience to authority. In the eighteenth century, a reaction set in and men began to look upon the absolute freedom of the individual as the chief end. Ever since then, the pendulum of human life has been swinging between the extremes of despotism and anarchism. But so far no serious attempt has been made to discover a method whereby men might act both interdependently and independently, and achieve the world to come through a harmonious interplay of individualism and collectivism.

The world to come is none other than this world redeemed from slavery and war, from want and suffering, from disease and crime. Bitter experience has made humankind realize that only by reckoning with the polarity of human nature will it be possible to achieve the better world-order, the world to come. Every human being is both an *ego* and an *alter,* a self and an other. The *ego* or the self hungers for the satisfactions that yield individuality and selfhood. The *alter,* or other, yearns for absorption in a larger self, in an enveloping permanence and order and meaning. This polarity is an inescapable part of the nature of things. Human life is most complete when it reckons with its double aspect. Then it approximates a mode of life which is in accord with the law of God as writ in the nature of man. In an ideally ordered world these two tendencies of human nature would find fulfillment.

All forms of the spiritual life are an organization and synthesis of conflicting tendencies and impulses in human nature, and the spiritually ordered world must provide for the realization of such a synthesis. For synthesis it must be. We cannot fulfill the two impulses alternately; we cannot first cooperate and then be free, and imagine that we have achieved the desideratum. In that case, freedom and unity would in the end destroy each other as they have always done. We must so order the world that the two impulses of human will may find complete expression in one and the same effort, in one and the same practical manifestations of our desire to establish the kingdom of God. The adjustment between individuals, classes and nations should be guided by this consideration. Good government depends upon the recognition of this functional principle. For only in a social order based on peace can the two impulses be expressed and synthesized.

Some will always assume a deprecatory attitude toward the attempt to reinterpret the Jewish values from a modern, functional standpoint on the ground that Jewish religion would attain a form that its Jewish forebears would not recognize. They argue that, since our aim is to maintain the continuity of Judaism, we are defeating that aim when we impose modern categories of thought upon the literature and institutions of Judaism. A basic error in approach is at the root of this contention. It proceeds from the assumption that those who are to determine whether or not the continuity of a culture is maintained are its founders or initiators, and not its spokesmen in the generations following. Those who make that assumption, therefore, believe that since the founders are no longer alive when the problem of continuity arises, we must be possessed by their spirit and act as their proxies in deciding whether the adaptation of the culture to the exigencies of the times preserves the identity of the culture or not. This is essentially the point of view of all the orthodoxies that have acted as a dead-weight upon human progress. The only ones to decide whether the continuity of a culture is maintained are those who are actually confronted with the problem. *The past or its proxies can no more pass judgment upon the present than the child can sit in judgment upon the man.*

Suppose we were to apply the orthodox criterion to the spiritual life of the Jewish people during the last three thousand years. Can we, for instance, assert that a Samuel or a David would have recognized in the Judaism of a Raba or an Abbaye, *Amoraim* of the fourth century, their own beliefs and practices? It is true that the *Amoraim* regarded the heroes of the Bible as living the life of Talmudic Jews. But we know that this was a gross anachronism. Fortunately, the sense of psychological continuity need not be based upon such an illusion.

Spirituality, or the aspiration toward the good life, is the common denominator of all civilization worthy of the name. They differ, however, in the particular form this aspiration assumes and in the emphasis it receives. The Judaism of the past was no doubt a spiritual civilization, but it was circumscribed in its spirituality by a limited knowledge of God and the world. The enlarged knowledge of God and the world will enable the Judaism of the future to function more completely and more effectively as a spiritual civilization.

Even those who believe in the finality of traditional truths will probably concede that today we can avail ourselves of a larger knowledge of the world than the Jews of the past could. The proposition, however, that correlative with enlarged knowledge of the world is an enlarged knowledge of God, seems absurd to them. To the traditionalists it is self-evident that the ancients knew more about God than we can ever hope to know, for did he not reveal and explain himself to them? Yet the proposition must stand, and it is basic to any attempt to construct the Judaism of the future as a spiritual civilization. Our knowledge of God is determined by our knowledge of reality. As our knowledge of reality is enlarged, our knowledge of God is deepened. Today we find it possible for a civilization to express itself spiritually and to feel the sense of destiny without claiming to have experienced theophany, without resorting to a conception of direct cause-and-effect relationship between obedience to God and the fortunes of the individual, and without having to assume that the only way a new world will ever emerge out of the present chaos will be through some supernatural cataclysm. The spirituality of the Jewish civilization in its fourth stage can dispense with all these assumptions. It will consist mainly in the effort to foster knowingly and deliberately the historical tendency of the Jewish religion to progress in the direction of universal truth and social idealism.

PART SIX

TORAH

JUDAISM AS A WAY OF LIFE FOR THE AMERICAN JEW

CHAPTER XXVII

INTRODUCTORY

TORAH AS A WAY OF LIFE

The ideal of Torah as the study of the sacred writings—The ideal of Torah as the practice of a specific mode of life—The need of evolving such values as will retrieve the spirit of the traditional attitude toward Torah.

IF THE Jews regarded themselves as more qualified for salvation than the rest of mankind, it was not because they believed that they possessed intrinsically superior mental and moral traits. Very few representative teachers or thinkers entertained such a belief.[1] The predominant teaching has been that the Jewish people owed the prerogative of salvation entirely to the particular way of life to which it had dedicated itself. In Jewish tradition that particular way of life is regarded as set forth in the Torah. The term "Torah" not only refers to the particular corpus of writings which include the Bible and the rabbinic literature, but also assigns a position of preeminence and authority to these writings. Upon them the Jewish consciousness has been riveted for the last two millenia. If the continuity of that consciousness depends, as was said above,* not so much upon retaining its beliefs unchanged as upon maintaining a live interest in certain specific *sancta,* then the Torah, or the sacred and authoritative writings designated by that term, should be accorded a position of primacy alongside the ideas of God and Israel. There can be nothing more paradoxical than a Torah-less Judaism. A Jewish life whose entire stream of consciousness from one end of the year to the next does not receive a single idea or impression directly from the Jewish writings which embody the great Jewish tradition would indeed be anomalous. It is, of course, impossible any longer to expect Jews to devote to those writings anything like the amount of time and attention their forebears were wont to spend. Present-day life is far too crowded to render that feasible.

See above, p. 325.

But so long as there is to be found any room in the contemporary scene for Jewish life, the knowledge of Torah must figure in it, or that life will be anything but Jewish.

In spite, however, of the obvious indispensability of such knowledge, the present apathy will continue so long as there prevails the assumption that the only way to know Torah is to know it in the traditional spirit, or not at all. The majority of thinking men and women, finding it impossible to approach the Jewish writings in the traditional spirit, neglect them altogether. It is therefore imperative deliberately to break down that assumption, and to promulgate the principle that *the primary requisite for the continuity of Jewish consciousness is not blind acceptance of the traditional beliefs, but a vital interest in the objects upon which those beliefs were centered.* If for the maintenance of interest in those objects it is necessary to abandon the traditional view concerning them, Jews should not hesitate to do so, and to replace those beliefs with whatever type of ideas is likely to sustain their interest.

This is what has actually been happening with the function of Torah in the life of the Jews during the last century. The Jewish consciousness has been gradually evolving a method whereby its interest in the Torah might be made compatible with the modern approach to reality. The rewriting of Jewish history in systematic and objective fashion is, in effect, a reinterpretation of the career of Israel as presented by the Torah. The Jewish scholars who belong to the Historical School, beginning with Nachman Krochmal, did not merely write history. By making accessible and intelligible numerous facts which seemed to have relevance only in the traditional setting, by furnishing the modern Jew with a connected and plausible account of the Jewish past, they have revitalized the ancient texts and have made possible the retention of the Torah in its widest sense as an object of Jewish consciousness. It is unfortunate that they contributed comparatively little to the scientific and objective study of the Bible, which is basic to a genuine understanding of the first stages of Judaism. The auspicious beginning made by Mendelssohn and the *Biurists* in the elucidation of the text of the Bible has not been followed up. That lack, however, has been made good by the vast range of biblical research pursued by Christian scholars during the last century. Jews should not allow the Christological hypotheses and theological prejudices which often vitiate this scholarship to stand in the way of utilizing whatever genuine light it sheds upon the Bible, its authorship and the historic background of its various books. It is highly important that the rabbinic texts should be subjected to the same kind of study as has revolutionized our appreciation of the Bible. It will then be possible to envisage the inner life of the Jewish people during the weary centuries of exile and persecution, in its struggle not merely for existence but for salvation. All this material should then be made available in popular form, to forestall the excuse of the Jewish layman that he has no time to wade through a mass of technical facts in order to acquire an appreciable knowledge of the Jewish past and its literature.

But of even greater importance for the reordering of Jewish life than the study of the sacred writings, is the fostering of a mode of life that will be animated by whatever in the traditional attitude toward the Torah is of incontestable worth. By analyzing the rationale which the Jewish consciousness has formulated to account for the position of pre-eminence and authority it assigned to the Bible and the rabbinic writings, we shall arrive at a knowledge of some of the important implications in the traditional attitude toward the Torah. That rationale contains beliefs which reflect the limited knowledge of the ancients about the manner in which human beings came upon new ideas and plans, and derived the urge and wisdom to execute them. These crude notions are responsible for the literalness with which they assumed the supernatural origin of the Torah. But included also in the rationale are implications which are still relevant, and which in their explicit form should be made part of a modern Jewish ideology.

In the first place, it is evident that when the ancients spoke of Torah they were very far from being as book-minded about it as we are. *We come nearest to experiencing how they felt about Torah when we realize that Torah was to them, in effect, the hypostasis of the civilization of the Jewish people. The writings, as visible objects, were important chiefly as symbols of that civilization, in the same way as the Temple and Ark were important as symbols of the reality and presence of God.* The sense of supreme advantage the Jews felt in possessing the Torah can best be understood if interpreted as equivalent to the belief that theirs was the only true civilization. The apotheosis of the Torah, which one encounters so frequently in the rabbinic literature, loses its bizarre character when read in the light of this equivalence of Torah to civilization. When the Sages say, "God created the world for the sake of the Torah," they say in their way that civilization gives meaning to reality. Or when they state that God in constructing the world followed the plan of the Torah in the same way as an architect follows his blueprints, they imply that God made the nature of the physical environment congenial to civilization. This apotheosis of Torah and the equating of it with civilization *par excellence* did not originate with the Sages. This attitude is expressed even in the Pentateuch where we read: "Observe therefore and do them; for this is your wisdom and your understanding in the sight of the peoples, that, when they hear all these statutes, shall say: 'Surely this great nation is a wise and understanding people.' " [2]

Moreover, the admiration of the Jews for the Torah, unbounded as it was, was not blind and unreasoned. The traditional belief that the Torah came directly from God might have given rise merely to a feeling of awe that would elicit obedience. But the glorification of the Torah, which we find expressed everywhere in traditional litera- ture, is undoubtedly motivated by some other virtue which the Torah is supposed to possess. It is the inherent power of conferring life abundant, or salvation, upon those who order their conduct in accordance with its precepts. The claim to the possession of this power is reiterated throughout the Scriptures, from the standpoint of life in this world, and throughout rabbinic literature, from the standpoint of life in the world to come.

The functional method of reinterpretation, as applied to the God- idea and to the Israel-idea, has been shown to consist largely in dis- engaging from the context of the ancient world-outlook those ele- ments which answer to permanent postulates of human nature and integrating them into the Jewish ideology that is in the making. By applying the same method to the traditional attitude toward the Torah-idea, we infer from it a number of significant corollaries.

We discern in the concept "Torah" the first attempt on the part of a people to detach itself mentally from its regimen of conduct, and to contemplate it as' something more than a matter of chance or accident, like the landscape one is born into. That regimen, it is implied, should not be treated as something arbitrary to which we must submit because we cannot do otherwise, but as inherently right and good which we should accept as an act of free choice. This is what entitles the social system of customs, laws and standards to be considered Torah, the law of God, or as the modern man would put it, a civilization or civilizing agency. Once a people can achieve such detachment from its routine, there is some likelihood of that routine undergoing modification as soon as it fails to keep up with the growing complexity of life. No doubt there will always be resistance to change, but so long as it is recognized that the way of life has to be accepted as a matter of free choice, the forces of intelligence and idealism will ultimately succeed in bringing that way of life in line with man's highest needs and capacities.

The concept "Torah" furthermore, by implication accentuates the highly important truth that human societies should differ from sub-human herds in having their bond of unity based not upon the blind forces of instinct or of consanguinity, but upon their common purpose to work out a way of life to which each member might conform as a free agent. In a sense, the church adopted that principle of organization when it made the basis of its unity a common faith instead of common race or common political interests. But with the organization of modern nations, there has been a return to the sub-human principle of the herd. The pretense of scientific plausibility is nowadays made for the theory of race as the chief determinant of the social life of man. The inevitable consequence of such a theory is a recrudescence of barbarism. This is tragically being demonstrated in the contemporary scene. A whole nation, which has hitherto been regarded as highly cultured, is suffering a moral relapse and is threatening the peace of the world as a result of having perverted the race theory into a claim to world-hegemony.

Finally, there is implied in the idea of Torah the crucial test of the value of a civilization. A civilization fulfills its function only when the people that lives by it, helps its individual men and women to achieve life abundant or salvation. All laws, customs, institutions and social arrangements that hinder the complete self-development of the individual are not civilization, but barbarization, and the peoples that uphold them are not civilized nations in the true sense of the term. To deserve the status of a civilized nation, a people must so order its way of life that all the possibilities in the natural and social environment which make for the complete self-realization of the individual shall be fully utilized.

It is not, however, the traditional Torah, or the Jewish civilization as it has come down from the past, that can any longer elicit the attitude that it is of supreme worth to the Jew and his people. The traditional Torah must be reinterpreted and reconstructed so that it become synonymous with the whole of a civilization necessary to civilize or humanize the individual. Individual self-fulfillment is possible only through affirmative and creative adjustments to a series of concentric and overlapping relationships within the human world, supplemented by a similar adjustment to the world as a whole. All relationships of the individual to his family, to the opposite sex, to friends, to community, to nation, to mankind and to the world as a whole, are potentially capable of evoking affirmative and creative adjustments. This process in every relationship that applies to a Jew is the career of Torah, or the career of the Jewish civilization.

Torah should mean to the Jew nothing less than a civilization which enables the individual to effect affirmative and creative adjustments in his living relationships with reality. Any partial conception of Torah is false to the forces that have made for Judaism's development and survival. Torah means a complete Jewish civilization. But to the Jew in the diaspora it must, in addition, spell the duty of beholding in the non-Jewish civilization by which he lives a potential instrument of salvation. He must help to render that civilization capable of enhancing human life as the Torah enhanced the life of Israel. If, like the Torah, it is to be worthy of fervent devotion, those whose lives it fashions must be convinced of its intrinsic righteousness.

The survival of Judaism in the diaspora depends upon whether the Jews outside Palestine will live Judaism as a civilization to the maximum degree compatible with their physical, economic and mental powers, as well as with the national spirit of the countries in which they live. With the infinite diversity of temperament, training, beliefs, callings and interests, and with their wide range of ideas about life, the universe and God, which prevail among Jews, the most pressing problem of Jewish life is how to render it sufficiently rich in opportunities for Jewish self-expression.

Not even under the most favorable circumstances can Jewish life in the diaspora create that rich variety in content which Judaism requires. All the constituents of Jewish civilization—language, literature, the arts, social standards and values—will be able to thrive creatively mainly in the Jewish National Home. But the Jews in the diaspora cannot afford to wait passively for whatever new values will be evolved in Palestine. Some degree of Jewish life and activity must be counted on as possible also in the diaspora, and with it a certain degree of creativity. Jews everywhere must deliberately strive to enlarge the scope of Jewish thought, increase the sphere of communal and intercommunal action, and widen the range of creative achievement. The future of Judaism is contingent upon its coming to possess an abundant, diversified and spiritually satisfying content. With that end in view, Jewish life in the diaspora must undergo considerable reconstruction in its folkways, in its ethics and in its educational postulates. What is involved in such reconstruction for Jewish life in America will be indicated in the chapters that follow.

CHAPTER XXVIII

JEWISH MILIEU

A. The Jewish family—The fundamental unit of Jewish life—The need for a constructive attitude toward intermarriage—The vitality of a civilization dependent upon functioning of family—Jewish family the backbone of Jewish civilization—Social and spiritual function of the family as fostered by Judaism—The community to be responsible for integrity of family institution.

B. The synagogue—The synagogue to be transformed into the Jewish neighborhood center—Its functions.

A

THE JEWISH FAMILY

WHAT native soil is to a plant, territory is to a civilization. Yet a tropical plant may be enabled to thrive in a northern clime by means of an enclosure within which the necessary conditions of temperature and sunshine are provided. Likewise, if Jewish life is to be cultivated outside its national homeland, it must be provided with a milieu congenial to its aims and modes of self-expression. The primary and indispensable *locus* of Jewish life is undoubtedly the home, where the child receives his first impressions, and where he obtains the basic layer of his cultural and spiritual life. It is there that the principal Jewish habits and Jewish values should be transmitted from one generation to the other. Therefore, whatever touches upon Judaism as a way of life has a bearing upon the Jewish home.

Since Judaism is more than a religion or a religious philosophy, it cannot even begin to function in the individual as such. The family is the smallest social unit through which it can articulate itself. A philosophy, whether religious or secular, presupposes a high degree of individualization and detachment from the heat and turmoil of life; but it is only some form of associated life with all its accompanying vicissitudes that gives rise to a civilization. The minimum unit of a civilization consists of man, wife and child, for no person by himself can be the carrier of a civilization, which depends upon social interaction as well as upon transmission of cultural content from one generation to the next. From that standpoint, the problem of adjusting the Jewish home to social conditions of modern life is at the center of the problem of Judaism. It is necessary, therefore, to consider the readjustment which the home must undergo in order that it may continue both to influence Jewish civilization, and to be influenced by it.

For the home to serve as the mainstay of Judaism, the man and wife who establish it must possess enough of positive Jewish background to create a milieu which will supply their children with that intangible and spontaneous quality of a civilization which is often referred to as "atmosphere." To meet that condition, both parents must be Jews. The possibility of intermarriage was so negligible in the past that it hardly entered into the discussions and responsa of the rabbis of former days. But now the freer social intercourse and the more numerous and varied contacts with Gentiles bring to the fore the problem of intermarriage. That intermarriages increase with alarming rapidity from one generation to the next has been shown by Zollschan, Ruppin, Drachsler and others. The conclusion which these students of Jewish life draw from the growing tendency to intermarriage is that diaspora Judaism will inevitably disappear. Their conclusion may indeed be proved by the event, if the present policy of ignoring the problem continues. Jewish leaders are as reluctant to probe into the status of Jewish mixed marriages as one who is ailing from disease is afraid to consult a physician lest he learn that his disease is fatal. It is certain that, if nothing is done to prevent the tendency to intermarriage, Judaism can barely survive another century, and, even if it does survive, it will have become hopelessly devitalized.

The inadequacy of the Reformist reconstruction of Judaism is most clearly evidenced by its vacillating policy with regard to intermarriage.[1] The fact that Reformism itself is a compromise between an avowed acceptance of Judaism as a religious philosophy and an unacknowledged and covert reckoning with it as a mode of social life has prevented any definite policy toward intermarriage. Some Reformists insist that the Gentile party to the marriage accept Judaism, while others have been known to solemnize marriages in which the Gentile remained unconverted. Neo-Orthodoxy still pretends to follow the principle which has been current for centuries, while in reality it grudgingly yields to the inevitable. It still avows that a Gentile who applies for proselytism is disqualified for that privilege, if the motivation be marriage. But since it is inexpedient to discourage a Gentile who wants to marry a Jewess from accepting Judaism, the motive of the applicant for conversion tends to be ignored. The consequence is that the Gentile is led to accept Judaism in the spirit of an empty formality which has no bearing upon the home to be established through the marriage. Rarely is it stipulated that the children born of the marriage be brought up under Jewish auspices. As a rule, therefore, such families are completely lost to Jewish life.

In contrast with either of the foregoing attitudes, Jews must be prepared to reckon frankly and intelligently with intermarriage as a growing tendency which, if left uncontrolled, is bound to prove Judaism's undoing. They must realize that the power and vitality of a civilization are put to the test whenever the members of different civilizations come into social contact with each other. When that contact results in intermarriage and children are born, the more vigorous civilization will be the one to which the children will belong. For Judaism to accept intermarriage between Jews and Gentiles as legitimate from its standpoint, it must be infinitely more sure of itself than it is at present. What else could urge it on to a revision of its values and a reconstruction of its outlook and mode of life, as much as the fact that it must be fully qualified to hold its own against competing civilizations? It must be able to imbue the Jewish partner to a mixed marriage with the willingness to maintain a Jewish home. Since this is the case, Judaism should meet all situations that might lead to mixed marriages not fearfully or grudgingly, but in the spirit of encountering an expected development. With such an attitude toward intermarriage, Judaism would avert the tragedy of Jewish parents who consider the child married to a Gentile as lost to them. With a belief in the integrity and value of his own civilization the Jewish partner to the marriage could achieve moral ascendency, and make Judaism the civilization of the home.

It is only an openly avowed policy of this kind that can make the position of the Jews tenable in America. For nothing is so contrary to the ideal of cultural and spiritual cooperation as the unqualified refusal of one element of the population to intermarry with any other. America should be open to the various cultures within her domains. But she is certain to look with disfavor upon any culture which seeks to maintain itself by decrying the intermarriage of its adherents with those of another culture. By accepting a policy which does not decry marriages of Jews with Gentiles, provided the homes they establish are Jewish and their children are given a Jewish upbringing, the charge of exclusiveness and tribalism falls to the ground. With such an attitude, there would no longer be any occasion for pointing to the racial pride of the Jews. What is valuable is the Jewish social heritage, or civilization, and not physical descent.

In considering the family as the principal field of operation for Judaism, we cannot lose sight of the fact that the Jew's interest in his heritage will depend largely upon the extent to which it will exert a moral and spiritual influence upon his life. Despite the failure of assimilation, the Jew will try to escape Judaism if it cannot help him to cope with the moral problems of his daily life. Yet, how can Judaism exert this influence, now that it lacks the authority it possessed when it was accepted as divinely revealed? No abstract code of ideals, however eloquently worded, can exercise a profound influence. Moreover, the ideals which the modern spokesmen of Judaism may formulate can scarcely surpass in power of authoritative appeal those which the spiritual geniuses of other civilizations, dead and living, have voiced. What more can these spokesmen do than work out a sort of anthology of ideals? But a civilization cannot live on anthologies. It must create and maintain social institutions which shape the character of the individual in accordance with certain ideals. *The difference in character between one civilization and another is not so much in the ideals they profess as in the social institutions they evolve as a means of expressing their ideals.*

The human being is civilized or socialized directly by the institutions, affiliations and modes of internal organization which a culture fosters. Social institutions are to the forces of human nature what machines are to the forces of the physical world. The machine is a medium of bringing physical forces into organization. A social institution like the family should be a means of so organizing the forces of human nature, particularly those of sex and parental love, that they further the self-realization of the individuals concerned, and raise the level of human life as a whole.

It is scarcely necessary to point out that the home gives the main bent to the character of the child. The family has been well described as the half-way house between the ego and society. There the child learns the first lessons in the meaning of social give-and-take. The habits he there acquires determine to a large extent the part he will play later in the larger relationships of life. *It must be remembered that in considering the potency of the family as an institution it is not only the family one is born into that counts, but also the family one looks forward to.* Normally, during the years of adolescence it is the prospect of family life that makes for self-restraint and purity in love. In married life it is the attitude toward the institution of the family on the part of husband and wife that determines not only their relation to each other, but their ambitions and achievements in every one of their other relationships.

What family integrity has contributed to the perpetuation of Judaism, and what in turn Judaism has done to perfect the institution of the family as a socializing and spiritualizing agency in the life of the Jew, are matters that should have been given scientific study. But we are on *terra firma* when we say that as a factor for moral purity Jewish family life has been without an equal. Judaism's influence upon the attitude of the greater part of mankind toward chastity has been more far-reaching, perhaps, than upon the attitude toward any other human, or cosmic, relationship. In contrast with the modern interpreters of the prophetic writings, who select the call to righteousness or fair dealing as the keynote of prophetic teaching, the ancients, both Jews and Christians, selected the denunciations of sexual immorality as the keynote of prophecy. The prophetic writings abound in rebuke of the sin of idolatry. That rebuke lost its relevance when polytheism gave way to monotheism. But as long as a message is considered divinely inspired, it does not lose relevance. The force of the rebuke of idolatry was, therefore, transferred to the sin of licentiousness. By this method of interpretation the Prophets became, to those who read their teachings in the light of tradition, more the exponents of chastity than of social righteousness.

The case of chastity affords an illustration of the principle previously referred to, that it is not the abstract ideal which counts, but rather the social instrument through which that ideal is actualized. While both Judaism and Christianity accepted the ideal of chastity as enunciated in the prophetic writings, they utilized different social instruments to achieve it. *Christianity evolved the institution of monasticism as a means of exalting the ideal of chastity. Judaism exalted the institution of the family, and made it the end to be served by chastity.* Of course, this did not come about consciously, any more than the butterfly developed its protective coloring consciously. But the lesson derived from the Jewish attitude toward family life emerges none the less clearly, the lesson that chastity is best furthered when it is treated not as an end in itself, but as a means for conserving the family.

If the family is to continue helping the Jew to live efficiently, its foundation must be rendered strong enough to withstand the disintegrating influences which at present threaten to undermine it. Large-scale migration has destroyed age-old habits, traditions and sanctions. Industrialism has created interests that cause the members of a family to drift apart. The emancipation of women has made it impossible for the home to continue on the quasi-patriarchal basis as in former days. All such influences, by weakening the sense of social obligation and destroying the balance between the self-seeking and the social tendencies in human nature, tend to give such predominance to the selfish impulses as to undermine the home. The proposed substitutes for the institution of permanent monogamous wedlock result merely in legitimatizing irresponsibility.

The family is both a natural formation and a social institution.[2] As a natural formation, it is the product of instinct. As a social institution, it is of the utmost significance for racial and social welfare. The mistake usually made is that in considering the family as a natural formation we regard the sex instinct as its sole or main motivation, whereas, for the true understanding of the family, even as a natural formation, we must reckon equally with the parental instinct. Thus, an objective consideration of the place of the family in human life enables us to appreciate why both its maintenance and permanent happiness depend upon giving its social function priority over the personal pleasure and comfort which each member expects to derive from it. The tendency to view marriage as a private affair in which society has no legitimate concern is at the root of the growing demoralization in Jewish life.

With regard to the family institution, the question of momentous import, not only to Jews but to all western nations, is the question as to which civilization—the civic or the historic—shall have control of the home. One thing seems certain, that the state is not qualified to preserve the home. In the effort to maintain the integrity of the family institution, the state has to depend largely upon the historic religious civilizations, upon Christianity for its Christian citizens, and upon Judaism for its Jewish citizens. The home will retain its wholesome influence provided the historic civilizations, with their moral and religious values, will make a serious effort to reenforce it by establishing better communal organization to act as the source of status and social standards, and by administering wise and systematic guidance in all questions that agitate the modern home.

It therefore devolves entirely upon Judaism, as far as Jews are concerned, to uphold the social and spiritual conception of marriage. Marriage must remain monogamous, and it must be entered into without any mental reservation about its permanence. *To further these ends, marriage amongst Jews must be treated as an event of significance to the Jewish community as a whole. It must, therefore, be solemnized by a representative of Jewish communal life, and recorded in a Jewish communal register.* A Jew and a Jewess, whose union is solemnized merely by an official of the city or state, should be regarded as reading themselves out of the Jewish community. There can be no stronger indication of how lethargic the communal spirit is at the present time among the Jews in western countries than the fact that for Jewish men and women to be united by a civil marriage is not even considered a serious infraction of Jewish duty. Even before any other communal activity be undertaken, the registry of Jewish marriages ought to be introduced immediately as a practical measure for fostering community-mindedness.

The Jewish community must further the integrity of the Jewish family by making itself responsible for the adjustment of any misunderstanding that may wreck it, and for the accommodation of the

Jewish divorce laws to the laws of the state. An organized effort must be made to reach the young people with a view to influencing them to look forward to home building, and to educate them for the purpose of marriage and the responsibilities of home life. Even after marriage, during the years when children are born and reared, Judaism can help the parents meet the problems that arise continually in the home. So long as the state is satisfied to leave the finer social adjustments of home making to the historic civilization, why should Judaism not avail itself of the opportunity to be of actual service to its adherents by helping them make their home life fruitful of the greatest good?

It will, of course, be said that Judaism never engaged in work of that kind. Neither did any country find it necessary to create broadcasting regulations before there was a radio, nor air traffic regulations before there were aeroplanes. The disintegrating forces that exist at present, the philosophies that sanction anarchic individualism and selfish indulgence necessitate deliberately devised measures to counteract them. In the bid for the future that all civilizations make, only those will survive that evince the wisdom and the foresight to look after the well-being of the family institution. Hitherto Judaism was a strong factor for social control through a vigorous public opinion, which was rooted in age-long tradition, and which placed a premium upon a well-ordered family life. Now it will have to engage in educating its men and women to appreciate the significance and sanctity of family life, and to meet the specific problems that arise in the home.

It is to be expected that, despite all efforts to fit the individual into the home so that it may function to his advantage as well as to that of the general community, maladjustments will arise. Cases of faithlessness or incompatibility are bound to present themselves, necessitating separation and divorce. Under present conditions, the state claims the principal right to decide what is to become of the home. Traditional Jewish practice, adhering to the laws which worked well as long as the Jewish community was the sole arbiter, not only does not help the parties to the ill-fated marriage, but even puts obstacles in their way. As a rule, the husband who is divorced by the law of the state, knowing that his divorced wife is not allowed to marry again according to Jewish law, unless he grant her a Jewish bill of divorce, uses her predicament to extort from her or her relatives as much as he can before granting her a Jewish divorce; or, what is worse, disappears altogether and compels her to remain unmarried the rest of her life. An even more deplorable situation arises as a result of adherence to the obsolete practice of levirate and *halizah* (release). Where a husband dies and has left no children, the traditional law requires that his wife obtain her release or *halizah* from his brothers, before she is permitted to marry again. This, too, is made occasion for extortion.[*]

The solution that the Reformists have adopted for all these difficulties will result in destroying the last vestige of organically associated Jewish life which is the matrix of Judaism. They have abrogated all Jewish divorce laws, and have totally renounced the right of the Jewish community to demand that those divorced by the law of the state also submit to Jewish divorce proceedings. This renunciation spells the death of Jewish communal life. From the Reformist standpoint, that the state has all to say in the matter of divorce and the Jewish community nothing, it is difficult to explain why the state should not be the sole authority in a Jewish marriage. If that is the case, why have the marriage solemnized by a rabbi? To be sure, the Protestants act likewise. But this is not the only instance where Christian Protestants and Jewish Reformists are equally paradoxical and inconsistent in their conception of the relation of church to state.

Granted that, if Judaism wishes to exercise authority in the matter of separation and divorce, it cannot afford to ignore the superior power of the state. But it can so adapt its laws that its authority will be felt by those who are faced with the problem of divorce and, at the same time, prevent either party from exploiting the other. We have an ancient precedent that, when a traditional law interfered with the economic life of the people, a way was found to circumvent the law. This is the well-known device of *prosbul* applied to loans which, according to ancient law, became void with the advent of the sabbatical year. It is apparent that this militated against obtaining financial credit. Hillel accordingly instituted the practice of turning over the debt to the court for, according to tradition, a court's debts were not voided by the sabbatical year. Why may not analogous power be assumed by a Jewish court nowadays to summon the husband who had been divorced by the court of the state to grant his wife a Jewish divorce? In case he fails to appear, or refuses to grant her the divorce, the Jewish court shall have the power to grant the woman her Jewish divorce. If Jewish law will thus overcome the obstacle presented by the primacy of the law of the state, it will preserve its authority in the life of the Jew. Through the modification of Jewish marriage laws, which were evolved under what was practically an autonomous Jewish life and on the basis of what is now the outgrown status of woman, to meet present needs and conditions, Judaism will regain a place of authority in the life of the Jew.

B

THE SYNAGOGUE

The Jewish milieu provided by the home, basic as it is to Jewish life, cannot suffice. There is need for some additional *locus* where the cultural and social aspects of Jewish civilization might find a far wider scope for expression and enjoyment than is possible in the home. That *locus* should be the synagogue, not the congregational synagogue which exists in American-Jewish life today, but the synagogue reconstructed to meet the new needs which have arisen in Jewish life. *To fulfill the comprehensive purpose called for by present-day conditions, a synagogue must not be monopolized by a particular congregation. It must belong to the entire Jewish community.* It should be a neighborhood center to which all Jews to whom it is accessible should resort for all religious, cultural, social and recreational purposes.

One of the main reasons why Jews have not made proper adjustments to the new social conditions under which they have had to live since the emancipation has been the failure to comprehend fully the new responsibility that devolves upon the synagogue. In olden times,[5] the synagogue was like a dynamo near a waterfall. As the power of the waterfall develops electric current in the dynamo, so did the social life that surged about the synagogue develop the spiritual power within the synagogue. The condition of the synagogue at the present time is similar to that of a dynamo when its water power is cut off and it has to resort to a fuel like coal or oil, which is kept within the power house itself. Now that the stream of Jewish social life has dried up, the problem consists in finding ways and means of storing up a substitute social energy within the synagogue itself.

When we survey the efforts that have been made during the last hundred years to infuse new life into the synagogue, we note that they have been directed mainly at modernizing or estheticizing the service. The chief interest is in introducing decorum, good music, sermons in the vernacular, and in modifying the type and language of prayers. All such efforts have been motivated by the fundamental error that the way to save the synagogue is to make public worship its primary purpose to a far greater degree than was ever contemplated in the past.

Reformism's conversion of the synagogue into a "temple" indicates that public worship which, until the emancipation, had been only one of the activities of the synagogue, was henceforth to be the chief, if not the only activity, of the synagogue. Strange to say, this attitude has been adopted by all the sections of Jewry, whether they agreed with or were opposed to the Reformist movement, and it is this attitude that has caused the progressive deterioration of the synagogue. Public worship should be one of the functions of the synagogue, but by no means the only one, nor even the principal one.

A number of causes at the present time make the desire for worship an insufficient motive for keeping the synagogue alive. In the first place, the economic difficulty involved in the observance of Sabbaths and festivals prevents a great many Jews from attending the services. Secondly, the obligation to take part in prayer, an act which was formerly considered indispensable to the salvation of the soul and to material well-being, has greatly weakened. Finally, there are the competing distractions. For many people, literature, music and the theater answer to the spiritual need which only public worship could once satisfy. It is, therefore, all the more necessary to include within the scope of the synagogue the cultivation of whatever workaday interests Jews have in common, and whatever leisure interests may form the basis of friendship and cooperation. The synagogue should not be displaced by, but it should evolve into, the *bet am*, or Jewish neighborhood center. Each center should be placed under the joint auspices of the *kehillah*, and of the Jews of the neighborhood where it is located. The cost of building and

maintenance should be shared jointly by the *kehillah* and the beneficiaries.

The *bet am* should have all of the spiritual sanction that formerly
rendered the synagogue dear to the heart of the Jew, and, in addition, should deliberately be developed to meet the broader humanist-
cultural needs that are included in a modern civilization. By upholding the spiritual sanction of the *bet am,* and by having the
responsibility for the establishment and maintenance of the *bet am*
shared between the *kehillah* and the Jews of the neighborhood, it
might be possible to break down the social barriers which prevent
Jews of different economic status from sharing their spiritual interests. Various attempts have been made by the synagogual organizations to enlist the wage-earning classes, but they have all proved
a failure. The bane of the synagogue in this country has been its
confinement to the middle class. Even professional men, unless
they can count upon deriving material advantage from affiliation
with the synagogue, somehow find themselves intellectually and
socially out of place in it. The feeling that the *bet am* is not the
private property of a small group, but belongs to the larger Jewish
community, and is intended to serve in even a more intensively social
and cultural capacity than the synagogue of old, would go very far
in breaking down the artificial distinctions of wealth that stand in
the way of the fusion of Jewish interests.

The primary humanist-cultural function of the *bet am* is the promotion of a cordial spirit of neighborliness and a community of feeling. The massing of Jews in large numbers has in our day produced
ghettos which differ from the ghettos of old mainly in being soulless. Even the ghettos of recent arrivals lack that intimate acquaintance and mutual interest which characterized the ghettos in
eastern Europe. How much of neighborly spirit can, therefore, be
expected among those who have reached the line of comfort, and have
moved into the so-called "gilded ghettos"? The lack of neighborly
interest and mutual responsibility among those who inhabit the
poorer districts has made these districts into hatcheries of gang-
sterism and racketeering. In the wealthier districts, it has produced
in large numbers Jews with no sense of communal responsibility, and
with no higher code than that set up by the narrow circle of friends
equally selfish and irresponsible. The larger cities, especially, are

conducive to individualism, which is the greatest menace that Judaism has to guard against in the new world. Hence the primary function of the *bet am* must be to combat this individualism and to weld the Jews who live in the neighborhood into a conscious communal unit.

If the *bet am* is to function as a means of generating Jewish atmosphere, it should aim to utilize existing needs for Jewish association, and to direct Jewish creative ability upon Jewish interests, projects and objectives.

The following are some of these needs: Jewish elementary school facilities; boys' and girls' clubs; recreational facilities such as gymnasia, showers, bowling alleys, pool tables and game rooms; adult study and art groups; communal activities; religious services and festival pageants and plays; informal meetings of friends and associates.

To live Judaism as a civilization is not only to pray as a Jew, but to work and to play as a Jew, that is, to carry on, as a Jew, activities which answer to fundamental human wants. Work and play answer organic needs. The character of a civilization expresses itself through both. "Pleasuring together favors the spread of the we-feeling," says Edward A. Ross. "Eating, drinking, acting, playing together, enjoying in common music, drama, are time-honored means of fostering friendship." Hence the importance of devising ways and means of giving a Jewish bent to recreational activities. In the very ghettos where the Jews suffered persecution, Judaism helped the Jew in his work and in his play. It gave him the language of social intercourse; it had a voice in the activities he pursued for the purpose of making a livelihood; and it provided him with the means of amusement and entertainment. Emancipation and industrialism have practically made it impossible for Judaism to influence the Jew in his work. All the more imperative, therefore, has it become for Judaism to influence the Jew in his leisure activities. The crowding and aggressive commercialism of our cities are jeopardizing the spiritual, no less than the physical, health of their inhabitants. To counteract this danger every community must give careful thought to the problem of directing the leisure time and energies of its members into channels of physical recreation and spiritual self-renewal.

The survival of Judaism in the diaspora as a civilization depends upon the extent to which the Jew will learn to utilize Jewish life and interests for the satisfaction of his recreational needs. How intimately the use of leisure is bound up with the problem of any civilization can best be understood, if we take into consideration that it is leisure that has brought man to the present stage of development. Moreover, the conditions of modern living have made man dependent upon leisure for the maintenance not only of his health, but even of his sanity. The Jew must learn to utilize his leisure in such a way that it shall enhance his life physically, mentally and morally. Jews should realize that they must impress their leisure life into the service of Judaism, as well as to use Judaism to direct and guide their leisure life.

The principal agency Jews will have to foster as a means of utilizing their leisure life to greatest spiritual advantage is the neighborhood center. Fortunately, it is not necessary to create such an agency *ex nihilo*. The various Jewish neighborhood centers in this country have received their initial impulse in the direction of such a goal as is here described. What is required is a technique whereby those who are to utilize these neighborhood centers shall catch the spirit and the intention of those who launched the general movement. This can be achieved by adopting a definite policy with regard to the hierarchy of activities carried on in these neighborhood centers. Everything will depend upon which activity will receive first consideration in the planning of the work. To the end that there be created a Jewish atmosphere, it is essential that primacy should be given to Jewish education in its most inclusive sense. Indeed, it is essential that Jewish education itself should be conceived in such comprehensive fashion as to include all forms of cultural activity, from the kindergarten to groups for the study of religion and the social sciences.

The one activity which is likely to present the greatest amount of difficulty is religious worship. Not only is there wide diversity of opinion concerning the proper form of worship, and concerning the need for worship altogether, but each opinion is held with such tenacity and heat as to give rise to serious conflicts which may wreck the communal center. The traditionalists insist on maintaining the old form of prayers and regard the least innovation as reprehensible. Yet we cannot expect those for whom the traditional service has lost its appeal, and who see nothing wrong in innovation, to submit to the dictates of the traditionalists. Some, therefore, conclude that the easiest way out of this dilemma is to omit worship and religious activities altogether. This, however, is a dangerous solution. Apart from the spiritual value which attaches to the experience of merging oneself with a body of people who unite for self-expression in worship, Jewish life must offer some visible outlet for folk spirit and self-expression; and nothing is so essential for that purpose as public worship. Sabbaths and festivals will not be celebrated in the home in a manner that will unite the Jew to his people unless public worship supply the incentive. If necessary, therefore, more than one type of service should be instituted at the neighborhood center. At the same time, a beginning should be made toward evolving a mode of worship which conforms with the conception of Judaism as a modern, spiritual civilization. A description of the kind of worship that would meet this requirement is given in the chapter on "Folk Religion."

These, in sum, are the means whereby the neighborhood center may supply the Jew in the diaspora with the milieu, which is essential to his experiencing the reality and worth of Jewish values.

CHAPTER XXIX

JEWISH FOLKWAYS

Why the term "folkways"—A. Religious folkways as religious poetry in action—As a means of emphasizing life's significance—Their character determined by the civilization to which they belong—1. Jewish dietary folkways—The spirit in which they should be observed—Recital of benedictions before and after meals—2. Sabbaths and festival folkways—How to observe the Sabbath—How to observe the festivals—The festivals reinterpreted—B. Cultural folkways—1. The Hebrew language—2. Jewish names—3. The Jewish calendar—4. Jewish arts.

IN Jewish tradition, all religious observances, civil laws and ethical principles are equally designated *miṣwot,* or "commandments." The implication is that they were all decreed by God. The distinction first met with in the *Mishnah,*[1] between "commandments (pertaining to the relations) between man and God" and "commandments (pertaining to the relations) between man and man," does not remove any law from the category of divine ordinances. Later, a further classification was introduced to distinguish those which were based upon some understandable reason from those which had no such reason.[2] Even though some of us no longer regard the traditional practices as commanded by God, we may still refer to them as *miṣwot,* provided we avowedly use that term in a metaphorical sense, in the sense that they arouse in us the religious mood. Should our spiritual well-being, however, require the change or abrogation of any of those practices, the fact that they are designated *miṣwot* ought not to exercise any inhibitive influence.

But it is of vital importance to have a significant term besides *miṣwot* for those customs which have been referred to as "commandments pertaining to the relations between man and God." A term is needed that would indicate a different approach from that with which we come to positive law or jurisprudence. The term "folkways" meets that requirement. In the traditional literature, the term *minhag* denotes a ritual practice for which there does not seem to be any basis in the authoritative writings, and which by the

431

mere reason of its being in vogue exercises a claim on conformity. It is never applied to the customary practices which are prescribed in the Torah, because it lacks the connotation of being as imperative as those practices. It therefore comes nearest to expressing what is conveyed by the term "folkways."

If we were henceforth to designate all "commandments pertaining to the relations between man and God" as *minhagim* or "folkways," we would accomplish a twofold purpose. First, we would convey the thought that they should not be dealt with in a legalistic spirit, a spirit that often gives rise to quibbling and pettifogging. They should be dealt with as the very stuff of Jewish life, which should be experienced with spontaneity and joy, and which can be modified as circumstances require. Secondly, we would convey the implication that not only should as many "commandments" or folkways as possible be retained and developed, but that Jewish life should be stimulated to evolve new and additional folkways. *Folkways are the social practices by which a people externalizes the reality of its collective being.* The more alive the collective being, the more it abounds in affirmative folkways. Of negative folkways, Judaism has plenty, but of affirmative folkways calculated to render Jewish life interesting and contentful, it has at present far too few.

The reinterpretation of "commandments pertaining to the relations between man and God" as folkways has been facilitated by their having been designated and treated in recent years as ceremonies. The very term "ceremonies" implies that they arise not by the command of God but through psychological necessity. Samson Raphael Hirsch was consistent in opposing the designation of the *miṣwot* as "ceremonies." In that designation he sensed the implicit denial of their supernatural origin. Although Moses Mendelssohn was a staunch upholder of the belief in supernatural revelation as the basis of Jewish law, he was too much influenced by the enlightenment to be content with the traditional conception of the *miṣwot*, and advocated their observance because they helped to maintain the solidarity of Jewish life.* But since the designation "ceremonies" stops halfway between traditionalism and modernism, the term "folkways" is preferable. It is more explicit with regard to the origin of the *miṣwot*, and more clearly suggestive of the course to be pursued with regard to them in the future.

It is evident, of course, that not all Jewish folkways are equally important. Evaluation will be simpler, if we classify them as religious or cultural, according to the interest about which they center. In the religious folkways, the main purpose is to emphasize the cosmic relationship implied in religious experience. Institutions like the Sabbath, the festivals and worship are intended for that purpose. The cultural folkways are the customs which emphasize the common life and interests of the group. The Hebrew language, the Jewish calendar, the wearing of the *talit* at services, belong to cultural folkways, insofar as they express the folk spirit. In actual life both cultural and religious elements are interwoven in the same folkway. Religious folkways are those in which the religious mood predominates; cultural folkways, those in which the folk spirit is emphasized.

A

RELIGIOUS FOLKWAYS

Of the two types mentioned, the religious folkways have always been considered the more imperative; yet, in non-orthodox circles those are the ones which are chiefly called in question. Ever since Judaism encountered the challenge of philosophy, opinion has been divided as to whether this species of religious precepts should be subjected to rational interpretation. Some hold that to subject any divine precept to the test of reason is to question the truth of tradition, or the wisdom of God; others assume that to give a rational interpretation of the religious precepts is to insure their observance. But even those who assume the need of rational justification for the religious ordinances have not been uniformly successful in the application of their method.

The one classic and large-scale attempt to establish a detailed rationale for the religious precepts was that of Maimonides. His attempt, however, utterly fails in the case of the sacrificial precepts, for although he maintains that the sacrificial system was a concession to the vestiges of barbarism in Israel, he nevertheless insists upon prayer for their restoration and perpetuation in a restored Jewish commonwealth, the reason being that the precepts of the Torah are meant for all time. The inconsistency is glaring. But since the Jewish philosophers held reason to be merely the handmaiden of faith, and her position one of sufferance, they were not greatly disturbed by the lack of logical consistency in their system.

The meaning of the religious precepts remained in this state of uncertainty until modern times. The effect of the challenge of enlightenment upon the leaders of the Reformist movement is evident in their proposal to abrogate the observances which are not strictly rational, or which do not symbolize some universal ideal. They could see no purpose to ritual observances other than the promulgation of the two main principles, the unity of God and the brotherhood of man, or some corollary derivable from them. There is remarkable unanimity between the Reformists and the Neo-Orthodox on this point. The only difference is that the Reformists find only a limited number of the religious precepts capable of serving that purpose, while the Neo-Orthodox claim that with the proper method of symbolic interpretation every religious precept can be shown to convey some moral or spiritual truth.

This attitude of both the Reformists and the Neo-Orthodox is bound to lead to the inevitable conclusion that the religious precepts are a superfluous means of furthering universal ideals and only complicate matters. We need but recall what happened to the religion of the Jewish community in Alexandria as a result of the tendency to seek a deeper meaning beneath the law. It soon became apparent that, if one could contemplate the pure meanings which the religious precepts were intended to convey, actual performance would only distract from contemplation. In vain did Philo protest against the inevitable tendency to do away with the observance of these precepts as a result of the symbolic interpretation to which they were subjected.[5]

Fortunately, there is an alternative to the traditional attitude toward the *miswot*—to treat them as religious poetry in action. *The normal human being is exhilarated by any kind of ritual which gives him a sense of unity with the larger life of some group. In sharing that life, his own is redeemed from its dull and drab routine.* This accounts for the prevalence of ritualism in the numerous secret fraternal orders which in many instances satisfy not only the need for association with one's kind, but also the need for experiencing the poetry of religion. Jews would have less reason to join such orders, if they realized that Judaism is not merely a universe of discourse, but also a universe of sense experience.

Jewish life should include a multiplicity of visible activities centered upon sense objects. Such activities would enable the Jewish world of discourse to be enriched with the necessary variety of sensory images. Jewish life should be treated as an end in itself, and not as a means to outside ends. Those visible activities and sense objects which delight one in and for themselves are the material of religio-poetic feeling, and such must be the content of self-justified Jewish life.

This does not imply that the visible activities which constitute Jewish folkways need remain meaningless, and impress merely the senses. They could not be the source for religio-poetic feeling unless they were invested with meaning. Let Jewish customs stimulate universal ideas and soul-stirring emotions, but let that stimulation emanate from individual reaction and not from external authority. Not authority but rather spontaneous creativity is required for the rehabilitation of Jewish religious folkways. Hitherto, there were only two alternatives: either to accept religious customs as authoritative forms which permit no deviation from the established standard, or to repudiate them as an obstacle to the free functioning of the spirit. But increased understanding of human nature and of the place of religion in human life has revealed a third course, that of accepting customs as essential to an emotional identification with the inner life of a people, and as a means of expressing the feeling of life's significance in the individual manner of that people. Stated in the language of religion, the purpose of religious observances in the past was twofold: first, to get a god to fulfill the wish of man; and, second, to have man enter into communion with his god. Though the former or magic function of religious observances is bound to disappear, the latter or spiritual function will keep alive the need for religious observances.

When people conceived of God's attributes as essentially human, though greatly magnified, there was no reason to question the value of religious observances, or to rebel at the performance of any ritualistic routine. But when we come to think of God in terms of infinity, and therefore as altogether beyond the power of human comprehension, we must either readjust our notion of communion with God, or do away altogether with religious observances. Some people, gifted with a spiritual insight that is usually identified with mysticism, are not in the least troubled by the realization of God's infinite nature. Can we not enjoy the light and warmth of the sun now, though we know that it is almost a million times the size of the earth, as when we thought that it was a large fiery chariot racing across the sky? Too many accounts of this direct communion with God have been given for us to doubt the genuineness of the experience.' Instead of dismissing such communion as an illusion, we may rather regard it as a more sensitive functioning of the human organism.

But even without the faculty for mystic experience, for direct communion with God, it is possible to be in rapport with those situations that seem to make God manifest. Any situation which has the power of enlarging our sympathies, widening the perspective of our thought, quieting our mind, sweetening our disposition and strengthening our will, should reveal God to us. The function of religious folkways would then be to direct our attention to those situations, and to induce that frame of mind which would enable us to evoke from them their richest spiritual values.

An outstanding instance is the marriage covenant. There is no civilization where marriage can take place without some kind of ceremony. What is the purpose of these ceremonies if not to render the man and the woman conscious that their marriage offers them a new means of enlarging their sympathies, developing their personality, widening the scope of their ideas and feelings, and adding purpose and strength to their will? This is what is meant by saying that God manifests himself in the home in which the purpose of marriage is fulfilled. In the words of the Sages, "The presence of God abides in the home in which man and wife live up to the spiritual significance of their wedlock." '

Likewise, we find among all races and religions elaborate customs to mark the transition from childhood to adolescence. The sudden influx of vital powers widens the child's mental horizon, increases his power of self-control, and enables him to enter into the thoughts and feelings of others. Such an enlargement of life is a manifestation of the divine. How can we direct the attention of the youth to the significance of his entry into the period of adolescence, if not by some kind of initiation ceremony? For this reason we shall always require some rite, like the *bar miṣwah,* or confirmation ceremony, to induct the youth into the new state.

We might go through the entire range of situations from the cradle to the grave to prove that the moment any one of them assumes spiritual significance it is attended with some kind of rite. Whether it be the meal that we eat, or the rest day that we enjoy, or the home that we enter, once there is some rite connected with it, we realize that the act or situation in question must be applied to higher ends than those of selfish gratification. We note that religious rites exercise the same psychological effect as social conventions, rules of etiquette, national customs and folkways—all of which direct attention to situations, experiences and institutions which help to humanize and socialize the human being. When a rite thus enlarges the scope of our sensitivity and imagination it becomes a means of relating us to the cosmos, or manifesting God to us. Some customs are trivial; others have a profound effect upon the life of the individual. But to the degree that they humanize and socialize the individual, customs and folkways accomplish the same spiritual result as religious rites. It is mere accident that they are no longer related to God, or to the manifestations of God. In a more devout age all customs and folkways were religious rites. In an age such as ours, religious rites are likely to be accepted only when they are regarded as customs and folkways.

The important fact to be borne in mind is that these customs or folkways give individuality and character to a civilization, just as its language and its history do. They give to every individual in that civilization the bent of mind, the cast of thought, the type of emotional reaction that distinguish him from the individual in every other civilization. The conception of Judaism as a civilization furnishes a plausible rationale for what are usually termed "Jewish ceremonies." Even the protagonists of the conventional conception of Judaism as a religion are forced to advocate the observance of Jewish ceremonies on other than purely religious grounds. Assuming that the Jew's first duty is to maintain Jewish separateness, Morris Joseph argues,

Creed alone cannot be a sufficient barrier, for it must needs be lowered at the invitation of Theism. We must rely, it is clear, upon the old safeguards, upon distinctive *practices*. But this is not to admit that the entire ceremonial system which has been slowly built into Judaism in the course of centuries ought to be preserved. That a law or an observance tends to keep up Jewish separateness is by itself no valid argument for its retention. To justify its continued existence it must show that it still serves a moral and religious purpose, that its spiritual vitality is unexhausted.[8]

As soon as a people loses its distinctive customs and folkways, its civilization begins to disintegrate. Customs, by their very nature, tend to retain their form long after the original meaning is outlived, and as long as they can bear new interpretation, it is proper that they should be retained. For, in addition to calling attention to the spiritual significance of the acts or experiences with which they are associated, they also give a sense of historical continuity, which in itself exercises a humanizing influence.

Thus also has the Jewish people maintained its historical continuity. Since the Jewish customs and folkways, however, have come to mean to the Jew infinitely more than English customs, for example, have ever meant to the Englishman, it is far less possible to be a Jew without Jewish customs and folkways than to be an Englishman without English folkways. Jewish customs were more consciously and deliberately a means of directing attention to the experiences in which the divine manifested itself than the customs of any other people. That is why the Jewish customs, to a degree immeasurably greater than the customs of any other people, have become so firmly knit with the rest of the Jewish civilization.

There is no gainsaying the fact that many of the Jewish religious folkways have outlived their usefulness, and no amount of reinterpretation will enable them to exert a spiritualizing influence upon the Jew. *A revision of the entire system of Jewish customs is imperative. Before any constructive attempt at revision can be made, however, Judaism must be accepted, both in theory and in practice, as a civilization.* Both from the standpoint of Neo-Orthodoxy with its belief that the religious practices are decreed by God, and from that of Reformism with its claim that Judaism is fundamentally a form of ethical monotheism, it is equally irrelevant to call for a revision and elaboration of the traditional system of observances. If Neo-Orthodoxy is right, Jews have no business to tamper with the observances. If Reformism is right, Jews ought to eliminate them altogether. But if Judaism functions as a civilization, Jews will be able to view the problem of ritual observance in an entirely new light. In the first place, the emphasis will be shifted from the negative observances, where it was in the past, to affirmative observances. The prohibitions in the traditional Torah far outnumbered the positive behests. In a modern Torah the reverse will have to be the case. The Jew will demand of his civilization many more meaningful and esthetic folkways and a greater variety and range from which to choose means of Jewish self-expression than it offers at present.

Accordingly, the principle that would then be adopted in the development of Jewish folkways would be that the elementary needs of human existence, and the significant events and turning points in a person's life should constitute an occasion for folkways to be practiced, whenever they do not involve an unreasonable amount of time, effort and expense. Of course, what is reasonable will depend upon how intensely Jewish one is. Augustine's saying, "Love and you may do what you will," is certain to prove true in this instance. In the last resort, one's Jewish selective sense must be the final arbiter. There need be no fears about anarchy resulting from diversity in the practice of folkways. Diversity is a danger when we are dealing with law. But, on the assumption that Jews would accept the *miṣwot* not as laws, but as folkways, spontaneity would not only help to foster the *miṣwot* but would also give rise to an unforced uniformity which would be all the more valuable because it was not prescribed.

Since folkways originally arose out of the basic needs of life, it was natural to prescribe what might and what might not be eaten. Since the folk ideas surrounded these basic interests with beliefs and sanctions of a religious character, the rules concerning diet became a part of religious practice. A few of the primitive folkways observed by *Bene Yisrael* in the pre-Judaic civilization survived in the various stages of the Jewish civilization, but a radical transformation took place in the folk sanctions that accompanied them. Ever since the theocratic period, the ancient folkways pertaining to food were elevated to the status of laws divinely ordained. To be sure, folkways had always been regarded as decreed not by man, but by some deity. But the significance of folkways decreed by some obscure deity could not be compared with the significance they came to possess when they were ascribed to the one and only God of the universe, who was believed to have commanded them through Moses, at Sinai, so that the children of Israel would know that they were set apart by God to be to him a kingdom of priests.

Granting that the dietary laws cannot be observed in the traditional spirit, the fact remains that because of the dietary inhibitions the Jewish civilization has acquired a high degree of distinction and dignity. The dietary practices have transformed the process of eating from a purely animal act to one in which spirituality plays a part. It may be said that all such attempts to hide or gloss over the animalism of human nature are forms of self-deception. It must be realized, however, that it is more natural for the human being to widen the distance between him and animal nature than to be assimilated with it. Since civilization is not an artifact but a natural fact, it is a perfectly natural development for the human being to move in the direction of more developed civilization. In the matter of diet, the process of civilization will not only affect the preparation of the food; it will also evolve a kind of religious etiquette which will minimize the animality of the act of eating. Why then should not the Jews avail themselves of those of their folkways which might energize the deeply ingrained habit of transforming the act of eating, as it were, into a sacrament.

In the next stage of the Jewish civilization, the distinction between animals that divide the hoof and chew the cud and those that do not, or between *kasher* and *treja,* or between fish which have scales and fins and those which have not, will not be observed as dietary "laws" commanded by God, or as mystic symbols of what man must do to qualify himself to enter into communion with God. But these distinctions should be maintained as traditional folkways which add a specifically Jewish atmosphere to the home. Such observances should not be regarded as intended to help one earn salvation in the here or in the hereafter, nor to produce a marked effect upon one's character. Maimonides' argument ° that the forbidden foods have a physiological effect which is prejudicial to the mind or spirit is scarcely worth considering. Equally untenable are the so-called hygienic reasons which are advanced in defense of the dietary laws.[10] Such arguments are not only contradicted by experience; they have the additional disadvantage of counteracting the spiritual effect which those practices were wont to exercise. By giving them a utilitarian purpose, their function as a means of turning the mind to God is bound to be obscured. Such justifications are gratuitous from the ancient point of view, and unacceptable from the modern point of view. But if Jews are not to exaggerate the importance of the dietary practices, neither should they underestimate the effect those practices can have in making a home Jewish. If the dietary folkways are capable of striking a spiritual note in the home atmosphere, Jews cannot afford to disregard them.

Once these practices lose their character as laws and become folkways, Jews will be able to exercise better judgment as to the manner of their observance.[11] There need not be the feeling of sin in case of occasional remissness, nor the self-complacency which results from scrupulous observance. Moreover, since the main purpose of these practices is to add Jewish atmosphere to the home, there is no reason for suffering the inconvenience and self-deprivation which result from a rigid adherence outside the home. From the standpoint urged here it would not be amiss for a Jew to eat freely in the house of a Gentile, and to refrain from eating *trefa* in the house of a fellow-Jew. By this means, dietary practices would no longer foster the aloofness of the Jew, which, however justified in the past, is totally unwarranted in our day. As for the fear that social intercourse between Jews and Gentiles may lead to the disintegration of Judaism, the reply is obvious: if Judaism is inherently so weak that it requires the artificial barriers of social aloofness fostered by dietary laws for its maintenance, the very need for maintaining it is gone. It is true that increased social contact with the Gentiles will prove a challenge to Judaism's inherent strength, but that challenge cannot be met by a defensive retreat.

Another difficulty created by the traditional observance of the dietary practices would be removed, were they maintained in the spirit suggested. The limitations which the conscientious observance of the dietary "laws" in the legalistic spirit places upon the scope of activities in which the Jew might engage, even upon his range of travel, would no longer exist. Since the question of home atmosphere is in no way affected by his dietary observances outside the home, there is no reason why he should on their account forego opportunities to enlarge the scope of his usefulness.

With these qualifications which permit a degree of latitude necessary to unhampered movement in regions where there are no Jews, and to free social intercourse with Gentiles, the dietary practices should be reinstated in every Jewish home as a means of contributing to the home that atmosphere in which national folkways are subtly combined with folk religion. Their observance in this spirit would not prevent them from furthering communal organization. They would even necessitate the retention of that unique functionary, the *shohet,* the man who is not a coarse butcher but who, besides being engaged in the business of killing animals for food, is also something of a scholar and a man of parts.

But the Jewish dietary practices alone cannot give to the home the atmosphere necessary to evoke the spiritual potencies of Judaism. They have to be supplemented by practices of a more articulate character. Hence the need for various utterances which make the partaking of food an occasion for cosmic orientation. To be sure, very few of those who recite the benediction over the breaking of bread or after meals pay attention to what they are saying. That is caused not by the benediction, but by the inertia of human nature. But once we have accustomed ourselves, through a process of self-education, to recite a prayer with a certain degree of awareness of what it implies, we can see how it is possible for an ordinary meal to become the occasion for cosmic orientation. With the increasing tempo of life it may seem absurd to be asked to pause sufficiently at each meal, or to take it so leisurely, as to allow ourselves to think of it in terms of the cosmos. Yet if we reflect a moment, does not the very rate at which we are living necessitate just such transcendence of the immediate, even more than the slow gait of life in the past? Are we not repeatedly urged to spend a few moments several times daily to relax?

Properly understood, to achieve, even if for a moment, a social or cosmic orientation to a commonplace act like eating is like filling one's lungs with fresh air. If permitted to interrupt the daily routine of hustle and bustle, it can afford the spiritual relaxation which is invaluable as a humanizing influence. A meal in a Jewish household where everyone washes his hands and recites the benediction, becomes not merely an occasion for satisfying hunger, but a social and spiritual act. The initial benediction can call to mind in a swift flash the cooperative process beginning with the plowing and the sowing to the moment the food is brought on the table. In the concluding benedictions, the same thought is dwelt upon at somewhat greater length, to be followed by a few words that remind one of Israel's yearnings and hopes. The meal thus becomes an occasion for Jewish religious folkways which should be acceptable to the modern-minded Jew.

Once we become actively conscious of profound religious truths and ideals, we feel the need for externalizing that consciousness by means of concrete acts. To forego the enlargement of spirit induced by the Jewish religious folkways that surround the meal is to deprive oneself of genuine esthetic delight.

A second group of religious folkways essential to giving the home Jewish atmosphere consists of the practices which center about the Sabbaths and festivals. The Sabbath is not only a means of collective self-expression; it is the principal institution through which each Jew individually can experience the spiritualizing influence of Jewish civilization. As a result of the mechanization and over-industrialism of present-day life, the human being has come to stand in greater need of the Sabbath than ever before. Modern technology may prevent men from becoming brutalized, but it cannot prevent them from becoming Philistines and Babbits. If the imaginative arts redeem life from ugliness, it is religion that redeems life from secularity. For the complete development of the imaginative arts and religion, a people needs both Sabbaths and festivals.

The first question which naturally arises is what constitutes the kind of work which conflicts with the spirit of the Sabbath. We cannot receive any guidance from the list of works forbidden by traditional Judaism. A consistent attempt to live up to it would be attended with unnecessary hardship and deprivation. We can very well conceive that here and there a person filled with zeal for the Sabbath would voluntarily submit to all the traditional regulations, because he has somehow come to feel that only by that regimen of abstention can he give full expression to his desire to honor the Sabbath. To rationalize his zeal, he may resort to such explanations as those suggested by Samson Raphael Hirsch for the many minutiæ of Sabbath observance, without necessarily subscribing to Hirsch's Neo-Orthodoxy.[12] In the light of those explanations, the function of the Sabbath is to prohibit man from engaging in work which in any way alters the environment, so that he should not delude himself into the belief that he is complete master of his destiny. One who observes the Sabbath in this spirit and abstains from all manner of work forbidden by tradition, would not be doing anything unreasonable. On the contrary, without such zealots life would be all too prosaic. But we cannot expect such Sabbath observance from the majority of Jews.

It is evident that those who during the rest of the week are engaged in a gainful occupation which can be interrupted on the Sabbath without interfering with the normal life of society, should not engage in any work connected with that occupation on the Sabbath. To do marketing and housecleaning and to prepare food in the same manner as during the week is not compatible with Sabbath observance. But as to activities which do not form part of the routine of the week and are definitely recreative, a sense of propriety ought to guide one in deciding whether they are in keeping with the Sabbath spirit. Claude G. Montefiore, in describing Jews who attend to their business on Saturday because they have no choice, as in no sense any the *worse* Jews because they do so, adds, "But if on Friday evening they voluntarily go to the theater or the music hall, then they *are* the worse Jews, then their consciences should be seared and sore, then they *are* guilty of deliberate wrong-doing." [13]

The principle underlying Sabbath observance is well stated by Morris Joseph:

The Sabbath is a sacred day, he says, and there are certain kinds of enjoyment which, by their very nature, are out of harmony with its inherent holiness. Participation in them on the Sabbath is like the sudden intrusion of a shrill street-organ on a beautiful melody sung by a lovely voice.

It is difficult, almost impossible, to lay down a definite rule on this point, to say 'This sort of amusement is allowable, that sort improper on the Sabbath.' The matter must be left to the individual conscience, to each person's sense of what is seemly. . . . There are people who see no harm in spending part of the Sabbath day in struggling with a crowd at some exhibition, or in rushing to and fro from a concert or a theatre. Surely these amusements cannot fairly be called recreation. They are certainly not a 'sanctification' of the Sabbath.

Another illustration suggests itself. It is a moot question how far athletic sports are legitimate on the day of rest. There are people who decide it offhand by saying that such exercises are necessarily permissible because they promote that bodily health and vigour which it is the aim of the Sabbath to induce. But the question is not settled so easily. Unfortunately, there is an almost irrepressible tendency toward excess in modern athletics, . . . this, of course, does not mean that outdoor sports are necessarily unlawful on the Sabbath any more than the danger of overwalking oneself makes it a duty to sit still all day. But it does suggest the necessity for caution and circumspection. Let us seek after recreation on the Sabbath, but let us choose it carefully and wisely, under an overmastering sense of the true character of the day.[14]

In the last instance, not what the Jew will refrain from doing will determine the spiritual influence of the Sabbath, but the affirmative conduct which the observance of the Sabbath will elicit from him. The Sabbath must make itself felt in the home. Only there can its observance be made attractive enough to impel the Jew to effort and sacrifice in its behalf. If it depends upon the home to render the results of Sabbath observance tangible, the Jew should take advantage of the Sabbath eve which, in most cases, is the only time when the home can be utilized for that purpose. Though the late Friday night services afford an opportunity for congregational worship to those who cannot attend synagogue on the Sabbath morning, they do not constitute an ideal way of spending the Sabbath eve. That should be a time for family reunion. Away from the routine of work and the thousand and one distractions of clubs, organizations and entertainments, the members of the family might learn to know one another. It is then that parents should become acquainted with their children, and children should interchange their experiences with their parents. The memories and impressions resulting from a Sabbath eve spent in this manner will have a far more permanent influence upon the happiness and character of the Jews than the most successful Friday night services and lectures.

During the Sabbath day, the home should have a distinct Sabbath atmosphere. How to spend the day outside the home should constitute the problem for the synagogue, or neighborhood center, which should provide the facilities for spending the day with physical and spiritual advantage. The forenoon must be set aside for worship, to be attended by all who do not work then. During that time Jews should refrain from all indoor and outdoor sports that might keep them away from the synagogue.

The Sabbath morning service should be the principal one of the week. Even the men who are engaged in business should be induced to absent themselves from their business at least for an hour once in every three or four weeks in order to attend the services. Jews must learn to overcome the mental resistance caused by the seeming inconsistency of men leaving their business to attend services on the Sabbath. If it were not for the unfortunate assumption that such conduct is self-contradictory, the synagogues would not have become depopulated. If the men accustom themselves not to attend synagogue from one end of the year to the other, growing indifference to the synagogue is an inevitable result. An hour of attendance once in three or four weeks on the part of the men is therefore absolutely imperative and feasible. For men who work and cannot take off any time in the morning, a special afternoon service should be arranged. It is essential for the Jew to retain a sense of duty in the matter of frequent attendance at synagogue services. It is assumed, of course, that the services are sufficiently vital and appealing to give those who participate in them a sense of spiritual recreation. Otherwise, they can have only a negative effect.

On Sabbath afternoons, the synagogue ought to conduct both educational and recreational activities. Under educational activities should be included lectures, round-table discussions of general problems, study circles, literary circles, reading in the synagogue library, and Sabbath school sessions for children.

From the standpoint of Sabbath restrictions as mere folkways, it seems not only futile but unwise to forbid outdoor sports on Sabbath afternoons. They are essential to young people. With the indoor existence most of them have to lead during the rest of the week, to say nothing of the mental and physical strain which they undergo the greater part of the time, outdoor exercise has become indispensable. Instead of permitting this healthier form of recreation to be carried on in violation of the Sabbath and in defiance of the synagogue, Jews must compromise with an inevitable need, and bring outdoor sports within the scope of synagogue activities, so that they contribute to the enjoyment of the Sabbath, instead of detracting from it.

According to the same principle, Jews should reckon with the question of riding on the Sabbath. Jews should refrain from riding on Sabbath eve and during the forenoon of the Sabbath day. The only exception should be made in case of those who cannot get to the services on Sabbath morning without riding. While all forms of physical recreation should be permitted on Sabbath afternoons, it is of the utmost importance that as far as possible the physical recreation be part of the activities of the synagogue or neighborhood center.

The late Sabbath afternoon should be utilized by the synagogues as an occasion for social gatherings. They afford excellent opportunities for entertainment, group singing, and an appropriate *habdalah* service.

The observance of the Sabbath in the spirit set forth in the foregoing is a matter of careful and deliberate cultivation. It can come only as a concomitant of a general transformation of the Jewish mind, which hitherto went to the one extreme of rigid adherence to the minutiæ of observance, or to the other extreme of complete repudiation of the Sabbath as a whole. Jews will have to acquire that power of mental adjustment and spiritual plasticity which is essential in an age of transition like ours. Only when there is no guiding or restraining principle does the surrender of one custom lead to the surrender of all the rest. But where the aim of readjustment is to enrich Jewish life, Jews need not fear that departure from certain traditional customs will undermine Judaism.

The observance of the festivals, like that of the Sabbath, should provide a deepened spiritual content to the Jewish consciousness. The Jewish people has manifested a unique faculty in making its Sabbaths and holidays contribute to the social and humane qualities of men. When the greater part of mankind made the religious experience of the Jews their own, they accepted the Jewish attitude toward periodic rest days and holidays, no less than the Jewish idea of God. In dealing with this type of Jewish religious folkways, Jews should aim to cultivate and even extend the application of this faculty.

In contrast with the Sabbath, which seeks to spiritualize the physiological need of rest, the festivals stress some of the principal phases of spiritual life itself. Originally, the three pilgrim festivals, *Pesaḥ, Shabuot* and *Sukkot,* were the occasions of thanksgiving for the bounties of field and flock, and they had the universal character of nature festivals. The festivals had a humanizing influence even then, despite the orgies associated with them. They widened the horizon of the individual and made him dimly conscious of the tribe or nation to which he owed his human attributes. But Judaism, by associating with the festivals the principal formative events of its history, events which evidenced God's guidance, rendered them far more significant spiritually and ethically than they were originally. The two holy days, *Rosh ha-Shanah* and *Yom Kippur,* were denuded of their former magical significance and became occasions for the probing of the soul, and for the contemplation of the kingdom of God. *Religious folkways which possess such profound and stirring implications give as much character and greatness to a civilization as a rich literature or a wealth of artistic achievement.* To prevent the festivals from falling into abeyance and to elicit their power and beauty should be one of the first tasks to which those who mean to render Jewish life intrinsically interesting should apply themselves.

The main requisite is to reinterpret the significance of the festivals and make their meaning relevant to current needs and ideals. The story of the redemption from Egypt, which is the traditional basis of the *Pesaḥ* festival, should be made the occasion for stressing the implications of the conception of God as redeemer. That festival should direct our attention to the need of utilizing the redemptive energies which exist in nature and in man, the energies to which we look to break the shackles of the human spirit. It offers an excellent opportunity for becoming conscious of the true significance and the proper uses of freedom. *Shabuot* became associated during the third stage of Judaism with the tradition of God's giving the Torah on Sinai. This meaning should be retained and adapted to the psychological implication of the doctrine of revelation, that the primary function of a civilization is to actualize man's highest spiritual potentialities. The practice of making *Shabuot* an occasion for the confirmation of the youth is entirely in keeping with the meaning of the day, and should not be confined to the Reformists who inaugurated it. The confirmation ceremony deserves to be elaborated and deepened in significance. *Sukkot*, which recalls the journeying in the wilderness, should give meaning to the strange destiny of Israel—in the beginning, a wanderer among the nations; now, a nation in dispersion.

The nature aspect of *Sukkot* as the festival of ingathering still retains its appeal. In olden times, when it marked the close of the ingathering season, it became the occasion for thanksgiving to God. Essentially, thanksgiving is accepting life as significant; it therefore constitutes the basic element of religion. This sentiment cannot be experienced in our day in the naïve and unqualified fashion characteristic of primitive man. "As soon as high consciousness is reached," says Whitehead, "the enjoyment of existence is entwined with pain, frustration, loss, tragedy." The problem then presents itself, how to retain the sense of life's worthwhileness in the midst of so heartbreaking a world. *Sukkot* should therefore have, as its secondary purpose, the cultivation of the appreciative mood and the affirmation of life's intrinsic worth. Koheleth, with his refrain, "Vanity of vanities; all is vanity," furnishes the text which now more than ever is in need of refutation.

Rosh ha-Shanah is traditionally dedicated to the affirmation of God as the sovereign of the universe and to the devout wish that his sovereignty be made manifest in the life of mankind. The traditional ideal of God as sovereign is, on the whole, synonymous with what is often referred to as the kingdom of the spirit. The prayer for the manifestation of God's sovereignty would, accordingly, find its moral equivalent in the earnest consideration of what men can do individually and collectively to further the kingdom of the spirit. Unlike the three pilgrim festivals which spring from the career of Israel and address themselves to the national consciousness, *Rosh ha-Shanah* takes into its purview humanity as a whole, and addresses itself to the function of the Jew as a member of the human race.

Yom Kippur is the day on which man should focus his attention upon the part that he plays as an individual in that world of which he is the center. The idea of repentance and consequent atonement, purged of its theurgy and anthropomorphism, has been incorporated in the modern conception of moral responsibility. The effect of some of the current scientific teaching is to weaken the sense of moral responsibility, for when the human being is studied and analyzed from the point of view of the factors that condition his life, he tends to be depersonalized. To counteract that tendency by accentuating the power of personality as a motivating and creative force should constitute the chief purpose of *Yom Kippur*.

The traditional religious folkways associated with each of the foregoing holidays, the *seder* and the *maṣṣot* with *Pesaḥ*, the confirmation ceremony with *Shabuot*, the four species of plants and the *sukkah* with *Sukkot*, the *shofar* with *Rosh ha-Shanah*, and fasting with *Yom Kippur*, are capable of appealing to the heart of the Jew. All that is necessary is that their full value be brought out by means of the appropriate religious symbol and esthetic expression.

Most of the suggestions with regard to making the Sabbath a means of giving atmosphere to the Jewish home also pertain to the festivals. The festivals in themselves, however, are enriched by customs and folkways which have all the charm and magic of religious poetry. The *Pesaḥ* festival, which is preceded by the usual spring cleaning, announces its coming long in advance. There is an air of expectancy in the household. Nothing could have so marked an effect upon the atmosphere as the absence of leavened bread for a whole week, and the substitution of the *maṣṣot*. No folkway could be more beautiful and at the same time so saturated with the ideal of self-realization through freedom. And the *seder* night—one has to seek far among the civilizations of the world to find a folkway so compact of pathos, wistfulness and mystic yearning, yet one that is human and simple enough to be loved by the youngest child, about whom the entire observance is centered. *It is the spirit of Israel trying to communicate its sufferings and its dreams to those upon whom its future depends.*

The last day of *Pesaḥ* is lacking in significant folkways. Some ceremony ought to be devised analogous to the *seder* of the first night. It ought to be the festival of song, a sort of consecration of the spirit of spring. Its present pointlessness makes it an encumbrance.

The *Shabuot* festival offers an excellent opportunity for Jewish self-expression. With the nature element as background woven into the Ruth theme, the significance of the Torah affords an appropriate occasion for various customs in the home, especially the one of staying up far into the night and engaging in such reading and discussion as may justly be called Torah. This by no means precludes entertainment of a lighter character, together with music and dancing.

Rosh ha-Shanah and *Yom Kippur* are mainly synagogue festivals. Nevertheless they can leave a deep impress upon the home surroundings. Atmosphere appropriate to these days has to be carried over from the synagogue. If there is no special effort made in the synagogue to give these days the proper interpretation, they will remain entirely characterless in the home. Their individuality should express itself in a subtle combination of festivity and solemnity.

The *Ḥanukkah* and *Purim* festivals should be observed with more *éclat* than at present. Since *Ḥanukkah* falls so near the Christmas season, it must be made as interesting and joyful for the Jewish child as Christmas is made for the Christian child. The *Ḥanukkah* festival should be the season for gifts. The children should look forward to gifts from their parents, and parents from their children. Receiving and giving gifts contributes to the festal air of the home. It should be the season for paying social calls, playing home games, and holding communal entertainments. *Purim* gifts, though prescribed by custom, will naturally grow rare as *Ḥanukkah* gifts will come more and more into vogue. But with masking, dancing, social entertainment, and the *seudah,* Purim can generate Jewish atmosphere in the home.

It may not be amiss to mention another folkway which contributes to the Jewishness of the home. The *mezuzah,* provided it is shorn of all associations with magic, has excellent potentialities for giving character to the Jewish home. Its contents, which emphasize the duty of allegiance to God and his law, should be more generally known. When the family moves into a new home and celebrates a housewarming, the reading of the *mezuzah*, the explanation of its contents, and the ceremonial attachment of it to the doorpost, might help to make the housewarming impressive.

B

CULTURAL FOLKWAYS

Traditional Judaism abounds in customs which were a means of fostering the Jewish consciousness. Those customs were not recognized as constituting a class by themselves but were treated as *miṣwot*, or divinely ordained institutions. Many of those customs are in the nature of prohibitions designed to discourage the tendency to imitate non-Jewish ways and practices. They all fall under the category of the commandment, "Ye shall not walk in their statutes." [16] *All such prohibitions, however, are out of place in the Judaism of the future, which will tend to assimilate whatever practices are congenial to its spirit.* On the other hand, there exist in Judaism many affirmative practices which, though not related to any ordinance in the Torah, have the effect of deepening the Jewish consciousness and promoting a sense of unity with the rest of Jewry. All such practices may be regarded as cultural folkways. Only those which deserve special consideration will here be discussed.

1. *The Hebrew language.* Chief among the cultural folkways, the cultivation of which has become imperative, is the use of the Hebrew language. The renascence of Hebrew as a vernacular in Palestine would not have been possible without the clear recognition on the part of a few enthusiasts of the indispensability of Hebrew to the fostering of the Jewish consciousness. In America and western Europe, however, the havoc wrought by the assimilationist tendencies which have dominated Jewish life is most evident in the practical elimination of Hebrew from the Jewish consciousness. *Once Hebrew becomes a foreign or an ancient tongue to the Jew, he ceases to experience any intimacy with Jewish life, and he begins to look for rational justification for being a Jew, with the consequent self-delusions and ultimate frustration.*

The first practical step in any effort to live Judaism as a civilization should be to learn Hebrew. It should be included among the languages that Jewish children are taught in the high schools and colleges, and it should be given the same academic credit as Latin and Greek. The impression received during the first years of infancy and childhood are strongest and most enduring. During the first years, the child should breathe and live in a Hebrew atmosphere. It would be far more appropriate if in the Jewish homes which can afford a governess, the children learn to laugh and play in Hebrew, rather than in French or German. The use of Hebrew in the religious services is natural and logical, as well as in the spirit of centuries of tradition.

In spite, however, of the urgent need of Hebrew as a means to a satisfying Jewish life, it is not likely that in the western countries the majority of Jews will possess a fair reading knowledge of it. Yet with the improvement in the technique of teaching the language, it is possible to reintroduce it as an important cultural factor in Jewish life.

The Sages intuitively grasped the value of folkways which could not be comprised within the category of divine precepts. They knew nothing of the anthropology and psychology of folkways, yet they said that the Israelites were redeemed from Egypt by virtue of four meritorious practices,[16] three of which were the use of their Hebrew language, the retention of their Hebrew names and the wearing of their national garb.[17] None of these practices is commanded, yet they were deemed so important as to have led to national redemption.

2. *Jewish names.* The matter of names is rarely included in a discussion of Judaism, yet if our aim is to enlarge the scope of Jewish folkways we cannot overlook the importance of names as a means of fostering Jewish consciousness. Except for the rabbinic statement quoted above, the sentiment of the past was not opposed to the adoption of non-Jewish names; Gentile names are known to have been used rather freely. It is easy to trace the changes in the cultural environment of the Jews by noting their names. Babylonia, Persia, Greece, Rome, and later the various European nations, left their stamp upon Jewish names.[18] In former times, Jews could permit themselves this laxity because it could not possibly jeopardize their Jewishness.[19] But circumstances have altered. Every possible meas-

ure that may fortify Jewish consciousness should be utilized, assuming that it is free of all anti-social bias. The name that a person bears carries with it cultural implications and associations, and identifies him with a particular civilization. Among the first evidences of the Jew's desire to escape Judaism is his adoption of a name that conceals his Jewish identity. *The self-respect which the Jews will regain when they succeed in rendering Judaism creative will no doubt be reflected in the names they will bear.*

In Palestine the conscious Jewish renascence is evident in the hebraization of both the personal and the family names. The names of Jews in the diaspora should normally be such as to reflect the fact that they are living in two civilizations. Their first names should be distinctly Jewish, and their surnames American, French or Polish, as the case may be.

3. *The Jewish calendar.* An important cultural folkway which deserves to be revived is the use of the Jewish calendar. In all probability there will come a time when all the nations of the world will adopt a uniform and simplified calendar. In the meantime, the Jews should be the last to give up their historic calendar. Although there would naturally be no occasion to employ it in dealings with non-Jews, it has a place in Jewish life, since so many religious folkways are based on it.⁹⁰

Two matters must be reckoned with in the use of the Jewish calendar. One is the designation of the months and days, and the other is the designation of the years. Although the traditional method of combining the lunar year with the solar year by adding seven intercalary months in the course of nineteen years is antiquated and awkward, the time is not yet ripe for a radical change in the calendar. On the other hand, the present method of designating the years is not complicated by too long a tradition and might be altered without causing any violent wrench. The practice of counting from the year of creation does not go back even to rabbinic times. In the light of modern astronomical and geological knowledge, the traditional mode of reckoning from creation has no point. The method of reckoning the year of the destruction of the Second Temple as the year "one" seems the most plausible, especially as it would have the effect of reminding the Jew that his people has been altogether too long a homeless wanderer among the nations.

4. *Jewish arts*. In the discussion of the relation of art to a civilization, it has been pointed out that Jewish life was never without its distinctive art forms, however limited in scope or crude in execution they may have been in certain periods. If there is good reason to believe that a Jewish Palestine will give the world a new Jewish art, it is because Jews always flowered in art as soon as they were liberated from the anxieties and fears of persecution. That a people which, in spite of circumstances most adverse to creativity, should be able to evince at present such talent and, in some instances, even genius, in the fields of music, drama [11] and painting, presages extraordinary achievement when Jewish life shall have become more normal.

The chief hindrance to be overcome is the failure to appreciate the importance of art to the survival of the Jewish civilization in the diaspora. Modern civilizations fascinate the cultured and sensitive person not because of their ethical or religious progress, but because of their esthetic achievements. At present, the power of esthetic values over the human mind is as strong as the hold which religious values had upon the human mind in the past. If, formerly, religion spoke in the language of art, the present tendency is to raise art to a religion. Jews who subscribe to the modern emphasis upon the esthetic as that aspect of the spiritual, which is a worthy end in itself, will lose all interest in Jewish civilization, unless it provide a field for abundant and variegated esthetic creativity.

While it is true that art is spontaneous and cannot be legislated or created to order, the conditions favoring it can be willed and prepared.

In the field of music, the first organized effort to conserve and develop characteristic Jewish music was the establishment, in St. Petersburg in 1912, of the Society for Jewish Folk Music. Its initial activity consisted in gathering all the Jewish folk music available. The war, unfortunately, put an end to the undertaking. [12] In the United States, especially in the large Jewish centers, this effort could be resumed.

Simultaneously with the preparation of the musical material there should be formed various choral societies, glee clubs, quartets, etc., to provide entertainment and develop a taste for Jewish music in the various synagogues, men's and women's clubs and centers. Ernest Bloch in his symphony, *Israel,* has given a foretaste of creativity in the field of Jewish music.

Theatrical art expressive of Jewish life is a very recent growth, and its medium has mainly been Yiddish. With the increasing numbers of those to whom Hebrew is a living language, it should be possible to foster the Hebrew theater in the diaspora. The achievement of the *Habimah,* the Hebrew theater established in Russia, is very remarkable. A noted critic had the following to say of the *Dybbuk,* one of the plays presented by the *Habimah;* "One felt that this totality, this astral body of weird beauty was so saturated with Hebrew tradition that every part and parcel of it, every curve, every contour, every note, every light and shadow, was flesh of the Hebrew flesh. Never since the Greek drama has anything appeared so autochthonous." [13] The Hebrew theater, like Hebrew music, is indispensable to the development of Jewish life in this country. Hebrew theater guilds or studios should be established to train people of talent, and authorities on stagecraft should be invited to make their several contributions to the development of Hebrew dramatic art. [14]

A conspicuous demonstration of what the Jews in this country can do to foster esthetic creativity was the production in the summer and fall of 1933 of the pageant entitled *The Romance of a People.* That pageant has in it the making of a stupendous spectacle which, from an esthetic point of view, might surpass the Oberammergau Passion Play. If, like that play, it should be performed periodically, it will not only help to articulate the Jewish spirit, but also serve as a colorful element in the American scene. It will probably not be able to counteract the poison of Jew hatred spread by the Oberammergau play. But there are enough fair-minded Gentiles who need just such a presentation of the Jewish case to catch a glimpse of the Jewish soul in all its grandeur and pathos. To the majority of the Jews who, under present conditions, are left without even an elementary outline of the Jewish past, this pageant is an invaluable means of conveying by a few bold strokes the highlights in the career of the Jewish people. The way in which that pageant brought out latent powers in artists who through it discovered unexplored fields for self-expression, the awakening in the several thousand men and women who took part in it of an unsuspected interest in things Jewish, the fusion into a throbbing unity of the throngs of men and women from all classes and conditions of Jewry—all these facts make the pageant itself part of *The Romance of a People*. Such are the unlimited resources for the enrichment of Jewish life that lie hidden in artistic creation.

Those who are entrusted with the construction of Jewish public institutions such as synagogues, institutions of learning, federation buildings, centers and schools, should possess a sufficient familiarity with Jewish life and aspiration to give a distinctly Jewish character to the architecture. An index of a civilization is its architecture; a civilization is most vital when it is architecturally creative. In a few instances in this country Jews have sought to express the individuality of their inherited civilization through the architecture of their public buildings. These public buildings are today a source of civic pride to the general community.

The same principle applies in beautifying the home. It is of the utmost importance that every available esthetic means of giving Jewish atmosphere to the home be utilized. Some who specialize in the art of interior decoration might be encouraged to design furniture, hangings and bric-a-brac in a manner that would reflect Jewish individuality. To do this successfully they must possess an adequate background of Jewish knowledge and emotion, and be stimulated by an increasing interest on the part of the Jewish public in this type of effort.

Another important step will be to release Jewish esthetic creativity in the field of Jewish religion. Public worship was once the mother of the fine arts, of architecture, sculpture, drama, music, song and the dance. While it is questionable whether the arts have had the same sublimity since their divorce from worship, it is certain that as soon as worship tries to emancipate itself from the arts it becomes arid and uninspiring. Though the plastic arts received but little stimulation from Jewish public worship, music and poetry owe their high development in Jewish life almost entirely to it. The

significance of this fact, however, has seldom been fully apprehended. Too much importance has come to be attached to uniformity. Legalism and endless repetition of prescribed formulas
have banished from Jewish worship all that freedom and spontaneity
without which art cannot flourish.

Assuming the value of worship, a completely new attitude toward
it must now be acquired. In organizing public worship, the aim
should be to utilize as much as possible of poetry, music, song, drama
and the dance. If these art forms will be congruous with the spirit
of Judaism, they will constitute an addition to Jewish values. This
by no means precludes the continuance and revival of ancient
liturgical formulas. Once those formulas are divorced from all associations with the theurgic attitude, they gain in esthetic appeal by
virtue of their historic association with a people's joys, yearnings
and martyrdom.

This conception of public worship would not only redeem it
from boredom; it would give a new impetus to Jewish art. Hebrew
poetry would again become the expression of man's deepest and most
passionate concern with the mystery of life, birth, love, suffering,
death. The themes of worship, man's various moods in the presence
of destiny, could again find their appropriate musical setting.
Dramatic presentations and pageants as part of public worship
would offer a rich field for esthetic creativity. Moreover, the aid of
the architect, the sculptor, the painter, the worker in glass, the
tapestry weaver, would be enlisted to beautify the place of worship.
The ancient interdicts against the use of human form are no
longer valid, since the original fear of idolatrous worship has become
totally meaningless. These are some of the measures necessary for
releasing the dormant capacities for art in Jewish life.

A statement made recently by Max Reinhardt, the eminent
authority on the theater, indicates that the place in Jewish life, which
is assigned in this discussion to art, is one which is recognized by anyone who has his eyes opened to the truth, as normally belonging to it.

For two thousand years, he said, we have been accustomed to lavish
our cultural gifts on other people, adapting them in each country, to the
national ideals, or to the racial mental and moral peculiarities of that
country. Conversely, our own Jewish culture has been influenced by the
ideals and the culture of the various nations who have been our hosts

throughout all these long centuries. That has made it very difficult for us to revive our own Jewish culture to achieve a cultural self-containedness, or even to define sufficiently closely what Jewish culture is.

I hasten to say that I am not advocating cultural isolation. That would be a calamity to us as well as to the civilized nations to whose culture we are proud to have contributed, and who appreciate our contribution. What I do advocate is a Jewish cultural renaissance in which Jewish achievements in the fields of literature, art, music and the drama should bear the unmistakable mark of their Jewishness, and in which Jewish genius should not be compelled to assume the disguise of another nationality. I am convinced that such a renaissance would stimulate us to ever higher attainments and would also benefit the rest of the world, perhaps to a far greater extent than at present.[25]

CHAPTER XXX

JEWISH ETHICS

A. Ethical motivation—The prophetic versus the philosophic attitude to ethical ideals —Ethical creativity presupposes the kind of ethico-intellectual activity represented by the study of Torah—Problems of social adjustment to be given priority by Jewish scholars. B. Jurisprudence, ethics rendered efficacious—The place of Jewish law in American-Jewish life. C. Economic justice—The moral fallacy of individualist economics—The spiritual fallacy of collectivist economics.

A

ETHICAL MOTIVATION

The worth of a civilization depends not only upon the ideals and values it professes, but upon its ability to energize them. Judaism formerly possessed that ability to an eminent degree. The concept of divine revelation reenforced the moral standards of Judaism so that they acquired the potency of physical causes. At a time when the disintegration of the ancient religions and loyalties shook men's faith in the values and standards essential to the stability of the social order, Judaism performed a much needed service to mankind. The nations were far less prepared than they are even today to be governed by an ethical code which is based on man's recognition of his spiritual nature. Men were still accustomed to look to extraneous authority for the sanction of the right. They were too heteronomously minded to be spiritually self-reliant. The philosophers and their schools were not able to inspire sufficient confidence in what they offered as sustaining certitudes, because they had no way of proving the objectivity and imperativeness of the moral law. It was at that juncture that Judaism saved civilization by supplying a transcendent sanction not only to the moral law as such, but even to some of the specific laws for the regulation of human conduct.

In place of the reasoned conclusions of the philosophers which pointed to the objective and categorical character of the ethical standards of human life, Judaism affirmed as a sanction of the higher life the historic fact of supernatural revelation. The fact that supernatural revelation is now questioned might mean that the human race will once more be plunged into the hopeless skepticism characteristic of the Roman world at the beginning of the common era, unless the human mind learn to free itself from dependence upon supernatural authority to validate moral law. It is imperative that men break away from the habit of identifying the spiritual with the supernatural. The reality of the spiritual should be conceived in terms of the supersensible which interacts with and functions through the sensible and perceptible world. The human mind, in sensing that reality, has with some already attained a mature form of spiritual grasp, the product of a first-hand realization that the world is not characterless, that it acts with a uniformity which gives meaning to existence, and that the salvation for which man strives is to live in rapport with that meaning. But this spiritual maturity is far from being general. The majority of mankind are still in the stage of spiritual adolescence. They have outgrown the traditional ideology, but they have not yet acquired an ideology which, taking into account the new knowledge, might help them achieve an affirmative and spiritual adjustment to life. *The Jews ought to realize the seriousness and extent of the spiritual maladjustment in their own lives and in those of the rest of mankind, and take a leading part in effecting the new orientation which is the only means of preventing the eruption of a new barbarism.*

Modern religiously minded thinkers are striving to construct a foundation of ethical values upon which the social structure might henceforth be reared. Kant inaugurated the movement in modern times to find in "practical reason" a sanction for values. But like the movement inaugurated by Socrates and Plato, or the school of the Stoics, this too will fail as long as it remains confined to the limited class of intellectuals.

The nations of the world are so preoccupied with their anxieties and ambitions that they do not realize that the very foundation of civilized life is being undermined. Though their traditional religious sanctions are decaying, there is no concerted effort on the part of their leaders to forestall the crash which must ultimately come. It is nothing more than fitting that the Jews should be among the first to reckon with this spiritual crisis. The rich residue of ethical passion and inspiration latent in the Jewish heritage should be called into action once more.

The spiritual reconstruction in which Jews of ethical enlightenment ought to engage should not be conceived merely as a task in rethinking the problem of spiritual adjustment along lines familiar to philosophers. The ethical teacher who promulgates his intuitions and experiences as though they belonged to man or mankind in the abstract, may develop a system of formal but not of living ethics. The ethical teachers who left the deepest impress upon mankind were those who came to save their own peoples, not mankind in general. By addressing themselves to their own civilization, their message had a concreteness and dynamic character which compelled attention. This explains why prophets have succeeded where ethical philosophers have failed. The ethical philosopher taught in abstract terms and failed to move men because he addressed himself to civilization in general. The prophet taught in concrete terms and moved men to action, because he addressed himself to his people's civilization, trying to change its course, opposing its idols and putting up before it new ideals. Ethical philosophers are dreamers and creators of Utopias. Prophets are practical revolutionaries. Only when the ethical reconstruction is incorporated into Jewish civilization will that reconstruction affect the lives of all Jews who want to remain Jews. They will want to remain Jews as soon as they feel that the best in them is being definitely challenged by and elicited through their civilization.

The only kind of ethical movement that is compatible with the genius of the Jewish civilization is a movement of the prophetic and not of the philosophic type.[1] This means that instead of taking the attitude that the new ethical structure should house only those who find themselves out of place in the traditional sanctions of social duties, all Jews should be aroused to the need of reconstructing their ethical and spiritual life. The reorientation should be advocated as a function of Jewish civilization as a whole.

The difference between the philosophic and the prophetic method becomes clear when we attempt to envisage the process of reorientation. Let us take the two main categories of human conduct whose ethical standards, in the light of recent social changes, require redefinition: sex and the will-to-power. It is essential that those who are intellectually qualified by their knowledge of Judaism and appreciation of present-day difficulties and problems, and who are spiritually qualified by their ethical attainments, should regard it their foremost duty to devote themselves to the study of these problems for the purpose of accomplishing the following twofold result: the discovery of an acceptable and effective sanction for whatever standards of conduct they shall have occasion to suggest, and the formulation of specific standards of right and wrong in these two categories of conduct.

Let us assume, for example, that after earnest research and reflection it is found that the one principle which must be accepted as normative of all human relationships is that human personality is too sacred to be treated otherwise than as an end in itself. The very foundation of the higher life is threatened every time a human being is treated as though he were other than an end in himself. That principle should then be adopted in Jewish life as a valid sanction, and urged with the same fervor with which the Prophets in ancient times urged their conception of YHWH as a God of righteousness. The traditional values of Judaism should be drawn upon to show to what extent the sanctity of the human person has implicitly played a part in shaping some of the most important laws and practices of the Jewish people.

This resort to the past for the confirmation of present values is not a sop to conservative minds. Ethical principles require the sanction of history not only to counteract the dogmatism they would otherwise possess, but also to show that they are in line with tendencies inherent in the very nature of man, and in keeping with that character of the world which expresses itself as the power that makes for righteousness. To this end, it is necessary to select from the Jewish heritage whatever will verify the validity of the sanction which Judaism is urged to adopt.[*]

No less important than finding standards that might serve as sanctions is the discovery of the norms which will provide specific guidance in concrete situations—in the sexual relations of men and women, and in the divers social and economic relations. Here the play of the new forces set afoot by modern conditions of life must

be taken into account. In sex relations, for example, the manifold
problems which have arisen in the wake of the widespread practice
of birth control must be dealt with in the light of specific ethical
objectives. If the Jews of the past were able to evolve high standards
of sex morality at a time when sex lust was sanctified by phallic
worship, the Jews of today will be able to avert the dangers of
promiscuity, provided their civilization maintain its wholesome chan-
nelling of the sex impulse in family life. A similar course should be
pursued with regard to the infinitely more complex problem of what
is wrong or right in our social and economic relationships. The
introduction of machinery has revolutionized not only the relations
of labor and commerce but even the more intimate relationships of
family life. Here again the process of formulating specific precepts
of ethical conduct should be applied and fortified by Jewish experience in the past.

We must not make the mistake, however, of assuming that
ethical creativity consists in building up elaborate systems of
"oughts" and "don'ts" supported by plausible rationales. The finality which seems to dominate some of the ethical systems, ranging
from the *musar* literature of the Middle Ages to the various collec-
tions of ethical sayings in Jewish literature which have been recently
published, has a paralyzing influence on the process of ethical creativity. The very notion of finished and rounded-out systems of
ethics is wrong. The abstractness and the banality common to ethical
systems may be traced to the fact that no two situations are alike,
and the only way of knowing the right and wrong in each situation
is to determine the ethics of it afresh in the light of all the known
facts that enter into it. The knowledge of a number of generalizations of past experience cannot make ethics alive and pertinent; a
vital ethics must be a process of individual or group reflection and
study carried on throughout life.* It is in this way that we look to
the renascence of the inherently ethical character of the Jewish
civilization.

It would be futile to hope for creativeness in the field of ethics
if there were no prospect for its realization. Fortunately, there
exists in Jewish life an institution or social habit which might not
only direct the energies of a self-conscious Jewry into the channels

of ethical creativity, but also contribute to the enrichment of every phase of Jewish life. The social habit of Torah-study, though dormant at the present time, has in it the potency of centuries of accumulated energy and devotion. If made to function again, it would revive the ethical genius of the Jewish people.

Torah as a habit of study was primary in traditional Judaism. It was not merely a form of intellectual activity; it was a spiritual experience. The study of phenomena as an end in itself, the interest in objective reality displayed by some of the Greek philosophers, was practically unknown among the Jews. The study of the Torah fascinated the Jew because he believed that the Torah was the revelation of God's will and purpose with regard to man. When a Jew was familiar with its teachings, he was certain of what he had to do to achieve salvation, or a share in the world to come. The importance of study was paramount because it led to the practice of the right. *Torah as study never meant detached contemplation of truth,* but group discussion with a view to arriving at a knowledge of the right in specific problems of human conduct.*

The naïveté which enabled the Jew to accept certain writings and traditions as supernatural revelation has departed. If, however, the continuity of the Jewish civilization is to be maintained, nothing is so sure to accomplish that end as the habit of study associated with Torah. To study human relationships with the purpose of rendering them a means of eliciting the best in human nature is to carry on in our day an activity similar in function, if not in form, to the study of Torah. That same ardent and inspired eagerness which the Jews brought to the study of a folio of the Talmud and commentaries can accompany the study of a chapter in history, in psychology, in ethics or in law for the purpose of comprehending the Jewish past or planning the Jewish future. The ideal of Torah can be most fruitfully translated into inspired intellectual activity in the form of adult education in the concrete problems of human life.

This transfer of spiritual enthusiasm from the old to the new content of Jewish civilization should be inaugurated by those who hold the position of intellectual and spiritual leadership in Jewry. The movement must begin at the top, from there spread to the rank and file, and then take effect in the education of the young. The reconstruction of Jewish life cannot be initiated merely through improvement in pedagogic technique. So long as there will be no change of mind and heart in the generation of adults, either the parents will be too indifferent to Judaism to give their child a Jewish training, or they will insist upon having their child learn what they regard as essential to his career as a Jew—the minima of a few Hebrew prayers—and will resist any serious attempt to train the child to be a Jew by means of an idea-content other than that upon which they themselves were brought up. *The primary and essential need at the present juncture is the reeducation of the adult Jew.*

As a prerequisite to this retrieving of the traditional zeal for study as an ethical and spiritual pursuit, it is necessary that scholars versed in ancient lore, teachers in schools of higher learning and rabbis in charge of congregations adopt the principle of priority in the kind of learning they cultivate. For the sake of their people's future they must be willing to forego the pleasure of living in the ivory tower of esoteric knowledge. Uppermost in their minds must be the consideration to advance the kind of learning that will help to upbuild Jewish life. Jews in the past glorified the knowledge of rabbinic lore, a knowledge which had nothing to do with the training of independent thought. The Gentile scholars in the present who are engaged in studies in the field of Jewish knowledge glorify the archeological ability to reconstruct the life and thought of the past. Both the command of the ancient texts and archeological research are of indisputable value to intellectual and spiritual leadership. But when they are exalted as ends in themselves, and are not made subsidiary to the broader and more inclusive disciplines such as psychology, sociology, ethics, religion, legal and political science, they cannot contribute to Jewish survival.

The failure of the Jewish people to reorient itself to the new world during the last hundred years has been due mainly to the failure of its intellectual and spiritual leaders to make Jewish knowledge relevant to the present problems of Jewish life and thought.

When Jewish scholars turned their eyes to the past, says Aḥad Ha-Am, they were not impelled to do so by something within them which demanded that the national spirit should continue to develop in the future. Zunz, who led the founders of the movement [for Jüdische Wissenschaft] regarded it as a means of converting the world to more friendly feelings toward the Jews. . . . Geiger threw himself heart and soul into "Jüdische Wissenschaft" in order to find support for *his* great ideal—religious reform—which was itself essentially a means to the acquisition of equal rights. Even Zacharias Frankel maintained that since the Jews have no longer a separate history, historical investigation of their past will have no connection with their life in the present and future, but will be purely a theoretical science.[5]

The failure to make Jewish learning relevant to living issues has been inherited by modern rabbinical institutions whose curricula are based on the method and spirit of the German-Jewish scholars of the nineteenth century.[6]

The training of the rabbi should aim to qualify him to be a Jewish teacher of both old and young. Not that any of the Jewish subject matter which is now taught in the rabbinic training school can be dispensed with. On the contrary, whatever ability the students acquire in the reading of ancient texts is so necessary that it should be a condition of entrance to a rabbinical training and not a qualification for assuming the rabbinical calling. The preparation for the rabbinical calling, however, should include an intensive study of the human sciences, and of their relation to Judaism as a civilization insofar as it must be transformed to meet unprecedented conditions of thought and life.

B

JURISPRUDENCE, ETHICS RENDERED EFFICACIOUS

In addition to the usual attributes of national life, what differentiates Judaism from a religious or ethical philosophy is the fact that its primary emphasis is on the translation of ethical theory into legalistic practice. Although Torah connotes among other things, moral and spiritual teaching, the connotation of law* is the most conspicuous. And with good reason, since the true index of a living civilization is not its ability to advise but its authority to command.

Even from a pedagogic standpoint, Judaism cannot exert any

---

* Throughout this discussion, the term "law" is used only in reference to jurisprudence, or to laws regulating human relationships. The need of departing from the tradition which applies the term law, *Halakah*, indifferently to torts and ritual practice has been discussed in the section dealing with folkways.

determining influence upon the character and life of the Jew, if it remain a mere system of teaching. It is recognized, for example, that by means of an adequate curriculum and methodology, the school can communicate a certain amount of knowledge to its pupils. Yet, despite courses in ethics and religion, it may not have the least influence upon their character and conduct. The only way to learn is by doing. If Jewish life is to exercise an educative influence upon the character of the Jew, it must possess the instrumentalities of Jewish self-government and the opportunity of law-making.

The formal distinction between ethics and law or jurisprudence may be stated thus: law is ethics plus the element of social efficacy. Like ethics, law is essentially a means of achieving a higher synthesis out of conflict, and not merely a means of settling disputes. When an ethical principle or precept is backed by approval and disapproval of the social group to which one belongs, it has entered the domain of law. It is immaterial what form the approval or disapproval takes. "Ideally, law embraces," says Felix Adler, "the totality of those conditions which are indispensable to the development of human beings toward personality, and which are capable of being enforced. Positive law is a transcript of the ideal in so far as the community at any time is intellectually and morally capable of willing such conditions." [7]

Jurists generally find it difficult to draw the line between ethics and law because their problem is the specific one of determining at what point social efficacy may take the form of physical coercion. So liable is individual freedom to be endangered by the exercise of physical coercion by the state, that the jurist must not permit society to exercise punishment for the infraction of ethical principles and precepts, even if these principles and precepts represent generally accepted ideals. The point in the ethical scale at which an act becomes sufficiently objectionable to be amenable to the social efficacy which takes the form of law must of necessity be far below the highest standard of ethical conduct. Nevertheless, the element of social efficacy constitutes an indispensable factor in a civilization. To whatever degree Judaism is to be lived in the diaspora, the element of social efficacy must supplement its ethical principles and precepts, and translate them into law or jurisprudence. This is no plea for coercion in the form of social ostracism or excommunication. Yet some means of approval and disapproval is necessary to lend efficacy to moral standards.

As long as we labor under the prejudice that law is an evil, though necessary, the importance of adding the element of social efficacy to Jewish life so that it evolve positive law will scarcely be admitted. Jews are likely to rejoice in the fact that they do not have to disturb the purity of their ethical ideals by the disputes and brawls of litigants, since the Gentile courts do the "dirty work" of adjusting quarrels among Jews. But a careful consideration of the function of law will make evident the truth that in surrendering the prerogative of putting into effect positive law, Judaism has surrendered the most civilizing function which it is within the power of any group or people to exercise. For through the exercise of law, the social group does not merely prevent the potential wrongdoer from injuring his fellow, but it creates a public opinion which helps every one of its members to overcome his anti-social tendencies.

Except for the few who are gifted with an extraordinary amount of self-control, the efficacy which a group gives to the ethical ideals is an indispensable means of checking the egoistic desires. A social group that does not exercise the prerogative of law ceases to be ethically creative and forfeits even the ethical standards inherited from the past. *The most important function associated with a civilization, that of setting up standards of action in our relations to one another, cannot be discharged by a people which is not in a position to pass judgment on the conflicting interests of its members.*

With a sure instinct the Jews in the darkest period of their career retained the right of exercising the power of juridical law, even when the nations which had conquered them would often prohibit the convening of Jewish courts. The Jews developed the institution of the improvised court which applied Jewish law as though the Jewish state had remained intact. If Jewish life is to be maintained in the diaspora, Jews must maintain courts to pass upon disputes in which only members of their own people are involved. Within the jurisdiction of these courts might come all cases of torts, contracts, agency and domestic relationships.

A more serious problem is the fact that Jewish law, in the form in which it has been handed down from the past in the *compendia* and the *responsa*, is largely unsuited to modern conditions. Palestine will undoubtedly contribute to the development of Jewish law in accordance with the new needs, but it would be a mistake to depend entirely upon Palestine. Judaism must function also in the diaspora. A practice which might be adopted with regard to cases not covered by ancient Jewish law is that the improvised court act in the same spirit as the circuit judges did in the early days of England. They had no fixed code to go by. They consulted the primitive laws which had existed for the most part as custom, but they relied on their own sense of justice. Their decisions have been handed down from generation to generation, and constitute the great *corpus* of common law which is the unique contribution of English civilization. Likewise the decisions rendered by the improvised Jewish courts should form the basis of Jewish common law in the future. The universal principles of reason and the desire to be just to both litigants would, undoubtedly, tend to give uniformity to the decisions of the various courts. In addition there should be appointed from time to time a group of competent people to pass upon and revise, if need be, the precedents set up by the decisions of those courts. In that way there would in time be evolved a *corpus* of Jewish law which would answer the needs of modern life.

The feasibility of fostering in America this element of Jewish civilization will undoubtedly be questioned. There seems to be nothing in American-Jewish life which might indicate the possibility of having the Jew resort to a Jewish court for the settlement of disputes which arise out of financial claims. Jews at present do not even expect their community to serve them in that capacity. The truth, however, is that among Jews whose consciousness is sufficiently alive to seek a communal outlet, the need is felt for adjudication under Jewish auspices of disputes between Jews. This need has actually given rise to a movement for the establishment of Jewish conciliation courts. To quote from the statement of one of these courts:

The Jewish Conciliation Court of America is more than an arbitration society. It is a Jewish communal institution. Its aim is to carry out the Jewish ideal of justice simply and directly without the incumbrances of complicated procedure. . . . It is performing a service to the city and state because in trying these cases it is relieving the congested calendar of the courts. Judges in civil courts often refer to the Jewish Conciliation Court of America cases which are of such a nature that they can best be tried before a Jewish court.

This court has been incorporated by the State of New York, is sponsored by a group of responsible men and women, and is making an effort to spread its policy and purpose to Jewish communities throughout the land.

C

ECONOMIC JUSTICE

The future of Judaism, even more than that of the other historical civilizations, depends upon its having the courage to commit itself to the cause of social idealism. The various religious traditions have by this time managed to come to terms with the challenge of the modern scientific and philosophic approach to reality. But a new and more serious challenge is either implied or expressed in the movements for the reconstruction of the economic order. Traditional religion, by its emphasis upon the ephemeral and relative worthlessness of the material aspect of human life, has at least indirectly condoned the evils of the present economic order. So imperious nowadays is the demand for economic justice that, if Judaism were to find itself without a message, and unable to canalize the trend of social and economic changes into a more equitable distribution of wealth, it would veritably admit its moral impotence.

Jews have become so implicated economically in the fortunes and misfortunes of the non-Jewish environment that the truth of Judah Ha-Levi's designation of Israel as the heart of mankind has been all too tragically demonstrated of late. As the heart responds to the least disturbance of the equilibrium of the body, so is Israel sensitive to the least that goes wrong in the life of the nations. Both collectively and individually, the Jews have been among the worst sufferers in the calamities that have befallen humanity since the World War. To no people has the world-depression which mankind has brought upon itself through its sins of avarice, exploitation and cruelty been so disastrous as to the Jews. *This should be sufficient reason for the Jews to realize that the only kind of a world which can be safe for them is one built on economic justice.*

The ethical contribution which Jews can make to the economic aspect of human life is to counteract the tendency to treat economic activity as though it were independent of considerations of right and wrong. Modern economics, whether of the individualist or the socialist type, is largely responsible for the dehumanization of economic problems. In former days men interpreted earthquakes and tidal waves as afflictions sent by God for the sins they had committed. The knowledge since acquired of the working of natural law has negated any connection between human sin and the tremors of the earth. But unfortunately this tendency to deny any relationship between human misery and human sin has been carried over to the domain of men's dealings with one another where the relationship is inextricable. Nineteenth-century economists of the individualistic school of thought, wishing to pose as masters of an exact science, sought to treat the process of exchange of goods and services as though it were fatalistically determined by external laws of nature, as are the forces of gravitation, heat and light. This conception of the economic activities, which constitute the major part of human conduct, has been humbly accepted as gospel truth by the teachers of morality and religion, and therefore as not within their sphere of judgment or guidance. Thus the producing, distributing and consuming of things have come to be regarded as inevitably subject to the law of the jungle. Accordingly, if there is to be such a thing as a law of the spirit, it has to be realized in those interstices of our life in this world which are not preempted by the economic struggle, or in some form of spiritual existence not bound up with the needs of the body. It is no wonder, therefore, that modern capitalism has been aptly described as being absolutely irreligious.

Most of the remedies which are being proposed at the present time by the various economic doctors are based upon this fallacious dualism between the problems of capital, labor, profit, interest and rent, on the one hand, and those of human welfare, justice and peace, on the other. They keep on evading the necessity of facing the absolute interdependence of the two sets of forces in that dualism. There has never been such vindication as there is today of the impassioned warnings sounded by the great Prophets of Israel, that any social order which is based upon exploitation of the weak, the helpless and the simple, by the strong, the resourceful and the cunning, is bound to be wrecked. The present economic order harbors within itself the seeds of its own decay. Based as it is upon the intense appeal to the money-making and money-loving propensities of the individual, it has to depend more and more upon the piling up of what is known as constant capital. As the nature of the constant capital is gradually improved through inventions, there is less need for human labor. This leads to over-population of wage-earners, which in turn results in decrease of wages and unemployment. The next inevitable link is the decrease in purchasing power, with its concomitants of under-consumption and over-production. Thus we may expect a series of ever-recurrent crises, each more violent than the preceding, with nothing but cataclysm as the direful end.

All who take the ethical view of life seriously must vigorously oppose the popular notion that business is essentially a struggle for advantage, in which considerations of right and wrong can play at best only a secondary rôle. They should even have the courage to question the economists' assumption that the law of supply and demand, with its corollary, the profit motive, is beyond human control. The professional economists still operate with the mid-Victorian doctrine, "Let each inform his mind, behave reasonably and look after his own interests; a society of such persons, each successfully minding his own business, will be a successful society." Current events have proved those Sages mistaken who said that to take the attitude of "Mine is mine and thine is thine" is to take a middle course, and have vindicated the opinion of those who maintained that such an attitude is worthy of the inhabitants of Sodom.

Those who are interested in the improvement of human life must learn to emancipate themselves from the domination of economic stereotypes which have been used to bolster up the profit system. One of these is the so-called law of supply and demand, which merely makes a law of lawlessness. In itself it is as likely to make for order and security as allowing the desire of each car driver to get to his destination as quickly as possible to govern present-day traffic. So long as the lawlessness and anarchy of supply and demand will be permitted to govern the production of goods and the employment of workers, it is futile to keep on urging what is termed "a just wage" in the exchange of services, and "a fair price" in the exchange of goods. Even a child ought to be able to understand that with the infinite complexity of factors which enter into the making of any product, or the buying and selling of any article, there is no possible way of determining what is fair or just from the standpoint of exchange based on *quid pro quo*. It may be that the whole price and wage system has become morally untenable and should be scrapped. What is true of price and wage is equally true of interest on capital, or rent on land. Surely there must be some justice to the contention of Henry George that rent on land is inherently indefensible from an ethical standpoint. A civilization which calls itself moral or ethical should delve beneath the surface of the commonly accepted standards and habits of our social order. It should ascertain whether the profit motive which is the fundamental source of most of the corruption and misery, and against which all teaching and preaching have spent themselves in vain, is the indispensable stimulus to human effort and productivity that it is trumped up to be. Such an assumption virtually implies that humanity is doomed to lead forever a life of violence, and that all the dreams and hopes of the great visionaries of mankind are a mirage. Such nihilism would confirm the description of man's world given by a modern economist who said that "in a universe of transmigrating souls, our particular planet must have been assigned to be the lunatic asylum of the universe."

No less unmoral than the thesis of the individualist economists is that of the socialist economists. Karl Marx, who was the implacable enemy of religion and philosophy, regarded all moral judgments and religious doctrines as the result rather than the cause of economic conditions. For him they were changing concepts, determined entirely by the economy at any particular time. Indeed, he said, all social values are the products of economic forces and the reflection of the economic system. Every "ought" is the outgrowth of an "is." This is known as the theory of "economic determinism," based, as Marx believed, upon true "science," and it is intended to demonstrate that far from being the source of sanctions and guidance, ethics and religion are no more than the passive by-product of social forces which can be controlled only through the scientific study of their operation.

Are the means of making a livelihood the only conscious movers in one's conduct? Nothing could be further from the truth. The case of the Jews and of all religious groups that sacrifice opportunities of making a livelihood out of loyalty to their historic tradition, are cases in direct refutation of this contention. The fallacy of economic determinism is that it confuses effective cause with indispensable condition. A foundation is indispensable to a house, and may even be responsible for certain features of the house; but it by no means explains the entire house. The exaggerated claims that Marx made for the economic factor may be explained by the tendency that has always prevailed to overestimate the significance of a discovery. Marx's outstanding discovery was the determining influence that economic factors have on human life. To Marx we are indeed indebted for his discovery that economic relationships play a great part in determining not alone the nature of the economic practices and institutions but of all social and creative activities. Nevertheless, the careful analyst of history cannot conscientiously accept Marx whole.

Marx's "scientific" study of economic history revealed to him that all human history shows an uninterrupted process of evolution, propelled inexorably by nature. This had been Hegel's conception of history, expressed in the doctrine of "historical necessity and continuity." The evolutionary process gradually and irresistibly unfolded the realization of a pre-existing idea. What has been, according to Marx, this single strain of history? It has been the struggle for supremacy between the economic masters and the mastered. At one time it was a struggle between master and slave, then between patrician and plebeian, later between feudal lord and serf, between squire and bourgeois, now between capitalist and wage-earner. The struggle has always been of the same character and for the same ends, modified in each age only by the means of production. The inevitable climax will come when the proletariat gain control over the world.

To interpret the entire history of civilization in terms of class struggle is to see nothing in the history of music, sculpture, religion, philosophy, education but evidences of the contest between exploiter and exploited. This is arrant dogma. What is perhaps true is that the struggle between exploiter and exploited that has always marked the life of peoples, accounts for most of the political history and for many of the laws and mores of mankind. It is true that those who possessed a greater degree of power and cunning than their fellows always took advantage of every opportunity to seize political authority and tried to translate their interests into laws and mores and religion. But to imply that the creative activity in religion and in the arts and sciences reflects merely class antagonism is to fail to realize that man does not live by bread alone.

But if class solidarity did exist and exert influence, it is also true that national, religious and a thousand and one other solidarities existed and functioned at the same time. Why did Marx insist upon the proletariat being made class conscious, since the dialectic of economic development would of itself bring about their ultimate victory? Is this not an admission that the psychological factors, the factors of mind and purpose are indispensable, if the class struggle is to result in a more equitable social order? *Exploitation and class struggle are entirely different phenomena.* The laws of Manu were laws for exploitation; but the history of Hindustan is far from being a history of class struggle. The weaker were not weak numerically; they were weak because they lacked knowledge, leadership, idealism and organization. What becomes then of economic determinism as the inexorable and all-embracing law of human history?

These inconsistencies in the Marxian "scientific" description of human history may be psychologically understood. All interpretations of history which claim to discover a continuity in the historical process are logical constructs to justify *anticipation of the future.* It is the expression of a wish rather than a reading of objective fact. This does not minimize interpretations of history. It only puts them where they belong—in the domain of values and not of science. "Every theory of social action is ultimately a philosophy of history. It attempts as best it may to read in the experience of mankind the lessons which would justify its own special urgency; it claims to be the objective toward which human development is tending."

The Jewish religion was, indeed, the first to enter the arena of world-affairs with an interpretation of history. That interpretation has no less claim to objective truth than the one given by Karl Marx. It is based on a dialectic which derives from the conception of God as the power that makes for righteousness. Jewish religion absolutely refuses to make peace with the *status quo* which it considers as godless because, despite the outward form of law and respectability, it is based upon the rule of might and not of right. That is the rule of violence, the original sin symbolized in the act of disobedience, on account of which human life is forever condemned to frustration. But God cannot permit this condition to exist forever. Human wickedness is allowed to overreach itself in order to bring on its own destruction. This is the history of the rise and fall of nations, which will terminate in the ultimate establishment of the Kingdom of God.

Translated into modern parlance this means that *Jewish religion sees in human history the same inevitability which the Marxists discern. But it is the inevitability of a process which makes for righteousness.* Ultimately, the forces for good that inhere in the world and in human nature will give rise to a just social order, one in which every human being will be able to achieve the full measure of self-realization and accord to his neighbor the same right and opportunity. The evolution of mankind, though marked by frequent and disheartening reactions, moves irresistibly in the direction of universal security and freedom. From the standpoint of the Jewish religion, ethical purpose does not emerge merely as an incident of social history, but is a directive and creative force. The social changes that occur as a result of mechanical inventions may be viewed as part of the divine plan. Achieved through the use of intelligence, the divine spirit at work in man, the machine precipitates the conditions that will create abundance, and thereby will remove forever the fear of scarcity and insecurity, which is the main cause of all social conflict. The machine is thus the instrument of the divine will. Through it God's attribute as provider will be completely fulfilled. If in the meantime it has given the exploiters added power to enslave the masses, it is only that they might overreach themselves as did all the arrogant rulers of mankind who set themselves up as gods, and thus brought about their own downfall.

Whether the security and abundance for all made physically possible by the creative intelligence and cooperative will of man is to come in our day or in some distant future is for us to decide. "All things are foreseen, yet freedom of choice is given," said Rabbi

Akiba.[10] This means that the ethical choice of man operates within the framework of a morally determined world. And it is in these areas of voluntary action that religion as a social force must fire the zeal of men and bring them to work ardently for the new day.

The Jewish interpretation of history, therefore, regards the contest between the exploiter and exploited not as a blind and purposeless one, nor does it regard the many changes in the social structure of mankind as meaningless and vain. It sees in them the striving for human equality progressively intensified and brought nearer than ever to realization by the industrial revolution. But whether this realization will be near or far, the inexorable law of God will prevail.

The only way in which any culture or civilization can come to possess significance and relevance in our day is by bravely grappling with all these problems. If Jews are in search of a mission, do they need one more urgent and imperative than the promulgation of economic justice? The behest of Jeremiah to the Jews who had been exiled to Babylon takes on an entirely new meaning in our day. When he urged them to seek the welfare of the city in which they dwelt because their welfare depended upon that of the city, he did not mean, as some interpret his words, that they should be demonstrative in their loyalty to the political régime. What he urged upon them was a participation in the furtherance of all those forces which made for the welfare of the general community. Translating Jeremiah's teaching into the duty for our day, it should be regarded by Jews as a plea to participate in all the forces and movements which make for the reconstruction and betterment of the social order to which they belong.

CHAPTER XXXI

THE MEANING OF JEWISH EDUCATION IN AMERICA

The need for a new philosophy of Jewish education in America—The aims of Jewish education from the standpoint of the community—The aims of Jewish education from the standpoint of the child—The Jewish educative process—1. Integration of the child into Jewish life—2. The teaching of Hebrew—3. The training of character—4. The transmission of Jewish values—5. The stimulation of esthetic creativity.

THE radical change in the life of the Jew could not but be reflected in an equally radical change in the historic functions of Jewish education. Formerly, when parents gave their child a Jewish training, they provided him with the means of making his way in this life and in the hereafter. The Jewish training was all that the child had to save him from absolute illiteracy. When he grew up, it helped him in the conduct of his daily affairs and qualified him for membership in the social group without which he would have had no status as a human being. It transmitted to him what he needed for the attainment of life eternal. That in turn gave worth to his life in this world. To this inner motivation for giving the child a Jewish training, there was added the outer pressure of the Jewish community which had long anticipated the modern principle of compulsory education.

If Jewish education is to be established in this country on a permanent basis, it must serve uses which are the equivalent of those it served in the past. In addition, there will have to be developed that communal support and social pressure without which no system of education can function. The Jewish child nowadays acquires through his general education enough literacy to get along in the world. The only *raison d'être* for Jewish education is the assumption that without it the Jew cannot possibly know what to make of his status as a Jew. To be illiterate as a Jew is to be the victim of unresolved conflicts, to be a source of irritation to oneself and to society. But this is only half the story. Some use for Jewish education must also be found that might correspond to the good it was formerly regarded as yielding in terms of other-worldly salvation. The modern equivalent for that good is self-fulfillment in the most socialized and spiritual sense. To be trained as a Jew should mean to be given habits that would help one function creatively in all of life's situations. Not unless Jewish education can at least approximate such results will the Jewish community assume responsibility for fostering it.

Those who subscribe to the Neo-Orthodox version of Judaism have no difficulty in supplying a rationale for Jewish educational effort. Neo-Orthodoxy takes for granted that a knowledge of Torah and of the traditional beliefs concerning God, the place of Israel in the world and the function of the human being, is a sufficient incentive to the good life. It assumes that the Jew who has been imbued with such knowledge will honor his parents, lead a life of chastity, provide for the material and spiritual needs of his children, speak the truth and be honest in all his dealings. As employer he will give his employees a fair wage; as employee he will be conscientious in the performance of his tasks. He will make a faithful husband, a true friend, a loyal citizen; he will be considerate in his treatment of strangers and generous to those who are in want. All these virtues will be crowned by fervent piety and trust in God. The study of Torah in its traditional sense has the power to call forth all these qualities of character and conduct.

Furthermore Neo-Orthodoxy furnishes the Jewish educator with a very simple rationale for wanting to supplement whatever character training the child receives from his non-Jewish environment with instruction in Judaism. That rationale is based upon the assumption that the humanistic approach which the public schools must of necessity adopt in their efforts to train the character of the child is inadequate, because it lacks the sanction and authority necessary to render the training effective. Man needs the authority which is validated by supernatural revelation to enable him to play his part worthily as child, as parent, as employer, as employee and as friend. Judaism possesses the requisite supernatural element to make it unsurpassed as an educative force in this sense.

There are other educational implications of a secondary character in the Neo-Orthodox view of Judaism. Such a conception of Judaism would advocate authoritative methods of education. Only in the first year or two, while the child is little more than an infant, is any indulgence to be shown to the weakness and playfulness of the child. But before long the child must be inured to strict discipline, for a rigorous training is essential to a mastery of the traditional text. Verbal memory is held in high esteem by the orthodox, who find intrinsic value in the mastery of words which originate from God, or from divinely inspired masters. Consequently a system of education based on orthodoxy is one that calls for a curriculum in which the emphasis is placed on formal studies, because of the great amount of time involved in acquiring the knowledge of the text.

An altogether different type of Jewish education would stem from the Reformist conception of Judaism as a religious philosophy based upon the history and literature of the Jewish past. Translated into educational terms, Judaism must supply the moral and spiritual elements in the civilization and socialization of the child. In order to be fully adjusted to the environment, the child requires a manifold culture, including the scientific, literary, esthetic and religious. Religion, like music, is simply one of the elements of culture. Just as the child goes to the music school to cultivate his musical faculty, so is he expected to go to the religious school to develop his religious sense or faculty. This conception of the function of the religious school is based on an antiquated notion of religion as something apart from any specific civilization.[1] It has been found unworkable in the Protestant system of religious education, despite the tremendous backing which it receives in a predominantly Protestant country like the United States. And it has produced very meager and unsatisfactory results in Jewish life.[2]

The unprecedented character of the social, the political and the intellectual factors of the environment to which Judaism must adjust itself calls not only for a new type of framework for the social life of the adult Jew, but also for a new type of Jewish upbringing and Jewish schooling for the child. Peoples rich in possessions and enjoying great political prestige are recasting their educational systems and planning new schools to take the place of the old. The Jewish people, which is passing through a crisis that may either spell death, or lead to a new lease of life, cannot afford to deal in haphazard fashion with the problem of education. The Jews must not only transmit their social heritage; they must also reconstruct it in the very process of transmission.

Moreover, the exigencies of life compel the Jews to give primary consideration in the upbringing of their children to the so-called secular training which those children receive in the public schools. The danger is not so much that the formal Jewish training will occupy a secondary place in the education of the child. Jews must be prepared for such an eventuality in countries like America, where political institutions are based upon cultural homogeneity. The danger is that the Jewish training might be altogether crowded out of the life of the Jewish child. The only way to prevent that danger is to make the Jewish training so effective in enlarging the mental scope of the child's life, in socializing his attitude toward his fellow-men, in inculcating in him an appreciation of life's worth and sanctity, that parents will rejoice to have such training imparted to their children. By rethinking the problem of Jewish education from the very beginning, we may arrive at a knowledge of what is necessary to render the Jewish training effective in that way.

The questions which will be dealt with in this chapter are: what is the aim of Jewish education from the standpoint of Judaism as a modern spiritual civilization, and what is the nature of the educative process by which that aim is to be achieved? *

Bearing in mind the elements into which it has been found convenient to analyze the Jewish civilization, the aim of Jewish education may be defined thus: to develop in the rising generation a desire and a capacity, (1) to participate in Jewish life, (2) to understand and appreciate the Hebrew language and literature, (3) to put into practice Jewish patterns of conduct both ethical and religious, (4) to appreciate and adopt Jewish sanctions and aspirations, and (5) to stimulate artistic creativity in the expression of Jewish values. It is almost superfluous to add that all of these objectives presuppose a type of Jewish life which is completely integrated into a progressive and dynamic American life. In view of the high ethical and spiritual implications of the Jewish civilization, an American-Jewish child who has the advantage of a Jewish training of the proper kind has his sympathies broadened, his tastes refined, and his striving socialized.

1. Primary is the objective of developing in the rising generation a desire and capacity to participate in Jewish life. Jewish life is represented in America mainly by institutions and organizations through which Jews function collectively, locally, nationally and internationally. The network of organizations—congregations, federations, Zionist groups, fraternal orders, young people's leagues, cultural clubs—is the concrete reality of the Jewish people, in which the young person must be accustomed to move and have his Jewish being. This must result from the Jewish education which the child, or the youth, receives. Toward that end all the other objectives must be directed. Their function is to qualify the child or youth to play his part, and cooperate with his fellow-Jews so that Jewish life, as represented by its network of institutions and organizations, will produce a wholesome, integrated and creative personality.

2. Hebrew can no more be omitted from the child's training as a Jew than English from his training as an American. If the child is to identify himself with the Jewish people, it is absolutely essential that he experience its reality as a living and functioning people. In an environment that is predominantly non-Jewish, the Jewish people is likely to appear to him remote and irrelevant. For the child to overcome the sense of remoteness and irrelevancy, he must learn the Hebrew language as a living vernacular. This will help to establish in his mind direct and immediate mental contact with the pulsating life and thought of the Jewish people. Hebrew is the thread that binds together all periods of Jewish history and all the Jewries of the diaspora. It is the only possible common denominator of Jewish cultural life throughout the world. To really know Israel's past, to gain an insight into the modern renascence of the Jewish people, to take part in this rebirth, to be fully sensitive to all that has happened, and to all that is happening in Jewish life, it is necessary to feel at home in the Hebrew language. In the degree that Jews approximate this sort of "at homeness" are they able to live intelligently and creatively as Jews.

3. The Jewish child, like every other child, depends for his development and happiness upon his ability to do two things: to use tools efficiently, and to function effectively in the various relationships which will constitute his life as a social being. Success in the former will give him a livelihood. Success in the latter will endow him with

character and personality. From the public schools and the non-Jewish social environment, the Jewish child acquires his ability in the effective use of tools, and a good deal of his ability to function normally as a social being. We must realize that if the American school, in addition to its formal content, were to give the child a complete social and spiritual training, if it were to aim at the training of character and the development of a religiously affirmative attitude toward life, it would need no supplementation. The American school, however, does not undertake to give the child such a training. It calls upon other agencies, primarily the home and the religious organizations, to complete the socialization of the child. The purpose of Jewish education in America should be to qualify the child to meet with an ethical and affirmative attitude all of life's situations and relationships—economic, sexual, civic, human and cosmic. Each of these relationships implies a certain set of ideals and habits, certain satisfactions and discontents, certain elements of permanence and of change. It should be the aim of Jewish culture to enable the human being to live in all of these relationships so as to elicit the best in himself and in those about him.

4. The heart of the problem of Jewish education and of Jewish life in the diaspora is the ability to motivate the conduct of the young by sanctions and aspirations which, while they are in direct descent from those which motivated Jewish life in the past, are at the same time in line with the most advanced ethical and spiritual strivings of man throughout the ages. The attainment of this objective involves the reinterpretation of the values which form part of the Jewish heritage. If the contents of the Jewish civilization were on the whole capable of transmission in the form in which they have come down from the past, the problem of Jewish education would be a comparatively simple one. The fact that Judaism must undergo a radical metamorphosis in order to survive complicates the task of the Jewish teacher, whose main function it is to furnish the inspiration for living a Jewish life. Due to the nature of the cultural environment, the content of Judaism must be transformed from a system of life based upon a theurgic and heteronomous conception of religion, of the Jewish people and of the moral law, to one based on a rational and experiential approach to all problems of morality and religion.

The specific task of Jewish education consists in freeing the cultural content from its adventitious or antiquated elements, and from the domination of outward authority, so that it can cultivate the individual conscience and be effective without the aid of outward authority and the sanctions of reward and punishment. As we now understand sanctions and aspirations, their operation in the life of a person is much like that of esthetic taste and creativity. If we did not believe that the capacity for responding to such sanctions and aspirations existed, education for the social and the higher life would be totally futile.

The history of all religions and of all ethical and philosophical systems is the history of man's striving to articulate the high worth of the individual human being, of the social group and of the world as a whole, and to render that worth manifest in conduct. These objectives would necessarily have to figure more prominently in a modernized Judaism. The Jew would undoubtedly come to feel the imperative character of these objectives through an adequate knowledge and appreciation of his people's heritage. If Jewish education is to furnish that knowledge and appreciation, it must so present the Jewish past to the child that he will feel its power to render his life as a Jew significant. This involves as a prerequisite to the proper teaching of Jewish traditions and ideals, a realistic, organic and psychological reconstruction of Jewish history, a history free from supernaturalism, a history every stage of which is understood in the light of all the preceding stages, a history in which as much importance is attached to the subtler forces of will and mind as to the more evident ones which operate in economic factors and political events.

5. Creativity is the result of whole-souled and organic reaction to life's values; of a reaction in which senses, emotions, imagination, intelligence and will are fully aroused. It is not enough for a civilization to be rich in values of a religious or esthetic nature. Unless its people respond wholeheartedly to those values, the civilization is artistically sterile. The validity of the present reconstruction of Judaism will be made evident, if the Jew will be able to live Jewishly, and satisfy every nerve and fibre of his being. Once Jewish life is capable of meeting the emotional, intellectual and social demands of human living, it will evoke the functional creativity of

the artist, and the secondary creativity of an audience conscious of art.

But the element of artistic creativity cannot be left completely to spontaneous achievement. It is a plant that must be carefully and tenderly nurtured. Far from being recognized as an indispensable element of Jewish education and living, a few schools grant it the tolerance extended to an extra-curricular fad. The very significance of Judaism as a civilization would be lost, if artistic creativity in the expression of Jewish values were treated as something secondary in the program of American-Jewish life. To give to this objective the place that it deserves in a program of Jewish education, it is necessary to extend the field of artistic creativity. Not only religious but other human values, not only those derived from the past of the Jewish people but those drawn from contemporary Jewish life, must find expression in art forms. Furthermore, the gamut of artistic expression must be widened to include poetry and song, music, drama, dance, painting, sculpture and architecture. *When Judaism has acquired the potency of multiple appeal, not even extreme diversity of belief will threaten its integrity.*

No whit less important than reckoning with the perpetuation of Jewish life and culture is it to reckon with the well-being and growth of the individual child. The Jewish educative process must start with the actual experiences of the child as he lives them in the present, and lead him constantly so to reorganize and reinterpret his experiences that he comes to identify his own good with the good of society in general, and do so in a manner that will indicate growth in mind and character. To achieve this end the child must be given increasing control over his own experience so that he will himself be able to shape and direct it toward aims freely and intelligently chosen. Restated from the standpoint of the child, the following should be the objectives of Jewish education: ‘

a. *To give insight* into the meaning of spiritual values and their application to different types of experience, religious, moral, social and political; Jewish life as a developing civilization; the spiritual character of that civilization; the relationships of Jewish to other civilizations in the past; the course that Jewish life must henceforth take in the different countries of the world, and especially in America.

b. *To foster an attitude* of respect toward human personality as such; tolerance toward other groups, races, faiths; intellectual honesty, open-mindedness and responsibility; social and international-mindedness; loyalty to and participation in Jewish life in this and other countries.

c. *To train appreciation* of individual and group creativity in the values of civilization; Jewish creativity in religion, ethics, language and literature, mores, laws and folkways, and the arts.

d. *To inculcate ideals* of justice and kindness in our social and economic relationships; peace and tolerance; a just, thriving, creative Jewish homeland in Palestine, a creative Jewish life in America.

e. *To condition habits* of reflective thinking; purposive experiencing; using leisure to develop personality; affiliation with the synagogue or *bet am;* celebrating Jewish Sabbaths, festivals, etc.; observing Jewish customs and ceremonies; reading Hebrew books and periodicals, Anglo-Jewish books, Anglo-Jewish press, Yiddish press, Bible, Talmud, etc.; contributing to the upbuilding of Palestine; helping to support social-service and educational institutions; attending Hebrew and Anglo-Jewish theaters, concerts, etc.; patronizing Jewish artistic endeavors; buying Jewish books, works of art, etc.

f. *To impart knowledge* of the Hebrew language; Jewish history; the outstanding selections from the Bible, the Talmud, and subsequent Jewish writings; history and meaning of Jewish customs and ceremonials, religious beliefs, ethical ideals; current Jewish problems, institutions, endeavors; Jewish arts and crafts, home-furnishing, cooking, etc.

The foregoing enumeration of objectives to be pursued in giving children a Jewish training may sound utopian. If the modest aims of the Reformist educators have had such disappointing results, how can these more ambitious objectives ever be realized? The answer is that the Reformist conception has failed not because of the modesty, but because of the abstractness, or irrelevance of its aim, which led to the narrow and limited conception of the entire Jewish educative process as a function which could be discharged by the congregational school, meeting on the average from one-and-a-half to two hours a week. There has been a tendency recently on the part of some congregations to increase the number of sessions to more than one a week. No doubt every increase will result in a more intensive knowledge of things Jewish, but that alone will not solve the problem.

It is necessary to change radically the very notion of what is to constitute the educative process through which the objectives of an effective and attractive type of Jewish education will be attained. If Jews will rely solely upon the Jewish school to achieve those aims, they are bound to fail. In the process of education, as in the other phases of social and spiritual activity, Jews cannot permit themselves the luxury of having practice lag behind theory. In all modern theories of education, it is reiterated again and again that we respond much more readily to activity than to ideas. The mind is normally motor-active rather than contemplative. Another truth which is continually emphasized is that education is not a process distinct from life in general, nor is it to be confined to the four walls of the schoolhouse. Education is the process of continuous growth, the result of present experience which modifies and reconstructs all previous experience. Every element in a person's environment is potentially educative, if the person, either through direction or initiative, focusses his attention upon the proper phase of that environment and reacts in a manner that makes for growth of knowledge and character.

If these educational commonplaces were acted upon, every civilization would realize that the school is only one link in a chain of educational agencies, and it would seek to bring agriculture, industry, business, government and amusement into its scheme of education. Every one of these activities would have a special department which would look after the educative and socializing effects upon those that carry on the activity, and would include ways and means of placing the educative and socializing aspects of that activity at the disposal of the growing youth. In the light of the harsh realities of modern life, however, such a plan must indeed sound utopian. With all activities of the various civilizations animated by a spirit of competition, to make them part of a comprehensive educative process would be an expensive luxury.

Strange as it may seem, what appears so visionary in other

civilizations is not beyond the reach of Jewish civilization, especially in America. From the educational point of view, the very fact that the latter has to be lived as an ancillary civilization is its redeeming feature, for its activities are inherently non-competitive, and the survival of Jewish civilization in America depends upon having all the activities that constitute Jewish life contribute to the educative process.

Jews must abandon the notion that the Jewish school, or the class for adults, is the primary conveyor of Jewish education. The mistake of limiting education to formal instruction is the primary cause of the complete failure and breakdown of Jewish educational endeavor. Were the school to be regarded as the only means of transmitting Judaism to the rising generation, Jews would have to follow the example of the Catholics, and establish a parochial system of Jewish education. Yet if the public school system, despite the unlimited financial resources, falls far short of some of its primary purposes, what could the Jews hope to accomplish with their limited resources, were they to be responsible for the entire education of the child? And even if such segregation of Jewish children were feasible, it is scarcely desirable. A Jewish parochial school system would be but a futile gesture of protest against the necessity of giving to Jewish civilization a position ancillary to the civilization of the majority. Jewish education must accordingly be supplementary to the general education which Jewish children receive in the American school. This limits their attendance in a Jewish school to but a few hours a week. Even with highly trained teachers and ideal facilities, there is no possibility of attaining any of the objectives of Jewish education, if Jewish education is to be limited to the training given the child in the religious or Hebrew school.

The solution lies in altering completely the conception of the Jewish educative process, and in learning to regard formal classroom instruction as only one link in a chain of agencies which must be instrumental in transmitting the Jewish heritage to the young. All organizations and institutions which represent the body of Jewish life and manifest the Jewish collective will-to-live should make provision for training the young so that they will ultimately take over these activities. This implies that the American Jew must learn to view every form of Jewish collective effort not only as a means of accomplishing its immediate purpose, whether it be relief, social service, or the upbuilding of Palestine, but also as a means of training the Jew in general and the Jewish youth in particular, in a sense of communal responsibility. All Jewish organized effort must be made consciously and purposively educative, an instrument for perpetuating Judaism through participation in the Jewish training of the young.

A second group of agencies which should be included in the Jewish educative process consists of the public elementary schools, the high schools and the universities. This is possible because no culture can be complete without the principal cultural values of the Jewish civilization, especially those identified with the Bible.[5] The Bible could be taught in the public schools as literature. Both Jewish and non-Jewish fundamentalists would undoubtedly object to treating the Bible as literature on the ground that such an approach to the Bible might make inroads into traditional religion. Were such objections taken seriously, even the sciences would have to be taught outside the schools. But the fundamentalist, if he possess any degree of common sense, must realize that the *sine qua non* of belief in the Bible is respect for it. To place the Bible on a level with other cultural subjects will do more to win respect for the Bible than the most successful instruction conducted under denominational auspices. This solution does not preclude the supplementary and interpretive instruction by religious schools and Hebrew schools; the interpretation will be facilitated, if the children will acquire a general familiarity with the contents of the Bible.[6]

Taking each of the five objectives enumerated above from the standpoint of Jewish education as a means of perpetuating Jewish civilization, the Jewish educative process should be envisaged as follows:

1. *The integration of the child into Jewish life:* Assuming that the objective of fostering in the child a desire and a capacity to play an active rôle in Jewish communal life is of primary importance, we shall have to consider through what kind of effort that result is most likely to be achieved. A practical training in Jewish communal life should constitute the most important phase of the Jewish

educational process. *The principle to bear in mind is that, if an activity is to develop in the child an interest in Jewish life, it must make him feel that he is a necessary part of the Jewish community.*

Jewish educational endeavor which confines itself to formal schooling and the teaching of texts is foredoomed to failure. If it is to achieve desirable and permanent results, it must reach the child not only from the intellectual angle, but from many angles besides. Of these, the social or gregarious interests of the child are perhaps the most important. Hence the need for club work. But in order that the club may function as a means of integrating the child into Jewish life, it is absolutely essential that it be fostered as a training ground for participation in the life of the Jewish community. It must be remembered that the child does not acquire a sense of loyalty by hearing loyalty preached to him. The fundamental weakness of Jewish classroom instruction is that it merely talks about the need for being loyal. In the club, however, where children must work together for a common purpose, they acquire the habit of loyalty. Only through the activity that the club or organization provides will Jewish ideals exercise an ethical influence upon the life of the child.

From the standpoint of character training such children's and youth's clubs are indispensable, for the character is developed through its contacts with some social group, and through the interplay of forces within that group. The "club" form of organization, where the child is permitted to exert his initiative, meets this condition to a greater extent than many a home, or school, where things are done for the child. If both the purpose of the club and the means employed in fulfilling that purpose were drawn from Jewish life and ideas, the part played by Judaism in the growth of character would be evident. It is therefore necessary to take the ethical function of the club clearly into account. Making character development a conscious purpose of the club will lead to the realization that it is important for the club leader to possess not only the quality of Jewish loyalty, but also a high sense of moral integrity. Nowhere does the power of example go so far as it does in the case of the club leader who is liked by the youngsters, for he inevitably comes to represent to them the ideal type of manhood. Unless the leader be qualified to translate the implications of Jewish loyalty into personal conduct of a highly ethical character, that loyalty is apt to degenerate into Jewish jingoism.

The Young Judæa movement, which was at one time fostered by the Zionist Organization of America, may serve as a practical illustration of the purpose and value of having communal organizations devote part of their energy to educational endeavor. The children who belonged to the Young Judæa club did not get much book knowledge there, but they caught the meaning of Palestine as they never could have done from formal instruction. From among them developed not only leaders of Jewish life in the United States, but also in Palestine. Other communal organizations should establish children's circles and youth's clubs on similar lines. These should devote themselves to practical tasks that would lead to an interest in the purposes and activities of the parent organizations.

If congregations, for example, were to turn over the synagogues to the children a few times during the year, permitting them to conduct their own services on the last day of *Sukkot* and of *Pesah*, and on one or two Sabbaths in the middle of the year, it would be an easy matter for children's and young people's clubs to organize themselves around such a project. These same congregational clubs could not only be entrusted with the care of the synagogue buildings and environs, but also with the various activities connected with the congregation, such as helping to secure attendance, acting as ushers, getting their friends to attend the congregational school, building up a synagogue and school library, and numerous other practical details, which, when added to the project of children's services, theatricals or pageants, would not only interest young people in congregational life, but would exercise an educative influence.' Even years of attendance at the religious school, as it is now constituted, seldom habituates the child to synagogue attendance, or gives him the ability to follow the service with interest. There can hardly be any doubt that synagogue clubs and circles for children would accomplish those ends.

It should not be difficult for the local federation to enlist the young in some form of practical work adapted to their capacities and understanding. Likewise organizations doing relief and reconstruction work across the seas could utilize the energies of the young.

Instances are multiplying, says George A. Coe, in which community service of great value has been done by the young upon their own initiative (with the constant help of teachers, of course). Not only have children shown eager willingness to relieve immediate distress; they have penetrated to the causes of one or more common infectious diseases, and have mastered some of the methods of prevention; they have worked intelligently and devotedly at the problem of parks and playgrounds; they have cooperated with police departments and fire departments. And in and through the whole there are glints of creativeness. Genuine creativeness, not merely naïveté that happens now and then to make a happy hit.[9]

It is evident that, if every organization put out an independent claim for the interest of the Jewish youth, a distracting confusion of aims and ideals would arise. To obviate this difficulty, it would be necessary to have a central educational bureau, maintained by Jewish organizations, direct the Jewish civic activity of children and youth. With the aid of experienced leaders in Jewish communal work, this bureau would enlist all Jewish children within its jurisdiction in some form of activity connected with the organizations that constitute Jewish communal life. The experience of the scout movement might serve as a guide in the building up of Jewish youth organizations with a view to integrating the young into Jewish life.

"Is there any likelihood," it may be asked, "that any of the Jewish organizaions which carry on their prescribed work with difficulty will engage in Jewish educational endeavor either directly or through some central bureau?" Not only the possibility, but also the actuality is at hand. The Independent Order B'nai B'rith has adopted, in the Hillel Foundation and in the Aleph Zadik Aleph movement, a large-scale Jewish educational program, the purpose of which is to foster religious, cultural and social activities among Jewish youth. The principle underlying these activities is that they must be carried on and organized as far as possible by the young people themselves.[10] There is no reason why other organizations in Jewish life should not follow the example of the B'nai B'rith.

2. *The teaching of Hebrew:* To cultivate the desire to understand, and the capacity to appreciate, the Hebrew language and literature is an objective which seems the most difficult to achieve. Much of the indifference to Hebrew has been due to the tendency to identify it with orthodox religiosity. The rich cultural and esthetic

possibilities of Hebrew are not even dreamed of by the masses of the Jews. This apathy, however, need by no means be regarded as incurable. The proper approach to Judaism should result in the development of new wants. Many Jews of cultured taste will undoubtedly want to enrich their esthetic experience by a knowledge of Hebrew.

In the meantime the use of Hebrew should be introduced wherever, and whenever, feasible. The Jewish school should employ every possible device which would facilitate the study of the Hebrew language, and every possible project that would make a knowledge of it necessary. It is essential to establish Hebrew kindergartens wherever feasible in order to implant in the child the proper conception of Hebrew as a living language and an instrument of general culture, as well as to utilize the years when learning a language is easiest. Hebrew-speaking nurses and kindergarten instructors are as yet not sufficiently available, but with an increased demand, and with the growing opportunities in Palestine, and even in this country, to acquire the necessary training for either calling, that problem too would be solved.

The summer camps offer an excellent opportunity to conduct Jewish educational work amidst ideal surroundings. There the children are free from the distracting influences that dominate their lives during the greater part of the year. Whatever advantages may be expected from a parochial system—and no one can deny that, while as a mode of all-year education it has its drawbacks, it has for a limited number of children very desirable possibilities from the standpoint of Jewish life—can be secured to a very large degree in the summer camp. Two objectives of Jewish education which are so difficult to attain during the regular school term—the ability to read Hebrew and the acquisition of Jewish interests—can easily be attained by these camps, which are yearly becoming more and more a necessary part of the child's life.[11]

Another very powerful factor for raising the prestige of Hebrew, and creating an interest in its study, is the establishment of chairs in Jewish history and literature in universities attended by large numbers of Jewish students. The awareness that the university recognizes Jewish studies and accords them credits on the same plane with other branches of learning is almost as much of an education for most Jewish young people as acquiring a knowledge of those studies. But apart from this indirect influence on the attitude of Jewish young people, the direct influence of stimulating a desire to learn the Hebrew language and literature will reach many more than can ever avail themselves of the Jewish courses in the university.

The one agency, however, which has hitherto been neglected as a means of spreading the knowledge of Hebrew is the public high school.[12] Only recently has a serious attempt been made to have a few high schools, in New York City and one or two other cities, introduce the teaching of Hebrew into their curriculum. At first the Jews in the educational system opposed the suggestion. Thanks, however, to cooperation of non-Jewish educators, who could not help seeing the cultural value of the knowledge of Hebrew, recognition has finally been won for Hebrew in the high school. It is now entirely a question with the Jews themselves whether the young people will avail themselves of the opportunity offered them. It may be that the Jews are still too much governed by conventional prejudices, fears and inertia to take full advantage of the opportunity. But from the few attempts thus far made to extend the knowledge of Hebrew, it is evident that, if Jews really want the Hebrew language to become a vehicle of Jewish life, they could easily achieve that purpose.[13]

3. *The training of character:* The objective of cultivating a desire and capacity for modelling one's life in accordance with the Jewish patterns of ethical and religious behavior can scarcely be entrusted solely to the Jewish school in its present form, for the simple reason that the child attends it only a few hours a week, most of which time is spent in giving him mainly factual knowledge. As with the objective of integrating the child into Jewish communal life, so with the training of his character, the problem is to direct the activities of the child so that he may acquire Jewish habits of life. The home is undoubtedly the most important determining influence in the formation of character. Scarcely any phase of the problem of Judaism could be more urgent than that of getting the Jewish home to instill into the child Jewish ideals and religion. It is necessary to devise some way of reaching the home and enlisting

its cooperation with Jewish educational endeavor conceived as an all-comprehensive communal undertaking.

The need for arriving at some method of energizing the moral and spiritual possibilities of the home is but part of the general problem of character training. All the schools and religious organizations and books on ethics aim to foster social efficiency, moral health and capacity for cooperation. Yet when the individual tries to translate their inspiration and advice into specific habits, he is left without help or guidance. In this respect Judaism fares no worse than the generality of organized attempts to improve human character and conduct. But this is no consolation for Judaism, since it cannot afford to remain morally impotent. Its survival as a civilization is contingent upon its power to mold character and personality. It must therefore help its adherents translate ideals into concrete acts.

The magnitude of the task is, to be sure, nothing less than baffling. Yet a beginning should be made, and the home seems to be the logical place where the good life might be taught not as a theory but as an art. To that end it is necessary to assign to the teacher of the child a new place in the scheme of Jewish life. The notion that the labors of the teacher begin and end with the school where he meets his pupils and has to impart to them some information and to preach to them on how good it is to be good should be entirely scrapped. In the general educational system, the contact of the teacher with the parents is not missed because all of the teacher's time is spent with the child. But the teacher who is to train the child for Jewish life comes in contact with the child only a few hours a week at the most. The limited time which Jewish children can give to Jewish schooling narrows the vocational possibilities of the Jewish teacher and deprives him of all incentive to devote himself to the mastery of all the knowledge and skill that are required to develop in the child an attachment to a civilization, which is not essential to his worldly success when he grows up. The field of the Jewish teacher's activity and influence must be enlarged, or there will soon be no Jewish teachers.

If Jewish education is to prove its worth in this country, the scope of the Jewish teacher must be enlarged to include the home of the child he teaches.[14] In fact, most of the influence he wishes to exert upon the child he must learn to exert through the medium of the parent. The teacher should be the one to establish the point of contact between the moral and religious generalizations and the specific situations and occasions in which they should be embodied. He should be the pastor to the families of the children in whom he has to inculcate the patterns of Jewish conduct. He should act as adviser to the parents in their training of the child, and through the opportunity thus presented to him, advise, instruct and guide the parents to enable them to evoke from the child the best that is in him.[16] The man or woman who teaches the child has Jewish cultural and religious interests in common with the parent of the child, and is in a position to use those interests as an aid in shaping the life of the home in accordance with the ideals of Judaism.

It will undoubtedly be a long time before this conception of the function of the Jewish teacher will take root. In the meantime every possible effort should be made to draw the Jewish child into the ambit of other agencies in Jewish life. The Jewish communal groups and the camps can help a great deal toward inculcating many of the Jewish folkways and the habits of Jewish religious life. It is possible even now to reach the child through the parent. Mothers might be guided in the Jewish upbringing of their children by means of correspondence courses. These courses might offer specific guidance centering about the various festivals of the year. They should include stories, songs and recitations, all formulated in a stimulating and systematic fashion. In addition, those who take these correspondence courses might organize into clubs, for the purpose of exchanging experiences, and calling in an instructor to help them solve the specific problems they encounter in the upbringing of their children. Sooner or later such courses will be recognized as an indispensable means of helping Jewish parents who live in rural districts, where there are too few Jews to establish Jewish schools. With the devices available at the present time, there is no difficulty in supplying the most detailed and effective guidance to parents concerning what they should do for their children. The main problem is how to get Jewish parents to appreciate the need of habituating their children in Jewish patterns of moral and religious conduct.

4. *The transmission of Jewish values:* The task of developing

in the Jewish child a capacity to appreciate and adopt Jewish sanctions and aspirations will have to be achieved, like all other objectives, jointly by the home and the Jewish communal groups with which the child, it is assumed, will be affiliated. Some kind of explanations and informative discussions to furnish background and incentive can be counted on to form part of the activities of those agencies. But, as a rule, the child is not likely to acquire an organized and integrated idea of Jewish norms and ideals from what he hears in this informal fashion. It is the task of the Jewish school to bring order into the impressions and ideas out of which the Jewish consciousness of the child is built up. Activity and participation in actual life, though of primary importance in the educative process, must not be permitted to crowd out the element of ideation. If action is the body of Jewish life, thought is the soul. The tendency in certain quarters to treat Judaism as though it were independent of body, or of the concrete manifestations of life, makes it necessary to emphasize the need of active participation in communal life as an indispensable element of the educative process. But once this need is recognized and provided for, attention should be turned to the ideological aspect of Judaism.

When the sanctions and aspirations of any civilization which constitute its ideological aspect are made an objective of education, they furnish the subject matter for history and religion. Since, for reasons which have been expatiated upon, the teaching of neither subject can be conducted along the lines demanded by Neo-Orthodoxy, or recommended by Reformism, it is necessary to indicate how the conception of Judaism as a modern spiritual civilization would affect the teaching of these two subjects.

Jewish education is inconceivable without reference to God. Either God, or the Torah as the law of God, is the central theme of practically all Jewish writings before the nineteenth century, and religion is the central interest of all but the recent events of Jewish history. The problem of the proper subject matter of Jewish religion is negligible for the teacher who is Neo-Orthodox in his convictions, for from his standpoint that subject matter consists of the literature and history as they have come down from the past. In the Neo-Orthodox system of Jewish education, religion is based upon the belief in the historicity of specific theophanies and miracles. In pre-enlightenment days, probably one in a thousand experienced a conflict between traditional religion and the general world of ideas acquired outside Jewish education, and even that one did not become aware of such conflict before he was mature and well grounded in Jewish teaching and practice. Then, when reason warred with tradition, it was comparatively easy to placate the former. The method of allegorical explanation resolved all the knotty problems in tradition.

Nowadays the position is reversed. Very few are immune to the modern intellectual climate, with its rejection of all religion based on theophanies and miracles. At the age of seven and eight, children begin to question the veracity of stories about miracles. Jewish teachers who find the conclusions of science and anthropology inescapable have given up the traditional religious beliefs. Yet most parents who send their children to a Hebrew school expect the teachers to indoctrinate their children with the belief in the historicity of the theophanies and miracles. A great many Jewish teachers, who find themselves in the predicament of having to teach what they cannot conscientiously believe, arrive at a kind of solution which may be ingenious, but hardly moral. It may be described in the words which Emerson used with regard to the English when he said, "Their religion is a quotation." They salve their consciences by completely depersonalizing themselves, as it were, and acting as mere transmitters of Jewish tradition. It is the function of Jewish education, they maintain, to expose the child to the influences of traditional Judaism, and then let the child work out his own religious adjustment. "Were we not," they add, "instructed in the traditional conception of religion, and have we not had to work out our own spiritual adjustment?"

The reasoning upon which that compromise is based is a desperate rationalization. If those teachers have been able to adjust themselves intellectually as Jews, it is due to their having been imbued with an ineradicable Jewish consciousness by the firm religious convictions and intensive piety of those who had taught them. But no child listening nowadays to his teacher's half-hearted avowals of belief and ambiguous explanations will be strongly influenced to remain a Jew. The actual effect of a Jewish education as it is conducted at present is to leave the child in a state of mental confusion. Either he intuitively realizes that he is not being taught what the teacher actually believes, or he inwardly revolts at the demand upon his credulity. With no alternative to the religion of theophany and miracle, he grows up with a prejudice against all religion. The ablest Jewish children trained in the so-called religious schools generally regard themselves as in some way cheated by their Jewish schooling. There can be no worse indictment against any method or system of education. If Jewish education is so indicted, the blame rests with the policy of evasion that dominates the teaching of religion in Jewish schools.

The teaching of religion must henceforth be conducted on rational lines, and the details of pedagogic method must be so planned as to render that kind of teaching feasible. The Jewish teacher will have to achieve an affirmative orientation to religion in general, and to the Jewish religion in particular, and he will have to reconstruct the curriculum so that religion will be taught in accordance with the new orientation. The aim in educating the child should be to develop his capacity to discern high worth in the individual human being, in the social group and in the world as a whole. More difficult than achieving a new religious orientation will be its application to educational practice. The attempt to teach Jewish religion as a modern religious orientation will be opposed by the general public whose conservatism is strongest in matters of religion. The fear of that opposition, however, is no excuse for continuing the present policy of evasion which alienates the child from Jewish life and thought, and defeats the very ends of Jewish education.

The first step in solving the problem of teaching religion is so to revise the curriculum of the Jewish school that the child will realize fully the distinction between Jewish history, Jewish religious folklore and Jewish religion. The teaching of the narrative parts of the Bible [1] cannot be postponed, as some suggest, to the time when the pupil is mature enough to understand those stories in relation to their historic setting and place in religious development. The stories of the Bible are so much a part of world culture that everyone, to a greater or lesser degree, has some idea about them. But the very popularity of the stories, and the blurred notion of their substance, background and meaning, leads to the false assumption that they constitute the principal, if not the only source, of Judaism's teaching about God. The average person imagines that he repudiates religion and all its works when he rejects the historicity of the Bible stories. If children were taught to dissociate religious folk-tales from the verities of religion, the cause of religion would be far better served. The mere distinction in name between folklore and religion would accustom the child to identify as religion not certain traditions about God but a particular type of personal reaction to life. The Bible stories as folklore belong to the elementary stage of the child's training, but as a source of religious teaching they belong to the training which cannot be imparted before the child has reached adolescence. It will accordingly be necessary to develop in the Jewish school curriculum two different types of approach to the teaching of Bible stories.

That was, indeed, a revolutionary change in Jewish education when the study of Bible and Jewish history was differentiated from the study of rabbinics, which until modern times constituted for most Jews the sole content of Jewish knowledge. With the exception of the portion read in the synagogue on Sabbaths and festivals, and the book of Psalms, the Bible was seldom studied apart from the rabbinic texts in which it is interpreted. Thus through the study of the *Talmud* and the *midrashim*, the Jew obtained his knowledge both of the Bible and of Jewish history. That method of obtaining knowledge conformed to the best pedagogic ideal; namely, that of having the source of educational subject matter as nearly a unit as life itself. When it became apparent that the contents of the Bible had a literal meaning, the *peshat*, which, as we understand the term, was practically ignored in the rabbinic literature,[17] Jewish education had to make room for the teaching of the Bible as distinct from rabbinics. Likewise, when it became apparent that rabbinics gave a very limited and distorted view of Jewish history, scholars rewrote this history. Its study consequently attained a position of importance in the training of the Jewish child.

But the process of differentiation has stopped halfway. Even though the past of the Jewish people is no longer taught as a series of detached stories, it is far from being presented as a connected history of a people. It is still marred by the inclusion of folklore. And even though some of the most conspicuous ideas in the Bible can no longer be regarded as religious or ethical truth in its final form, all parts of the Bible are still indiscriminately taught as though they were meant to be immediately translated into belief and action. Most children remain mentally maladjusted to all religion for the rest of their lives as a result of the confusion created in their minds between fact and fiction, between outlived and permanent values. To forestall such confusion, it is necessary to continue further the process of subject differentiation until Jewish ideational content will be so set forth that the learner will be able to distinguish between the factual and the normative.

The teaching of religious folklore should be kept apart from the teaching of history. Even if they both deal with the same subject matter, the difference should make itself felt in the type of approach. All that comes under the head of folklore should be treated as poetry, and as the product of the imagination. In the course of his general education, the child is told stories to which he does not apply the measuring rod of actuality. In order to spare the Jewish child the struggle and readjustment, the narrative parts in which God figures as a participant, or as an interlocutor, should be presented as ancient religious folklore, and not as historic fact. If the stories of creation, the flood, the Patriarchs, Moses, the exodus, Israel in the wilderness, the conquest of Canaan as described in the book of Joshua and most of the stories about Elijah and Elisha, were told in this spirit, there would be once and for all an end to that mental conflict which has alienated Jewish youth from their religion. People are so accustomed to associate religion with dogmatic affirmation that they overlook the cardinal importance of intellectual honesty. They fail to realize the baneful influence upon character that the very conflict to which the confusion between fact and fiction in the matter of religious belief is bound to exert.

Instruction in history should not begin before the child is ripe enough to grasp the meaning of collective life and of evolution. It has been pointed out that the things one learns too soon one runs the risk of never knowing. The purpose governing the teaching of history should be to convey to the pupil a realization that the Jewish people started with a background of life and thought which they possessed in common with other branches of the human family, and that in time it developed a civilization with an individuality of its own. The adolescent grows disinterested in the career of the

Jewish people, if he is allowed to labor under the impression that the history of the Jews is not history in the ordinary sense of the term, because of the part played in it by the intervention of the supernatural. It never attains for him that reality which the history he studies at public school possesses. The result is that the Jewish people comes to figure in his mind as a vague abstraction, as a bodiless soul or ghostlike entity, that has never managed to make a place for itself in the world of live and effective nations.

Jewish history, therefore, must be presented as realistically as possible. This involves accepting in broad outline the reconstruction of the beginnings of Jewish history achieved by biblical scholarship, and connecting the events of Jewish history with those of the nations whose life touched that of Israel. Considerable use should be made of all such archeological details as help to render vivid the scene and atmosphere of ancient life in Palestine and the surrounding countries. It is only then that the pupil will appreciate those factors, forces and institutions in the life of the Jewish people which brought about its unique religious and ethical development. Only thus will he realize the significance of the process whereby the limited world-outlook of the nomad tribes of Israel grew into a conception of a single humanity governed by God, the creator of the world. Thus would Jewish history enlarge his mental and moral horizon, and create in him the desire to continue the career of his people.

But neither the history of the Jewish religion, nor Jewish religious folklore, constitutes religion. Those two subjects are necessary to clear the ground for the teaching of religion proper, which consists not in talking or thinking about what other people believed, felt or acted, but in personal reaction. The problem is how to elicit from the child the kind of reaction which makes for the growth of personality and the capacity for wholesome adjustment to life. Recalling that religion finds expression in the appreciation of life's intrinsic worth and sacredness, the task with the child is to foster in him those attitudes which will render such appreciation an integral part of his character and capable of withstanding the shocks of tragic experience.

The training in religion may be divided into two parts, instruction and practice. Where the purpose is to produce not merely verbal knowledge but a desirable mental attitude, textbooks are of little value, because such an attitude can be called forth only by establishing a point of contact with the actual knowledge and interests of the child. The point of contact to be utilized in teaching religion is the child's inherent capacity for thankfulness, which is to develop later into the power to discern the elements of life that give meaning to human striving for self-fulfillment. The instruction should consist mainly of discussion between teacher and pupil. The purpose of the discussion should be to articulate the feeling of thankfulness, to socialize it and to relate it to the conception of God.

These three purposes cannot be considered as disparate aims. They constitute the elements indispensable to the translation of the capacity for thankfulness into religious experience. To articulate the feeling of thankfulness is to have the child identify the specific facts in his experience he has reason to be grateful for, and to acquire a sense of indebtedness to all the personal and impersonal factors that contribute to his well-being and growth. But he should be made to realize that gratitude for advantages one enjoys always carries with it the responsibility for extending those advantages to those who are without them. *The worship of God, though desirable as an end in itself, can somehow never be in the right spirit, unless it impel one to the service of man.*

The child should be trained to experience thankfulness not only for the good which he himself enjoys, but also for that which falls to the lot of his family and playmates. It is important that the child cultivate an attitude of thankfulness for the good fortune of all with whom he learns to identify himself so that, as the ambit of his life grows, the spirit of thankfulness grow with it. In the hands of an able teacher, the child's capacity for thankfulness and for converting that thankfulness into creative energy will be reenforced by his studies and social contacts. The entire range of things true, good and beautiful will be appreciated by the child in a spirit that will impel him to augment them in accordance with his abilities.

As the occasions and factors in life that arouse the sense of gratitude are seen in terms of ever-widening relationships, they come to impinge more and more upon the conception of God. There can be no single explanation or definition that can once and for all answer the question: what is meant by God. The conception of

God is intrinsically such as to call for continual restatement in an infinite variety of ways. In each such restatement the teacher will have to counteract the child's tendency to anthropomorphize, and will have to accustom the child to sense reality in those tendencies in the world which deserve appreciation. Conceived as belonging to the one organically inter-related world, those tendencies will come to spell for him the reality of God. After the pupil has become habituated to such a presentation of religious ideas, the question of how religions in general, and the Jewish religion in particular, have approximated this conception of God, would naturally form an important part of instruction in religion.

It should be remembered that religion is as much a progressive unlearning of false ideas concerning God as it is the learning of the true ideas concerning God. The mind is full of distorted images, wrong conclusions, misleading notions. It works even when asleep. When we are awake we correct the vagaries of our dreaming minds. As regards the conception of God, the average human mind is half asleep even when awake. It is the function of the teacher of religion to translate intelligence into action, to clear the mind of all theological and psychological dreams, and to fill it instead with such ideas about God and self as would eliminate all inner conflict.

Should the reader protest that it is impossible to expect all this of the average teacher, who must have his subject matter clearly worked out for him in textbooks and divided into lessons, and who is helpless the moment he has to organize the subject matter himself, the answer is that the teaching of religion should be entrusted only to one who is specially qualified. There is no reason why the average teacher should teach a subject which requires so much specialized knowledge and technique. We have special teachers for music and for arts and crafts. To master the main results of research in religion and to communicate them to others requires an intensive training in the science and the pedagogy of religion. Since such training must accompany a sense of concrete reality, a poetic sense and a highly ethical disposition, it is no easy matter to be a teacher of religion. The problem of teaching religion in Jewish schools will not be solved unless the Jewish community, through its rabbinical and teachers' training institutions, make provision to have young people of ability and character concentrate on studies that would give them an understanding of the place of religion in human life, and of the Jewish religion in the life of the Jews, and that would acquaint them with the art of communicating that understanding to children and adolescents at the various stages of their mental development.

The instruction of religion should culminate in religious practice. Apart from translating the attitude of thankfulness into conduct, it is necessary to train the child to translate that attitude into the practice of worship. In the light of the distinction that has been drawn between the religion of the past and the religion of the future, worship will henceforth have but the one function of imbuing the human being with the God-consciousness, or the consciousness of life's significance and momentousness. It will therefore express itself in words and gestures of *tehillah* rather than *tefillah*, of praise rather than of prayer. If the sense of life's significance and momentousness is to become potent enough to function in times of stress and temptation, it must be cultivated by practice, religious rites and religious service. This is the intent of the benedictions which formed part of the religious regimen of the Jew. Though it may not be necessary to recite a hundred benedictions a day, as the traditionalists advised, the frequent recital of benedictions in the new spirit of religion should be encouraged. We need not fear that the practice of reciting benedictions might become routinized and lead to mechanical religiosity. Such religiosity was the concomitant of the traditional conception and practice of religion, when religion was for the masses a form of theurgy, and when the religious act was supposed to possess an inherent virtue, independent of any spiritual meaning the act may have had for the one who performed it. But with the tendency to treat religion as essentially the conscious affirmation of those elements in life that validate the belief in God, the danger that the repetition of a religious act might reduce the awareness of its meaning and deaden all spontaneity is lessened.[18]

The spirit of thankfulness, whereby the child first experiences the sense of life's inherent worth, should be expressed through religious service participated in by large numbers of children, so that religion will become a vital and interesting experience to him. It is through religious service that Jewish education can bring to bear upon the child all of those factors in Jewish life which have an emotional appeal. All the artistic skills of the children should be enlisted in rendering the religious service an occasion of joyous self-expression, and the distinctive mark of that joyousness would be the attitude of reverence. This implies the need of organizing religious services for the children as an integral part of their Jewish training.

A new generation of Jews brought up to look upon religion not as a matter of unassimilated and irrelevant tradition, but as a living personal experience, will be able to carry through the great spiritual reformation that Jewish life must undergo, if it is to justify itself to the millions of Jews in the diaspora.

5. *The stimulation of esthetic creativity.* Children are entitled to esthetic experience in their own right. Their spontaneous feelings should be focussed about Jewish values and directed into the channels of expression through song and music. Songs dealing with themes which the child can appreciate, and which satisfy his esthetic bent must be taught as part of the Jewish school curriculum. The celebration of festivals, of birthday parties, of events in the general or Jewish community, should become occasions for the children to express themselves in song and music.

But song is only one of the many art forms which the religious school can cultivate. Jewish folklore and history afford rich background for dramatization, composing poems, modeling, paper construction, drawing, painting and designing of costumes. If the project method in education owes its value to the fact that it is based on the interests and needs of the child, then arts and crafts must hold a position of primacy in the religious school curriculum. The making of things furnishes the avenue of approach to the average child's heart and mind.[1]

One wonders why modern congregations spend such vast sums on professionally trained choirs. If the congregation were to use the money it spends on professional singers in organizing and conducting children's choirs, the problems of religious school attendance, attendance at services, and in general the participation of the young in the work of the congregation, would almost be solved. To carry out this purpose successfully, it would be necessary to make instruction in the music of the religious service a part of the religious schooling, and not a mere adjunct or extra-curricular activity. Only inertia and academic prejudice hinder the establishment of direct and immediate connection between learning a thing at school and making practical use of it forthwith. In the Jewish educative process only such connection between education and life will secure and maintain the child's interest in Jewish content.

But neither the school nor the congregation can be the main agency for cultivating in the child the capacity to express Jewish values through the medium of the arts. The congregation is interested in the esthetic only as it is an aid to worship, and the school only as it helps the educative process. To foster an art-consciousness and to achieve an art tradition, it is necessary to add to the institutions that go to make up Jewish life, art schools, museums and dramatic societies.[20]

The foregoing program represents, to be sure, a desideratum rather than an immediate possibility. But it has at least the merit of proposing a goal which is certain to set in motion the creative forces in Jewish life, because it proposes a workable synthesis of the claims of the environment with those of the Jewish heritage. Jewish education has suffered long enough from the lack of any guiding philosophy. It is true that the exigencies of the practical situation in the near past were so pressing that temporary palliatives and mechanical devices and techniques had to do duty for a comprehensive and basic conception of the aims and methods of Jewish education. The time has come, however, for the formulation of a philosophy of Jewish education, as part of a philosophy which holds the greatest promise of a worthwhile future for Jewish life in this country. A beginning toward such a formulation has been attempted in this chapter.

CONCLUSION

CHAPTER XXXII

CREATIVE JUDAISM—A PROGRAM

THE differences between the world from which the Jew has emerged and that in which he now lives are so sharp and manifold that they almost baffle description. The Jew shared with the rest of the ancient world the universal belief that salvation meant the attainment of bliss in the hereafter as a result of having lived according to the will of God in this life. Consequently he was free from all self-questioning and doubt. He was sure of his privileged position in the scheme of divine redemption. But all such conceptions together with the reasoning upon which they are based are alien to the modern world. In the short time that the Jew has lived in the modern world, these conceptions have become almost unintelligible to him. He thus finds himself deprived of what had been the principal justification for his loyalty to Judaism.

The only adequate substitute for other-worldly salvation which formerly motivated the loyalty of the Jew to his social heritage is a creative Judaism. This means that Judaism must be so reconstructed as to elicit from him the best that is in him. It must be so conditioned as to enlarge his mental horizon, deepen his sympathies, imbue him with hope and enable him to leave the world better for his having lived in it.

The Jews who are likely to assume the task of thus conditioning Judaism are they who cannot do without it, and yet cannot do with it as it is. As a rule, they are those with whom Judaism is a habit. Coming from intensely Jewish homes, they have had Judaism bred into their very bones. Jewish modes of self-expression and association with fellow-Jews are as indispensable to them as the very air they breathe. They would like to observe Jewish rites, but so many of those rites appear to them ill-adapted to the conditions and needs of our day. They are affiliated with congregations, but they are bored by the services. They take an active part in Jewish organization, but are revolted by the futility, waste and lack of sincerity. They cannot help feeling that many an opportunity for reaching into the soul of the Jew, improving his character and eliciting his powers for good is thoughtlessly neglected. Anachronisms abound where cogency and relevance could prevail. Much that might be rendered beautiful and appealing is allowed to remain stale and flat. The teachers and scholars, instead of following the example of Moses, the teacher of all teachers, who went down to the people, ensconce themselves in the ivory tower of abstract learning.

Others, again, cannot do without Judaism because it is a nostalgia with them. It haunts them and gives them no rest. But as it is constituted at present, it offers no field for the expression of their innermost selves. Such Jews may never have seen anything Jewish in their homes, but some atavistic yearning or childhood memory has awakened within them. Now they want to become reunited with their people. If they are of a romantic temperament they may idealize their people's failings. Otherwise they may be repelled by the petrifaction of many of its lauded traditions and institutions and the aimlessness of most of its collective activities.

What must these Jews do to render Judaism creative?

1. In the first place they must rediscover Judaism; they must learn to know its true scope and character. The rediscovery of Judaism implies the lifting of the fog of pious sentimentalities and the mists of wish-thoughts which have enveloped it since the days of the emancipation. For fear lest Jews be charged with hyphenating their loyalties to the countries in which they are citizens, timid leaders and teachers have made it appear that Judaism is nothing more than a religion, or a cult. The Neo-Orthodox have taught that it is a revealed religion which so transcends all laws of social life as to be in no way affected or determined by them. As a revealed religion, Judaism is final and authoritative, destined to transform the environment but not to be transformed by it. The Reformists have interpreted Judaism as a historically evolved religion. According to them, the only bond which unites Jews is the mission to promulgate the truth about the unity of God and the brotherhood of mankind. These conceptions of Judaism have so emptied it of content that it has come to mean to most Jews nothing more than a medley of anti-

quated ideas and archaic practices which persist as an irrational hangover from the past.

A number of Jews who could not reconcile themselves to the vacuity of Reformism, or the intransigeance of Neo-Orthodoxy, are advocating the elimination of religion from Jewish collective life, and are staking the future of the Jewish people upon the spirit of nationalism. They point to nationalism as the most potent social energy in the modern world, and therefore conclude that it should be fostered as a means of solidifying and fructifying the life of the Jewish people. They forget, however, that, if nationalism is to unite the Jews, it must be rooted in the history and spirit of the Jewish people, otherwise the Jews would be merely playing at the kind of nationhood which has balkanized the world. Thus have the Secularists added to the general confusion of ideas which has obscured the true character of Judaism.

There must be an end to all these misconceptions and misunderstandings. The quality and quantity of life that spell Judaism must be rediscovered and reemphasized. It must be recognized as nothing less than a civilization. It must figure in the consciousness of the Jew as the *tout ensemble* of all that is included in a civilization, the social framework of national unity centering in a particular land, a continuing history, a living language and literature, religious folkways, mores, laws and art.

As a civilization, Judaism is that dynamic pattern of life which enables the Jewish people to be a means of salvation to the individual Jew. In the past when salvation meant attainment of bliss in the hereafter, the Jewish civilization was other-worldly in its entire outlook, content and motivation. Now when salvation depends on making the most of the opportunities presented by this world, the form of social organization, the language, literature, religion, laws, folkways and art must so function that through them the Jewish people will help to make the life of the Jew creative and capable of self-fulfillment. Jewish life must not depend upon syllogistic rationalization. It must have body and substance. It must function through vital institutions and articulate itself in a plastic and creative ideology.

The only way in which Jews will ever be able to coordinate their own mode of life satisfactorily with the life which they must share with their neighbors will be by rethinking their beliefs, reorganizing their institutions and developing new means of self-expression as Jews. To that end it will be necessary for them to operate with Judaism not merely as a religion but as a civilization. If Jews will apply themselves to each specific problem with this truth in mind, they will bring to bear creative intelligence upon whatever task they will undertake, whether it be the upbuilding of Palestine, the campaign against discrimination, the organization of communal life, the establishment of congregations, the fostering of religion or the encouragement of Jewish art. They will then no longer content themselves with half-thoughts and compromises which are responsible for the present chaos and demoralization in Jewish life. Their hearts will then be set upon so revitalizing their social heritage, so reconstructing their mode of life, so conditioning their future, that the Jewish people might become once more a source of spiritual self-realization to the individual Jew.

For Judaism to become creative once again, it must assimilate the best in contemporary civilizations. In the past this process of assimilating cultural elements from the environment was carried on unconsciously. Henceforth that process will have to be carried on in deliberate and planned fashion. Therein Judaism will, no doubt, have to depart from its own tradition. But conscious and purposeful planning is coming to be part of the very life process of society. No civilization, culture, economy or religion that is content to drift aimlessly has the slightest chance of surviving. It is in the spirit, therefore, of adopting the best in other civilizations and cooperating with them, and not in the spirit of yielding to their superior force or prestige, that Judaism should enter upon what will constitute a fourth stage in its development.

This development in Judaism necessarily presupposes many changes in its ideology, sanctions, practices and social organization. The criterion which is to determine whether a suggested change is beneficial or detrimental to Judaism is the extent to which it helps Judaism to retain its *continuity*, its *individuality* and its *organic character*.

The continuity of Judaism is maintained so long as the knowledge of Israel's past functions as an integral part of the Jew's personal memory, and is accompanied by some visible form or action symbolic of that fact. An organism has been defined as "an object which develops and maintains a unified pattern of response to changing situations." Unless, therefore, we can insure some degree of continuity between the past and the future of Jewish life by means of "a unified pattern of response to changing situations," the very notion of the Jewish people as a social organism is absurd.

The individuality of Judaism is maintained so long as the newly instituted custom, sanction, idea or ideal helps to keep alive the element of otherness in the Jewish civilization. Not separatism must henceforth be the principle of living as a Jew, but otherness. Separatism is the antithesis of cooperation, and results in an ingrown and clannish remoteness which leads to cultural and spiritual stagnation. Otherness thrives best when accompanied by active cooperation and interaction with neighboring cultures and civilizations, and achieves an individuality which is of universal significance.

The organic character is maintained so long as all the elements that constitute the civilization play a rôle in the life of the Jew. Any attempt to live or transmit only certain elements in Judaism to the neglect of others is bound to end in failure, since in Judaism as a civilization the normal functioning of each element is bound up with and conditioned by the normal functioning of every other. Even though it may not be possible in the diaspora to foster each element to its full extent, there is a minimum below which it must not be allowed to fall, lest all the other elements of the civilization be jeopardized.

2. To render Judaism creative it is essential to redefine the national status and reorganize the communal life of the Jews. Fundamental to the reorganization of Jewish life is national unity. That unity is not determined by geographic boundaries; it is cultural rather than political. The Jews are an international nation, functioning as such by virtue of their consciousness of a common past, their aspiration toward a common future and the will-to-cooperate in the achievement of common ends.

Palestine should serve as the symbol of the Jewish renascence and the center of Jewish civilization. Without such a center upon which Jews throughout the world might focus their interest, it is impossible for Jews to be conscious of their unity as a people. Without the spiritual aid and example of the adjustment of Judaism to modern life in the new Jewish environment possible only in Palestine, the efforts at similar adjustment by other Jewries of the world would be without impelling stimulus. Judaism cannot maintain its character as a civilization without a national home in Palestine. There essential Jewish creativeness will express itself in Hebraic forms not so easily developed in other lands. There Jews will attain sufficient autonomy to express their ideas and social will in all forms of organized life and thought.

In fostering their collective life, Jews must reckon with the circumstance that they live under varying national and political conditions. The development of Judaism as a modern spiritual civilization will vary in different lands. The chief variations will correspond to the three zones of Jewish distribution—Palestine as the Jewish National Home, eastern Europe with its recognition of minority nationalities, and western Europe and America with communal organization as the form most consistent with their political institutions.

As a result of a peculiar conjuncture of historic forces, the citizen of a modern state is not only permitted but encouraged to give allegiance to two civilizations: one, the secular civilization of the country in which he lives, and the other, the Christian civilization which he has inherited from the past. He turns to the civilization of his country for his literary and esthetic values. From his national life arise those duties of civic allegiance which are the substance of patriotism. He turns to the Christian civilization for his moral and spiritual sanctions. The separation of church from state has put into the class of hyphenates all who adhere to both organizations. The necessity which justifies the Christian in hyphenating his Christianity with Americanism, justifies also the Jew in hyphenating his Jewishness with Americanism.

Jewish communal life is the *sine qua non* of cooperation among Jews. In America, particularly, Jews will need a measure of communal autonomy if American-Jewish life is to develop along broad and inclusive lines. Jewish organization should embrace all the activities of Jews, and integrate those activities into an organic unity. To such communities will belong all Jews who feel physical or spiritual kinship with the Jewish people, no matter what their personal philosophy may be.

Congregations will be units in these communities, units consisting of groups of Jews who wish to express their Judaism through common worship. The community, however, is larger than its congregations and must of necessity provide for needs and activities that do not fall within the scope of the congregation. There should also be other units consisting of groups and individuals who wish to express their Jewishness and their creativity through literature, the arts and activities for the furtherance of social welfare and social justice.

The community should direct Jewish economic life into productive occupations. The position of middleman, which history has imposed upon the Jew, is becoming economically insecure and unsound. For the sake of greater economic security, and because of the dignity and moral worth of engaging in productive labor, Jews should endeavor to enter the fields of industry and agriculture wherever opportunities permit.

The community should establish centers where the religious, philanthropic, social and educational problems of each neighborhood would be dealt with specifically. These centers, subsidized by the community, will stimulate Jewish creative effort among writers, scholars, artists, musicians and social workers.

The community should institute such civic activities as the establishment of Jewish arbitration courts, the recognition and recording of births, marriages, divorces and deaths, the representation of Jews before the non-Jewish community and the defense of Jewish rights.

Among the functions of Jewish communal life, priority should be given to Jewish education. In relief work and social service, the community discharges nothing more than an elementary human duty. But it is in the socialization of its members through the transmission and enrichment of a spiritual heritage that a community lives up to the highest purpose of its existence. Jewish education in its widest sense as applying to children, adolescents and adults must become one of the main functions of the Jewish community. The Jewish training of the young must be planned on a far more comprehensive scale than hitherto. This training must be continued by a systematic development of adult Jewish education. The school must be further supplemented by the home. If the home is to possess the requisite Jewish atmosphere, the adults as well as the young must continue their interest in Jewish study.

The Jewish community must foster institutions of higher learning. It must so apportion the duties of those engaged in communal work as to leave time and leisure for them to grow in the knowledge of their respective callings. It must stimulate in the home, in the synagogue and in the construction of Jewish public buildings the creative arts expressive of Jewish interests and ideals.

3. To render Judaism creative, its tradition must be revitalized. The main reason Jews display such a negative attitude to their tradition is no doubt the fact that they labor under the assumption that it is inextricably bound up with a theology which has ceased to have any vital meaning for them. They conceive tradition as a series of fixed and static ideas which either have to be accepted in the form in which they have come down, or be let alone entirely. This erroneous idea must be offset by the realization that the only way tradition will ever come into its own as an active factor in the Jewish consciousness is to disengage from it the element of past interpretation, and to get at the reality behind the interpretation.

The future of Judaism is contingent upon the formulation of a Jewish ideology which will make it possible for Jews, despite their unlike-mindedness, to accept the intrinsic value of Jewish life. Only through a participation in Jewish interests and aspirations which elicits the best that is in him will the individual Jew find salvation through his people. But if such participation is to have a truly redeeming or saving influence, it must be accompanied by a clear perspective of the whole of Jewish life.

The crux of the problem of how to foster a constructive and unifying Jewish ideology at the present time is to disabuse the average person of the deeply rooted preconception that for a people or community to function as an instrument of salvation, all who compose it must think alike and behave alike. Out of this preconception stems the intolerance which is by no means confined to the historic churches. Modern nations are no less adept in intolerance. An inference which some wrongly draw from this hitherto unquestioned assumption is that, since it is impossible to get people to think and behave alike, there can be no such thing as a group acting as an instrument of salvation. Salvation, they maintain, is purely an individual achievement. Such a conclusion is tantamount to nihilism, yet it is the inevitable one to which any sincere and conscientious person is driven, so long as the churches and nations continue in their refusal or inability to reconcile the salvation they proffer with tolerance of credal differences. It is doubtful whether they will change their attitude. With the Jewish people, however, this synthesis is a matter of life and death. Its very existence depends upon its making a virtue of the necessity of giving its individual men and women wide scope in views, and at the same time extending salvation to all of them alike.

A people does not offer itself to the individual as an instrument of salvation, in the same way as a system of philosophy usually does, by appealing to his reason to accept certain general principles or abstract truths. It always comes to him with a story about itself which he is made to feel is in a deeper and truer sense his story than the experiences that are confined to his person. In the course of that story there figure certain events, persons, places, objects, or, in brief, *sancta*, which come to possess a vital interest for him, since they belong to a history that he comes to look upon as his own. These *sancta* the people interprets, and these interpretations form the ideology and rationale of its existence and strivings. In the past, when everybody thought alike, one type of interpretation or ideology was enough to enable the *sancta* to help the individual orient himself to the world about him. One ideology, uniform and unchangeable, thus came to be regarded as indispensable to salvation.

Now that such uniformity is no longer possible, there is the alternative of permitting different ideologies to be developed whereby the *sancta*, which have played an important part in the history of the people or church, may retain their place as sources of and occasions for ethical motivation and spiritual exaltation for individuals with different philosophies of life. The sense of unity and even of likemindedness is not contingent upon the sameness of interpretation, but upon the sameness of the constellation of realities interpreted. The latter sameness is far more unifying than agreement in abstract generalizations. If Jews will thrill to the *sancta*, or constellation of historical realities which figure in their tradition, and maintain those realities as centers of ethical and spiritual reference, no matter how far apart they are in their views about life—they will be sufficiently united to function in their collective capacity as an instrument of salvation to the individual Jew.

Assuming, therefore, that multiple ideologies are compatible with unity of group spirit, there remains the task of formulating in outline, at least, an ideology for those Jews who cannot align themselves with any of the existing groups, and who experience the need of such salvation as the Jewish people in its proper capacity might afford them. Such Jews are sufficiently numerous and influential to deserve this consideration.

The principle underlying the ideology that would meet their need is that the traditional *sancta* must be kept within the focus of the Jewish consciousness. The interpretation, however, which is to be given to those *sancta* cannot be the one which they received in the past. Since any interpretation, to be valid, must coincide with the rest of one's thinking, it is essential that the ideas which form part of the Jewish social heritage be reinterpreted in the light of the modern world-outlook. If such reinterpretation is to succeed in bridging the gap between tradition and modernism, it must seek out from among the implications of tradition those which would reenforce the highest social and spiritual strivings of our day—the complete self-realization of the personality of the individual and the maximum cooperation among human beings irrespective of racial, political and historical divisions.

It is from the standpoint of the foregoing postulates with regard to the need of revitalizing Jewish tradition that religion must continue to be the central identifying characteristic of Jewish civilization. The Jewish genius has always sought to express itself in religious terms; it has always sought to interpret every individual act and process, both natural and human, in the light of reality regarded as creative and meaningful. Like all other phases of human life, religion is subject to the process of evolution. Jewish religion should ally itself with the modern orientation toward religion as the spiritual reaction of man to the vicissitudes of life, and as the expression of the highest needs of his being.

The problem of Jewish religion will be considerably clarified, if we will take into account the distinction between personal religion and folk religion. Jewish folk religion consists in all those expressions of Jewish life, and all those forms of custom and law, through which the individual identifies himself with the life and strivings of his people. It is therefore to be expected that Jews will find in folk religion a common spiritual denominator. Personal religion, on the other hand, is essentially the world-outlook which each one is taught and encouraged to achieve for himself. Such an outlook every individual Jew should be free to develop in accordance with his own personal convictions regarding life and the universe.

Jewish religion as a folk religion should find expression in the practice of the maximum possible number of Jewish religious customs and folkways compatible with one's circumstances. There can be no Jewish life without the use of Jewish symbols in the home and without the observance of Sabbaths, festivals and customs connected with birth, marriage and other vital events.

Yet traditional Jewish customs and folkways must be subject to modification, both in form and in motive, so that they may be observed sincerely and wholeheartedly by modern Jews. New folkways and customs should also be developed and sanctioned to give Jewish significance to numerous occasions in individual and social life at present not invested with spiritual meaning.

Jewish folk religion should find expression in the endeavor to render public worship as significant as possible by relating it to the ideology of the modern Jew and basing it upon the Jewish traditional forms as far as they are consistent with spiritual appeal.

It is a far cry from the simple Judaism of the past to the intricate program called for by Judaism as a civilization. Accustomed to think of Judaism as a form of truth, whether divinely revealed or humanly achieved, we conclude that complexity is a sign of artificiality. It is therefore necessary to recall that Judaism as a civilization is not a form of truth, but a form of life. The higher the organism is in the scale of life, the more intricate and complex its structure. To survive, Judaism must become complex. It must absorb some of the very forces and tendencies that threaten it, effect new syntheses on higher levels of national life, and enter upon a career which will set up new goals in the evolution of civilizations.

In sum, those who look to Judaism in its present state to provide them with a ready-made scheme of salvation in this world, or in the next, are bound to be disappointed. The Jew will have to save Judaism before Judaism will be in a position to save the Jew. The Jew is so circumstanced now that the only way he can achieve salvation is by replenishing the "wells of salvation" which have run dry. He must rediscover, reinterpret and reconstruct the civilization of his people. To do that he must be willing to live up to a program that spells nothing less than a maximum of Jewishness. True to his historic tradition he should throw in his lot with all movements to further social justice and universal peace, and bring to bear upon them the inspiration of his history and religion. Such a program calls for a degree of honesty that abhors all forms of self-delusion, for a temper that reaches out to new consummations, for the type of courage that is not deterred by uncharted regions. If this be the spirit in which Jews will accept from the past the mandate to keep Judaism alive, and from the present the guidance dictated by its profoundest needs, the contemporary crisis in Jewish life will prove to be the birth-throes of a new era in the civilization of the Jewish people.

NOTES

ABBREVIATIONS

C. C. A. R.	Central Conference of American Rabbis.
J. S. S. Q.	*Jewish Social Service Quarterly*.
N. C. J. S. S.	National Conference of Jewish Social Service.
S. A. J.	Society for the Advancement of Judaism.
Y. M. H. A.	Young Men's Hebrew Association.

NOTES

CHAPTER I

[1] Kayserling, M.: *Moses Mendelssohn*, Leipzig, 1862, 543.

[2] *Jewish Encyclopedia*, VI, 330.

[3] Cf. Lessing, Theodor: *Der jüdische Selbsthass*, Berlin, 1930, note 11, 238-247.

[4] Cf. Ravich, Jessie: "Relative Rate of Change in Customs and Beliefs of Modern Jews," *Papers and Proceedings of the American Sociological Society*, Chicago, 1925, XIX, 171-176.

[5] Symposium: "What Judaism Means to Me," *Temple Emanuel Chronicle*, San Francisco, November 8, 1929.

[6] Cf. *Authorized Daily Prayer Book*, translated by Rev. S. Singer, 5. The original text of all the traditionally authorized prayer books read *goy*, which is the rabbinic term for "Gentile," in place of *nokri*, which is rendered here "heathen." Cf. *Abodat Yisrael*, Rödelheim, 1868, 40, commentary.

[7] Kassel, Louis: "Do Jewish Undergraduates Attempt to Disguise Their Jewishness?" *Jewish Tribune*, New York, February 26, 1926.

[8] Wolfson, Harry Austryn: *Escaping Judaism*, Menorah Pamphlets, New York, 1923, no. 2.

[9] Lasker, Bruno: *Jewish Experiences in America*, New York, 1930, 111 f.

[10] Cf. Ginzberg, Louis: *The Legends of the Jews*, Philadelphia, V, 67, note 8.

[11] Cf. *Tosefta Sanhedrin* XIII, 2; *Sanhedrin* 105a.

[12] *Mishnah Sanhedrin* X, 1.

[13] This is implied in the allusions to Judaism by the Christian and the Mohammedan interlocutors of the Khazar king, Cf. Judah Ha-Levi: *Kitab Al Khazari*, translated by Hartwig Hirschfeld, New York, 1927, par. 4, 9.

[14] Cf. Maimonides: *Commentary on Mishnah Sanhedrin* X.

[15] *The Authorized Daily Prayer Book*, London, 285.

[16] Translated by M. Samuels, London, 1838, II, 13.

[17] *Ibid.*, II, 47, note.

[18] *The Merchant of Venice*, act III, scene 1.

[19] Heine, Heinrich: "Prinzessin Sabbat," *Confessio Judaica*, Berlin, 1925, 205-209.

[20] *The Authorized Daily Prayer Book*, 139.

[21] *Berakot* 57b.

[22] *The Authorized Daily Prayer Book*, 284.

[23] *Ibid.*, 68.

[24] "Jerusalem," *Gesammelte Schriften*, Leipzig, 1843, III, 316.

[25] Maimon, Solomon: *An Autobiography*, Translated by J. Clark Murray, Boston, 1888, 25.

CHAPTER II

[1] An interesting contrast between the medieval and the modern conceptions of national life as affecting the Jews is presented within the French colonial empire. In Morocco the Jews retain their ethnic individuality, their schools and their language. André Spire writes, "The Jews of Algeria—which, as far as administration is concerned, is a sort of extension of French territory—were naturalized *en bloc* in 1870 under the sole condition that they accept the French civil code without reservation as it was accepted by French Jewry after the convocation of the Grand Sanhedrin by

Napoleon I in 1807. In Tunisia and Morocco—which are not French colonies, but autonomous countries under French protectorate, the Jews, like the other native groups, have preserved their own regulations of personal status. In other words, their family relations are based upon traditional Jewish law, and their civil suits are judged by tribunals of their own." *New Palestine*, June 7, 1929, XVI, 489.

In a single issue of the *Jewish Daily Bulletin*, February 13, 1929, the ambiguity in the political status of the Jews was reported as making trouble for the Jews in three European countries where they were supposed to be enjoying political equality.

1. In Italy, the Italian-Vatican Agreement on the Enforcement of Canon Law raised the question, how will Jews fare in a country where Catholic instruction is obligatory. The proffered information that Jewish children attending Italian public schools will not be affected by this compulsory measure, as the parents of the children have a right to ask for their exemption during religious instruction, is hardly satisfactory, in view of the fact that the basic principle of Catholic education is not to confine the instruction of religion to any specific hour, but to have it dominate the entire curriculum.

2. In Greece, the main issue that was then being debated among the Jews was the establishment by the government of a separate Jewish Electoral College. The position taken in government circles was that the Jews of Salonica and Macedonia, in general, were not yet sufficiently identified with the Greek state to be admitted to the body politic without reservations. In the discussion between representative Jews and the government, neither side states frankly and specifically what it understands by assimilation. The only item mentioned in passing is adequate teaching of the Greek language in the Jewish schools.

3. In Poland, there was a continuation of the struggle to get the government to live up to its constitution, and to remove the numerous disabilities and restrictions which were a heritage from the Czarist times.

In contrast with the unsolved problem of the status of the Jews in the foregoing countries, the *Jewish Daily Bulletin*, February 13, 1930, gives the complete text of the Jewish Community Law adopted by Jugo-Slavia, which is an instance of a satisfactory *modus vivendi* worked out for the Jews in one of the states created by the Peace Conference.

[2] Dohm, Christian Wilhelm: *Ueber die bürgerliche Verbesserung der Juden*, Berlin, 1781.

[3] Cf. Dubnow, Simon: *Dibere yeme yisrael badorot ha-aḥaronim*, Berlin, 1923, I, Ch. XIV, XV.

[4] Mirabeau, Comte de: *Sur Moses Mendelssohn, sur la reforme politique des juifs*, London, 1787; cf. Riesser, Gabriel: "Vertheidigung der bürgerlichen Gleichstellung der Juden" *Gesammelte Schriften*, Frankfort a. M., 1867, II, 91-194.

[5] Mendelssohn, in *Jerusalem*, rejects the proposal made by C. W. Dohm that the Jews exercise the right of ecclesiastical excommunication. *Gesammelte Schriften*, Leipzig, 1843, III, 197 ff.

[6] Ilfeld, Zebi Hirsh: *Dibere negidim*, Amsterdam, 1799.

[7] Some regarded that superiority as inherent, and others as conditional. According to Judah Ha-Levi, *Kitab Al Khazari*, I, par. 47, the Jews alone inherited from Adam a capacity for spiritual life. According to Saadya, it is only the possession of the Torah that confers distinction upon the Jews. Cf. *Emunot W'Deot*, III, 7.

[8] *Sanhedrin* 74a, b.

CHAPTER III

[1] Cf. Dubnow, Simon: "Vos felt in unzer ekonomishe geshichte?" Yiddish Scientific Institute: *Schriftn far ekonomik un statistik*, Berlin, 1928, I, 180-183.

[2] On basis of figures in Linfield, H. S.: "Statistics of Jews," *American Jewish Year Book*, XXXIII, 277.

[3] Cf. Leiserson, M.: *Adjusting the Immigrant in Industry*, New York, 1924.

[4] "When tailorism began to assert itself, it was anti-religious, permeated by the spirit of vulgar atheism. The tailor organized Yom Kippur Balls and morally pogromed the Orthodox Jew. He has no national hopes, and no religious expecta-

tions. He is extravagantly immodest, nor is he silent. So far as he has survived, he is an exhibitionist of the first order. His philosopher is Feigenbaum, his publicist the late Louis Miller and Mr. Abe Cahan. The late Mr. Pfeffer was his chief litterateur. Messrs. Szolotherefsky, Gable and Lateiner are his playwrights and a host of vulgarians, his actors." Melamed, S. M.: "The Rise and Fall of the Sadowsky Empire," *Reflex*, August, 1927, 6.

⁵ "The Keren Hayesod in this country depends largely upon the Jewish bourgeois which is strongly represented in its counsels. This is due to two circumstances: (a) The Jewish middle class, which has money to give, is on the whole sympathetic to the movement and has more readily responded to the call of Palestine than any other groups; (b) the great mass of Jews, namely, the working classes, are, as a group, under non-Zionist or anti-Zionist influences and have thus far not been won over to our ideal. These are facts which neither the Keren Hayesod nor the Keren Kayemeth can overlook or change in one day." Neuman, Emanuel: "Artificial Issues," *New Palestine*, July 24, 1925, IX, 82.

CHAPTER IV

¹ Whitehead, Alfred North: *Adventures of Ideas*, New York, 1933, 348.
² Judah Ha-Levi: *Kitab Al Khazari*, I, par. 95.
³ Pope Pius XI: *Encyclical Letter on the Christian Education of Youth*, January 11, 1930.
⁴ *Abot* II, 1.
⁵ Judah Ha-Levi: *op. cit.*, II, par. 48.

CHAPTER V

¹ Ruppin, Arthur: *Soziologie der Juden*, Berlin, 1930, I, 75 ff. Linfield, H. S.: "Statistics of Jews," *American Jewish Year Book*, XXXIV, 247.
² *Ibid.*, XXVIII, 96.
³ Wirth, Louis: *The Ghetto*, Chicago, 1928; Drachsler, Julius: "The Trend of Jewish Communal Life in the United States," *Jewish Social Service Quarterly*, November, 1924, I, 1-21; Park, Robert E. and Miller, Herbert A.: *Old World Traits Transplanted*, New York, 1921; *Jewish Communal Survey of Greater New York*, Bureau of Jewish Social Research, New York, 1928.
⁴ "As they have lived throughout their dispersion, so, for the most part, they live at the present day—in communities. These communities are, with very few exceptions, of an urban character; those of a rural character comprise little more than a quarter of a million Jews altogether." Cohen, Israel: *Jewish Life in Modern Times*, New York, 1914, 32.
⁵ Soltes, Mordecai: *The Yiddish Press*, New York, 1925, 115.
⁶ Since the days of Ezra and Nehemiah, the interdict against intermarriage has been associated in traditional Judaism with the law in Deut. vii, 3, forbidding intermarriage with the native Canaanites. Reformism, realizing the need for a new basis for the prohibition of intermarriage has formulated the rationale that the Jews are a race, and would therefore lose their spiritual potency through intermarriage. Cf. Kohler, K.: *Jewish Theology*, New York, 1918, 445-46.
⁷ Cf. Ruppin, Arthur: *op. cit.*, I, 209.
⁸ Cohen, Israel: *op. cit.*, 216.
⁹ Young, Pauline V.: "The Reorganization of Jewish Family Life in America . . .," *Social Forces*, December, 1928, VII, 238-244.
¹⁰ Cf. Ogburn, William F.: "The Changing Family," *Papers and Proceedings of the American Sociological Society*, Chicago, 1928, XXIII, 124-133.
¹¹ Golub, Jacob S.: "Attitude Toward Intermarriage," *Society for Advancement of Judaism Review*, January 4, 1929, 20; Pool, D. De Sola; *Intermarriage*, Jewish Welfare Board, New York.
¹² Berger, Graenum: *Jewish Center Publications*, Thesis, Graduate School for Jewish Social Work, New York, 1932.

[13] Leo, S. N.: "The Beginning of the Y. M. H. A.," *Y. M. H. A. Bulletin*, XXV, 12.

[14] 92nd Street Y. M. H. A. *Annual Report*, 1900, 34.

[15] [Bogen, B. D.]: "Jewish Settlements," *Jewish Charities*, August, 1911, II, 10.

[16] Robinson, A.: "Development of Jewish Center Philosophy," *Jewish Center*, June, 1930, VIII, 12.

[17] Cf. Jewish Welfare Board: *Report of Second Biennial Convention*, Philadelphia, 1924.

[18] The philosophy underlying the Jewish Center is formulated, from the standpoint of American democracy, by Berkson, I. B., *Theories of Americanization*, New York, 1920, 177-272; the progress of the movement is described in numerous reports and articles in the *Jewish Center* and *Jewish Social Service Quarterly*.

[19] Glucksman, H.: "Program of the Jewish Welfare Board," *Jewish Center*, October, 1922, I, 12.

[20] Cf. "Synagog," *B'nai B'rith Manual*, Cincinnati, 1926, 20-23.

[21] Golub, Jacob S.: "Jewish Youth and Tradition," *S. A. J. Review*, New York, April 19, 1929, 19, 20.

[22] Cederbaum, David I.: *The Story of Jewish Education in the United States in 1927 in Figures*, Bureau of Jewish Education, New York, 1928 (mimeographed); Linfield, H. S.: "A Survey of the Year . . .," *American Jewish Year Book*, XXVII, 43; XXVIII, 42; XXIX, 40.

[23] Hexter, Maurice B.: "Evolutionary Tendencies in the Jewish Federation Movement," *Proceedings National Conference Jewish Social Service*, 1926, 9-29.

[24] Cahn, Louis: "The Federation and Community Funds," *Proceedings N. C. J. S. S.*, 1928, 197.

[25] "Federations Throughout the United States," *American Hebrew*, July 9, 1926, CXIX, 270.

[26] Jacobs, Herman: *Some Aspects of the Federation of Jewish Charities Movement in the United States*, Thesis, Graduate School for Jewish Social Work, New York, 1933.

[27] *Proceedings N. C. J. S. S.*, 1923, 195-199.

[28] Bogen, B. D.: *Proceedings N. C. J. S. S.*, 1925, 197; Bernstein, Ludwig: *Ibid.*, 4 ff.; Lowenstein, Solomon: "Federations and Local Non-Affiliated Societies," *J. S. S. Q.*, March, 1926, II, 145-151.

[29] Waldman, M. D.: "New Issues in Federation," *Proceedings N. C. J. S. S.*, 1925, 220; Hexter, M. B.: "Evolutionary Tendencies in the Jewish Federation Movement," *Ibid.*, 1926, 26 f.; Lipsitch, I.: "Community Chests," *Ibid.*, 1927, 143-149; Goldsmith, S.: *Ibid.*, 159; S. C. Kohs and others: "Jewish Community Chests," *Ibid.*, 1927, 112-160.

[30] Soltes, Mordecai: *The Yiddish Press;* Rubin, Philip: "The Yiddish Press," *American Mercury*, March, 1927, X, 342-353.

[31] Report by the president of the Society, *American Jewish Year Book*, XXVII, 487-88.

[32] Goldberg, Isaac: "Modern Trends in Drama," *Special Bulletin of Yiddish Art Theatre on Tenth Anniversary*, New York.

[33] De Haas, Jacob: "The Provisional Executive Committee," *Jewish Communal Register*, 1917-1918, 1401-1405.

[34] "The supreme question is: whether the time has come to secure a safe refuge for the race, whose sufferings seem to be increasing rather than tending to their end; and this is a problem to which the Jewish reformation cannot close its eyes without becoming faithless to its own profession." Gottheil, Gustav: "The Jewish Reformation," *American Journal of Theology*, 1902, VI, 284.

[35] Circulars and Bulletins of the Yiddish Culture Society, New York; Yiddish Scientific Institute: *Di ershte idishe shprach-konferentz. Barichtn, dokumentn un opklangn fun der Czernowitzer konferentz, 1908*, Wilno, 1931.

[36] Article "B'nai B'rith," *Jewish Encyclopedia*, III, 275.

[37] Sachs, A. S.: *Di geshichte fun Arbeiter Ring*, New York, 1925, 2 vol.; Burgin, Hertz: *Geschichte fun der idisher arbeiter bevegung in Amerike, Rusland un England*, New York, 1915.

CHAPTER VI

[1] Mommsen, Th.: *Auch ein Wort über unser Judenthum*, Berlin, 1880.

[2] Belloc, Hilaire: *The Jews*, New York, 1922.

[3] The term anti-Semitism was first used in 1879 when Wilhelm Marr published his book, *Der Sieg des Judenthums über das Germanenthum*, Berlin, 1879.

[4] Belloc, Hilaire, *op. cit.;* Chamberlain, Houston Stewart: *Foundations of the 19th Century*, translated by J. Lees, New York, 1912.

[5] *Ja-sagen zum Judentum, eine Aufsatzreihe der jüdischen Rundschau zur Lage der deutschen Juden*, Berlin, 1933, 148.

[6] Lasker, Bruno: "Jewish Handicap in the Employment Market," *Jewish Social Service Quarterly*, March, 1926, II, 174.

[7] The Hitler program, which was written by Gottfried Feder in February, 1920, is given point by point in the Nazi party's official statement published in Alfred Rosenberg: *Wesen, Grundsätze und Ziele der N.S.D.A.P. Das Programm der Bewegung erweitert durch das Agrarprogramm*, Munich, 1930.

The points that affect the Jews, as given in the translation of the program made by the *Information Service of the Foreign Policy Association* for January 21, 1931, VI, are as follows:

"IV. Only a member of our own people (*Volksgenosse*) may be a citizen (*Staatsbürger*). Our own people are *only* those of German blood without reference to confession. Therefore, no Jew may be a member of our people.

"V. He who is not a citizen may live in Germany only as a guest and must be governed by laws regulating foreigners.

"VI. Only citizens may decide on the leaders and laws of the State. Therefore, we demand that every public office, no matter of what sort, whether in the Reich, the states or the communes, shall be filled only by citizens. "We fight against the corrupting parliamentary system which is composed only of people chosen for their party politics without reference to character or ability.

"VIII. All further immigration of non-Germans is to be stopped. We demand that all non-Germans who have immigrated to Germany since August 2, 1914, shall be forced to leave the Reich.

"XXIII. We demand a legislative battle against certain political lies and their propagation in the press. In order to make possible the creation of a German press, we demand that:

"1. All editors and workers on newspapers which appear in the German language must be citizens.

"2. Non-German newspapers require the specific permission of the State for publication. They may not be printed in the German language.

"3. Any financial participation or influence in a German newspaper by a non-German is to be forbidden by law and punished by confiscating the paper as well as by the immediate expulsion from the Reich of the non-German in question.

"Newspapers which work against the common good are to be prohibited. "We demand laws against tendencies in art and literature which have a bad influence on our life as a people, and the closing of institutions which offend our people.

"XXIV. We demand freedom for all religious sects in the State so far as they do not endanger the State or work against the customs and morals of the German race. The party as such represents the point of view of a positive Christianity without binding itself to any particular confession. It fights the spirit of Jewish materialism in us and outside us and is convinced that a lasting convalescence of our people can only take place from the inner conviction of 'common usefulness before individual usefulness.' "

[8] Spengler, Oswald: *Decline of the West*, translated by Charles F. Atkinson, Alfred A. Knopf, New York, 1930, II, 320.

[9] Berkson, Isaac B.: *Theories of Americanization*, New York, 1920; Kallen, Horace Meyer: *Culture and Democracy in the United States*, New York, 1924.
[10] Cf. *Encyclical on Education*, January 11, 1930, Ch. XXVIII, note 1.
[11] Cf. Smith, Gerald Birney: *Principles of Christian Living*, Chicago, 1924, Ch. XVII.

CHAPTER VII

[1] A striking illustration of the prevailing perplexity is a recent division of opinion among the Jews of Pittsburgh over the project of having a Jewish Room in the Cathedral of Learning which was constructed under the auspices of the University of Pittsburgh. Questionnaires were sent to one hundred persons, Jews and non-Jews, for their opinion. Of these, forty four returned replies. The following replies give a true picture of the ideas, fears, hopes and predilections of the majority of American Jews with regard to Judaism:

"Twenty-five expressed themselves as believing that the Jews should have a room in the long heralded Cathedral of Learning. Seven were opposed to a Jewish Room. Six were non-committal, and six were unable to answer. Of the affirmative replies, nine were received from Pittsburghers.

"The reasons given for abandoning the project of the proposed Jewish Room were as follows:

"1. The only purely Jewish contribution to the culture and civilization of the world is in the field of religion. No other religious group is considering such a project, so that a room devoted to religion would be out of place.

"2. Jewish scientists, musicians and painters have not done their work as Jews. It has been produced through and as a result of their national environment. In medicine, science and art there is nothing typically Jewish.

"3. The expense of such a room would be great and the money invested could be used to better advantage in the work of our local social and philanthropic institutions.

"4. The room would not be used. It would be a showpiece to our vanity.

"5. We should not place our contribution, which is purely spiritual, beside the tangible contributions of other peoples.

"6. Owing to the widely different opinions as to whether the Jews represent a race, a nation, a religion, the room and the idea behind it would need constant interpretation.

"7. The fact that Jews disagree so greatly in regard to the project would make the room a monument to our differences.

"8. Jewish students at the University of Pittsburgh would not want the room.

"9. Neither the Jews of the Community nor the Jewish student body have been approached by the University in regard to this room. The idea of a Jewish room did not originate at the University and should the project be endorsed by all Pittsburgh Jewry, there is no authority for the assumption that the University of Pittsburgh is ready to grant such a room.

"The following reasons were advanced as reasons why the Cathedral of Learning should include a Jewish Room among the fifty-six rooms set aside to represent the cultural contributions to civilization of the various peoples of the world:

"1. Monotheism, the basic unity of mankind. The three monotheistic religions are all of Jewish origin.

"2. Culture—Jewish culture is a unique culture based on the Bible, the Talmud, and ideas contained therein. Jewish culture is not limited by national boundaries.

"3. Social justice is articulated through the Prophets.

"4. In view of our civilizing influence, our contribution to the Cathedral of Learning would be incomplete and unhistorical without a Jewish Room.

"5. Jewish culture is consistent with American ideas. The immigrant may shed his social habits but not his culture.

"6. Jews are taken to task as Jews when we have a Jewish criminal. Why not place in the Jewish Room memorials to the great Jewish personalities?

"7. The Jewish Room would promote good will and understanding.

"8. It would be a source of pride to Jewish students.

"At the conference's meeting [Pittsburgh Conference of Jewish Women's Organizations], the vote by organizations was taken, with the following results: of 20 constituent organizations belonging to the Conference, sixteen groups sent written notes as requested. Thirteen voted in the affirmative, and three in the negative." *Jewish Daily Bulletin*, April 25, 1930.

[2] Friedlaender, Israel: *Past and Present*, Cincinnati, 1919, 263-267.

CHAPTER VIII

[1] Hertz, J. H.: *Affirmations of Judaism*, London, 1927, 125, note 10.

[2] Philipson, D.: *The Reform Movement in Judaism*, New York, 1931, 351, 352.

[3] Margolis, Max L.: "The Theological Aspect of Reformed Judaism," *C. C. A. R. Yearbook*, 1903, XIII, 294.

[4] Additional presentations of Reformist Judaism; Hirsch, E. G.: *Jewish Encyclopedia*, X, 347-352; "Reform Judaism from the Point of View of the Reform Jew"; Deutsch, G. and Mielziener, M.: "Principles of Judaism," *C. C. A. R. Yearbook*, 1900, X, 148-164; Margolis, Max L.: *op. cit.*, 185-308; Montefiore, C. G.: *Outlines of Liberal Judaism*, London, 1923; Hirsch, Emil G.: "The Philosophy of the Reform Movement in America," *C. C. A. R. Yearbook*, 1895, 90-112.

[5] Philipson, D., *op. cit.*, 357.

[6] *Ibid.*, 355.

[7] The Sages interpreted the scripture "They have forsaken me and have not kept my law," Jer. vi, 11, as meaning that God would not have minded being forsaken by Israel if Israel had only kept the Law. *Lam. Rabba Proem* 1. This would imply that to the Sages the study of the Torah and the observance of its laws were more important than the worship of God. Elsewhere, the question is raised whether the Torah exists for Israel or Israel for the Torah, and the tendency is to favor the idea that the Torah exists for Israel. *Ecc. Rabba* I, 4.

[8] Kohler, K.: *Jewish Theology*, by permission of The Macmillan Company, publishers, New York, 1918, 36.

[9] Philipson, D.: "Beginnings of Reform Movement in Judaism," *Jewish Quarterly Review*, 1903, XV, 481.

[10] Margolis, M. L.: *op. cit.*, 192, 193.

[11] Kohler, K.: *op. cit.*, 158.

[12] *Ibid.*, 165.

[13] Montefiore, Claude G.: *Outlines of Liberal Judaism*, The Macmillan Company, London, 1912, 160.

[14] Kohler, K.: *op. cit.*, 38-39.

[15] *Ibid.*, 326.

[16] *Ibid.*, 328.

[17] *Ibid.*, 6.

[18] *Ibid.*, 446.

[19] *Ibid.*, 340.

[20] C. G. Montefiore elaborates further on the doctrine of the mission. He makes it evident that the mission-idea as interpreted by Reformism played but a relatively insignificant rôle in the consciousness of the Jew until modern times. He recognizes that even the few passages in the Bible which dwell upon the election of Israel were always understood in a national sense. Messianism meant less the universal adoption of the truth concerning God than the prosperity of Israel and its spiritual preeminence. The glory of God was identified with the glory of Israel. Moreover, the limited scope that has hitherto been given to Jewish worship and ceremonial, whereby their uses were regarded as confined to those born in Israel, stood in the way of the Jews grasping fully the universal character of their mission: *op. cit.*, 167.

[21] Kohler, K.: *op. cit.*, 46.

[22] *Ibid.* 352; Montefiore, *op. cit.*, Ch. XV, takes, in the main, the same attitude as Kohler, although he attaches somewhat more value to legalism than Kohler. "Liberal Judaism," he says, "is still in a certain, modified sense . . . a legal religion." *op cit.*, 220. The modification consists in giving to the term "legal" the connotation not of specific juridical or ceremonial laws, but of law-mindedness as a trait of the ethical life.

[23] Kohler, K.: *op. cit.*, 482.

²⁴ *Ibid.*, 490.

²⁵ Montefiore looks forward to the universal adoption not only of the doctrine of Judaism but also of its ceremonies. "It is not sufficient," he says, "to offer to outsiders excellent doctrines without also offering to them forms and ceremonies. Religion is a whole, and the doctrines need a form. Men cannot do with doctrines (however excellent) alone. They require an historic ceremonial as well. Judaism must offer them both." *op. cit.*, 168.

²⁶ Montefiore, C. G.: *op. cit.*, 165 f.

CHAPTER IX

¹ Philipson, David: *The Reform Movement in Judaism,* 470, note 32; Bernfeld, Simon: *Toledot ha-reformazion ha-datit be-yisrael,* Warsaw, 1923, 21, 25.

² Cohon, Samuel S.: "The Theology of the Union Prayer Book," *C. C. A. R. Yearbook,* 1928, XXXVIII, 249, 250.

³ *C. C. A. R. Yearbook,* 1926, XXXVI, 300.

⁴ Morris Joseph, whose theology is in substantial agreement with that of the Reformists, attempts to show why onè cannot further the "universal truths" of Judaism as a Theist or Universalist. In answer to the question, "what does it matter by which particular race or sect the great task is accomplished?" he says: "The Jew owes allegiance to Judaism as well as to his mission, just as every Englishman owes loyalty not only to England's civilizing task but to England herself. . . . Loyalty is the first duty of the citizen and of the Jew alike. But, in the second place, the maintenance of Judaism as a distinct religion is itself faithfulness to the mission. . . . To disregard our distinctive Judaism . . . is to rob Theism of a powerful ally in the task she shares in common with Israel." *Judaism as Creed and Life,* New York, 1903, 186. The first reason approximates that nationalism which, while tolerated by Morris Joseph, is regarded by him as a survival of traditionalism, inconsistent with the more spiritual interpretation of Judaism. The second reason merely begs the question. Both reasons are advanced as an argument for prohibiting marriage between Jew and Gentile.

⁵ Philipson, David: *The Reform Movement in Judaism,* 356.

⁶ Cf. Maimonides: *Yad, Hilekot teshubah* III, 7 and comment of Abraham ben David (RaBaD).

⁷ Kohler, K.: *Jewish Theology,* 447.

⁸ Montefiore, C. G.: *Outlines of Liberal Judaism,* 66.

⁹ "To argue in general whether brotherhood, race equality, respect for personality, democratic participation, industrial democracy, are practical and desirable often means that no party to the discussion knows what the other person is talking about. . . . It often happens on the other hand, that members of a group say they agree in their belief in brotherhood, respect for personality, loyalty to the country, good will to other races, and at the same time it is discovered that they disagree radically as to what they would do in the concrete. This shows that when the principle is defined, they really disagree on the principle." Elliott, H. S.: *The Process of Group Thinking,* Association Press, New York, 1928, 56.

¹⁰ Committees have been appointed and resolutions drawn up bearing on the strife between capital and labor. *The Union Prayer-Book,* 1922, II, 314-17, contains a trenchant statement on the question to be recited once a year. All these measures are, however, about as potent as whistling at a thundering express train. The frequent appeals for cooperation between workers and employers are mere verbiage. "Cooperation toward what?" it has been asked. Each has his dominant objective: The employer asks for cooperation toward increased production; the worker toward increased wages. Just what, then, is implied in the appeal to cooperate?

¹¹ Dewey, John: *Human Nature and Conduct,* New York, 1922, 28.

¹² Montefiore, C. G.: *op. cit.,* 165.

¹³ "The conception of a Jewish *race,* in the biological sense, seems to be based on a misunderstanding. The word race is often used very loosely, but there is both anthropological and historical evidence against the existence at the present time of a Jewish race in the biological sense." Singer, Charles: "The Jewish Factor in Medieval Thought," *The Legacy of Israel,* Oxford, 1927, 180, note 1.

[14] Cf. Hertz, Friedrich: *Race and Civilization*, New York, 1928, 135.

[15] Kohler, K.: *op. cit.*, 446; Cf. Mielziener, M.: *Jewish Law of Marriage and Divorce*, Cincinnati, 1884, Ch. VII; Feldman, Ephraim: "Intermarriage Historically Considered," and Schulman, Samuel: "Mixed Marriages in Their Relation to the Jewish Religion," *C. C. A. R. Yearbook*, 1909, XIX, 271-335.

[16] Kohler, K.: *op. cit.*, 6.

[17] Joseph, Morris: *op. cit.*, 8.

[18] Kohler, K.: *op. cit.*, 447. He admits that "the cultivation of the Torah . . . effected more even than the preservation of monotheism," *op. cit.*, 362.

[19] *Protokolle der ersten Rabbiner-Versammlung*, Braunschweig, 1844, 61.

[20] *Protokolle und Aktenstücke der zweiten Rabbiner-Versammlung*, Frankfort a. M., 1845, 33.

[21] Reinhart, Arthur L.: *The Voice of the Jewish Laity—A Survey of the Jewish Layman's Religious Attitude and Practice*, Cincinnati, 1928, 29-30.

[22] "What are the Reform Sunday Schools spending today on the religious education of their children and how do these expenditures compare with expenditures made by other types of Jewish schools? The amount of money that congregations spend on the religious education of their children is certainly an index of the interest they have in this problem . . . whereas all the Jews of America are spending \$8,779,933.00 . . . we Reform Jews are only spending \$507,310.00 or 5.8 per cent of this amount. . . .

"Do our curricula, textbooks and methods reflect the changed conditions, and the new demands of American Jewish life? A study . . . shows that there is very little difference between the curricula of forty years ago and the curricula of today. . . . We have not developed courses of study which deal with many problems and difficulties which confront our children and young people. Our materials are extrinsic, and do not touch their lives; our worship services are often routine and stereotyped. . . . We will be unable to give our children the minimum essentials of Jewish education until we substitute the two-day a week school for our present Sunday school." Pollak, J. B.: "Forty Years of Reform Jewish Education," *C. C. A. R. Yearbook*, 1929, XXXIX, 408, 409, 417, 432.

[23] Haydon, E. Eustace: *The Quest of the Ages*, New York, 1929, 26.

[24] Matthews, Shailer: "Doctrines as Social Patterns," *Journal of Religion*, January, 1930, X, 1-15.

CHAPTER X

[1] Philipson, David: *The Reform Movement in Judaism*, 393.

[2] London, 1920.

[3] Friedlander, M.: *The Jewish Religion*, New York, 1923.

[4] New York, 1903, Preface, p. viii.

[5] *Ibid.*, p. ix.

[6] "For no authority," he says, "is greater than that which is wielded by the truth, and for the apprehension of the truth there is no instrument so trustworthy as reason." Joseph, Morris: *Judaism as Creed and Life*, 19.

[7] *Ibid.*, 40.

[8] *Ibid.*, 46.

[9] *Ibid.*, 44.

[10] *Ibid.*, 51-59.

[11] *Ibid.*, 22.

[12] *Ibid.*, 166.

[13] *Ibid.*, 186.

[14] *Ibid.*, 170.

[15] *Lam. Rabba*, I, 16.

[16] *Jer. Berakot* II, 5a.

[17] Joseph, Morris: *op. cit.*, 10.

[18] *Ibid.*, 11.

[19] *Ibid.*, 12.

[20] London, 1907.

[21] *Ibid.*, 153 f.

[22] *Ibid.*, 87, 89.

CHAPTER XI

[1] Cf. Philipson, D.: *The Reform Movement in Judaism*, Ch. I, and notes.

[2] S. R. Hirsch is the only one among the defenders of orthodoxy whose presentation is lucid, logical and consistent. One may disagree with his fundamental premise, but once his premise is granted, for argument's sake, the majority of his conclusions are inevitable. Cf. Hirsch, S. A.: "Jewish Philosophy of Religion and Samson Raphael Hirsch," *A Book of Essays*, London, 1905, 167-218.

[3] New York, 1899.

[4] In his writings, he frequently indicates that his appeal is mainly to the younger generation of his day. This is significant insofar as it shows that the Neo-Orthodoxy advocated by Hirsch is a conscious and deliberate attempt to meet the challenge of modernity. In every instance, he urges the young to overcome the anti-Judaistic tendencies of an age which is marked by a complete upset of traditional human values, and to anchor themselves to the one certainty amidst the sea of doubt, to God and his word.

[5] *Peninè SHaDal*, Przemśl, 1888, 410-421.

[6] Hirsch, S. R.: *Horeb, Versuche über Jissroel's Pflichten in der Zerstreuung*, Frankfort a. M., 1899, Introduction, xii.

[7] S. R. Hirsch states emphatically that it is wrong to believe in God as a result of personal experience and study. God, according to him, should serve as the very premise by virtue of which the world and the self possess reality. He reminds the reader that the God of the Torah is the creator, whereas the human mind is qualified to understand only the created world, and even the created world only to the extent to which man can bring it within the sphere of his influence. The Torah reveals only what God must mean to man, not what God is in himself. Whatever has no direct bearing on life, it is futile for the understanding to try to grasp, and even if grasped, would be of no consequence. Before you set out upon any investigation, be sure that its object is attainable and that it is a means to the furtherance of life. The search which is prompted solely by curiosity without regard to the value for human life or the object sought for, is a denial of God's transcendence and an audacious transgression of the bounds set up by God. It is harmful because it leads to doubt and discontent. Only such knowledge as has no relevance to the way in which we should serve God and obey his will is outside the province of the human mind. *Ibid.*, Introduction.

[8] Hirsch, S. R.: *Nineteen Letters of Ben Uziel*, translated by Bernard Drachman, Funk and Wagnalls, New York, 1899, 37.

[9] *Ibid.*, 47.

[10] 1854-55, I, 17-18.

[11] *Ibid.*, 18-19.

[12] "Grundlinien einer jüdischen Symbolik," *Jeschurun*, 1857, III, 615-630.

[13] Hirsch, S. R.: *Horeb*, Introduction, vii.

[14] *Ibid.*, 72.

[15] Hirsch, S. R.: *Nineteen Letters of Ben Uziel*, 103 f.

[16] *Ibid.*, 132.

[17] Judah Ha-Levi: *Kitab Al Khazari*, I, par. 103; Cf. Margolis, Max L.: "The Theology of the Old Prayer Book," *C. C. A. R. Yearbook*, 1897-98, 1-10.

[18] *Sanhedrin* 59a.

[19] *Emunot WeDeot*, III, 7.

[20] Hirsch, S. R.: *Nineteen Letters of Ben Uziel*, 67.

[21] *Ibid.*, 66.

[22] *Ibid.*, 69.

[23] *Ibid.*, 80, 82.

[24] *Ibid.*, 84.

[25] *Ibid.*, 84.

[26] *Ibid.*, 86.

[27] *Ibid.*, 162; Cf. Hertz, J. H.: *Affirmations of Judaism*, London, 1927, 128. Dr. Hertz is an avowed adherent of the orthodox school of thought. Yet he is an ardent Zionist, and places the participation in the rebuilding of Palestine on a par with religious observance and synagogue affiliation as the principal manifestation of loyalty to God and to Israel.

CHAPTER XII

[1] Gotthard Deutsch published in 1898 a critique of orthodoxy, centering his arguments upon the one specific principle then avowed by the representatives of the Union of Orthodox Jewish Congregations: "We affirm our adherence to the acknowledged codes of our rabbis." Deutsch maintained, "There is no Orthodoxy.

"1. Because there is no authority to decide what is orthodox and what is not.

"2. Because our codes have never been recognized as official and authentic interpretations of Judaism.

"3. Because they contain superstitious views which are untenable.

"4. Because they pre-suppose that the fundamental views of sciences are false.

"5. Because their ritual practices are impracticable in our days.

"6. Because in many instances they provoke our feelings by trickery.

"7. Because dogmas like all human knowledge have to be revived by enlarged experience." *Modern Orthodoxy*, Chicago, 1898, 26.

[2] Cardinal Newman is quoted as having said, "If I must submit my reason to mysteries, it is not much matter whether it is a mystery more or a mystery less."

[3] Cf. Birnbaum, Nathan: *In Dienste der Verheissung*, Frankfort a. M., 1927; Herrmann, Leo: *Nathan Birnbaum, sein Werk und seine Wandlung*, Berlin, 1914; *Vom Sinn des Judentums, Ein Sammelbuch zu Ehren Nathan Birnbaum*, Frankfort a. M., 1925.

[4] *Shulḥan Aruk*, fly leaf of Vilna edition.

[5] *Baba Batra* 54b.

CHAPTER XIII

[1] *Protokolle und Aktenstücke der zweiten Rabbiner-Versammlung*, Frankfort a. M., 1845, 18-19.

[2] Holdheim and Einhorn resented Frankel's charge that the rabbinical conferences at Brunswick and Frankfort paid no attention to principle and retorted that his principle concerning "positive historical Judaism" was meaningless. Cf. *Ibid*, 161.

[3] Greenstone, Julius H.: *The Jewish Religion*, The Jewish Chautauqua Society, Philadelphia, 1929, 180.

[4] *Ibid.*, 216.

[5] *Ibid.*, 221.

[6] *Ibid.*, 222.

[7] *Baba Batra* 15a, Cf. *Sanhedrin* 99a.

[8] Greenstone, *op. cit.*, 219.

[9] *Ibid.*, 220.

[10] Güdemann, Moritz: *Jüdische Apologetik*, Glogau, 1906, 3.

[11] Greenstone, *op. cit.*, 219.

[12] *Ibid.*, 233.

[13] *Ibid.*, 222.

[14] Nu. xxxi, 17.

[15] Greenstone, *op. cit.*, 196.

[16] *Ibid.*, 197.

[17] *Ibid.*, 198.

[18] *Ibid.*, 2.

[19] *Ibid.*, 32.

[20] *Ibid.*, 184.

[21] *Ibid.*, 269.

[22] *Ibid.*

[23] *Ibid.*, 270.

[24] *Ibid.*

[25] *Ibid.*, 226.

CHAPTER XIV

[1] Kohler, K.: *Jewish Theology*, 6.

[2] This definition of a civilization is a paraphrase of the definition of ethos in Sumner, William Graham: *Folkways*, Boston, 1906, 36.

[8] The realization that the conventional conception of Judaism as a religion is untenable has been expressed at various times. Cf. Immanuel Wolf's opening essay, "Ueber den Begriff einer Wissenschaft des Judenthums" in Zunz's *Zeitschrift für die Wissenschaft des Judenthums*, Berlin, 1822, I, 1-24; definitions of Judaism in *Zeitschrift für die religiösen Interessen des Judenthums*, Leipzig, 1846, III, 83. To Graetz Judaism was a synthesis of Jewish national life and religious truth. The Torah, the Jewish nation and the Holy Land, according to him, are in miraculous *rapport* with one another; they are bound together with an invisible cord. Without a firm foundation of Jewish national life, Judaism is like a hollow, half up-rooted tree, which continues to put forth leaves on top, while it is no longer capable of supporting branches and twigs. Cf. "Jewish Theses," by Bernard Felsenthal—Felsenthal, Emma: *Bernard Felsenthal, Teacher in Israel*, New York, 1924, 212-227. Gotthard Deutsch in his polemic against orthodoxy wrote "Judaism is a historic body, a body of people who belong together by community of sentiment, based on the community of history and who have the aims of their self-improvement in common. We wish to pursue the moral and intellectual aims of humanity within the limits of the Jewish people." *Modern Orthodoxy in the Light of Orthodox Authorities*, 26; Cf. Zangwill, I.: "The Position of Judaism," *The Voice of Jerusalem*, London, 1920, 131-44.
[4] Spengler maintains that the difference extends even to science. *The Decline of the West*, II, 172.
[5] Friedlaender, Israel: *Past and Present*, Cincinnati, 1919, 269-270.
[6] Haffkine, W. M.: "A Plea for Orthodoxy," *Menorah Journal*, April, 1916, II, 71, 76.
[7] A casual remark made in the course of a discussion often gives a truer summary of existing conditions than many volumes of lectures and essays. In the *C. C. A. R. Yearbook*, 1927, XXXVII, 270, one of the speakers who discussed a paper that had been read on "Adult Education in Religion" is quoted as saying: "During the last year, I found a surprising interest of my people, i.e., the adults, in subjects of Jewish concern. You know we have often to be apologetic when we bring a subject of Jewish interest, or shall I say Jewish non-interest, before our people—anything but that! We have to move carefully and 'walk softly' when we approach our young people as to the advisability of some Jewish problem." The experience of the speaker is no doubt shared by the overwhelming majority of American rabbis. There is nothing more discouraging than to be confronted with the attitude of complete un-interestedness in Judaism. The first step in breaking down that attitude is to abandon the very approach to Judaism as essentially a religion, and to stress its character as a civilization.
[8] Ahad Haam: "Imitation and Assimilation," *Selected Essays*, translated by Leon Simon, Philadelphia, 1912, 107-124.

CHAPTER XV

[1] Hirsch, S. R.: *The Nineteen Letters of Ben Uziel*, 75.
[2] "A Treatise Against Flaccus," *Works*, translated by C. D. Yonge, IV, par. 7.
[3] Cf. Dubnow, Simon: "Council of Four Lands," *Jewish Encyclopedia*, IV, 304-308; Lewin, Louis: *Die Landessynode der grosspolnischen Judenschaft*, Frankfort a. M., 1926; Vishnitzer, Mark: "The Lithuanian Vaad," *Menorah Journal*, March, 1931, XIX, 261-270.
[4] Cf. Baer, Fritz and Gelber, N. M.: "Gemeinde," *Encyclopœdia Judaica*, VII, 191-210; Nübling, E.: *Die Judengemeinden des Mittelalters*, Ulm, 1896, 25-52, 241-261; Scherer, J. S.: *Die Rechtsverhältnisse der Juden in den deutsch-österreichischen Ländern*, Leipzig, 1901, 1-105.
[5a] Burke, A. B.: *The Opus Majus of Roger Bacon*, Philadelphia, 1928, I, 75 f. I am indebted for this reference to Rabbi Herman Hailperin.
[5] Cf. *Anthropologie in pragmatischer Hinsicht*, Königsberg, 1800, 130, note.
[6] Spiegel, Shalom: *Hebrew Reborn*, New York, 1930. 21.
[7] Zangwill, Israel: "Language and Jewish Life," *The Voice of Jerusalem*, 245.
[8] *Decline of the West*, II, 120.
[9] Neh. xiii, 23, 24.
[10] Isa. xix, 18.

[11] *Canticles Rabba* IV, 12. An elaborate discussion of the question when Hebrew ceased to be the vernacular of the people is contained in Schneider, Mordecai Bezalel, *Torat ha-lashon b'hitpathutah*, Wilno, 1923-25, 11-59.

[12] Cf. Juster, Jean: *Les Juifs dans l'Empire Romain*, Paris, 1914, I, 365-68.

[13] Shulman, Eliezer: *Sefat yehudit-ashkenazit v'safrutah*, edited by J. H. Taviov, Riga, 1913.

[14] Cf. Steinschneider, Moritz: *Die hebraeischen Uebersetzungen des Mittelalters und die Juden als Dolmetscher*, Berlin, 1893; A. Leroy-Beaulieu: *Israel Among the Nations*, translated by Frances Hellman, New York, 1895, 275.

[15] The following conversation is revealing:
"I find the followihg conversation jotted down in my diary: Scene: Outside a Jerusalem *Bet Hamidrash*. A boy about nine or ten years old stares hard at me.
"Myself: 'Do you learn at the *Bet Hamidrash?*'
"Boy: 'Yes.'
"Myself: 'How old are you?'
"Boy: 'If God is willing I will be *bar-mizvah* in two years.'
"Myself: 'What are you learning?'
"Boy: 'Gittin (divorce).'
"Myself: 'Do you find it interesting?'
"Boy (aghast): 'Interesting? It is the word of God.'
"Myself: 'I suppose you study the Talmud in Hebrew?'
"Boy: 'Certainly not. In Yiddish. Only the atheists and Zionists learn and speak Hebrew.'
"Myself: 'How is it, then you speak Hebrew?'
"Boy: 'I have learned it from my sister.'
"Myself: 'Is she allowed to go to the schools of the Zionists?'
"Boy: 'Ach! She is only a girl.'"
Goitein, E. David: "The Little Things. . . ." *New Palestine*, December 30, 1927.

[16] Spiegel, Shalom: *Hebrew Reborn*, charmingly describes that revival.

[17] Cf. Fowler, W. Warde: *Religious Experience of the Roman People*, London, 1911.

[18] Deut. iv, 6.

[19] Gulak, Asher: *Yesode ha-mishpat ha-ibri*, Berlin, 1923, IV, for a description of the organization and procedure of the Jewish court.

[20] Lev. xviii, 5.

[21] Cornill, C. H.: *Music in the Old Testament*, Chicago, 1909, 2; Horodetzki, S. A.: "Ha-rikud ha-ḥasidi," *Moznayim*, January 28, 1932, III, for the important part played in Jewish life by the dance.

[22] Idelsohn, Abraham Zebi: *Jewish Music in Its Historical Development*, New York, 1929.

[23] Exod. xv, 2, and rabbinic interpretation in *Shabbat*, 133b.

[24] Cf. Asaf, S.: *Bate ha-din vesidrehem aḥare ḥatimat ha-talmud*, Jerusalem, 1924, and, *Ha-oneshin aḥare ḥatimat ha-talmud*, Jerusalem, 1922; "Gemeinde," *Encyclopædia Judaica*, Berlin VII, 191-210.

CHAPTER XVI

[1] Exod. xv, 11.

[2] Amos iv, 7; Isa. iii, 10, 11; Mal. iii, 10, etc.

[3] *Mishnah Abot* IV, 16.

[4] *Hilekot teshubah* IX, 2 f; *Hilekot melakim* XII, 4.

[5] *Religio Laici Judaici*, Bloch Publishing Company, New York, 1907, 78.

[6] *Ibid.*, 53-54.

[7] Neuman, Abraham A.: "The Keys of the Sanctuary," *Jewish Exponent*, Philadelphia, June 14, 1929.

[8] Apropos of the general question whether Jewish life is compatible with diversity of religious beliefs, the following is quoted as stating the modern view with regard to fellowship:
"It has been assumed that the greatest fellowship comes between people who are likeminded. Consequently, we tend to associate with persons who have the same

interests and who look at life the same way that we do. This is a relationship easier to secure, but it is not the highest form of fellowship. The fellowship out of which creative results emerge is that between persons concerned in the same area of life, but who have varying attitudes, convictions and experiences. Such a fellowship is an achievement worth while because it demands first, mutual respect; second, an attempt to understand the other person's point of view; and third, an effort to find a way out in which all can join wholeheartedly. It is creative because of the very richness of the contribution of diverse points of view." Elliott, H. S.: *Process of Group Thinking*, 183-184.

[9] Burgess, E. W.: The Family as a Unity of Interacting Personalities," *Family*, March 1926, VII, 4.

CHAPTER XVII

[1] Cf. Gen. xi, 1-9; Isa. x, 5-6, 13-16; Jer. xxv, 15-31; xlvi-xlix.

[2] Cf. Hayes, C. J. H.: *The Historical Evolution of Modern Nationalism*, New York, 1931.

[3] Cf. Baron, Salo: "Nationalism and Intolerance," *Menorah Journal*, June, 1929, XVI, 503-515; November, 1929, XVII, 148-158.

[4] *Decline of the West*, II, 363.

[5] Miller, Herbert Adolphus: *The Beginnings of Tomorrow*, New York, 1933, 45.

[6] *The Promise of American Life*, New York, 1909, 212 ff.

[7] Neumann, Fr. J.: *Volk und Nation*, Leipzig, 1888; Zangwill, Israel: *The Principle of Nationalities*, New York, 1917; Renner, Karl: *Das Selbstbestimmungsrecht der Nationen*, Leipzig and Vienna, 1918; *Der Kampf der oesterreichischen Nationen um den Staat*, 2nd edition, Leipzig, 1918; A summary of Renner's ideas will be found in Bauer, Otto: *Die Nationalitätenfrage und die Sozialdemokratie*, Vienna, 1924, 324-366.

[8] Stoyanovsky, J.: *The Mandate for Palestine*, London, 1928, 54.

[9] "The status of the Jews no longer constitutes a mere political issue within certain States, or a diplomatic issue between States, on the ground of humanitarian protection afforded them by such Powers as Great Britain, France and the United States; Jews as such have become subjects of rights and duties provided for by international law. This change was rendered possible by the widening of the scope of the law itself, as since the establishment of the systems of protection of minorities and of mandates international law may be said to begin with nations while previously it began with States. It is through this extension that Jews, constituting at the present time a nation without a corresponding State, could directly be dealt with by international law across the boundaries of the various States in which they reside." *Ibid.*, 55.

[10] If it is true that the Jews in Eastern Europe "played a decisive part in the enactment by the Paris Peace Conference of provisions for the protection of minorities," it is due to the agitation that had been carried on among them for almost a quarter of a century in behalf of the new cultural conception of nationhood. Janowsky, Oscar I.: *The Jews and Minority Rights*, 1898-1919, New York, 1933, 7.

CHAPTER XVIII

[1] Renan, Ernest: "Qu'est-ce qu'une nation?" *Discours et Conférences*, Paris, 1887, 306, 307.

[2] An interesting case in this connection is that of the eleven year old boy in the state of Washington who was taken away from his parents and placed out for adoption in another family because he had been taught by his parents to refuse to salute the flag. Van Waters, Miriam: "Parents in a Changing World," *Survey*, November 1, 1926, 140.

[3] The fact that the individual conscience can come into conflict with the state seems to have been overlooked. Cases have arisen recently of applicants for American citizenship who refused to take up arms in case America went into war. In the decision of the MacIntosh case rendered by Judge Martin T. Manton of United States Circuit Court of Appeals, June 30, 1930, Judge Manton, taking up at the same

time a similar case of a woman applicant, says: "This appellant said that she would promise to defend the Constitution as far as her conscience as a Christian would allow. The government, by its Constitution and its acts of Congress never exacted more from any applicant." *The New York Times*, July 1, 1930, 31. It appears that the conscience fares better when it is Christian than when it is non-sectarian.

[4] "Shifting the National Mind-Set," *The World Tomorrow*, February, 1924; Snedden, David: "Sociology, a Basic Science to Education," *Teachers College Record*, March, 1923, enlarges upon this point; Dickey, Louise Atherton: "Democracy in the Home," *World Tomorrow*, September, 1922, 267-268.

CHAPTER XIX

[1] The pragmatic interpretation of "election" which we here suggest in no way precludes the psychological interpretation of the idea as the religious experience of grace. We subscribe fully to the following description of the individual's inner experience of "election." "The recipient of divine grace feels and knows ever more and more surely, as he looks back on his past, that he has not grown into his present self through any achievement or effort of his own, and that, apart from his own will or power, grace was imparted to him, grasped him, impelled him, and led him." Otto R.: *Idea of the Holy*, translated by J. W. Harvey, London, 1928, 91. In the pragmatic interpretation we merely make explicit how the "elect" conceives the present self into which he has grown.

[2] Joseph, Morris: *Judaism as Creed and Life*, 156.
[3] I *Chron.* xvii, 21.
[4] Sumner, W. G.: *Folkways*, 14.
[5] *Authorized Daily Prayer Book*, 4.
[6] *Decline of the West*, II, 174.
[7] *Ibid.*, II, 24.
[8] *Ibid.*, II, 27.

CHAPTER XX

[1] Zimmern, Alfred E: *Nationality and Government*, London, 1918, 52.
[2] *Gen.* xii, 7.
[3] *Gen.* l, 24.
[4] *Ex.* iii, 8.
[5] *Ex.* vi, 7-8.
[6] *Ex.* xv, 16-17.
[7] Cf. *Isa.* xlix, 18.
[8] *Sifrè* on *Deut.* xxxvii, xxxviii.
[9] Statement by R. Eliezer b. Pedat, *Jer. Rosh ha-shanah* 58b.
[10] *Baba Batra* 91a.
[11] *Ketubot* 110b.
[12] *Pesahim* 87b.
[13] Macaulay, Thomas Babington: *Essay and Speech on Jewish Disabilities*, edited by I. Abrahams and S. Levy, Edinburgh, 1910, 53-54.
[14] *Sur Moses Mendelssohn, sur la reforme politique de juifs*, London, 1787.
[15] Ilfeld, Zebi Hirsh: *Dibere negidim*, Amsterdam, 1799.
[16] Cf. Hirsch, S. R.: *Nineteen Letters of Ben Uziel*, 159-168; Rapoport, Solomon Judah: *Tokahat megulah*, edited by R. Kirchheim, Frankfort a. M., 1845, 13.
[17] Cf. Gelber, N. M.: *Zur Vorgeschichte des Zionismus*, Vienna, 1927, 42-48.
[18] Series of League of Nations, *Publications*, 1930, VI A, 37, 38.
[19] "The report made for the government of which I was the head in 1919, by competent and experienced engineers stated that by well-planned schemes of irrigation one million acres could be added to the cultivatable area of Palestine and that by this plan sixteen persons could be maintained for every one there now." David Lloyd George: "Britain Facing Grave Imperial Crisis," *New York American*, Sunday, April 13, 1930, E-4.
[20] "A national home," says Norman Bentwich in "The Mandate for Palestine," *British Year Book of International Law*, 1929, 139, "connotes a territory in which a

people without receiving the rights of political sovereignty, has, nevertheless, a recognized legal position and receives the opportunity of developing its moral, social, and intellectual ideals." Felix Frankfurter, in "The Palestine Situation Restated," *Foreign Affairs*, April, 1931, IX, 415, states: "Authoritative Jewish demand is not for a Jewish state; it does not ask the right to govern others. Jews desire only the opportunity of national development within their ancestral land. What kind of polity will eventually emerge from the interplay of the two dominant cultures and races in Palestine, further complicated by Protestant and Catholic Christian influences, what place such a polity may assume in the British Commonwealth of Nations or in a possible federation of eastern peoples, no man is shrewd enough to foresee."

The effects of Jewish immigration into Palestine on the economy of the country in general, and on the prosperity of the Arab population in particular, is set forth with considerable detail in a pamphlet, *Immigration and Prosperity*, Tel Aviv, 1930. This pamphlet contains the evidence prepared for the Palestine Commission of Inquiry by S. Hoofien.

CHAPTER XXI

[1] Ross, E. A.: *Foundations of Sociology*, New York, 1920, 238.

[2] The chaos existing at present in Jewish communal life is revealed in the symposium conducted by the *Jewish Social Service Quarterly* in its issue of September, 1930. Two tendencies find expression in this symposium: one which holds that Jewish life is valuable and should be conserved, the other which regards Jewish life as unpromising and valueless and favors assimilation and ultimate dissolution.

The extremely negative attitude toward Jewish life is expressed in an anonymous article, "Facing Reality." The writer holds that there is nothing unique or different in Jewish life. It contains nothing which may not be obtained by assimilating in world humanity. Jewish "distinctiveness" is a result of definite economic and social restrictions; upon removal of these restrictions the Jew and his "distinctiveness" have disappeared. In America especially these artificial differences are being "mainstreeted" out of existence. With a vague vision of the time when all social work will be unnecessary, the writer indicts Jewish social work for forming a barrier to intergroup good-will.

Without the directness of the former article, H. L. Lurie, "Evidence from a Social Agency," expresses the same assimilationist tendency. He finds that although Jewish agencies serve Jewish clients, in technique and function these agencies possess little Jewish content. Although they strive to be tolerant of Jewish ceremonial, folkways and culture, they possess little understanding of the religious and cultural milieu of the various groups, and the tendencies point away from a specific Judaism toward what he calls a "modern social viewpoint." When Jewish custom is in conflict with American life, they favor the abandonment of Jewish custom. The adjustment that the agencies effect is not the adjustment of the Jewish heritage to another culture. It is the negation of the Jewish heritage.

Other writers take an affirmative attitude to the problem of the perpetuation of Jewish life in America. Jewish life is seen as a positive and valuable entity, which the Jewish communal agencies should foster. The agency should concern itself with the adjustment of Jewish family life to the American community, holds Violet Kittner, "As the Case Worker Senses It." It should contribute to Judaism and to Jewish survival in America. The writer feels that Jewish life should function effectively in America not by discarding its individuality, but by accepting that individuality and developing it.

The writer of the most vigorous article, John Slawson, "Communal Aspects," does not approach the problem of Jewish life from any polemic point of view. Jewish life exists, he argues; therefore, it should be reckoned with. It is active, varied, functioning; therefore, it should be encouraged to develop that experience. He considers as one of the chief aspirations in Jewish communal endeavor a *common underlying purpose* permeating all its activities: the purpose of raising Jewish life to as highly functioning a plane as possible. That implies self-adjustment to American culture along with the retention of what is significant in the heritage. This objective may be achieved by an integrated yet multiple approach, which takes cognizance of the many elements in the Jewish community, and of the many elements—religious, political, social, cultural—in Jewish life. It is an approach essentially Jewish in character, one that recognizes the value of Jewish education, and understands the meaning of Jewish group life in America. The Jewish community should not consider itself self-sufficient, but must develop an *international interest* in Jewish life, which should take the form of a concern with the upbuilding of Palestine, with east-European relief, with the protection of the civil, political, and religious liberties of Jewish minorities throughout the world. The writer proposes federation as the agency most fitted to achieve the realization of these aims, because it unites within itself many elements of the Jewish community, and can approach Jewish problems from their multiple aspect.

³ Purvin, J. F.: "My Synagogue Dues," *Opinion*, August, 1933, III, 13-15.

⁴ Sackler, H.: "The Kehillah of New York," *Communal Register*, New York, 1918, 47-73; Waldman, M. D.: "Cooperation Between All Groups in a Community," an address to the National Conference of Jewish Charities, Indianapolis, May 9, 1916, *Jewish Charities*, September, 1916, VII, 92-99.

⁵ *New York Kehillah Archives*, February, 1919 (mimeographed).

⁶ On page 543 is a chart of the Jewish Community Council of Pittsburgh, Pennsylvania, reprinted with the permission of Dr. Ludwig B. Bernstein. This was prepared in the spring of 1933. Mr. Israel A. Abrams suggested the plan of financing. The plan is proposed to take the place of the present community organization, the Federation of Jewish Philanthropies of Pittsburgh. The federation was felt to be primarily interested in a philanthropic program and as such fell far short of what the sponsors considered was an articulate desire for a new type of community-controlled and well-integrated Jewish organization. Some of the more interesting features of this plan are:

1. The General Assembly would be the ultimate governing body. It would be composed of representatives from the communal agencies and organizations. These latter would send delegates in accordance with their budgets. An agency having a budget from $5,000 to $25,000 a year would be entitled to one delegate. One with a budget from $25,000 to $50,000 would send two. The maximum number from any one agency would be four. Labor organizations, professional groups and others who work without budgets are allowed to send one delegate provided they have a minimum of twenty-five members.

2. The General Assembly would meet three times a year to discuss general policies and to designate one fourth of its numbers to serve as an Administrative Council. The Administrative Council will elect an Executive Council of fifteen to carry on the actual work.

3. There are to be four main divisions of the communal organization (see chart).

4. The division of religious organizations will have the following subdivisions:
    a. Temple and Synagogues.
    b. The Board of *Kashruth*.
    c. The *Beth Din* (court of arbitration, domestic relations).
    d. men's, women's and alumni organizations attached to the Temples and Synagogues.
    e. Committee on Cemeteries.

5. The division of cultural and educational organizations will be composed of the following sub-committees:
    a. Committee on Intensive Jewish Education, including *Talmud Torahs, Ḥedarim*, Hebrew Schools, Institutes and Training Schools for Teachers.
    b. Committee on Jewish Education of the non-intensive character (Sabbath Schools, Sunday Schools and Training Schools for Teachers).
    c. Committee on Extension Education, including the communal celebration of Jewish festivals and holidays (*Ḥanukah, Purim* and Passover) and on lectures of larger Jewish import to the community, possibly through the development of a Jewish lecture bureau.

6. Perhaps the most significant and revolutionary aspect of this plan is the democratic form of support which it provides. The total estimated budget of $270,000 is to be derived from the following sources:
    a. A sales tax on kosher meats, poultry and *maṣot* to yield.... $155,000
    b. An admission tax of $1.00 per person attending high holiday services in Synagogues and Temples to yield........   15,000
    c. Membership fees from the entire community ranging from $3.00 a year to a more generous fee for wealthier people   100,000

In a community of some 50,000 Jews the more generous fees at their best will be nowhere near the munificent gifts from the few wealthy, which federations still depend on, with all the attendant evils of patronage and absent control.

7. The budget is to be expended among the following:

a. Administration, complete executive staff offices	$ 25,000
b. Maintenance of spiritual heads of whole community	20,000
c. Maintenance of *Shoḥetim* and *Mashgiḥim*	30,000
d. Maintenance of cattle *Shoḥetim*	18,000
e. Maintenance of Jewish education	35,000
f. Cultural activities, forums, extension education, lecture courses	30,000
8. Maintenance of minor organizations	5,000
h. For all types of national and international organizations devoted to religious, educational and philanthropic objectives	100,000

The Jewish Welfare Board inaugurated on November 17, 1933, a plan for the Jewish community of Harrisburg, Pennsylvania, which though not so ambitious as the Pittsburgh plan is motivated by the same desire for a fully integrated, total expression of Jewish needs. The prospectus of the plan for which I am indebted to Mr. Harry Glucksman of the Jewish Welfare Board, New York, explains its aims as follows:

"It is proposed to form a new, all inclusive Jewish community organization, to be known as 'The Jewish Community of Harrisburg, Inc.,' to succeed the present Federation and to serve as the central agency for the support of the communal program of Harrisburg Jewry.

"While one of the purposes will be to raise the funds necessary to meet the present needs of Jewish education, relief and Jewish Center work, the new organization has larger objectives. It aims to aid in uniting all elements and groups in the community, the congregations, lodges, women's organizations, Workmen's Circle, as well as the beneficiary organizations of the Federation. It will be the one democratic body, expressing the will and the best interests of the Jewish community. It expects that every Jew in the community will become a member and have a voice in the affairs of the organization.

"It will utilize the existing organizations in the planning and conduct of a broad cultural and Jewish program for the benefit of the members.

"The new organization will plan for the orderly development of necessary institutions and activities essential to a dynamic and constructive development of Jewish life.

"The difference between the present Federation and the proposed organization is best illustrated by the fact that whereas under the existing arrangement a contributor received no direct benefits himself, under the new plan he and his family will.

"In the first place, every contributor will be a participating member with a voice in the Assembly.

"Secondly every contributor will be privileged to attend lectures and cultural meetings arranged by the organization.

"Every contributor will, if he so desires, be privileged to enroll his children in the Hebrew school.

"Each contribution will be credited towards full or partial membership in the Jewish Community Center, for himself, his wife and children.

"A community publication will be issued monthly, or more often, if funds permit, to each member of the new organization.

"These are tangible services. Much more important perhaps, is the value of this plan in establishing and continuing a firm basis upon which Jewish life in Harrisburg shall exist. The appeal for support of every Jew in Harrisburg is primarily an appeal for the support of a necessary and sound community program as a matter of duty to Jewish institutions.

"In addition, it appeals for the affiliation and identification of every Jewish citizen with a movement that strives to promote to the highest degree and in the largest measure the welfare of Harrisburg Jewry. It calls for intelligent action upon problems of local importance and of general Jewish significance."

A report, *The Federation As the Vital Community Agency*, submitted by the Committee on Finances and Governmental Welfare Policies of the National Council

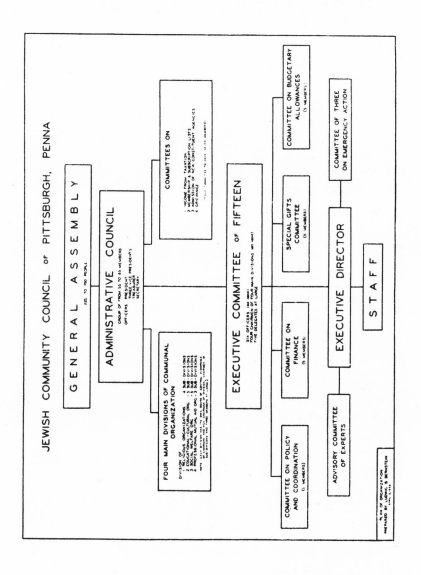

JEWISH COMMUNITY COUNCIL of PITTSBURGH, PENNA

GENERAL ASSEMBLY
225 TO 240 PEOPLE

ADMINISTRATIVE COUNCIL
GROUP OF FROM 55 TO 65 MEMBERS
OFFICERS
PRESIDENT
THREE VICE PRESIDENTS
TREASURER
SECRETARY

COMMITTEES ON
1 INCOME FROM TAXATION
2 MEMBERSHIP & SUBSCRIPTION LISTS
3 ADMISSION OF NEW CONSTITUENT AGENCIES
4 GRIEVANCE

FOUR MAIN DIVISIONS OF COMMUNAL ORGANIZATION
DIVISION OF
1 RELIGIOUS ORGANIZATIONS   4 SUB DIVISIONS
2 EDUCATIONAL-CULTURAL ORG.   3 SUB DIVISIONS
3 SOCIAL WELFARE ORG.   5 SUB DIVISIONS
4 PROFESSIONAL MUTUAL AID ORG.   3 SUB DIVISIONS

EXECUTIVE COMMITTEE of FIFTEEN
SIX OFFICERS (SEE ABOVE)
FOUR CHAIRMEN OF FOUR MAIN DIVISIONS (SEE ABOVE)
FIVE DELEGATES AT LARGE

COMMITTEE ON POLICY AND COORDINATION
(5 MEMBERS)

COMMITTEE ON FINANCE
(5 MEMBERS)

SPECIAL GIFTS COMMITTEE
(5 MEMBERS)

COMMITTEE ON BUDGETARY ALLOWANCES
(5 MEMBERS)

ADVISORY COMMITTEE OF EXPERTS

EXECUTIVE DIRECTOR

COMMITTEE OF THREE ON EMERGENCY ACTION

STAFF

PLAN OF ORGANIZATION
PREPARED BY LUDWIG B. BERNSTEIN

543

of Jewish Federations and Welfare Funds, prepared for discussion at the General Assembly, meeting at Chicago on January 6-7, 1934, lists nine factors which determine the demands upon Federation and then proceeds with the question:

"What reconstruction in the Federation program do these factors demand?

"1. An increasing emphasis upon those functions which will help Jewish families and individuals in the grave problems of social and economic adjustment arising out of our developing economic life.

"2. An increasing emphasis upon those functions which are so specifically Jewish that none but Jews can be expected to deal with them.

"The welfare of the Jewish group as a whole, with all that this involves in the furtherance of economic, social, political, religious, and cultural needs of the entire group, is the definite objective of organization in the Jewish community. The Federation has an important, if not primary responsibility in organizing the community for these objectives.

"May we not, therefore, formulate as working principles:

"1. That where public social work and the protective devices of social legislation are in operation, Jews will participate as citizens in the general community.

"2. That Jews will retain and foster services to help fellow-Jews make their adjustments in a new and rapidly changing American society.

"3. That Jews will shoulder the full and sole responsibility for distinctly Jewish community work.

"How would such a realistic approach affect our present procedure? Budgetary practice until now has allocated the bulk of Federation's funds to relief, health and child care; a small residuum for character building, Jewish culture and Jewish education; and little, if any, toward constructive projects for social and economic adjustments or for Jewish work of national and international character.

"Public agencies are steadily assuming responsibility for Jews, as for other citizens, who may need services in relief, health, and child care. This is exactly as it should be. We should encourage and strengthen it into accepted governmental policy. We should support all efforts for constructive programs which seek to improve the economic position of the masses. With the Federation gradually freed of primary relief demands, *should we not correspondingly release Federation funds for the support of constructive projects for economic and social welfare of the Jewish group and for other distinctively communal activities?*"

[7] Gordis, Robert: "Jewish Education in New York City," *Menorah Journal,* November, 1929, XVII, 133-144.

[8] Waldman, M. D.: "Federations in Jewish Philanthropy," *Menorah Journal,* IV, 111-122.

[9] Hexter, Maurice: "Certain Tendencies in Federation Movement," *Proceedings N. C. J. S. S.,* 1923, 127-137.

[10] Lowenstein, S.: "Federations and Local Non-Affiliated Societies," *J. S. S. Q.,* March, 1926, II, 151.

CHAPTER XXII

[1] Durkheim, Emile: *Elementary Forms of the Religious Life,* Allen and Univin, London, 430.

[2] Freud, Sigmund: *The Future of an Illusion,* New York, 1928.

[3] *Ibid.,* 43.

[4] "Religion and Science," *The New York Times Magazine,* November 9, 1930, 1.

CHAPTER XXIII

[1] Montefiore, C. G.: *Outlines of Liberal Judaism,* 78 f.

[2] Job xiii, 7.

[3] *Decline of the West,* II, 266.

[4] Montefiore, C. G.: *op. cit.,* 168.

[5] *Ibid.*

[6] As the historic religions are at present interpreted, even from the most liberal standpoint, there is no room in any of them for the frank renunciation of their ambi-

tion to become the religion of mankind. Universalism, messianism, spiritual imperialism, call it what you will, is the logical deduction from their basic premises about themselves. Christian thinkers of the most liberal schools would hesitate to concede permanency to Judaism. Surely, no one will accuse Claude Montefiore of being narrow, yet even he maintains that "Christianity itself seems to Jews only a state in the preparation of the world for a purified, developed and universal Judaism." *op. cit.*, 163. How far this is the case at the present time even in Christian liberal circles is evident from the question: "Is a 'Tolerant' Christianity Possible?", Eakin, Frank: *Christian Century*, February 26, 1930, 267-269. So integral to Christianity does intolerance appear to him that he cannot part with it unless he can be assured of some "moral equivalent."

CHAPTER XXIV

[1] Durkheim, Emile: *Elementary Forms of the Religious Life*, 348-349.

[2] Cf. Ames, Edward Scribner: *Psychology of Religious Experience*, Boston and New York, 1910, 280.

[3] "Magic Science and Religion," *Science Religion and Reality*, New York, 1928, 40.

[4] Cf. Durkheim, Emile: *op. cit.*, 47.

[5] The papacy went still further in insisting upon loyalty to the Pope as a prerequisite to salvation. "To be subject to the Roman pontiff we declare, say, define and pronounce to be absolutely necessary to every human creature to salvation." Boniface VIII, *Unam Sanctam*.

[6] Hayes, Carlton J. H.: *Essays on Nationalism*, New York, 1926, 93-125.

[7] Cf. Haydon, A. Eustace: *The Quest of the Ages*, 18 ff.

[8] *Decline of the West*, II, 69.

[9] Fichte maintained that Christianity was presented to the Teutons as part of the desirable equipment of the Romans. *Addresses to the German Nation*, translated by R. F. Jones and G. H. Turnbull, Chicago, 1922, Ch. VI.

[10] "Roman imperialism . . . ended by destroying the spirit of nationality. . . . Yet the empire, though it decayed as a fact, survived as an idea. It had a new and very remarkable lease of life in an idealized form, as the Roman Church. . . . In Christianity we may say with Seeley that the Jewish nationality had a new and boundless extension. The civilised world has adopted Jerusalem as its spiritual capital, and David and the prophets." Inge, W. R.: *Outspoken Essays*, Second Series, New York, 1923, 61-62.

[11] *National Character*, New York and London, 1927, 185.

[12] Saluting the flag is one of the rituals of patriotism. Like the ritual of traditional religion it is subject to abuse, the chief one being the facility with which the flag ritual is employed as a means of arousing a war spirit. Instead, however, of demanding the discontinuance of the ritual we should make it the means of purging patriotism of its selfishness. Cf. Guthrie, William Norman: *Religion of Old Glory*, New York, 1919.

[13] Keynes, J. M.: *Essays in Persuasion*, New York, 1932, 297.

[14] *Megilah* 29a.

[15] It is interesting to note that among the so-called radical elements in Palestine, there is a distinct yearning for religious self-expression. Cf. Schweiger, Izhak: *Yesod ha-hevei shelanu viyesirato, Ha-poel ha-sair*, April 11, April 25, May 1, 1930, XXIII.

[16] "Synagogue is a place for prayer, as is every other place—the open field or the bed-chamber—where man attunes his mind to communion with God. But Synagogue is first and foremost the place of public worship, a central meeting-place and a resting-place for the scattered congregations of the Jews. There they assemble to use, to display, and to assert their last common possession of religion, with the aid of a book of common prayer. Certain expressions in that book may or may not appeal to this or that member of the congregation. His feeling, however, may be disregarded, for the fault most probably lies in his own imperfect realization of the purpose which the Synagogue fulfils. Most probably he misses the sanction in history or tradition which attaches to the usage; and the remedy should first be sought in a careful study of the Prayer-book. Even so it is inevitable that the forms of public worship will not exactly correspond to the needs of the individual soul. Public

worship is bound in a certain degree to be crystallized by sentiment and made rigid by convention. Its 'atmosphere,' to use a stock phrase, is necessarily different from that of personal prayer, and any experiment which aims at a coalescence of the two must end in destroying the purpose for which the Synagogue exists." Magnus, Laurie: *Religio Laici Judaici,* 30-32.

We subscribe fully to the clearly stated distinction in function between private prayer and public worship, but we take exception to the inference that public worship is doomed to rigidity and conventionalism. This inference is in line with the philosophy of Conservative Judaism as expounded in that book.

CHAPTER XXV

[1] Bernfeld, Simon: *Mabo lekitebe ha-kodesh,* Berlin, Tel Aviv, 1923-1929, I-IV for a summary of the results of the critical study of the Bible; Schürer, Emil: *Geschichte des jüdischen Volkes im Zeitalter Jesu Christi,* Leipzig, 1901-11, ed. 4; Moore, George Foote: *Judaism,* Cambridge, 1927-1930, 3 vol., for the centuries after the period of Ezra through that of the Tannaim.

[2] To the extent that the *Aggadah* deals with the characters and incidents recorded in Scripture, it is a reconstruction of Israel's early past in terms of Torah and *miṣwot* as current values. The Sages conceived of Adam as having been given the six elementary laws of morality, *Gen. Rabba* XVI, 6 and *Sanhedrin* 56a. These were reiterated to Noah. Shem and Eber are credited with having conducted academies for the study of Torah, and Jacob is said to have fled there from the wrath of Esau, *Gen. Rabba* LXVIII, 5. Abraham is pictured as an elder presiding over an academy, and as having observed the details of the oral law, *Yoma* 28b. The three hundred and eighteen men who fought with him against the four kings, Gen. xiv, 14, were scholars of the law, *Nedarim* 32a. During Israel's sojourn in Egypt the study of Torah was maintained, *Yoma* 28b. Joshua, Saul, Doeg, Ahitophel, David, etc., were all immersed in the study of the Torah. In this vein the *Aggadah* reinterprets the beginnings of Israel.

[3] Jud. xi, 24.
[4] Jud. xi, 31.
[5] Jud. viii, 27; xvii; xviii.
[6] Gen. xii, 6-7; xviii, 1-19; xxvi, 23-25; xxviii, 10-22; xlvi, 1-3.
[7] Jer. xiv, 22.
[8] I Sam. v, 6 ff; xxv, 38; II Sam. xxi, 1 ff; xxiv, 1, 12 ff.
[9] I Sam. xxvi, 19; II Sam. xvi, 10 ff; xv, 31; I Kings xii, 15.
[10] II Sam. vii, 14-15.
[11] II Sam. xxiv, 1.
[12] The prophetic point of view also found expression in psalmody. It is therefore not surprising to find a psalm like the 82nd where YHWH is represented as taking the other gods to task for showing partiality to the wicked.
[13] Jer. vi, 16 f; Hos. viii, 12.
[14] Mic. iii, 11.
[15] Amos v, 18, 20.
[16] Theocracy is the term used by Josephus in describing the organization of the Jews. *Cont. Apion.* ii, 165.
[17] Cf. Josh. xxiv, 19.
[18] Cf. I Kings viii, 29, 33, 35; Dan. vi, 11.
[19] Cf. Ps. xix, cxix, etc.
[20] Is. xlix, 14-23; li, 3; lii, 7-12; liv, 1-8; xiv, 7; xviii; xlvii; liii, 7; lxix, 36-37; lxxx; lxxxv; lxxxix, 20-52; cvi; ix, 36-37; Dan. ix, 4-19; xii.
[21] Sanhedrin 90a.
[22] Sam. i, 28; Is. viii, 19, etc.
[23] Cf. "State of the Dead," Hastings: *Encyclopedia of Religion and Ethics,* XI, 841-843. The attitude of the present-day spiritists who affirm that the dead can and do commune with the living is a modern illustration of the way the belief in the continued existence of those who died need in no way influence one's religious beliefs and practices.
[24] Ps. vi, 6.
[25] Is. xxxviii, 18.

²⁶ Cf. Ezra iv.
²⁷ Ps. i; lxxiii; xciii.
²⁸ Dan. xii.
²⁹ Moore, G. F.: *op. cit.*, I, 110-121, 357-442; II, 279-396.
³⁰ In the numerous instances in *Targum Onkelos* and in the occasional passages in rabbinic literature in which anthropomorphic passages of the Scripture are translated or interpreted by some circumlocution that seems to steer clear of the anthropomorphism it is not the ascription to God of human qualities or attributes that accounts for the circumlocution, but the wish to avoid expressing an idea which is inconsistent with the supreme power and majesty of God. Cf. Luzzatto, Samuel David: *Oheb ger*, Vienna, 1830, 3-5.
³¹ Cf. *Gen. Rabba* I, 13; XII; *Mishnah Sanhedrin* IV, 5; *Jer. Berakot* IX; *Halakah* I, R. Eleazar b. Pedat.
³² *Abot* I, 14; IV, 13, 22; *Shabbat* 153a.
³³ *Yalkut* Ps. XXV.
³⁴ Ps. i, 2; xii, 7; xvi, 11; xix, 8-10; cxliii, 8-10; cxlvii, 19-20.
³⁵ *Lam. Rabba, Proem.; Jer. Hagigah* 76c.
³⁶ *Berakot* 5a; *Sifra*, ed. Weiss, *Behukotai*, VIII.
³⁷ Deut. xvii, 11-13.
³⁸ "Moses was apprised at Sinai of what every faithful disciple was destined to discover." *Jer. Hagigah* I, 76d.
³⁹ The Hasidic "Rebbi" is a resurgence of an institution which had long grown defunct in Judaism.
⁴⁰ Compare the status of R. Yohanan ben Zakkai with that of Hanina b. Dosa, *Berakot* 34b.
⁴¹ *Sifrè*, Deut. 154.
⁴² *Jer. Horayot* 45d.
⁴³ Cf. *Yad*, Hilkot Mamrim, III, 4.
⁴⁴ *Abot* II, 9.
⁴⁵ Cf. *Kiddushin* 39b.
⁴⁶ *Jer. Peah* 15d.
⁴⁷ *Kiddushin* 70b; Cf. *Yebamot* 47a.
⁴⁸ *Sifrè*, Behaaloteka 78; *Gen. Rabba* XXXIX, 14; *Num. Rabba* X, 1; *Cant. Rabba* V, 16.
⁴⁹ *Authorized Daily Prayer Book*, 48.
⁵⁰ *Tanhuma*, Lek leka, VI.
⁵¹ *Cant. Rabba* I, 6; Cf. Play on names of Jeremiah and Amos, *Ecc. Rabba* I, 2.
⁵² *Megilah*, 29a.
⁵³ *Gen. Rabba* I, 4; *Shabbat* 88a.
⁵⁴ *Berakot* 32b.
⁵⁵ Ahad Ha-Am: "Shilton ha-sekel," *Al parashat derakim*, Berlin, 1913, IV, 1-37.

CHAPTER XXVI

¹ "Individuality in Our Day," *New Republic*, April 2, 1930, LXII, 187.
² Rabinowitz, Saul Pinhas: *R. Yom Tob Lipman Zunz*, Warsaw, 1896; Rabinowitz, Saul Pinhas: *R. Zekariah Frankel*, Warsaw, 1898-1902; Ginzberg, Louis: *Students, Scholars and Saints*, Philadelphia, 1928, 195-251.
³ Bernfeld, Simon: *Mabo lekitebe ha-kodesh*, Berlin, 1923, I, 13.
⁴ "A Talmudic Problem," *Jewish Quarterly Review*, New Series, 1911-12, II, 88.
⁵ *Debir*, Berlin, 1924, II, 6.
⁶ Klausner, Joseph: *Yahadut va-anushiut*, Warsaw, 1910, I, 136.
⁷ *Jewish History*, Philadelphia, 1903, Ch. III.
⁸ The tradition recorded in I Kings xii, 28, is that Jeroboam set up two golden calves, one at Dan and the other at Beth El. "Calf" is a term of derision used by scriptural writers for the image of the bull, which was adopted by the Israelites. The Pentateuch assigns the origin of bull worship to the Israelites at Sinai. Another tradition recorded in the Book of Judges xvii, xviii, traces the origin of the worship at the sanctuary of Dan to the invading Danites. The image that Gideon made was probably also a bull, Jud. viii, 22-28. The inference to be drawn from all of these

traditions is that the worship of the bull was not known to the Israelites during their nomadic stage, and that they adopted it as part of agricultural civilization.

[9] Torczyner, Harry: "Die Bundeslade und die Anfänge der Religion Israels," *Festschrift . . . der Hochschule für die Wissenschaft des Judentums*, Berlin, 1922, 219-297.

[10] Cf. Abraham b. David of Posquières: Comment on *Hilekot teshubah* III 7. Cf. Graetz, H.: *Geschichte der Juden*, Leipzig, 1894, VII, 28-58, for the activities of the Anti-Maimunists.

[11] Powys, John Cowper: *The Meaning of Culture*, W. W. Norton, New York, 1929, 7-8.

[12] Barnes, H. E.: *Twilight of Christianity*, New York, 1930.

CHAPTER XXVII

[1] Judah Ha-Levi: *Kitab Al Khazari* I, 47.

[2] Deut. iv, 6.

CHAPTER XXVIII

[1] Montefiore, C. G.: *Outlines of Liberal Judaism*, 298-299.

[2] Popenoe, Paul: *The Conservation of the Family*, Baltimore, 1926.

[3] A form of legal procedure has been worked out by Rabbi J. L. Epstein in his *Lemaan takanat agunot*, New York, 1930.

[4] In 1931 there were at least 10,000 cases of Jewish women in eastern Europe whose husbands had abandoned them, had journeyed to other countries and had re-married. These women are compelled to abide all their life in a thraldom from which the Jewish community does nothing to free them. The existence of such a condition contributes largely to the spread of prostitution and white slavery. The facts disclosed at a recent conference in London to deal with the problem of white slavery among Jews reveal the tragic effects of the unwillingness of orthodox authorities to deal with the situation in an enlightened manner.

[5] Cf. Abrahams, Israel: *Jewish Life in the Middle Ages*, London, 1932, Ch. I, II.

CHAPTER XXIX

[1] *Mishnah Yoma* VIII, 9.

[2] The term *hok* (statute) is interpreted as a law which is issued as a decree the reason for which is not intended to be revealed, *Pesikta derab Kahana* IV.

[3] "The ceremonial law was to offer inducements to personal and social intercourse between teacher and pupil, the inquirer and the instructor, and to excite and encourage competition and emulation." Mendelssohn, M.: "Jerusalem," *Gesammelte Schriften*, Leipzig, 1843, III, 350.

[4] *The Guide for the Perplexed*, translated by M. Friedlaender, London, 1910, Ch. XXVI-XLIX.

[5] Cf. Bentwich, Norman: *Philo-Judaeus of Alexandria*, Philadelphia, 1910, 40.

[6] Cf. James, William: *Varieties of Religious Experience*, New York, 1919.

[7] *Sotah* 17a.

[8] Joseph, Morris: *Judaism as Creed and Life*, 189.

[9] Maimonides: *op. cit.*, Ch. XXV, XLVIII.

[10] Cf. Aronstam, N. E.: *Jewish Dietary Laws from a Scientific Standpoint*, Detroit, 1904; Macht, David L.: "Scientific Aspects of the Jewish Dietary Laws," *The Jewish Library*, New York, 1930, II, 203-225.

[11] A detailed discussion of the dietary laws and specific suggestions as to the manner of their observance is contained in Wiener, A.: *Die jüdischen Speisegesetze nach ihren verschiedenen Gesichtspunkten*, Breslau, 1895.

[12] *Versuche über Jissroel's Pflichten*, Frankfort a. M., 1899, 57-85.

[13] *Outlines of Liberal Judaism*, 249.

[14] Joseph, Morris: *op. cit.*, 208.

[15] Lev. xviii, 3; Cf. *Sifra* on verse; Maimonides: *Yad.* Hilkot abodat koka-bim, XI.

[16] *Cant. Rabba* IV, 12.

[17] Cohen, A.: "The Jewish Garb," *Jewish Chronicle Supplement,* November 29, 1929, p. iv; Abrahams, Israel: *Jewish Life in the Middle Ages,* 302 ff.

[18] Among the survivals of medieval persecution in the early nineteenth century was the attempt of some European governments to prohibit the adoption of Gentile names. Leopold Zunz, "Namen der Juden," *Gesammelte Schriften,* Berlin, 1876, II, 1-82, brought to bear his extraordinary learning and memory upon the history of names to prove that Jews have always been in the habit of using foreign names. They ought, therefore, to be permitted to continue that habit.

[19] Bills of divorce which contain Gentile names are valid "because Jews who live outside of Palestine bear Gentile names." *Jer. Gittin,* Ch. I, Halakah I.

[20] The Reformists have ignored the calendar in their educational work and in their prayer-book. The only means the layman has of knowing when the festivals of the year occur is to consult the calendar in use by the orthodox.

[21] Gorin, B.: *Geschichte fun idishn teater,* New York, 1923, 2 vol.; Schipper, I.: *Geschichte fun idisher teater kunst un drame,* Warsaw, 1923-25, 2 vol.; *Archiv far der geshichte fun teater un drame,* edited by J. Shatsky, New York and Wilno, 1930, I.

[22] Cf. *Prospectus of the Society,* St. Petersburg, 1912.

[23] Powys, John Cowper: "A Modern Mystery Play," *Menorah Journal,* August, 1927, XIII, 361.

[24] Cf. Kedem-Hebrew Theatre Guild of America, *Prospectus,* New York.

[25] *Jewish Daily Bulletin,* July 16, 1933.

CHAPTER XXX

[1] Cf. Lazarus, M.: *The Ethics of Judaism,* Philadelphia, 1900, I, 95 ff.

[2] *Ibid.,* 1-107.

[3] It is now generally recognized that for character formation and improvement it is not enough to set up an ideal, and then urge the individual to live up to it, regardless of his heredity, environment and circumstances. These elements that enter into the formation of character offer sufficient variety and scope for adult study.

[4] *Berakot* 63b, the statement of R. José b. Ḥanina.

[5] Aḥad Ha-Am: *Al parashat derakim,* Berlin, 1904, II, 123.

[6] A striking evidence of the failure of Jewish scholarship to relate its learning to the troublesome questions of Jewish life is its timidity in dealing with the question of the modern scientific attitude toward the Bible. Although most of the modern Jewish scholars tacitly assume that attitude toward the Bible, not one of them has made any attempt to face the issue squarely and to point out the implications of the scientific conception of the Bible and of the origin and development of Jewish religion, for belief, practice, and the education of the young. There are rabbinical institutions which omit the teaching of the Pentateuch and of the modern period in Jewish history in order to escape the need of dealing with current issues that are vital to Judaism. An attitude of this kind in institutions of advanced Jewish learning is one of the most serious obstacles to the reconstruction of Jewish life.

[7] "Personality: How to Develop It," *Essays in Honor of John Dewey,* New York, 1929, 15.

[8] Shohet, David M.: *The Jewish Court in the Middle Ages,* New York, 1931.

[9] *Abot* V, 13.

[10] *Ibid.,* III, 19.

CHAPTER XXXI

[1] This view is seldom articulated by the Reformists. Other religious bodies have a more sound philosophy of the relation of religion to education. In referring to modernist educators the Pope says, "But many of them with, it would seem, too great insistence on the etymological meaning of the word, pretend to draw education out of human nature itself and evolve it by its own unaided powers. . . . Hence, every form of pedagogic naturalism which in any way excludes or weakens super-

natural Christian formation in the teaching of youth is false. Every method of education, founded wholly or in part on the denial or forgetfulness of original sin and of grace, and relying on the sole powers of human nature, is unsound." Pope Pius XI: *Encyclical Letter on the Christian Education of Youth,* January 11, 1930.

In 1927, a bill was introduced in the California State Senate to release children from public schools, known as the Cobb Release Bills Nos. 145, 146, 147. A similar bill known as the Miller Bill had been introduced and defeated in 1925.

The following from the resolutions of the Liberal Ministers of Los Angeles County is indicative of what is coming to be regarded as the place of religion in education:

"The measure, if carried out, would give to the children what we hold to be an entirely erroneous idea of religion—teaching them that it is something apart from the rest of life, a subject to be learned like arithmetic or geography. Whereas we hold that it is a spirit that should permeate all life, something that cannot be taught, but can be communicated by the contagion of a person who himself possesses it. Wherever you have a consecrated teacher, there religion is being taught, no matter what the subject. Our position is well represented by the following quotation from L. P. Jacks, Principal of Manchester College, Oxford, England.

"In his book on *A Living Universe,* L. P. Jacks relates a conversation with a schoolmaster. 'Where in your time-table do you teach religion?', asked Mr. Jacks. 'We teach it all day long,' replied the teacher. 'We teach it in arithmetic by accuracy. We teach it in language by learning to say what we mean. . . . We teach it in history, by humanity. We teach it in geography, by breadth of mind. We teach it in handicraft, by thoroughness. We teach it in astronomy, by reverence. We teach it in the playground by fair play. We teach it in kindness to animals, by courtesy to servants, by good manners to one another, and by truthfulness in all things. We teach it by showing the children that we, their elders, are their friends and not their enemies.' "

² Cf. Gamoran, Emanuel: *A Survey of 125 Religious Schools Affiliated with the Union of American Hebrew Congregations,* Cincinnati, 1925.

³ Cf. Dushkin, Alexander M.: *Jewish Education in New York City,* New York, 1918, Ch. I; Gamoran, Emanuel: *Changing Conceptions in Jewish Education,* New York, 1924, book II.

⁴ The classification is based on the one formulated by Samuel Dinin, *Judaism in a Changing Civilization,* New York, 1933, 202-204.

⁵ Jews remember what church-ridden states formerly did to their ancestors, and in their effort to keep the public educational institutions free from all sectarian influences, appeal continually to the fundamental law of the United States, which demands the complete separation of state from church. The resistance which Jews everywhere display to the introduction of Bible reading into the schools is perfectly understandable and justified, because the spirit in which those who seek to make Bible reading a part of the school curriculum is sectarian. It is strange, however, that those who are so violently opposed to having the Bible read in the school should be so complacent about the fact that the public schools make churchly religion so prominent a part of the school curriculum on Christmas and Easter.

On the other hand, the Jews allow themselves to be maneuvered into a position which prevents their own children from ever gaining a knowledge of the Bible. Obviously, Jewish children will not get to know the Bible, if they are to depend solely for that knowledge upon their religious or Hebrew schools. Some constructive plan must be worked out that would keep inviolate the American ideal of separating state from church, and provide a means of having Jewish children know the Bible. The solution must consist in urging that both the Old and the New Testament be taught in the public schools as literature, and not as religious texts.

⁶ Another practical task which will have to be performed as a prerequisite to the teaching of the Bible as literature will have to be the writing of textbooks and the training of teachers with that end in view. This will involve considerable discussion and planning. Greater tasks, however, have been accomplished, and it would be to the credit of the Jew if he were to contribute to the enrichment of the American mind by helping in the movement to render it acquainted with the great human values contained in the Bible. By advocating such a solution, Jews would give proof of their desire to integrate their life as Jews into their life as Americans. They would demonstrate their ability to draw moral inspiration not only from their own institu-

tions but also from the institutions of the land. Through that solution Jews would come to include the American school system in the educative process whereby they want to train their children to live as Jews as well as Americans.

[7] The point of view implied in the above conception of Jewish civic activity is different from the one recently developed in certain quarters, which makes the club a form of extension education. The idea at the basis of extension education is that under present circumstances only a limited number of Jewish children can be given an intensive Jewish education. It is therefore considered advisable that those, who would otherwise remain completely ignorant, have an opportunity of getting some knowledge about Judaism. The trouble with this point of view is that it makes knowledge, instead of participation in Jewish life, the criterion of Jewish education. Nevertheless, some very excellent suggestions can be obtained from the experiments in extension education for Jewish civic groups. Cf. Emanuel Gamoran: *Changing Conceptions in Jewish Education*, New York, 1924, book II, 163-168. Of a more direct bearing is the work done by the Tzophim Jewish Civics Club, under the auspices of the Board of Jewish Education in Chicago. Cf. Manual and other mimeograph publications on the subject, by the Chicago Board of Jewish Education.

[8] An interesting experiment is being tried out in the little community of Walden, New York. A church known as a Cathedral for All Children was established by the Episcopal Church of St. Andrews in that town. The architecture of the church is designed entirely to appeal to the imagination of the children. The children constitute a congregation, which duplicates in every respect the congregations of their elders. They have their own officials, deacons and preachers, and conduct their own services, which are adapted to their own tastes and understandings. They present, in addition, the old mystery plays which give them an opportunity to express their religion in a natural and child-like way. Anne Lee: "A Cathedral for Children . . ." *New York Times Magazine*, May 2, 1926, 6.

[9] Coe, George A.: *The Motives of Men*, Charles Scribners, New York, 1928, 107.

[10] Cf. *C.C.A.R. Yearbook*, 1925, XXXV, 332.

The Aleph Zadik Aleph of the B'nai B'rith is composed entirely of young men between the ages of 16 and 21. In the few years it has been organized, it has spread all over the United States and into Canada. It professes Jewishness in all its aims and cultural activities. Its program is commonly referred to as being "Five Fold and Full." It consists of activity which tends to:

> First, advancement of religious observances
> Second, revival of Hebrew
> Third, participation in communal efforts
> Fourth, advancement of Jewish culture
> Fifth, participation in social and athletic activity.

From the circular letter sent out February 25, 1931, from office of the Executive Secretary, Omaha, Neb.

[11] Cf. *1933 Directory of Summer Camps under the Auspices of Jewish Communal Organizations* compiled by the Jewish Welfare Board, New York City.

[12] It ought to be more generally known than it is that the various European national groups in some of the larger cities have succeeded in having their language, literature, history and art recognized as part of the public and high school curricula. This is the case with such national groups as the Poles and Czecho-Slovakians in Chicago, the Germans in Omaha, the Irish in Boston, and likewise with other European groups. Cf. Cotton, Thomas L.: "Tetigkeit fun kulturele grupen in Amerike," *Yidishe Kultur Gezelshaft Buletn*, New York, no. 3, January, 1930.

[13] The memorandum presented by a number of Jewish leaders to the Board of Education of New York City meets effectively the objections advanced against the introduction of Hebrew as an elective into the high school curriculum. The main objection which had been raised against including Hebrew in the curriculum was that Hebrew could not be taught except as a religious subject. The following is an extract from the memorandum:

"Objection Raised

"In the two memoranda received from Associate Superintendent Campbell, certain hesitations or so-called objections to the inclusion of the study of Hebrew as an elective subject are indicated. They seem to grow out of two main assumptions which are founded upon incomplete facts, and therefore lead to strange and erroneous conclusions. The first assumption is that Hebrew has primarily religious values, and the second is, that college requirements are the chief criteria for the determination of the high school curriculum.

"Universal and Cultural Values of Hebrew

"Hebrew, too, has its non-religious values. It, too, contains a very rich and significant body of non-religious literature. It is the language of an historic people which has classic origins, and which has continued to develop its literature through medieval and modern times. It is the language of a living people which is international and constitutes about one-third of the community of New York City. The language and literature of such a people must have its universal cultural values. . . .

"He who speaks only of the religious literature which has been expressed in Hebrew is evidently ignorant of the many poets, novelists, essayists, historians and even scientists who have used Hebrew as their vehicle of expression. Today in Palestine and in certain parts of Eastern Europe, Hebrew is the language of instruction in the three R's, in nature study, in mathematics, physics, in chemistry, medicine, engineering, architecture, philosophy, jurisprudence. It is the language of commerce and newspapers. Every year sees hundreds of new volumes in Hebrew on all subjects produced in Palestine, Eastern Europe and America. In Palestine and Eastern Europe, young people get their knowledge of Shakespeare, Mark Twain, Goethe, Tolstoi, Anatole France and others only through the medium of Hebrew. In this country, there are young Americans with college degrees singing of the beauties of the Hudson, of the Catskills and of the grandeur of the great Western scenes, in Hebrew poetry and prose. . . .

"While it is true that more Jewish than non-Jewish pupils in New York City may be expected to elect Hebrew, this fact does not render the language sectarian any more than the fact that Italian children may elect Italian or German children, German. Democracy demands the recognition of all cultural values, and the free opportunity for all pupils whatever their origin, to elect the studies which prove of interest and value to them. . . .

"Sociological Values of Studying Hebrew in New York Public High Schools

"There are, however, certain other important reasons for the introduction of Hebrew as an elective subject in the public high schools, which should recommend themselves to the modern educator. Not only has Hebrew universal cultural values and some utilitarian values, but it has certain definite sociological values in the community of New York City. In his memorandum, Dr. Campbell refers to the modern conception of culture, as follows:

'Our modern conception of culture represents the possession of a mental equipment that enables one to participate in the daily affairs of life to the fullest degree of self-realization and to the greatest contribution to Society.'

This thought is quite correct. Let us face the facts frankly. About 53% of the pupils in the high schools of New York City are of Jewish parentage. To what degree is the public school system helping these children towards a 'self-realization and towards the greatest contribution to society.' The student of social and educational conditions amongst the Jews in this city is repeatedly confronted with the physical and psychological maladjustments among the Jewish youth which can be traced to the effects of public school education, which have estranged child from parent. The Jewish child has been given a new set of values and has grown up in ignorance of those of his forebears. He has frequently grown up not only to misunderstand his parents and the people from whence he sprung, but to dislike them and to consider them a burden. The Jewish child who might have had the benefits that come from values in an historic culture has been denied those benefits because of a peculiar attitude towards the teaching of his people's history and his literature. The teaching of Hebrew may reestablish for the Jewish child a harmonious relationship between himself and his parents. It may help him to get rid of certain sources of unhealthy psychologic and social complexes. It will restore his self-respect and the respect for his past and his people. He will discover a rich cultural heritage which should give him greater strength of character and psychological poise. It may develop in him a sense of 'noblesse oblige' and a desire through further study to contribute to the cultural values of America.

"The Modern View

"The American educator recognizes the cultural values which immigrant groups may contribute to the civilization of America. The modern educator who regards self-realization for the individual as an aim in education is compelled to reckon with the family connections, the social and cultural background of the individual, as inherent factors in the process of education. The progressive educator will regard the introduction of Hebrew as an elective subject in the public high schools of New York City as an expression of current sociologic and democratic tendencies in education. The modern philosopher and statesman can view such a gesture as another evidence of the movement towards goodwill and mutual understanding amongst all classes of society, as well as amongst the various peoples of the world." . . . [MS] *Reasons . . . for the Introduction of the Teaching of Hebrew as an Elective Subject in the High Schools of the City of New York.* . . . *Prepared by Israel S. Chipkin,* 1-5.

[14] Ultimately the function of the Jewish teacher would resemble somewhat that of the social worker. "I do see the time coming when the functions and duties of the social worker will be more far-reaching than they are today—when they will include the problems of education and home conditions. In this manner we may be able to bring about a rejuvenation of those contacts that should exist among the synagogue, the school and the home." Frankel, Lee K.: "American Jewry," *Jewish Tribune,* February 7, 1930, XCVI, 30.

[15] At present, the function of pastor included among the numerous other duties of the rabbi must resolve itself into an invitation to dinner, which is followed by a card game. The rabbi is thus deprived of time which he ought to employ in study, writing, and communal work, while his pastoral duties are limited to perfunctory and formal visits at the homes of his congregants.

[16] Cf. Scharfstein, Zvi: "Traditional versus Historical Approach in the Teaching of the Bible," *Jewish Education,* January, 1930, II, 4-16.

[17] The literal meaning referred to in the Talmudic dictum, "No scripture is to be deprived of its literal meaning," (*Shabbat* 63a) is not the same as to a modern exegete.

[18] Claude Montefiore meets the question of the effect of routine in prayer somewhat differently. "It is very important that teachers and parents should tell children that they cannot expect to find and possess and receive all the benefits of prayer at once or very soon. But they must not relax or abandon the habit, which in later life it may be difficult to acquire again. Let them not be *too greatly* troubled because at any time they think that their prayers are mechanical, or that they do not *experience* all the happiness or satisfaction which it is said that prayer can give or has given. It is not prayer that is at fault, and it is not necessarily themselves. The experience and the help and the satisfaction may come gradually. The best persons do not *always* feel the benefit of prayer. . . . Here, as in other departments of religion, let them learn to *look forward*. The expectant—the humbly waitful—attitude of mind is so much more wholesome than the idea that everything ought to be realised all at once. . . . The perfect prayer may sometimes be the crown, the fruition of a long life of humble and strenuous endeavor. But let not even imperfect prayers, vague prayers, stumbling prayers, inarticulate prayers be despised." *Outlines of Liberal Judaism,* 98.

[19] The following extract from a statement introducing an exhibit held at the Community House of Congregation Emanu El in New York, on April 20, 22, 23, 1930, illustrates the possibilities in Jewish education of the project method in general, and of art work in particular:

"When the work was first begun, . . . the aim of both teacher and pupil was to develop the ability of the Jewish child to make beautiful things with his hands. The emphasis was more on the artistic expression of the child than on the learning of Jewish history. . . . However, as the work with 'arts and crafts' continued, it became clear that manual activity of all sorts was extremely interesting to the children. . . . The question which naturally arose was: Can we devise a curriculum which will retain the motivation inherent in the 'arts and crafts' and at the same time give the child all the learnings known as Jewish History, Customs and Ceremonies, etc.

"The first step was to conduct the experiment under normal school conditions. The old 'arts and crafts' groups were extra curricular but the two experimental groups were regular classes of the Council House School. . . . In the first group, the ages of the children ranged from seven to eleven years. The children in the second group were a little older, but here also there was a range of ages from nine to thirteen years. No attempt was made to select the groups on the basis of age or their abilities to do manual and artistic work. The children had been classified according to their knowledge of Hebrew, as is the custom in Hebrew Schools, and this classification had no relation to their ability to carry on an experiment in the Project Method of teaching history. The project work was therefore made part of the regular curriculum in the school. The two groups met during school hours while the rest of the school was in session, and the children received no other instruction in Jewish history. . . .

"The experimental work was called 'A Project on the Life of the Early Hebrews.' The project began with reconstructing the life of the early Hebrew nomads. During the first meeting, the children were orientated in the general life of the people they were to study. Each child was then given a set of directions to guide him in making an object which related to the life of the nomads. Each child made a different object, until the whole project was completed. In this manner, all the objects were made entirely by the self-activity of the children.

"The manual activity, however, was but incidental to the real purpose of the project which was to motivate the children to an interest in the life of the early Hebrews. As the children were working to complete the objects in the nomadic home, they were reading especially prepared literature which explained the significance of the things they were making. Thus, the two pupils who were making the tent, studied the significance of the tent to the life of a desert people; the children who constructed the desert also made an exhaustive study of the geographic and climatic conditions of the ancient Orient; the pupils who drew the nomadic family studied the various types of clothing, occupations and social customs of the early nomads, etc. As each object was completed, it was presented to the class for criticism. During the discussion which followed, the child who made the object reported upon what he had learned about it. By this procedure the manual work was integrated with the readings on the Jewish history of Bible times.

"Although the manual work was the basis of the curriculum, it was by no means its central feature. The materials were simplified so that the manual work consisted merely of fitting together prepared pieces of wood, paper, etc. The principal emphasis was upon the historical significance of the objects under construction. Whereas the 'arts and crafts' groups were interested primarily in making beautiful pictures, statues, pottery, etc., the most important feature of the experimental work was the transfer of the interest in manual work to an interest in the life of the Jewish people. Some meetings were devoted entirely to discussions of the life which the class was reproducing. The children themselves were on the lookout for more and more reading material to explain the objects they were making, and on several occasions they organized a complaint to the effect that they were unable to find enough literature to keep them busy at home. . . .

"The underlying philosophy of the experimental work is that the child is an active and not a passive being, that he learns by doing. Through activities of various kinds, the children enter into the past and live it. Thus the nomadic life of their fathers is not merely a vague blurred picture to them. It becomes a reality. They study about that life; they make a tent in which their nomadic ancestors lived; they people it with nomads. History becomes a part of their lives."

[20] Cf. *Catalog First Exhibition of Acquisitions of the Jewish Museum Association of Chicago.* Jewish Peoples Institute, Chicago, November 10-27, 1928.

INDEX

Abraham ben David of Posquières, critic of Maimonides, 115.

Activities, Jewish, *desiderata* of, 219 ff.; as educative processes, 489 f.; as inherent factors of conservation, 52 f.; and objectives of Jewish education, 483.

Activities, leisure, in proposed *bet am,* 428.

Adams, J., opinion of emancipation, 21.

Adjustment, Jewish, attempt of Frankel at, 176-177; and function of Jewish scholars, 466; and guiding principles of Frankel, 160; and religious groups, 176. *See also* Civilization, Judaism as; Conservative Reformism; Hirsch, S. R.; Joseph, M.; Functional Interpretation; Neo-Orthodoxy; Left Neo-Orthodoxy; Reformism; Religious Culturism; Secular Culturism; Zionism.

Adler, F., on interpretation of law, cited, 468.

Adler, N. M., opponent of Reformism, 134.

Adolescent, the, and teaching of Jewish history, 502 f.

Affiliation, Jewish, prerequisite of community membership to, 296 f.; reasons for in the U. S. A., 511 f.

Agency, Jewish for Palestine, created by mandate, 277 f.

Aggadah, the, beginnings of Israel in, 546 n. 2; election of Abraham in, 264; Moses in, 547 n. 38; reconstruction of Scripture characters in, 546 n. 2; Reformist view of, 105. *See also* Rabbinic literature.

Aggregation, Jewish, as a conserving factor, 49. *See also* Ghetto.

Agnostic Jews, and Jewish group life, 230 f.

Agriculture, elements of, in early Israelitish religion, 354.

Agriculture and Jews, community, Jewish, and farm settlement, 289, 517; educational opportunities, 49; historical reasons for neglect, 49; social opportunities, 49.

Agudat Yisrael, disagreement with Zionism, 326; opposition to Zionism and to the *Jewish Agency,* 174.

Agunah, problem of, 423; and Orthodoxy, 548, xxviii n. 4; solution of Epstein, 548, xxviii, n. 3.

Ahad Ha-Am, on assimilation and imitation, 185; critique of his theory, 282; on Jewish scholarship, 466.

Akiba, on free will, 477 f.

Al Khazari, compared to *The Nineteen Letters,* 135.

Aleph Zadik Aleph, educational activities of, 493; program of, 551 n. 10.

Alexander the Great, religious and cultural imperialism of, 339, 212.

Alexandria, Jews in, citizenship rights of, 19; conflict with Hellenism of, 382; group life of, 189; interpretation of observances and subsequent fate of, 434.

Alexandrian school, influence on Jewish religion, 393.

Algeria, Jews in, 525 n. 1.

Allegiance, divided, and moral sanctions, 251 f. *See also* Hyphenism, cultural.

Allegorical method, of Hirsch, 383; in religious reinterpretation, 380.

Alliance Israélite Universelle, 286.

Allied powers, and mandate system, 277.

America. *See* United States of America.

American Revolution, and Jewish equality, 19.

Americanism and Judaism, a coordination of, 216 f., 293, 516.

Americanization and anti-Semitism, 73; and Jewish family, 50.

Americanization, concept of, Chicago Hebrew Institute on, 53; Council of Y. M. H. A. and Kindred Associations on, 53.

Amoraim, anachronistic view of biblical heroes, 405; authority of God-idea, 397; as religious interpreters, 370; on reward and punishment, 156; view of Hirsch, 141.

Amos, reinterpretation of the Day of the Lord, 357, 380.

Anglo-Jewish books and press, in Jewish education, 487.

Animism, in early Israelitish religion, 353.

Anthropocentrism, in humanist stage, 214.

Anthropology, and concept of God, 39.